Dictionary of Contemporary French Connectors

Connecting words and phrases are essential for discussion, clarity and fluency in any language. French is particularly reliant on connecting language: *also* and *in fact* have more than fifteen equivalent words and expressions in French.

This is the first French–English dictionary to focus on this fascinating and crucial part of the language. The dictionary presents nearly 200 full entries in alphabetical order, including:

au demeurant	*en l'occurrence*
au final	*et ce*
c'est dire que	*or*
de plus	*par ailleurs*

Entries define, discuss and exemplify a whole range of connecting language in French. In addition to these full entries, the dictionary includes some 400 other connecting structures. More than 2,000 authentic examples, chosen from a variety of registers and many different contexts and written mainly in contemporary prose, add further clarity.

This dictionary is the ideal reference for advanced students, teachers and translators of the French language.

James Grieve is a Senior Lecturer in French at the Australian National University, Canberra.

Titles of related interest

Modern French Grammar
Margaret Lang and Isabelle Perez

Manual of Business French
Stuart Williams and Nathalie McAndrew-Cazorla

The French Language Today
Adrian Battye and Marie-Anne Hintze

A History of the French Language
Peter Rickard

A History of the French Language Through Texts
Wendy Ayres-Bennett

French: From Dialect to Standard
R. Anthony Lodge

Dictionary of Contemporary French Connectors

James Grieve

London and New York

First published 1996
by Routledge
11 New Fetter Lane, London EC4P 4EE

Simultaneously published in the USA and Canada
by Routledge
29 West 35th Street, New York NY 10001

Typeset in Times by
Florencetype Ltd, Stoodleigh, Devon

Printed and bound in Great Britain by
Mackays of Chatham PLC, Chatham, Kent

British Library Cataloguing in Publication Data
A catalogue record for this book is available from the
British Library

Library of Congress Cataloguing in Publication Data
Grieve, James, 1934–
   Dictionary of contemporary French connectors / James Grieve.
      p. cm.
   Includes bibliographical references and index.
   1. French language – Connectives – Dictionaries.   I. Title.
PC2395.G75 1996
443'.21–dc20   95–42785

ISBN 0–415–13538–9 (hbk)

L'idée que la langue est fixée reste debout, dans sa fausseté séculaire.

Ferdinand Brunot, 1926

Contents

Acknowledgments

I am pleased to thank the following friends, colleagues and helpers:

Anton Alblas, who worked with cheerful efficiency and initiative as my research assistant in 1993 and 1994, and Sonia Wilson who did the same in 1994.

Graeme Clarke, the Director of the Humanities Research Centre at the Australian National University, who was good enough to ask me to be *his* assistant for a happy and busy twelvemonth, 1993, in which I made much progress on this work.

Iain McCalman, the Associate Director of the Humanities Research Centre at the Australian National University, who housed me there as a Sabbatical Writing Fellow for some further months in 1995, enabling me to complete the work.

Jacqueline Mayrhofer, of Troyes and Canberra, whose patience and generosity as a friend and cooperativeness as a colleague have not only endeared her to me for many a year but have much benefited the present work.

Jacques Thiériot, who helped with *au final* and handsomely housed me at the Collège international des traducteurs littéraires, Espace Van Gogh, Arles (Bouches-du-Rhône), of which he is the Director.

Alain Arnaud and Gloria Ruhmer, also of Arles, who offered in abundance words, wine and good cheer.

Mlle Marie-Thérèse de Fiévreuse of the Bibliothèque nationale, Paris, and Mlle Fabienne Martin of the Médiathèque d'Arles.

Angus Martin, of the University of Sydney, and Carol Sanders, of the University of Surrey, who gave the project vital support in the right quarter.

Jeannie Gray, who for the love of me read the whole text and made it better than it was.

And last but far from least, la parfaite bibliothécaire, Mme Irène Rouanet of the Médiathèque d'Arles, qui, malgré le fait de travailler dans la bibliothèque sans doute la plus bruyante de France, sait être gentille, serviable, efficace et... silencieuse.

Preamble

« La langue écrite qui recherche la précision et qui a le loisir d'une prépara-
tion réfléchie complique volontiers l'expression de la relation entre les phrases
suivant les nuances de la pensée. »

> J. Vendryes, *Le langage : introduction linguistique à*
> *l'histoire* (La renaissance du livre, 1921, p. 174)

This dictionary is intended for any speakers of English who wish to
improve their ability to read and write discursive, dialectical or analytical
French prose. I assume it will be consulted both by those seeking a French
equivalent for an English structure and by those who seek clarification of
the functioning of a French structure.

Perhaps the latter will find the dictionary more informative than the
former, if only because of the difficulty of giving a useful list of English
equivalents from which to start. I do give such a list, 'Some English structures', at page 19. Whether it will prove very useful in practice remains
to be seen. By virtue of the way we speak our language and pronounce
it, English expository connectors tend to be much less precise than French.
There are, if not fewer of them, at least fewer that are necessary and
specific in their function: one could almost get by in English with a basic
half-dozen, 'actually', 'also', 'anyway', 'but', 'however' and 'in fact'. There
is far less consensus among English-speakers about, say, the difference
between 'indeed' and 'in fact' than among the French about the difference between *en effet* and *en fait*. And if one starts from what is sometimes
called a *charnière-zéro* (Vinay & Darbelnet, 225), meaning the lack of an
explicit connector, a common feature of English, how does one find an
appropriate French structure? How can you list a more or less non-existent English equivalent for the *points de suspension* as used to hint at a
coming pun or joke, especially when English-speakers are also ignorant
of the existence and special role of this connector in French? Or, starting
from a single English structure such as 'on the one hand ... on the other',
how is one to direct English readers both to *d'un côté... de l'autre* and to
d'une part... d'autre part, without warning them that each of these two

structures, which usually work in quite distinct ways and tend not to be interchangeable, is an equivalent for only one of the two functions combined in the English structure? This versatility, these absences and the comparative imprecision of the functioning of many English connectors lessen the potential usefulness of any attempt to cross-list them with straightforward French equivalents. Indeed, were it possible to pair off English and French connectors in that way, other dictionaries would have done it long ago.

Another problem with connectors, from the conventional lexicographer's point of view, is that many of them have subtleties of usage which make their conceptual functions difficult to define without extended excursions into that semi-philosophical realm known as discourse analysis. For one thing, proper elucidation of these functions requires more space than traditional dictionaries have been inclined to allot to it. For another, the way some lexicographers give their examples is often unsuited to a clear explanation of a connector and its functioning: they commonly choose a quotation which begins not with the sentence preceding the connector but with the connector itself. This, by extracting the latter from the conceptual process that it is part of, prevents one from seeing the link of thought it makes and the emphasis it distributes. And if one does not grasp those, one cannot see how it acts as a connector.

This dictionary does not aim to be exhaustively authoritative. Its definition of what constitutes a connector will undoubtedly be seen by some as idiosyncratic, by others as eclectic and by yet others as elliptic. It is demonstrably all three. It takes scant account of spoken French. If it pays some attention to *alors*, *enfin* or *justement*, it is largely despite their role as spoken connectors. It discusses French use of the colon and the *points de suspension* while ignoring *bon ben* and all those other quasi-verbal utterances known as MSC (*marqueurs de structuration de la conversation*, Roulet, 93ff) which rarely see print, for the very reason that they do rarely see print, whereas punctuation marks are integral to it. For a similar reason I include (p. 14) 'A comment on italics', as italicization is a feature of printed English which shows a difference in the way argumentative connectors usually function in the two languages.

My definition of the connectors which lie within the compass of this work derives from the restrictions set out above. They are, for the most, 'inter-assertional connectors' (Gray, 12). They are structures which are used in writing expository or argumentative French; they are aids to persuasion and to making points; rather than expressing a meaning, they link meanings together and relate them to each other; they help to articulate a point of view by distributing emphases. And I include especially those which can be most troublesome to English learners of French. This troublesomeness comes partly from the fact that connectors are rarely dealt with as such in grammars and dictionaries, and more rarely dealt with satisfactorily. Seek in Mansion for the principle that makes the difference between *en fait* and *en effet*, in Robert for the very existence of *d'un côté ... de l'autre* or in Grevisse for, say, the distinction between *en l'occurrence* and *à savoir*, and you will know the meaning of the expression 'a wild goose chase'. This is not to criticize the compilers of those standard works; it is to recognize that connectors belong wholly neither to the grammarian nor to the lexicographer. Connecting words or phrases that are unproblematical to the English speaker, which can be found in any grammar or dictionary, are of little interest to me: *quoi qu'il en soit* and *en particulier* are undoubtedly connectors by any definition, and are usable by anyone who knows their straightforward equivalents in English or who can look them up in existing works of reference. The same goes for *mais* and *et*: except in certain functions, they afford little difficulty to the English-speaking learner of French. Which is why the entries given to them here concern not the full gamut of their uses but only those particular functions. This applies also to *il* and *ce*: although pronouns are among the most ubiquitous and indispensable of connectors, they are comprehensible to any beginner. Only two sorts of pronoun structure are included in this compendium: the tonic pronouns as distributors of contrastive stress; and some structures made from common demonstrative pronouns, like *cela dit, cela étant* or *et ce*. Similarly, *évidemment, par exemple* and *par conséquent*, in their unproblematic familiarity to any speaker of English with access to the smallest of dictionaries, do not require the attention that their less visible variants such as *bien évidemment, ainsi* and *du coup* do require. As for many conjunctional phrases ending in *que*, such as *à condition que, en sorte que, sous réserve que, si bien que*, I include them only if they are commonly used as connectors, especially at the beginning of dependent sentences, and if there are subtleties or difficulties in them for the speaker of English. There are also many common adverbs – *accessoirement, curieusement, positivement* and the like – which function as expository connectors, in that, placed usually at the beginning of a sentence, they enable a writer to comment on an idea. Some of these are so similar in their functioning to their most apparent English equivalents that it seems redundant to include them. Others, such as *assurément, décidément* and *également*, being more problematic for the speaker of English, are included. Some, not included as separate entries, are discussed or mentioned in the entries for other connectors. They can be found in the End-list (p. 518).

The great majority of my connectors can be found linking two major statements such as sentences or even paragraphs. Different words, such as 'pragmatic' and 'lexical', are sometimes used to define connectors. I use words like 'functional' or 'persuasive'. They help one see that a connector's role in a statement is often important by what a writer makes it do rather than by what it means. Its interest lies in the fact that it serves a function in a written argument, by connecting a second idea to a first as a consequence, by way of confirmation, by making it more precise, by setting it in parallel with another, or else by objecting to it, explaining it, restricting it while certifying its basic validity, exemplifying it, giving it comparative emphasis, summing it up with others and so on. It may show the author's own attitude to a subject rather than convey information. This authorial functionality of many connectors is another thing that makes it difficult for lexicographers to define them by meaning and even to give examples of their use. I discuss some of the major functions in the section 'Some common functions' (p. 1).

Strictly speaking, a few of the structures which I include, such as *aura* and the one I call *l'idée que*, do not wholly meet my own definition of a connector. These ones usually serve to shape statements that stay within a single sentence. None the less they too are integral to the persuasive style, they are important in structuring the discursive sentence and through them an author can make a point. And a mastery of them is essential for any who would write contemporary analytical French. They are also at times difficult for the English-speaking writer of French to grasp, both in theory and in practice.

A word on technical terminology. In defining the functions of connectors, my use of terminology may appear inconsistent. It can be pointless, at least for my purposes, to draw lines between any two categories of connectors' functions. Is *en tout cas* a restricter or a certifier? If the first, does it belong with *du moins* or with *ne serait-ce que*? If the second, does it go with *en tout état de cause*? What if it is at times more the one, at others more the other and on occasion both, certifying a previous affirmation while limiting its scope? When it restricts, I call it a restricter; when it certifies, a certifier. *Si je ne comme bien,* as Montaigne says, *qu'un autre comme pour moy.* However, my preference for untechnical language does not go so far as to rule out the words 'anaphoric' and 'cataphoric'. I use them rather than say 'referring back to a previous word or element' and 'referring forward to a word or element following' or as some put it 'a statement lying immediately to the left' and 'the statement to the right' (MacNamara, 110, 112, etc.).

Most of my examples are taken from today's discursive prose. This is the prose of rational argument and persuasion, the prose in which expository connectors are in their element. No writer who discusses anything in French can do without them entirely. Those who make do with many fewer of them than others must take pains to express their meaning clearly – outstanding examples from our time being Philippe Boucher, François de Closets, Maurice Duverger and Marc Fumaroli, and from an earlier period Alain, Henri Bergson and Remy de Gourmont. It is known that Alain took pains to eliminate from his prose what he saw as the redundant *mais: il y en a un de bon sur quatre, les autres ne sont que des échos dont on cherche vainement le sens* (Alain, 1970: 1111). One of his editors speaks of *une chasse aux* mais *méthodique* (ibid., 1265). Readings in the discursive prose of fifty to a hundred years ago suggest that writers nowadays use many more connectors than their predecessors. Now and then a voice is raised against the use of them in an unthinking way:

> ...parasites, les conjonctions (en effet, du reste, au surplus, d'autre part, de fait...) quand elles servent de béquilles à un raisonnement lâche. Les phrases doivent se lier non par des amorces factices mais par la logique des idées.
>
> (Bénéton, 48-49)

Despite such injunctions, the great majority of writers of discursive prose use these days an abundance of connectors. Some of them use two where one would apparently do; some use two or even three in a single sentence. I have found my examples in newspapers and books, learned articles, obituaries, the financial pages, weather reports, television guides, parish magazines, book reviews, editorials, advertising bumf from savings-banks, public announcements, essays and critical works in many different fields: discussions of social and moral matters, literary theory, history, human geography, the vulgarization of science, satirical sallies and commentaries on political events. A very few of my examples are taken from writers of that other form of prose: fiction, whether in the form of autobiography, novel or short story. In selecting all of them, I have tried to remain aware of the obvious fact that some writers are much more given than others to the use of particular connectors; that the idiosyncrasy that affects all writers in certain ways can run to what may appear to be aberrant usage; and that conclusions may mislead as much as they enlighten if they generalize too readily from findings arrived at by methods as random as mine.

A word on newspapers and the French written by journalists. I know of no derogatory French word for 'journalese'. It may be that French journalism has a tradition of intellectual pedigree lacking in the English-speaking world or now lost to us. Are there analogues in the English-speaking world for the defence of journalism mounted by Chateaubriand, Lamartine and Hugo? It can claim to have been the detonator of the revolution of 1830. The image of the journalist given by Balzac in *Illusions perdues* or by Maupassant in *Bel-Ami*, compounds of talent, opportunism and scurrility, are caricatures. In any case, the men and women who write in the dailies and weeklies from which I have taken most of my examples are far from that caricature. They write mainly in *Le Monde*, in *Le Nouvel Observateur*, *L'Événement du jeudi*, *Le Figaro* (and in the now defunct *Figaro littéraire*), *Le Point*, *Libération*. They write, for the most, standard French, often rich in expressiveness, pregnant with intellectual stimulation and in accordance with stylistic criteria of taste and elegance beyond the ken of *Time* magazine or *The Sun*. Journalists are no doubt among the most important vectors of linguistic change these days. And as such they are the first to naturalize many of the Americanisms that some of their compatriots find objectionable. But that is a feature of prose that affects mainly items of vocabulary such as nouns and features of style such as metaphor. Few of the writers I have used are noted for the use of such neologisms. And even in the prose of those who do use up-to-the-minute features of style, their shaping of thought by the use of connectors is largely unaffected by that. Many of them are writers of the calibre of Jean Daniel, André Fontaine, Michel Polac, Jean-François Revel, Françoise Giroud, François de Closets, Philippe Boucher, Jean-François Kahn, Dominique Jamet, André Chambraud, Albert du Roy, Alain Duhamel, Jacques Julliard. Many are writers, historians or academic specialists of other kinds who contribute to newspapers: Max Gallo, Michel Winock, Bertrand Poirot-Delpech, Bernard-Henri Lévy. If 'journalese' is written by hacks, debasing the language and their trade, impoverishing the minds of their readers, writing in some trendy tricksy lingo, in which no sentence shall have more than twelve words and from which anything smacking of true sophistication of thought or construction is banned, devised to be read at speed by someone whose reading-age is set for ever at twelve, then it is plain that this is not what these journalists write. They are, for the most part, the inheritors of a tradition which sees the journalist not as hack but as intellectual, and rightly so. The prose they write in newspapers differs little, if at all, from the prose they write in their books and their specialism. Perhaps the very nature of discursive prose, made for the discussion of ideas – made *by* the discussion of ideas – requires qualities of clarity, pertinence and stimulation which are incompatible with a certain conception of journalese.

A word, too, on 'contemporary'. The great majority of my examples are of connectors as used nowadays. But today's usage can sometimes be clarified by comparison with that of a generation or more ago. In the field of French connective structures, evolution is clearly at work. New connectors come into usage; some older ones become obsolete. This evolution is not always made apparent by dictionaries; by and large French lexicographers have paid little attention to this sort of structure. But it is a fact that *en fait*, probably at some time during the nineteenth century, came to supplant *en effet* in the latter's earlier adversative function. Towards the end of the century, *du coup* and *du même coup* seem to have made their appearance at about the same moment. It is certain that in the first half of the twentieth century, *pour autant* came to take the place of *pour cela* in negative structures. In about the same period, *par surcroît* has all but died out in favour of *de surcroît*; and *au lieu que* has been replaced almost entirely by *alors que*. One could quote other examples of this development: the obsolescence of *par suite*, the advent of *par ailleurs*, the comparative decline of *en un mot*. In this connection, *au final* and, possibly, *pour le reste* show the process continuing at the present time. When it seems apt, so as to show change or continuity, I advert to this history and use examples from authors of former times which illustrate it.

All of my examples have been found in print; a very few of them are transcriptions of speech. Penned by many different hands, most of them not well known, the examples were selected as samples of forms, which belong to no particular writer, rather than as ideas bearing the intellectual stamp of an individual. With very few exceptions, they are authentic. And most of those exceptions are inauthentic only in that, shorn of their wider context, they required a minimum of editorial intervention so as to be fully intelligible. I use few of them more than once. That I have plied some authors more than others will be evident.

Some common functions

In this chapter, I discuss some of the most common of the French connectors, seeing them in sets according to the function they serve in articulating an argument: adding, contrasting, conceding, restricting, precising, etc. (The word 'precising' and the verb 'to precise' are used throughout the text in the sense of 'making/to make (more) precise') Structures *italicized in bold* in this chapter are considered at greater length in the corresponding entries in the dictionary.

Adding a second point to a first

Reinforcers

At the simplest level, a conjunction like 'and' can add a second point to a first. Its most direct equivalent, *et*, often functions like 'and'. However, in important respects it does not. Take this sentence with its unexceptional and unexceptionable English 'and' linking a confirmatory example back to a sort of hypothetical principle:

> It has been said that a creative writer can only expect to remain at the top of his form for about fifteen years, and the bibliography which is included in the Everyman reprint of Conrad's short stories seems to bear this out.
>
> (Orwell, 1968: III, 387)

In written French, it is unlikely that the two statements joined by that conjunction would be joined in the same way. The conceptual link between them is that between generalization and particular illustration, between principle and instance. This is not a link that *et* would make immediately clear. The French writer might well make the two assertions in separate sentences. In that case, the second of them could begin either with *Ce principe semble être confirmé par la bibliographie...* or with *C'est là une hypothèse que semblerait confirmer la bibliographie....* Alternatively, a noun in apposition following the full stop would make an apter link than *et* between the principle and the instance: *Idée qui est confirmée, dirait-*

on, par la bibliographie.... On the other hand, if the writer did choose to structure these two statements as a single sentence, the noun in apposition could still be used, following a comma. The fact is that English 'and' can function in ways which are not those of *et*. For example, it is often used to link two actions which are cause and effect, as in this sentence from a historian's discussion of the beginnings of the Dreyfus Affair: 'The judges of the court martial had not been discreet and it soon became known that they had been shown secret documents.' In French, this pair of statements would most likely not contain *et* at all. If it did, it would obscure that very cause-effect relationship made by 'and', by presenting the two actions as consecutive, but not necessarily as consequential. More likely would be a construction with present participle: *Les juges du conseil de guerre ayant manqué de discrétion, on sut bientôt que...* or even *Parce que les juges avaient manqué à leur devoir de discrétion....* This illustrates a principle often remarked upon: that English sentences are often structured by coordination (two main clauses joined, say, by 'and' or 'but'), whereas French sentences are often structured by subordination (a single main clause, often placed late in the sentence and preceded by subordinate clauses).

Another point about *et* compared to 'and' is that it will be placed first in the sentence more often. This means that within French expository style there may be an implicit assumed norm about the form of the sentence which is not the same as that usually assumed in the equivalent style in English. The French discursive sentence is often shaped by a single idea. Which means that writers often link ideas by separating the sentences which express them. And that French conjunctions often stand first in sentences.

In a simple statement like 'He said x and he also said y', the second point is parallel to the first, is of equal importance and tends towards the same conclusion. It might well be written in French as two sentences. The connective function is served by two words, 'and' and 'also'. The 'and' could be dropped as redundant; and 'also' could be expressed by ***aussi*** or ***également***. In this function of adding a second point to a first, either in the same sentence or in consecutive sentences, these two connectors are more or less interchangeable. Being adverbs and French, they tend, unlike some English adverbs which wander about the sentence, to accompany the word they bear upon. So they will not be placed first in the sentence but, in this case, with the verb: *il a dit aussi que*. They are often used with paired points each of which has the same subject and verb, as in 'he said' in the example given above: *Nos fromages sont le premier des desserts. Ils sont aussi l'honneur de notre pays.* Sometimes the verb in the second point is not quite the same as in the first; but has a similar meaning: *sembler* and *paraître*, for instance, *annoncer* and *déclarer* or *il y a* and *il s'agit*. Or a pair of quite different verbs may have the same subject: *Elle* *fait de la musique. Elle apprend aussi à nager.* The subjects may be different while the acts are similar: 'X did that and so did Y'. There *aussi* or *également* could still be used, placed beside the subject: *George Sand faisait des fautes d'orthographe, et Lamartine aussi.* The equality of importance in the points can be seen in structures like *non seulement... mais aussi.* In that structure, *aussi* may be replaced again by *également* or by **encore**.

We tend to place 'also' loosely in sentences. If spoken or written today, this sentence from the New Testament 'For this cause the people also met him' (John, xii, 18) could have two meanings: not only the people, but others as well, met him; or the people did not only meet him, they also did something else to him. This type of adverbial wandering is common in the English we speak and write. French adverbs cannot be treated in that way: their place in the sentence is much more determined by the place of the word they modify.

If the two points are not quite as cognate as those instanced above, as in, say, 'He said x and he also did y', some thought is required: compared to x, is y of equal or lesser importance? If it is of similar importance, if it tends towards the same conclusion, then one of the modes of **de plus** (for example, *qui plus est* or simple *plus*), **de surcroît** or **en outre** may be required. A common English habit with 'also' is to place it first in a sentence in the function of, say, *de plus* or *de surcroît*. If this habit is transposed directly into French and *aussi* is placed first, the meaning is not 'also' but 'therefore' or 'so'. A study of divorced couples makes two points about possible ill effects on a child if the relationship with a parent has been very close. The second of these points, linked here with *en outre*, could conceivably be made in English with initial 'also':

> Être séparé d'un être si attentif et si aimant apparaît souvent à l'enfant comme totalement inacceptable. En outre, si la rupture aboutit à des rapports conflictuels, l'enfant court deux risques graves.

If the added point is to be presented as stronger than the first one, *bien plus* or *plus encore* may be appropriate. If it is presented as going one better than what precedes, leading towards a favourable conclusion, perhaps it should be introduced by **mieux** or one of its variants such as *mieux encore*. And if, conversely, it is presented as worse than what precedes, then one of the modes of **pis** can be used:

> En quelques mois, Jacques Delors a vu sa maison saccagée deux fois par des agriculteurs en colère. Pis, ils s'en sont pris à celle de sa mère.

Accessories

If the added point is seen as having a different importance, more supplementary or accessory, or not tending as necessarily as the first towards the conclusion, it may be that one of the set containing **d'ailleurs, au reste** and ***du reste*** will be more apt. An article on prehistoric cave-paintings in a grotto under the sea in one of the *calanques* near Cassis describes the difficulties it poses to anyone who might want to see it:

> La grotte est inaccessible à quiconque n'est pas un plongeur très entraîné et expérimenté. Trois plongeurs curieux ont d'ailleurs trouvé la mort le 1er septembre 1991 en voulant aller la voir.

It is not that the deaths of the divers are in themselves unimportant, only that in relation to the writer's main intention – to describe the grotto and the paintings – they serve to support a point in passing. A somewhat similar link could be made with ***au surplus***.

Another structure which sometimes functions rather like *au surplus* is ***d'autre part***. However, both of them can also introduce points which are of comparable importance to the first one and in no way accessory. The latter one can function either by itself or as the second element in the binary structure ***d'une part... d'autre part***, where the equality of the two points linked is made clear. The announcement by the first element of this binary that two points follow may make for clarity of exposition, as the reader knows what to expect of the ensuing sentences. This advantage of announcing paired points can be extended to ***sequences of points*** by the addition of *encore*, *enfin*, *ensuite* or *puis*, adapted to a three-part structure such as the standard *d'abord... ensuite... enfin*.

Contrasters

In another of its modes, *d'autre part* is similar to ***au demeurant*** and ***par ailleurs***. All of these structures can add a point which reinforces what precedes. But as well as functioning roughly like *et*, they can also function rather like ***mais***, when a second point is linked not as parallel but as contrastive. *D'autre part* and *par ailleurs* can actually combine with *mais*.

Stronger contrasts between two points can of course be made with variants of *mais*, such as *cependant*, *néanmoins*, *pourtant* and *toutefois*. Close to *pourtant*, both in derivation and present functioning, is ***pour autant***, often used in negative structures: *Le français perd du terrain au Canada, mais l'anglais ne progresse pas pour autant.* And there is a rich range of other contrastive or oppositive connectors to draw upon. Among the most commonly used, in senses like 'however' and 'nevertheless', are ***en revanche*** and ***par contre***. Much used, too, is ***au contraire***: *L'ulcère gastrique n'est pas un mal rare ; au contraire, c'est le plus répandu sur la terre.* Others which are close to it in function are ***à l'inverse***, ***inversement*** and ***à l'opposé***.

Another useful means of defining direct contrasts in viewpoints, attitudes or behaviour is the ***pronom tonique disjoint***, as in this comparison setting out a difference between the *révolutionnaire* and the *révolté*: *Le* *révolutionnaire sait ce qu'il veut construire, les révoltés, eux, ne savent que ce qu'ils veulent détruire.* The longer form of this connector, **quant à [lui]**, can do much the same thing, as can **pour [sa] part** and **de [son] côté**. Some of these structures are used not only to shape contrasts between two points but to distribute emphases in longer sequences of comparative viewpoints.

Here too binary structures have a valuable clarifying function, making for a fluent cohesive text: **autant... autant** and **d'un côté... de l'autre** can not only set two ideas in direct antithesis to each other but warn the reader to expect something more. This is also one of the clearest functions of indispensable structures like **alors que** and the **si d'opposition**. Obviously the four basic structures *bien que, malgré que, quoique* and *encore que* are also there to be used. But *alors que* and the *si d'opposition*, which are often interchangeable, are probably more common nowadays in any 'although' type of relation between statements. A mastery of them is integral to the discursive style.

More specialized oppositions can be made with **encore faut-il (que)** and **seulement**: after a statement of relative satisfaction, the first of these may introduce a requirement for something more, as in this comment on the view some Corsicans take of their rights and duties in relation to the mainland French:

> S'il appartient à l'État de garantir l'égalité de tous, encore faut-il que les insulaires ne cherchent pas à être moins égaux devant les obligations et plus égaux devant les droits que les continentaux.

And *seulement* too can function as a specialized type of 'but', to raise an overlooked unfavourable point in a preceding situation presented as favourable:

> Il existe en France des dizaines d'entreprises méconnues, championnes mondiales dans leur spécialité. Elles participent au rétablissement de la balance commerciale tout comme Airbus ou le TGV. Seulement, elles sont petites.

Similar objections can be raised by **n'empêche** and by **reste que**. These two can not only raise objections but restate them after the intervention of a concession.

As well as the non-adversative **or**, which draws attention to an important point, there is an adversative mode for which 'but' or 'yet' can often be apt English equivalents. For instance, it can structure an opposition between a statement deemed to be false and a truer one, as in this extract from Durkheim's discussion of an untenable theory on the reasons why people commit suicide (in which *elle* refers to the theory and *il* to suicide):

> Elle suppose, en effet, qu'il a toujours pour antécédent psychologique un état de surexcitation, qu'il consiste en un acte violent et n'est possible que par un

grand déploiement de force. Or, au contraire, il résulte très souvent d'une
extrême dépression.

(Durkheim, 1930: 88–89)

That combination of *or* with *au contraire* is sometimes replaced by a
combination with ***en fait***, which can be strongly adversative (see more on
en fait below). For another of the modes of *or* it can be difficult to find
an English equivalent: it sometimes puts into words a link of thought
which in English remains tacit. In a pair of sentences about profound
economic and social changes affecting Italian peasants during the 1960s,
a writer uses this type of *or* to link a concrete historical statement to a
following generalization:

> Les ruraux abandonnent leurs villages pour se diriger vers les pôles industriels
> du Nord. Or de telles migrations ne vont jamais sans déchirement humain.

There, English might simply omit the connector. Or it might make the
link with 'of course'.

Concessives

The sentence above 'Obviously the four basic structures *bien que*, *malgré
que*, *quoique* and *encore que* are also there to be used' states a concession. In its context, it is accessory to the main point about the importance
of *alors que* and the *si d'opposition*. The 'obviously' introduces a point
the validity of which should not be forgotten. It is followed by a sentence
introduced by 'but' restating the greater pertinence of the point about
alors que and the *si d'opposition*. In such contexts, 'obviously' is replaceable by other concessive statements, some of them more overt, such as
'admittedly', 'granted', 'true', 'to be sure' or 'of course'. Often an English
concession is not marked by the presence of an explicit connecting word:
George Orwell, discussing filth in the kitchens of French restaurants,
accepts in the second of the following sentences that there may be something to be said in favour of a French cook:

> It is not a figure of speech, it is a mere statement of fact to say that a French
> cook will spit in the soup – that is, if he is not going to drink it himself. He is
> an artist, but his art is not cleanliness.

(Orwell, 1961: 80)

The first part of the second sentence, going against the trend of the author's
argument, could be expressed in French as in English without an explicit
concessive structure. But it is likely that it would begin with ***certes*** or ***sans
doute***. These are two of the commonest in a range of connectors which
function by temporarily accepting a point which may be restricted or over-
ruled soon after. Among others are ***assurément***, ***bien entendu***, ***bien sûr***
and ***soit***. The first function of them all is to express more or less agree-

ment with a possible objection to what precedes; their second function can be to foreshadow a countervailing point which may well annul the objection and reinforce what precedes it. Some of them, ***admettons*** and ***peut-être***, for instance, express less agreement than others. Some, such as ***il est vrai que***, are followed less often than others by a cancellation of the agreement. Some, such as ***oui***, may express total agreement with the objection; but they may still be followed by a point seen as more important. This point is often introduced by a connector of which *mais* is the paradigm: *cependant, pour autant, n'empêche,* ***quand même***, *reste que, seulement,* ***tout de même***, the ***n'en... pas moins*** construction: *Certes, c'est un artiste. Seulement, l'art qu'il exerce n'a rien à voir avec la propreté.*

Confirming and precising

Among the most common of the French connectors is one which can stand as the paradigm of the confirmer and preciser: ***en effet***. It should not be thought of as meaning 'in effect'; and the meaning sometimes given in dictionaries, 'indeed', may also be unreliable, as many speakers of English use 'indeed' in ways which do not correspond to the function of *en effet*. Take this example of 'indeed', used by Aldous Huxley in discussing the difficulties entailed in writing tragedy nowadays:

> To impose the kind of arbitrary limitations, which must be imposed by anyone who wants to write a tragedy, has become more and more difficult – is now indeed, for those who are at all sensitive to contemporaneity, almost impossible.
>
> (Huxley, 16–17)

There 'indeed' could not be *en effet*. It not only confirms what precedes, it goes well beyond it. Its function could be rendered in English by 'in fact' and in French by *en fait*, by ***même*** – or even by ***voire***. Often, instead of using an equivalent connector, English would omit a lexical link between sentences joined by *en effet*. This is the phenomenon, common in English when compared to French practice, known as the *charnière-zéro* or the tacit connector. The value of *en effet* can be seen in pairs of English sentences where the lack of a connector may make for some indeterminacy in the reader's grasp of the author's meaning. The following instance of this comes from a paragraph in which the subject is the beginnings of the relationship between Arthur Symons and Havelock Ellis, who was then editing a series of Jacobean play-texts:

> [Ellis] wrote to Symons, a correspondence ensued and a commission was arranged. It was agreed that Symons would prepare a volume of five Massinger plays for Ellis.
>
> (Sturgis, 67)

The English reader who is informed about the subject or who is following the drift of this writer may well deduce from the context of these two sentences that the commission mentioned in the first is the preparation of the Massinger volume mentioned in the second. However, it would be quite possible to read the second sentence as speaking of something different from the first one. It is this type of potential ambiguity which *en effet* serves to obviate: placed either at the beginning of the sentence or after the first verb, it would make plain that the Massinger volume was in fact the same as the commission. Like ***effectivement***, which when used as a connector is interchangeable with it, *en effet* usually corroborates what precedes by making it more exact. What it introduces is often little more than a sort of translation: an apter form of words in which to express what precedes. This translational function is well seen in this pair of sentences about the proportion of the rented accommodation in Paris which is controlled by the municipal authorities:

> Un quart des logements locatifs de Paris (23,45 % exactement) est contrôlé, directement ou indirectement, par la Ville de Paris. Elle en possède, en effet, en ce tout début d'année 1989, près de 163 000, alors qu'il n'y en a au total que 694 800.

The two sentences actually say much the same thing in three different ways: the information in the second sentence, announced by *en effet*, just translates into a cardinal number the fraction and percentage given in the first sentence. Though this connector's function is usually close to that of ***de fait***, it should not be confused with *en fait*, which in most contexts functions more like an opposite of it. Indeed, the differences between *en effet* and *en fait* are marked and profound, a point not always clarified by some dictionaries, which can give the impression that the two structures are close to interchangeable. Two of the main differences are that *en effet* never structures an opposition, whereas *en fait* often does; and that *en fait* introduces new material, whereas *en effet* normally does not.

Other precisers include ***à savoir (que)*** and ***en l'occurrence***, the functions of which can be difficult for the English-speaker to distinguish between: the first of them, like 'namely', introduces a closer identification of what precedes; the second one, like 'in this instance', normally defines what follows as a particular exemplar of a broader set preceding. At times *à savoir (que)* could be replaced by punctuation: its function could be served by a ***deux-points***. But one could not say the same of *en l'occurrence*.

The pair ***c'est dire (que)*** and ***c'est-à-dire (que)*** are also close to each other in function: what the former introduces is usually of the order of an explanation or a consequence of what precedes; what follows the latter is often a clearer restatement of what precedes. The latter functions as a single word; the former also lends itself to a range of variants like *c'est* *peu dire* and *c'est assez dire*. As precisers, they belong to the same set; but they can also be seen as belonging to different sub-sets: *c'est dire (que)* is at times close to **autant dire (que)**, whereas *c'est-à-dire (que)* is closer to **autrement dit**. The latter can be replaced in one of its modes by other precisers such as **en d'autres termes**. Similarly, modes of *mieux*, *même* and **plutôt** can serve to introduce a better way of saying what has just been said. In another more conclusive mode, *autrement dit* can function rather like **en clair**, much favoured nowadays by journalists.

Concluders and recapitulators

Precisers such as *autrement dit* and *en clair* may not only introduce an apter word; in so doing they may also introduce a more telling analysis of an argument. For putting a finer point upon an idea, making unapparent implications visible, summing up a development in fewer words and a more pregnant meaning, there is a range of concluding and resuming connectors.

As mentioned above, *enfin* can introduce the last in a sequence of points. It does not usually recapitulate the force of the points preceding it, unlike some of the other concluders. Almost as versatile as *enfin* is **en définitive**, although it does not have the same explicit concluding value and, unlike *enfin*, it always accompanies a judgment. Among those which tend to be used both to mark conclusion and to resume what precedes are **bref** and **en un mot**. These two connectors are always used to introduce what the writer sees as the last word on a subject, both in the sense that it ends a development and in the sense that it is the aptest formulation of a concept. One difference between them is that *bref* is by far the more common nowadays, *en un mot* being less used than it was even in the earlier years of the twentieth century.

A somewhat similar dual role is played by **en somme**. As for **somme toute**, it too is close to these other concluders; but it may be more often used than they are to introduce a judgment not supported by arguments, somewhat after the manner of **après tout**. With such connectors, the reader is assumed to agree with an unstated reasoning or is implicitly reminded of an idea supposed to be shared by both writer and reader. This is one of the ways in which conclusive structures like **au fond**, **décidément**, **en fin de compte** and *finalement* are sometimes used: as well as being placed towards the end of a development, they can be placed first, anticipating the discussion which they have in a sense already recapitulated. Others, like **en résumé**, a less common replacement for *bref*, do not usually anticipate in that way. In very recent years, this set of conclusive connectors has grown by the addition of **au final**, a structure used by some journalists as a replacement for standard concluders and resumers like *enfin* or *finalement*. It can also function like **au total**, which often accompanies a

literal adding up of amounts, as in this extract from a discussion of the
Grand Palais, part of which is slowly subsiding:

> En novembre dernier, on a constaté un affaissement du bâtiment de 2
> millimètres, côté fleuve. Au total, quelque 2,5 centimètres séparent les deux
> ailes du Grand Palais.

Other resumers, **au bout du compte** and **tout compte fait**, originate like
au total and *somme toute* from nouns meaning literally the sum total of
an addition. They have evolved far from that original arithmetical sense
and now usually introduce a definitive judgment.

Two other commonly used structures, slightly longer than your average
connector, also have concluding and resuming functions: **force est de** and
tout se passe comme si. Both of them introduce judgments drawn from
a preceding discussion or demonstration: those introduced by the former
are presented as being grounded on more conclusive evidence than those
introduced by the latter. What follows the latter is less of a certainty,
more of an informed conjecture.

Explanations of causes and reasons

The differences between **car** and **parce que** can be difficult to grasp – in
certain modes, some native French-speakers do not distinguish between
them. Strictly speaking, the former introduces a reason, the latter a cause.
With *car* a writer explains why the preceding statement was made. With
parce que, the cause of the previously mentioned action is identified.
The answer to a question asked with *Pourquoi ?* would not be given
with *car* – and yet it could be given with **c'est que**, which in many contexts can replace *car*. Explanations may also be introduced by **c'est
pourquoi**, by **là** (in, say, *C'est là la raison pourquoi...*), by **tel est** (as in
Telle était l'explication que...) or by **voilà**: *Et voilà pourquoi votre fille est
malade !*

Consequence and concomitance

A link of logical consequence can be made with **alors** and **dès lors**. Both
of these structures derive from expressions of time meaning roughly 'then'
in the sense of 'next' or 'at that time'. They have evolved to mean also
'then' in the sense of 'so'. In discursive prose their usual function is, like
'in that case' or 'because of that', to introduce a point which follows logically from what precedes. This point can be an assertion or a question.
In a statement like the following, taken from a discussion of public health
measures such as screening for cancer, the link between the two sentences
could be made by either of these connectors:

> Au-delà de 50 ans, 40 % des hommes ont des cellules cancéreuses dans leur prostate, mais seulement 8 % en souffriront à un moment quelconque de leur vie. Alors, faut-il les obliger tous à un dépistage qui présente certains risques ?

In certain contexts, such as that one, *dès lors* could be replaced by one of the modes of ***cela étant***, by ***de ce fait*** or by one of the range of variants of ***par conséquent***.

Among the variants of *par conséquent* is ***du coup***, a very commonly used structure these days in the worlds of journalism and academia. It is close, both in origin and in its contemporary functioning, to ***du même coup***. The first of this pair, rather like *de ce fait*, is used to speak of a direct consequence, something which is the result of a previous act or state. Thus a historian uses it in discussing the economic consequences for the southern parts of France in the sixteenth century of two coincidental events, an increase in population and a lack of increase in gross product:

> La population augmente très vite, récupérant ses niveaux d'avant la peste noire. Mais les rendements du blé restent stables, la production agricole et la productivité sont bloquées. Du coup, des processus de paupérisation se déclenchent.
>
> (Le Roy Ladurie, 31)

The link made there is one of consecutiveness. The link usually made by *du même coup* is one of simultaneity, similar to that made by ***ce faisant***, as in this comment, published in 1918, on the possible future of Yiddish spoken at that time by Jews in Russia and the newly independent states of eastern Europe:

> L'avenir montrera si cette langue est capable de résister à des institutions démocratiques qui, accordant aux juifs l'égalité avec les autres citoyens, briseront l'isolement où ils sont, mais, du même coup, les obligeront, s'ils veulent exercer leurs droits, à être maîtres de la langue commune des pays dont ils seront des citoyens normaux.
>
> (Meillet, 266)

Another pair of consequencers, quite close at times to *dès lors* and *de ce fait*, are ***de là*** and ***d'où***. Each of these could be seen at times as equivalents of English 'hence', although , unlike 'hence', they are normally used without a verb and followed directly by a noun-structure, as in this extract from an essay on the relations between sex and power, speaking of the power-defying effect created by anyone who discusses sex:

> Qui tient ce langage se met jusqu'à un certain point hors pouvoir ; il bouscule la loi ; il anticipe, tant soit peu, la liberté future. De là cette solennité avec laquelle aujourd'hui, on parle du sexe.
>
> (Foucault, 13)

There the writer could have used *d'où*.

Two other consequencers which need to be distinguished are *aussi* and **ainsi**. This mode of *aussi* is different from the adverbial one discussed above with *également* as an equivalent for 'also'. It is not an adverb but a conjunction. As such, it is usually placed first in the sentence and followed by an inversion of subject and verb; and it means not 'also' but 'so' or 'therefore'. The report about three divers drowning in a dangerous grotto near Cassis, quoted above in relation to *d'ailleurs*, continues like this:

> La grotte est inaccessible à quiconque n'est pas un plongeur très entraîné et expérimenté. Trois plongeurs curieux ont d'ailleurs trouvé la mort le 1ᵉʳ septembre 1991 en voulant aller la voir.
>
> Aussi a-t-il fallu imaginer un système très spécial pour que les quelques préhistoriens capables de plonger et les sept nageurs de combat « prêtés » par la marine nationale fassent les prélèvements pour analyses et le relevé par images vidéo et photographies sous la direction directe de Jean Clottes installé en surface sur une vire des calanques.

This function could sometimes be served by one of the modes of *ainsi*, which is also often followed by an inversion of subject and verb when placed first in the sentence. But at the same time as it introduces a consequence, *ainsi* can have a shade of exemplifying function as well. In this example, the writer is pointing out that three founding principles of modern societies (*la méritocratie individuelle*, *la solidarité sociale* and *l'utilité collective*) have not prevented in any of them the inequitable distribution of wealth; of these three principles he says:

> On les retrouve d'ailleurs dans les différentes formes d'États modernes, du capitalisme libéral aux sociétés socialistes, chacun les organisant différemment. Ainsi est-ce en fonction de cette trilogie : mérite, utilité, justice, qu'un partage inégalitaire de l'argent a pu être légitimé.

> (Closets, 1983: 177)

In the French written by some speakers of English, the English habit of beginning a sentence with 'so' can make for sentences beginning with **donc**. But in the sense of 'so', the usual place for this connector is after the first element of the sentence: *Tout concourt donc à prouver que...*; *Il ne faut donc pas chercher à...*. Initial *aussi*, to be avoided in the sense of 'also', is to be cultivated in the sense of 'so'.

Consequences or results of what precedes are quite often placed in a separate sentence beginning with a structure like **de sorte que** or **si bien que**. The grammatical function of these structures is adverbial: they introduce a modifier of the preceding verb. And their syntactical function is conjunctional. The sentence they begin is a **phrase dépendante**: it has no main verb and its grammar, syntax and meaning are all determined by the sentence before. Such sentences are often made with other conjunctional phrases such as *alors que* and **au point que**.

Restricters

Dependent sentences are also made in ways which restrict what precedes. A restricter can modify a preceding statement by admitting an exception to it, by attenuating its force, by reducing its scope. This can be done with a conjunctional phrase such as *à ceci près que*. A writer, having made a first statement which needs to be limited in some direction, adds a second statement which reduces the ambit of the first. In this example, the writer first generalizes about the rough similarity that he sees between politicians' ways of exercising power nowadays and in former times; he then particularizes an aspect of his initial statement, introducing it with this restrictive structure and sharpening the focus of his idea:

> Au fond, on ne gouverne pas, aujourd'hui, de manière très différente de ce qui se faisait voilà cent ou deux cents ans. À ceci près que, depuis peu, disons une trentaine d'années, les hommes politiques doivent compter avec la télévision, qui les révèle ou les étouffe.
>
> (Boucher, 445)

Preceding affirmations can be restricted in other ways. Two of the most common connectors that enable this link to be made are *du moins* and *en tout cas*. At times, as when they combine with *sinon*, they may be interchangeable, as in this extract from an editor's discussion of the rough draft of an author's manuscript:

> Il semble avoir été écrit sinon d'un seul jet, en tout cas dans un court laps de temps, une dizaine de jours peut-être.
>
> (Malicet, 51)

Often what they restrict is uncertainty, as in that example where the hypothesis of *un seul jet* becomes the lesser but firmer affirmation *un court laps de temps*. The writer vouches for what they introduce as a statement of minimal validity. A mode of *toujours est-il que* also comes close to this function.

Similar in some respects to *en tout cas*, but different in others, are *en tout état de cause* and *de toute façon*. The first of these, probably more contrastive than *en tout cas*, rather than restricting what precedes may introduce a certainty which coexists with it and is seen as more important. After an attempt to interpret conflicting evidence or a dilemma posed by differing but possibly valid hypotheses, the writer does not resolve these but introduces a statement of what *can* be accepted as valid. In the following example, having canvassed two conflicting theories of political economy as solutions to the difficulties of North Yemen, the writer concludes that, whichever of them prevails, the situation will still be difficult:

> La décentralisation, estime le premier ministre, permettra d'atténuer progressivement les différences et la méfiance. Certains observateurs pensent, au

contraire, que le salut pourrait venir d'un État autoritaire, très centralisé, dans un premier temps.

En tout état de cause, les problèmes économiques restent considérables.

Certainties of this sort may also be introduced by *de toute façon* or by its variant *de toute manière*. In certain contexts, most of these restricters and certifiers could be replaced by *quoi qu'il en soit*.

A comment on italics

A sentence above, containing italicized English *can* (p. 13), illustrates an important difference between the two languages. The functions served by italicization in English are often not those which are served in French. To say of General Gallifet that 'he was for the friends of the Commune, *the* man of blood' (Brogan, 201) or of Communists and Russophiles during the 1940s 'I consider that willingness to criticise Russia and Stalin is *the* test of intellectual honesty' (Orwell, 1968: III, 203), is to translate a specialized English intonation into a convention of print. Although a French writer occasionally italicizes the definite article in this way: *Aucun parti (sauf les extrêmes) ne peut s'imaginer détenir à lui tout seul* la *solution politique*, a more usual analogue for it is the addition of the expression *par excellence*, placed either before the noun, *La Champagne reste par excellence le pays des contrastes violents*, or after it, *une couverture de limon, terrain meuble par excellence* (Braudel, 43 & 274). Similarly, when the Red Queen says to Alice, '*I've* seen gardens, compared with which this would be a wilderness', the writer is giving a visual analogue of an audible feature of English speech (Carroll, 206). That is, the tonic accent of unstressed spoken English can be strengthened and used in emphasis; and this emphasis alters the meaning of what is said. A sentence such as 'He used to pick me up on the way home from work', in addition to the straightforward meaning it has when spoken unstressed, could have at least six different other meanings when pronounced with stress, depending on whether the emphasis was put on 'he', 'used', 'me', 'up', 'home' or 'work'. Each of these emphases precises what the meaning of the statement is by implying a contrast with what the meaning is not. In French, a form of words expressing the unstressed meaning, *Il me ramenait en voiture en rentrant du travail*, say, would not usually suffice to express the six other meanings. Each of them could well be signalled by a different form of words and a different order of words according to what meaning is to be stressed: *C'est lui qui...*; *C'est moi qu'il ...*; *C'est en rentrant du travail qu'il...*, etc.

So, this changing of meaning through distributive stress is something which typography can adapt to written English. Many writers try to make visible this function of audible stress. The point about the Red Queen's italicized word, too, apart from the fact that it shows her sedulous smugness, is that it is essentially comparative. That is, it makes a link, however implicit, to some other part of her utterance: in this case, it implies a contrast with her interlocutor who has not seen such gardens. French, which does not have such a tonic stress, does not use contrastive emphasis of this kind. Instead of increasing stress on a syllable or a word, French usually adds a word or words. The Red Queen would not say « *J'ai* vu ... » but « Moi, j'ai vu » or « J'ai vu, moi qui vous parle ».

In English discursive prose, italics can be connectors. This is quite different from the way in which italicization normally functions in written French. What has been said about Stendhal's use of *l'italique* could by and large be said about its general use in French: *Stendhal se fie à elle pour inciter le lecteur à comprendre que le mot souligné est révélateur* (Wagner, 180). French italics usually focus attention on a special feature of the word or phrase underlined. They may even enable a writer to sharpen a point or to exclaim. But they rarely make a conceptual link between the text italicized and some other part of the text. Occasionally a French writer does italicize in this way, as in this statement about the workings of the British political system:

> Dans cette Angleterre où l'on ne peut jamais gouverner *par* le centre, on est toujours incité à gouverner *au* centre.
>
> (Duverger, 285)

This use of italics for contrastive effect is unusual in French. Its relative frequency in the prose of this author may be related to the comparative infrequency with which he uses procedural connectors.

However, in printed English this is a very common main function of italics: they not only emphasize, they distribute emphasis, they define an idea in relation to another. And this they do in different ways, either contrastive or confirmative, which in French is done by the use of a range of different connectors. Sometimes the connective link made by English italics is similar to that made in the quotation from Duverger above, that is by emphasizing a preposition in relation to another: in my 'Preamble' I say of discursive prose that it is 'made for the discussion of ideas – made *by* the discussion of ideas' (p. xvi). Rather than italicizing the preposition *par*, it is much more likely that a French writer would reinforce the link between the two ideas by adding a connector like *voire* or one of its variants such as *que dis-je !*

This connective mode of italics is common in English when a negative point and a positive one are contrasted: 'Kipling not only wrote about India, but was *of* it' (Said, 160). The echo of the speaking voice is clear. The sentence was written for the ear as much as for the eye. A similar thing can be seen in an essay on the poetry of Peter Porter:

> For Porter, the loss of historical continuity is not to be seen as a means of disowning the past and sharpening one's focus on the present: it *destroys* the present.
>
> (James, 63)

Here the writer's point is to clarify and define a distinction between what 'the loss' does and does not do. In structuring such a contrastive point, the French writer might replace the colon with a full stop, make two sentences of the English one and begin the second of them with *Non, cette perte détruit plutôt le présent* or *Au contraire, elle...* or *En fait, elle....* That is, here again, instead of increasing an existing stress, French would add a word, in this case a contrastive connector.

In the following example, the writer discusses a view expressed by an Englishman writing in the 1920s about India:

> Indians 'lie' because they are not free, whereas he (and other oppositional figures like him) can see the truth because they *are* free and because they are English.
>
> (Said, 249)

In a context like that, again a contrast between a negative and a positive, instead of italicizing to signal a contrast the French writer might well choose a connector like ***précisément***, often used to sharpen contradictions or paradoxes, and structure the second part of the contrast with the mode of the *si d'opposition* which introduces a cause or reason: *alors que, si lui et d'autres figures oppositionnelles sont à même de voir la vérité, c'est précisément parce qu'ils sont libres....*

Sometimes the contrast made in English by italics would be shaped in French by the *pronom tonique disjoint*. In this extract from a discussion of nationalism, the English writer contrasts 'word' and 'thing':

> Somewhere or other Byron makes use of the French word *longueur*, and remarks in passing that though in England we happen not to have the *word*, we have the *thing* in considerable profusion.
>
> (Orwell, 1968: III, 361–362)

There the French writer, again using the *si d'opposition*, might shape the second part of the sentence like this: *que si en Angleterre il se trouve que le mot nous manque, la chose, elle, abonde.* Or with different syntax, possibly without the *si d'opposition*, another adversative connector such as *en revanche* or *par contre* could be used: *par contre la chose nous l'avons à profusion.* Such oppositive relationships can also be made in English by italicizing not a noun but a verb. A writer, discussing Fascist intellectuals in Europe in the 1930s, says of the Nazi ideologue Bronnen:

> he was simply weak, and had to spend most of the thirties trying to prove that he was not a Jew because his father had not sired him, which implied that his father *was* a Jew, and put *him* on the hook.
>
> (James, 256)

This time, for the part of the sentence beginning 'which implied', the French writer would have the choice between using an adversative structure such as *à l'inverse* or *à l'opposé*: *ce qui donnait à penser à l'opposé que...* and using a structure like **bien** to underline a confirmation of the suspicion: *ce qui laissait supposer que son père était bel et bien juif.* As for 'him' in the final words, italicized so as to clarify its proper antecedent, either simple *celui-ci* would suffice to resolve this indeterminacy of English as it is sometimes written nowadays; or else *à [son] tour* could be added to the verb.

In other contexts, rather than underlining a contrast between separated elements of the text, English italics aim at confirming an earlier statement. In these cases, it is usually a verb which is italicized.The same writer, looking back on his first book, which was called *The Metropolitan Critic*, links two paragraphs in this way:

> There were pages dedicated to what a Metropolitan Critic was, or is.
>   Well, what *is* a metropolitan critic?
>
> (James, xiii)

Instead of italics, the French writer might use **au vrai** if wishing to give a slightly literary tone to the text, or **au fait** if keeping the more familiar register of the English: *Mais au fait, un critique métropolitain, ça représente quoi ?* In the following example, a writer talks about the contempt of the historian and politician Thiers for Napoleon III. Here the italics function as a connector between two developments which are more sizeable than paragraphs: the first of the sentences is the last in chapter four; the second of them is the first in chapter five:

> That contempt was deepened as the historian of the Consulate and the Empire saw Napoleon III dissipate his resources and those of France in enterprises more and more romantic.
>
>   v
>
> The Empire *was* dispersing its forces in an alarming manner, spending its peasant soldiers and marines all over the globe.
>
> (Brogan, 131)

There, instead of italicizing, the French writer might begin his new chapter with *il est de fait que* or use **il faut dire que** or **c'est un fait (que)**. Or else, to serve the italics' function of reminding, confirming and precising, he could use *en effet*. In a somewhat similar example, Orwell tells what he calls a 'brain-tickler' about a businessman who was warned by a superstitious person not to take his usual train because it might be wrecked in a crash:

> The businessman was sufficiently impressed to wait and take a later train. When he opened the newspaper the next morning he saw that, sure enough, the train *had* been wrecked and many people killed.
>
> (Orwell, 1968: III, 190)

There, clearly, it is *de fait*, *effectivement* or *en effet* which would make the link back to the writer's previous paragraph.

Among the most frequently italicized words in English prose are negatives. The effect aimed at is usually one of contrast. However, as can be seen in the next example, taken from an essay on popular American fiction and on the people who should read it but do not, the italicized negative too may have a confirming function:

> There is evidence that a recent best seller by a well-known writer was never read by its publisher or by the book club that took it or by the film company that optioned it. Certainly writers of book-chat for newspapers *never* read long books and seldom do more than glance at short ones.
>
> (Vidal, 79)

The function of the second sentence is to reinforce the first one by restricting its scope to a single group of those professionals who might be expected to read these books but never do. In French, the restriction could be done with *en tout cas*; and rather than structuring the sentence to stress the negative, it would make more sense to stress the 'writers of book-chat', by using either the *pronom tonique disjoint* or its longer form *quant à [lui]*: *Ce qui est sûr en tout cas c'est que les échotiers littéraires, quant à eux, ne lisent jamais....*

English italics can also function like the redundant connectors with which French writers quite often support other connectors: they reinforce. In the example above about the businessman and the train-crash one might say that 'sure enough' is the operative connector and that the italics do no more than reinforce it. That may be what they do to 'in fact' in the following extract from a discussion of women's supposed 'moral deficiencies' as defined in Victorian times by Otto Weininger:

> and women today might well find that what Weininger describes as defects might be in fact *freedoms* which they might do well to promote.
>
> (Greer, 106)

In this function of underlining an opposition, 'in fact' quite often attracts italics, as in this comment on much twentieth-century art:

> By pretending that certain things are not there, which in fact *are* there, much of the most accomplished modern art is condemning itself to incompleteness, to sterility, to premature decrepitude and death.
>
> (Huxley, 31)

It may be that the connector reinforces the italics, or vice versa, or that they reinforce each other. What is pretty certain is that a French writer who shaped those oppositions with *en fait* or *au contraire* would not also italicize the noun or the verb.

Some English structures

Warning

Unlike some other dictionaries, this list does not try to give simple and straightforward French equivalents for the English connectors. Different contexts make for different functionings of certain connectors, especially in English. Generally speaking, English connectors in common use are few and versatile, and do many different jobs; French ones are many and specific, and do particular jobs. Take 'actually': in current English usage, the different intonations that the voice can give to it enable it at least to confirm, deny, rectify, precise, restrict, resume, exemplify, stress, hint a polite warning of disagreement and probably play many other roles. In the list below, 'actually' has seventeen French equivalents; it might have more than seventeen: only an analysis of the function it serves in an English context can determine which of the possible equivalents will serve that function in a given French sentence. Much the same goes for 'in fact', as one can see by glancing at the twenty 'equivalents' given in the list below, and for 'also' with its nineteen. The French connectors given for each of the English ones in this list do no more than direct the reader to the entries for those different structures. It may be necessary to consult more than one entry before finding an appropriate French connector for a particular function of an English one in a certain context. As for the many tacit connectors of English speech and writing...

absolutely: assurément; bien évidemment; bien sûr; effectivement; en effet

a case in point: par exemple; voyez

accordingly: ainsi; de ce fait; de sorte que; donc

actually: à la vérité; après tout; au contraire; au demeurant; au fond; au vrai; à vrai dire; d'ailleurs; du reste; effectivement; en définitive; en fait; en vérité; même; or; précisément; somme toute

admittedly: assurément; à vrai dire; bien entendu; certes; fût-ce; il est vrai (que); sans doute

after all: après tout; finalement; somme toute; tant il est vrai que

again: à [son] tour; encore; et; puis

against that: au contraire; d'autre part; d'un autre côté; en contrepartie; en revanche; inversement; par contre

albeit: à vrai dire; fût-ce

all in all: à tout prendre; en fin de compte; tout compte fait

all right: en vérité

all that said: cela dit

all the same: n'empêche; quand même; toujours est-il que; tout de même

all things considered: à tout prendre; au final; au fond; au total; bref; en définitive; en fin de compte; en somme; finalement; somme toute; tout compte fait

also: ajoutons que; à [son] tour; au reste; aussi; aussi bien; au surplus; avec cela; d'ailleurs; d'autre part; de même; de plus; de [son] côté; de surcroît; du reste; également; encore faut-il (que); ensuite; par ailleurs; puis

alternatively: ou bien ... ou bien

although: alors que; si d'opposition; tandis que

altogether: au total; en fin de compte; tout compte fait

and: et; or; puis

and even then: encore; et ce

and so: de sorte que

and that: et ce

and then again: d'autre part; de plus; de surcroît; d'un autre côté; du reste; également; ensuite; puis

and this: et ce

and yet: cela dit; mais; or; pourtant

anyhow: au demeurant; d'ailleurs; de toute façon; de toute manière; en tout état de cause; puis; n'empêche; reste que; toujours est-il que

anyway: au demeurant; d'ailleurs; de toute façon; de toute manière; en tout état de cause; puis n'empêche; reste que; toujours est-il que;

apart from: sauf à

apart from that: à ceci près que; au-delà (de); pour le reste; si ce n'est (que)

as: car; parce que

as a matter of fact: à la vérité; aussi bien; au vrai; à vrai dire; en vérité

as a result: ainsi; de sorte que; donc; par conséquent

as far as he's/she's concerned: de [son] côté; pour [sa] part; pronom tonique disjoint; quant à [lui]; s'agissant de

as for: à [son] tour; de [son] côté; pour [sa] part; pronom tonique disjoint; quant à [lui]; s'agissant de

as is well known: tant il est vrai que

as it happens: au demeurant; d'ailleurs; en fait; en la circonstance; en l'espèce; en l'occurrence; finalement

as I was saying: donc

assuredly: assurément; bien entendu; bien évidemment; bien sûr; sans doute

as well (as that): ajoutons que; au-delà (de); au reste; d'ailleurs; d'autre part; de plus; du reste; encore faut-il (que); en plus; ensuite; et; et ce; mieux; par ailleurs; pis; puis

at all events: de toute façon; de toute manière; en tout état de cause

at any rate: de toute façon; du moins; en tout cas; en tout état de cause; mieux; plutôt

at best: tout juste

at least: du moins; en tout cas

at one and the same time: ce faisant; du même coup

at one fell swoop: du même coup

at that: et ce

at the end of the day: au bout du compte; au final; au total; en définitive; finalement

at the most: tout juste

at the risk of: quitte à

at the same time: alors que; du même coup; mais; pour autant

basically: au fond; en résumé; en somme

because: car; c'est que; parce que

because of this: de ce fait; donc; par conséquent

beside: au-delà (de)

besides: au-delà (de); aussi bien; d'ailleurs; du reste; en plus

be that as it may: de toute façon; de toute manière; en tout cas; en tout état de cause

better still: mieux

briefly: bref; en résumé; en un mot

but: encore faut-il (que); en revanche; mais; n'en... pas moins; n'empêche; or; par contre; pour autant; reste que; seulement

but that is not all: de plus; mieux

but then: au reste; d'autre part; du reste

but then again: d'autre part; d'un autre côté

by the same token: ce faisant; du coup; du même coup

by the way: au reste; d'ailleurs; du reste

certainly: assurément; bien entendu; bien sûr; en effet; en tout cas

clearly: assurément; bien entendu; bien évidemment; certes; force est de; tout se passe comme si

colon: antithèses sans charnière; à savoir (que); deux-points

come to think of it: après tout; au fait;

consequently: alors; donc; du coup; du même coup; par conséquent

consider: ainsi; voyez

conversely: à l'inverse; à l'opposé; en retour; inversement

correspondingly: à l'inverse; à l'opposé; de même; en retour; inversement

definitely: assurément

despite that: ce faisant; cela dit; n'empêche; pour autant; pour cela; reste que

despite the fact that: alors que; et ce; n'empêche; n'en... pas moins; si d'opposition

either ... or: ou bien... ou bien; soit... soit

equally: de même; également

especially (because): d'autant que; précisément

even: au point que; fût-ce; même; ne serait-ce que; voire

even if: fût-ce; quitte à

even just: ne serait-ce que

even so: ce faisant; cela dit; encore; malgré tout; n'empêche; n'en... pas moins; pour autant; pour cela; quand même; reste que; toujours est-il que; tout de même

even the slightest: ne serait-ce que

even though: alors que; fût-ce; ne serait-ce que; quitte à

eventually: au bout du compte; au final; en définitive; enfin; en fin de compte; finalement; tout compte fait

everything points to the conclusion that: tout se passe comme si

except for the fact that: à ceci près que; si ce n'est (que)

finally: au final; enfin; finalement; reste; reste à; sequences of points; tout compte fait

for: car; parce que

for all that: au demeurant; au reste; malgré tout; n'en... pas moins; pour autant; pour cela; quand même

for another thing: d'autre part; de plus; d'une part... d'autre part; en outre; ensuite; puis; sequences of points

for example: ainsi; c'est le cas de; par exemple; soit; voyez

for his/her part: de [son] côté; pour [sa] part; pronom tonique disjoint; quant à [lui]

for instance: ainsi; c'est le cas de; par exemple; voyez

for my part: de [son] côté; pour [sa] part; pronom tonique disjoint; quant à [lui]

for myself: de [son] côté; pour [sa] part; pronom tonique disjoint; quant à [lui]

for one thing: d'une part... d'autre part; sequences of points

for that matter: aussi bien; même; voire

for the rest: pour le reste

for this reason: de ce fait; pour autant; pour cela

frankly: pour tout dire

fundamentally: au fond

furthermore: au surplus; de plus; en outre; ensuite

given that: alors; cela étant; dès lors

granted: admettons; assurément; bien entendu; bien évidemment; bien sûr; certes; il est vrai (que); oui; sans doute; si l'on veut; soit

had it not been for: n'était

having said that: cela dit

hence: ainsi; de ce fait; de là; d'où; du coup

here: là

however: au contraire; ce faisant; cela dit; en revanche; mais; n'empêche; or; par contre; pour autant; pronom tonique disjoint; quant à [lui]; reste que; seulement

I agree entirely: assurément; bien évidemment; bien sûr

I daresay: admettons; oui; sans doute; si l'on veut

if (concessive): alors que; si d'opposition

if for no other reason: ne serait-ce que

if only because: fût-ce; ne serait-ce que

if only so as to: ne serait-ce que

if so: alors

if you like: sans doute; si l'on veut

I mean: après tout; c'est-à-dire (que); enfin

in actual fact: en fait; en réalité

in addition: ajoutons que; au-delà (de); au reste; aussi; avec cela; d'ailleurs; d'autre part; de plus; de surcroît; du reste; également; encore faut-il (que); en outre; en plus; ensuite; et; mieux; par ailleurs; pis; puis

in a few words: au total; bref; en résumé; en somme; en un mot

in another development: par ailleurs

in a nutshell: bref; en un mot; pour tout dire; somme toute

in any case: au demeurant; aussi bien; d'ailleurs; de toute façon; de toute manière; en tout cas; en tout état de cause

in any event: au final; de toute façon; de toute manière; en tout cas; en tout état de cause

in a word: au total; bref; en résumé; en somme; en un mot; pour tout dire; somme toute

in brief: bref; en somme; en un mot; pour tout dire

incidentally: au fait; d'ailleurs; du reste

in consequence: cela étant; du coup; par conséquent

indeed: au contraire; au point que; de fait; effectivement; en effet; en fait; en réalité; même; voire

in effect: c'est dire (que); en clair

in fact: au contraire; au point que; à vrai dire; bref; de fait; du reste; effectivement; en définitive; en effet; en fait; en réalité; en somme; en vérité; même; or; plutôt; pour tout dire; sinon; somme toute; voire

in his/her case: de [son] côté; pronom tonique disjoint; quant à [lui]; s'agissant de

in other words: autant dire (que); autrement dit; bref; c'est dire (que); en clair; en d'autres termes; en somme

in short: au total; bref; en résumé; en somme; en un mot; pour tout dire

in so doing: ce faisant; du même coup

instead: au contraire; bien; plutôt

in sum: au total; bref; en résumé; en somme; en un mot; tout compte fait

in that case: alors; cela étant; dès lors; du coup

in the case of: de [son] côté; pronom tonique disjoint; quant à [lui]; s'agis-sant de

in the end: au final; en définitive; enfin; en fin de compte; finalement; tout compte fait

in the event: au bout du compte; au final; en fait; en fin de compte; en réalité; finalement; tout compte fait

in the first place: d'une part... d'autre part; sequences of points

in the last analysis: à tout prendre; au final; au total; en définitive; en fin de compte; finalement; somme toute; tout compte fait

in these circumstances: cela étant; de ce fait; dès lors

in the second place: d'autre part; de plus; de surcroît; en outre; ensuite; mieux; pis; puis

in this case: en la circonstance; en l'espèce; en l'occurrence

in this instance: en la circonstance; en l'espèce; en l'occurrence

in this way: ainsi

into the bargain: au surplus; en plus

in truth: à la vérité; au vrai; à vrai dire; de fait; en fait; en réalité; en vérité

in view of this: cela étant; de ce fait; dès lors; par conséquent

in which case: alors; cela étant; dès lors; du coup

it goes without saying that: ajoutons que; bien entendu; bien évidemment; bien sûr

it is a fact that: assurément; certes; c'est un fait (que); de fait; il est vrai (que); oui; sans doute; tant il est vrai que

it is common knowledge that: tant il est vrai que

it is obvious: bien évidemment

it is true: admettons; assurément; certes; c'est un fait (que); il est vrai (que); oui; sans doute; tant il est vrai que

it is undeniable that: assurément; bien entendu; bien évidemment; bien sûr; certes; c'est un fait (que); il est vrai (que); oui; sans doute; tant il est vrai que

it must be said: à vrai dire; c'est un fait (que); de fait; il est vrai (que); il faut dire que; tant il est vrai que

it remains to: au final; encore faut-il (que); enfin; reste à

just as ... so: autant... autant; de même

lastly: au final; enfin; finalement; reste; reste à; sequences of points

let's face it: après tout; malgré tout; quand même

let us consider: soit

likewise: de même

looking beyond: au-delà (de)

meanwhile: ce faisant

mind you: cela dit

more importantly: au-delà (de); de plus

moreover: au reste; aussi bien; d'ailleurs; de plus; de surcroît; du reste; en outre; ensuite

more precisely: à vrai dire; au vrai; en fait; en réalité; mieux; plutôt; si l'on veut

namely: à savoir (que)

naturally: bien entendu; bien évidemment

needless to say: ajoutons que; brief interpolated main clause

nevertheless: mais; malgré tout; n'en... pas moins; quand même; toujours est-il que

no doubt: bien entendu; certes; sans doute

none the less: mais; n'en... pas moins; toujours est-il que

nor was this all: de plus

not only ... but also: aussi; au-delà (de); de plus; également; encore; en outre

not only that: ajoutons que; au surplus; avec cela; de plus; mieux; pis

not to mention: ajoutons que

not to put too fine a point on it: pour tout dire

not to say: mieux; plutôt; pour tout dire; sinon; voire

notwithstanding: n'en... pas moins; reste que

now: or

obviously: assurément; bien entendu; bien évidemment; bien sûr; certes; du reste; il est vrai (que); oui; sans doute; soit; tant il est vrai que

of course: admettons; assurément; au reste; bien entendu; bien évidemment; bien sûr; certes; d'ailleurs; du reste; il est vrai (que); oui; sans doute; soit; tant il est vrai que

on balance: à tout prendre; au final; au total; en fin de compte; en somme; finalement; tout compte fait

one could be forgiven for thinking that: tout se passe comme si

one could go so far as to say that: au point que

one might even say: au point que

one should add that: le fait est que

on second thoughts: après tout; au fait; mieux; plutôt

on the one hand ... on the other: d'un côté... de l'autre; d'une part... d'autre part

on the other hand: à l'inverse; à l'opposé; au contraire; d'autre part; de [son] côté; d'un autre côté; en contrepartie; en retour; en revanche; par contre; pour [sa] part; pronom tonique disjoint; quant à [lui]; reste que

on the question of: s'agissant de

on the whole: à tout prendre; au final; au total; en fin de compte; en somme; finalement; tout compte fait

or else: ou bien... ou bien; soit... soit

or even: même; voire

or rather: à la vérité; à vrai dire; mieux; plutôt; si l'on veut; voire

other than: sauf à

otherwise: pour le reste; sinon

overall: au total; tout compte fait

presumably: sans doute

rather: au contraire; plutôt

really: à la vérité; au fond; au vrai; à vrai dire; bien; décidément; en clair; en définitive; en fait; en réalité; en vérité; finalement; pour tout dire; quand même; somme toute; tout compte fait

right enough: en vérité

say: par exemple; voyez

secondly: d'autre part; de plus; en outre; ensuite; mieux; puis

short of: sauf à

similarly: de même

so: ainsi; alors; aussi; de sorte que; donc; du coup; du même coup; par conséquent; si bien que

so much for: voilà

so much so that: au point que; si bien que; tant il est vrai que

so true is it that: tant il est vrai que

still: cela dit; n'empêche; reste que

strictly speaking: au vrai; à vrai dire

suffice it to say that: bref; pour tout dire

sure enough: de fait; effectivement; en effet

surely: assurément; bien entendu; bien sûr

take: par exemple; soit; voyez

taking all things together: à tout prendre; au fond; au total; en fin de compte; finalement; somme toute; tout compte fait

taking one thing with another: à tout prendre; au fond; au total; en fin de compte; finalement; somme toute; tout compte fait

tantamount to: autant dire (que); c'est dire (que)

that apart: à ceci près que; pour le reste

that being the case: alors; cela étant; de ce fait; dès lors; du coup; par conséquent

that having been said: cela dit; cela étant

that is: à savoir (que); autrement dit; c'est-à-dire (que); c'est dire (que); deux-points; en clair; en d'autres termes

that is to say: à savoir (que); autant dire (que); autrement dit; c'est-à-dire (que); c'est dire (que); deux-points; en clair; en d'autres termes

that is why: c'est pourquoi

that said: cela dit

the conclusion is inescapable that: force est de

the difference is that: à ceci près que

the fact is: c'est que; c'est un fait (que); de fait; il faut dire que; le fait est que; reste que

the fact is, though: il faut dire que; n'empêche; reste que

the fact remains that: n'empêche; n'en... pas moins; reste que; toujours est-il que;

the idea that: deux points; l'idée que

then: ainsi; alors; dès lors; donc; par conséquent

then again: d'un autre côté

the point is: c'est que; le fait est que

the reason is: c'est pourquoi

thereby: ce faisant; de ce fait; dès lors; du coup; du même coup; là

there can be no doubt that: de fait; en effet; en fait

therefore: ainsi; alors; aussi; de sorte que; donc; du coup; du même coup; par conséquent; si bien que

there remains: reste; reste à

there's no doubt about it: décidément

the trouble is, though: mais; seulement

the very thing: précisément

this may mean: quitte à

this means: autant dire (que); autrement dit; c'est-à-dire (que); c'est dire (que); en clair; en d'autres termes

though: aussi bien

three dots: points de suspension

thus: ainsi; aussi; donc

to be blunt: pour tout dire

to be precise: à la vérité; à savoir (que); au vrai; en la circonstance; en l'espèce; en l'occurrence; mieux; plutôt; pour tout dire; si l'on veut

to be sure: bien sûr; bien entendu; bien évidemment; certes; il est vrai (que); sans doute

to cap it all: avec cela

too: aussi; également; encore

to put a finer point upon it: pour tout dire

to such an extent is this true that: tant il est vrai que

to sum up: bref; en résumé; en un mot

to tell the truth: à la vérité; au vrai; à vrai dire; en fait; en réalité; en vérité

to that can be added: ajoutons que

to that end: pour ce faire; pour cela

true: admettons; assurément; bien entendu; bien évidemment; bien sûr; certes; il est vrai (que); oui; sans doute

ultimately: au final; enfin; finalement; tout compte fait

undoubtedly: assurément; bien entendu; bien évidemment; bien sûr; certes; il est vrai (que); oui; sans doute

unfortunately: seulement

unless: sauf à

well: or

were it not for: n'était

whatever the case may be: de toute façon; de toute manière; en tout cas; en tout état de cause; toujours est-il que

what's more: d'autre part; de plus; en plus; même

when all's said and done: au bout du compte; au final; au fond; au total; bref; en définitive; finalement; somme toute; tout compte fait

whereas: alors que; autant... autant; en revanche; là; or; si d'opposition; tandis que

which: ce qui

which is why: c'est pourquoi

which means that: aussi; c'est dire (que); de là; d'où; si bien que

while: alors que; là; si d'opposition; tandis que

with: avec; de [son] côté; en effet

with the difference that: à ceci près que; si ce n'est (que); sinon

with the exception that: à ceci près que; si ce n'est (que); sinon

with the proviso that: quitte à

with the result that: de là; de sorte que; d'où; si bien que

witness: par exemple; voyez

yet: malgré tout; or; pour autant; quand même; tout de même

you might even say: au point que

Explanatory notes

1   All entries are in simple alphabetical sequence, letter by letter. Thus *décidément* will be found between *de ce fait* and *de fait*; *d'autant que* will be found not under *autant* but under *d'*, *le fait est que* not under *fait* but under *le*, *n'en... pas moins* not under *moins* but under *n'*, *s'agissant* not under *agir* but under *s'*, and so on. A group of structures based on *plus* is to be found at *de plus*.

2   Within the alphabetical list, all headwords of entries are in French, except for 'brief interpolated main clause' and 'sequences of points'.

3   All headwords are the structures themselves, except for a few, which are names of categories of structures, such as: *antithèses sans charnières*, *inversion du verbe*, *transitions mécaniques*.

4   Within entries, first references to other entries are ***italicized in bold***.

5   An asterisk placed beside a headword (e.g. *en effet* *) means that the connector so marked is also mentioned or discussed in the chapter 'Some common functions'.

6   The End-list contains structures mentioned or discussed in the dictionary but not given as separate entries.

7   Quotations which are sourced are given in the form (Truc, 146), which means page 146 in the book by Truc to be found in the list of sources. If the list of sources contains two or more books by Truc, the reference includes a date, as (Truc, 1988: 146)

Dictionary

à ceci près que *

This structure usually functions as an inter-assertional connector, being most often placed first in a **phrase dépendante** – in probably fewer than 20 per cent of cases is it found inside the sentence, after a comma. Whether linking two sentences or two parts of a single sentence, it always introduces a statement which slightly restricts the scope of a main clause. The most common variant is *à cela près que*.

The connector functions in the semantic field of *à peu près* and other expressions in which the combination *à... près* marks a difference, a shortfall, an exception. It could often be replaced by *sauf que*. It introduces a minor objection, a shade of difference; it puts a finer point upon something. Quite often this finer point is put upon a comparison of two things which are seen first as like then as less like. An author discussing certain French critics, having identified a particular defect in Sainte-Beuve, goes on to make a similar point about Thibaudet, which he then modifies: *Il y a chez Thibaudet un défaut du même genre, à ceci près qu'il a moins de méchanceté et plus d'ingéniosité verbale que Sainte-Beuve.* An article about a Paris street sees it first as similar to others, then defines a dissimilarity: *Une petite rue semblable à des milliers d'autres petites rues. À ceci près qu'elle possède une histoire.* What precedes often contains words like *même chose, comparer* or *comme*: *Une équipe organisée comme un véritable Samu. À ceci près qu'il n'y a pas de gyrophares.* / *Breiner a composé quelque chose comme des* Brandebourgeois *modernes. A ceci près que leurs thèmes sont des chansons des Beatles.*

à cela près que

Dictionaries continue to give *à cela près* as the paradigmatic form, which may have been the case in real usage at some past period. But *à ceci près* predominates nowadays. This evolution, if that is what it is, consists with the rule said to be observed in the usage of the *démonstratifs lointain et prochain*:

> Les formes en *-ci* annoncent ce qui suit (fonction *cataphorique*), et les formes en *-là* rappellent ce qui précède (fonction *anaphorique*).
>
> (Grevisse, 1988: 1059)

But it puts this structure at variance with two others containing *cela*, **cela dit** and **cela étant**: in both of them, spoken usage seems to favour the form with *ceci* and written usage the form with *cela*.

Variants

The demonstrative pronoun may be replaced by a noun expressing the idea of a minor restriction or disparity such as *nuance, particularité* or *exception* plus a definite article or a demonstrative adjective: *à ce détail près que, à la différence près que, à cette parenthèse près que*. An essay on the Socialist governments of the 1980s says they exercised power *de la même façon que leurs prédécesseurs, au style près* (Duverger, 10). A discussion of the proposal to route the new A89 motorway down the valley of the Isle makes two points, one of them that people living in the Gironde favour the idea, the other that people living in the neighbouring *départements* do not:

> Ce tracé présenterait le triple avantage de délester du trafic poids lourds la RN 89 saturée, d'irriguer la vallée de l'Isle, pôle économique en péril, et de ne point empiéter sur le vignoble. Solution quasi idéale aux yeux des Girondins. À cette nuance près cependant qu'elle élude un aspect du dossier cher aux Périgourdins voisins.

A concession–objection type of link is made evident between the two points, underlined in this instance by *cependant*. In this function, *toutefois* is also common. In such contexts, where the connector functions as a more pointed form of **mais**, it could sometimes be replaced by **seulement**. And when what precedes is a negative structure in the same sentence, it is at times replaceable by **si ce n'est (que)**.

Other variants are constructed with **avec**, either in the form *avec ceci que* or with nouns: *Avec cette différence, toutefois, que...*; *Avec des nuances d'un pays à l'autre...*; *Avec cette particularité que...*; *Avec cette restriction que....*

Main clause following

Almost always the main clause precedes the restriction and the connector functions anaphorically. Occasionally that order is inverted and the connector, first in the sentence, restricts what follows, as in this extract from an essay on the survival into our own day of certain discriminatory attitudes towards women common in the nineteenth century:

Quel âge avez-vous ? Dix-huit ans ? Vous avez donc encore cinq ou six ans pour être aimée, huit ou dix pour aimer vous-même, et le reste pour prier Dieu, dit Musset à la capricieuse Marianne.

À cela près que les étapes, de nos jours, sont un peu plus longues, les choses n'ont peut-être pas tellement changé.

(Giroud, 386)

English has no neat equivalent for this connector. Its function would be served by 'except that' or 'with the difference that' – except that neither of these would commonly be placed at the beginning of a sentence as a complement to a main clause in the sentence before. However, they could restrict a main clause following them in the same sentence, as in the last example.

admettons *

This is one of the less frequently used concessives, a set of which *certes* may be seen as the model. Like others, such as *bien sûr*, *oui* or *soit*, it is adapted from a word which has as its primary function to affirm, to agree, to certify. Also like them, in conceding agreement with a preceding proposition, it can foreshadow a counter-argument, frequently introduced by *mais*, which will have the effect of overruling the concession. More sceptical in tone than most of the others, this one expresses less agreement with what precedes than they do. It merely entertains a hypothesis and is closer to *peut-être* or *si l'on veut*. It accepts a point provisionally, while hinting doubt about it – after all, the verb *admettre que* is sometimes followed by a subjunctive. An example comes from a discussion of the principle of whether public funds should be spent on church schools:

Selon Mgr Ducourtray, archevêque de Lyon : « L'enseignement catholique est un service public, il est normal qu'il y ait des fonds publics pour ce service public. » Admettons. Mais que penser alors des directives de l'épiscopat aux responsables de l'enseignement catholique selon lesquelles, « dans la perspective d'une nouvelle évangélisation », la mission des écoles chrétiennes consiste à apprendre aux enfants « à vivre en fils de Dieu » ? Est-ce bien là la mission d'un service public ? Les fonds publics doivent-ils être affectés à ce genre d'activité ?

That example is typical of two features of the usage of this connector: it usually stands as a sentence in itself; and what follows it, the objection to the concession, is often framed as a question. Sometimes it is also preceded by a question. All three of these features can be seen in the following example, taken from an article discussing the relativity of human measures of time:

L'an 1994 aura commencé samedi à zéro heure, qui en douterait ? Et pourtant, cette évidence est pour le moins trompeuse. C'est ainsi que, décalage

horaire aidant, les Australiens de Sydney fêtent la Saint-Sylvestre avec neuf
heures d'avance sur nous et les Américains de Los Angeles avec neuf heures
de retard. Un détail ? Admettons. Mais que dire, alors, des musulmans prati-
quants qui, eux, se considèrent à la mi-1414, et célébreront leur « nouvel an »
(l'hégire) le 10 juin ? Quant aux juifs, leur année 5754 a débuté le 16 septembre.

Variants

An occasional variant for this concessive is *accordons-le*. In the following
example, taken from a discussion of the need to protect Salman Rushdie
against the threat of murder by Islamists, the writer first accepts the standard view, then defines a dissatisfaction with it:

> L'Occident doit montrer qu'il n'est prêt à céder ni sur le droit ni sur les principes
> fondateurs de ses démocraties, et tout le reste, pourrait-on dire, est littérature.
> Une telle position, accordons-le, ne manque pas de cohérence [...].
> Et pourtant cette argumentation, pour nécessaire qu'elle soit, n'en est pas
> pour autant, me semble-t-il, suffisante.
>
> (Scarpetta, 2)

A different mode, with *que*, can introduce an objection which is not
cancelled out by anything following. In this example, the writer combines
it with *néanmoins* to sum up a review of two dictionaries, the *Grand
Larousse* and the *Trésor de la langue française*, which he finds valuable –
but less valuable than they might be because they draw on sources which
are too literary:

> Il reste que, tels quels, ces répertoires sont des instruments de travail indis-
> pensables. Ne nous plaignons donc pas que la mariée soit *trop* belle. Admettons
> néanmoins qu'en sacrifiant à l'excès à la beauté ces ouvrages perdent un peu
> d'efficacité.
>
> (Wagner, 134)

However, the objection introduced by this mode can also be cancelled,
by a following *mais*, say, as in this extract from Camus's discussion of
whether the death penalty is a punishment commensurate with the crime
of murder:

> Admettons qu'il soit juste et nécessaire de compenser le meurtre de la victime
> par la mort du meurtrier. Mais l'exécution capitale n'est pas simplement la
> mort. Elle est aussi différente, en son essence, de la privation de vie, que le
> camp de concentration l'est de la prison.
>
> (Camus, 1965:1039)

In English, 'admittedly', 'granted', 'true', 'to be sure' or 'of course' could
sometimes serve as equivalents. In some contexts, 'that's as maybe' or 'all
right, for the sake of argument' would be preferable.

ainsi *

Aspects of this connector may be slightly problematical for some speakers of English. Basically a demonstrator of the validity of a point, it has two main functions: while confirming what precedes, it introduces an explanation or an example of it. It can be difficult, possibly pointless, to say which of these functions is being served by a particular exemplar. It may serve both.

Explanatory

In the following extract from a history of violent death, the connector could be replaced by *en effet*, or possibly even by *car*:

> Jusqu'à l'avènement de l'ère automobile, les chevaux et les véhicules hippomobiles présentent un danger surprenant. Ainsi, en France, durant la période 1861–1865, cinq mille quatre cent cinquante-neuf hommes et six cent femmes (soit deux fois plus que de victimes d'homicides) auraient été tués de leur seul fait.

> (Chesnais, 316)

This basically explanatory function can be seen too in the following extract from an article on legislation protecting the copyright of creative artists:

> La législation qui protège financièrement le créateur et ses ayants droit limite la diffusion de l'œuvre au « cercle de famille ». Ainsi, un professeur qui utilise l'enregistrement d'une émission de télévision dans sa salle de classe est dans l'illégalité.

There the connector would be replaceable by *par conséquent* or one of its variants.

The explanatory function is at times explicit in the words used, as in the common sequence *Ainsi s'explique* plus a noun or *Ainsi s'explique que* plus a verb. And either the explanatory or the exemplifying function can be denoted by *C'est ainsi que*.

Exemplifying

The exemplifying mode is clearly seen in *C'est ainsi par exemple que....* In this mode, what precedes often contains a general rule or a plural; and what follows is an instance:

> Dans la vallée du Rhône, le mistral a soufflé à plus de 90 km/h, entraînant l'annulation de plusieurs spectacles sous chapiteaux prévus hier, pour des raisons de sécurité. Ainsi, à Gordes, le festival des Pastorales a dû être reporté.

Sometimes the connector could be exactly replaced by *par exemple*, as in this extract from a discussion of vestiges of Arab occupation of the south of France during the early Middle Ages, especially in Quercy and Provence:

> Quelques villages gardent la trace de cette présence musulmane dans ces provinces : ainsi Ramatuelle en Provence dont le nom est la transcription de l'arabe *Rahmat-Allah.*
>
> (Lamand, 22)

Followed or not by inversion

The connector is often placed first in the sentence. Some writers follow it with a comma, others do not. It is sometimes, though not as often as some grammarians would have us believe, followed by an inversion of subject and verb. In the explanatory mode, it may attract an inversion more often than in the exemplifying one. This sequence of repeated explanatory inversions comes from a consideration of the judgment handed down in the trial of two doctors, Garretta and Alain, found guilty of having presided over the distribution of AIDS-contaminated blood:

> Le jugement du tribunal présidé par M. Jean-Louis Mazières répond de manière simple à quelques-unes des questions généralement soulevées.
>   Ainsi explique-t-il ce qu'il faut penser de « l'état de la science » concernant le sida en 1985. Ainsi situe-t-il l'exact niveau de responsabilité auquel se trouvaient les docteurs Michel Garretta et Jean-Pierre Alain, tous deux dirigeants du Centre national de la transfusion sanguine (CNTS). Ainsi évalue-t-il aussi l'ampleur de la « tromperie sur les qualités substantielles d'un produit » reprochée aux dirigeants du CNTS.

Sometimes the question of whether to invert does not arise, as the verb is omitted. This mode being clearly the exemplifying one, *ainsi* could be replaced by *témoin* or one of the other variants of *par exemple*:

> Parmi les prix littéraires qui fleurissent dans l'Hexagone, un petit nombre récompensent exclusivement des textes écrits dans des langues régionales, principalement le breton et l'occitan. Certains concours concernent cependant des aires linguistiques encore plus réduites. Ainsi, le concours de textes en langue morvandelle (les lauréats gagnent des jambons, ainsi que le droit d'être publiés dans *l'Almanach du Morvan*).

Variants

Among structures sometimes used as variants are *de cette façon* and *de la sorte.* In the following example, a writer speaks of Mallarmé's denial of the reality of the real world:

> Mallarmé se paye le luxe d'échapper au réel et de remplacer ce qui est par ce qui n'est pas. De la sorte, au lieu d'être l'esclave docile de la vérité matérielle qui partout s'affirme, il peut se constituer comme le libre monarque de sa propre pensée.

To introduce a conclusion, *Ainsi donc* is still used.

English equivalents include 'for example' and 'for instance', as well as 'in this way', 'so', 'therefore' and 'thus'.

ajoutons que

Like other injunctions to the reader (*Disons, Prenons le cas de, Qu'on nous permette de*), this connector can be seen as one of the overtly procedural gambits which I call *transitions mécaniques*. However, in virtue of its versatility and the frequency of its use, it also justifies an entry to itself.

Replacing *de plus*

Like the other injunctions, this one can serve to shape large tracts of text and to guide the reader through them, it can announce whole developments, it can be one in a sequence of similar verbs. But it can also serve a more punctual function, as in the following example in which a social scientist speaks about possible future developments in French family relationships:

> La quasi-totalité des naissances seront désormais voulues et comme programmées par le couple. Il ne faut donc plus tabler sur des naissances accidentelles. Par contre, comme cette élimination est déjà très avancée, la baisse brutale survenue au moment de la diffusion de la pilule est pratiquement terminée. Désormais le facteur principal de l'évolution réside dans le désir des parents. Ajoutons que probablement les méthodes contraceptives seront d'un emploi de plus en plus aisé et que l'état de stérilité artificielle permanent continuera à être perçu comme une situation normale pour le couple.
>
> (Roussel, 259)

There, the structure has little if any function as injunction to reader. It is closer to being a simple variant for *en outre* or *de plus*. This is a role which it often plays: it merely warns the reader to expect a further or last argument going in the same direction as the ones immediately preceding. Depending on what structure that preceding argument has, this connector is also to be found in the variants *ajoutons-y que* and *ajoutons* followed by a noun. This example comes from an essay on spoken French:

> La société la plus éloignée de Paris parle à peu près comme à Paris dès qu'elle se surveille, prêtres avec leurs paroissiens, instituteurs avec leurs élèves, fonctionnaires avec le public, ajoutons : esbroufeurs avec esbroufés.

In sequences of points

The connector may be used near the end of a development in the form *Ajoutons pour finir que...* It sometimes replaces *enfin* in the standard tripartite **sequence of points**: *D'abord... Ensuite... Enfin.* Or it can round off and reinforce a longer list of similar points. Much of this applies too to the different modes of the related expression *Si l'on ajoute à cela* or *Si l'on ajoute à tout cela*, as in this catalogue of ills facing France and the world in 1993:

> Effritement des idéologies et des projets globaux, balkanisation des nations resurgies, lutte des classes muée en compétition des corporations, rebond de l'égoïsme américain, dépression des campagnes où l'homme se fait rare et stress des villes mal bâties où certaines banlieues sont des additions de solitudes, de pauvretés et, parfois, de peurs. Si l'on ajoute à ce sombre tableau la hantise du sida, les emballements du système médiatique, la révélation des « affaires » où certains politiques ont perdu leur âme, on ne saurait dire que la France de 1993 se porte nettement mieux que celle de 1983.

Other variants

The same goes in large measure for the numerous other variants of the basic structure such as *Ajoutons à cela que, À quoi il faut ajouter, À quoi j'ajoute, Ajoutez que, J'ajoute enfin que, J'ajouterais volontiers que, Il faut ajouter que, Nous ajouterons, On y ajoutera, Qu'on nous permette d'ajouter* and the rhetorical interrogative form *Faut-il ajouter que,* usually printed without a question mark.

The related pronominal verb *s'ajouter* is also used, in a way which makes it an example of **inversion du verbe**, either in the forms *À cela s'ajoute* or *À quoi s'ajoute* or in the form *S'y ajoute le fait que.* These can, of course, also be found in the plural forms *À quoi s'ajoutent* and *S'y ajoutent.*

Occasionally *ajouter* is replaced by *joindre*: *À quoi il convient de joindre; Joignez à cela.* Other expressions that sometimes see service as variants are *Inutile d'ajouter que, Inutile de dire que, Est-il besoin de dire que, Et que dire de, N'oublions pas, Pour ne rien dire de, Sans oublier, Sans compter que* and *Sans parler de.* It is usual for all these structures, whether formed from *ajouter* or not, to be placed first in the sentence. With some of them, that sentence is a **phrase dépendante**.

Among possible English equivalents for this connector would be 'as well as that', 'in addition', 'not only that, but also', 'to that can be added' or 'not to mention'.

à la vérité

Unlike **en vérité**, which tends to be adversative, this connector usually introduces a precision or restrictive clarification of what precedes, appended sometimes in a supplementary way.

The structure often restricts and clarifies explicitly, by accompanying a reminder of some of the words already used in the preceding statement. And it is these words which are made more precise. In the following example, the *satisfaction* mentioned is occasioned by an attempt by the European Community to resolve the war in Bosnia-Herzegovina:

> Paris et Bonn ont eu la satisfaction de voir un projet de règlement élaboré par leurs ministres des affaires étrangères respectifs, Alain Juppé et Klaus Kinkel, entériné par l'unanimité des Douze.
>
> Satisfaction bien mince, à la vérité, puisque, malgré une première réaction plutôt positive des trois présidents serbe, croate et bosniaque, l'espoir est vite retombé.

In such contexts, the connector could be replaced by *à vrai dire*. In the next example, it comes just as close to *ou plutôt* or to a mode of *mieux*: it precises what precedes by rectifying it, by replacing it with what follows, as in this comment on France's place in the world after the resignation and death of President de Gaulle:

> Depuis la disparition du Général, la France se vendait mal. À la vérité, elle ne se vendait plus du tout, et l'on se demandait si elle se revendrait de nouveau.
>
> (Dutourd, 1985: 86)

In other contexts, it is closer to *il faut dire que*, as in the following extract from a reminiscence of the *événements* of May 1968 and the new relationships based on *participation* formed between teachers and students at the Censier premises of the University of Paris:

> Il se noua là et pour quelque temps des rapports excellents, comparables à ceux de partenaires de bonne foi dont le premier et le principal souci est d'apprendre à se connaître, de s'informer mutuellement sur leurs positions concernant des problèmes qui leur sont communs et d'amorcer ainsi une politique de « participation ». À la vérité ce mot ne circulait pas encore dans les débats de Censier. Il fut lancé un peu plus tard par le pouvoir et dès ce moment d'ailleurs il fut assez mal reçu par les étudiants et par ceux des enseignants qui rejetaient l'idée d'une réforme *imposée* par le ministère.
>
> (Wagner, 164)

There, as in many other contexts, an English equivalent for this structure could be 'to tell the truth' or 'to be precise'. It is also one of the diverse French equivalents of 'actually'.

à l'inverse *

The single function of this structure is to introduce a statement which stands in direct opposition to the one preceding it. It is one of a set of connectors, which also contains *à l'opposé*, of which the paradigm can be said to be *au contraire*. In some contexts, it functions differently from the paradigm; but in certain other contexts, it is replaceable by the more contrastive mode of *au contraire*. That is to say, it could often be replaced by *en revanche* or *par contre*, as in this extract from a discussion of different attitudes to nakedness, both in art and in life, at different periods:

> La Renaissance, le XIX⁽ᵉ⁾ siècle, s'ouvrent à la nudité artistique en enfermant la vie quotidienne dans une pudibonderie plus stricte. À l'inverse, le Moyen Âge, le XVIII⁽ᵉ⁾ siècle, s'ils font « des tableaux voiler les nudités », ont plus de goût pour « les réalités ».
>
> (Bologne, 10)

Dual contrasts

Beloved of economists and writers of financial reports, and often found in technical contexts which bristle with statistics, this connector is often used to structure contrasts which are, if not exact and quantifiable, at least very concrete. Such contrasts often oppose more than a single element on each side. A dual comparison between the working conditions of *employés* and *ouvriers* speaks of how each of them are treated with regard to absences from work and flexibility of working-hours:

> La répression de l'absentéisme est bien plus rigoureuse à l'usine. Dans 24 p. 100 des cas, l'absence donne lieu à retenue sur le salaire, contre 5 p. 100 des cas seulement pour l'employé. À l'inverse, 7 p. 100 des employés jouissent d'horaires à la carte, contre 1 p. 100 seulement des ouvriers.
>
> (Closets, 1983: 393)

An English equivalent could often be 'on the other hand' or even 'conversely', particularly when the contrast is more than a single one:

> La France consacre 1,92 % de son PIB aux allocations, l'Allemagne 1,16 % et la Suède 0,67 %. À l'inverse l'Hexagone ne dépense « que » 0,73 % de son PIB dans les actions dynamiques de réinsertion, contre 1,02 % pour l'Allemagne et 1,58 % pour la Suède.

However, conversely, many writers use the basic *au contraire* to structure antitheses which are just as complex:

> En 1924, lorsque Lénine meurt, Trotsky est d'avis de mettre fin à la NEP et de reprendre la révolution mondiale. Staline, au contraire, veut prolonger la NEP et consolider le socialisme en URSS.

Inverse symmetries

In some contexts, this connector is used to mark not duality or complexity of contrast but a degree of inverted symmetry. In this example, a writer makes a contrast between Christian names and surnames:

Les enfants de personnages célèbres ont généralement des difficultés à se faire un prénom. À l'inverse, M. Olivier Lapidus, le fils du couturier Ted, a dû, lui, batailler pendant des années pour utiliser son patronyme.

In the following example, dealing with risks of cancer, the connector underscores the fact that different scientists have shown a similar thing in two different groups going in opposite directions:

Les chercheurs australiens ont démontré que les immigrants arrivés après l'âge de 15 ans en Australie ont moins de grains de beauté que les personnes nées sur place. Ils ont aussi un risque diminué de mélanome. À l'inverse, des chercheurs écossais viennent d'observer que des adolescents venus d'Australie en Grande-Bretagne après l'âge de 15 ans ont un risque de mélanome aussi élevé que ceux restés dans leur pays d'origine.

Variants

Like *au contraire*, this connector can be reinforced by the addition of *tout*, as in the following extract from a discussion of abstract painters such as Marc and Kandinsky: *Leur abstraction n'est pas refus de la nature, mais, tout à l'inverse, communication plus étroite avec elle.*

A frequent variant is ***inversement***. An infrequent one is *en sens inverse*, which some writers may think has a more concrete feel. This example is from an article contrasting attitudes to the continuation of testing of nuclear bombs in the circumstances of the early 1990s:

Le contexte international devient de plus en plus défavorable à la poursuite des tirs où que ce soit et par qui que ce soit. En sens inverse, la menace d'une prolifération « sauvage », les ambitions nucléaires de la Corée du Nord, de l'Iran et d'autres pays encouragent dans de nombreux pays les partisans d'une dissuasion minimale, mais maintenue en état de marche pour un avenir indéterminé.

à l'opposé *

Like *inversement* and *à l'inverse*, this is a variant for *au contraire*, albeit less common than any of those other three contrastives. Like them, it underlines binary oppositions, especially those which show a marked or direct antithesis or which compare two extremes. English equivalents could often be 'on the other hand' or 'conversely'.

Strong antitheses

The opposition may be reinforced by the fact that the structure is almost always placed first in the sentence or paragraph. In the first example, an author discussing the great range of modest and immodest behaviour to be found in historical personages, speaks first of the renowned *pudicité* of the Emperor Maximilian and Isabella of Castille, then goes on to say:

> Et que dire d'Anne d'Autriche, qui fit détruire pour plus de cent mille francs de tableaux « indécents » ; de Louis XIII, qui barbouillait les fresques de sa chambre ; de Mazarin, qui mutilait les statues ?
>
> À l'opposé, que dire de la baronne de Montreuil-Bellay, qui demandait à un de ses vassaux, quand elle se rendait chez lui, de la porter sur ses épaules là où lui-même allait à pied et de lui tendre la mousse qui tenait lieu de papier ?
>
> (Bologne, 9)

Sometimes there is a marked inverse symmetry in the two elements contrasted, as in this extract from a debate on whether or not Europe should set limits on the importing of American television programmes, a debate which, says the author, has *longuement opposé deux stratégies antagonistes*:

> Dans une optique ultralibérale, la Grande-Bretagne, le Luxembourg, appuyés par nombre de chaînes commerciales, voulaient démanteler les systèmes de quotas nationaux pour faciliter le lancement de nouvelles télévisions européennes largement approvisionnées par des programmes américains. À l'opposé, la France et l'ensemble des organisations de créateurs rêvaient d'imposer des quotas européens pour susciter automatiquement une demande accrue de production à l'intérieur de la Communauté.

Less strong contrasts

Despite one of the dictionary definitions of *opposé* as *totalement différent* (*Trésor de la langue française*), the connector often structures simple comparisons in which there is no extreme oppositiveness. It is then just a substitute for ***en revanche*** or ***par contre***, as in this contrast between the interest to be found in the letters of Stendhal and those of Taine:

> Stendhal intéresse pour lui-même, en train de s'examiner dans ses lettres. À l'opposé, celles de Taine sont d'un intérêt considérable pour le cheminement et la critique des idées chez un philosophe.

Sometimes, too, the structure functions as little more than a substitute for *au contraire*, to avoid repetition. The following example contains both of these connectors, in consecutive sentences, where they could probably be interchanged. The extract comes from an article about a new surgical technique to combat deafness:

> Le chirurgien estime que, dans la moitié des cas, les résultats sont très bons, que 25 % des malades ont des résultats moyens et sont contraints de s'aider en lisant sur les lèvres de leurs interlocuteurs. Dans un quart des cas, au contraire, les résultats sont franchement mauvais. À l'opposé, un quart des opérés arrivent à suivre une conversation téléphonique, ce qui signifie un vrai succès.

Variants

Much like *tout au contraire*, the connector is sometimes reinforced by *tout*, to signal the importance of a contrast, as in this extract from a discussion of Jean-Paul Sartre urinating on the grave of Chateaubriand:

> À part Claudel, dont quelques tarés sont allés, il y a quelques années, déranger les ossements, ce genre de délassement n'est heureusement pas devenu l'habitude.
>
> Tout à l'opposé, nous sommes respectueux des écrivains du passé, nous les commémorons volontiers, d'autant plus que nous avons trouvé le moyen de nous débarrasser de les lire.

And occasionally a possessive mode, *à son opposé*, is used, as in this comparison between two women novelists, in which it is particularly their differing attitudes to the past which are set in contrast with each other:

> Mme Sallenave se passionne pour l'humanité, pas pour des individus. Elle préfère le corpus au corps. Elle écrit tout au présent, comme par haine du passé, et de sa nostalgie. Mme Sallenave est très intelligente, très pessimiste, mais elle n'est pas romancière.
>
> À son opposé, Mlle Chérer ne déteste pas la tradition, ni les souvenirs, ni les modèles classiques.

alors *

In spoken French, this can be one of those ubiquitous and versatile markers of conversation like *Eh ben* or 'Well, actually', so common and multifarious in their applications as to be minimal in meaning. In written French, where it is used less often, and with greater precision, than in the spoken language, it can retain something of its conversational familiarity of tone.

Temporal *alors*

Like *dès lors* and *or*, this connector is formed from a word which has temporal functions. And it is from one of these that its main reasoning function – to introduce a logical consequence – derives. That temporal function is the one which helps structure a narrative in a way similar to temporal *ensuite* or *puis*. This derivation is analogous to what one finds in English with one of the most direct equivalents of *alors*, 'then' in the sense of 'next'. The temporal shade can be inseparable from the functioning of the connector, especially when the verb which *alors* accompanies is in the future or the conditional. This is seen in an extract from an article urging the French government to commemorate the *déportés* of 1940–44 not just by words but by coming to the aid of a political prisoner who, having once been decorated as a member of the French Resistance, is now being tortured in Brazil:

> La France fera-t-elle un geste, un effort pour l'arracher au supplice ? Alors on pourrait parler d'hommage aux déportés qui, en leur temps, subirent semblables outrages.

> (Giroud, 434)

English 'then', expressing this link, would mean 'at that hypothetical time' as much as 'in that hypothetical case'.

Initial *alors*

When *alors* is first in the sentence, its temporal function, though possibly present, may be less important than its function of making a link of reasoning. In this example, part of a lament for the fact that the intellectual elite of a former generation has now been replaced by a different breed of 'communicators', there is of course a chronological aspect to the contrast between the two groups of people. But more important to the author is the point of view which the connector puts upon an argument about the moral consequence:

> On ne distingue plus ces élites constituées qui encadraient la société grâce à leur savoir, leur pouvoir et leur communauté de vues. Elles ont été déstructurées comme toutes les autres couches sociales par l'explosion de notre société et par la fragmentation vertigineuse du savoir. Le temps des généralistes est bien terminé. Alors il reste des « vedettes », créées par les médias, et en particulier la télévision.

When introducing a logical consequence, when its English equivalent could be 'so', this mode can retain some of the expressive force it has as a spoken connector to make a combative affirmative statement. In the following example, the writer combats the view that the nation's present ill humour has simple economic causes:

> De grâce, n'exagérons pas : la France est devenue aujourd'hui l'un des pays les plus riches de la planète. Le franc est fort et l'inflation contenue. Elle a, c'est vrai, trois millions de chômeurs, mais cette gangrène n'épargne pas nos voisins. Alors, pitié, pas d'amalgame abusif : le mal-être des Français, leur ras-le-bol général, résulte moins d'éléments strictement économiques que de la morosité délétère qui accompagne toutes les fins de règne.

Initial *alors* can introduce a consequence of a hypothesis postulated in the previous sentence, in which case it is sometimes replaced by *Auquel cas* or *Dans ce cas*. Possible English equivalents for certain modes of initial *alors* would be 'Well' and 'In that case': *Ils ne savent donc pas ce qu'ils font ? Alors, il faut le leur dire.* In that statement, the connector could of course be placed at the end: *Il faut le leur dire, alors*. It would have a spoken tone, like English 'then' at the end of a statement instead of 'Well' at the beginning.

Interrogative *alors*

The initial mode can also introduce interrogative statements. It can question what might appear to be a consequence of a preceding proposition, as in this extract from a discussion of René Bousquet, a high police official under Vichy, who had Jews sent to Nazi death-camps:

> « Bousquet n'était absolument pas antisémite », confirme Me Serge Klarsfeld. Alors, pourquoi a-t-il pu organiser, sans haine ni idéologie mais avec tant de méticulosité, la rafle des enfants juifs, allant même au-delà des exigences de l'occupant ?

This interrogative mode sometimes combines with ***mais***, either giving more point to a consequential objection or introducing a question, as in Monsieur Martin's celebrated line in Scene IV of *La cantatrice chauve*:

> Mais alors, mais alors, mais alors, mais alors, mais alors, nous nous sommes peut-être vus dans cette maison, chère Madame ?
>
> (Ionesco, 29)

The four interrogative combinations of *alors* which are most common in discussion are: *Alors, faut-il* (sometimes in the variant form *Fallait-il alors* or *Faut-il alors*); *Mais alors*; *Alors pourquoi*; and *Que faire alors ?* Quite common, too, among journalists is the use of this connector not to begin a question but to constitute of itself a whole question about the consequences of what precedes. It is then sometimes followed immediately by an answer which begins with the same word: *Alors ? Alors, il va falloir....*

Non-initial *alors*

When placed later in the sentence, one of the most frequent functions of the connector is to introduce the arguing of a conclusion from a preceding *si*, whether hypothetical or a ***si d'opposition***:

> Si l'exercice du pouvoir est d'abord un face-à-face sincère avec la réalité, alors le nouveau président américain, le démocrate Bill Clinton, ne s'y dérobe pas.

In such contexts, an English equivalent could be 'then'. In others, it could be 'in that case' or 'that being the case'. But when *alors* presents the consequence of a preceding *comme*, it would probably have no equivalent in English, as in this discussion of the alleged incompetence of the French taxation system:

Les Français n'y comprennent plus rien. Et comme ils ont peur du chômage, de leur retraite, des économies sur la santé, de la guerre en Europe, alors ils épargnent et ne consomment plus.

ou alors

This mode, quite common, can serve two different functions. Either it can restrict a consequence, as in this extract from a discussion of the scarcity of biographical or autobiographical writing about or by peasants and workers:

Aussi n'est-ce pas dans le chapitre des vies individuelles qu'il faut chercher trace du « vécu » des paysans et des ouvriers. Ou alors seulement dans les récits de gens qui sont sortis de ces milieux, et dont l'expérience laborieuse ou campagnarde est reléguée dans un récit d'enfance ou de jeunesse : mais alors ils n'écrivent plus en tant que paysan ou qu'ouvrier.

(Lejeune, 253–254)

Or it can introduce an alternative consequence, thus acting as a substitute for *ou bien*:

Face à la crise que traverse la représentation politique, et que personne aujourd'hui ne nie, deux attitudes sont possibles. Le catastrophisme, avec la description apocalyptique d'une République bafouée, qui serait menacée à court terme dans ses fondements, dans ses valeurs essentielles. Ou alors, la relativisation du mal qu'accréditerait une plongée dans les livres d'histoire et dans le souvenir de tant d'autres périodes tourmentées – et surmontées – de notre vie politique.

alors akin to *dès lors*

When what precedes is a principle or a definition, either of these consequencers could be used. In this example, the writer first isolates the defining characteristic of the European novel. It deals, he says, with the relationships between individual and polity and with the individual's discovery of the lack of freedom this entails:

Il n'y a qu'un seul sujet de roman : l'existence de l'homme dans la cité et la conscience qu'il prend des servitudes entraînées par le caractère social de cette existence. La nature et la portée d'un roman dépendent alors des rapports qu'il institue entre l'auteur, les personnages et le public.

(Caillois, 165)

alors que *

Along with the *si d'opposition*, which it can replace in some functions, this is probably the most common contrastive structure in contemporary

French, both spoken and written. The two statements which it links often form a single sentence; but it can also link two sentences. One can define four different modes of this connector: purely temporal; temporal-contrastive; purely contrastive; and combined with *même*.

alors que and *tandis que*

Both of these structures are sometimes used in a purely temporal sense, sometimes in a more contrastive way. Of the two, *alors que* is more often used contrastively; *tandis que* is more usual in temporal statements. It can at times be difficult to say whether they serve only one of these functions or both simultaneously. In this example, which contains both of them, a writer alleges that French trades union movements are backward, out of touch with important aspects of contemporary social and political life:

> Les organisations syndicales restent installées dans leurs tranchées creusées par l'histoire, tandis qu'autour d'elles tombent tant de murs que l'on croyait immuables. Alors que la démocratie prône la participation de tous et le choix du plus grand nombre dans les orientations politiques, économiques, sociales, tout se déroule à présent dans une passivité grandissante.

In the first sentence, the link structured by *tandis que* is both temporal and adversative: the antithesis of *restent installées* and *tombent* describes what is happening now. In the second sentence, *alors que* introduces a contrastive binary statement, an antithesis made of theory (*participation*) and practice (*passivité*), in which the temporal element is important only in so far as it reinforces the contrast of the ideal with the actual.

Purely temporal

In this mode, the structure is a simple variant of *quand, lorsque* or *pendant que*, as in this statement about a journalist and a war-criminal: *Maurice Denuzière, alors qu'il était grand reporter au* Monde, *avait interrogé Touvier en octobre 1975.* Another example is seen in the following report about a Soviet submarine which sank off the coast of Norway:

> Le *Komsomolets* a été victime d'un grave incendie, au large des côtes norvégiennes par 73° de latitude Nord, alors qu'il enregistrait le bruit caractéristique – la signature – produit par les hélices et la machine des sous-marins adverses patrouillant dans la région.

In those examples, two things are clear: *alors que*, saying little more than that two events took place at the same time, structures no conceptual contrast between them; and consequently there is a strong if implicit narrative quality to the statements, detectable also in the use of the past tenses. Despite the frequency of this temporal usage in contemporary written French, Robert says it is *vieilli en ce sens*.

Temporal-contrastive

Here too, the present tense is less common. The difficulty of separating the temporal function from the adversative is seen in this example (in which the present is a historical narrative present):

> Voilà un point acquis : alors que Racine a vingt-quatre ans, aucun déplacement de tendresse n'a encore eu lieu de la mère à la jeune fille.
>
> (Mauron, 221)

The statement appears at first sight to be a purely temporal statement of (Freudian) fact, which could have been made with *quand*. But made with *alors que*, it hints a comment on that state of affairs; and that comment at least implies a contrast, between the state of Racine's heart and the inferrable view that, for the author, this state, at the age of twenty-four, is at least noteworthy, if not abnormal.

In the following example, this structure occurs twice: first in a simple temporal usage where it could be replaced by *au moment où*; then, two sentences later, as a temporal-contrastive in which the two different functions reinforce each other and which could be replaced by *tout en sachant*. The subject is Boris Yeltsin, the President of Russia, making rash promises to his compatriots about the economic outlook:

> « Ce sera dur, mais ce ne sera pas long, six ou huit mois », a-t-il déclaré alors qu'il s'expliquait sur la réforme des prix. Les habitudes sont dures à perdre. Alors qu'il sait que la transition sera longue et douloureuse – la population ne devrait pas en ressentir d'effets positifs avant dix ans, selon l'un de ses conseillers, – il promet une amélioration pour très bientôt.

It is no doubt this combination of functions that makes for the strong adversativeness of the statement, which in English might be variously made with 'At a time when', 'Although he knows very well' or 'Despite the fact that'.

A variant for this temporal-contrastive mode is simple *quand*, as in this contrast between two painters, one who studies old masters and the other who shuns them: *Quand Giorgio de Chirico prêche l'adoration des musées, Sironi repousse la tentation du pastiche.* And here a writer compares the interest of Flaubert's letters to that of his novels:

> D'abord cette correspondance est spontanée, au jour le jour, quand l'œuvre faite à tant d'effort et de travail pour être imprimée a quelque chose de volontaire et de tendu dans sa beauté qui a pu faire dire que cette perfection d'objet d'art était un peu stérilisée.
>
> (Henriot, 1954: 69)

Sometimes, exchanging a temporal expression for a topographical one, a writer will use *là où*, a mode of *là*, equivalent to the English use of 'where' instead of 'whereas'.

Purely contrastive

This mode can be placed first in the sentence; more commonly, it introduces the second element of the contrast; and the tense of the verbs linked is, overwhelmingly, the present. The function is similar to English 'whereas', 'though' or untemporal 'while'. This mode can structure very antithetical statements made of two similar parts, in which each element of the second part stands as a visible contrary to a corresponding element in the first, as in this example defining the difference between fission and fusion:

> Dans la fission, l'énergie est produite par l'éclatement, sous l'impact d'un neutron, de noyaux d'atomes lourds, (uranium, plutonium), alors que dans la fusion, elle provient de la réunion d'atomes légers.

There, the similarity of the two halves of the binary shows in the *produite par/provient de*, while the strong opposition between them is made by the three elements: *fission/fusion*; *éclatement/réunion*; and *atomes lourds/ atomes légers*.

When the connector introduces the first part, the second may be introduced by another oppositive term, such as the **pronom tonique disjoint** or, as in this contrast between wage-earning work and non-wage-earning work, **au contraire**:

> Alors que le salariat a commencé sous le signe du libéralisme total, de l'insécurité absolue et n'a conquis son statut que progressivement, le travail non salarié, au contraire, s'est développé au fil des siècles dans un cadre protégé : celui des corporations.

Sometimes a writer reinforces the second part even when it is introduced by this structure: *La mesure paraît modeste alors qu'en fait elle porte atteinte à un principe juridique fondamental.*

alors que and *si d'opposition*

It is this purely contrastive mode which would often be replaceable by a concessive *si*. However, this is the case only when it begins a sentence and makes a contrast which is wholly contained within that sentence. At other times, when it functions anaphorically, it would not be replaceable by *si*, which normally does not introduce the second part of an opposition. The two anaphoric modes differ only in the punctuation which precedes them. One of them introduces the second part of a sentence and therefore shapes a contrast with the first part of the same sentence, as in this comparison between successful and unsuccessful attempts at suicide among young people:

> De la veille de la Première Guerre mondiale à la fin des années soixante, la suicidité chez les jeunes a très sensiblement reculé alors que, parallèlement, les tentatives de suicide se sont multipliées.

The other anaphoric mode is the one placed after a full stop, completing a contrast begun in the preceding sentence. That is to say, unlike the *si d'opposition*, this structure is used to begin a **phrase dépendante**.

alors même que

The addition of *même*, by reinforcing the temporal coincidence of the two events, also sharpens the contradiction between them. Expressions of time are common with this mode. It says 'At the very moment when ...' or 'Even though ...' and usually denotes coincidences which are more monstrous or surprising than the norm. This example comments on the trial of two medical directors of the CNTS, the French national blood bank, charged with knowingly distributing contaminated blood for transfusion:

> Or, il apparaît de plus en plus clairement que le silence observé par ces deux directeurs dès le début de l'année 1984 – alors même qu'ils possédaient la preuve de la nocivité de leurs produits et donc, du risque patent des transfusions – a eu pour conséquence de retarder la prise de conscience collective du danger.

The dominant tense with *alors même que* is frequently not the present. Like the purely temporal mode mentioned above, this one is rarely placed first in the sentence.

Some writers use this mode with less of a temporal dimension, to stress directness of contrast, as in this extract from a discussion of the bad reputation of Paris taxi-drivers:

> Une profession respectable se sent mal aimée, victime trop souvent de préjugés injustes, alors même qu'elle est la principale victime de toutes les pollutions de la société moderne.

alors même que and quand bien même que

According to Robert, *alors même que* means *quand bien même que* or *même dans le cas où*, another definition which does not seem to be in close accord with current usage. Examples of it with this meaning date mainly from the late nineteenth and early twentieth centuries. In 1897, Durkheim speaks of the times of year when most suicides happen:

> ...dans les grandes villes, contrairement à ce qui se passe dans le reste de la société, c'est généralement au printemps qu'a lieu le maximum. Alors même que le printemps est dépassé par l'été (Paris et Francfort), l'avance de cette dernière saison est légère.
>
> (Durkheim, 1930: 105)

It is clear that the structure functions hypothetically and that the author's meaning is 'even if' or 'even in cases where'. This fundamental difference of meaning can be seen in many writers of the same period. Other differences are that this variant was more often placed first in the sentence, as in the previous example, and that, like *quand bien même que*, it usually accompanied the conditional or the conditional perfect:

> Il suffit pour bien faire, ou pour en avoir le mérite, d'en avoir l'intention ; au lieu qu'un péché de langage reste un péché, alors même que le pécheur aurait sa conscience pour lui.
>
> (Hermant, 202)

As can be seen in that example, this mode dates from a time when *au lieu que* was used in the adversative functions now served by this connector.

antithèses sans charnière

A common feature of French discursive style is the construction of neat binary sentences, acute contradictions put in lapidary form, visible parallelisms in structure. Because this sharpens contrasts and shows paradoxes, it aptly accompanies irony, polemic and comedy; because it enables the meanings to set the relationships between statements, it is brief; because it is analytical, it lends itself to striking definitions; because it lets the words speak for themselves, it can have dramatic power or a sort of solemnity. The importance of antithesis to this style has often been noted:

> L'antithèse est la force du style abstrait... En dehors du style descriptif, elle est la grande ressource de l'art d'écrire.
>
> (Antoine Albalat, quoted by Gourmont, 1902: 126)

The force of antithesis comes only from the juxtaposition of its two parts. Neither of them is important in its own right, even if they stand as separate sentences, but only in relation to the other. This is the point made by La Bruyère in his definition: *L'antithèse est une opposition de deux vérités qui se donnent du jour l'une à l'autre* (La Bruyère, 90).

Antithesis with connector

In contemporary English, writers can give the impression that their aim is to disguise such binaries or at least not to mark their presence. Take a common-or-garden English sentence like this, the subject of which is Albert Camus: 'In Anglo-Saxon countries his reputation has not fallen but young Frenchmen have almost ignored him' (McCarthy, 6). The English reader, unaccustomed to binary and antithetical statements, could be forgiven for not noticing that it is one. Its binariness is shaped mainly by the conjunction 'but', placed after the first of its two components. Its antithetical quality is marked by two features: the mention of two groups of Camus's readers and the fact that, among them, his reputation has had opposite fortunes. Yet the point of that binary antithesis is not only not abetted by the structure of the English sentence, it is even slightly blunted. The lack of punctuation makes the sentence look like a single statement. The inattentive reader could even have the momentary impression that the 'young Frenchmen' are in Anglo-Saxon countries. If the same statement was made in French, the writer might begin with an overtly contrastive structure such as ***alors que*** or the ***si d'opposition***, thus apprising the reader from the outset that a binary is to be expected; might also reinforce the second element with a connector such as ***au contraire*** or ***en revanche***; might well shape the parts about languages or countries ('In Anglo-Saxon countries' and 'young Frenchmen') with a similar grammatical structure rather than in two different ways; and would very likely show the binariness of the structure in another way, by placing a comma:

> Si dans les pays anglo-saxons sa réputation s'est maintenue, en France au contraire les jeunes ne le lisent plus guère.

A French writer might even try to choose two verbs whose oppositeness would make the antithesis more apparent than the pair used there.

The four structures named in the last paragraph, two of them used in my translation of the sentence, are among the commonest ways of making binary antitheses in French. Among others are ***à l'inverse***, ***par contre***, ***au lieu que***, ***autant... autant***, ***d'un côté... de l'autre***, ***n'en... pas moins***, ***plutôt***, ***pour autant***, ***pour cela***, ***pronom tonique disjoint***. To this list one could add obvious binary structures not included in this work, such as *tantôt... tantôt* and *plus... plus*.

Antithesis without connector

French writers often eschew procedural connectors and let the substantive meaning shape their antitheses. This can have the advantage, of course, of making a statement more pointed because it is briefer. Remy de Gourmont, who disliked antithesis when it was *voulue et appuyée*, was himself a master of the antithesis uncluttered by connectors:

> Voulue et appuyée, l'antithèse est une manière de discourir assez fâcheuse ; ingénue, elle est une nécessité. Rien n'existe en soi ; tout est relatif. Décrire un objet, c'est le comparer ; exposer une idée, c'est la comparer...
> (Gourmont, 1902: 126)

In those three sentences, Gourmont's pithy brevities and the oppositive meanings of the words he chooses are aided only by punctuation (a comma to shape each half of the binary, a semicolon to set the halves in relation to each other) and by similarity of grammatical structure in both halves: initial adjectival clause balanced by initial adjectival clause; verb *être* by verb *être*; *Rien* by *tout*; infinitive structure with object by infinitive structure with object. Those same two features, strategic placement of commas and semicolons, parallel grammatical forms, are noticeable in the antitheses made without procedural connectors by many other writers. The style, consisting of the juxtaposition of two statements rather than coordination or subordination of them, is as old as Rabelais in the 1530s: *Oignez villain, il vous poindra ; poignez villain, il vous oindra* (Rabelais, I, 123), or as Montaigne in the 1580s:

> J'achette les imprimeurs en Guiene, ailleurs ils m'achettent. [...] Je conçois aisément Socrates en la place d'Alexandre ; Alexandre en celle de Socrates, je ne puis.
>
> (Montaigne, II, 227, 228)

It is as recent as Sartre in the 1960s: *Plus absurde est la vie, moins supportable la mort. / Lecteur, je sautais ces passages didactiques ; auteur, j'en bourrais mes romans. / Je riais de malice, je pleurais d'attendrissement. / Je n'avais pas choisi ma vocation : d'autres me l'avaient imposée* (Sartre, 1964: 78, 118, 142, 172). Some of the most memorable sentences written in the seventeenth and eighteenth centuries are couched in similar antithetical form:

> Les femmes s'attachent aux hommes par les faveurs qu'elles leur accordent : les hommes guérissent par ces mêmes faveurs.
>
> (La Bruyère, 116)

> Dans cette partie si inégale, notre fortune est de ne pas perdre, et votre malheur de ne pas gagner. [...] je veux l'avoir, et je l'aurai ; il veut le dire, et il ne le dira pas.
>
> (Laclos, 173, 181)

> À Annecy, j'étais dans l'ivresse ; à Chambéry, je n'y étais plus. [...] Rien d'absurde ne leur paraît incroyable dès qu'il tend à me noircir ; rien d'extraordinaire ne leur paraît possible dès qu'il tend à m'honorer.
>
> (Rousseau, 225, 766)

Antithesis within a sentence

The tradition of the antithesis-by-juxtaposition prospers to this day among journalists. Sometimes this antithesis without connector is structured in a single sentence, its two parts signalled only by a comma, although they are independent clauses, neither of them more important than the other. Often each part will have the same subject and verb: *C'est très contestable, ce n'est pas impossible.* Or the subjects will be the same and the verbs different: *On s'inquiète encore, on se rassure déjà. / Ils souhaitaient préserver le rôle du Parlement, ils l'ont abaissé jusqu'à l'affaissement.* Or else subject and verb will both be different, as in this triad of short antitheses, written by the journalist Anne Sinclair about the minister Simone Veil, all three of which shape the same contrast between popular misconceptions about her character and her truer nature: *On la croit posée, elle est violente. On la croit paisible, elle est ardente. On la croit sage, elle est rebelle.* In the following example, it is the object of the verbs, *la tête* and *celle*, and the identities of two Communist leaders in East Europe, which shape the antithesis: *On attendait la tête de Milos Jakes, le dirigeant tchécoslovaque, c'est celle de Todor Jivkov, son homologue de Sofia, qui est tombée.*

Instead of a comma, sometimes a mode of the colon is the structuring punctuation: *Elle croyait faire la révolution : elle fait naufrage.* This is infrequent and akin to the English usage 'in gnomic contrasts (Man proposes: God disposes)' (Fowler, 589):

> Sous le prochain septennat, la France aura peut-être de nouveau à sa tête un socialiste président : elle n'aura plus un président socialiste.

This mode of the colon is mentioned neither by Grevisse nor by Drillon (387–403). See also *deux-points* and, above, an example from La Bruyère and one from Sartre.

Much more usual than the colon is the semicolon (preceded, like some other French stops, by a space):

> Le roman du dix-septième siècle s'est noyé dans le synthétisme ; le roman du dix-neuvième s'est brisé sur le particularisme.
>
> (Gourmont, 130)

> Les Perses d'Hérodote pensaient que tout le monde avait tort sauf eux ; nous autres Occidentaux modernes, nous ne sommes pas loin de penser que tout le monde a raison sauf nous.
>
> (Revel, 1988: 117)

Antithesis in two sentences

Sometimes the antithesis without connector occupies two separate sentences. These are usually brief. If the subject is the same in each half, the predicates may differ: *La manœuvre est délicate. Elle n'est pas impossible.* Or the same verb may have two subjects which are opposites of each other, as in this statement about *mal* and *remède*: *De la royauté était venu le mal. Du roi vint le remède.* Or else both elements, subject and verb, may be opposed, as in this pair of sentences written by a critic of the policy of the SNCF, which closes down local lines while extending its high-speed services: *Le TGV file. Les lignes secondaires disparaissent.* The opposition may be between the same thing at two different periods, as in this comment written by an anti-Communist on Louis Aragon, once a living Communist, hence detestable, now a dead poet, hence admirable: *De son vivant, c'était le camarade de Marchais. À présent, c'est celui de Victor Hugo* (Dutourd, 1985: 28).

Visible similarities and differences

The similarity of grammatical structures runs sometimes to the repetition of similar words in both parts of the binary, sometimes to the very same words: *Tout cela est vrai. Tout cela n'est pas suffisant.* / *Cela peut n'être qu'un avertissement. Cela peut aussi annoncer un grand déballage.* This type of sequence fits very well with lapidary definitions: *Sans conflit, il n'y a plus de politique. Sans coexistence, il n'y a pas de démocratie.* / *Exprimer une opinion, c'est voter pour le souhaitable. Exprimer une volonté, c'est voter pour le possible* (Duverger, 249).

More often, the same grammatical structure contains words which have opposite meanings. Paired opposites, having a visible likeness in form, beginning with the same word or letter, are common: *Autrefois... Aujourd'hui*; *À priori... À posteriori*; *Avant la diaspora... Après la diaspora*; *Dans le premier cas... Dans le second*; *En principe... En pratique*; *La droite... La gauche*; *Les uns... Les autres*; *Leur avantage... Leur inconvénient.* As many of the examples already used show, these words are usually placed at the beginning of the two elements, as in this pair of sentences about the life and prospects of the unskilled worker: *Commencer à la chaîne, bien des travailleurs l'acceptent. Savoir qu'on y finira, c'est intolérable* (Closets, 1983: 394); and in this comment on a play which reads well but which is a disaster on stage: *À lire*, le Régent *est un texte plein de belles choses. À voir, c'est une catastrophe.*

Among these paired opposites, the sequence negative-positive is common, as in this comment on an aspect of the poetry of Paul Valéry:

> Le vague valérien n'est pas un flottement indolent ni une lassitude ; c'est une façon de se découvrir les coudées franches et de s'apprêter à agir.

The contrastive words may be placed for effect not at the beginning but at the end of each part, as in this comment on a suspicion that the integrity of a Prime Minister, Pierre Bérégovoy, had been compromised by having received a large loan without interest: *Il a emprunté de l'argent, c'est banal ; ses explications n'ont pas convaincu, c'est embêtant.*

This type of contrastive structure combines well with a **question**, and sometimes with sequences of them: *L'amnistie ? C'est l'oubli accordé à des coupables. La grâce ? C'est le pardon accordé à des condamnés.*

> Longtemps l'Europe fut impérialiste ? Elle ne l'est plus. Longtemps elle fut belliqueuse ? Elle a cessé de tuer les autres et de s'entretuer. Longtemps elle fut minée par la lutte des classes ? Elle a eu la sagesse de tempérer les excès du capitalisme en redistribuant une partie des revenus par l'impôt et un système de protection sociale d'inspiration socialiste.

Such sequences of similar construction are found also in non-interrogative antitheses:

Il avait promis de sauver le pays de la catastrophe économique. La catastrophe est là, sans précédent. Il avait annoncé la fin de la corruption généralisée et de la gabegie. Ces maux n'ont pas disparu. Il s'était engagé à rendre le pouvoir aux civils en 1990. L'échéance a été reportée quatre fois.

Longer statements

Most of these unconnected antitheses shape short statements. They can also make longer or more complex ones, while retaining the parallelisms and verbal similarities which help give the antithesis its contrastive force and perceptible form. The first of these two examples, written by Albert du Roy, dates from the moment in September 1992 when it was announced that President Mitterrand had just had an operation for cancer:

Si Mitterrand avait décidé d'écourter son mandat, chacun, hier, aurait disserté avec cruauté sur les raisons politiques de sa décision. Si cela se produisait demain, chacun en admettrait sans discuter les nobles raisons personnelles.

La démocratie ne peut pas vivre sans la vérité, le totalitarisme ne peut pas vivre sans le mensonge ; la démocratie se suicide si elle se laisse envahir par le mensonge, le totalitarisme s'il se laisse envahir par la vérité.

(Revel, 1988: 33)

après tout *

This connector usually persuades by introducing not a reason but a fact, true or assumed to be true. It is a fact which, by reminding the reader of shared knowledge and inviting agreement on it, tends towards confirmation of what precedes. Sometimes the fact is a plain statement of a known event; sometimes it is the reminder of a general principle.

After an assertion

In this affirmative mode, the role of the structure is to remind the reader of shared knowledge; the invitation to agree with the preceding proposition remains implicit. In the first of the following examples, the author's purpose is to defend an Italian political activist called Bossi against the suggestion that he belongs to the extreme or anti-democratic Right:

Bossi assume son « populisme », mais il n'est pas du genre à marcher sur Rome ou à uriner sur le Parlement, comme l'écrivain D'Annunzio à l'orée du fascisme. Après tout, dans sa jeunesse, il était de gauche, faisait des sit-in contre Pinochet et manifestait contre le totalitarisme de l'Est.

The other basic features of this connector, in this function, are that usually it begins a sentence, or even a paragraph, and is followed by a comma. In the second example, the writer uses it to introduce a fact which supports her tentative doubt about the proper and improper use of language:

> À trop considérer les vicissitudes de l'histoire des langues, on risquerait parfois de douter qu'il y ait un bon ou un mauvais usage, ou qu'une langue puisse avoir des qualités qui la distinguent. Après tout, le français n'est jamais que du latin mal employé, mêlé d'éléments celtiques ou germaniques, et rempli d'anciens solécismes devenus peu à peu la norme.

After a question

After a *question*, the fact which is introduced by the connector can do one of two different things: it can serve to validate the doubt expressed in the question:

> Sommes-nous si sûrs que l'immigration soit la cause de cette crise morale que nous traversons ? Après tout, le nombre des étrangers avait depuis longtemps atteint son niveau actuel quand s'est déclenchée cette crise que nous avons un peu vite baptisée crise de l'immigration.

Or, conversely, it can doubt the validity of the objection raised by the question, as in this extract from an article on the need to restrict international trade in weapons:

> D'abord, c'est une urgence absolue, réglementer le commerce des armes à l'échelle mondiale. Utopie ? Pourquoi donc ? Après tout, les deux Grands sont bien aujourd'hui sur la voie d'un désarmement concerté et contrôlé, notamment en matière nucléaire.

Introducing a question

Questions introduced by this connector are usually couched in the negative. This mode takes one or other of two different forms. The first of these behaves, in interrogative form, exactly like the basic mode exemplified above. That is, it introduces a reminder of a fact already known to both writer and reader and invites the latter to see that as a reason for accepting what precedes. Thus, in the following example, the suggestion is made that the parliamentary Left, though in a precarious position, may manage to benefit from the support of the President:

> ...grâce à une cohabitation qui reposera, en effet, sur les seules épaules présidentielles, si tant est qu'elle puisse s'engager. Après tout, la droite ne donne-t-elle pas des signes avant-coureurs des erreurs qu'elle s'apprête à commettre, sous l'empire d'un esprit de revanche et de surenchère ?

The author's suggestion that such a period of constitutional *cohabitation* between President of the Left and parliament of the Right may, however, prove unworkable is supported by the reminder, after the connector, that the Right may shoot itself in the foot.

In the other type of negative question, the connector is combined with **mais**. It introduces an implicit rejoinder which says 'Well, so what?' to the objection raised in the preceding sentence. A discussion of the idea that all schools be required to teach to all pupils a *savoir minimum garanti* accepts first that it will be difficult to reach agreement on such a controversial proposal; then, introducing a negative interrogative with this mode of the connector, it counters that objection:

> ...on a toutes les chances de voir s'opposer les acteurs sociaux concernés : les spécialistes des diverses disciplines, les parents d'élèves des différents milieux, les employeurs et les syndicats de salariés, les enseignants et les maîtres d'apprentissage. Mais, après tout, n'en va-t-il pas de même pour le niveau du SMIC ou la Sécurité sociale ? À l'école aussi, il faut se risquer aux compromis polémiques.
>
> (Baudelot & Establet, 198)

Affinities with other connectors

By its invitation to agree, the function of this connector is akin to that of *n'est-ce pas ?* Because of its confirming function, it is often close to being a variant for **car**, **de fait** or **en effet**. It says 'Don't forget the following'; and it implies 'What I have just said must be accepted, in view of what I am about to say'. In this, it is very close to 'after all' in one of the registers of English; and in another register it is close to the very common 'I mean' or 'Let's face it' which appeal to a listener's sense of logic: 'He's a right wally, that bloke – I mean, he went and sawed off the branch he was sitting on.'

In some contexts, it can function rather like **au fait**. In the following example, where it introduces a question, the relation it makes between what precedes and what follows is very different from those described above. In this passage, the author tries to remember clearly the circumstances in which M. Richard, to make up for having killed some mice, gave him as a present a pair of other animals:

> Ce fut un couple de tourterelles. Après tout, fut-ce bien lui qui me les offrit, ou simplement les toléra-t-il ? Mon ingrate mémoire abandonne ce point [...]
> (Gide, 1954: 446)

There, it is clear that the connector introduces not a confirmation, not an invitation to a reader to agree with a shared assumption, but a doubt about the accuracy of the statement preceding. If not by *au fait*, it could be replaced by *ou plutôt*. In English, its function could be served by 'on second thoughts', 'come to think of it' or the multifarious 'actually'.

When combined with *mais*, it functions rather like *mais enfin*. In other contexts, especially when referring to a possible outcome, it can be close to *en fin de compte* or *tout compte fait*: in the first quotation above, about Bossi and D'Annunzio, neither of these would fit; but in the second one, about the origins of the French language, only a very slight shade of difference prevents them from being interchangeable with *après tout*. At times, too, it comes very close to *somme toute*, as in this extract from an article about the future European role of a reunited Germany, based on the experience of the former Federal Republic (*la RFA*):

> Les propositions allemandes pour l'organisation future de l'Europe sont tirées de l'expérience, après tout plutôt bien réussie, de la RFA, comme si ce qui a été bon pour l'Allemagne devrait être bon pour l'Europe.

à savoir (que) *

This connector, rather like a more pointed form of *c'est-à-dire (que)*, introduces an explanation or precision in other words of whatever immediately precedes. In current English, many writers make this link without a connector: a statement like *le principal témoin, à savoir Mme Palme* would usually be in English 'the main witness, Mrs Palme'. However, the link can also be made by 'namely' or the abbreviation 'i.e.'; and in older English there used to be an exact equivalent of this French structure, still surviving in legal parlance, namely 'to wit', a verb which once meant the same as *savoir*.

The form without *que*

Like *c'est-à-dire*, this mode is used when what follows is a complement of what precedes. What precedes is usually a noun or a pronoun; what follows is usually a similar grammatical structure. In this excerpt from a historian's discussion of the Reformation, the noun-group formed on *possibilité* precises the noun *cœur du système religieux*:

> La Réforme est née du rejet radical de ce qui était peut-être le cœur du « système religieux de sécurité » bâti par l'Église, à savoir la possibilité d'abréger, voire d'effacer, les terribles et infinies peines purgatoires promises aux pécheurs, qu'ils soient encore vifs ou déjà morts, grâce à l'obtention d'indulgences à temps ou plénières.

In this example, the pronoun *ce* and the noun *l'essentiel* are amplified by the nouns *les succès* and *la façon*:

> « Ô rage, ô désespoir... » Manifestement, M. Mitterrand, plus « démonté » qu'il ne l'admet par l'affaire Habache, plus remonté qu'il n'était raisonnable, enrage

de voir l'opinion tourner le dos à ce qu'il considère comme l'essentiel, à savoir les succès qu'il rencontre sur la scène internationale et la façon dont la France, finalement, tient son rang.

The form with *que*

This mode is used when what follows is a complete statement, introduced by a subject and verb. What follows *que* could always be detached and stand as a main or independent clause. It is often an amplification, longer than what follows the other mode. What precedes is still often a structure based on a noun or a pronoun. The first of these examples comes from a discussion of certain women's magazines: very dependent on tobacco-advertising, they rarely publish articles on the World Health Organization (*l'OMS*) and its warnings about the dangers to health caused by smoking:

> Ces journaux féminins cachent à leurs lectrices ce que l'OMS ne cesse de répéter, à savoir qu'il y a de plus en plus de femmes qui meurent de maladies liées à l'usage du tabac ; que le cancer du poumon tue davantage de femmes que le cancer du sein ; que partout dans le monde les femmes qui fument risquent trois fois plus que les autres d'être atteintes du cancer du col de l'utérus ; que leur ménopause se produit deux ou trois ans plus tôt ; [...]

> Cela me fait mal au cœur de vous rapporter ce que j'entends dire et répéter par ma clientèle, à savoir que la France serait magnifique sans les Français.
> (Frischer, 25)

Punctuation

Even when what follows is a complete and independent statement, an author occasionally dispenses with *que*, replacing it either with a comma or a *deux-points*, as in this extract from a discussion of the history of cultural relativism:

> Avec Montaigne, par exemple, et, bien sûr, encore plus avec Montesquieu, se développe pleinement le thème de la relativité des valeurs culturelles. À savoir : nous n'avons pas le droit de décréter une coutume inférieure à la nôtre simplement parce qu'elle en diffère, et nous devons nous rendre capables de juger notre propre coutume comme si nous l'observions du dehors.
> (Revel, 1988: 116)

This connector is usually preceded by a comma or a colon; but, as in the last example, it can also begin the sentence if the author feels that what it introduces is important enough to be dramatized in this way. Whether with *que* or without, such a sentence is a *phrase dépendante*. This example comes from a discussion of the paradoxical nature of Jacobinism: freedom is its aim, loss of freedom is its outcome:

Le paradigme jacobin, comme toute idéologie totalitaire, crie et cache à la fois son secret. À savoir que toute révolution accomplie selon le modèle jacobin, au nom de la liberté, accroît en fait le pouvoir de l'État et détruit la liberté de la société civile.

à savoir and *en l'occurrence*

There is an important difference between this structure and *en l'occurrence*. With *à savoir*, one goes not from the general category to a particular case, but from a particular case to a more precise reference to the same particular case. Thus, what follows *à savoir* is an exact equivalent, semantic and grammatical, of what precedes. However, on occasion some writers use *en l'occurrence* in a way which is little different from *à savoir*:

Nous n'examinerons ici que les conflits majeurs du XXe siècle, en l'occurrence les deux guerres mondiales.

(Chesnais, 385)

The conceptual closeness of the structures is seen too in the fact that sometimes, instead of *en l'occurrence*, a writer will use a sort of conflation of both: *à savoir, dans ce cas.*

Variants

The use of *savoir* in this function may once have been more common than *à savoir*:

Il faut deux facteurs pour que la couleur existe, savoir : un état particulier de ce que les physiciens appellent l'éther et un homme clairvoyant.

(Le Dantec, 29)

This form is common in the prose of a century ago. Hanse (1983: 848) still gives it as current. But it would be apter to say that it is nowadays so rare as to be obsolete. As for *c'est à savoir*, it too is archaic – although Jules Romains could use it as late as 1966:

Si profonde et, hélas ! si légitime que soit notre défiance envers l'avenir, nous ne devons jamais perdre de vue une considération qui remet les choses à leur place.
    C'est à savoir ce que l'aventure totale de l'humanité, depuis les origines, a d'incroyablement minuscule à l'échelle du cosmos.

(Romains, 1966: 21)

The expression *je veux dire* could at all times replace this connector, at least in the mode without *que*. This example comes from a discussion of the diaries of Stendhal:

> L'achèvement de la publication du *Journal* a éclairci l'un des points obscurs de la biographie, je veux dire la nature des rapports qui lièrent la comtesse Pierre Daru à notre héros.
>
> (Blum, 465)

Another formulaic expression, *j'ai nommé* followed by a proper name, which can function as a ***brief interpolated main clause***, is sometimes used in place of this connector to identify a person:

> Les « crânes d'œuf » de Rocard et Fabius, nous avons nommé l'historien Alain Bergougnoux et le sociologue Henri Weber, soulèvent des objections.

à [son] tour*

As in *de [son] côté* or *pour [sa] part*, the possessive adjective varies depending on the person of the subject. The main dictionaries are notably uninformative on this structure's connective function, which is usually to signal an added point reinforcing something in what precedes. This it does by underlining, between what precedes and what follows, a sequential or an accumulative similarity

The connector is usually placed with the verb or between commas after the first element of the sentence. It can be used to denote a change of subject, usually the second of a pair, whose turn it is now to act or be mentioned. The point made is often that the paired acts are identical. The structure may denote mere sequence, as 'also' or 'now' might if this statement about the spread of AIDS from one continent to another were made in English: *L'Asie, jusqu'ici épargnée, est à son tour aux prises avec l'épidémie.* A somewhat similar example comes from a report of separate meetings held by Palestinians and Israelis to consider the Taba agreement:

> Hier soir à Tunis le comité exécutif de l'organisation palestinienne a adopté dans ses grandes lignes l'accord de Taba. Ce matin, le gouvernement israélien se réunit à son tour pour ratifier l'accord.

As is at least implicit in these examples, there is a narrative quality to the acts described, despite the fact that the tense used is often the present. This quality is at times visible too in the presence of *après* in the sentence stating the second of the paired acts. The following example comes from a report of a speech in which the Prime Minister, Alain Juppé, having earlier warned civil servants and doctors of the need to curb public spending, repeated this message to a gathering of mayors of large cities:

> Ses propos traduisaient sans doute le souci de faire comprendre aux responsables des collectivités locales qu'ils devaient accepter leur part de sacrifices.

Après les fonctionnaires, les médecins et bien d'autres en cet automne, voilà les Maires à leur tour avertis : plus question de projets somptuaires avec financements à tiroirs.

Sometimes the structure denotes reciprocity of action, as in this extract from an article about a television advertisement, where English might say 'she roars too' or 'she roars back':

Une créature de rêve marche à quatre pattes dans la savane et tombe nez à nez avec un lion qui rugit. Elle rugit à son tour.

The expression is often used in contexts where, in spoken English, a mere inflection of voice would serve its function, and in written English, possibly italics. Take Orwell's piece about the disgusting things done to customers' steak in the kitchens of expensive restaurants, first by the head cook, then by the waiter:

He picks it up in his fingers and slaps it down, runs his thumb round the dish and licks it to taste the gravy, runs it round and licks it again, then steps back and contemplates the piece of meat like an artist judging a picture, then presses it lovingly into place with his fat, pink fingers, every one of which he has licked a hundred times that morning. When he is satisfied, he takes a cloth and wipes his fingerprints from the dish, and hands it to the waiter. And the waiter, of course, dips *his* fingers into the gravy ...

(Orwell, 1961: 80)

There, even if Orwell had not italicized 'his' the reader could hear the emphasis which helps the writer make the cumulative effect of revolting-ness. To achieve the same effect, the French writer would certainly not italicize *ses*, but would probably reinforce the verb with *à son tour*; and the last two sentences might read as follows:

S'estimant satisfait, il s'empare d'un torchon pour effacer les empreintes que ses doigts ont laissées sur l'assiette, laquelle il tend au serveur. Celui-ci, bien entendu, trempe à son tour ses doigts dans la sauce [...]

A similar thing may be seen in the following extract from a discussion of countries which chose to develop thermonuclear weapons. The author, having considered the USA's and the ex-USSR's varying fortunes in respect of atomic armaments, then asks this question: *La France a-t-elle agi sagement en s'en dotant à son tour ?* In spoken English, a slight stress on 'France' in 'And was it wise for France to aquire them?' would suffice to make the link of thought to the author's theme. Written, the question might begin with 'As for France ...'.

Depending on register, English could also make the link between the two statements with 'again' or a variant of 'in [its] turn', as might be the case in the following extract from Camus's discussion of three works by Kafka. Having defined a double point with reference first to *The Trial*, he goes on to speak of a similar duality in the other two texts:

De même, *Le Château* est peut-être une théologie en acte, mais c'est avant tout l'aventure individuelle d'une âme en quête de sa grâce, d'un homme qui demande aux objets de ce monde leur royal secret et aux femmes les signes du dieu qui dort en elles. *La Métamorphose*, à son tour, figure certainement l'horrible imagerie d'une éthique de la lucidité. Mais c'est aussi le produit de cet incalculable étonnement qu'éprouve l'homme à sentir la bête qu'il devient sans effort.

(Camus, 1964: 171–172)

assurément *

This adverb frequently does service as a connector, functioning as one of the confirmers-cum-concessives of which *certes* or *sans doute* can be seen as models. In its confirming mode, it may be stronger than either of those structures. Like them and other confirmers which lend themselves to the role of concessives, it can be found in three modes.

Confirming

In this mode, it can make a more or less explicit reference to a foregoing statement, which it confirms without in any way hinting at a concession. Thus, an article alleging that President Mitterrand intends to remain in office despite a landslide electoral victory for the Right in 1993, goes on to say this:

La Constitution, assurément, lui donne le droit de se maintenir : elle est faite pour lui, c'est-à-dire pour le titulaire de la charge.

There the connector bears out the implication made earlier in the article that the President intended to see out his term. The affirmation it makes is similar to but stronger than that made by *il est vrai que*. It could almost be replaced by *de fait* or *en effet*. In this mode it can replace *bien* in sentences beginning with the *si d'opposition*:

S'il est un homme dont raffolèrent, au XVIIIe siècle, deux continents, dont la sagesse fut prônée comme l'évangile des temps nouveaux, c'est assurément Benjamin Franklin.

(Rougier, 215)

It is also used not to confirm a statement but merely to stress it, but with something of the force of *décidément* in implying agreement between writer and reader about the aptness of the statement, as in this extract from a film review:

Un gag toutes les dix secondes. Le charme, la finesse, la drôlerie mêmes. Assurément, le film le plus divertissant que nous ayons vu depuis long-temps.

There, the writer of English might say 'definitely', 'without a doubt' or 'quite the most'.

In this mode, the connector quite often introduces an answer to a *question*, as in this example where Durkheim wonders about the role played by heredity in suicide:

> L'observation démontre-t-elle l'existence d'une telle hérédité ? Assurément, on voit parfois le suicide se reproduire dans une même famille avec une déplorable régularité.
>
> (Durkheim, 1930: 70)

Concessive in sequence of two

The connector can be placed in the first of two consecutive statements, to make an affirmation which will be attenuated or qualified in the following one. And this second statement is frequently introduced by *mais* or some other objector. In this mode, the connector could be said to have an implicit concessive function – even in its confirmation, an anticipated objection is perceptible. In the first of these examples, a reviewer speaks of a collection of pieces by Maurice Barrès, posthumously published:

> Si ces « Barresiana » ne constituent assurément plus, pour un esprit de la fin du XXe siècle, un manuel d'« énergie nationale », ils n'en demeurent pas moins parfois un réservoir de vitalité.

In the second, a French politician speaks in the early 1930s of what is happening in Germany:

> « C'est bien notre droit, à nous, Allemands, me dit-on, de nous administrer comme nous le voulons. » Assurément. Mais c'est bien notre droit, à nous, Français, d'observer ce qui se passe outre-Rhin.
>
> (Herriot, 22)

Concessive in sequence of three

In this mode, common to most of the concessives, the connector is placed second in a sequence of three propositions. Conceding an objection to the first one, it foreshadows the third one, which will begin with *mais* or an equivalent and reaffirm the gist of the initial statement. In this sequence of three sentences on three plays by Jules Renard, a drama critic first says they are different; next, with the connector, he mentions similarities; then, in the third sentence he refines the point of his first:

> *Monsieur Vernet* ne ressemble ni à *Poil de Carotte* ni au *Plaisir de rompre*. Les mêmes habitudes, les mêmes préférences d'écrivain s'y retrouvent assurément. Mais chaque œuvre est différente par la conception et l'exécution.
>
> (Blum, 204)

A book reviewer, praising an annual guide to good food-shops, *À vos paniers* by Jean-Pierre Coffe, first says it is *formidable*; then with this connector he adds a slight restriction; finally he more or less restates the initial point:

> Coffe fournit là un formidable travail d'investigation gastronomique. Toutes les bonnes adresses ne sont assurément pas citées, mais, dans l'ensemble, *À vos paniers* 1995 permet d'accéder dans toute la France aux points de vente d'une nourriture saine, naturelle et authentique.

As can be seen from the examples, this connector can occupy different positions in the statement it accompanies. As the example from Herriot shows, it can also constitute a whole sentence.

English equivalents include 'admittedly', 'clearly', 'granted,' 'I agree entirely', 'it is a fact that', 'it is true', 'to be sure', 'obviously', 'of course', 'really', 'surely' and 'true'.

à tout prendre

Rousseau says of himself: *moi qui me suis cru toujours, et qui me crois encore, à tout prendre, le meilleur des hommes* (Rousseau, 608–609). This old expression belongs to the set of resumers and concluders which contains also **somme toute** and **tout compte fait**. Some dictionaries define it as *à tout considérer* or *tout bien examiné*; some cross-reference it with **en fin de compte**. It is one of those connectors for which an English equivalent could often be 'all things considered', 'on balance' or 'on the whole'.

Inside the sentence

The structure is usually placed inside the sentence, beside a verb or an adjective. This example refers to the *principale occupation* of a middle-class girl writing up her diary in the Victorian period:

> Rêver à l'idéal « mariage d'amour », au terrifiant « mariage de raison », ou encore à l'enviable – à tout prendre – « mariage de raison tournant à l'amour ».

The second example is an extract from an article describing how the names of defunct noble families can be acquired by non-nobles, a case in point being the Giscard family:

> Les Giscard avaient porté leur choix sur le patronyme « de la Tour-Fondue ». Las, une descendance oubliée s'opposa à l'annexion. La famille se rabattit alors sur l'amiral-comte d'Estaing, héros de la guerre d'indépendance des États-Unis – ce qui, à tout prendre, sonnait mieux pour un futur président !

In this position, it is quite often used with the verb *préférer*: *Se sentant menacé de licenciement, il préfère, à tout prendre, les honneurs de la démission* (July, 97); and with the verb *être*, usually structured with *ne... que*:

> J'ai abordé ce problème dans *Le Degré zéro de l'écriture*, qui n'était, à tout prendre, qu'une mythologie du langage littéraire.
>
> (Barthes, 1957: 221)

First in the sentence

The structure is also found at the beginning of the sentence or paragraph, where its connective function is more clearly conclusive and anaphoric than in other positions. Thus a writer discussing the relative demerits of petty racism and non-racist tyranny concludes that the former is preferable:

> Si intolérable soit le racisme, reste que subir un manque d'égards, essuyer un comportement injurieux dans les rapports personnels de la part d'un raciste, dans une société de droit, est moins irréparable pour moi, comme individu, lorsque j'en suis victime, que d'être assassiné par un despote, même si la couleur de sa peau est la même que la mienne. À tout prendre, je préfère la discrimination sans meurtre au meurtre sans discrimination.
>
> (Revel, 1988: 114)

au bout du compte *

This connector is one of the set of resumers or synthesizers which also contains *en fin de compte* and *tout compte fait*. Some dictionaries define it as having a 'familiar' tone; some equate it with *tout compte fait*; some differentiate it from *en fin de compte*. The structure has as much of a semantic as a procedural function: rather than linking to identifiable words or structures in the development which precedes it, it refers to the whole of a preceding exposition, to the facts of a situation that often entails complications, disagreement, set-backs, difficulties, a time-consuming process. It says, roughly, 'all things considered' or 'on the whole'. Other English equivalents would be 'eventually', 'when all's said and done' or the expression beloved of televised trades union officials and politicians: 'at the end of the day'. Also like those English expressions, this one has a quasi-narrative quality which can be seen in the fact that the verbs accompanying it are quite often in a past or a future tense, such as the one discussed at *aura*. Thus, a discussion of Korean politics which stresses long-drawn-out conflicts and the failure of great efforts made by an influential entrepreneur, contains this sentence:

> L'homme qui, au péril de sa vie, a lutté toute son existence pour la démocratie aura, au bout du compte, été bien mal récompensé de ses efforts.

There the connector does not link to any identifiable structure in what precedes; it underlines the magnitude of the struggle, seen from its end.

Often the failure is more contrastively signalled by the connector in a reference to a preceding intention or expectation. It may then be combined with *mais*, as in this extract from an article about an attempt by the national athletics federation to improve young athletes' performances: *L'objectif était d'aguerrir des jeunes, pour qui le niveau mondial est encore hors d'atteinte. Mais, au bout du compte, très peu se seront révélés.*

In this respect, the connector is used too in combination with verbs like *finir par*, which enable the reader to view the final outcomes of processes, especially if they contradict earlier judgments, as in this comment on Antoine Pinay, a Minister of Finance in the 1950s, whose great achievement, a government loan, later turned out to be not so great: *Au bout du compte, l'emprunt Pinay finit par coûter très cher à l'État, notamment dans les années 70.* Similarly, an article discussing American attempts to discourage illegal immigration from Mexico, first emphasizes the *gigantesques moyens répressifs* used, then speaks of its final outcome:

> Barbelés, dispositifs électroniques les plus sophistiqués, patrouilles d'hélicoptères à vision nocturne : tout fut mis en œuvre pour contrer la montée des Chicanos vers l'Amérique du Nord. Échec. Au bout du compte, les gouvernements américain et mexicain ont finalement enterré la hache de guerre pour s'orienter vers un partenariat pragmatique.

Again, it is not to any particular word that the connector relates. It sums up an idea: the eventual futility of the lengthy complicated process described in the preceding sentences. That example also shows a not infrequent feature of the usage of some writers, the redundant reinforcement of a connector by another, in this case *finalement*.

As the examples show, this connector can be placed either first in the sentence or with the verb.

au contraire *

This is one of the most common of the adversative connectors of French. It has two distinct modes. On the one hand, it can play the contradictive role of English 'on the contrary'; and in that mode, it can be seen as belonging to the set of structures which also contains *à l'inverse*, *inversement* and *à l'opposé*. On the other hand, it can serve a different function, more simply contrastive, served in English by some other structure such as 'on the other hand', 'however' or even 'actually'. And in that mode, it is akin to the set of less oppositive structures which contains *en revanche* and *par contre*. In either mode, the connector can be placed in a variety of different positions in the sentence.

Contradictive

This first mode usually follows a statement in the negative. In this example, a writer argues in favour of the study of the history of ideas, language and culture:

> Un enseignement moderne ne doit en aucun cas sacrifier l'histoire des langues et des littératures, des cultures et des religions, des philosophies et des sciences. Il doit au contraire se mesurer et travailler sans cesse à ces histoires, de façon de plus en plus subtile et critique.

This mode not only follows the negative structure but introduces an affirmation which either directly contradicts it or establishes a strong contrast with it, or both. In so doing, it can combine with **mais**: *Non seulement les Occidentaux n'exigent rien des « vaincus », mais au contraire ils leur offrent leur aide.*

Sometimes the negativity of the statement is not framed with *ne* but expressed in words meaning refusal, failure or distance: *Loin d'avoir souffert des attaques virulentes dont ils étaient l'objet, ils en ont au contraire bénéficié. / L'émirat refuse de se voir attribuer un quota. Au contraire, il ne cesse d'augmenter sa production.*

The connector can be placed not only first in the sentence and in the middle, but at the end, as in this extract from an article about Bob Hawke, a Prime Minister of Australia, who shed a tear on television as he owned up to unhappiness within his family circle: *Les Australiens ne lui en avaient pas voulu de sa sincérité médiatique, au contraire.* There, rather than introducing a contradiction of the foregoing negative structure, the connector constitutes the contradiction. However, in this position it more usually functions as though placed at the beginning of the next sentence, foreshadowing a contradiction of what precedes. An article discussing the recent and massive urbanization of traditionally rural Muslim populations says:

> Cette évolution ne s'est pas traduite par un recul religieux, au contraire. En 1978, ce furent les paysans déracinés des faubourgs de Téhéran qui manifestèrent sans réserve pour l'instauration de la république islamique.

A similar usage is seen in sentences which are constituted by nothing but the connector, as in this sequence of sentences from an account of the complicated trial of a police inspector:

> Dix jours après son ouverture, le procès du commissaire Jobic n'a pas gagné en limpidité. Au contraire... Au fil des audiences, la « vérité » semble se diluer.

In most of the features outlined above, this mode could be replaced by one of the modes of **là**, *loin de là*.

In English, if 'on the contrary' is not used, the contradiction between the two statements may be structured without recourse to an explicit connector: 'I am not suggesting that the stories about Nazi atrocities are untrue. To a great extent I think they are true' (Orwell, 1968: III, 317). In the reader's mind, the contradiction would be carried by the echo of spoken stress on 'are' in the second sentence, which might even be italicized.

Less contradictive contrast

This second main mode could not usually be replaced by *loin de là*. Instead of contradicting a preceding negative statement, it structures a less oppositional contrast between two statements of similar form. This can be done within a single sentence, as in this extract from a discussion canvassing possible alternative strategies for disarmament:

> Par quoi faut-il commencer un désarmement ? Dans certains domaines bien délimités, de manière à traiter les problèmes cas par cas et par étapes, ou, au contraire, selon une méthode globale et sur plusieurs « fronts » en même temps ?

Or it can be done in two consecutive sentences of symmetrical structure, such as: *Faut-il faire ceci ? Faut-il au contraire faire cela ?* or *S'agit-il d'une improvisation ? S'agit-il au contraire d'une sorte de résumé vulgaire ?* or *S'il s'enlise, il échoue. Au contraire, s'il aboutit, il retrouve le goût de l'action.* Sometimes the similarity between the structures is less visibly symmetrical, but still grammatically identical:

> Au XVIIIe siècle, et même pendant la Révolution, les juifs étaient très peu nombreux à Paris. À partir de 1814, au contraire, se développe un milieu juif parisien actif et de plus en plus nombreux.

In some of these contexts, this connector would be replaceable by *par contre* or *en revanche*. Like them, it is often used to accompany the second element in the common paired contrasts *Certains... D'autres* (as in *Certains estiment... D'autres au contraire soulignent...*) and *Les uns... Les autres*:

> Les uns tiennent que le changement a été bénéfique. Les autres au contraire estiment que les mouvements récents ont été néfastes.

a contrario

Lately, some writers have taken to using the Latin expression *a contrario*. The conventional usages of this expression are adverbial (*raisonner a contrario*) or adjectival (*un raisonnement a contrario*); and it has a technical usage in logic, defined thus by the *Petit Robert*:

> Se dit d'un raisonnement qui conclut d'une opposition dans les hypothèses à une opposition dans les conséquences.

Nowadays some writers adapt the expression as a variant for this connector. Sometimes they italicize it, sometimes not. In the first of these examples, the subject is the vanity of certain writers, who choose pen-names which suggest their family is of noble origin:

> Naguère, le duc de Castries, historien de renom, membre de l'Académie française, ne s'est-il pas vu reprocher de s'être paré d'un prestige excessif, attendu qu'il ne pouvait en réalité prétendre au-delà d'un marquisat de la Croix de Castries ?
>
> *A contrario*, il est vrai, on connaît au moins un exemple d'un écrivain se choisissant modestement pour nom de plume un pseudonyme roturier, et masquant ainsi son indubitable appartenance à une maison ducale.

The following example comes from an article discussing allegations that, during the 'cultural revolution' in China, cannibalism was practised:

> Il y eut de grands meetings pour proscrire le cannibalisme, mais on a aussi retrouvé des directives précisant qu'« il ne fallait pas manger de la chair humaine sans raison »... ce qui signifiait, a contrario, qu'on pouvait le faire si on avait une bonne raison !

Reinforced forms

In addition to its two basic modes, the connector is used in combinations reinforced by **bien**, *tout* and **même**. The first of these is used mainly to strengthen the first mode of the connector, that is when it contradicts a preceding negative structure. It can be placed at the end of the sentence; but usually it is placed first, as in this extract from an article about the alleged discovery in the early 1990s that the lost *fichier des juifs*, compiled by the Vichy authorities fifty years before and supposedly destroyed long since, was really still being held by a government department:

> Lorsque Serge Klarsfeld avait annoncé avoir la certitude que le fichier du recensement des juifs d'octobre 1940 se trouvait dans les archives du secrétariat d'État aux anciens combattants, nul ne l'avait sérieusement contesté. Bien au contraire, M. Louis Mexandeau, ministre en titre, avait authentifié la découverte en déclarant à l'Assemblée nationale, le 13 novembre 1991 : « Je suis en mesure, quant à moi, de confirmer l'existence de ce fichier. »

As for *tout au contraire*, it is used in either mode, placed either first in the sentence or beside the verb. In this comparison between two ways of seeing the ecological movement, one negative, the other positive, it reinforces the second mode:

> Les pessimistes diront que le mouvement écologiste n'est que le sous-produit d'une Europe repue, décadente, qui, n'aspirant plus à rien, en arrive à vouloir autolimiter ses désirs et ses besoins, comme si elle programmait inconsciemment son vieillissement puis sa mort. Les optimistes pensent tout au contraire

que le souci de sauvegarder notre terre nourricière marque une nouvelle étape
de l'aventure des hommes qui, jusqu'ici, la pillaient sans vergogne.

The form with *même* is less frequent than those with *bien* and *tout*.
Unlike them too, *même* is usually placed after the connector, as in this
extract from an article about politically motivated atrocities committed in
certain countries against children:

Dans certains pays, la terreur n'attend pas le nombre des années et l'enfance
ne constitue pas une circonstance atténuante face à la violence délibérée de
l'État. Au contraire même. Le dernier constat d'Amnesty International sur
cette question estime que les enfants de ces pays sont souvent des « cibles »
privilégiées des tueurs et des tortionnaires officiels.

Other combinations

The second part of a sentence beginning with a *si d'opposition* may be
accompanied by this connector, thus reinforcing the contrast, as in this
comparison between two groups of Russian parliamentarians:

Si certains réformateurs, à Moscou, se préparent à passer à l'opposition, d'autres
estiment au contraire qu'un premier ministre « conservateur » est mieux à même
de protéger la poursuite d'une politique d'essence finalement réformatrice.

This structure, in one or other of its variants, can also reinforce adversative *or*. This example comes from an article about the mood in the West
after the fall of the Berlin wall:

Les Occidentaux vivent un curieux paradoxe : depuis la chute du mur de Berlin
et l'effondrement du communisme, ils devraient respirer plus librement, mettre
un peu d'ordre dans ce monde qu'ils dominent militairement et matériellement,
connaître une période d'expansion sans précédent puisqu'il y a tant à construire
et à reconstruire. Or, tout au contraire, ils broient du noir.

It should perhaps be added that this connector is a close relative of the
grammatical structure *au contraire de*, which has the sense of *à la différence
de* or *contrairement à*. In the following quotation, defending the former
Prime Minister Pierre Mendès France against the charge that he was a
distant technocrat, inimical to open government, it structures a contrast:

Le président du Conseil, au contraire d'un pouvoir abstrait et occulte, s'attacha
tout au long de son mandat à définir en toute clarté sa politique.

au-delà (de)

In recent times, the mode without *de* has begun to be used in ways which
appear to suggest that it might be becoming an inter-assertional connector.

Traditionally, one of its functions has been to designate a length of time or distance, a tract of space, a degree of intensity, etc, which goes beyond that preceding or implied. An example comes from an article about two politicians, François Léotard and François Bayrou, who have struck an alliance with the aim of eliminating possible competitors within their own parties who might spoil their chances of becoming Prime Minister and eventually possibly President of the Republic:

> Les deux François s'entendront donc pour écarter les gêneurs, Valéry Giscard d'Estaing et Alain Madelin. Au-delà, ce sera chacun pour soi.

A mode of this use is often found in tandem with *et*: *En attendant l'an 2000 et au-delà... / Pour Belgrade et au-delà, le message est clair... / M. Le Pen et son Front national vont appliquer tout leur programme et au-delà./ L'architecte recouvrira l'ensemble de l'édifice, et au-delà, d'une structure de mâts et de toiture vitrée.* In all of these usages except the temporal, the idea expressed is close to the English 'but also' which follows 'not only'.

Close to this combination, too, are other usages which designate neither time, space nor intensity. Of Jacques Chirac, standing as a candidate for the presidency in 1995, it was reported that he first commended his rival, Édouard Balladur, for his idea of a pact for the stability of Europe, then went further, to propose a form of partnership between the European Union and Russia:

> « Cette initiative, à la réalisation de laquelle la diplomatie française a beaucoup œuvré, va dans la bonne direction, a-t-il dit, mais, au-delà, il revient à la France de promouvoir une vision globale de l'équilibre de notre continent, pour prévenir les risques de conflits liés à l'expression des nationalismes et à l'existence de minorités. »

There, it is evident that the structure stands for *au-delà de cela* or *au-delà de cette initiative*. Its function could be served in English by 'but even more importantly'. The point it introduces may not be of greater immediate import than what precedes. It broadens out discussion of a point to canvass farther reaching implications of it, as in a statement like *Mais au-delà, il y a un enjeu plus large.* As is partly perceptible in the quotation from M. Chirac, the structure may be used contrastively to link a short-term advantage to a longer-term disadvantage. An example comes from a discussion of recent trends in the French economy: the loss of many jobs in the industrial sector; the creation of many fewer jobs in other sectors; expenditure by companies on research and development about one third less than by companies in Germany. All this gives the following results, some briefly favourable, others at length unfavourable:

> Ce choix trouve aujourd'hui sa traduction dans l'offre française. L'industrie a retrouvé une compétitivité en termes de prix. Mais au-delà, ses produits se différencient peu de ceux de ses concurrents. Ils n'en sont que plus sensibles aux variations monétaires.

Some journalists have taken to using the structure in a way which brings it close to being replaceable by additive formulae such as *en plus*, *de surcroît* or *en outre*. In this mode, an article discusses the separate reactions of four parliamentarians of the Right (Léotard, Poncet, de Villiers and Le Pen) to President Chirac's announcement, in June 1995, of the resumption of French nuclear explosions in the Pacific:

> L'ancien ministre de la défense, François Léotard (UDF) a jugé cette décision « nécessaire », et Jean-François Poncet, sénateur UDF et ancien ministre des affaires étrangères, a approuvé une mesure « qu'il était difficile de ne pas prendre ». Au-delà, Phillipe de Villiers a estimé la reprise des essais « indispensable » tandis que Jean-Marie Le Pen, president du Front national, assurait le gouvernement « de son total soutien dans cette perspective ».

Something similar is seen in the following extract from an article on the government's plans for privatization of public instrumentalities, whether financial or industrial. The writer, having said that the choice of financial institutions open to the government was restricted, then says the choice of industrial institutions was also restricted:

> Côté industriel, le choix du gouvernement n'était pas beaucoup plus large. Il compte sur la cession de sa participation de 10 % dans Elf Aquitaine (10 milliards de francs), comme sur celle de ces 5 % dans Total (environ 3,5 milliards). Au-delà, deux groupes publics sont encore « présentables »: Renault et Pechiney.

There, English might say 'In addition', 'As well' or even 'Apart from these two'.

This mode of the structure is not always placed first in the sentence. An article about the purchase of Intuit, a financial software program, by Microsoft says that it will have two advantages for the latter, the second of which the writer introduces with *au-delà* between commas:

> Pour Microsoft, ce rachat permet de combler un retard. Son propre programme, Money, n'est pas un grand succès et n'arrive qu'en lointaine deuxième position dans les ventes américaines, avec 7 % du marché. Mais l'aquisition est, au-delà, d'une grande importance pour Bill Gates, son président, dans le cadre de ses ambitions dans le multimédia.

au-delà de

Like the mode without *de*, this one has simple adverbial applications in spatial and temporal statements, as in this comment on a soprano's performance in *La Bohème*:

> Ses *si* et son contre-ut sont assez terrifiants et son timbre plutôt métallique. Car elle a malheureusement des difficultés à monter au-delà du *la*.

But in addition to that simple adverbial role, this mode usually links two points in a 'not only ... but also' relationship. This it usually does in a single sentence, which it often begins. It is followed by a noun-structure; and its function could often be served in English by 'looking beyond'. That is, either it is used like 'in addition' to bring two points together, as in this sentence which says there are two problems to be solved, one of timetabling, the other more important: *Au-delà du calendrier, le gouvernement doit trancher une question de fond.* Or else like 'apart from', it can mark off a point from another, as in *Au-delà de cette différence essentielle, plusieurs points communs émergent* or *Au-delà de leurs différences, les deux films partagent une volonté de tout dire* and in this extract from an article about President Chirac and his first Prime Minister:

> Au-delà de leur différence de tempérament, Chirac l'officier de réserve et Juppé le diplomate sont en parfaite harmonie.

par-delà

The form mentioned above, *au-delà de* followed by a noun-structure, is sometimes replaced by *par-delà* (without *de*). Thus the final sentence of an obituary article on an eminent and controversial scholar reads as follows: *Par-delà les controverses qu'il suscita, il allait à l'essentiel : tel est son legs, tel est son défi.* And a discussion of apparent differences between Nazi practices towards those imprisoned in their concentration camps, as revealed by the ambiguous language of surviving documents, uses this structure to say that despite disparate appearances, the language reveals the same thing: an inability to tell the truth about what was being done in the camps:

> Les oppositions d'intérêt entre ceux qui se souciaient avant tout de tuer et ceux qui voulaient avant tout utiliser la main d'œuvre, même juive, sont attestées aussi bien par les documents de l'époque que par les témoignages postérieurs. Par-delà les oppositions de clans et de couches sociales, on retrouverait pourtant, chez ceux qui parlent, une même peur devant le réel, un même langage masqué.
>
> (Vidal-Naquet, 1987: 24–25)

The structure also at times replaces *au-delà* (without *de*) in some of its other functions: *Dans le monde arabe et, par-delà, dans l'espace musulman....*

The hyphen

The statement in the Quillet-Flammarion dictionary that *Au-delà s'écrivait autrefois sans trait d'union* appears to be accurate. On whether the structure is written nowadays with or without a hyphen, both the Robert and the *Trésor de la langue française* speak of the co-existence of forms with and without. Robert goes so far as to say that *l'usage reste très libre* and that *la plupart des écrivains l'omettent*. This is a statement which flies in the face of the evidence: few contemporary writers, and hardly any of the dictionaries, omit the hyphen. As for the hyphen of *par-delà*, there is no disagreement.

Some other ways of linking sentences with structures such as 'Besides', 'In addition', 'As well' or 'Apart from that' include *à côté de cela, en dehors de* and *outre*.

à côté de (cela)

This structure is used in two ways, one additive (like 'Besides'), the other comparative (like 'Beside'). It can introduce either the first or the second element of a statement. In its additive function, the more common of the two, *à côté de* could often be replaced by *outre* or *en dehors de*. It usually links two points of comparable significance: *À côté de ses besoins d'action, le XVIIᵉ siècle eut ses besoins d'esprit* (Leygues, 50). A theorist of political thought uses it when defining the origins of modern capitalism: having stressed the importance of the Reformation, he then adds that other developments also contributed to it:

> Il n'en résulte pas que la Réforme calviniste soit la cause première et suffisante de l'avènement capitaliste. Ce serait outrageusement simplifier les données de l'histoire : à côté de ce facteur moral de premier ordre, des circonstances purement matérielles ont joué.
>
> (Rougier, 223)

The comparative mode may be more often used than the additive to introduce the second part of the statement. This example comes from an article on the relative ferocity of pre-Communist and post-Communist forms of oppression in Russia, the latter being seen as bloodier by far:

> La répression de la révolution de 1905 donnerait même une image d'indulgence à côté de la destruction de Grozny et de la sauvagerie des troupes spéciales de Boris Eltsine en pays tchétchène.

The structure is quite often used in the form *à côté de cela* (or in speech, *à côté de ça*). In this example, taken from an account of the auctioning of the estate of Jean-Louis Barrault and Madeleine Renaud, the link made is contrastive:

> La Bibliothèque nationale a largement usé de son droit de préemption. Elle a emporté la majeure partie des documents d'écrivains – avec une enchère maximum de 29 000 francs pour treize lettres de Beckett à Madeleine Renaud, estimées à 6–8 000 francs. À côté de cela, les livres des Renaud-Barrault se sont vendus par caisses – 4 500 F pour une centaine d'ouvrages de « La Pléiade », soit 45 F l'exemplaire !

en dehors de

This structure has simple adverbial uses like those of *au-delà* – an article on hooliganism in a *cité* (called *la téci* in the youths' inverted slang) says: *En dehors de la téci, du territoire, il y a danger et on s'y aventure rarement.* When linking two parts of a statement, the structure most often has the force of 'in addition to'. A sentence in a death-notice on the racing driver Juan Manuel Fangio shows it in this mode:

> En dehors d'une fortune en espèces estimée, lors de sa retraite, à 1 million de dollars, Fangio était propriétaire de biens immobiliers et fonciers à Mar del Plata, le Deauville argentin.

However, sometimes it is used like 'apart from', to mark a disparity, as in the following sentence from a discussion of the theory of the early nineteenth-century naturalist, Étienne Geoffroy Saint-Hilaire, that the vertebrae of vertebrates and the segments of insects derived from a common origin. The author of the article, having accepted that the theory can appear to have a certain validity, then objects to it in a paragraph beginning: *Reste que vertébrés et insectes, en dehors de cette segmentation, semblent avoir bien peu en commun.* And sometimes it introduces neither addition nor divergence but only a different point, after the manner of *à côté de.* In this example, taken from an early twentieth-century discussion of the theory of genetic mutations, the authors having just discussed a type of mutation which they call *lente ou continue,* go on to discuss a different type:

> Mais, en dehors de ce mode de variation, il en existe un autre auquel on a donné le nom de variation *brusque* ou *discontinue.*
>
> (Delage & Goldsmith, 317)

At other times, the structure could be replaced by *au-delà de.*

outre

Like *au-delà*, this structure derives from an adverb meaning 'beyond'. Like it too, it is used to express the idea of 'in addition to'. The point which it introduces does not necessarily go farther than what it precedes. It says that what follows should be seen in conjunction with what precedes, as in this sentence describing two components of the Right-wing movement opposed to legal abortion, one of them belonging to the government of Alain Juppé, the other not belonging to it: *Outre un courant gouvernemental ultra-droitier, on trouve dans les rangs des anti-IVG une partie du Front national et quelques religieux.* In the following extract from an article on the Rapid Reaction Force (*la FRR*) sent to Bosnia in 1995, this equality of the two points linked is reinforced by **aussi** in the second half of the sentence: *Outre sa puissance en matière d'intervention terrestre, la FRR est aussi dotée d'une capacité aéromobile importante.*

The related conjunctional expression *outre que* also links two propositions of similar importance, as in this statement defending the Organization for African Unity (*l'OUA*) against criticism by pointing out two of its relative successes

> Outre qu'elle a sans doute empêché, par son existence même, que de nombreuses disputes ne dégénèrent gravement, l'OUA – qui regroupe aujourd'hui cinquante-trois pays – a entrepris, ces dernières années, un salutaire examen de concience.

au demeurant *

This expression is made from a noun no longer in current use, *le demeurant*, which meant 'the remainder'. With a literal meaning, therefore, close to that of ***au reste***, expressing something like 'as to the remainder' or 'as far as other things go' and hence intrinsically anaphoric, this connector has two basic functions: either it makes a contrast with what precedes or it reinforces it. At times, it may do both.

Contrastive

In this mode, the structure introduces a statement that is something of an opposite of, or corrective to, the one preceding. In English, its point could often be made by 'For all that'. Thus, an article discussing the likely outcomes of a gross blunder made by the government of the ephemeral Prime Minister Edith Cresson makes two points:

> Cette situation conduit immanquablement à s'interroger sur la survie de l'attelage exécutif, tel qu'il a été constitué autour de Mme Edith Cresson.
> Au demeurant, le premier ministre n'est pas en première ligne.

On the one hand, the future of the governing team is seen as problematical; on the other, the Prime Minister is not directly threatened. The connector could have been ***pour autant***. A similar relation between two statements, this time within a single sentence, can be seen in this excerpt from an editorial deploring an assassination by the IRA:

> Au-delà de la suppression d'un adversaire particulièrement déterminé – dont les arguments, au demeurant, n'avaient pas prévalu, – le meurtre de Ian Gow paraît relever d'une stratégie beaucoup plus générale de « terreur pour la terreur ».

In that sentence, the connector points the obvious contrast that, despite being a formidable adversary, Ian Gow had not been formidable enough to persuade others to his views.

In this contrastive mode, the structure quite often modifies adjectives by adding to a list of qualities one which hints at a disparity with those already mentioned. A journalist singles out a criticism of France made by a foreign newspaper in *un éditorial, au demeurant assez favorable.* An author discussing the newspaper sources drawn on by a writer for the plot of a novel refers to *une sinistre et, au demeurant, banale affaire d'assassinat.* A critic writing about a character in a play mentions his *goût un peu trop vif – au demeurant tout à fait platonique – pour la compagnie des adolescents.* A review of a recital by a singer combines praise for her voice with criticism of her technique:

> La soprano Dawn Upshaw, très belle voix au demeurant, nous dévoile tous ses problèmes techniques : aigus ouverts à l'extrême, bouche quasiment fermée tant dans les aigus que dans les graves (donc pratiquement absents).

An article about poor attendance of some French MPs at the then Chambre des Députés, and others' criticism of them for this, speaks of a certain Adolphe Chauvin:

> Depuis des années des élus s'indignent : l'un des plus virulents, aujourd'hui décédé, le centriste Adolphe Chauvin, homme au demeurant tolérant et placide, prenait de bien belles colères en constatant la désertification de l'hémicycle.

There the structure underscores the contrast in the man's character between occasional virulence and general easy-goingness. It could be replaced in this context by *par ailleurs*. In English, one could express the same relation between qualities with 'in other respects'. Also like *par ailleurs*, this structure can be placed, as can be seen from some of the examples, either at the beginning of sentences (and paragraphs) or in the middle of statements. In the former position, it is usually followed by a comma; in the latter, it is often flanked by commas.

Reinforcing

This second mode, reinforcing what precedes, is not mentioned by some of the linguistic authorities, who see the connector as having only a contrastive function. Indeed, Le Bidois defines no function for it. And the only function that the earlier Grevisse defined was as marking *opposition, restriction*; the revised Grevisse has deleted even that small mention (Grevisse, 1964a: 970; 1988: 1500). The older large Robert gave neither definition of meaning nor mention of any function. The fact is, many writers nowadays use *au demeurant* without marked contrastive or restrictive force, at times after *et*, like a simple variant for the supportive mode of *du reste* or *d'ailleurs*. A discussion of inter-tribal politics in the African state of Burundi says this:

> Le pouvoir politique central reste un monopole tutsi. C'est une dictature et, au demeurant, cela ne saurait être autre chose.

Similarly, a report on negotiations between Denmark and the French aircraft manufacturer Dassault-Breguet says, first, that the Danes had been interested in the Mirage 2000 and the Rafale, then adds this:

> Tout en reconnaissant les qualités du Mirage 2000, l'état-major de l'armée de l'air danoise l'estime trop cher et, de leur côté, les négociateurs de Dassault-Breguet ne croient pas aux chances du Rafale au Danemark.
>
> Au demeurant, à la fin du mois dernier, l'état-major de l'armée de l'air danoise a fait savoir qu'il avait sélectionné une version modernisée du F-16 de General Dynamics et le Gripen suédois [...]

There it is clear that the connector serves no oppositive function, but rather introduces an additional fact that makes it unlikely that the outcome of the negotiations will be favourable for the French company. The same goes for the following exemplar, taken from a discussion of massive disruptions to French road traffic caused by drivers opposed to new licences with deductible points for traffic infringements:

> Résumons : le 1er juillet entrait en application le principe du permis à points, dûment légalisé par un vote massif de l'Assemblée nationale. Il y était, entre autres, précisé que l'entrave ou la gêne à la circulation valait retrait automatique de trois points sur six. Au demeurant, cet aspect de la réforme n'était contesté par personne.

In that last sentence, what follows the connector in no way contrasts with or restricts what precedes. On the contrary, in clarifying what was known and commonly accepted about the new points-system, it reinforces the *dûment légalisé* and the *précisé* of the previous sentences. In such a sentence in English, this function might well be served by 'anyhow', 'anyway' or 'And in any case'.

A dual mode

Sometimes, the connector functions in a dual mode, introducing both a contrast and a reinforcement. An article on the delayed advent of take-over bids in the French financial world during the mid-1980s says this:

> Il faudra attendre avril 1986 pour en connaître une première spectaculaire avec l'offensive de l'Italien Carlo De Benedetti sur le premier équipementier automobile français Valeo. Au demeurant, les principales entreprises françaises de l'industrie et de la finance étaient préservées de toute attaque par leur statut de nationalisées.

In that example, the structure at one and the same time marks a contrast and reinforces a point: although take-over bids had begun to become prevalent at that time, even so the nationalized industries were not at risk. A similar dual usage occurs in the next example, which deals with what the writer sees as the duty incumbent on Germany's present and future leaders:

> Les dirigeants actuels et futurs de ce pays devront, plus que jamais, renoncer à leur péché mignon : le provincialisme, qui est, au demeurant, infiniment moins dérangeant que les maléfices d'un autre temps.

There, the connector, bearing partly on the adjective *mignon* and partly on the noun *péché*, both confirms that the sin, though venial, is still a sin and contrasts it with the enormity of German sins in the past.

The views of some authorities

Recent developments in the usage of this connector may be seen in the comments of some authorities. In the middle of the nineteenth century, Littré saw in it *une certaine nuance de familiarité*. A century later, the Le Bidois' book says of it: *ne s'emploie plus guère que dans une intention plaisante* (Le Bidois, II, 628), possibly because the authors were thinking of its tongue-in-cheek tone in Marot and Rabelais, who use it to append a favourable coda to a list of unfavourable qualities, as in the celebrated description of Panurge, who is not only a thief, a drunkard, a cheat and a layabout but a good son to his father:

> malfaisant, pipeur, beuveur, bateur de pavéz, ribleur s'il en estoit en Paris...; au demourant, le meilleur filz du monde.
>
> (Rabelais, I, 301)

There, its comic effect comes mainly from its indeterminacy: if it means 'despite that', it acknowledges a disparity between what precedes and what follows; if it means 'as well as that', it suggests that what precedes is a list of admirable qualities. It could be replaced in that mode by **avec cela**.

Conversely, Dupré takes the view that, apart from a single difference, the structure is indistinguishable from *au reste*; and that each of these structures is the equivalent of the expression *à part ça*. The single difference is as follows:

> Il y a plutôt une différence de ton : [...] *au demeurant* est un archaïsme qui s'emploie avec une nuance un peu solennelle et ironique [...]
>
> (Dupré, I, 639)

Contemporary uses of *au demeurant* do not appear to bear out these views. Most writers use it without apparent archaism or jocular intention. Nor is any trace of familiarity or tongue-in-cheek tone to be detected in the usage of a writer from an earlier part of this century who was very fond of it, André Gide – in the following example, he clearly uses it contrastively: his description of Anna Shackleton's flat gives first its disadvantages, then, with the connector, an advantage:

Elle habitait, rue de Vaugirard, entre la rue Madame et la rue d'Assas, un petit appartement de quatre pièces exiguës et si basses que presque on en pouvait toucher de la main le plafond. Au demeurant l'appartement n'était pas mal situé, en face du jardin ou de la cour de je ne sais quel établissement scientifique, où nous pûmes contempler les essais des premières chaudières solaires.

(Gide, 1954: 368)

au fait *

This structure, which has a largely spoken flavour, is sometimes used in texts of familiar or conversational tone. As a connector, after the manner of *à propos*, it sometimes links less to a previous word or statement than to an assumption left latent or implicit in what precedes. Sometimes it serves to recall in passing a point which is of tangential importance, of momentary interest but inconsequential in its present context; at other times, it can introduce the development of a more important point.

The point in passing

In this mode, the connector makes a sort of direct apostrophe to the reader. It usually accompanies something like an aside, very possibly a question. After the manner of 'incidentally' or 'come to think of it', it reminds both writer and reader of something which, though of minor importance in the present circumstance, should not be neglected. What it accompanies is often placed inside brackets, as in these examples, the first of which comes from a review of a performance of Wagner's *Ring*:

À commencer par la merveilleuse Léonie Rysanek, voix flamboyante, Sieglinde tout entière à son frère attachée : on n'oubliera plus le cri qu'elle a poussé lorsqu'il s'est effondré, frappé à mort. Nadine Denize, Fricka superbe d'autorité vocale et dramatique, a confirmé la forte impression qu'elle avait laissée dans *Parsifal* au Palais Garnier (au fait, pourquoi l'y voit-on si peu ?). Les fameux « Hoïo-toho » de Birgit Nilsson, au deuxième acte, ne sont plus ce qu'ils furent [...]

The second example, combined with *mais*, comes from Roland Barthes's essay on the mythological significance of Albert Einstein's brain:

Une image le montre étendu, la tête hérissée de fils électriques : on enregistre les ondes de son cerveau, cependant qu'on lui demande de « penser à la relativité ». (Mais, au fait, que veut dire exactement : « penser à... » ?) On veut nous faire entendre sans doute que les sismogrammes seront d'autant plus violents que la « relativité » est un sujet ardu.

(Barthes, 1957: 92)

A more important point

In its second mode, this structure does not just comment on a point in passing. It reminds the reader of something mentioned earlier, a more substantial point on which discussion may run to a paragraph. Sometimes combined with *donc* or *car* and again often asking a question, it is usually placed at the beginning of a sentence or paragraph. This extract from a study of François Mitterrand describes the moment during the presidential election of 1965 when he became recognized as the leader of the Left:

> Le leader de la gauche n'a certes pas de doctrine très assurée. Ainsi, entre les deux tours, à la télévision, plaidera-t-il à la fois pour la liberté de l'entreprise et la renaissance du rôle de l'État, qui est de « décider » – notamment pour les investissements.
> Au fait, qu'est-ce donc que la gauche, à ses yeux ?
> Le 22 mai, il s'explique à la télévision [...] : « La gauche, c'est tout ce qui se bat pour les libertés individuelles, pour la justice, l'égalité sociale... »
>
> (Nay, 288)

This development introduced by *au fait* continues for two paragraphs. Similarly, an article dealing with the difficulties faced in France by Algerian intellectuals whose lives would be threatened by Islamic fundamentalists if they were to return home, discusses first the *bienveillance* with which, it is hoped, French consular officials will treat them:

> Cette bienveillance a également été recommandée aux préfectures sur le sol français. Elles ont consigne de prolonger sans trop de difficultés les visas de plusieurs semaines. Mais l'information est-elle vraiment passée ? Tout dépend, dans tel ou tel service, de l'interprétation des consignes face à cette catégorie inédite d'immigrés. Car au fait, administrativement, qu'est-ce qu'un Algérien qui fuit aujourd'hui l'Algérie ?
> On le définit d'abord par ce qu'il n'est pas. Et ce n'est pas un réfugié politique. Selon les normes internationales [...]

This mode may also be preceded by *mais*, also usually introducing a question. The author of a discussion of French foreign policy towards the war in Bosnia-Herzegovina, having canvassed several points of view in as many paragraphs, begins a new paragraph of discussion which will broach a pertinent consideration not yet mentioned: *Mais, au fait, quelle cause devons-nous défendre en Bosnie ?* In such contexts, saying something like 'Look, let's be clear about this', suggesting that it is time to make explicit an assumption shared by writer and reader which, though basic, should not have been left so long unstated, the connector comes close to being replaceable by *après tout*.

At times, too, it is used in place of *en fait* or *à vrai dire*, to define a preceding point more accurately, like one of the modes of 'actually':

Voici un cas singulier : Mlle Ying Chen, comme son patronyme l'indique, est chinoise. Elle est d'ailleurs née à Shanghai il y a trente-quatre ans. Mlle Ying Chen, au fait, n'est plus une Chinoise mais une Québécoise pur sucre.

In English, 'in fact' or 'so' might be used for this second mode, possibly accompanied by italics. The example above about Algerian refugees from fundamentalism might be phrased: 'So what *is* an Algerian ...' English-language journalists might well fall back on their tic of adding 'just' or 'exactly' to any interrogative word: 'Just what do we mean by ...?'

au final *

This connector is of very recent coinage, dating possibly from the early 1980s (Grieve, 1995a). It has become common among some journalists and people in performance industries. It has joined the set of concluders or resumers such as *bref*, *enfin*, *en fin de compte*, *en somme* or *finalement*.

History

The connector derives from the common noun *le final(e)* (Grieve, 1995b). The original form *le finale*, borrowed from Italian *il finale*, is now rare. The form which now dominates is the shorter *le final*. Certainly the connector seems never to have the spelling *au finale*. The original meaning of the noun was the climactic conclusion of an act in an opera or a movement in a piece of music, the meaning which came into English as 'finale'. In recent times the noun has come to be used for the climax of stage-shows given by dancers and pop-singers, the endings of ballets, plays and films, the closing or climactic scenes of novels, the final stage of fashion parades and car rallies. In the usage of some writers, *le final* would appear to have little more semantic content than *la fin*. It may be in that shift of meaning that one can see the origin of the connector *au final*, which usually designates 'end' rather than 'climax'.

As connector

The connector summarizes a development, introduces a conclusion, puts a finer point upon a preceding argument, saying something like 'finally' or 'when all's said and done' or 'in the last analysis'. At times it is clear that it replaces *enfin* in one of its modes; at others it replaces *finalement*; on occasion, it can be seen to be an equivalent of *somme toute*, *tout compte fait*, *en fin de compte*, *au fond* or even *au total*. This example comes from a review of a production of *La main verte* ('collage de textes sur les jardins mis en scène par Gilbert Tsaï'), in which the settings both of the stage and the auditorium are described like this:

> [Le spectateur] emprunte de petites allées de sable au milieu de centaines de très hauts bambous, et de lauriers du Portugal avant d'aller s'asseoir autour du vaste plancher carré (avec bancs... de jardin). Le décor simple conçu par Lou Gouaco est circulairement environné d'une sylve au final assez japonisante, aménagée par le paysagiste Gilles Clément [...]

There the neologism appears to stands for *finalement* or *somme toute*. It underscores the slight comment made by the writer on a contrast or an incongruity which she perceives between the Japaneseness of the woodland scenery and, presumably, the Portugueseness of the laurels. In English, that slight comment might be made with 'actually'.

The next example shows the structure replacing *enfin* in its most basic sense of 'lastly'. Taken from a discussion of the recent history of the French Communist Party, it refers to the steep and flagrant decline of the Party's fortunes; and it links this decline to the continuing Stalinism of practices within the central committee aimed at eliminating any dissenters from the reigning orthodoxy of 'democratic centralism'. The verb has four direct objects, in the form of a list of nouns, detailing the unfavourable outcomes of the twenty-fifth and twenty-sixth congresses of the Party; and the fourth and last of these it introduces with *au final*. It is the combination of the connector with *et* which makes plain that its role is to announce the final element in the list, rather than sum up the preceding three:

> Les vingt-cinquième et vingt-sixième congrès en 1985 et 1987 ont permis un nettoyage en règle du comité central, la remise au pas des fédérations dissidentes, l'exclusion des élus trop autonomes et, au final, l'établissement d'un pouvoir sans partage sur des décombres.

This substitution for *enfin* is evident, too, in the combination with **reste**, at the beginning of a paragraph and introducing the last substantive point in a discussion: *Reste au final une question sans réponse à ce jour...*

In some contexts the connector could be replaced by *quoi qu'il arrive*. In others, the tone is closer to 'taking everything together', to *au total*. In the following example, taken from an article on the working life of a young lawyer, it begins the final paragraph summing up the previously detailed day of overwork: *Au final, de dix à quinze heures de travail par jour, sans compter les permanences du week-end.*

At the moment, the connector is something of a trendyism, comparable to 'at the end of the day'.

au fond *

This structure functions either like a simple adverb, that is, within a single sentence, or as an inter-assertional connector. Its function is always to introduce a more accurate definition either of what precedes or of what is implied. For example, when a character says of Swann, *Moi je crois qu'au fond il n'aime plus cette femme* (Proust, I, 34), the simple adverbial function is clear enough: it defines the truth about Swann's feeling. But Swann's *coquine de femme* has just been spoken of some lines before; and this *au fond* accompanying the new mention of her functions also at a more intuitive level as a sort of anaphoric link. Conversely, the connective function is explicit when Zola writes *Les Coupeau, devant le monde, affectèrent d'être bien débarrassés. Au fond, ils rageaient* (Zola, 392). There the structure marks, after the manner of *en fait*, the contrast between the pretence of the Coupeaus' appearance and their genuine feelings. But the simpler adverbial function, defining the truth of their feeling, is no less present. English equivalents, depending on contexts, might be 'really', 'at heart', 'basically', 'fundamentally'. The link made is sometimes adversative, sometimes confirmative.

Confirming

Whether this structure is placed first in the sentence or accompanies the verb, it can serve either the adversative or the confirming function. An example of it in the latter mode is this extract from an article dealing with Pierre Mendès France's high-minded conception of the proper relation between governments and governed:

> Antidémagogique par principe, au lieu de flatter le peuple il exige de celui-ci sa participation continue.
> Cependant, cette éthique si élevée repose sur un optimisme probablement excessif sur [sic] la nature humaine. Au fond, Mendès France, comme tant d'autres hommes de gauche, croyait non seulement dans la perfectibilité de l'homme – celui-ci parvenant à subordonner ses intérêts propres à ceux de la Cité – , mais dans une sorte de coïncidence nécessaire entre les progrès de la démocratie et les progrès de l'efficacité du pouvoir.

There, if there is an adversative quality to the proposition introduced by the connector, it is probably no more than an implicit echo of the preceding *Cependant*; and this exemplar of the connector could almost be replaced by *en effet*. And in the next example, combined with *même*, it confirms that Camus was really a writer, while going beyond that definition in a way which is quasi-adversative:

> Alors que Sartre est d'abord un philosophe hanté par l'image de l'écrivain, Camus est d'abord un écrivain, hanté par l'image du philosophe. C'est même, au fond, un homme de théâtre.

Adversative

The adversative link is often one between appearance and a deeper reality, sometimes made explicit in what precedes by a word such as *apparence* or *surface*. In many of these contexts too, the link could be made with *en fait*: *La tentative d'aujourd'hui est plus modeste en apparence, et plus ambitieuse au fond.* / *Des faits qui, malgré des dissemblances apparentes, sont, au fond, identiques.* / *Que se cache-t-il derrière ces apparences anec-dotiques ? Au fond un dépit amoureux.*

In making this link to the idea of misleading appearances, it can be seen that the connector also serves to introduce an interprétation of what precedes, a translation of it into a more reliable statement. In the following example, the writer translates the word *classe*, used as praise in a wine-guide, into a more fitting form of words to describe a great Champagne. An apter version of truth is opposed to one seen as inaccurate:

> Un vieux régisseur, une technique éprouvée – vinification en petits fûts de chêne – et la rénovation progressive d'un vignoble vétuste : le Clos du Mesnil atteint, quand le millésime le permet, ce que le guide Hachette baptise la « classe » et qui n'est au fond rien d'autre qu'une superbe apogée, l'expression sublimée d'une parcelle champenoise extraite du métissage végétal.

There, the author might have used *en réalité* or *en vérité*. This analytical or simplifying function is seen in another way in a reduction of many considerations to a single pertinent one: *Au fond, les questions posées dans les pages qui précèdent pourraient se ramener à une seule.*

This translative function is also analogous to that of *bref* or *en un mot*, which could be used in this discussion of Sartre's notion of the *salaud*:

> Le salaud, au sens sartrien du terme, c'est celui qui se croit, qui se prend au sérieux, celui qui oublie sa propre contingence, sa propre responsabilité, sa propre liberté, celui qui est persuadé de son bon droit, de sa bonne foi, et c'est la définition même, pour Sartre, de la mauvaise. Le salaud, au fond, c'est celui qui se prend pour Dieu (l'amour en moins), ou qui est persuadé que Dieu (ou l'Histoire, ou la Vérité...) est dans son camp et couvre, comme on dit à l'armée, ou autorise, ou justifie, tout ce qu'il se croit tenu d'accomplir.

Variant

The expression *dans le fond*, perhaps a little more familiar in tone, is sometimes used as a variant for this connector. In this example, transcribed from an interview, the speaker comments on the vogue for chefs who theorize and pontificate on television, not only about cooking, and tries to give an accurate definition of their attitude to the world:

Je me demande si chez ces gens de la cuisine, il n'y a pas une vieille revanche
à prendre sur toute la société. Dans le fond, les cuisiniers n'ont jamais été
estimés. Ils ont toujours été bien en deçà, même des travailleurs manuels.

(Sédouy & Bouteiller, 235)

au lieu que

Here is an obsolescent connector which once functioned much like *alors
que* in its adversative applications. Indeed, much less used nowadays
than it once was, it has been almost completely replaced by *alors que*.
This view was voiced as long ago as the 1950s: *Cette locution paraît
aujourd'hui archaïque ; on dit plutôt tandis que, alors que* (Thomas, 1956:
241–242).

History

The structure was favoured by writers of prose and verse in the seventeenth century. It was very well suited to shaping the antithetical sentences
of the eighteenth, as in this contrast that a writer makes between his
different reactions to two women:

J'abordais Mlle de Vulson avec un plaisir très vif, mais sans trouble ; au lieu
qu'en voyant seulement Mlle Goton, je ne voyais plus rien ; tous mes sens étaient
bouleversés.

(Rousseau, 30)

Until about a century ago, the structure was common, as in this extract
from a discussion of different versions of the folk-tale Puss-in-Boots:

La version donnée par Perrault du Chat Botté est très ancienne, car le chat
parle et agit comme tel, au lieu que dans d'autres versions, c'est un homme
métamorphosé en chat, ou même un ami humain qui tirent d'affaire le fils du
meunier.

(Van Gennep, 218)

And in the first half of this century, it was still widely used: Alain, for
instance, uses it often – sometimes on the same page as he uses its then
competitor *alors que* (Alain, 1956: 444 & 1254). Camus was still using it
in the 1950s (Camus, 1965: 1060)

Contemporary usage

Despite the more recent view of Dupré: *la locution conjonctive* au lieu
que *[...] n'est pas si désuète que le pense A. V. Thomas* (Dupré, II, 1475),
it must be said the structure is rare in the second half of the twentieth
century. It is probable that the few writers who use it began to write at

a time when it was still extant or do not object to a flavour of archaism. One of the former would be Sartre, who must have been one of the last generation of French writers to use it with any frequency. In 'Le procès de Burgos' (1971), considering the Basque country as a colony of Spain, he identifies

> ce paradoxe que le pays colonisateur serait pauvre et surtout agricole au lieu que le pays colonisé serait riche et qu'il offrirait le profil démographique des sociétés hautement industrialisées.
>
> (Sartre, 1976: 17. See also 1949b: 42)

Nowadays the connector is sometimes used in the academic or literary world. A preface (1967) to *Manon Lescaut* contrasts the novel with the tragedies of Racine:

> Mais la tragédie racinienne se déroule entre des dieux et des princes, au lieu que le roman de Prévost a pour héros, selon les termes de Montesquieu, « un fripon » et « une catin ».
>
> (Coulet, 23)

About the same time, the Le Bidois brothers use it in their discussion of the distinction that can be made between the functioning of two pairs of adverbs and conjunctions, on the one hand *pourtant* and *cependant*, on the other *néanmoins* and *toutefois*:

> Comme l'a bien vu Lafaye, *pourtant* et *cependant* ont cette caractéristique commune de détruire ou d'exclure ce qui a été dit, (le premier, d'ailleurs, avec plus de force que le second); au lieu que *néanmoins* et *toutefois* ne le renversent pas [...]
>
> (Le Bidois, II, 242)

The structure is almost completely unused in the world of journalism. Once in a while it turns up, as in this extract from an obituary article published by *Le Monde* in January 1994 on the death of Jean-Louis Barrault, in which the writer contrasts the sort of after-life enjoyed by a dead film-actor with the utter finality of the death of the theatre actor:

> Le comédien de cinéma peut jouer les revenants de ciné-clubs ; les arrière-petits-fils de Jouvet connaissent ses pommettes et ses hennissements comme s'ils avaient flirté à l'Athénée en 1947, ou au cinéma Champollion. Au lieu que l'acteur de théâtre, quand il meurt : plus rien, le vide des coulisses un soir de relâche !

And in a review of a naturalistic play, a critic who finds naturalism crude and wanting uses this connector to define what it is about it that is crude and wanting. The play, he says, about incest, is a mere imitation of a sordid *fait divers* reported in any newspaper, utterly lacking in what Greek tragedy or Shakespeare would have made of it:

Le théâtre n'a pas lieu. Pas le moindre commencement de théâtre. Du toc. C'est que l'inceste, à Delphes, à Londres en 1600, n'est pas jeté comme ça, comme des bas morceaux de carne à des chiens, à la face d'autrui. Les faits participent d'une fable, d'un imaginaire, d'une invention spirituelle, ils sont sublimés par la lumière d'une éternité de conscience. Au lieu que le théâtre de la contrefaçon naturaliste ne décolle pas du sordide. Surtout si l'acteur reproduit gestes et voix par une démarche réaliste.

(Cournot, 17)

As the examples show, this structure, again like *alors que*, can either function within a single sentence or be placed first in a ***phrase dépendante***. Its most evident English equivalents are 'whereas' and non-temporal 'while'.

au point que *

Like other modifiers ending in *que*, such as *à ceci près que* or *si bien que*, this one links two propositions either as parts of the same sentence or as separate sentences. When it does the latter, it stands first in a ***phrase dépendante***.

Six modes

Au point que is one of six variant structures based on the noun *le point*. The others are *à ce point que*, *à tel point que*, *à un tel point que*, *à un point tel que* and *C'est au point que*. The most frequently used nowadays are *au point que* and *à tel point que*. All six variants mean roughly *tellement que*. In English, an expression like 'so much so that' would cover most of their applications. However, convention makes it unlikely that an English sentence would begin with 'so much so that' – in that position, 'indeed' often serves the function of this connector. Inside the sentence, the structure is preceded by a comma.

All six are probably interchangeable in most contexts, except for *C'est au point que*. It would be unusual for it to be placed inside a sentence; and it is the only one able to introduce a grammatically independent sentence. An example comes from a discussion of the distinction made in Indo-European languages between noun-forms and verb-forms:

La morphologie indo-européenne présente en effet pour l'un et pour l'autre des séries de suffixes et de désinences qui ne sont pas les mêmes. C'est au point que neuf fois sur dix on peut reconnaître du premier coup si une forme du sanskrit ou du grec ancien appartient à un nom ou à un verbe.

(Vendryes, 139)

In English, the second sentence might begin 'One might even say' or 'One could go as far as to say'.

Standard functioning

Whether placed internally or initially, what precedes may express ideas such as growth and expansion, aggravation or difficulty, development for better or for worse; what follows states the outcome or effects of this development. In the next two examples, these ideas are conveyed by *effervescence, de plus en plus, vagues* and *violence*:

> Après plus d'une année de calme dans les milieux scolaires et universitaires, une certaine effervescence tend de plus en plus à se manifester, au point que les autorités ont choisi récemment d'arrêter les cours durant trois jours dans l'espoir d'apaiser les tensions.

When placed first in the sentence, it may be a convenient way to break a sentence which would otherwise be too long, as in this extract from a discussion of the growth of strikes during the *belle époque*:

> Plus brève, plus fréquente et plus extensive (on dénombre 1 600 conflits en 1890–1893, et très souvent pour cause de 1er Mai), plus offensive aussi en période de hautes eaux économiques, moins violente et peu à peu autodiscipilnée, déferlant par vagues, la grève fin de siècle entête tous ses acteurs, dégage un étrange parfum d'espoir qui est, lui, d'une rare violence. Au point que ses théoriciens, renforcés il est vrai par des transfuges de l'anarchisme et flattés par quelques bons apôtres du socialisme, en feront l'Idéal, l'annonce du « grand soir », le signe et le signal d'une Révolution inéluctable, celle de la grève générale.

Closeness to *même*

The function of the structure could often be served by *même*, placed beside the verb. Indeed a combination, *au point même que*, is not unheard of. The following example shows how a sentence that is not split into two, though just as intelligible as one which is, may give an effect of untidiness or disparateness – it starts by speaking of Donizetti's opera, *Lucia di Lammermoor*, goes on to a mention of a soprano, and ends with a reference to another soprano who has nothing to do with the opera under discussion:

> Inspiré de *la Fiancée de Lammermoor* de Walter Scott, il devait être créé au San Carlo de Naples en 1835 avec, dans le rôle-titre, une soprano, Fanny Persiani, qui, à 23 ans, avait déjà gagné ses galons de diva, au point même que, l'année précédente, à l'issue d'une représentation au San Carlo, elle avait eu la visite dans sa loge d'une autre immense star, la Malibran elle-même, venue la féliciter pour la beauté de sa voix !

à telle enseigne que

The variant structure *à telle(s) enseigne(s) que* can link two parts of the same sentence, as in this lament on the disappearance of good bread written by the gastronome Jean Ferniot:

> Je suis un amateur de pain et, par conséquent, un homme malheureux. Cette denrée, essentielle, surtout pour nous, Français, réputés mangeurs de pain (nous en consommons, en moyenne, à peu près notre poids en une année) est traitée par la plupart des boulangers de façon scandaleuse, à telle enseigne que bien des restaurateurs, et pas toujours avec succès, se sont mis à le fabriquer eux-mêmes.

But it is probably more often placed at the beginning of a *phrase dépendante*, as in this extract from an essay on lobsters by another gastronome, James de Coquet:

> Dans le monde fermé des crustacés, rien ne vaut le homard. L'inconvénient de celui-ci c'est que, pour le bien déguster, il faut être outillé comme un dentiste et se livrer à une chirurgie peu ragoûtante. En outre, le morceau de choix de cet animal c'est la pince. À telle enseigne que ceux qui ont perdu au combat une de leurs redoutables cisailles, ou les deux, valent beaucoup moins cher que les sujets d'élite ayant su conserver l'intégrité de leur armement.

au point de

The related construction *au point de* is always followed by an infinitive. It too is placed either internally or initially, as in this example, which speaks of the greatly increased budget of the French Ministry of Cultural Affairs during the tenure of Jack Lang as minister:

> Grâce à Jack Lang, ce portefeuille a été doté d'attributions financières sans précédent, ce qui a permis de mener une action réelle dans tous les secteurs de la culture. Au point de se poser non seulement en interlocuteur mais aussi en interprète du monde artistique.

aura

This structure, although not a connector, is sometimes combined with connective structures such as *finalement* and *au bout du compte*. And it is part and parcel nowadays of the discursive style to which procedural connectors belong. It consists merely in the use, for a special purpose, of a compound tense, variously known as the future perfect, the future anterior or the compound future. This tense, made of the future of an auxiliary verb, either *avoir* or *être*, and the past participle of a main verb, is frequently used, especially by journalists, in ways which may appear to have little to do with the time-zone of the past future to which, in the logic of tenses, it belongs. According to that logic, this tense would be used to refer 'to a past in relation to some point in the future'; and a simple example of this straightforward use would be: *J'aurai fini ce travail dans trois jours* (Judge & Healey, 112). However, the tense is nowadays very often used to describe actions which are in the past when seen not from the future but from the writer's present. In fact, this is one of the three most common tenses by means of which French writers recounting a series of past events avoid using a simple past tense, the others being the future and the historical present.

The writer who uses this compound tense for a simple past gives, or tries to give, to what it describes an aura of awe. The sentence in which it occurs is often either the first or the last of an article. It may talk of the beginning of something seen as pregnant with the promise of peril, as in this comment on the Danes' rejection of the referendum on the Treaty of Maastricht:

> Le « non » des Danois au traité de Maastricht n'aura été que l'explosion de la première mine d'un champ qui en compte beaucoup d'autres.

Or it may speak of the end of something important in the shared experience of the nation at large or the human race, an era, a tradition, a life, a phase of government, as in this extract from a reflexion on the closing years of the twentieth century:

> Cette fin de siècle aura été riche en événements inouïs qui auront vu se succéder l'euphorie et l'inquiétude : chute du mur de Berlin et effondrement du système et de l'empire soviétiques, fin de l'apartheid en Afrique du Sud, aujourd'hui éclaircie au Proche-Orient.

The sentences read as though the events described are being seen not from the point in the present at which they are being written about but from that more remote point in posterity at which History will make its gnomic judgments. The writer not only gives himself the superior acumen of one who evaluates the public act described, but also adopts the profound and prophetic view of one who can decipher the meaning of present events as they will have come to be seen in the retrospect of wiser men than we. The tone of solemnity befits the valedictory article on a former Prime Minister who commits suicide:

> Le dernier acte de Pierre Bérégovoy, acte intime s'il en est, aura d'une certaine manière été son dernier acte politique.

Final sentences

This tone, befitting exceptional circumstances, is heard in the final sentence of a review of an outstanding work of poetry: *Rarement la douleur aura été à ce point énoncée dans son émouvante nudité*. It is a tone to be heard in the last sentence of obituaries, that sentence which sums up a life or in which a way of dying is seen in relation to a whole life. Here are two examples of final sentences, the first from an obituary on a politician of the Centre, the second from an obituary on a President of Algeria, assassinated by Muslim extremists:

> Et pour tous, après plus de quarante ans de combat politique, il faisait figure de père du centrisme, même s'il avait pris quelques distances avec le mouvement lui-même. Il aura disparu sans avoir vu son grand rêve d'un centre autonome se réaliser.

> Singulière destinée, en tout cas, que celle de Mohamed Boudiaf : l'homme avait déclenché, avec la lutte armée, le terrorisme, pour donner l'indépendance à son pays. Il aura péri par le terrorisme.

In these examples, as in all exemplars of this usage as a *de facto* past tense, the verb's meaning is the one it would have in the simple past or the perfect: *Il disparut* or *Il a péri*. But the compound tense speaks that grave meaning in the voice of expectant destiny. An English equivalent, if a certain solemnity is felt to be apt, might be 'He was to die ...'.

Opening sentences

Opening sentences, like final sentences, lend themselves these days to this sententious voice of history. Sometimes, the compound tense is still used in accordance with the simple logic of its two points of reference: the present, at which it is written, and the future point at which a foreseeable act will have been accomplished:

> En quatre jours de visite officielle en Chine populaire, M. Gorbatchev aura achevé, la semaine prochaine, de réconcilier l'URSS et le monde.

And, even when the act described has already taken place, a reader can often see that the circumstances may be important enough to warrant the use of such a ceremonial tense – the fact, for instance, that fifty years after the *rafle du Vel' d'Hiv'* the French, in the view of the writer, have still not adopted a proper attitude to their complicity in the Nazis' Final Solution: *Un demi-siècle n'aura pas suffi à la France pour porter sur son passé un regard lucide et juste.*

A journalist's tic

One must assume that when this tense is used in an opening sentence a reader hears in it a hint that the article it heads will have something portentous to say. However, the fact is that many examples of its use are mere attempts by journalists whose motto is hyperbole to appear to be saying more than they do and to give to trivia a trendy pretence of durability. As a tic of style, this one is now endemic in French journalistic culture. The circumstances which it dignifies are often not worth it: *Pour la presse quotidienne nationale, les années 1991 et 1992 auront été des années difficiles.* The most common verbs used are undoubtedly *falloir*, accompanied by an expression of time, and *être*:

> Quarante-cinq ans ! Il aura fallu presque un demi-siècle pour qu'un gouvernement ose prendre le risque de soumettre au Parlement la réforme du statut des dockers.

> L'année passée, dont on tire à présent les bilans, aura été pour le moins, en matière d'architecture, une année contrastée, agitée.

It is remarkable that Grevisse, commonly so aware of twentieth-century usage, having noted this use, has nothing to say about the epidemic of it among journalists. The most recent of the examples he quotes dates from 1899. Nothing is added to the entry in the revised 12th edition; but a few things are subtracted (Grevisse, 1964a: 661; 1988: 1299).

au reste *

Some authorities define a difference in force between *au reste* and ***du reste*** akin to that between *au moins* and ***du moins***:

> La forme en « du » annonce une division plus tranchée, une restriction plus forte que la forme en « au ».
>
> (d'Harvé, 275)

This view is not confirmed by other authorities. Hanse, while seeing the two structures as synonymous, discerns only a slight difference of tone between them: au reste *est aujourd'hui plutôt littéraire [...];* du reste *est plus courant* (Hanse, 1983: 824). This view supersedes a very different entry in Hanse (1949: 636).

Relation to *d'ailleurs*

This connector, like *du reste*, is something of a variant for ***d'ailleurs***. According to Le Bidois:

> *Au reste* et *du reste* sont à peu près synonymes de *d'ailleurs*, mais marquent plus de détachement encore, (« en laissant de côté les autres choses »).
>
> (Le Bidois, II, 628)

It usually introduces an additional point or argument which, though tending in the same direction as the one preceding, is supplementary to it. Thus, a discussion of an international rugby match lost by the French gives two reasons for not jumping to the conclusion that this defeat marks the end of a period of French hegemony in the Five Nations Championship:

> Cette défaite est-elle dès lors le début de la fin de la domination française en Europe ? Compte tenu des conditions exceptionnelles dans lesquelles ce match a été disputé, il est trop tôt pour l'affirmer. Au reste, le sélectionneur tricolore a pu être rassuré sur au moins un point : après avoir surmonté la tension nerveuse du début du match, Didier Camberabero s'est bien affirmé comme le buteur (trois transformations et trois pénalités, soit 15 points) qui a fait défaut ces dernières années à l'équipe de France.

The first reason given, the poor weather, would be sufficient to discount the hypothesis raised in the opening question. The second reason, the advent of a good goal-kicker, merely confirms the first by adding a further argument to what is in itself a convincing reason for not accepting the hypothesis.

The argument introduced can also be an afterthought or a coda, merely appended and leading to no further development. A writer, setting out an exposition of Marxist economic theory, says that it combines

> l'analyse scientifique et la condamnation morale. La force de travail est payée à sa valeur mais celle-ci, dans un système de propriété privée, laisse au propriétaire des moyens de production la plus-value. Au reste, qu'y a-t-il de plus répugnant qu'un régime qui traite le travail humain en marchandise ?
> (Aron, 1977, 39–40)

That being the end of a paragraph, the author has nothing more to say on this point. A similar thing is seen in an extract from a discussion of whether André Malraux, searching for the legendary capital of the Queen of Sheba, ever flew over the right part of Arabia:

> Quant à la géographie... Malraux, apparemment, ne s'en souciait guère, ce qui a toujours fait dire aux « spécialistes » en la matière que, venant de la côte française des Somalis (à présent État de Djibouti), il n'a pas atteint la zone même de Mareb mais survolé seulement les villages situés un peu au nord de Sanaa, au reste fort spectaculaires avec leurs gratte-ciel d'allure babylonienne.

This coda has often the nature of an aside, expressing the author's own view, tacked on to a preceding proposition which is deemed to be more objectively true. Something of this can be seen in the last two examples and more plainly in this, which deals with the Futurists: *ils ne sont pas des artistes, ce qui est au reste leur droit et leur devoir.*

However, again like *d'ailleurs*, this connector is also used to introduce points which are much longer and more substantive than mere codas or asides. Léon Blum, discussing Stendhal's novel *Le rouge et le noir*, comes in the last sentence of a paragraph to the vexed question of whether or not the hero, Julien Sorel, is motivated by ambition:

Julien Sorel alors se fait prêtre, par déception, par nécessité, nullement par ambition.

Au reste, c'est dans ce mot d'ambition que gît le malentendu véritable.

(Blum, 519)

The ensuing discussion of this question, linked to what precedes by this connector, occupies the next two pages of the work.

Place in the sentence

It is commonly assumed that one difference between *au reste* and *du reste* is that the former is more usually placed first in the sentence: Au reste *se met d'ordinaire en tête de la phrase* (Le Bidois, II, 628). This does seem to be true in about 60 per cent of cases. The others are placed either after the first element or with a verb, as in this excerpt from a discussion of the sexual life of married women in late-Victorian times:

Le corps nié des femmes honnêtes préserve ses secrets, même sous les assauts réguliers d'un devoir conjugal dont rien ne nous prouve, au reste, qu'il ait toujours été monotone ou fastidieux.

English 'also' and *aussi*

Depending on circumstances and register, English equivalents could be 'besides', 'moreover', 'anyway' or 'actually'. There might be no satisfactory equivalent – in translating the quotation above about Marx's economic analysis or the one about the Futurists, the link between statements might be made without a connector. But often the English speaker or writer would fall back on the vaguer and versatile 'also'. Herein lies a difficulty for the English-speaker trying to master this type of connector: the temptation to link additive propositions of all sorts with *aussi*. One of the main differences between *aussi* and the set of connectors including *d'ailleurs*, *du reste* and *au reste* is that *aussi* would add a point of greater importance. In all of the examples given above, *d'ailleurs* or *du reste* could replace *au reste*; in none of them could *au reste* be replaced by *aussi*.

aussi *

In the guise of this word, there are two, if not three, quite separate connectors. There is adverbial *aussi*, which can be a rough equivalent for 'also' or 'too', is rarely placed at the beginning of statements and could often be replaced by *également*. And there is the conjunction *aussi*, which means 'therefore' or 'so', is usually placed at the beginning of statements and can never have the meaning of *également*. In addition to that, this initially placed *aussi*, rather than expressing consequence, sometimes acts like **aussi bien**, when the latter structure has the function of **du reste** or **d'ailleurs**.

aussi as adverb

This mode can link two parts of a single sentence which tend in the same direction and are of equal value: *Il est clair qu'au bout de la route de la solidarité européenne il y aura aussi une solidarité nucléaire*. It can link in the same way two statements made in consecutive sentences, as in this pair of deductions from a survey of the development of Western art:

> Un coup d'œil panoramique sur le parcours de l'art montre les glissements accélérés de la communion vers l'individualité, de la tradition vers la modernité. Il suggère aussi que l'accomplissement de l'art occidental implique son achèvement.

In those examples, one notices first that the French adverb, unlike many adverbs in English, accompanies the verb that it modifies. Secondly, it is clear, in each of them, that *aussi* introduces a second proposition or element which is of no less magnitude than the one which precedes it. This equality of importance is often to be seen in the fact that the second proposition contains a verb with the same subject as the first one. And this second verb will have a very similar meaning to the one in the first proposition, such as *montrer* and *suggérer* in the last example or *apercevoir* and *constater* in the next. The subject of the following pair of sentences is the alleged Germanic bent of the diarist Amiel's ways of writing French:

> En étudiant la phrase d'Amiel, on aperçoit à quel degré le germanisme l'avait possédé. On constate aussi combien certaines idées de formation allemande sont irréductibles au verbe français.

In fact, this second verb is frequently the same verb as the first, as is seen in the repetition of *Il s'agit de... Il s'agit aussi de* in the next example, taken from a discussion of the 'Human Genome' project:

> Il s'agit d'établir la cartographie du substrat, de la mémoire et de la spécificité de l'espèce humaine, voire au-delà, de l'ensemble du vivant. Il s'agit aussi de disposer d'un ensemble de données permettant de comprendre l'intimité moléculaire des mécanismes physio-pathologiques de l'ensemble des maladies.

The same repetition, in the sequence *on sait que... On sait aussi que*, is seen in this extract from an article on Rotomagus, a Gallo-Roman town, freshly excavated:

> Par les amorces de rues est-ouest, on sait que Rotomagus était découpée en grands îlots carrés de plus de 100 mètres de côté, subdivisés ou non en îlots

d'une cinquantaine de mètres de côté. On sait aussi que les rues ont gardé le même tracé du premier siècle avant Jésus-Christ jusqu'au troisième ou quatrième siècle de notre ère.

This similarity of structural elements in the paired propositions can lead to the use of more than one *aussi* in a sequence of sentences, or even in the same sentence. However, more usually, writers do not repeat *aussi* but vary it with **encore** (*Nombreux sont ceux qui... Nombreux sont ceux aussi qui... Nombreux sont ceux encore qui...*) or with *également*:

> Les sièges de la quinzaine de sociétés du Groupe Pierre Botton ont tous fait l'objet d'une ou plusieurs perquisitions par les policiers du SRPJ, qui ont également visité, à Lyon, deux filiales de la Lyonnaise des eaux, émettrice de deux importantes factures litigieuses. Le juge d'instruction s'est aussi rendu en personne dans les résidences parisienne, lyonnaise et cannoise de M. Pierre Botton.

In all of these statements this mode could be replaced by *également*. This holds true also of two other structures in which *aussi* is common: *non seulement... mais aussi*; and *d'abord... aussi* as in: *Comprendre le présent, c'est d'abord voir d'où il vient. C'est aussi chercher où il va.*

This mode can link ideas not only in consecutive phrases or sentences, but also over much longer distances of print. The author of an article about a United Nations conference in New York focussing on ways to exploit intelligently the world's reserves of fish, having said the meeting is timely, having gone on to say in a later paragraph *La réunion de l'ONU est opportune pour un autre motif* and having discussed this *motif* for three further paragraphs, begins the next one like this: *Propice, la rencontre de New-York l'est aussi pour une raison de calendrier.*

It is this mode of *aussi* which is sometimes used in the second part of contrastive binary sentences structured by the **si d'opposition**:

> Si cette réforme avait pour objectif de réduire les impôts directs, elle a aussi eu pour conséquence un certain nombre de mesures impopulaires.

Other common uses of this mode, such as *là aussi* and *aussi* supporting a pronoun (*lui aussi*), are intelligible enough to the speaker of English. However, English-speakers do need to avoid transposing to French the vagaries of function and positioning noticeable in 'also'. This *aussi* always accompanies the word it bears upon and never leads to uncertainties or ambiguities such as are found every day in English structures like 'She also said', where only the context can enlighten us on whether it means *Elle aussi dit* or *Elle dit aussi*. The other widespread practice of beginning a sentence with 'Also' should also be avoided in French, if it entails using *aussi*. The fact is that initial *aussi* does not usually mean 'also'. Its proper uses are discussed in the next paragraphs.

aussi as conjunction

This mode is placed first in the statement, usually first in the sentence or paragraph. In that position, it functions in one or other of two slightly different conjunctive modes. The more common of these makes a link of consequence between the two statements. It means 'So', not 'Also'. In some French dictionaries, one finds it defined as a synonym for *c'est pourquoi* and *en conséquence*. It says 'Thus' or 'Therefore' and is always the first word of the statement which constitutes the consequence, logical or chronological, of the one before it. Another article about Pierre Botton, who allegedly devised an ingenious tax-evasion scheme, says this:

> C'est M. Botton lui-même qui, afin d'échapper à un redressement fiscal apparemment inéluctable, n'a pas hésité à compromettre ses amis et relations, notamment médiatiques. Aussi n'y a-t-il aucune raison de le croire sur parole.

A paragraph detailing an American poetess's liking for travel is immediately followed by another which begins: *Aussi passe-t-elle, à vingt-quatre ans, tout un été en Bretagne, et l'hiver à Paris.* A writer says that the only real writers are those who write for themselves, not for a readership:

> Poussé par une nécessité intérieure, l'homme de lettres écrit d'abord pour se chercher, pour se trouver ensuite et se réaliser enfin dans son œuvre. Aussi qui dit homme de lettres dit non point exhibitionnisme, mais conscience.

As some of these examples show, this mode is usually followed by an inversion of subject and verb. *Pace* the view of Judge and Healey: 'When used as a conjunction it must be followed by the inversion of verb and subject' (Judge & Healey, 387), some writers do not observe this practice. The view of the new Grevisse is: *L'inversion est assez fréquente* (Grevisse, 1988: 618). It does not distinguish between this mode of initial *aussi* and the following one. It must be said that most authorities fail to make this distinction. However, the newer Hanse dictionary does give an interesting entry to it (Hanse, 1983: 122; see also Mauger, 325).

aussi in the function of *aussi bien*

It is with this second mode of the conjunctive *aussi*, functioning like a replacement for *aussi bien*, that one sees the force of the Le Bidois' statement about the word's elastic qualities: Aussi *doit à l'élasticité de son sens de se prêter à des emplois divers, et quelques-uns fort délicats* (Le Bidois, II, 247). Strictly speaking, in so far as one can speak strictly about such a versatile structure, *aussi bien* introduces an explanation or a confirmation of a preceding proposition. Unlike the previous mode of *aussi*, this one, although it too stands first in the sentence, is usually followed by a comma rather than an inversion. Practice probably varies from one writer to another, but certainly some examples of initial *aussi* without inversion are ambiguous enough in their contexts to appear to function either like this one or the former one. In any case, the shades of reasoning which separate consequence from confirmation, or explanation from consequence, are at times faint; and in many contexts little would change in the link of thought made by this connector if it was replaced by ***ainsi*** rather than by *c'est pourquoi* or *en conséquence*. Thus, a discussion of budget strains caused by the increasing costs of social security payments and old-age pensions links two sentences in a way which could appear to mean that the second expresses either explanation or consequence, or both:

> Le poids de ce passif sur la trésorerie ne pourra être indéfiniment absorbé par les avances réglementaires de la Caisse des dépôts (11,7 milliards de francs l'an passé) ou les coups de pouce du Trésor. Aussi, on voit mal comment éviter une mesure – immanquablement présentée comme « exceptionnelle » – de financement dès cette année.

If the link between those two sentences is both explanatory and consequential, it may be the relation of consequence which predominates. Both consequence and confirmation are perceptible in this extract from a discussion of the parlous state of Ukraine's economy:

> Les réformes n'ont jamais vraiment commencé, l'inflation adopte le rythme de 50 % par mois et la production a chuté beaucoup plus qu'en Russie, car les entreprises locales sont handicapées par le manque d'énergie. Cette dernière, fournie par la Russie (et par le Turkménistan pour le gaz), doit désormais être payée à des cours proches de ceux du marché mondial. Aussi, Kiev a accumulé une dette de 2,5 milliards de dollars vis-à-vis de Moscou.

On the other hand, in the following example, dealing with an architectural project to redesign part of the Musée de l'art moderne, the relation is probably closer to that made by ***en effet*** or ***car***:

> Le projet entre dans le registre du paradoxe dans la mesure où les nouveaux équipements du palais ne semblent pas *a priori* demandeurs des mêmes performances lumineuses. Aussi, une fois retenus la définition des espaces dévolus aux divers occupants et le principe d'un « mur » technique commun qui formera la colonne vertébrale du nouvel édifice, le projet laisse tout à la fois admiratif et perplexe.

There, the function of the connector is to link the beginning of the first sentence with the very end of the second sentence. The two adjectives *admiratif et perplexe* confirm and give clearer focus to the initial idea of *paradoxe*. In all of these examples, the connector could probably be replaced by *aussi bien*.

aussi bien

Of all French connectors, this may be the most versatile, hence problematic. It is probably the only one with applications as multifarious as those commonly found with certain English connectors, for instance 'actually'. This indeterminacy of function may be why its usefulness as a connector is sometimes questioned:

> Les contours de l'expression sont assez indécis. C'est pour cela justement qu'elle se prête à des emplois de demi-utilité ; ajoutons : d'inutilité, dans plus d'un cas.
> (Grevisse, 1964b: 287)

Not only have its functions evolved over time – in the seventeenth century, it did service for *d'ailleurs*, in the nineteenth for *en fait* – but nowadays it is used quite variously by different writers.

The views of authorities

Lexicographers and grammarians give a wide range of different meanings for this connector. Littré, for instance, defined a single function or meaning for it: *dans le fait*. And for Littré *dans le fait* meant *réellement, effectivement.* Robert actually gives no definition. What it does give is cross-references: not only to *d'ailleurs* and *au surplus* but also to *en tout état de cause* and *tout compte fait*. The *Trésor de la langue française*, in its entry for *mais aussi bien* adds *au demeurant, dans le fait, somme toute* and *après tout*. Bescherelle sees it as an equivalent at times of *au surplus* and *d'autant plus que*. And Grevisse, while agreeing with much of this, says the connector is also close to *en somme*, *en effet* and *quel que soit le cas*! As for *aussi*, there is a mode of it which sometimes coincides with the most usual function of this connector. However, most dictionaries consider this structure to be quite distinct from *aussi*. On the other hand, the *TLF* gives a single entry to the two structures, confused and confusing. In some measure the *Petit Robert* too conflates them without clarifying them.

Usage of writers

It is apparent that in the usage of some authors, this structure means little more than *aussi*, whether conjunctive or adverbial; in the usage of others, its meaning appears to be influenced by the usually unrelated structure *aussi bien que*, which means roughly 'as well as'. To some, it has a dated flavour; to others, a literary one. Among native speakers of French, many educated people see it as belonging solely to a written register and would never use it. This intuition is confirmed by Le Bidois, whose discussion is, as far as it goes, acute and enlightening: a *gallicisme*, it expresses *un rapport d'égalité* between two terms, has something of the value of *après tout, en somme* and *tout compte fait*, and

> paraît tenir le milieu entre *d'ailleurs* et *en effet* ; comme *d'ailleurs*, il marque une transition, (ou plus exactement l'addition d'une perspective ouverte sur quelque chose d'externe) ; comme *en effet*, il appuie, il confirme une déclaration, mais d'une façon autrement délicate, autrement souple et nuancée.
>
> (Le Bidois, II, 248–249. See also p. 23)

The most usual function

This connector's most usual function nowadays is to introduce a second point or reason, supplementary to a first one. It is nearly always placed at the beginning of the statement which it links to what precedes. The statement that it begins is usually a sentence or a paragraph; but it may follow any sort of stop. A writer comments first on some subtleties of French grammar, then adds two points on its general simplicity:

> Mais les règles essentielles sont élémentaires ; aussi bien sont-elles les premières que l'on montre aux enfants, qui ordinairement les comprennent.
>
> (Hermant, 162)

There, it is clear that the connector could have been *après tout* or even *du reste*. This is consistent with the view of at least one grammarian:

> **Aussi bien** exprime une cause accessoire, et a souvent le sens de : d'ailleurs, du reste :
>
> « Laissez cette affaire, aussi bien, je la connais mieux que vous. »
>
> (Mauger, 325)

Many exemplars of this structure do accord with that view: it adds a point which, though not as central as the one before it, can be seen as confirming, justifying or corroborating it. Thus a discussion of the crises of the 1930s, and their effects on birth-rates, adds a final sentence which supports the author's main idea, namely that population growth is greatly affected by economic and political outlooks:

> L'Espagne républicaine fut vaincue. Rien ne semblait pouvoir s'opposer aux desseins de l'Allemagne nazie. Le chômage, la pauvreté, le désarroi s'installaient en Europe. L'évolution démographique exprimait à sa manière la situation générale ; la fécondité était faible, la divortialité montait. Aussi bien ceux qui se risquaient à tracer des perspectives croyaient-ils à un déclin rapide des populations, au moins dans les nations démocratiques.
>
> (Roussel, 199)

Something of the problematical nature of this connector can be seen in this extract from a discussion of the common origin of *lois* and *mœurs*:

> [Les lois] ne sont rien d'autre que des mœurs mieux définies ; or personne n'ignore que les mœurs ne sont pas d'institution volontaire, mais qu'elles sont

engendrées par des causes qui produisent leurs effets à l'insu des hommes eux-mêmes. Aussi bien l'origine de la plupart des lois n'est-elle pas différente.

(Durkheim, 1953: 86)

There, the connector could be held to stand either for *en effet* or *en fait*, perhaps even for **et**.

Punctuation and inversion

A minority of writers put a comma after this connector when what follows is a noun or a pronoun; almost all follow it with an inversion of subject and verb. Some writers invert in some circumstances but not in others. Occasionally, it precedes a structure which cannot be inverted, such as an infinitive: *Aussi bien, comment refuser l'occasion qui nous est fournie ?* At times, too, this connector, perhaps redundantly, accompanies another (**car**, **c'est pourquoi**, most commonly *puisque*) which explicitly introduces either a justification or an explanation of what precedes. It would then be unlikely to find it followed either by a comma or by an inversion: *N'insistons pas, car aussi bien nous serions facilement entraînés trop loin.*

> Rien n'était moins fiable que les déclarations que j'aurais pu faire. C'est aussi bien pourquoi je n'en faisais aucune.

> On dira enfin que nécessité fait loi ; l'un après l'autre tous les pays de la planète se mettent au nucléaire, puisque aussi bien il est admis que les combustibles fossiles n'existent qu'en quantité limitée.
>
> (Fontaine, 1978: 257)

This combination with *puisque* could often be replaced by **tant il est vrai que**.

As can be seen, it is in these combinations that the connector does not stand first in the statement. At other times, although none of these expressions is used, it is clear that the connector could be replaced by something like *voilà pourquoi*, as in this example taken from an essay on Fustel de Coulanges in which the writer tries to account for this historian's comparative lack of popularity:

> On aperçoit facilement la raison de sa situation à l'écart, dans le groupe de nos historiens : c'est un savant, c'est un penseur, un homme grave et sérieux, sans concession ni sourire, pour tout dire un peu janséniste, incapable de chercher à plaire, et uniquement soucieux de proclamer la vérité. Aussi bien, l'essai nourri de citations de M. Tourneur-Aumont rendra-t-il un fécond service à sa mémoire, en introduisant au plus près de sa pensée critique et moralisatrice le lecteur lettré qui n'aurait pas eu le loisir de l'étudier à sa source [...]
>
> (Henriot, 1954: 214–215)

There, the connector could also be replaced by one of the modes of **ainsi**, a relation that can be seen in a statement like the following: *Il est un* *bédéphile invétéré. Ainsi il n'a pas pu s'empêcher d'acheter les dernières parutions* (Zenone, 190).

English equivalents of different registers are 'in any case', 'so' and 'moreover'. Harrap adds 'for that matter', 'besides', 'and as a matter of fact' and 'though'. Even 'also', with its imprecision and versatility, could often act as an equivalent.

au surplus *

This is one of the set of connectors which serve to introduce a point additional to a preceding one. The dictionary of the Académie saw in this structure the meaning of *au reste*, an adversative function and the possibility of combining with *mais*. On the alleged adversativeness of the structure Dupré says:

> En fait, [la locution] n'a plus guère cette valeur dans l'usage actuel, mais elle indique au contraire un renchérissement comme *de plus : il n'est pas intelligent ; au surplus, il est méchant.*
>
> (Dupré, III, 2478)

For Littré, it meant *au reste* or *d'ailleurs*. For the larger Robert, it seems to be more versatile: it gives as equivalents *au reste, d'ailleurs* and *mais aussi* and it cross-references to *après tout* and *aussi bien*. It follows from all of this that what is added by this connector is sometimes of comparable importance to what precedes it, sometimes less important. It could be variously rendered in English by 'moreover', 'furthermore' or 'what is more'.

Adding a statement of equal value

In a discussion of possible IRA reactions to the British and Irish governments' offer of a cease-fire in Northern Ireland, an author uses it as he might *en plus*:

> L'IRA et sa branche politique, le Sinn Fein, pourraient considérer qu'en acceptant de renoncer à sa souveraineté sur la province, la Grande-Bretagne avoue sa faiblesse et reconnaît implicitement que la violence paie. S'ils ont, au surplus, le sentiment que Londres essaie de les duper par le biais d'un référendum d'auto-détermination sur la réunification, une partie des « nationalistes », jusque-là modérés, pourraient bien sombrer eux aussi dans l'extrémisme.

There, English might even say 'into the bargain'. In the following judgment on the political advantages of the Parti socialiste over its adversaries of the Right, the connector could be replaced by *et puis*.

> Le PS conserve et même accentue sa large avance sur ses points forts tradi-
> tionnels : la capacité de faire les changements et les réformes, de réduire les
> inégalités sociales, de défendre les intérêts des gens.
>   Au surplus, il devance pour la première fois la droite sur la capacité à bien
> gérer l'économie.

The equality of the two statements is seen when the connector replaces
aussi or *en outre* in the second half of the binary structure beginning *non
seulement*. In this example, the writer, speaking of the ambivalent attitude of the Communists, part of President Mitterrand's first government
in 1981 yet critical of him, sees two equally important consequences:

> En prenant une attitude oppositionnelle vis-à-vis de Mitterrand tout en parti-
> cipant au gouvernement, les communistes veulent mettre l'action présidentielle
> en péril. Non seulement Mitterrand est contraint de subir cette opposition, ce
> qui prouve qu'il a bel et bien besoin des communistes, mais, au surplus, il fait
> preuve d'incohérence.
>
> (July, 161)

Adding a statement of lesser importance

The structure is often placed first in the sentence or paragraph; and just
as often after the first element of a sentence or after the verb. Placed at
the beginning of a paragraph, as in one of the examples above, it functions more like *de plus* than like *d'ailleurs*, which does not usually
introduce an element important enough to warrant a new paragraph. It
may be closer to *d'ailleurs* when linking briefer statements. Sometimes
these contain adjectives: *Peut-être n'est-il pas inutile, ni au surplus malaisé
de dire ce qui constitue la nouveauté de ce roman.* Sometimes the two
structures linked contain nouns:

> Un philosophe, comme au surplus un artiste, a-t-il le droit de se désintéresser
> des conséquences pratiques qu'un disciple tire de son enseignement ou de ses
> œuvres ?

> On devine beaucoup de largeur d'esprit et de gentillesse chez la jeune madame
> Renan, au surplus admirable épouse et mère parfaite.

In some of these briefer statements, the connector could probably be
replaced by the non-contrastive mode of *au demeurant*. The older form
pour le surplus, to be found in Littré, was still used in the early twentieth
century (e.g. Blum, 498, 504, 521)

autant... autant *

Here is one of those binary structures much favoured by French writers
who wish to make marked antithetical comparisons within a single

sentence. It structures a relation between ideas in ways very similar to the *si d'opposition*.

That relation is essentially adversative. The structure usually stresses the contradictoriness there is in differences between things which might be expected to be similar – words like *paradoxe* and *paradoxal* sometimes occur in its vicinity. Most authorities make no mention of this oppositive function, seeing the structure as only comparative: for Le Bidois, it indicates *des grandeurs du même degré* (Le Bidois, II, 262). The same goes for Robert. The earlier Grevisse said it marked *égalité de degré, de nombre ou de quantité* (Grevisse, 1964a: 128, 807, 1089). This view may derive from Littré's: *Autant... autant, mettant en regard et en comparaison deux membres de phrase.* Yet the examples they all give are themselves clearly adversative, including even *Autant de têtes, autant d'avis*, since what that saying stresses is disparity or divergence, rather than mere comparison. The revised Grevisse adds *inversement proportionnel* to the definition (Grevisse, 1988: 1440).

Visible parallelism and English equivalents

The structure was much used in the eighteenth century. With it, Jean-Jacques Rousseau contrasts his first impression of Paris in 1731 and his second, some ten years later: *Autant à mon précédent voyage j'avais vu Paris par son côté défavorable, autant à celui-ci je le vis par son côté brillant* (Rousseau, 327). The visible parallelism of the dual *autant* is reinforced in each of the halves of the sentence by three elements, each of which is in a sense the opposite of its counterpart: *précédent voyage* and *celui-ci*; two different tenses of the same verb *voir*; and the same noun, *côté*, qualified by disparate adjectives. There would appear to be no fully satisfactory English equivalent adapted to the expression of such symmetrical antitheses. One might translate Rousseau's sentence as: 'Whereas on my previous journey I had seen the seamy side of Paris, on this one I saw its finer side'. Or perhaps: 'Just as I had seen ... so this time I was to see ...' Neither of these has the pointed oppositiveness of the French construction. The same goes for the common English construction 'as ... as': 'At my second visit, Paris was as brilliant as it had been unsightly at my first.' French has, of course, a similar adversative structure, the *aussi... que* which contrasts qualifiers: *Ce témoignage-pamphlet de X est aussi violent, moderne, inventif que celui de Y est sage, traditionnel.*

Place in the sentence

Binary antitheses continue to be common in the prose of many contemporary French writers. Almost always this structure is placed first in the sentence: *Autant les pères abondent dans les livrets d'opéra, de Mozart à*

Verdi, autant les mères y sont rares. The next example describes Colette's speaking voice: *Autant la prononciation et le rythme ont une saveur provinciale, autant la langue elle-même est raffinée et hypercorrecte* (Lejeune, 135). However, sometimes it is preceded by a brief connector, such as *car* or *mais*, or a noun in apposition:

> Cela dit, autant les propositions gouvernementales sont tardives, floues, timides et étriquées, autant elles ne justifient pas la réaction psychanalytique de rejet qu'elles ont suscitée au sein de l'opposition.

> Ultime paradoxe : autant le choix des électeurs est clair, autant sa traduction dans les faits reste obscure.

Punctuation

The usual punctuation, as can be seen from all examples used so far, is that recommended for parallelisms by Jacques Drillon: a comma separating the halves of the binary (Drillon, 164). Jules Vallès, or his editor, preferred the semicolon:

> Autant j'aimais les prairies vertes, l'eau vive, la verdure des haies ; autant j'avais le dégoût de cette campagne à arbres courts, à plantes pâles, qui poussent, comme de la barbe de vieux, dans un terrain de sable ou de boue, sur le bord des villes.
>
> (Vallès, 62)

Inversion of subject & verb

Inversion of the subjects and verbs following is not usual; but it is not unheard of, as in this extract from a discussion of the difficulties entailed in trying to teach spelling to today's children as though it were somehow a subject in its own right, distinct from general culture:

> L'instituteur se trouve devant une tâche paradoxale : autant est-il nécessaire, autant est-il impossible d'enseigner de façon autonome une discipline qui ne peut en aucune façon être séparée de la culture qui la fonde.

The lapidary & the lengthy

This structure almost always occupies the whole sentence which it begins, especially when it is a lapidary antithesis: *Autant le second reste rare, autant le premier est fréquent. / Autant on accueille difficilement les idées nouvelles, autant on se débarrasse difficilement des idées admises* (Bohn, 237). On the other hand, it can shape and point not only the lapidary and the simple but also the composite:

> Autant l'efficacité de notre menace stratégique est-elle fonction d'un nombre et d'une puissance minimale des armes qui la mettraient à exécution, autant

l'ultime avertissement est-il indépendant de ces contraintes puisqu'il ne s'agit pas d'influer sur le cours des opérations mais d'« avertir » que l'on change de registre et que l'on est au seuil de l'impensable.

And occasionally this compositeness can lead to a third *autant* being added to the binary opposition, as in this ironic comment on the comparative garrulousness of politicians, depending on whether they speak of the past, the future or the present:

Autant ils sont prolixes sur le passé, à plus forte raison s'il s'agit de celui des rivaux, autant ils sont diserts pour dépeindre (à la constante exception de M. Barre sur certains terrains) le futur lumineux qu'ils sauraient bâtir pour leurs concitoyens si ceux-ci avaient le bon goût de les élire, autant, pour commenter les événements du moment, ils sont tout de retenue, c'est-à-dire taciturnes, c'est-à-dire muets, autrement dit prudents.

(Boucher, 649)

Similarity to the *si d'opposition*

With minimal rearrangement of syntax, most of these contrasts could be made with the *si d'opposition* in the first part and **alors** or an adversative structure such as **en revanche** or the **pronom tonique disjoint** in the second. Take this antithesis between the frequency of subordination in written language and the frequency of juxtaposition in speech: *Autant le langage écrit se sert de la subordination, autant la langue parlée pratique la juxtaposition.* The sentence could be rewritten: *Si le langage écrit se sert de la subordination, la langue parlée, elle, pratique...* or *...la langue parlée, en revanche, pratique...*

An obsolete form

A form *autant que... autant*, discussed by Littré, with examples from authors of the seventeenth and eighteenth centuries, and by Grevisse, is no longer used.

autant dire (que) *

This is a specialized mode of a standard construction: *autant* followed by the infinitive of almost any verb, which has the meaning of English expressions like 'might as well' or 'just about'. Thus, *Autant rentrer à la maison* can be 'We might as well go home' and *Ils ont autant dire fini* can be 'They've just about finished'. When used as a connector, *autant dire que* is functionally related both to *c'est-à-dire (que)* and to *c'est dire (que)*. Going not quite as far as either in defining a logical consequence of what precedes, it means, strictly speaking, 'what I have just said is almost tantamount to saying what I am about to say'.

The form with *que*

What immediately follows this mode is always the subject and verb of a full independent statement. In any context, the structure could be replaced by *ce qui revient à dire que*. Like *c'est dire que*, and for similar reasons, it is almost always placed first in the sentence or paragraph. In practice, it is often given the value of *c'est dire que*, as in this extract from an article questioning Strasbourg's suitability as the seat of the European Parliament:

> Dès les élections européennes du printemps 1994, les parlementaires seront au nombre de 567. Un chiffre qui peut encore grandir si, d'ici là, la Communauté accueille un, deux ou plusieurs nouveaux États membres.
> Autant dire que Strasbourg pourrait avoir dans deux ans des difficultés à accueillir les élus supplémentaires dans l'hémicycle actuel (loué au Conseil de l'Europe) où les 518 représentants actuels estiment déjà être à l'étroit.

The connector often has something of the value of **autrement dit**, as in the following extract from an article about the dangers caused to aviation by birds near airports, especially if there are rubbish-dumps nearby:

> Les mouettes viennent y lisser leurs plumes après avoir festoyé sur les décharges avoisinantes. Dans certains pays, les aéroports se trouvent aux portes de réserves ornithologiques, comme celui de Kennedy à New-York, ou proches de la mer. Autant dire que la gent ailée abonde aux endroits où les avions circulent en plus grand nombre et que cette proximité peut se révéler dangereuse.

What follows the connector is often a sort of translation, a recasting of what precedes in a clearer or more analytical form. In that sense it could sometimes be seen too as a variant for **bref**. Indeed, this mode is sometimes combined with *bref*, as in this extract from a review of *Pulp*, the posthumously translated last novel of a crime-fiction writer:

> Polar délirant, désopilant, *Pulp* est une occasion de récapituler toute sa philosophie de la vie et aussi, avec beaucoup de classe, de mettre en scène sa propre mort, rôdant si près de lui qu'il en devine l'haleine. Bref, autant dire qu'il nous a légué une manière de chef-d'œuvre testamentaire.

The form without *que*

This mode introduces not a proposition based on a verb but a substitute complement of what precedes. It is probably rarer than the equivalent modes of *c'est-à-dire* or *c'est dire*. It can be placed inside the sentence, like the former, as in this extract from a comment on the two novels of Raymond Radiguet:

> Après *le Diable au corps*, *le Bal du comte d'Orgel*, dont Radiguet a corrigé les épreuves in extremis, sera son passeport pour l'éternité, autant dire pour la fable flamboyante et définitive qui lui vaut d'occuper une place parmi les statues
> [...]

Or like *c'est dire*, it can be placed at the beginning of the sentence, as in this extract from an article about Polish treatment of a girl suffering from AIDS:

> De Gdansk à Cracovie, bien peu de gens ont prié pour Kristina ce dimanche. Kristina est maudite, elle est malade du sida. Autant dire une sorcière dans cette Pologne qui vient d'exorciser le communisme mais pas encore la peur du sexe, de la drogue et de tous ceux qu'on nomme ici les « déviés », avec un curieux vocabulaire d'autoroute.

As in that example, what follows this mode is usually a noun, as in *Autant dire une Bérézina*, describing a landslide defeat for a politician, or in *Autant dire tout le monde*, a comment on the number of French people who have telephones. But the part of speech which follows it will always be the same as the one which precedes.

The *Trésor de la langue française* says of a mode of the form without *que*: *souvent employé dans la conversation courante pour apporter une précision, rectifier sa pensée*. This mode too is used in written French, as in this excerpt from a discussion of the creation of new surnames in rural France through nicknames that stick:

> Dans bien des endroits les noms sont autant dire hors d'usage, on ne connaît que les sobriquets vieux ou neufs : *Cartille, Napoléon, la Baronne, Barbe de bigue*, etc.
>
> (Brunot, 44)

Other forms

Occasionally the verb *dire* is replaced by some other verb of similar meaning. A writer discussing other writers and intellectuals who use their moral authority to ill effect, as Jean Genet did in 1977 by publicly praising the Baader-Meinhof gang of terrorists, uses *plaider*:

> Va-t-on prétendre que ces vilenies sont vénielles parce qu'elles émanent d'écrivains de réputation mondiale ? Autant plaider que plus on est écouté, moins on est comptable de ce qu'on dit.
>
> (Revel, 1988: 331–332)

A writer disputing the notion that there exists a single form of spoken French substitutes the verb *croire*:

> L'erreur capitale du faux savant est de croire que les jeunes gens, et de style apache, sont tout le peuple, qui est tout Paris, qui est toute la France. Autant croire que la bourgeoisie parle comme dans la cour du lycée.

Some dictionaries still give *autant vaut dire (que)* and *autant vaudrait dire (que)*. Living forms a century ago, they are rarely used nowadays. In the first example, Jules Renard speaks of ageing peasants: *Dès qu'ils n'ont plus le goût de gagner de l'argent, autant vaut dire qu'ils sont morts* (Renard,

1965: 772). / *J'ai donc tâché d'esquisser une sociologie pure. Autant vaudrait dire une sociologie générale* (Tarde, xxii).

au total *

Like other resumers or synthesizers, this connector is often found near the end of a paragraph, a development or a discussion. It usually introduces a brief conclusion to be drawn from an analysis which precedes, after the manner of, say, 'all in all'. In certain contexts, other English equivalents might be 'altogether' or even 'overall'. Examples of this structure tend to be lengthy, as the analysis that precedes it is often detailed or long, or both – unlike these two: *En trente ans de carrière, il n'aura produit que peu de films. Moins d'une dizaine au total !* / *Au gratin, Michel Simon préfère les filles. Elles servent, les fesses à l'air, justes vêtues d'un tablier. Il les connaît toutes, une soixantaine au total.*

Literal totals

What precedes often has a strongly numerical flavour; the context can be formidably technical; percentages or amounts abound; and the connector's function is then more clearly semantic than in other contexts, as it introduces the round number that these figures add up to. This can be seen even in the two examples above and more evidently in the following extract from an article celebrating the commercial success of a chain of department stores:

> Neuf magasins à Paris et en province, 24 millions de clients par an, 76 millions d'articles vendus chaque année, dont 5 millions de paires de collants, 1 million de slips, 28 000 robes de mariée. Au total, les magasins font 1,7 milliards de francs de chiffre d'affaires, avec des marges bénéficiaires de 5 %.

Sometimes, however, this totalization is a translation into numerical terms of amounts or factors that are not quantified in the preceding analysis but merely described, as in the following example, which lists the various ways in which losses are incurred in the production of gaboon, a hard wood (*l'okoumé*) from equatorial Africa:

> Si l'on se réfère à l'Europe, l'exploitation « minière » (par prospection) de l'okoumé apparaît au premier abord comme un vilain gâchis. Les pistes sont souvent jonchées d'arbres inutilisés, brisés ou broyés. En bord de route forestière, on voit les énormes « culées » qui restent de la « purge » (on ne conserve que la partie droite de la grume, seule utilisable en déroulage) et aussi des grumes éclatées à l'abattage ou maltraitées au débardage. Les pertes augmentent aussi au flottage, lorsqu'une grume oubliée pourrit, ou sur les parcs à bois, quand les insectes attaquent sous l'écorce. Au total, pour 1 mètre cube

de bois qui sera utilisable dans les scieries de Honfleur ou Lisieux, on aura perdu 20 à 25 m³ entre l'abattage et la livraison !

After a list

In the previous example, what precedes the connector is less an enumeration than an accumulation of factors, a list in fact. The role of the connector in such paragraphs is to introduce a conclusion that rounds off or clarifies the idea being developed in this list. In the following extract from a discussion of a series of cumulatively adverse economic developments affecting French farmers in the twentieth century, the list is in the form of a sequence of short sentences:

La ferme est devenue une entreprise qui achète pour produire et vend pour survivre. La consommation « maison » s'est réduite comme peau de chagrin. Les dettes ont remplacé les réserves et les vicissitudes économiques se sont ajoutées aux aléas climatiques. Au total, les incertitudes se sont accumulées sur des exploitations plus fragiles.

Clearly, in that context the connector could have been *bref* – or even, without altering much in its function, one of the set of explicators such as *en clair* or *autrement dit*.

Combined with *soit*

When the final synthesizing statement contains a numerical total and when its syntax requires no verb, the structure is quite often accompanied by *soit*, as in the following paragraph discussing the planned relocation of the holdings of certain Paris libraries:

La future Bibliothèque nationale des arts sera constituée grâce à plusieurs fonds. D'abord les départements spécialisés de la BN : estampes, monnaies, manuscrits, photographies, qui conserveront leur mission traditionnelle de dépôt légal. Ce fonds considérable sera enrichi par l'apport de plusieurs collections : la Bibliothèque d'art et d'archéologie Jacques-Doucet, la Bibliothèque des musées nationaux, dite Bibliothèque du Louvre, et le fonds d'architecture de la Bibliothèque de l'École des beaux-arts. Soit, au total, près d'un million et demi de volumes.

In such a verbless context, and when the connector functions numerically, journalists sometimes replace initial *au total* by *total* used as a noun in apposition, followed by a colon: *Total : une garantie de chiffre d'affaires supérieure à 100 millions de francs par an.*

Place

This structure is most often placed at the beginning of sentences, frequently at the beginning of paragraphs. But it can be found, as some examples already used show, at the end of the sentence. And it can accompany the verb, in which case it is usually put between commas:

> Ce bonhomme, instruit aux systèmes et féru d'idées personnelles sur l'univers et sur l'homme, n'est, au total, qu'un grand ignorant, candide et prétentieux.

As this example shows, too, this structure is used at times as a variant for *au fond, finalement, pour tout dire, somme toute* or *tout compte fait*, when the statement it accompanies is in no way a quantification but more a vaguely synthesizing or summing up type of remark, equivalent to English expressions such as 'in the last analysis', 'all things considered', 'when all's said and done' or 'taking one thing with another'. In this mode, it is also sometimes replaced nowadays by the new trendyism *au final*.

en tout

The structure is sometimes replaced by *en tout*. A reinforced form of the latter, *en tout et pour tout*, is used to stress the meagreness of a total, as in this extract from a discussion of the Church's response to the pandemic of AIDS in Africa:

> Pour la première fois, se tiendra à Rome dans quelques semaines un synode d'évêques africains. Mais l'épais document de travail qui prépare cette assemblée ne consacre, en tout et pour tout, qu'une ligne à un fléau qui ravage l'Afrique.

This expression is sometimes used in the sense of 'once and for all', as in this extract from a discussion of the morphology of certain languages such as French in which nouns and verbs are conceived of as strictly distinct categories (*espèces*):

> Or, l'existence d'espèces strictement grammaticalisées engendre une astreinte fort gênante. Elle condamne un signifiant à assumer en tout et pour tout les fonctions de l'espèce à laquelle il appartient.

(Wagner, 107)

autrement dit *

The function of this connector is as plain as its meaning: 'in other words'. It belongs to the set of precisers and resumers of which the paradigm could be said to be *en d'autres termes*. This is a set which also includes, among other variant structures, *à savoir (que)*, *autant dire (que)* and *en clair*, some of which, depending on circumstances, can replace this one. It is normally placed at the beginning of a sentence, although on occasion it is preceded by *ou*. Bringing both precision and amplification to what precedes, it introduces an explanation of it, an inference to be drawn from it or even a conclusion.

With *que*

A mode with *que* is sometimes used. What follows it, as with *c'est-à-dire (que)*, is always a subject and verb beginning a new independent statement, as in this extract from a discussion of ways and means of reducing the disparity between rich peoples and poor:

> Cela suppose évidemment que l'Occident accepte le principe d'une réduction de son train de vie au profit du tiers monde. Autrement dit qu'il ne considère pas seulement celui-ci comme une vaste zone où acheter le meilleur marché possible et vendre le plus possible de biens de consommation, mais qu'il lui donne, avec les moyens de s'équiper, ceux d'acheter moins et de vendre plus.
> (Fontaine, 1978: 243)

But in fact the analogy with *c'est-à-dire* is a false one, as this *que* is always a repetition of a *que* in what precedes – in that example, it repeats the *que* of the first sentence.

Without *que*

The mode without *que* usually introduces both independent statements and alternative complements of what precedes. The first of the following examples shows the standard way of introducing an independent statement. It is taken from a discussion of the economic principles which are inseparable from the concept of a government loan:

> L'emprunt donne à l'économie ce qui allait à la finance. Seulement, il a aussi des inconvénients. Le premier, c'est qu'il faut le rembourser avec des intérêts. Autrement dit, il rapporte sur l'instant, mais coûte plus cher après. En d'autres termes, il contribue à creuser un déficit exactement comme lorsqu'on laisse filer « l'impasse budgétaire ».

In this mode, if not followed by *que*, the connector is almost always followed by a comma. When it introduces a substitute complement of what precedes, the comma is less usual, as in this extract from an article on socio-economic tensions in Turkey:

> Les Turcs sont impatients : ils voudraient avoir à la fois le « beurre », autrement dit le développement, et l'« argent du beurre », c'est-à-dire la consommation immédiate.

In both of these examples, one can see, too, how this structure is sometimes varied by the use of another resumer: *en d'autres termes* in the first and *c'est-à-dire* in the second.

Variants

Variants of the basic structure are sometimes used: *Disons les choses autrement*; *Pour le dire autrement*; *Pour dire la même chose autrement*; or *dit autrement*, as in the following example, which discusses a book by a German theologian, known for his radical criticism of churchmen:

> Drewermann démonte tous les mécanismes d'autodéfense dont s'entoure l'appareil de l'Église, et c'est en cela que ce livre unilatéral, coulée de lave contre la mentalité cléricale, est atypique. Il touche moins que ses précédents ouvrages à la question religieuse, mais plus au système ecclésial. Ou, dit autrement, après avoir sapé les fondements, il s'attaque à la superstructure.

Other variants, less common but used in the same functions, are *Entendez* and *Comprenez*. An example of the first comes from an essay on certain books by different authors, all published in the space of a few years in the late nineteenth century:

> De ces livres, apparemment divers par le sujet qu'ils traitent, se dégage une manière d'inspiration générale, un esprit commun, ce que Spuller appellera, du haut de la tribune, « l'esprit nouveau », – entendez, le sentiment, nouveau à cette heure, ou si l'on préfère, renouvelé, de la complexité de la vie, de son sérieux, de sa gravité, de la place qu'y occupe le mystère.

And this example of the second is taken from an ironic description of extremes of riches and poverty in certain West African countries:

> ...le journaliste a d'abord traîné ses guêtres derrière la « façade » des gratte-ciel du « Paris de l'Afrique de l'Ouest ». Comprenez Abidjan.

In some contexts *je veux dire*, a replacement for *c'est-à-dire*, can function as a variant for this structure too. So can **au total** in tandem with a mode of **soit**, *soit au total*.

au vrai *

This structure, meaning *pour être tout à fait précis*, has at times a function close to that of **à vrai dire**, at others to that of **en fait**: it restricts and makes more precise a preceding affirmation. It is usually placed first in the sentence, sometimes preceded by **et** or **mais**.

Some dictionaries describe this connector as *vieux*; some as *littéraire*; others give no usage label. According to the most recent edition of Hanse, it is *Assez courant* (Hanse, 1983: 1006). This seems something of an exaggeration. But one does find it, albeit not often in contemporary French, in the prose of twentieth-century writers. Alain, for instance, used it commonly, as did other writers of his generation:

> La guerre n'effraie pas plus l'homme que n'importe quel métier qu'il sait faire. Car la fatigue et l'accident sont dans tout métier. Et au vrai toute la vie humaine est combat.

> (Alain, 1956: 430)

André Gide, too, favoured both this form of the connector and its rarer variant *de vrai*:

> Mon père avait rapporté de [Nîmes] une indisposition qu'on affectait d'attribuer aux figues. De vrai, le désordre était dû à de la tuberculose intestinale [...]

> (Gide, 1954: 409)

Albert Camus was given to using it (Camus, 1964: 69 & 80)

Contemporary usage

Nowadays, this rather old-fashioned connector is used occasionally, as by an octogenarian Academician writing about Maupassant:

> Poussé par un mystérieux besoin de déserter les lieux de ses succès, il multiplie les voyages, en Corse, en Algérie, en Tunisie, en Italie, en Sicile... Au vrai, ce qu'il cherche à fuir, c'est lui-même.

> (Troyat, 72)

Some academics use it, as in this extract from an essay on Raymond Radiguet, a writer who died at the age of twenty, and whom Jean Cocteau bracketed with Rimbaud as young, gifted and doomed:

> C'est bien une gloire de maudit que Cocteau revendique pour le tout jeune homme, en rapprochant son cas de celui de Rimbaud.
> Au vrai, les rapprochant, Jean Cocteau tendait surtout à les opposer.

There the precising function is clear: what follows makes a more accurate statement than what precedes. Sometimes the precising is done by introducing an affirmative statement in contrast to a preceding interrogative one, as in this extract from an article about how the French government should respond to the spate of Islamic terrorism in Algeria:

> Que doit faire la France ? Choisir le camp répressif de l'armée contre le camp terroriste ? Ou bien s'en tenir à une position de « non-ingérence » en affirmant sa solidarité avec le peuple algérien ? Ou encore manifester son indifférence ? Attendre ? Au vrai, en Algérie, nous sommes impuissants.

Sometimes the connector puts a finer point upon an idea, as in the previous example. Sometimes it introduces a word deemed to be apter than the one which precedes and which it supersedes, as in this comment on a character in a novel – the writer has second thoughts about the expression *regain de jeunesse*: *Elle s'effare du regain de jeunesse de son mari : au vrai, une boulimie sénescente, ou présénescente, de voyages.*

The structure is also sometimes used by writers who, despite straying into journalism, are not averse to a faint flavour of literariness or archaism: Françoise Giroud, Max Gallo, Philippe Boucher (366, 628) or Bertrand Poirot-Delpech, speaking of the coming of peace to places where violence recently reigned, apparently fortuitous but really an outcome of human will:

> La satiété de sang, qui sait ! En Afrique du Sud, au Proche-Orient, c'est venu tel un cadeau de Noël, dans le même temps où reprenait en Europe, comme si un don de l'enfer compensait celui du ciel, la fièvre nazie des années 30.
> Au vrai, la fin des conflits n'est pas un beau hasard, mais l'œuvre de quelques hommes lucides et résolus.
>
> (Poirot-Delpech, 2)

English equivalents might be 'actually', 'really', 'to tell the truth' or 'to be precise'. An expression like 'in truth' might have an aptly dated flavour.

avec *

This preposition has many modes, possibly as many as its most apparent English counterpart 'with'. I deal only with those which may prove problematical or be adapted to a connective function.

With a present participle

It used to be taught to English-speaking students of French that, unlike 'with', *avec* was not used in structures with present participles. This is a very common construction in contemporary English prose, especially that written by journalists, as in this sentence taken from a discussion of a difference between the attitudes of two decades towards sexual behaviour:

> The late 1980s seem to be a period of confused sexual mores with the crisis of sexually transmitted diseases upsetting the mood of liberation which pervaded the 1970s.

The semantic and grammatical relationships between the two statements linked by 'with' are indeterminate. Only on reflection is it seen that the statements are close to each other in meaning, the first one being less a fact than an interpretive comment on the fact mentioned in the second one. This problematical relation is more evident in the following extract from a blurb put out by an insurance company, Perpetual, about an award it received for its success in investing its clients' monies:

> Perpetual has once again featured prominently in *Money Management*'s 1992 Fund Manager of the Year Awards with this leading industry magazine ranking Perpetual number one in 'Equities'.

There is a perfect example of an apparently binary sentence making a single statement, but needing two linked propositions to do it. In French, the preposition, the present participle and the indeterminacy of the link made can all be avoided: either by placing a ***deux-points*** instead of the preposition and using a finite verb; or by making two sentences, the second of which would be linked to the first by ***en effet*** and would again contain a finite verb. Not only journalists and investment agents make sentences with this combination of 'with' and a present participle: the following example is taken from an eminent historian's work on marriage and divorce in England:

> The desertion clause was accepted by the Lords on a narrow vote of 66 to 48, with all fifteen bishops and archbishops present voting against it – and almost as many absentees.

> (Stone, 395)

There, the indeterminacy of the link being made by 'with' is of a different sort. Perhaps it means 'and'; perhaps it means 'although' or 'despite the fact that'.

Structures made with *avec* and a present participle, though not common in contemporary French, are far from unknown. An article about lorry-drivers who decided to paralyse communications by road throughout great parts of the country says: *Avec ces camions bloquant les autoroutes et assiégeant les villes, les Français ont eu le sentiment de vivre un événement exceptionnel.* A sociologist writing on the statistics of divorce says this:

> « À long terme, écrit Jean-Louis Rallu, environ 18 % des enfants de 16 ans seraient enfants d'un divorcé, avec un divorce stable affectant 31 % des mariages ».

> (quoted by Roussel, 174)

And the structure even occurs in sentences like the one of Lawrence Stone's quoted above in which the link is 'despite' or 'although', as in this one where it is *avec* plus a present participle which makes the contrastive link between the electoral power of the Communist Party and the comparative weakness of the party's newspaper:

> Avec 20 % des Français votant pour le PC, *L'Humanité* connaît un tirage dérisoire et la plupart des journaux communistes ont dû suspendre leur publication.

The relative clumsiness of the construction, its potential for indeterminacy and the fact that *avec* can be redundant are three reasons for structuring such sentences as the writer has done in the following extract from a discussion of the European Monetary System (*SME*), in which the subject is the recovery of some ground against the German mark by other currencies: *D'autres monnaies se trouvent aussi en phase de convalescence, les taux d'intérêt restant élevés partout.*

With a past participle

Likewise, it used to be and possibly still is taught to English-speaking students of French that *avec* is not used in structures with past participles. This too is a common construction in contemporary English-language journalism: 'Little was stolen, with valuable equipment left untouched.' / 'In all, forty-seven sheep died, with three cases diagnosed as positive in the laboratory'. The latter example shows again the potential of this construction for creating indeterminacy in the reader's mind: were the three which were diagnosed among the forty-seven which died or were they in addition to them? For after all, 'with' is also used to add facts and figures: 'About 350 Aborigines were killed up to 1850, with the number of Europeans murdered perhaps 10 per cent of that.' Structures like this are also written in French, and not only by journalists in a hurry. A historian of language, writing in the early 1920s about the spread of northern French influence to the south of the country in the fifteenth and sixteenth centuries, says this:

> Le Languedoc perd le caractère d'exception que sa position géographique lui donnait auparavant : avec la Guyenne, la Gascogne et la Provence devenues françaises, il n'est plus un monde hétérogène, presque étranger, une sorte de « protectorat » dont le roi peut avoir intérêt à respecter les institutions, les coutumes : il n'est plus un État-adjoint.
>
> (Brun, 79)

In the same decade, a writer on sex education speaks of the risks run by women who try to abort their own pregnancy:

> Avec des procédés chirurgicaux employés sans habileté, au mépris des règles de l'antisepsie la plus élémentaire, c'est merveille que des patientes en réchappent.
>
> (Marestan, 219)

And any day of the week, journalists write that sort of sentence, placing *avec* first and following it with a noun plus a past participle, as in this extract from an article on Europe's affluence compared to the poverty of most inhabitants of the earth: *Avec 18 % du revenu mondial réparti entre 6 % de la population du globe, la Communauté européenne apparaît comme un îlot de paix et de prospérité dans un monde tourmenté.*

For reasons similar to those mentioned above with regard to *avec* and present participle, this construction can be avoided, either by replacing 'with' by a colon and the past participle by a finite verb, or in some cases by making two sentences, the second of them containing *en effet* and a finite verb. The following example of an English sentence would lend itself to the latter form. It is one of those in which 'with' links two statements saying much the same thing in slightly different ways, the first a gloss, the second a fact:

> The Canadian fishing industry has been hard hit with thousands of jobs lost in recent years and boats deliberately kept at dockside to allow a gradual return of fish numbers.

avec, à la clé

One of the many modes of *avec* is very similar to the 'with' which speaks of the results, risks or consequences, actual or potential, of what precedes. In the following sentence, the *avec*-structure could be transposed directly into English as 'with'. It comes from a discussion of the abortifacient drug RU 486, the focus of a recent public debate similar to the one in the early 1970s about the legalization of medically assisted termination of pregnancy (*l'IVG*):

> Le remake du débat sur l'IVG ignore une autre nouveauté intervenue depuis quelques années : l'épidémie du sida qui est en train de banaliser l'usage du préservatif, avec d'évidentes conséquences sur la contraception, la natalité et les comportements sexuels en général.

It is this mode of *avec* which is now often combined with the trendy little expression *à la clé* (or *à la clef*), with the sense of a side-effect or an additional consequence, possibly unforeseen or unintended. The structure has two forms: either *avec* + *à la clé* + noun-structure, when the noun-structure is long; or *avec* + noun-structure + *à la clé*, when the noun-structure is shorter, as in this extract from a report about the amalgamation of two German radio networks and the job losses among musicians this will entail: *Les ensembles musicaux et choristes des deux radios vont également fusionner avec des compressions de personnel à la clé.*

In the sequence *avec* + *à la clé* + noun-structure, some writers flank *à la clé* with commas, some omit them. In this example, part of a spoken interview, a police officer forebodes the consequences of a time when local authorities may have their own police forces:

> Le vrai danger, c'est que la sécurité devienne un jour un service payant, que les maires créent des polices municipales, avec à la clef de grandes disparités entre zones riches et zones pauvres.

This mode of *avec* is quite often placed first in a **phrase dépendante**. Some writers even drop *avec*, as in this adverse comment on two measures taken by the government in its effort to combat terrorism in the mid-1980s:

> Le rétablissement des visas ne convainc pas. L'affichage des suspects, récompense à la clé pour qui les dénoncera, inquiète.
>
> (Boucher, 297)

There, the *avec*-less structure functions in place of *avec* – albeit in a position, after the noun, that *avec* could never adopt. In the following example, taken from an article about a controversy between two medical researchers, it functions not in place of *avec* but in place of an expression of consequence:

> Un conflit opposant deux chercheurs du Centre d'étude du polymorphisme humain (CEPH, hôpital Saint-Louis, Paris) – le professeur Daniel Cohen et le docteur Philippe Froguel – agite depuis plusieurs semaines la communauté scientifique française. À la clé, l'avenir de la recherche en génétique du diabète et de l'obésité.

avec, en prime

A mode with *en prime*, meaning roughly *en plus*, functions in a very similar way to the mode with *à la clé*. This example comes from an article on reasons for disquiet within the police force, as revelations are made about the illegal activities of some officers:

> C'est toute la brigade de répression du banditisme qui se trouve montrée du doigt lors du procès de trois de ses anciens membres, condamnés pour hold-up, voilà deux ans. Avec, en prime, le brûlot que s'apprête à publier un ancien de ce service, Dominique Loiseau : de nombreux commissaires de la PP, la Préfecture de police de Paris, devraient en prendre pour leur grade.

Variants of this mode are *Avec, en plus...*, *Avec, par surcroît...* and this, with *en outre*, from an admiring essay on the diaries of Stendhal and on the personal qualities of the diarist which they show:

> La jeunesse, l'amour de la vie : aussi bien, tout Stendhal est là ; et c'est tout ce que nous aimons chez Stendhal, joint à un particulier privilège de s'enthousiasmer et de s'attendrir qui lui est propre, avec, en outre, une lucidité merveilleuse à se rendre compte, qui double le plaisir de jouir, n'y ayant de bonheur qu'à connaître.
>
> (Henriot, 1924: 9–10)

With *ceci*

A mode of *avec* is sometimes combined with *ceci* to make a restrictive structure which can replace *à ceci près que* in the sense of 'except for the fact that', as in this excerpt from an essay on the history of the French definite article and demonstrative adjectives:

Dès son origine, le français était en possession de ces morphèmes avec ceci, toutefois, que le rôle de l'article y était bien moins étendu qu'aujourd'hui et que *le*, dans bien des cas, pouvait alterner avec *cil*.

(Wagner, 30)

avec cela

This structure is commonly heard in spoken French. Written, it retains a certain familiarity of tone. It is usually seen as replaceable by **en outre** or **en plus**. However, it has a rather specialized function, in that usually it does not introduce just a further element but rather a remarkable one which it adds to already remarkable others. This, especially when the structure has the form *avec tout cela* or when it is preceded by **et**, gives it something of the force of English 'not only that' or 'to cap it all'. In the first example, the author's subject is Protagoras, the Greek philosopher, a man of great and diverse abilities:

Arrivé à Athènes, il y fit en effet cette profession d'agnosticisme : « Touchant les dieux, je ne suis pas en mesure de savoir ni s'ils existent, ni s'ils n'existent pas, pas plus que ce qu'ils sont. » Ce qui lui valut aussitôt une condamnation à mort, à laquelle, moins héroïque que Socrate, il échappa par la fuite.

Avec cela, un auteur très encyclopédique. Il fut sans doute le premier à s'intéresser aux genres des noms, aux temps des verbes [...]

(Reboul, 19)

There, the connector could probably be replaced by a mode of **au demeurant**.

Sometimes, also like a mode of *au demeurant*, it can add a final element as a sort of climax to a more lengthy listing of features. It is usually placed first in the sentence, as in the example above; but it can be placed elsewhere. In the next example, a writer casts an ironic eye on his contemporaries and the period they are living through, one of precarious employment, redundancies and unfavourable working conditions; his first paragraph, with its repeated *normal*, constitutes the list which will be capped by the first sentence of the next paragraph:

...il faut désormais les persuader qu'il est normal, sinon légitime, de ne pas avoir de travail, normal d'en être privé d'un instant à l'autre si l'on en possède un, normal qu'il faille revenir aux heures supplémentaires obligatoires, mais à la garantie de l'emploi facultative, normal de se voir attribuer un succédané d'emploi qui [sic] rétribuera un succédané de salaire, normal d'être décrété vieux et parasitaire à cinquante-cinq ans, et, enfin, normal d'entrer dans la vie en sachant que la vie sera cette vie.

Et il faudrait avec cela que les jeunes gens aient le goût de vivre, qu'ils aient le sens des valeurs civiques, le respect de la loi, des bonnes mœurs et de la propriété, qu'ils soient bons fils et bons époux, qu'ils procréent trois enfants, qu'ils aient de la considération pour la police, la justice, la fiscalité, les hauts-de-forme et les tourniquets de métro.

(Boucher, 313–314)

A sort of contrastive shade can also be perceived in the structure, *avec* having something of the force of *malgré*, as can be sensed in the two examples above. Indeed, this is the only sense which Littré sees in it. The following example, also structured as an accumulation, speaks of the contradictions of the typical Parisian of the late nineteenth century:

> Il passe pour égalitaire, et il court risquer sa vie au bout du monde avec l'espoir d'un petit morceau de ruban rouge ; – pour spirituel, et pas de saison où il ne se délecte à quelque refrain inepte de café-concert ; – pour ingouvernable, et il subit, sans révolte, les pires tracasseries et paperasseries des bureaux. Tout s'explique de ces contradictions, par l'abus constant et héréditaire de la vie nerveuse qui fait la force et la faiblesse, la grâce séduisante et redoutable de cette ville, la plus féminine de toutes, la plus conduite par ses impressions, mais aussi la plus capable d'élans désintéressés, d'intuitions lumineuses, d'ardeurs magnanimes. Avec cela le Parisien est de tous les animaux politiques le plus complètement dépourvu d'initiative. La cause en est aisée à comprendre [...]

Unlike some other structures which include a demonstrative pronoun *ceci* or *cela*, such as *à ceci près que*, *cela dit* and *cela étant*, this one has no variant form in *ceci*. The form *avec ceci que*, discussed above under ***avec***, is not related.

Other English equivalents might be 'in addition' or the ubiquitous 'also'.

à vrai dire

This structure exists in two forms: *à vrai dire* and *à dire vrai*. Of the two, the second seems nowadays a little less prevalent than the first and it may be slightly more literary in tone. In either form, the structure usually functions as a restrictive: it introduces a statement which attenuates or limits the scope of a preceding one.

Restricting a word

It often introduces what a writer sees as simply a more accurate form of words than what precedes, as in this sentence where, as though on second thoughts, the writer redefines the *très jeune femme* as nothing more than *une enfant*: *Une très jeune femme, à vrai dire une enfant précipitée dans l'âge adulte par la découverte de sa séropositivité*. The meaning, as that example shows, is often 'to be more precise'. A similar modification is seen in the following extract from a discussion of the expansion of science late in the eighteenth century into areas previously not seen as scientific. The author explicitly reinforces this function of the connector with *plus exactement*:

> On sait qu'à la fin du XVIIIe siècle, les sciences s'étaient annexé des domaines tels que leurs investigations ne pouvaient désormais laisser indifférent quiconque était à l'affût de l'aventure spirituelle. À vrai dire, elles ne les avaient pas annexés : plus exactement, des audacieux s'étaient mis à leur école ou couverts de leur prestige pour s'y aventurer.
>
> (Caillois, 25)

There it is the verb *annexer* which the author sees as not quite accurate enough. The structure could almost be replaced by *ou plutôt* or one of the modes of **mieux**.

Restricting an idea

In a slightly different mode, sometimes the restriction introduced is less of a word than of an idea; and then the connector can be seen to have a function akin to that of **il faut dire que**, as in this extract from a historian's essay on the alliance between France and Russia reinforced under Félix Faure in 1896, in which Russia is seen as an improbable ally:

> Oui, fascinant pays « éternellement prostré devant la guipure d'or de ses icônes, peuple loin de nous de mille ans et que le tsar a fait notre frère » ! Cette fraternité soudaine, à dire vrai, c'est l'alliance contre nature de l'eau et du feu.

A more concessive mode

At times, the restriction is more overtly concessive and the connector functions in a way that is akin to **certes** or **il est vrai (que)**. The first of these examples comes from an article by Sartre on conflictual aspects of French society during the Occupation, in which he restricts *la bourgeoisie* in the second sentence to *une poignée de « collaborateurs »* in the third:

> Le gouvernement attisait la querelle par des discours qui, tantôt portaient les agriculteurs aux nues et tantôt leur reprochaient de cacher leurs récoltes. L'insolence des restaurants de luxe dressait les ouvriers contre la bourgeoisie. À vrai dire, ces établissements étaient surtout fréquentés par les Allemands et par une poignée de « collaborateurs ». Mais leur existence faisait toucher du doigt les inégalités sociales.
>
> (Sartre, 1949b: 40)

The second example is from a discussion of Henri Bergson's concept of musical time:

> Le temps musical n'est donc ni le temps homogène, ni la pure interpénétration, la pure fusion de la durée bergsonienne. Bergson écrit que les notes d'une

mélodie sont fondues ensemble et que nous les apercevons les unes dans les autres. Il ajoute, à vrai dire, qu'il en est ici comme de l'organisation de la vie où la distinction accompagne la solidarité. Mais très vite il revient à la succession sans distinction, à la pure pénétration, à la multiplicité indistincte et qualitative, image de la durée pure.

(Delacroix, 1927: 254)

In each of those examples, as is often the case with *certes*, the connector is followed soon after by *mais* introducing a statement which at least partly invalidates the concession. Here English might use 'strictly speaking', 'as a matter of fact' or one of the multifarious pair 'actually' and 'in fact'. As for the apologetic use of the structure in the following example, where the writer uses it to excuse his use of a word, English might use a differently concessive expression such as 'albeit' or 'admittedly'. The writer's subject is the French origins of sociology as a social science:

Et pourtant ce n'est pas seulement le Français Aug. Comte qui a été le premier à lui donner son fondement propre, à en distinguer les parties essentielles et à lui donner un nom particulier, à vrai dire un peu barbare : le nom de *sociologie* ; mais tout cet élan qui nous porte aujourd'hui vers les problèmes sociaux, est venu de nos philosophes du XVIIIᵉ siècle.

Place

The connector is usually placed first in the sentence. But it is also placed elsewhere, even at the end, as in this extract from a discussion of the very favourable working conditions enjoyed by certain employees of the Banque de France, who need only threaten to strike for their demands to be met – well, some of the employees, that is:

Le personnel a tous les atouts dans la manche : un patron qui peut payer et des arguments qui ne peuvent être négligés. Les récompenses vont donc pleuvoir sur nos « banquedefrançais ». Pas sur tous, à vrai dire. Ainsi les balayeurs ne verront-ils rien venir.

(Closets, 1983: 72)

Variants

Occasionally, writers use variants of the two basic forms of this structure. Some of these variants are probably old-fashioned, like *pour dire plus vrai* (Guignebert, 141). But one or other of them turns up from time to time in the prose of contemporary journalists: *à dire le vrai*; *pour dire le vrai*; *pour dire vrai*; *pour dire la vérité*. The most frequently used of these variants, rather literary in tone, is no doubt *au vrai*.

bien *

The main functions of *bien* as connector derive from its simpler functions as adverb, as in *nous avons bien travaillé* or *c'est bien difficile*. As a connector, *bien* can signal emphasis and confirmation, but also contradiction or concession. It can accompany any verb; but more often than not it is used with one or other of two verbs: *s'agir* and *être*. In any of its modes, it can have the reinforced form *bel et bien*.

Emphasizing and confirming

The most common functions of this connector are to emphasize or confirm an idea expressed or implied in a previous statement. It can be difficult to distinguish between these functions. An example of each can be seen in the following extract from a discussion of the last days of East Germany and the unwillingness of the country's leaders to abandon Marxist economic orthodoxy:

> S'il y a une chose qu'on ne peut reprocher aux dirigeants est-allemands, c'est bien un manque de suite dans les idées. Exposés en permanence au triomphe économique de l'autre Allemagne, soumis à la formidable pression que les réformes soviétiques exercent dans tous les pays de l'Est, ils seront bien les derniers à démontrer que le centralisme planificateur a encore de beaux jours devant soi.

In the first sentence, combined with a non-contrastive mode of the *si d'opposition*, *bien* merely emphasizes the anaphoric *c'est*; it is not even necessary to the meaning. In the second sentence, it is itself anaphoric: it reminds the reader of the general proposition, put forward in the first sentence, that East Germany's leaders cannot be accused of changing their minds, and introduces a confirming example of it.

In this confirming function, the connector sometimes recalls what precedes by underlining the aptness of a particular word used; in which case, the verb it accompanies is usually introduced by *car*. The word thus underlined may or may not be repeated in what follows. In this example, taken from a discussion of the social circumstances which a politician of the extreme Right such as Jean-Marie Le Pen might be able to exploit so as to establish an authoritarian regime, the word reinforced is *identité*:

> Le processus est connu. On fustige la « décadence ». On appelle les citoyens à réagir contre l'« invasion ». On désigne les boucs émissaires : étrangers, « communistes », « instituteurs barbus », etc. On convainc les masses que la « catastrophe » est imminente et que le pays a besoin d'un sauveur. Et l'on a d'autant plus de chances d'y parvenir que la société est en crise et que son identité est en jeu.

> Car c'est bien d'un problème d'identité qu'il s'agit, révélé par un nouveau coup d'accélérateur de l'histoire. La « crise » venant interrompre les certitudes de la croissance [...]

In this mode, the connector is often combined with *en effet* in the formulaic sequence *c'est bien en effet... qu'il s'agit.* In this example, the underlined and confirmed word, *réaction*, is not repeated: *J'ai parlé de réaction contre le romantisme : et c'est bien, en effet, de cela qu'il s'agit.* In this combination, *bien* often has the force of 'really'.

In this confirming mode, the connector is very commonly used to corroborate a possibility canvassed in the preceding statement. This is sometimes done in the form of question and answer. However, it is more usually done in a single sentence introduced by *si* as in the very first quotation of this entry: in the second half of the sentence, *c'est bien* reinforces a point raised in the first half as a hypothesis. In this sequence, the sentence usually begins with *S'il est* rather than *S'il y a*, as in this comment on the vexed question of which cheese should be eaten with which wine: *S'il est un sujet sur lequel les gourmets se cassent la tête, c'est bien celui des épousailles des fromages et des vins.*

In statements which give an explanation or a reason, the emphatic structures *c'est bien pourquoi* and *c'est bien pour cela que* are commonly used to confirm what precedes. An English equivalent would be 'this is the very reason why'. This example comes from an essay on the personality cult built by the Vichy régime on the popularity of Marshal Pétain:

> Rétrospectivement, les formes du culte rendu à Pétain laissent pantois. Il était déjà incroyablement populaire en 1940, et c'est bien pour cela que Paul Reynaud l'avait mis en avant pour essayer de rassurer les Français.

This mode is also combined with *là*, in the reinforcing expressions *C'est bien là* and *Il s'agit bien là de*. In this example, we see the end of a paragraph and the beginning of the next one:

> La France ne peut pas espérer limiter un conflit atomique au territoire de l'Allemagne fédérale.
> Il s'agit bien là d'une communauté de destin conditionnée par la géographie, à l'avant du champ de bataille.

Contradicting

This mode may accompany a statement refocussing a debate, insisting upon a point or an analysis which the writer sees as truer than what precedes. In the following example, the author, having set forth the collaborationist view that, during the Second World War, the Vichy régime of Marshal Pétain was not collaborating with fascism but really helping France to withstand the fascism of its Nazi invaders, now rebuts that view:

Or cela est totalement et indiscutablement faux. Et il ne s'agit pas ici d'opinions, mais de faits. Le régime de Vichy, issu d'un coup d'état légal (comme ceux de Hitler et de Mussolini), fut bien la version spécifiquement française des systèmes qui s'installèrent un peu partout en Europe dans le sillage des triomphes fascistes.

This contradictive mode often immediately follows a negative statement. It is then usually accompanied by *mais* and functions much like *plutôt* or one of the modes of *au contraire*. The subject of this example is the *baccalauréat*, which the writer fears is being devalued because too many pupils pass it:

L'inflation des candidats le démonétise. Le problème n'est pas, vieux serpent de mer, celui du niveau de l'examen, objet de tant de gloses et de controverses. Mais bien celui de sa place dans le paysage général des formations.

This mode following a negative is also used without *mais*, as in this extract from a discussion of the homosexuality of Henri III:

À la manière de Bluche, d'autres historiens respectueux prétendent qu'Henri III n'était pas homosexuel. Il l'était bien, et on possède d'indéniables témoignages de contemporains qui le disent le plus clairement possible.

The longer form *bel et bien* is often used in this mode. Its added force aptly accompanies a rectification, a statement setting right a historical record, say, as in this writer's denial of the view abetted by President Mitterrand in his declining years, that the Vichy régime had not been as black as some have painted it:

Sans doute est-ce ainsi que le jeune François Mitterrand vécut ses années vichyssoises. Mais le président d'aujourd'hui, si féru d'histoire, ne saurait ignorer qu'il s'agit là d'une illusion historique. L'État français de Vichy avait bel et bien son idéologie – nationaliste, élitiste, corporatiste, antirépublicaine, antiparlementaire, raciste, liberticide.

This strengthened form often accompanies the positive redefinition of a proposition which the preceding statement has defined negatively. Thus it is used after structures like *il ne s'agit pas de... mais*. With a similar structure, Proust adds a satirical touch to his portrait of the duc de Guermantes:

...on n'avait jamais entendu le duc de Guermantes se servir de l'expression assez banale « bel et bien » ; mais depuis l'élection du Jockey, dès qu'on parlait de l'affaire Dreyfus, « bel et bien » surgissait : « Affaire Dreyfus, affaire Dreyfus, c'est bientôt dit et le terme est impropre ; ce n'est pas une affaire de religion, mais *bel et bien* une affaire politique. »

(Proust, III, 40)

Conceding

When this connector reinforces a verb other than *être* or *s'agir*, it can have a concessive function, as in this extract from an article about the then President of the USSR:

> La majorité des Soviétiques pensent que M. Gorbatchev voyage trop à l'étranger. Le président soviétique peut bien rétorquer que ces visites internationales ne sont pas gratuites et qu'il les utilise de plus en plus pour quémander une aide des pays riches, il ne convainc pas.

There, the connector functions as a variant for *a beau rétorquer* or has the force of *certes*, conceding a point which will prove unavailing in the face of the final *il ne convainc pas*. In this concessive function, in which the concession is at least weakened by the following statement introduced by an objector such as *mais*, the connector often has the form *fort bien*. Usually directly followed by the objector, this structure can occupy different positions in the sentence, or even constitute a sentence by itself:

> Que l'intellectuel se serve des médias, fort bien. Mais, trop souvent, il ne s'en sert pas pour faire passer ses idées : il modifie ses idées pour qu'elles puissent passer dans les médias.
>
> (Revel, 1988: 332)

Long-distance connecting

Like some other connectors, *bien* does not link only to what immediately precedes it; it can refer back to statements from which it is separated by much intervening wordage. The author of an article about the difficulties faced by astronomers and physicists looking for evidence of the action of neutrinos, begins like this: *Pour eux, chercher une aiguille dans une botte de foin est un défi presque quotidien.* Ten paragraphs later, he reminds his reader of these difficulties with a repetition of the same metaphor introduced by the confirming mode of this connector: *Il s'agit donc bien pour les scientifiques de trouver une aiguille dans une botte de foin.* In this function, the connector could be combined with, or replaced by, *décidément*.

Bien is also combined, as a reinforcer, with certain modes of other connectors such as *au contraire*, *plus* and *plutôt*, and is an integral part of structures such as *bien entendu*, *bien évidemment* and *bien sûr*.

bien entendu *

This is one of a set of structures, which contains among others **bien sûr**, **sans doute** and **certes**, that can function either as whole-hearted affirmatives or as half-hearted preliminaries to an apparent concession.

Affirmative

In this mode, the connector does no more than state the obvious while confirming the author's agreement with what precedes, as in this extract from an article celebrating the ratification of the Treaty of Maastricht by both houses of the parliament:

> La victoire est totale ; elle est même plus large que ne pouvait l'espérer le président de la République. Elle est, bien entendu, celle de tous ceux qui pensent que la construction d'une Europe unie est le préalable indispensable aux autres débats, qu'ils soient diplomatiques, militaires, économiques ou sociaux.

Concessive

This mode begins like the affirmative one: it agrees with a supposed interlocutor's view. But now it also foreshadows a disagreement, a lessening or even a retraction of the concession, which is usually introduced by **mais** or a similar objecting word. In English discourse, this function is often served by connectors such as 'of course' or 'obviously'. Thus, a discussion of the intellectual dishonesty of certain eminent scientists and intellectuals who have been known to endorse and disseminate pernicious opinions which have nothing to do with their undoubted expertise makes the following point:

> Nul ne songe, bien entendu, à contester à ces grands hommes, pas plus qu'à tous les scientifiques, le droit de professer toutes les opinions qu'il leur plaît dans tous les domaines qui les intéressent, sans se confiner dans leur spécialité. Ils ont la même liberté de le faire que les autres humains. Mais l'imposture commence lorsqu'ils impriment le cachet de leur prestige scientifique à des prises de position qui paraissent découler de leur compétence, alors qu'en réalité elles n'en découlent pas du tout.
>
> (Revel, 1988: 186)

Instead of *bien entendu*, to express agreement with the initial principle, this author could have used *bien sûr* or **bien évidemment**.

A variant

A variant of this structure can be seen in the **brief interpolated main clause** *c'est entendu*. In the following extract from an article discussing

general elections in Algeria, arguing that the victory of the fundamentalist *FIS* (*Front islamique du salut*) is not as great as it might appear, the
cancelling out of the apparent concession is done by *or*:

> Le FIS, c'est entendu, a remporté un triomphe électoral. Non seulement il
> obtiendra la majorité absolue dans la future Assemblée, mais il n'est pas impos-
> sible, en outre, qu'il atteigne la majorité des deux tiers qui lui permettrait de
> procéder à une réforme constitutionnelle.
>   Or, en réalité, 25 % seulement des Algériens ont voté pour le FIS, soit
> 3 260 000 électeurs sur plus de 13 millions d'inscrits [...]

bien évidemment

Like a cross between *évidemment* and **bien entendu**, but used less often
than the latter, this is one of the set of structures, of which **certes** can be
seen as the paradigm, which can serve either as affirmative or concessive
connectors.

Affirmative

This mode introduces a statement which in the author's view is a self-
evident truth. Its function could be served in English by 'quite clearly',
'naturally', 'obviously' or 'it goes without saying that':

> La Chine, avec un revenu annuel moyen par habitant de 150 dollars, c'est-à-
> dire égal à celui de l'Égypte ou de la Bolivie, mais inférieur à ceux de la
> Côte-d'Ivoire ou de l'Iran, déverse environ 8 à 9 % de son produit national
> brut dans ses armements. Bien évidemment, les populations dont ces choix
> compromettent si gravement le présent et l'avenir n'ont pas la possibilité de
> participer aux décisions qui les tuent ni même d'entrevoir ce qui est en ques-
> tion [...]
>
> (Revel, 1970: 105–106)

Concessive

When it functions as a concessive, this strongly affirmative tone is still
present, albeit foreshadowing a statement which may cancel it out. In the
following example, one can see the sequence of three propositions which
is sometimes customary with concessives: initial affirmation; second statement, introduced by the connector, reducing the scope of the first; then
third statement, presented by *mais*, reaffirming the main importance of
the first. The importance of this relation of the second and the third propositions to the first is underscored by the presence of the word *expliqué* or
explication in all three. It should be pointed out that the Gulf War in
question is the first one, between Iran and Iraq:

En soutenant l'Irak pendant la guerre du Golfe, la France entendait se ranger du côté du monde arabe, qu'elle jugeait menacé par l'intégrisme du régime iranien de l'époque, a expliqué en substance M. Mitterrand. Ce n'est bien évidemment qu'une explication partielle, mais c'est une explication nécessaire pour faire comprendre aux peuples arabes que la décision de la France de se doter aujourd'hui des moyens d'une intervention militaire dans la région n'est pas dirigée globalement contre eux.

Variants

Two variants of this connector, both of them functioning affirmatively and concessively, are *de toute évidence* and of course *évidemment*. In this example, the first of them functions affirmatively:

> On ne peut pas parler d'un village français typique. Il y a de toute évidence des types nombreux de villages : la diversité, le pluriel garde ici tous ses droits.
>
> (Braudel, 112)

There is little difference in practice between the form with *bien* and the form without, as can be sensed from this extract, containing concessive *évidemment*, from an article in which the writer, foreseeing a win for the Right in the presidential election of 1995, begins to glimpse a chance for the candidate of the Left, Lionel Jospin:

> Une droite à 60 % au premier tour ; une gauche démoralisée, décérébrée, désorganisée, dévitalisée, décrédibilisée ; un Parti socialiste à l'agonie. Le seul espoir du PS en ces mois difficiles ? Faire de la figuration plus ou moins intelligente. Et puis, soudain, le miracle, le retournement de ce début de campagne : Lionel Jospin peut espérer l'emporter !
>
> Un triomphe socialiste n'est évidemment pas l'hypothèse la plus vraisemblable. Mais, alors même qu'il n'avait quasiment rien dit (ou peut-être grâce à cela), le candidat du PS s'est soudain retrouvé en situation d'être présent au second tour. Entre 20 % et 24 %, selon les sondages !

bien sûr *

Like **bien entendu** and **bien évidemment**, this connector is one of a set of similarly functioning structures of which **certes** may be seen as the model: originally affirmative, they have developed in addition a concessive function. The tone of this one is quite different from that of other concessive connectors such as **admettons** or **sans doute**, which are much less wholehearted in the agreement they express with what precedes.

Affirmative

This mode functions like the two others containing *bien*, by implying that the statement it accompanies is as axiomatic to the reader as it is to the writer. The first of these examples speaks of the value of certain organizations and organizers to the life of the community:

> Les anciens combattants (il s'agit aujourd'hui, bien sûr, de ceux de la guerre d'Algérie) et les animateurs sportifs jouent un rôle essentiel dans la société civile.

And the second of them comes from an article about the assassination of a President of the Algerian Republic:

> Il est difficile, aujourd'hui, de montrer du doigt ceux qui ont commandité l'assassinat de Mohamed Boudiaf. Un crime que, bien sûr, personne ne prendra le risque de revendiquer.

The tone of this structure may be slightly more conversational than that of the other two. Occasionally its affirmativeness is strengthened by an exclamation, as in this extract from an essay on dandies, English and French, during the 1830s, in which the author stresses

> la différence qu'il y a entre les brummelliens de Regents Park et de Piccadilly, et nos dandys du boulevard de Gand. Eh ! bien sûr, comme toujours, notre Jeunesse dorée a eu sa crise d'anglomanie, que Balzac a peinte dans son *Traité de la vie élégante*.

On occasion, too, a writer may stress the adjectival quality of *sûr* by preceding the structure with *c'est*, as in this contribution to the debate that raged on the emergence of ***par ailleurs*** in its connective function:

> Mais ce sens de *par ailleurs* est nouveau, objecte-t-on, et on n'en trouve aucun exemple chez les classiques ! Littré l'aurait su !
> Que ce sens soit récent, c'est bien sûr; il date apparemment du début du siècle. En tout cas, il est largement admis par les bons écrivains d'aujourd'hui ; les puristes le reconnaissent [...]

Concessive

In concessive mode, this connector functions much like the others in the set. That is, on the one hand it retains all its affirmative force in agreeing with the preceding statement, while on the other foreshadowing at least a clarification of it. This modification is usually introduced by ***mais*** or one of its variants, as in this extract from an article about President Mitterand's decision not to make an official pronouncement dissociating the Republic from the pro-Nazi acts of the Vichy régime during the Second World War:

> Dans un de ces moments de vérité qui lui sont propres, Simone Veil avait demandé au chef de l'État « un geste d'apaisement pour notre souffrance ». Elle évoquait, bien sûr, la souffrance des juifs. Mais aussi celle de tous ces Français trahis par d'autres Français et par leur pays.

Also like *certes* and the others, this concessive can function as a link between three consecutive statements: occupying second place in the sequence, it accompanies an objection to the first, which objection is in turn invalidated by the third in its confirmation of the first. This tripartite sequence is visible in the two sentences of this extract from a comparison between Yves Montand, a singer and film-actor whose political sympathies were with the Left, and Jean-Marie Le Pen, the leader of the Front national of the extreme Right:

> Je souhaite que M. Montand ne se formalise pas si je hasarde que, d'une certaine façon, il offre aux Français un pareil sujet de satisfaction que M. Le Pen. Ils ne disent pas la même chose l'un et l'autre, bien sûr, et je vois aussi bien que n'importe qui la distance qui les sépare, mais ils ont en commun ce qui attire les gens d'aujourd'hui : ils parlent comme l'homme de la rue. Leurs paroles touchent directement les cœurs.
>
> (Dutourd, 1985: 65)

Like other concessives, this one can make a sentence on its own, as in this example from an article on the economic strength of Germany in which the author tries to explain why a certain decision has been taken affecting the whole European Community:

> Pourquoi, comment ? Parce que l'Allemagne est la première puissance économique du continent. Bien sûr. Mais cela n'eût pas suffi. En réalité [...]

bref *

This connector is one of a set of resumers which includes, among others, *en résumé*, *en somme* and *en un mot*. What is recapitulated by this one is usually a sentence, sometimes a paragraph. Unlike some other resumers, what follows this one tends to be much shorter than what precedes. Thus, a paragraph listing in detail the multifarious commercial interests of the *Compagnie générale d'électricité* concludes with a short verbless sentence:

> La CGE produit des turbines, des trains, des métros avec Alsthom. Mais elle est surtout le numéro deux mondial du téléphone (derrière le géant américain ATT) avec Alcatel, ce qui ne l'empêche pas de contrôler des chantiers navals (Chantiers de l'Atlantique), des forêts américaines (Générale occidentale), un grand groupe d'édition (Presses de la Cité), le premier news magazine français (*l'Express*) et le leader des centrales nucléaires (Framatome). Bref, un vrai conglomérat.

Introducing a sentence

This connector shares a feature or two with *autrement dit* and *c'est-à-dire (que)*: it could at times be replaced by one or other of these structures; and it can introduce either a whole sentence or part of a sentence. When it does the former, it is placed first and is usually followed by a comma. The following example comes from a discussion of the view that the contraceptive pill has had huge social, moral and demographic significance for the last generation of the twentieth century:

> Tous nos changements viendraient donc de là. En effet, grâce aux nouveaux moyens contraceptifs, la cohabitation sans mariage pouvait se diffuser : elle était désormais sans risque et la crainte d'une conception entraînant un mariage forcé n'avait plus de raison d'être. La dissociation entre activité sexuelle et risque de fécondité favorisait une « émancipation sexuelle » qui touchait jeunes et adultes, hommes et femmes. Enfin, changement fondamental dont on ne parle pas assez, cette maîtrise de la fécondité était cette fois, assurée, non plus par l'homme mais par la femme. Bref, cette petite pilule, à elle seule, aurait suffi à déclencher une révolution.
>
> (Roussel, 190)

Often this complete sentence is a *phrase dépendante* composed of nothing but the connector followed by a noun in apposition, as in this description of a donation of works of art made to the museum of Toulouse:

> Plus de 40 tableaux anciens, 80 tableaux et dessins modernes et une centaine de bronzes, coupes, cruches, livres anciens et objets divers des XVIe et XVIIe siècles. Bref, une merveille.

Introducing part of a sentence

When what follows is a substitute complement of what precedes, an alternative subject or object, the connector is usually placed inside the sentence, often towards the end, and the comma is omitted. What follows is probably most often a noun, as in this statement about the importance of 'packaging' in politics:

> L'« emballage » joue un grand rôle en politique. L'« accompagnement » d'un programme, ou d'un projet, la façon dont il est présenté, bref la forme, compte beaucoup.

The sentence frequently has the form of a list or a repetition of similar structures; and whatever follows the connector is the same part of speech as what precedes, such as the infinitive in this extract from a guide to good style:

> Il faut sabrer les épithètes superflues, biffer les adverbes inutiles, débûcher les conjonctions parasites, émonder les redondances, résorber les pléonasmes naïfs et les tautologies, bref retrancher toutes les excroissances verbales, indice d'une mauvaise santé du style.

In the following example, it is the preceding *à* which is repeated in what follows:

La très grande majorité des Français se déclare attachée à la liberté, à la tolérance, aux droits de l'homme, à l'antiracisme, bref aux valeurs de la République.

This mode can of course combine with *que*, as in this extract from a discussion of what distinguishes 'Arab' from 'Muslim':

Il faut rappeler que quelques millions de chrétiens égyptiens, syriens, libanais, sont aussi des Arabes, qu'il fut une époque où de nombreuses tribus arabes étaient de confession juive, bref, que la désignation d'« Arabe » ne renvoie pas à une famille spirituelle, celle de l'Islam.

Combinations

This connector is sometimes used in combination with another belonging to the same set: *Bref, en un mot*; *Enfin, bref*. The latter combination, common in speech, is rarely written; and when it is written, it is usually in a text of markedly familiar tone, as in the following excerpt from a review of a video featuring a pop group called Noir Désir. What particularly distempered the reviewer was the style of filming, which he found old-hat, derivative from a scene in Antonioni's film *Blow-Up*:

Je m'étonne simplement que l'on ait encore le goût de ces exercices échevelés aussitôt qu'apparaît dans le champ une guitare électrique, ou même Dieu sait quoi. Il est difficile de ne pas penser à ces types qui se recoiffent et s'aspergent la bouche d'un jet mentholé avant de s'approcher d'une femme. On aimerait pouvoir leur épargner une conduite un peu ridicule. On se dit que cette scène de *Blow-Up* n'a pas fini de nous empoisonner la vie. Enfin bref, il n'aurait plus manqué que la vidéo du concert de Noir Désir n'ait été confiée aux mains d'une de ces bandes d'épileptiques qui font dans le genre déstructuré et fiévreux. Nous avons bien assez des émissions de télé pour ça.

en bref

This is a less common variant of the connector. In 1975, the *Trésor de la langue française* said it was *senti comme un néologisme*; and it had already been objected to as superfluous a quarter of a century before: *On a tendance aujourd'hui à substituer en tête d'une phrase* en bref *à* bref *qui en dit tout autant* (Georgin, 1951: 100). It functions, in its various modes, exactly like the shorter form; and, *pace* Georgin, it is not only placed first in the sentence:

Comprendre un texte, n'est-ce pas discerner ce qui se cache derrière les mots, aller des mots aux choses, en bref séparer le contenu de sa propre expression ?

The only difference between the two forms may be one of tone – the Robert dictionary sees the longer variant as *littéraire*. But then it also sees it as a simple adverb and ignores its connective function. Yet it is much commoner as a connector than as a simple adverb.

In his study of Stendhal's *Lamiel*, Léon Blum uses a variant of this variant, *au bref*:

> Une enfance méconnue, puis une vie dépendante au milieu de gens du monde qui raillent son patois et ses manières, mais subissent peu à peu son ascendant, telle est, au bref, l'histoire inachevée de Lamiel.

> (Blum, 521)

English equivalents

English writers who wish to announce a summing-up also have plenty of choice: 'in short', 'in brief, 'to sum up', 'in other words'. They may adapt a more versatile connector such as 'so'. But this point in a discourse is one of those where modern English prose, unlike French, often does without a specialized connector. An example of this difference may be seen in the following extract from Gowers' discussion of 'rules of grammar and syntax' as they apply to the writing of 'good English'. He reaches a sort of sub-conclusion like this:

> The golden rule is not a rule of grammar or syntax. It concerns less the arrangement of words than the choice of them. 'After all,' said Lord Macaulay, 'the first law of writing, that law to which all other laws are subordinate, is this: that the words employed should be such as to convey to the reader the meaning of the writer.' The golden rule is to pick those words and to use them and them only.

> (Gowers, 3)

At the beginning of that last sentence, where a French writer might well have placed *bref*, the English author might have placed a conclusive 'so'. Gowers chose, instead, to exemplify the prevalence in English of what, from a French point of view, has been called the *charnière-zéro*.

brief interpolated main clause

If a connector is a structure which sets discrete ideas or whole statements into a dialectical relationship with each other, pointing out a link of emphasis between them, then it is clear that this is one. In the following example, the authors make such a relationship between the *sous-phrase* or brief sentence *ceci est une vérité banale* and the longer sentence into which they insert it. Their subject is the necessary requirements of a good definition: *Une bonne définition, ceci est une vérité banale, doit convenir à tout le défini, ne s'appliquer qu'au défini* (Hovelacque & Hervé, 9–10).

In a statement like 'He said – it was not true – he had been to the cinema', spoken English can intelligibly make such a link, by means of pause and intonation. In written English, because of the versatility of some of its punctuation and our habit of omitting 'that', greater care would have to be taken than in written French to avoid ambiguities.

Two types of *sous-phrase*

In speaking of *sous-phrases*, some grammarians define no practical distinction between incidental clauses like *cria-t-il* and the very different *je le répète* (Grevisse, 1964a: 122). One can see three main differences between them. First, apart from *semble-t-il*, the incidental has little function in expository prose. Second, the *je le répète* variety, being a main clause, could stand by itself as a separate sentence. Third, it comments on the clause into which it is put. That is what makes it a connector. This structure is in fact a short complete sentence, containing usually a subject and a verb, often an object and sometimes an abverbial complement, placed like a parenthesis inside a more important statement, itself usually a main clause, on which it expresses a view. It can be a rapid means of editorializing, by which a writer comments on the information conveyed in the host clause. It can separate subjects from verbs and verbs from objects. It can function as a form of tmesis. It can be a kind of **transition mécanique**, a procedural injunction to the reader or a reminder of a point dealt with earlier.

Punctuation

The structure is most often placed between two commas, as in the example given above. Brackets or dashes draw attention to the insertion in a more emphatic way:

> C'est en ce sens (Edwy Plenel, qui vient d'y consacrer un ouvrage passionnant, ne nous démentira pas) que l'on peut soutenir qu'une grande partie de l'information se vole.

> ...les innombrables troupes aguerries d'un Saddam Hussein prêt à tout, y compris – il l'a prouvé – à l'usage des armes chimiques.

With a conjunction

As this type of clause is joined to the host clause by punctuation rather than by syntax, it could be removed from it without altering either the syntax or the meaning of either itself or the host. It is true that occasionally its first word is a conjunction which may appear to be a syntactical link: *Cependant, et c'est là tout le problème, cette monnaie est étrangère.*

But the two statements can usually be made as separate sentences: *Cependant, cette monnaie est étrangère. Et c'est là tout le problème.* Apart from *et*, the conjunction most commonly used in this way is *mais*, as in *Parfois, mais il faut un ou deux siècles pour s'en apercevoir distinctement, on prend conscience que....* Rather than making a syntactical link, the function of the conjunction in such interpolations is to obviate the grammatical indeterminacy which would follow from *Cependant, c'est...* or *Parfois, il....* Also used in this way are *car* and *d'ailleurs*.

Beginning with a pronoun

When not linked by a rare conjunction, the clause usually begins with a subject pronoun, often *je*: *L'origine organique de la schizophrénie, j'y reviendrai plus loin, illustre bien cette « dérivation ».* / *Nous autres commentateurs, sociologues et historiens, nous pouvons très bien, je l'ai fait la semaine dernière, comprendre le rôle dévastateur de l'humiliation.* Other pronouns are quite common: *il, on, nous, ce*: *M. Chirac, il n'est personne pour l'ignorer, est un homme dont les qualités humaines sont profondes.* / *Les critiques visent la mise en œuvre du traité, mais aussi, c'est plus nouveau, le fond.*

Meaning 'this is common knowledge'

As some of the examples show, the structure often means roughly 'what I say is obvious', 'everybody knows this' or 'needless to say'. This is probably the most common comment made by these clauses: *Leur indolence faisait d'eux, on le comprend sans peine, de dociles véhicules de la désinformation.* / *La fréquence des échecs et des ruptures scolaires caractérise, c'est presque une évidence, le parcours de ces jeunes délinquants.* / *Les années Mitterrand, c'est une lapalissade que de le rappeler, ont mis fin à la culture politique militante et batailleuse héritée de l'été 1789.*

The following ones, more or less commonly used, express a similar meaning: *cela va de soi; cela va sans dire; c'est clair; c'est assez clair; c'est connu; c'est bien connu; c'est indiscutable; c'est le moins qu'on puisse dire; c'est une banalité de le dire; chacun vous le dira; évidence que de le rappeler; est-il besoin de le dire?; je ne l'ignore pas; n'en doutons pas; ne l'oublions pas; nul n'en doute; ne nous lassons pas de le répéter; on en conviendra; on l'a dit cent fois; on ne le répétera jamais assez; on ne sait que trop; on s'en doute; on l'a compris; on l'aura compris; on le devine; on le sait; on le sait, mais on l'oublie trop souvent; tout le monde le sait; d'illustres exemples sont là pour le démontrer; il y aurait quelque mauvaise foi à le nier; il ne s'agit là que d'un secret de Polichinelle.* In interrogative forms, such as *faut-il le rappeler* and *qui l'ignore*, the question mark is often omitted.

Author's addresses to reader

As can be seen, some of these inserted clauses are modes of the *transition mécanique* by means of which the author directly addresses the reader or speaks not of the content of the text but of its forms, of his or her procedures in composing it, as in *A mes yeux, je le répète pour qu'on ne se méprenne pas sur ma position, c'est...*; *La question, j'y insiste, n'est pas de savoir si...*; and *Le texte de cette édition, je crois pouvoir le dire, est d'une entière fidélité.* Many of these clauses begin with *je* or *nous.* They include: *croyons-nous*; *j'en ai donné plusieurs exemples*; *nous aurons tout loisir d'y revenir*; *nous venons de le dire*; *j'y reviens*; *nous y reviendrons*; *je le répète*; *je répète le mot*; *je le montrerai plus loin*; *je crois l'avoir montré.* Sometimes they take a slightly different form, an imperative, say, as in *rappelons-le* and *sachons-le* or as in this writer's passing apology for using a crudish expression while discussing the subject of sexual harassment:

> Nous lisons, de temps à autre, des articles où un patron ou un petit chef est accusé de faire systématiquement passer à la casserole, excusez le terme, son personnel féminin.

Other common clauses

Other main clauses more or less commonly used are: *c'est là que le bât blesse*; *c'est le cas de le dire*; *c'est la moindre des choses*; *c'est tout dire*; *ce n'est pas rien*; *c'est vrai*; *il est vrai*; *il faut bien le dire*; *il faut être juste*; *il s'en faut*; *il s'en faut de beaucoup*; *loin s'en faut*; *tant s'en faut*; *je crois pouvoir le dire*; *je l'ai constaté plus d'une fois*; *je ne l'ignore pas*; *n'en déplaise à...*; *on l'imagine*; *on l'oublie trop souvent*; *on le voit*; *on l'a vu*; *on ne sait jamais*; *on s'en souvient*; *passe encore*; *qui sait*; *soit dit entre parenthèses*; *soit dit en passant*; *une fois n'est pas coutume*; *ne jurons de rien*; *excusez du peu.* Some of these, such as the last four in the list, can neatly express a passing criticism or irony:

> Les gouvernements américain, britannique et français ont répondu, une fois n'est pas coutume, avec promptitude et vigueur.

> L'annonce d'une baisse de 0,5 % de l'indice des prix de gros a éloigné temporairement, ne jurons de rien, la perspective d'un relèvement des taux par la Réserve fédérale.

And the proverbial saying *Noblesse oblige* not only lends itself to interpolation but adapts to the requirements of different contexts:

> Il dressait ensuite, à l'intention de son compère Peyrefitte, un tableau de chasse des plus scrupuleux – à ceci près que, prudence oblige, les missives étaient codées [...]

Voter ou ne pas voter pour lui dans un jury dont on fait, notoriété littéraire oblige, partie ?

Alors, cette fois, il en a ras le bol. Pourtant – devoir de réserve oblige – il se tait.

As a coda

Quite common also, though lacking the verb that would make them true main clauses, are *sauf erreur* and *loin de là*. The latter, instead of being inserted inside a host, is sometimes appended to the end of the sentence as a coda: *Car l'accord de Minsk ne règle pas tout, loin de là.* The same goes for *tant s'en faut* and some of the others: *Le pouvoir de la presse ne milite pas toujours au seul service de la vérité, tant s'en faut.* Sometimes this appending is done in the form of a separate sentence: *Bien sûr, le sida n'est pas le monopole des homosexuels. Loin de là. Mais tout de même [...] / Ce n'est pas à dire que cette édition soit irréprochable. Il s'en faut de beaucoup.* And this postpositioning is sometimes done with clauses of more standard form: *Ce sera l'épreuve de vérité pour 1984, tout le monde le sait* (Closets, 15).

First in the sentence

The structure is sometimes neither interpolated inside the sentence nor appended to the end but put at the beginning of the sentence, where it is followed by a comma:

On l'a constaté avec François Léotard, zombi poli de la cohabitation, succéder à Jack Lang n'est pas une sinécure.

Élection présidentielle oblige, il est virtuellement exclu qu'une mesure de financement (hausse de la CSG ou de la TVA) intervienne d'ici avril 1995.

In this position, *On l'aura compris, On le voit* and **C'est un fait** are not uncommon. Others sometimes used in this position are *Avouons-le* and variants of those which mean 'this has often been said': *On l'a dit cent fois : l'écrivain français est moraliste* (Boisdeffre, 20). / *Nous l'a-t-on assez dit ? Corneille nous peint tels que nous devrions être, Racine, hélas, tels que nous sommes* (Mauron, 256).

Tmesis

In 'absobloodylutely' a word is split by the insertion of another word. If one stretches the definition of tmesis to include not just words but also structures, this interpolation of a main clause may be seen as a mode of it. This may be most evident in separations of common syntagms, such as *cru devoir* in this (double) example:

> Ayant eu à relire mes lignes, je n'ai pas cru, c'est la moindre des politesses sitôt qu'on a en vue l'agrément du lecteur, devoir, il eût fallu, davantage, peut-être, leur éviter maintes retouches à cet égard.

> (Ricardou, 9–10)

It is seen too when the clause is inserted between the two parts of a structure such as **alors que**: *Alors, répétons-le, que le suicide n'est pas un délit légal, il est traqué comme un crime.* French use of the comma has by and large remained clear enough for even these to cause no great ambiguity. In the following example, discussing wealth-creation under the French socialist governments of the 1980s, **quitte à** is split:

> Quoi qu'en dise la droite, le pouvoir socialiste a joué dans cette longue chaîne un rôle non négligeable et même essentiel. Quitte, et c'est son grand échec, à assumer, en définitive, la répartition la moins égalitaire des fruits de la richesse collective dont il a favorisé la création.

Less brief clauses

As is obvious from some of the examples already quoted, the 'brief' main clause may be not all that brief:

> Dans les travaux scientifiques, j'entends par là ceux qui constituent actuellement nos sciences ou qui ont contribué à leur développement, au cours de l'histoire, la méthode est toujours ou mathématique, ou expérimentale.

> (Rey, 17)

> Les fidèles du Festival d'Avignon – ils sont chaque année plusieurs dizaines de milliers, venus de tous les coins du monde pour ce qui est le principal rendez-vous du spectacle vivant – auront certainement été saisis de vertige à la lecture du programme de l'édition 93.

This goes, too, for sentences in which two of these clauses rub shoulders, as in this extract from an article discussing an interest-free loan arranged by the then Prime Minister, Pierre Bérégovoy, and the exaggerated chorus of disapproval it aroused, although it was nothing more than

> une « imprudence » fautive qui ne méritait pas cette implacable mise en scène. D'autant, et nous l'avions écrit à l'époque (il se trouva des lecteurs pour nous le reprocher), que plus de 90 % des personnes qui feignaient de s'indigner eussent sans aucune hésitation accepté, si elles en avaient eu besoin pour s'établir, un prêt sans intérêt d'un ami fortuné.

car *

Those who enjoy silly bilingual jokes may find it apt that an authority on *car* is Voiture. In 1637, he wrote to Mlle de Rambouillet to assure her that *car* is *une diction qui marche toujours à la tête de la raison, et qui n'a point d'autre charge que de l'introduire* (Voiture, 294).

When *car* and when *parce que*?

The only real difficulty with this conjunction is caused by the fact that it is sometimes replaceable by *parce que* and sometimes not. Most often *parce que* introduces the objective cause of an action (and thus relates conceptually to a verb) whereas *car* presents a writer's own reason for having said what precedes, a justification or explanation of it (and thus it relates usually to a whole statement).

It is not only foreign learners of French who can have difficulty in differentiating some of the functions of the two conjunctions. Some French writers do not respect the distinctions which authorities on usage define. In the two following sentences, written by a novelist, there are three exemplars of *car*:

> Quand elle est gentille avec lui car elle a vu l'autre homme (le mardi, généralement) ; quand elle est froide car elle ne l'a pas vu et que, sans doute, elle lui reproche d'être là, à sa place. (Franck, 65)

> Au réveil, elle lui a dit qu'elle a très mal dormi car il n'a cessé de toucher son corps [...] (Franck, 111)

In all three of these statements, where the connector introduces causes and not reasons, *parce que* rather than *car* would have been more in accord with conventional practice. Clearly, some distinctions between the conjunctions will be difficult to make; and in many statements, either of them will function adequately. But in many other contexts one of them will be apter than the other. A clear instance of this can be seen in the second of the two quotations above (Franck, 111): the cause of her sleeping badly was that he kept touching her; yet *car* momentarily seems to mean that the reason *why she said so* was that he had kept touching her. It is only when the boggled mind resolves this illogicality that the author's meaning, and the preferability of *parce que*, become apparent.

Anaphoric *car*

All authorities make the point that a question asked by *pourquoi* cannot be properly answered with *car*, but only with *parce que*. In any statement, *parce que* could replace *car* without introducing a great ambiguity (thus, in the words of the missal, one can find *Bénissez-moi parce que j'ai péché* alongside *Pardonnez-moi, car j'ai péché*); but the opposite would not always be true. It is of course possible to place *car* at the beginning of a statement; but, being solely anaphoric in its function, it can only ever introduce an explanation of a preceding statement. On the other hand, *parce que* can function both anaphorically and cataphorically: placed at the beginning of a statement it can either account for a preceding action or it can present the cause of a following action, as in this sentence taken from a discussion of the differences between the sounds of prose and those of poetry:

> Les caractères de niveau phonique ont été codifiés et nommés. On appelle « vers » toute forme de langage dont la face phonique porte ces caractères. Parce qu'ils sont immédiatement visibles et rigoureusement codifiés, ils constituent aujourd'hui encore aux yeux du public le critère de la poésie.
>
> (Cohen, 9)

In accordance with this principle, it would be possible to reshape one of the examples quoted above (Franck, 65): *Parce qu'elle ne l'a pas vu, elle est froide*. But the same statement could not be made using *car*: *Car elle ne l'a pas vu, elle est froide*.

Register of *car*

One of the ways in which *parce que* can function like *car* is that it too can introduce not a cause but evidence or an argument in favour of believing what precedes. In the following example, taken from an editorial deploring a decision by the Security Council of the United Nations, both conjunctions are used without violence being done to logic and in the same register:

> Cette décision n'est pas courageuse, car elle est hypocrite. Elle n'est pas courageuse, parce que, bien loin de contribuer à établir la vérité, elle va aggraver un désastreux contresens.

There, the implicit meaning of *parce que* is *Je dis « pas courageuse » parce que*. Similarly, in a spoken utterance like *Il est intelligent, ce gosse, parce qu'il sait déjà lire*, the connector precedes not a statement of the cause of the intelligence, but the observation on which the initial deduction about intelligence is based. In this, *parce que* acts as does *car* in a different register. For another difference between *parce que* and *car* is that the latter is more formal or educated. Both of them belong to spoken and printed discourse; but it is the logician, the explainer, the writer, the persuader who find *car* indispensable. It is one of the most didactic of the French connectors, perhaps a reason why Voltaire lampoons it in the speech of Pangloss the pontificator:

Car, dit-il, tout ceci est ce qu'il y a de mieux ; car s'il y a un volcan à Lisbonne, il ne pouvait être ailleurs ; car il est impossible que les choses ne soient pas où elles sont ; car tout est bien.

(Voltaire, 148)

In combination with *enfin* and *en effet*

As part of the reasoner's repertoire, *car* is sometimes used in combination with *enfin* and *en effet*. In fact, at times its function is identical with that of *en effet*, which could replace it in the following statement about the relativism of Montaigne:

Son relativisme protège contre l'intolérance autant que contre le nihilisme. Car Montaigne est relativiste, et d'un relativisme radical : pas de valeurs absolues, pour lui, pas d'universel qu'on puisse imposer à quiconque.

There, it is clear that the role of the second sentence is to make more precise and to amplify the sense of the first; and that is exactly the usual function of *en effet*. As for *car enfin*, it makes a step in reasoning akin to that made by *après tout*, by which the writer implicitly invites the reader to be reminded of something that is self-evident or known to them both, as can be seen in Durkheim's famous statement about sociology:

La méthode sociologique, telle que nous la pratiquons, repose tout entière sur ce principe fondamental que les faits sociaux doivent être étudiés comme des choses, c'est-à-dire comme des réalités extérieures à l'individu. Il n'est pas de précepte qui nous ait été plus contesté ; il n'en est pas, cependant, de plus fondamental. Car enfin, pour que la sociologie soit possible, il faut avant tout qu'elle ait un objet et qui ne soit qu'à elle.

(Durkheim, 1930: ix)

The extra emotional charge given by *enfin* is sometimes denoted these days, at least in journalistic practice, by the addition of an exclamation mark at the end of the sentence. The combination *car après tout* is also used, in ways which at times make it a replacement for *tant il est vrai que*.

Three other differences

Three other differences between *car* and *parce que* should be noted. First, whereas *parce que* can be preceded by *mais* or *et*, the same does not hold for *car*. Also, although both structures can introduce a negative statement (*Car elle n'est pas venue...*; *Parce qu'elle n'est pas venue...*), only *parce que* can introduce a non-reason – in the second sentence of the following example, say, *non car* and *ni car* would be inconceivable. The extract comes from a discussion of the absence of extra-textual referents in a text by Rousseau:

Il n'y a pas de hors-texte. Et cela non parce que la vie de Jean-Jacques ne nous intéresse pas d'abord, ni l'existence de Maman ou de Thérèse *elles-mêmes*, ni parce que nous n'avons accès à leur existence dite « réelle » que dans le texte et que nous n'avons aucun moyen de faire autrement, ni aucun droit de négliger cette limitation.

(Derrida, 227–228)

Third, in a sequence of propositions, *parce que* reduces to *que* – as in the last *que* of the previous quotation – which *car* does not usually do, at least not when written. Or rather, that is the view of prescriptive grammarians:

Le sens de la construction de la phrase se perd. On commence à exprimer l'idée de cause par *car*, et emploie *que* en tête de la proposition suivante. Or *que*, conjonction de subordination, lien très fort, ne peut remplacer *car*, conjonction de coordination moins forte ; il peut ici représenter seulement *parce que*.

(Georgin, 1951: 151)

However, an example quoted above (Franck, 65) contains *que* apparently used in that way. Another example can be seen in the entry for ***points de suspension***, the quotation beginning *À quinze bonnes minutes par orateur* (p. 393–4).

Linking two adjectives

Nowadays, some writers use either *car* or *parce que* without a verb to make a causal link between two adjectives or adjectival phrases. A discussion of unresolved contradictions in the attitudes of political parties of the Right, which can be tolerated while they are in opposition and while no presidential election is imminent, says this:

Mais une fois au gouvernement il faudra bien résoudre ces contradictions, choisir et affronter des débats internes qui, la perspective présidentielle aidant, devraient être plus rudes encore, parce que plus larges, que ceux qui ont divisé la droite au moment de la ratification du traité de Maastricht.

There, what follows *parce que* is the cause of the increased difficulty of managing the disagreements: they will be wider. It is that function of introducing a cause which makes it illogical to see *car* being used in the same structure. Perhaps its brevity is what recommends it to its users: *...cette période heureuse, car choyée par les Muses*; *...la solution la plus confortable pour le chef de l'État, car la plus porteuse de continuité.* One senses that what the authors mean to do is to explain why they use the first adjective; and that a clearer connector would be a mode of ***c'est-à-dire (que)***. One even finds this sequence being used to link to a following noun or verb-structure:

Birgit Nilsson se montre très prudente la première journée mais telle une lave en fusion, car personnalité hors du commun, elle emporte tout dans *Siegfried* et le *Crépuscule des Dieux* [...]

Le 6 juillet 1993, une ordonnance déclare le SNJ irrecevable car ne pouvant justifier d'un « préjudice direct résultant de la lésion d'un intérêt collectif de la profession ».

Similar sequences are sometimes made with *puisque*: *Jacques Duquesne, homme quasiment universel, puisque à la fois romancier, historien et journaliste.*

Closeness to *c'est que*

Car is semantically close not only to *parce que* and *puisque*. In addition, in many contexts its explanatory function is close to that of ***c'est que***:

L'encre de certaines dispositions législatives ou réglementaires n'est pas sèche qu'un texte nouveau est déjà à l'imprimerie... C'est que chaque ministre voudrait laisser son nom à une loi.

Jusqu'en 1914, les Français payaient beaucoup moins d'impôts que les Britanniques et les Allemands. C'est que leur administration était nettement plus légère que dans les deux grandes nations voisines.

Broadly speaking, this connector and *c'est que* are interchangeable, except when the latter is preceded by the ***si d'opposition*** or *mais*.

Introducing a brief interpolated main clause

Like some other conjunctions, this connector is sometimes placed at the beginning of a ***brief interpolated main clause***:

La religion de Montaigne, car il n'y a pas lieu de douter de ses professions de foi, était une arme contre le fanatisme.

There, *car* supports only the initial part of the statement, viz. that Montaigne did have a religion; if instead it had been added as a separate sentence after *le fanatisme*, it would have required its author to devise a more complicated syntactical procedure.

English equivalents

Nowadays, explanatory 'for' can still be an English equivalent for most modes of this connector, as it was in George Ade's irony: '"Whom are you?" said he, for he had been to night school.' Another is 'as', in a statement like the following:

In the name 'Swann' which Proust gave to this character, there may be echoes of allegory or Wagnerian themes, as the narrator says it is a *nom presque mythologique.*

ce faisant *

This structure is one of a set of formulaic expressions (***pour ce faire*** and ***et ce*** are others) in which *ce* stands for *ceci* or *cela*. Its nature as a fossilized anomaly is apparent in the fact that *ce* precedes the verb, while being its object. The structure has two distinct modes. In the first of them, it should be one of the least problematic of French connectors; but it does sometimes lend itself to a problematic usage.

Linking of convergences

The function of this mode, no more difficult to grasp than that of English equivalents such as 'thereby' or the more literal 'in so doing', is usually inseparable from the manifest meaning of the two words that make the structure. It says that what follows is an outcome of what precedes, more or less simultaneous with it and tending in the same direction. The connector comes close to being replaceable by ***ainsi***. The following example refers to the publishing of a report on François Mitterrand's first operation for cancer:

> Il faut saluer la manière dont le chef de l'État aura levé, dans la vie publique de la France, le tabou du cancer. Ce faisant, il est en phase avec l'évolution de la société elle-même, où les cancéreux ne cachent plus leur maladie.

In a more conventional form, the structure would be *en faisant cela*. Variants including *en* used to be commoner than they have now become:

> C'est ce qu'a fait Claude Bernard; et, en ce faisant, il [...]
>
> (Dastre, 15):

> [La supériorité de l'homme] est de penser, il faut qu'il pense ; sa supériorité est de travailler, il faut qu'il travaille ; sa supériorité est de chercher, il faut qu'il cherche ; sa supériorité est d'aimer et de se dévouer, il faut qu'il aime et se dévoue. En le faisant, il entraîne avec lui tous ceux qui l'entourent et sur lesquels son exemple peut influer [...]
>
> (Launay, 232)

If the connector is placed after the verb, it is always between two commas; if placed first in a statement, it is always followed by a comma. At times it is preceded by ***certes***, ***mais*** or *et*; at others, it is placed in the heart of the sentence, as in this extract from an article about the Danes' rejection of the Treaty of Maastricht in 1992:

Fallait-il opposer aux électeurs danois la rigidité absolue d'une Europe à une seule vitesse et renoncer, ce faisant, non seulement à l'appartenance du Danemark à la Communauté, mais aussi, à coup sûr, à celle de la Grande-Bretagne ?

In this first mode, as can be seen in the quotations, the connector's function can come close to that of *de ce fait* or *du même coup*.

Linking of divergences

A closeness to *cependant* is apparent in this second mode. Neither *du même coup* nor *ainsi* would interchange with it. The connector, slightly adversative, is used in tandem with *n'en... pas moins*. What this mode denotes is an act which, though simultaneous and directly related, is somewhat at variance with what precedes. Instead of 'in so doing', English would more likely say something like 'meanwhile' or even 'despite this'. The first example of this mode is from a reviewer's comment on saloon cars produced by BMW. It speaks first of a partly new range of vehicles just coming into production; then the connector introduces a new paragraph discussing the Z13, a wholly new concept to be developed at the same time:

Un seul moteur sera proposé sur cette nouvelle version, le 4 cylindres de 1 600 cm^3 infatigable que l'on connaît en base des berlines. Il a été retouché et délivre 102 ch. Mais le 1,8 litre et des versions diesel vont suivre.
Ce faisant, la marque de Munich n'en poursuit pas moins l'étude de la Z13. Cet engin, nouveau, lui, n'excédera pas 3,44 m de long. Il aura un 4-cylindres en ligne de 1 000 cm,^{3} (à 16 soupapes) [...]

There, the connector is not saying that the Z13 project is a by-product or a consequence of the earlier models. It helps to stress the fact that both projects are going forward simultaneously and that the second is not prevented by the first. It has a quality of 'however' in it, a shade of 'even so'. Another example comes from a demographer's discussion of whether the unexpected changes in birth-rates and in attitudes to marriage and family relationships, evident from the middle-1960s, were attributable to the wide availability of *nouveaux moyens contraceptifs*:

Ceux-ci, incontestablement, furent un facteur essentiel de la baisse de la natalité puisqu'ils réduisirent l'intensité de la fécondité à la seule fécondité désirée, ou peu s'en faut. Du coup, des dizaines de milliers d'enfants qui n'avaient pas été souhaités, mais qui auraient été acceptés et finalement aimés, ne sont pas venus au monde. Westoff et Ryder avaient bien montré que cette cause n'avait pas été la seule ; ce faisant, ils n'en confirmaient pas moins le poids de ce facteur.
(Roussel, 190)

There, the link established between the two propositions by the connector is closer to being the adversative sort expressed by 'although'.

As unattached participle

In this structure, *faisant* usually has the same implicit subject as the main verb to which it conceptually links, as is usual with present participle constructions; and this main verb with its subject either immediately precedes or follows the connector: *Ce faisant, le gouvernement savait...* or *Il serait, ce faisant,...* With the first mode, however, some writers contradict the rule and construct the sentence in such a way as to create what Fowler calls an 'unattached participle', that is one which, though semantically related to one noun, is grammatically related to another (Fowler, 1918: 112–115). An example of this more problematic usage comes from an article on a film in which the director Fellini recounts his early days as a newspaper reporter; in the third sentence, the subject of the main verb is *nous* but the implied subject of *faisant* is Fellini:

> C'est le fil qui traverse tout le film et relie une séquence à l'autre. Fellini évoque sa découverte de Cinecittà dans les années 40, lorsque, journaliste imberbe, il venait interviewer, le cœur battant, une diva du péplum. Ce faisant, nous sommes transportés sur le plateau de ces années-là et assistons à ladite découverte de l'univers baroque des studios.

Another example comes from an article about differences of policy between the USA, France and other Western allies on the war in Bosnia-Herzegovina. In the third sentence, the subject of the main verb is *Paris*; yet the implied subject of *faisant* is *les alliés*, two sentences before:

> Les alliés ont suivi, entraînés par un double revirement, français et américain. Les États-Unis, qui depuis longtemps défendaient l'idée de frappes aériennes, mais sans l'accompagner de rien d'autre que la levée de l'embargo sur les armes au profit des Musulmans, récusaient le plan de règlement sur la table des négociations, qui prévoit un découpage de la Bosnie en trois entités ethniques. Paris leur reprochait, ce faisant, d'encourager les Musulmans à poursuivre la guerre pour modifier par les armes les contours de leur futur État.

There, if the writer had placed the connector after *d'encourager*, instead of before it, the participle would not be unattached. This usage suggests that the connective function of this mode is not reducible to its semantic function. Some writers use it as though it replaces *cependant*. On this point, it may also be worth noting that some French grammarians can be more lenient towards makers of 'unattached participles' than some of their counterparts in English (Grevisse, 1964a: 739; 1988: 548–549).

dans la foulée

This expression, formed from a noun meaning 'stride', is often used to link either two actions done simultaneously or two actions one of which is an automatic if subsidiary outcome of the other. In certain contexts, it partakes of the value of *ce faisant* and *du même coup*, as in this extract from a comment on an encyclopedia:

> Ainsi, pour tout savoir de la querelle des Fourons qui rebondit pour la énième fois en Belgique, suffit-il de se reporter à la page 237 du livre. Le lecteur apprendra dans la foulée que la Belgique n'est, officiellement, pas bi- mais trilingue, du fait des soixante-dix mille germanophones qui peuplent les « cantons de l'Est ».
>
> (Boucher, 309)

In that example, a familiar English equivalent could be 'while you're about it' or 'while he's at it'.

cela dit

The *dit* is, of course, a past participle. A variant with *ceci* is also used. The grammar of this connector is that of the *complément absolu* type of structure deriving from the ablative absolute of Latin and quite common in modern French: *Réflexion faite, il... / Toutes proportions gardées, je... / Le café bu, elle est repartie. / Le dictateur disparu, son culte s'abolit. / Ce point éclairci, reste à en tirer les conséquences.*

With this connector, a writer can express a reservation or a difference of opinion, define the significance of a fact relative to another, clarify a shade of difference between points of view, concede agreement with what precedes and foreshadow disagreement with what follows. It says 'Having said that', 'Even so' or, in a more conversational register, 'Mind you'. It frequently shapes a contrast as much as it makes a concession:

> Que les choses soient claires. Je considère Saddam Hussein comme un dicta-teur. Ce qu'il a fait au Koweït est inacceptable. Il doit s'en aller. Cela dit, je constate qu'au lieu de traiter ce problème comme un problème arabe régional, les États-Unis l'ont transformé en combat opposant les États-Unis et le « mal ».

Place in the sentence

The structure is most usually placed at the beginning of a sentence, very often of a paragraph. This frequent positioning at the head of a paragraph is explained by the fact that the connector usually relates not just to a previous statement but to the entirety of a fairly lengthy development, as in this end and beginning of two paragraphs from an article about the dismantling of the former Soviet secret police:

> Le démantèlement du KGB, annoncé vendredi 11 octobre à Moscou, ne fera pas pleurer dans les datchas. D'abord parce que cette décision était attendue depuis l'échec du putsch du mois d'août. Ensuite parce qu'il n'y a sans doute

pas une seule famille soviétique qui n'ait eu, en plus de soixante-dix ans, à pâtir de ce monstre inventé par Lénine, qu'il se soit appelé au fil des ans GPU, NKVD ou KGB.

Cela dit, même découpé en tronçons, le KGB risque de peser lourd pendant longtemps sur la vie politique de la nouvelle Union.

Similarly, in a Parisian weekly, a writer, asked his opinion on a literary matter of pregnant topicality, prefaces his answer with two long paragraphs, nearly six broad column-inches, of clarification of the implications concealed in the questions, then says: *Ceci dit, je réponds à vos questions.* Not that his opinions are in marked contrast to this clarification; it merely expresses his reservations, which are then underscored by the connector. Sometimes the lengthiness of what precedes is explicitly designated in a slight variant of the basic structure, *Tout cela dit.*

Sometimes the connector is not placed first in the sentence. On occasion it is preceded by **mais**. Some writers place it after the first element of the sentence: *Reste, cela dit, l'essentiel*; *Mais le plus intéressant, cela dit, c'est...*; *Il souffre, cela dit, c'est certain.* Bernard-Henri Lévy, who enjoys placing it anywhere but at the beginning, even likes to place it at the end of the sentence, as in this extract from one of his reports on the war in Bosnia in early 1994:

Dîner, le soir même, au PTT building avec quelques-uns des officiers du bataillon français. Atmosphère plus sympathique. Plus franche, surtout. Avec un parti pris de débat « à la loyale » qui me change de la conversation précédente. Mais quel étrange univers, cela dit ! Quels singuliers arguments !

The verb following

Any verb-structure, with any type of subject, may follow *cela dit*. It is not uncommon to find it followed by an impersonal construction: *il n'est pas certain que*; *il faut bien constater*; *force est d'admettre*; *il reste que*; *il reste à*; *il serait erroné de.* Whatever follows it is a main clause: *Cela dit, tout est dit.*

However, occasionally a writer uses this structure for a function which is quite different from any of those mentioned above and in a way which comes closer to being one of the modes of **et ce**. In this form, usually followed by an infinitive and lacking the comma, it is itself part of a main clause which gives either a reason for a preceding statement having been made or a comment on it; and it usually has only a resuming function: *Cela dit sans rire*; *Cela dit pour répondre aux critiques.* As well as that, it is probably part of a narrative and implies a finite verb: *Cela fut dit sans rire.*

Used with overtly adversative structures

Sometimes, this connector is used rather like *mais*, to restrict a concession introduced by **certes**, as in this extract from a discussion of the coexistence of subtle and unsubtle forms of censorship in a general climate of freedom of the press:

> Certes, il existe une autonomie réelle des journalistes. Cela dit, le fait que la direction du *Figaro* se permette de censurer un dessin de Faizant pour ne point déplaire à Balladur montre bien que ceux qui nient le rapport presse-argent sont bien naïfs.

And sometimes the contrastive nature of the sentence introduced by this structure is underlined by an explicitly adversative expression such as *cependant*, **tout de même**, **pour autant** or **n'en... pas moins**: *Ceci reconnu, il nous faut cependant voir aussi les autres conséquences. / Cela dit, ils n'imposent pas pour autant la solution inverse. / Ceci dit, il n'en est pas moins vrai que... / Cela dit, cette carte est tout de même significative.*

cela dit or *ceci dit*

On the question of whether *cela dit* is more or less common than *ceci dit*, Grevisse quotes the view of André Thérive, who believes that the form with *ceci* is by far the commoner:

> *...ceci dit* a presque évincé *cela dit*. C'est que le paragraphe précédent est considéré non pas comme fini, mais comme encore tout proche. (Grevisse, 1964a: 459)

This may have been a defensible view of the structure a generation or two ago, as may Thérive's other opinion, that *ceci dit* is preferable: *Presque personne, hormis des écrivains très ou trop délicats, n'emploie* cela dit (Thérive, 1962: 210). But it is likely that these views were informed by insufficient observation and a modicum of personal preference; and against them one could put the different views of others, Michel Polac for instance, who speaking of the *traduction lamentable* of a book by Julian Jaynes, says: *« ceci dit » revient deux fois par page et j'aurais moins souffert avec « cela dit »* (Polac, 99). Although Thérive's opinion may have some validity as a comment on spoken usage – the form with *ceci* may perhaps be heard nowadays more often than it is read – as a comment on written usage, it appears to have little. An empirical finding, based on a random but probably quite reliable sample of current usage (several dozen written exemplars), deriving almost entirely from contemporary journals, newspapers and monographs, and containing *dit* rather than the past participle of some other verb, is that over 80 per cent of exemplars are constructed with *cela*. If structures using *posé* instead of *dit* are included in the sample, this percentage rises, as *posé* seems to be used even more rarely with *ceci*.

This finding contradicts the view, still prevalent, that *ceci* is the dominant form (see for example Dupré, I, 388; *Trésor de la langue française*; Grevisse, 1988: 1059). It also shows that this preference for the form with *cela* contrasts with the dominant usage of *à ceci près que*. Some writers use both *ceci dit* and *cela dit*, and that on facing pages (Goldmann, 352, 353). And despite his views on this, André Thérive himself used the form with *cela* (Thérive, 1962: 14, 17).

Used with other verbs

Not only the *cela* can vary but the *dit* as well; the connector exists in a range of variants: *Cela précisé*; *Ceci mis à part*; *Cela fait*; *Ceci éclairci*; *Cela reconnu*; *Cela su*; *Ceci admis*; *Tout cela accordé*. Of these variants, the most common nowadays is no doubt *Cela posé*; it often introduces a statement which is barely contrastive in relation to what precedes: *Cela posé, les conséquences s'ensuivent nécessairement.*

Relation to *cela étant*

Some writers appear to use ***cela étant*** as a variant for this connector in its more adversative mode. This interference between the two structures seems to have produced another variant, *cela étant dit*, something of a cross between the two: *Cela étant dit, considérons d'abord...*; *Ceci étant posé, et pour revenir à la question, disons que...*; *Cela étant posé, il est clair que....*

The structure containing a noun

This structure functions as a connector even when it contains not *cela* or *ceci* but a noun. The latter necessitates a grammatical agreement, of course, with the past participle: *Ce préalable posé*; *Ces principes posés*; *Ce premier point acquis*; *Ce constat dressé et ces questions posées*; *Ces réserves faites, il n'en demeure pas moins que*; *Ces précautions prises, venons-en à*; *Ce point admis, bien des directions fécondes s'ouvrent aux recherches.* Some writers even invert the noun and the participle: *Admis le fait que*; *Posées en effet les finalités de ces modèles...*; *Part faite aux nomenclatures,...*. The variant arising from the cross with *cela étant* is found in this form too: *Ces précisions étant faites, il reste que...*; *Cette remarque étant faite, disons que...*:

> Étant admises la légitimité, l'utilité efficace de la nouvelle grammaire, peut-on penser que ses descriptions épuisent tout ce que les linguistes et les grammairiens ont à dire sur un état de langue donné ?
>
> (Wagner, 79)

Some English equivalents of *cela dit*, in addition to those mentioned above, are: 'that said', 'all that said' or 'that having been said'; 'despite all that'; 'that is true, but the fact remains'.

cela est si vrai que

The form which I give as the paradigm of this structure has a dated flavour for some contemporary speakers and writers of French. Albert Camus was not averse to using it (Camus, 1965: 1021). And in forms like *c'est si vrai que* it is still occasionally used. Its usual function is hardly different from its most evident meaning: what follows is a supportive proof of the assertion preceding. At times, it could be replaced by **au point que** or even possibly by **si bien que**.

Up to the early years of the twentieth century, the form with *cela* was commonly used. A theorist of political thought, discussing the idea of the natural equality of all human beings, an idea which he sees as *anti-scientifique, irrationnelle et dangereuse*, maintains the view that as society progresses and becomes more complex, inequality increases among individuals:

> On pourrait même facilement établir qu'avec la division croissante du travail social, la nécessité de la spécialisation qui en résulte, le progrès industriel et scientifique, l'inégalité des aptitudes tend à s'accroître avec la diversité des fonctions. Cela est si vrai que tous les apôtres de la justice égalitaire l'ont toujours entendue comme un *retour à un état de faible différenciation sociale*, qui constitue, pour le sociologue, un phénomène de régression.
>
> (Rougier, 84–85)

The mode with *c'est* is seen in this extract from an article on new appointees in the Trésor and the Direction générale des impôts (*la DGI*) and on what the writer sees as a corresponding decline in efficiency of those financial bodies:

> Partant à la Banque de France, Jean-Claude Trichet cède à son collaborateur, Christian Noyer, son poste de directeur du Trésor ; M. Lemierre fait de même à la DGI avec M. Barilari ; dans l'un et l'autre cas, c'est une page qui se tourne : les seconds n'ont ni l'aura ni l'autorité de leur prédécesseur.
>
> C'est si vrai que, depuis le passage de relais, la direction du Trésor traverse une grave crise d'identité, qui pourrait conduire le ministre à redéfinir son rôle et à en changer le responsable.

A slight variation of this mode is seen in this extract from an article on the likely admission of Eastern European countries to the European Union:

> Il faut parfois faire un effort pour se rappeler que ces pays sont encore dans l'antichambre : c'est tellement vrai que leur demande d'adhésion à l'Union passe désormais inaperçue.

cela étant *

This structure exists also in a form with *ceci*, which is more common in spoken than in written French. It has been pointed out that no systematic description has been given of the structure (Roulet, 55). Few dictionaries define it. Those that do, see it as making a relation of consequence between two statements. For the *Trésor de la langue française*, it stands for *cela veut dire que*; for Littré, *vu que la chose est ainsi*. Thus defined, the connector seems to correspond unproblematically to English equivalents such as 'That being the case', 'That being so', 'In view of these circumstances' or 'In that case'. However, there is more to it than that. It is possible to define three modes of this connector.

Littré's mode

This first mode, saying roughly 'because of that', is more or less replaceable by *dès lors*. It links directly to the preceding sentence and is possibly becoming less common nowadays. It seems likely that it is the oldest of the different modes. Certainly, the older the exemplar of this connector, the more it seems to conform to the dictionaries' definitions. Littré gives two examples, shorn of contexts which might illustrate the function. Put back into those contexts and preceded by the statements which they originally linked to a following one, they show the function. The first is in fact taken from a sycophantic paragraph in a letter sent to Richelieu by Jean-Louis Guez de Balzac:

> Vous estes destiné pour remplir la place de ce Cardinal qui fait aujourd'huy une des belles parties du Ciel, & qui n'a point de successeur, quoy qu'il ait eu des héritiers & des frères. Et cela estant, qui doute qu'il ne falust faire des prières générales pour une santé si nécessaire, et si précieuse que la vostre ?
>
> (Balzac, I, 7)

It is clear that in its context, the connector means, 'That being so'. The same goes for Littré's second example, which comes from a scene in Lesage's play *Crispin rival de son maître* in which a marriage is under discussion; Damis is expected be the bridegroom, Valère will be the unlucky suitor:

> La Branche: Oui le contrat est déjà signé des deux pères et de Mme Oronte. La dot, qui est de vingt mille écus en argent comptant, est toute prête : on n'attend que l'arrivée de Damis pour terminer la chose.
>
> *Crispin*: Ah ! parbleu ! cela étant, Valère, mon maître, n'a donc qu'à chercher fortune ailleurs.
>
> (Lesage, 63)

A third example confirms the functioning of this mode. It occurs in Rousseau's celebrated story about the Princesse de Talmont reading *La nouvelle Héloïse* while preparing to go to the Opera ball:

> A minuit, elle ordonna qu'on mît ses chevaux, et continua de lire. On vint lui dire que ses chevaux étaient mis ; elle ne répondit rien. Ses gens, voyant qu'elle s'oubliait, vinrent avertir qu'il était deux heures. Rien ne presse encore, dit-elle, en lisant toujours. Quelque temps après, sa montre s'étant arrêtée, elle sonna pour savoir quelle heure il était. On lui dit qu'il était quatre heures. Cela étant, dit[-elle], il est trop tard pour aller au bal ; qu'on ôte mes chevaux. Elle se fit déshabiller, et passa le reste de la nuit à lire.
>
> (Rousseau, 646)

This first mode is still found in the twentieth century, albeit infrequently, as in this extract from an essay on Flaubert's attempt to keep his personal views out of his novels:

> Exaspéré, tout romantique qu'il était, de l'effusion, de la confidence et pour tout dire de l'indiscrétion romantique, Flaubert s'était fait une loi de cacher sa personne et sa vie, tenant que les affaires privées ne regardent pas le public et ne doivent pas l'intéresser. Il y a l'art, et c'est tout. Cela étant, Flaubert, qui malgré sa réputation d'impassible a mis beaucoup de lui-même dans ses livres, s'est largement exprimé et étalé dans sa correspondance [...]
>
> (Henriot, 1954: 69–70)

Yet even there, the relation made by the connector can be read as being slightly ambiguous, if only because it appears to link what follows to more than the sentence before.

Concomitance rather than consequence

This mode, linking conceptually to more than the preceding sentence, says not 'in view of these circumstances' but merely 'in these circumstances'. The implausibility of replacing the connector by Littré's *cela veut dire que* or *dès lors* is seen in the following extract from a discussion of rice production in Europe and in particular in the Camargue region of the Rhône delta:

> Quant à notre douce France, c'est la Camargue renaissante qui lui fournit, désormais, un tiers de son riz (pour une moyenne de 4 kilos par an et par tête) et qui pourrait, même, en faire un peu plus en portant à 26 000 hectares la superficie des rizières et en accroissant leur rendement. Aujourd'hui, le riz se sème au printemps, se récolte à l'automne et ne se repique même plus, mais il n'est pas toujours rentable. Cela étant, en repoussant les eaux salées de la Grande Bleue, en évitant les remontées de sel, les rizières sauvent la Camargue, ce qui n'est pas si mal.

As appears to have happened with *ce faisant*, this mode may have been affected by the temporal value of *cependant*, which could certainly replace it in that example.

A more adversative mode

This mode, rather than 'that being so', says something like 'despite that', as though the connector's function was now sensed as the adversative mode of *cependant*. An apparently unproblematical example, yet lending itself to ambiguous readings, is found in an article about a terrorist attack against Tunisia (*le coup de Gafsa*) and its implications for French policy in North Africa:

> Si le coup de Gafsa confirme que des commandos tunisiens comprenant des ressortissants libyens s'entraînent en Libye et attendent, pour se manifester, que la succession de Bourguiba soit ouverte, on ne voit guère pour l'instant quel courant politique ces commandos seraient susceptibles de soutenir.
> Cela étant, le gouvernement français suit l'affaire de très près.

There appears to be nothing ambiguous in that writer's usage: because of these circumstances, given the situation, the French government is keeping an eye on events. However, this very exemplar has been commented on as follows: *le connecteur interactif* cela étant *[...] semble se rapprocher d'un* pourtant (Roulet, 55). Roulet has further postulated the existence of:

> des emplois comme celui-ci: *Ce film est un peu long ; cela étant, la mise en scène est remarquable*, qui se laissent moins paraphraser par *vu que la chose est ainsi* que par *néanmoins*.
>
> (Private communication, 3.5.93)

Whatever the case may be on that exemplar, it is clear that many writers do use this connector in ways which correspond neither to the dictionary definitions nor to Littré's examples, as in this extract from a discussion of signs of economic confidence and recovery coming from the USA:

> Wall Street, en ce sens, ne s'y est pas trompé, inscrivant cette semaine un nouveau record à la hausse après l'annonce d'une hausse, plus importante que prévu, de 1,5 % des commandes de biens durables pour le mois de janvier. Ce chiffre confirme un certain redressement propre à rassurer les investisseurs de part et d'autre de l'Atlantique.
> Cela étant, s'il avait été mauvais, l'assurance que M. Greenspan était prêt à stimuler l'économie par un relâchement de la politique monétaire si néces-saire n'était pas pour leur déplaire.

Here the value of the connector appears to be *cela dit.* Here too, it seems clear, partly from its placing at the beginning of a new paragraph, that it does not link merely to the sentence immediately preceding. All this is true also of the following example, taken from a discussion of fax-mail seen as serious competition for the Post Office and of the possibility that some senders will be influenced by cost in choosing a means of despatch:

> Pour Jean-Philippe Ducasse, responsable des études marketing à La Poste, « le courrier pourrait reprendre du poil de la bête dès lors que l'arbitrage fax/

> courrier se fera aussi sur des questions économiques ». Effectivement, si dans certaines applications le fax est nettement plus économique, son coût augmente par contre rapidement avec le nombre de pages envoyées, surtout en province ou à l'international. Cela étant, à La Poste, on prend ce concurrent très au sérieux.

There, the writer's meaning is something like 'even so'. It is apparent that, in such a context, the combination with *et* seen in the first quotation of this entry would be impossible. In the following example, taken from an article on the Channel tunnel, the author first makes a distinction between the rolling-stocks used for goods trains and for the passenger shuttles:

> Si les rames des TGV Eurostar et les convois des trains de marchandises sont tout compte fait analogues à ceux qui circulent sur nos voies, il n'en va pas de même des navettes de transport rail-route. Pour ce service, Eurotunnel a dû développer des matériels spécifiques. Cela étant, le principe de base commun à tous ces matériels roulants est celui de wagons en inox totalement fermés.

There the writer could have used *pour autant* – in fact, this connector is sometimes used in tandem with *pour autant*, as in this account of a phase in a lawsuit between the newspaper *Le Monde* and a company called Microfor, won by the newspaper:

> Pour l'anecdote, signalons que Microfor réclamait au *Monde* la somme de 1 298 290 dollars canadiens pour... « atteinte à la réputation de son produit ». Le dollar canadien vaut 5,50 francs. Pour sa part, *Le Monde* réclamait 20 000 francs et en a obtenu 7 500.
> Cela étant, *Le Monde* n'a pas pour autant définitivement gagné la partie.
>
> (Boucher, 136)

The link made is a sort of 'however'. The existence of the structure *cela étant dit* may affect the usage of some writers in this. This may be seen in the next example, taken from an editorial on a controversial meeting between President Mitterrand and the then leader of the Palestinian Liberation Organization, Yasser Arafat:

> La poignée de main entre le président français et son hôte représente, pour ce dernier, sinon un sacre diplomatique, du moins un formidable succès médiatique.
> Cela étant, l'événement aurait gagné à être dédramatisé.

The absurdity that would be created by replacing the connector in that context by, say, *dès lors*, is manifest.

Nowadays, in whichever mode, the structure is always placed first in the sentence, and frequently in a paragraph; the comma is integral to it.

In spoken French, the form *ceci étant* occurs. It is rarely written. The only example I have found, in the more adversative mode, dates from 1942 (Henriot, 1956: 182).

ce qui

This structure can be said to exist in two forms: *ce qui* and *ce que*, depending on whether it relates to a subject or an object. The functioning of both of these forms is familiar to anyone who has mastered the grammatical distinction between the relative pronouns *que* and *qui*. However, because they are often placed at the beginning of sentences, they can have a connective function; and under those circumstances, a modicum of care must be taken with each of them. When placed in the middle of a sentence, usually after a comma, it is plain enough that they function anaphorically, that is they introduce a comment on what precedes: *On m'accuse de mentir, ce qui est faux. / On m'invite à sortir de là, ce que j'ai refusé de faire.* But if those two exemplars were preceded not by commas but by full stops, a degree of momentary indeterminacy would be engendered: it might not be immediately apparent whether the structure was introducing in the form of a ***phrase dépendante*** a comment on what precedes or was functioning cataphorically, that is as a new subject at the beginning of an independent statement. The fact is these structures can do either. And many writers place them first in the sentence.

ce que

With *ce que*, this potential for indeterminacy is not great. When the structure is anaphoric, the sentence following is often quite short. The first example comes from an article on one of the practices of the national blood-transfusion service, collecting blood from donors in prison, which was to contribute to the distribution of HIV-infected blood to French haemophiliacs, many of whom later died:

> Prélever le maximum de sang en un minimum de temps. C'est pour cette raison que certains transfuseurs demandèrent à Myriam Ezratty, alors directrice de l'administration pénitentiaire, d'augmenter le rythme de ces collectes. Ce qu'elle accepta de faire par une circulaire en janvier 1984.

> Certains souhaitent le retour d'un « homme fort » à la tête de la région. Ou une intervention massive de l'État. Ce que les lois de décentralisation rendent difficile, voire impossible.

And when *ce que* is cataphoric in function, ambiguity can be avoided by the inversion of subject and verb, as is seen at the beginning of the second sentence of this extract from a discussion of some of the ideas on personal responsibility underpinning Michel Foucault's history of sexuality:

> C'est aussi dans cette perspective que doit se déchiffrer le projet qui sous-tend l'*Histoire de la sexualité*. Ce que montre en effet la philosophie de l'Antiquité

tardive, c'est que l'individu est d'autant plus proche du souverain bien – c'est-à-dire de la possibilité de « faire de sa vie une œuvre d'art » – que les pouvoirs s'occupent moins de lui et qu'il doit donc se prendre lui-même en charge.

ce qui

It is mainly with *ce qui* that a possibility of momentary indeterminacy arises; and there is no avoiding it by inverting subject and verb. The first of the following examples shows the anaphoric mode, opening a *phrase dépendante*:

> L'opposition est dans le potage. Bien au fond. Ce qui, surtout en période estivale, n'est pas la plus confortable des situations.

The second illustrates the cataphoric mode, placed first in a fully independent sentence. It is an excerpt from a critical discussion of an aspect of French nuclear defence policy:

> Précisons que nous ne critiquons ni ces systèmes d'armes, ni le concept de frappe unique, ni celui d'ultime avertissement. Ce qui fait problème, c'est l'absence de cohérence entre le but annoncé, les moyens programmés et la doctrine de leur emploi.

Indeterminacy about the function of this structure rarely lasts long in statements like the last quotation: the structure completing the cataphoric *ce qui* and thereby disambiguating its function, which in the last example is *c'est l'absence*, is usually placed close to it. Nor does it last long in the dependent sentence if the latter is short, as in this extract from a parish magazine dealing with a bishop's advisory committee for the selection of a new priest:

> Puis, une équipe de quatre prêtres a été nommée avec mission de préciser l'enjeu de cette nomination et d'en rendre compte à l'évêque. Ce qui a été fait.

> (Anon, 1994a, 3)

There are, of course, some syntagmas which occur so frequently in a given function that the indeterminacy they cause is minimal. Among the most common of these, normally found only in the anaphoric mode, are the different combinations of *ce qui* and the verb *être*; as well as *Ce qui implique*, *Ce qui signifie*, *Ce qui revient à dire que* and *Ce qui suppose*. Another is *ce qui* with *empêcher*, usually in the negative:

> Paris ayant décidé de geler ses contacts au niveau ministériel avec la Chine à la suite des massacres de la place Tiananmen, les conversations ont porté pour l'essentiel, selon un porte-parole du Quai d'Orsay, sur le Cambodge. Ce qui n'a pas empêché M. Qian Qichen d'aborder les questions bilatérales, regrettant le « refroidissement » des relations entre Pékin et Paris.

Other examples of similar potential ambiguities could be given for related structures made from *ce*, like *ce dont* or *ce à quoi*, which also function at times anaphorically at the beginning of a *phrase dépendante*. Let one suffice: in the article from which the previous example came it is immediately followed by this sentence:

> Ce à quoi M. Dumas a répondu que ce « refroidissement » n'avait d'autre cause que les récents événements de Pékin.

English convention

'Which' placed first in a dependent sentence, an English enough habit in speech, is no doubt found less often in writing, where no adequate legible analogue of interrogative intonation, other than the question mark, can warn the reader of which function 'Which' is serving. English 'which', already doing some of the jobs of *que* and *qui* as well as of *ce que* and *ce qui*, must also serve as an interrogative. And as such its most usual position is first in the sentence. Which may be why dependent sentences beginning with 'Which' are frowned on by some English grammarians – and not only grammarians:

> Non-interrogative sentences starting with 'which' are usually relative clauses with delusions of grandeur: the insertion of a preliminary dash or colon can, and nearly always should, restore them to their rightful position in the preceding sentence.
>
> (James, 117)

And yet, were convention to be open to reason, it might be pointed out that such a beginning makes for less indeterminacy in an English sentence than in a French one, although such structuring is in fact much more frequent in French. Non-interrogative 'which', being invariably followed by a verb, makes for no indeterminacy at all when compared to an interrogative 'which' followed by a noun, say, as in 'Which twin has the Toni?' Nor is there any indeterminacy in a sentence beginning 'Which may be why', like the one just before the last quotation, even though it contains initial non-interrogative 'which' followed by a verb. It is no doubt as important to treat the conventional style of one's language with a cautious creativity as not to transpose too readily a convention, however reasonable, from one language to another. Certainly, when *Ce que* and *Ce qui* function anaphorically in the initial position, they are behaving like many other structures in a language whose speakers (and readers) are more accustomed than we are to encountering sentences that depend on what precedes for their form, some of their grammar and the burden of their meaning.

certes *

As an affirmative adverb, this word is sometimes defined by dictionaries as regional, archaic, literary or affected. However, as a concessive, which is its main function as a connector, it is none of these. It is in fact an indispensable and ubiquitous connector, one of the most common of the set of concessive gambits – **assurément**, **sans doute**, **il est vrai**, etc. – without which little lucid discussion of anything could take place in the language. In an English discussion, this concessive role is sometimes played by 'admittedly', 'of course', 'granted' or 'I grant you'. That is, it acknowledges the validity of an objection to the main point and may also foreshadow a demonstration that the objection is not as valid as the objector thinks.

Affirmative

Like the other concessives, this one is adapted from a word which has as its primary function to affirm, to agree, to certify. Plenty of writers still use it in that affirmative way, with little or no concessive function, as in this statement about the influence that the geography of Besançon has had on the history of the town ever since its origins:

> Peu de sites urbains sont plus nets, plus propices, au premier coup d'œil, que celui de Besançon. De ce site, tout a dépendu, le meilleur et le pire ; le déterminisme géographique, ici, n'est certes pas un vain mot.
>
> (Braudel, 169)

A writer composing a little celebration of wine, both red and white, wonders whether the former is better with meals and the latter between meals:

> L'un ne serait-il consommable qu'accompagnant des mets, l'autre délectable qu'entre les agapes ? Certes, non. Je suis de ceux qui préfèrent, et je ne suis pas le seul, un déjeuner conçu harmonieusement, avec deux vins au lieu d'un.
>
> (Ferniot, 1995a: 96)

And if there is something archaic about this affirmative mode, an ironist can exploit it, as in this extract from an article having a spoonerism for its title 'Le gratin et le lec', commenting on somebody's suggestion that the study of Greek and Latin should once more be made compulsory at secondary schools:

> Il est indispensable d'apprendre ces langues mortes parce qu'elles nous donnent l'étymologie de mots français, assure-t-on. Certes. Étymologiste, c'est un métier d'avenir ; on embauche beaucoup dans ce secteur.

Concessive

As a concessive, although it always introduces a second proposition, it can be seen to have two main modes: either second in a sequence of two propositions or second in a sequence of three. In the first of these two modes, the connector signals only a restriction of the preceding proposition, as in this example about Georges Marchais's long tenure of the general secretaryship of the Parti communiste français (PCF), in which the second sentence reduces the achievement suggested by the first:

> Le PCF, sous la direction de Georges Marchais, a joué un rôle décisif, au cours des années 70, dans l'émergence d'une opposition de gauche au régime mis en place en 1958. Certes, ce faisant, le secrétaire général ne faisait que poursuivre dans la voie ouverte par Maurice Thorez dès le début des années 60 et explorée ensuite par Waldeck Rochet. Il n'a rien inventé.

This restrictive function is often seen, too, in a brief qualification by an adjective inserted inside a sentence:

> Des nutritionnistes américains qui étudient les habitudes alimentaires françaises saluent l'efficacité des « bonnes graisses » contre le cholestérol et l'usage – certes modéré – du vin rouge comme facteur de longévité cardiovasculaire !

In its other concessive mode, the connector occupies second place not in a pair of propositions but in a close-knit sequence of three: initial assertion; qualification, attenuation or restriction of that assertion, introduced by *certes*; and revalidation in whole or in part of the initial proposition, usually introduced by **mais** or some other objecting connector. This extract is from a discussion of the constitutionally republican origins of the anti-republican Vichy régime of Marshal Pétain in the summer of 1940:

> Vichy, avant d'assassiner la République, fut intronisé par son Parlement. Il se trouva, certes, quatre-vingts députés pour refuser les pleins pouvoirs à Pétain, mais beaucoup plus pour les lui accorder.

Sometimes, as that example shows, the second and third propositions occupy the same sentence. Sometimes, the three stages make three separate sentences, as in this extract from an article on what is known and not known about the leaning tower of Pisa:

> Curieusement, la forme de la tour penchée est mal connue. Certes, elle a été équipée dans le passé d'instruments de mesure. Mais on ne sait pas toujours quand ceux-ci ont été installés et il n'existe que très peu de relevés et de plans.

Place in the sentence

The connector is often placed first in the sentence or paragraph. Some writers even repeat it at the head of three or four consecutive sentences, each one granting a separate attenuation of the main point, in combination with **encore** and **enfin** as in *Certes... Certes... Certes encore* or *Certes... Certes... Certes enfin*. A reinforced variation of this triple mode is seen in the following example, commenting on one of a series of *bavures policières*, in which a young man was killed by a policeman:

> [...] cela commence à transformer les bavures en statistiques.
> Certes, trois fois certes, le jeune homme, qui était âgé de vingt-deux ans, a été tué alors qu'il tentait de franchir un barrage de police. Certes, trois fois certes, Aziz Bouguessa n'était pas un enfant de chœur.
> Mais il faut rappeler : 1) que la peine de mort est abolie ; 2) qu'elle n'a jamais été prévue à l'encontre de cette petite monnaie de la délinquance à laquelle appartenait, paraît-il, Aziz Bouguessa.
>
> (Boucher, 486–487)

The concessive is sometimes not only placed in the same sentence as the following *mais* but juxtaposed to it: *Quel homme politique ne se satisferait pas d'être le maire de Paris ? Certes, mais pas Jacques Chirac*. It can be placed after the words it bears upon. To appreciate the humour of the following example, it helps to know that Édouard Balladur, as Prime Minister and candidate standing against Jacques Chirac for election in 1995 to the presidency of the Republic, was said to be worried by being thought to not have the common touch, to be po-faced and stilted, to be too well dressed in clothes made by only the very best By-Royal-Appointment tailors (such, no doubt, as Façonnable):

> Le pire, ce serait de donner raison à Chirac qui ironisait depuis si longtemps sur sa délicatesse de plante d'appartement. Alors, Édouard Balladur s'est acheté une parka – chez Façonnable, certes. Et, ainsi vêtu, il est parti barouder, tâter le cul des vaches au Salon de l'agriculture et les pognes calleuses des pêcheurs bretons sur l'île de Houatt.

As happens with certain other concessives, some writers make a sentence of the connector unaccompanied, as in this comment on a practice of government which the writer sees as possibly traditional and certainly intolerable:

> Il en a toujours été ainsi, à travers tous les gouvernements, s'agissant des affaires dites « sensibles » ? Certes. Ce n'est pas recommandable pour autant.

First in a discussion

Concessives being almost by definition anaphoric in function, it is rare for this one to open a discussion, unpreceded by a proposition to which it can introduce an objection. However, it is sometimes used in that way. An article in *Le Monde* opens thus:

> Certes incomplet, et encore en pointillé, l'accord intervenu le 25 juin entre les ministres des affaires sociales à Luxembourg constitue, plus qu'il n'y paraît, un événement.

There the connector, though the first word in the discussion, still introduces a partial acceptance of a possible objection – that this agreement, because it is incomplete, is not very important. But that objection remains virtual, implicitly shared by writer and reader. Similarly, a critic reviewing a book by an old woman about a homosexual love affair, rather than beginning with a general exclamation of surprise, opens his first sentence with the first reason why this should not be seen as unusual – albeit the reader must wait till the fourth sentence to learn what the sequence of objections are objections to:

> Certes, il y a eu avant elle Marguerite Yourcenar et la passion d'Hadrien et Antinoüs. L'Anglaise Mary Renault a également consacré la quasi-totalité de son œuvre aux amitiés masculines passionnées de l'Antiquité. Et la Japonaise Mari Mori ne pouvait concevoir d'autres héros de roman que deux beaux garçons qui s'aiment. Mais on a lieu de s'étonner que, pour ses débuts tardifs, une vieille dame sicilienne ait choisi de raconter l'amour fou du prince Hamid El Ghazi pour un jeune esclave.

c'est-à-dire (que) *

This structure exists in two modes, quite grammatically distinct: *c'est-à-dire* and *c'est-à-dire que*. It usually introduces what a writer sees as a more precise restatement of what precedes, either an apter substitute for a form of words or a finer point put upon an idea. In some respects it is similar to **c'est dire (que)**; in others, it is very different. A discussion of the main similarities and differences will be found in the entry for that connector.

This is one of a set of structures which correspond in some measure to English 'that is' or 'that is to say'; others are **à savoir (que)**, **autant dire (que)**, **autrement dit** and **en clair**. It could often be replaced by one or other of these – except when beginning the answer to a spoken question: *Vous venez ? – C'est-à-dire que je ne suis pas libre.* Indeed, it is sometimes combined nowadays with *en clair*, as in this extract from an essay on nineteenth-century learned attitudes to the sexuality of young females, seen as a root-cause of disorders for which the only cure is regular sexual intercourse in marriage:

> La nuit de noces est donc l'exutoire d'une sexualité de plus en plus obsédante qui ne peut se satisfaire que « par ces si tristes et si funestes habitudes », c'est-à-dire, en clair, par l'onanisme [...]

(Adler, 40)

Two preliminary points

English-speakers should be reminded of two small but essential features of this structure. First, the spelling: with or without *que*, the hyphens are integral parts of it – it is they which make it a lexical unit, with its own entry as such in dictionaries. Second, the syntax it requires when followed by a finite verb accompanied by its subject: then, and only then, the *que* is indispensable. (That is a point which may well require emphatic repetition for speakers of English, who may feel that 'that is that' or 'that is to say that' contain too many 'that's.) When the structure is followed by a finite verb unaccompanied by a subject, *que* would be inappropriate:

> Tout écrivain qui se respecte, c'est-à-dire respecte sa langue, a dans sa bibliothèque, à portée de la main, le *Dictionnaire* de Littré.

It should be added that in speech the *que* preceding the finite verb is sometimes omitted, as in this transcribed excerpt from a spoken interview with a journalist who, having written a book critical of some journalists, was asked whether any of his colleagues had taken offence and who answered: *Pas du tout... C'est-à-dire, j'ai surtout eu des réactions en direct de ceux à qui le livre avait plu.*

The two modes: with *que* and without *que*

The essential grammatical difference between the two modes is that the form without *que* introduces only a substitute completion of what precedes, whereas the structure of subject and verb which follows the form with *que* is always the beginning of a new main clause confirming and precising the other main clause preceding the connector. This is no doubt why many exemplars with *que* are placed first in separate sentences, as in this example taken from an obituary about a respected art critic:

> Disons qu'il était dans notre siècle d'une espèce bien rare : un homme de cette Renaissance pour laquelle il s'était tant passionné. C'est-à-dire que, non content de connaître admirablement son sujet préféré, il étendait sa curiosité à l'Art de tous les temps, et notamment du nôtre.

And conversely it is also why many of those without *que* merely introduce the final element in a sentence. Often this final element is a substitute object of the preceding verb, hence a noun-structure, as in this extract from an article about negotiations between Iraq and three Western governments:

> Les États-Unis, la Grande-Bretagne et la France ont rejeté le nouveau marchandage proposé par le président irakien, M. Saddam Hussein, c'est-à-dire le retrait des forces américaines en échange de la libération des milliers de ressortissants occidentaux retenus en Irak et au Koweït.

L'éditeur des dreyfusards publia en 1898 les *Lettres d'un innocent*, c'est-à-dire les lettres de Dreyfus à sa femme.

And, of course, even if the mode without *que* does begin a sentence, it will only ever be a ***phrase dépendante***, one of those sentences detached from but completing a main clause in the preceding one, as in this example which talks of the historical sources of the 'presidentiality' of the constitution of the Fifth Republic as opposed to the 'parliamentary' constitutions which had preceded it:

> C'est un peu sur cet arrière-fond que la Constitution fut élaborée. C'est-à-dire édifiée en système dont la clef de voûte reposait sur un président détenteur d'un nombre de pouvoirs suffisants pour s'opposer aux excès du parlementarisme qui n'avait que trop déstabilisé la France.

Linking of similar grammatical structures

In either mode, this connector always links a statement back to an antecedent of like grammatical structure. With *c'est-à-dire que*, statements containing main clauses are linked to statements containing main clauses. What follows the form without *que* often begins with the same word as what precedes, as in this statement of basic principle about the methods of sociology:

> La méthode sociologique, telle que nous la pratiquons, repose tout entière sur ce principe fondamental que les faits sociaux doivent être étudiés comme des choses, c'est-à-dire comme des réalités extérieures à l'individu.
>
> (Durkheim, 1930: ix)

But the important thing is that this connector makes links between similar structures and parts of speech, such as the repeated preposition (in this case *de*): *Un vice inhérent à la notion même du mariage, c'est-à-dire de la monogamie*; the relative pronoun (in this case *que* and *dont*): *Une vie qu'on a coutume de dire réussie, c'est-à-dire dont le ratage essentiel a été caché à tous*; an adverbial expression of time (*vers 1868* and *après...*): *Ce processus avait commencé vers 1868, c'est-à-dire après la révolution commerciale*; a subsidiary verb-structure (*en* + present participle): *En fixant un repère à la rémunération des agences, c'est-à-dire en rétablissant une forme de commission*; an adjectival structure: *Les salaires sont à l'unisson de la situation économique. C'est-à-dire déprimés*. And many more.

Interrogative modes

Three different interrogative forms also exist. The first is *Est-ce à dire que...?* A discussion of the future of the former USSR, having mentioned some favourable circumstances, begins a paragraph thus: *Est-ce à dire que l'avenir soit pour autant rose ? Nullement*. It should be noted that this interrogative structure is always, by its very nature, to be found at the beginning of statements, frequently of paragraphs. It exists only in the form with *que* and a following finite verb, which is sometimes in the subjunctive, as in the previous example, sometimes in the indicative: *Est-ce à dire qu'ils sont tous prêts à jouer aux terroristes ? Non, et loin s'en faut.*

The second interrogative form is *Qu'est-ce à dire ?* It can be seen as the interrogative form of *c'est-à-dire* without the hyphens and without *que*. Of itself, it normally makes a whole sentence, as in this excerpt from a discussion of the double meaning of certain paintings:

> C'est cette contradiction, nous dit-on, qui révèle la nature allégorique de ces tableaux. Qu'est-ce à dire ? Qu'à côté du sens évident il en existerait un autre ?

And in a conversational register one can hear a third interrogative mode (through intonation) of *c'est-à-dire*, as in this extract from the transcript of an interview with a geneticist exhilarated by working at the Généthon among geniuses in their twenties:

> – Mais il y a d'autres raisons à ce succès : j'ai été entouré de petits génies de tous âges !
>
> – C'est-à-dire ?
>
> – Commençons par parler des plus jeunes : au Généthon, la moyenne d'âge est de 27 ans.

A negative mode

Just as this connector has interrogative forms, so it has a negative form: *ce n'est pas à dire que*, which is usually followed by a subjunctive. An example comes from an editor's preface to a work by the sixteenth-century writer Joachim du Bellay:

> J'ai naturellement gardé comme texte de base celui de l'édition *princeps* parue au mois d'avril 1549. Ce n'est pas à dire que cette édition soit irréprochable. Il s'en faut de beaucoup.

Variant

A variant of the mode without *que*, possibly more familiar in tone, which can put a finer point upon an expression used in what precedes, is *je veux dire*. Although it consists of a subject and verb beginning a new and apparently independent statement, it usually follows a comma. An example comes from a discussion of one of the cruder forgeries in the Dreyfus Affair: *les révisionnistes, je veux dire les artisans de la seconde révision*

(Vidal-Naquet, 1982: 49). A biographer tries to define the beauty of Judith Gautier: *souverainement belle ; je veux dire : belle à la façon d'une souveraine* (Guichard, 15–16). A historian uses it to define what he means by saying that a problem is *insoluble*:

> Un problème diffus en vérité, bien que souvent abordé. Sans doute insoluble, je veux dire dont les racines, dont les causes, nous échappent en grande partie.

> (Braudel, 114)

A variant of this variant is *s'entend*, usually appended after the words it bears on: *On connaît le résultat négatif du premier procès, négatif pour les accusés s'entend.*

c'est dire (que) *

This structure says implicitly: *dire ce que je viens de dire entraîne ce que je vais dire*. It is one of a set of connectors which introduce explanations of preceding statements or elaborations on the consequences of preceding statements. The set contains, among others, **à savoir (que)**, **c'est-à-dire (que)**, **autant dire (que)** and **en clair**. This one is akin to *autant dire (que)*. Literally, it goes farther than *autant dire (que)* in that it equates the value of what follows with what precedes; but in practice, the two connectors are often used interchangeably.

Primary function

A paradigm of this structure may be seen in Haraucourt's line: *Partir, c'est mourir un peu*. When the first infinitive in that sequence of two is a verb of speech such as *Dire*, this connector may introduce the second part of the statement, as in the following celebrated sentence on the theory of justice from the opening chapter of *De l'esprit des lois*. It is a sequence which shows clearly the logic of the connector's primary function:

> Dire qu'il n'y a rien de juste ni d'injuste que ce qu'ordonnent ou défendent les lois positives, c'est dire qu'avant qu'on eût tracé de cercle tous les rayons n'étoient pas égaux.

> (Montesquieu, 4)

There, *c'* recapitulates, as the subject of *est*, everything preceding it in the sentence.

Contemporary usage

Writers still make sentences in that two-part form:

> Dire que le roman est l'art des situations, c'est dire que, dans le roman, la vérité est vue à la lumière de l'instant.
>
> (Boisdeffre, 291)

This sequence sometimes includes ***du même coup*** or ***aussi*** in the second part: *Dire ceci, c'est accepter du même coup cela. / Remarquer que le parlementarisme a raté son adaptation aux média, c'est aussi constater son incapacité à dialoguer en dehors des cadres institutionnels* (Julliard, 224). However, the connector is much more often used nowadays at the beginning of a separate sentence; and that separate sentence does not usually link to a preceding infinitive as in the example from Montesquieu, but to a complete and independent statement of any structure, as in this excerpt from an essay on the prehistory of the Middle East:

> Quelques millénaires plus tard, vers 3300–3100 avant notre ère, les habitants de la Mésopotamie ont inventé l'écriture ; pendant des siècles, ils ont élaboré des civilisations brillantes et ont constitué des royaumes puissants. C'est dire que l'Irak est particulièrement riche en sites archéologiques.

There, the structure could be replaced by *Il s'ensuit de là que*. It can often be seen as a variant for *Cela veut dire que* or *Ce qui signifie que*:

> Aujourd'hui, 2 360 Renault sortent des chaînes chaque jour et 211 700 unités avaient déjà été livrées au 1er mars. C'est dire que le modèle, qui n'était pas apparu comme un champion de l'innovation, a trouvé son public.

Occasionally the structure combines with *là*. In the following example, the subject is André Gide's novel *Les faux-monnayeurs* (in which one of the characters is a novelist writing a novel also called *Les faux-monnayeurs*):

> Portant le même titre, traitant un sujet identique, obéissant à des principes esthétiques communs, les deux romans ne peuvent que glisser et se renverser l'un dans l'autre, brouiller leurs traces, confondre leurs auteurs et nous introduire dans un espace ambidextre où le principe d'identité est soumis à d'incessants dommages. C'est là dire que le miroir-espion a moins à charge ici d'intégrer au roman une réalité « extérieure » que d'abolir l'antithèse du dedans et du dehors [...]

c'est dire and *c'est-à-dire*: similarities

This connector can function in ways very similar to those of *c'est-à-dire*. The main similarity is that both are used to explain the meaning of a foregoing statement or to spell out its latent consequences. They are thus, in some contexts, interchangeable, especially when they make explicit a logical consequence of what precedes. Both can be followed either by *que* and a verb, or by a noun without *que*. If *c'est-à-dire que* could almost always be replaced by ***autrement dit***, and be expressed in English by 'that is' or 'that is to say', much the same could be said of many examples of *c'est dire que*. However, frequently a better English equivalent for this structure would contain 'This means ...', 'in effect' or 'is tantamount to'.

c'est dire and *c'est-à-dire*: differences

There are two main differences between the structures. The first is that, although *c'est dire* is in some ways more adaptable, it cannot serve some of the functions of *c'est-à-dire*. The form without *que* cannot qualify in the following way: *Un livre, c'est-à-dire un ami*. And when it is followed by a noun-structure, it is rarely an unaccompanied noun like *un ami* in that example, but normally a fuller proposition including not only the noun (usually with definite article) but at times also a verb. The noun often expresses an idea of importance or extremity, as in *C'est dire l'importance de* or *C'est dire la nécessité de*. The first of these examples comes from a discussion of French workers' political organizations in the late nineteenth century:

> Le Parti ouvrier français de Guesde compte péniblement 2 000 membres en 1889 et 16 000 dix ans plus tard. C'est dire l'extrême faiblesse numérique du socialisme français dans l'Internationale.

The second is an extract from an article on the spread of AIDS to Asia:

> L'Asie, jusqu'ici épargnée, est à son tour aux prises avec l'épidémie. C'est dire l'urgence avec laquelle tous les pays attendent les résultats des recherches qui n'ont pas encore abouti à la mise au point d'un traitement ou d'un vaccin.

Nor could this structure be used in place of *c'est-à-dire* to give the meaning of *je veux dire* or *à savoir* in the following: *Il travaille efficacement, c'est-à-dire avec sérieux et professionnalisme*. And it would be impossible to use it to introduce the explanatory excuse given in answer to this sort of question: *Tu viens à la plage ? – C'est-à-dire que je ne suis pas libre.*

The second difference is that *c'est-à-dire* functions as a single word, in which neither the verb nor the tense ever change, whereas in *c'est dire que* all three elements that make up the structure can vary. Thus, the tense of *être* can change: *C'était dire que* is the commonest variation. The verb too can differ – *dire* is sometimes replaced by a synonym, as in *C'est affirmer que*. But the verb need not even be one expressing the idea of speech: verbs of understanding or reasoning, in sequences such as *C'était reconnaître que*, *Ce serait ne pas saisir l'enjeu*, *C'eût été là mal apprécier la nature de*, are not infrequently used. Two quite common variants of this mode are *C'est oublier que* and *C'est aller un peu vite en besogne*.

And even *que* is at times replaced by *si* in a way that emphasizes the importance of what follows, adding emotive force or drama to it. This example refers to Yves Montand, the Italian-born singer and actor, whose real name was Ivo Livi:

> Du temps qu'Ivo Livi grandissait à Marseille, on y traitait les « macaronis » comme on traita les Arabes pendant la guerre d'Algérie. C'est dire si devenir français était un acte d'espoir contre toute raison.

This more emotive or dramatic quality is seen in the fact that the statement introduced by *C'est dire si* is sometimes closed by an exclamation mark. That exclamatory tone is also seen when this variant is abridged to only *C'est dire*, as in the following extract from a stock exchange report commenting on a welcome upturn in trading after a lean week. Here the exclamatory mode is justified by the fact that the report dates from 1975:

> C'est bien, c'est même très bien, car l'on s'est littéralement « battu les flancs » cette semaine sous les colonnes du Palais Brongniart. Il faut remonter à la période s'étendant du 9 au 13 août 1971 pour retrouver des volumes de transactions aussi faibles. C'est dire !

An extension of this exclamatory mode may be seen in *C'est tout dire*, which can also do service as a ***brief interpolated main clause***. In the following example, the subject is the unpopularity of the Prime Minister, Alain Juppé, in late 1995:

> Le Premier ministre est dans une situation sans précédent. Cinq mois après son arrivée à Matignon, il bat les records d'impopularité. Son crédit personnel est fortement entamé. Seule Édith Cresson avait connu pareille Berezina. C'est tout dire !

Other variants of *C'est dire que*

Other variants include expressions of quantity: *C'est assez dire si*, *C'est peu dire*, *C'est dire combien*. A critic, deploring a performance of a play by Victor Hugo, adds a further complaint to those he has already expressed:

> Le style même de Victor Hugo s'y trouve réduit, dans les scènes d'amour, aux bégaiements lyriques qu'échangeaient le « Toto génial » et la « Juju mon ange » dans les milliers de billets que s'écrivaient Victor et Juliette Drouet. C'est assez dire que c'est souvent consternant.

An article on Albania since the end of its Communist regime describes a night-club in the capital:

> À l'Artisti, dans l'ancien quartier réservé aux dignitaires du régime, où il était rigoureusement impossible d'entrer, les amoureux écoutent maintenant des airs d'opéra.
> C'est donc peu dire que Tirana a changé.

A report of the ceremony in Oslo at which the Prime Minister of Israel and the leader of the Palestinian Liberation Organization received the Nobel Peace Prize speaks of the security arrangements:

> Il a fallu abriter les lauréats derrière une vitre à l'épreuve des balles, pour saluer la foule massée dans la rue. C'est dire combien la paix qu'Israël et l'OLP ont mise en route le 12 septembre 1993 demeure précaire et combien l'escapade à Oslo ne pouvait être que fugitive.

All three of these forms with *peu, assez* and *combien* exist in variants. The one with *assez* is sometimes varied to *C'est là suffisamment dire que*. Nineteenth-century writers, including Berlioz, say *C'est dire assez que, Ce n'est pas assez dire que* and *Est-ce assez dire que*. The one with *combien* is sometimes replaced by *C'est dire à quel point*. The one with *peu* has more variants than the others. The most common is *C'est peu de dire que*, as in this extract from a discussion of two dictionaries which the writer compares to a museum:

> On entre dans ces ouvrages comme au Louvre. Les pièces du trésor ici, sont des mots, et c'est peu de dire qu'eux et leurs visiteurs sont traités avec le maximum d'égards et de soins.
>
> (Wagner, 131)

It is sometimes used without *que*: *C'est peu dire, le Président syrien s'est même payé le luxe d'enliser les Américains et les Français* (July, 137). It has a negative form *Et ce n'est pas peu dire*.

The form with *peu* is also elliptical. A fuller statement of the meaning expressed by the example about Albania used above would be *Dire que Tirana a changé, c'est donc peu dire* or *C'est donc peu dire que de dire que Tirana a changé*. Perhaps it should be noted that the latter form with *que de* is a sort of more formal or literary inversion of this structure: the first infinitive is cataphoric, anticipating the second; whereas the basic connector, in any of its modes, is by definition anaphoric. Musset's alexandrine *C'est imiter quelqu'un que de planter des choux*, could be reshaped in complete accordance with this structure: *Planter des choux, c'est imiter quelqu'un.*

Occasional variants

Occasionally a writer uses an interrogative form of this structure: *Est-ce dire que*. It could usually be replaced by the more usual *Est-ce à dire que*:

> Pour Sartre, la conscience critique ne peut ni pénétrer ni se maintenir dans la conscience critiquée. Une identification en profondeur, une identification avec la profondeur de l'être, telle qu'on la trouve chez Rivière, chez Du Bos, ou plus récemment, chez Marcel Raymond, est de la part de Sartre, inconcevable. Est-ce dire cependant que toute identification des deux consciences est impensable ?

c'est le cas de

This is one of a set of connectors, including *ainsi* and *par exemple*, which are used to introduce illustrative examples of a point just made.

What typically precedes the structure is a statement about a category; what follows it is an instance or instances of the category. In this example, the category is that of clever cooks during the Revolution:

> La multiplication des restaurants de qualité à Paris date de la Révolution. Il est vrai, comme on l'a dit bien souvent, qu'un certain nombre de cuisiniers talentueux ont alors perdu leur maître, émigré ou guillotiné. C'est le cas de Méot, cuisinier du prince de Condé, qui s'établit en 1791 rue de Valois.

The category may be designated by a noun in the plural, as in that example, or by a noun in the collective singular, as in the following one, taken from an article discussing criticisms of the Polish Catholic hierarchy's handling of a dispute over the propriety of establishing a convent in the former death-camp at Auschwitz:

> La responsabilité de l'épiscopat polonais est en cause, mais de tels propos visent aussi la partie la plus ouverte de l'intelligentsia catholique, qui a joué un grand rôle dans les négociations sur le carmel. C'est le cas de personnalités comme Stefan Wilkanovicz ou Jerzy Turowicz, amis personnels du pape.

Variation of parts

A writer can adapt this structure to different contexts by varying one or other of its components. The tense of the verb is variable, as in this example (which also includes *notamment*, a quite frequent combination) from a daily stock exchange report:

> Sur le plan des valeurs, quelques titres ont retenu l'attention. Ce fut le cas notamment de Cap Gémini, très recherché après l'annonce de l'accord avec Matra.

Sometimes it is *de* which changes, usually to *pour*:

> Toutes les choses humaines vieillissent, mais il n'est pas dit qu'elles meurent à la façon des humains, en se dissolvant, en disparaissant de la scène du monde. C'est le cas pour une langue.

And even *C'est* can become a variant for *tel est*, as in this pair of sentences from a report on local politics:

> Dans plusieurs villes où les communistes ont perdu, en six ans, de 40 % à 50 % de leur électorat, ils refusent qu'il en soit tenu compte dans leur représentation municipale. Tel est le cas à Arras (Pas-de-Calais), où les socialistes leur proposent de passer de huit à six conseillers ; à Boulogne-sur-Mer [...]

Sometimes the whole structure is reduced to *C'est*, especially in a sequence of similarly shaped examples, as in a historian's evocation of the towns along the Rhône:

> Trafics, échanges, transbordements, magasinage, créent au long du Rhône, autant que possible à l'abri de son eau dangereuse, une série de villes actives, éblouissantes souvent quand l'histoire a bien voulu les favoriser. C'est Arles, qui survit longtemps aux splendeurs de la Gaule romaine ; c'est Avignon, longtemps centre de la Chrétienté et qui alors brille de tous ses éclats [...]
>
> (Braudel, 248)

n'est-ce pas le cas ?

This is a negative-interrogative mode, one of those rhetorical forms of the *question* requiring no answer which functions similarly to the affirmative form. This example comes from the same historian's discussion of the Massif Central, its strategic and structuring function in the history of France:

> Finalement, et plus qu'on ne le pense, la France s'explique par ces hautes terres centrales, à être ainsi partagée, bloquée et protégée aussi par elles. N'est-ce pas le cas, pour prendre un seul exemple, lors de la dernière phase de la guerre de Cent Ans, à l'époque désespérée du roi de Bourges qui y trouve d'opportuns défenseurs ?
>
> (Braudel, 49)

Combined with *là*

The combination with *là* can increase the demonstrative force of the example introduced, as in this extract from a discussion of whether or not formal instruction in grammar is appropriate at primary school:

> ...on s'aperçoit que l'on peut faire l'économie de presque toute la grammaire scolaire dans la mesure où la langue que l'on cultive à l'école n'est pas autre chose que celle que l'enfant apporte avec lui. C'est là le cas dans les pays de langue anglaise où les distinctions grammaticales qu'il faut respecter lorsqu'on écrit la langue sont celles que fait tout un chacun en parlant : quiconque prononce le *-s* de *he gets* ne sera pas tenté de l'oublier lorsqu'il écrit le mot [...]
>
> (Martinet, 22)

Place in the sentence

The connector is nearly always first in the sentence. Occasionally it is preceded by a *deux-points*, as in this extract from a discussion of the increasing variety of roles played by military forces under the auspices of the United Nations:

Leurs missions se diversifient de plus en plus. Au début, il s'agissait essentiellement d'interposer, tant bien que mal, un écran entre des forces hostiles : ce fut le cas dans le Sinaï, ce l'est toujours à Chypre, au Liban sud, à la frontière entre l'Irak et le Koweït.

Occasionally, too, rather than replacing *par exemple*, this connector reinforces it, as in this final point from an article about certain good wines and fanciers of them who had the foresight to buy up stocks while they lasted:

Reste l'avantage de posséder des bouteilles que l'on n'est pas sûr de retrouver actuellement chez un caviste. C'est le cas, par exemple, du Gruaud-Larose millésime 1979 (saint-julien).

The negative-interrogative form is also used in tandem with *exemple*, as can be seen in the extract from Braudel used above.

Comparative

In a way, this mode is a sort of inversion of the exemplifying one. Instead of the instance following the category, it precedes it, as in this statement about the relation between a medieval town and the countryside surrounding it:

...il est clair que, vers 1300, Besançon ne contrôle guère que son territoire propre. Que celui-ci ne compte que des villages et des hameaux, on ne s'en étonnera pas outre mesure. C'est le cas de toutes les villes, aussi bien Toulouse, où la vigne monte la garde autour des murs, que Paris lui-même.

(Braudel, 174)

With very little syntactical rearrangement, the statement could be made with *de même*. The discussion, rather than going from the general to the particular, goes from the particular to the general.

A negative mode

Despite its fixed formulaic quality, the structure can, like any verb, have a negative form. Although this mode no longer functions as a variant for *par exemple*, it can still serve to single out an instance in relation to a preceding plural category, as in this historian's statement about what makes the Rhône different from other French rivers:

D'ordinaire, on dit des fleuves qu'ils sont, plus que des séparations, des traits d'union ; qu'ils sont faits pour que l'homme aille d'une rive à l'autre de l'eau courante, au gré de ses intérêts ou même simplement de sa fantaisie. Ce n'est pas le cas du Rhône.

(Braudel, 253)

c'est pourquoi *

This connector could be replaced, indeed often is, by *C'est pour cette raison que*. It is so straightforward that, if it did not also exist in a slightly problematical variation of its basic form, it would hardly deserve inclusion in this work.

The basic form functions, as does its literal English counterpart, exactly in accordance with what its meaning is: it introduces a consequence, or an explanation of a consequence, of what precedes. Given its syntax, it is most usually placed first in the sentence. In some contexts, it could be replaced by *de sorte que*. In this example, a writer argues that the socio-economic functioning of a democratic state will be improved if governments make a habit of consulting organizations of employers, workers, farmers and the like:

> [Cette participation] doit être l'un des paramètres essentiels de la préparation des décisions et de la conduite de la politique économique et sociale. C'est pourquoi je me refuse absolument à prendre mon parti du déclin du syndicalisme, parce qu'il est indispensable à la démocratie.

In a more emphatic mode of the basic form, *c'est* is replaced by *voilà*. In another, it combines with *bien*, as in this excerpt from an essay on political régimes based on authoritarianism and *le règne de l'ordre*:

> Mais l'ordre ne peut être une fin en soi. Il doit être au service d'une idée, d'une politique, d'une ambition, sinon il risque de se trouver sans défenseurs à l'heure de l'épreuve. C'est bien pourquoi Hitler et Mussolini se sont lancés l'un et l'autre dans la conquête, pourquoi, avant de s'effondrer, la dictature des colonels grecs s'est engagée dans la criminelle aventure de Chypre.
>
> (Fontaine, 1978: 187)

A variant: *ce pourquoi*

The slight variation mentioned above consists of omitting the verb: *ce pourquoi*. This version functions just like the form with verb, with the slight exception that the dropping of the verb can make for momentary ambiguity. This may also make it more likely that the connector will not be placed first in the sentence, as in this extract from an essay on the traditional strong point of the Right in politics:

> Le thème le plus porteur pour la droite a toujours été la défense du libéralisme, opposé à l'étatisme centralisateur des socialistes : ce pourquoi, en 1986, elle remporta les élections sous les doubles auspices de Reagan et de Thatcher.

However, perfectly competent and careful writers do place this abridged mode of the structure first in the sentence:

[Je crois savoir que Barbey d'Aurevilly] aurait promis à Mme de Bouglon de laisser par son testament la propriété de ses œuvres au fils de cette dame. Ce pourquoi, par la suite, ayant appris l'influence prise, à Paris, par Mlle Read sur le romancier vieillissant, Mme de Bouglon jeta les hauts cris et intervint de façon véhémente pour réclamer de Barbey l'exécution de sa promesse.

(Henriot, 1954: 237)

And some of them even spell it as three words:

La politique agricole commune recèle des inconvénients qui se sont aggravés avec le temps. Elle coûte extrêmement cher, ce pour quoi nos partenaires ont l'impression de toujours payer pour nos paysans.

In this spelling, the structure may have been influenced by the substantive meaning of *ce pour quoi*, which would denote, not the explanation of a consequence, but the aim or intention of an act: *Ce pour quoi nous nous battons depuis cinq ans, c'est la paix en Europe.* There, *ce* is the grammatical object of the verb *se battre (pour).* And the structure's form is similar to that of *ce à quoi* and *ce avec quoi.* In its full form, with verb, this structure can only function anaphorically. But the verbless mode, especially when spelt in three words, can cause ambiguity when placed first in the sentence. This comes from the reader's uncertainty about whether the writer intends it to function anaphorically or cataphorically. The reader may have to finish reading the whole sentence which begins with the connector before being able to resolve the ambiguity. This example comes from a discussion of the working-class origins of football, seen as a symbolic transformation of warlike impulses:

Non seulement une confrontation simulée se substituait à des affrontements réels, mais une activité de groupe échappait aux impératifs du profit et au mécanisme de l'exploitation. Ce pour quoi les matchs se déroulaient généralement le dimanche, jour du Seigneur réservé au temps « libéré ».

Hanse, who chides those who write *pourquoi* instead of *pour quoi*, lets pass unchidden this converse habit of writing *pour quoi* instead of *pourquoi*, which may make for greater ambiguity (Hanse, 1983: 747).

English equivalents for this connector, in either of its modes, might be 'That is why', 'The reason is' and 'Which is why'.

c'est que *

There are two main modes of this structure: one which introduces the second part of statements of cause made with the *si d'opposition*; and one which functions separately as a connector. Only the latter is treated here. Unlike the mode used with the *si d'opposition*, this one is never found in any tense other than the present.

This connector is usually placed at the beginning of a sentence or even of a paragraph. Its function is predominantly anaphoric: to introduce an explanation of a preceding statement or longer development, possibly by putting it in a wider context. In English, these explanatory statements could begin with 'The point is' or 'The fact is'. In this example, a writer comparing red wine to white justifies the implication that it is only the former which can properly deserve the adjective *gros*:

Le langage populaire serait-il révélateur ? On peut se le demander quand on entend parler de « petit blanc » et de « gros rouge ». C'est que l'assommoir, le sang du clochard, le pousse-à-l'assaut du fantassin, c'est le pinard, le rouquin, le casse-poitrine, le reginglard, celui qui laisse des ronds sur le bois.

(Ferniot, 1995a, 96)

Like other constructions with *que*, this one can govern more than one statement, as in this example where it is prolonged by a ***phrase dépendante***. The subject is threatened litigation between the wine authority of the Champagne region and the Yves Saint Laurent company:

Le comité d'appellation des vins de Champagne a fort mal pris (ou feint de mal prendre) que l'ultime parfum d'Yves Saint Laurent s'appelle ou veuille s'appeler « Champagne ». C'est qu'il y a une affaire de sous et de gros sous en jeu. Qu'il y a de l'argent à tirer, sans procès ou avec procès.

Similarity to *car*

The structure is often an equivalent of *car*. It can introduce a justification of the content of a preceding statement, by explaining why the latter was made. A historian discussing the death penalty as applied differently to men and women says this:

Qui sont, ou plutôt, qui étaient les condamnés ? Presque exclusivement des hommes. En Angleterre, comme en France, la proportion des femmes est minime (trois pour cent par exemple, vers 1900) ; elle est du même ordre que la fraction féminine aujourd'hui détenue dans nos prisons. C'est que la grande criminalité, et notamment la criminalité de violence est, avant tout, le fait des hommes.

(Chesnais, 147)

A writer uses it to amplify his poor opinion of leading French communists:

Je me suis souvent demandé pourquoi la direction du Parti communiste français était, humainement, intellectuellement, si médiocre. C'est que je l'ai côtoyée d'un peu près.

In these types of statement, too, the connector could often be replaced by ***il faut dire que***.

The grammar of the structure allows it to be used not only in affirmative statements, but also in the negative, as is shown by the second sentence in the following quotation:

> Si le basculement de l'Europe centrale ne prend effectivement pas l'allure d'un mécanique retournement d'alliance, c'est que cette Europe, elle aussi, a des intérêts d'État. Ce n'est pas seulement qu'elle perdrait beaucoup à rompre du jour au lendemain tous ses liens économiques avec l'URSS. C'est avant tout que les nouveaux équilibres européens ne peuvent se trouver – sauf à marcher droit aux guerres – dans la constitution d'un déséquilibre.

Here too the affinity with *car* is clear, as the writer could have structured her sentence *Car non seulement.*

Differences from *car*

Among the few differences of functioning between *car* and this structure is the fact that *car* would never be preceded by *mais* in a statement like the following excerpt from an essay on the German Occupation of 1940–1944:

> Les Français qui parlent entre eux des Allemands, de la Gestapo, de la Résistance, du marché noir s'entendent sans peine ; mais c'est qu'ils ont vécu les mêmes événements, c'est qu'ils sont pleins des mêmes souvenirs […]

> (Sartre, 1949b: 16–17)

Nor would *car* introduce the answer to a ***question*** like the one in this example taken from a discussion of the influence of Bob Wilson on the composer Philip Glass:

> Mais en quoi Bob Wilson est-il un déclencheur ? C'est qu'il amène Phil Glass à la croisée de pratiques multiples : musique, théâtre, danse.

What makes the main difference with *car* is the fact that in some constructions, *ce* has a more markedly anaphoric function, linking to what precedes in a way akin to the normal relationship of pronoun to antecedent:

> Je tiens à insister sur un fait à mes yeux plein d'enseignements : c'est que le plus ancien syndicalisme européen est le syndicalisme anglais.

> Ces systèmes sont parfaitement admissibles à une condition essentielle : c'est qu'ils ne servent pas à gagner sans rien risquer.

In such statements, *c'est* could clearly be omitted without detriment to the meaning. However, there are others in which this structure functions partly as an inter-assertional connector, but partly also as a straightforward grammatical amplification of an antecedent, as in *Ce qui importe, c'est que...*, *Le plus triste, c'est que...* or in:

> Je ne veux plus vous voir, plus vous entendre ! Et il y a quelque chose d'encore plus fort que ma haine et que mon dégoût. C'est que je meurs d'ennui, madame, à côté de vous !
>
> (Anouilh, 90)

> L'ennui pour M. Ben Bella, c'est que le parti islamiste a aujourd'hui les moyens, sinon le désir, de se passer des services d'un homme « providentiel ».

Thus, in that last example, it could be argued both that *c'est que* introduces an explanation of *L'ennui* and that the latter is also the antecedent of *ce*.

In conversation, *c'est que* can be heard as an explanation not of a preceding utterance but as an comment on an act or a manifest situation: *Mais, c'est qu'il est malin, celui-là !*

c'est un fait (que) *

The meaning of this structure is as plain as the words which make it. Its functions are less plain. It states a fact. But it is a fact against which another more pertinent fact may be conceded. Or else, conversely, it is a fact which may counter a concession.

Concessive

The structure usually functions as one of the set of concessive connectors: *certes*, *il est vrai que*, *sans doute* and others. Like them, it can not only introduce an argument conceded against the substantive point but may also foreshadow the reaffirmation of the latter in a proposition introduced by an objector such as *mais*. In this mode, it can either accompany one of a pair of propositions or introduce the second in a close-knit sequence of three. An example of the first of these comes from a discussion of the effects of a possible war on the economies of the then USSR and the USA:

> La guerre mondiale n° 2 a rapporté d'immenses bénéfices aux producteurs américains, c'est un fait. Mais la guerre mondiale n° 3 pourrait les ruiner, comme la précédente a ruiné les Allemands, à partir de 1943, et avant qu'un seul kilomètre carré de leur territoire ne fût envahi.
>
> (Frédérix, 264)

Two modes: with *que* and without *que*

Like other concessives, this one is used in different positions, one of which, seen in the previous example, is the end of a sentence. It can also be placed at the beginning of the sentence, with or without *que*. This example, taken from a discussion of the work of the photographer Robert Doisneau, shows the tripartite sequence (assertion: Doisneau was not 'anecdotal'; concession: yes, he liked anecdotes; reassertion: but there was more to him than that):

> Après cinq livres, le « style Doisneau » est en place. Un peu trop même. De là vient cette étiquette – fausse – de « photographe anecdotique » qui lui colle toujours à la peau. C'est un fait, Doisneau aimait le canular et l'anecdote. Un écolier qui fourre son doigt dans la bouche du voisin ; le propriétaire qui repasse son gazon au rouleau à pâtisserie. Mais l'anecdote n'a de sens, à ses yeux, que si l'on peut « rêver » sur l'image, si elle accorde à celui qui la regarde une large place à l'imaginaire.

Also like some other concessives, this one can constitute a whole sentence. In the following example, discussing the claim made by *notaires* that since their profession is efficient the government should not tamper with it, the author points out that this defence, though true, enables them to go on making huge profits. In this case, at the beginning of the third sentence the objecting function is done by the implicitly ironic **aussi**:

> Le notariat assure un service public dans des conditions satisfaisantes. C'est un fait. Il permet aussi de vivre en P.-D.G., à la tête d'une entreprise qu'on a trouvée toute faite et qui navigue paisiblement sur les eaux lisses d'un étang à jamais préservé des tempêtes concurrentielles.
>
> (Closets, 1983: 260)

The form without *que* can function as a **brief interpolated main clause**, as in this extract from an article on a new funding mechanism of the Ministry of Culture, known as *l'aide au lieu*, applicable to regional *maisons de la culture*:

> Grâce à une subvention mise en place par Bernard Faivre d'Arcier alors directeur du théâtre au ministère de la culture, l'aide au lieu est susceptible d'être attribuée à tout établissement dont la programmation allie risque et qualité. Ambition que tout ministère affiche, et qui, c'est un fait, n'avait jamais dépassé le vœu pieux.

Cancelling a concession

Sometimes the connector, instead of introducing the second element in the three-part sequence, combines with *mais* in the third part to counter the preceding concession. The following example, in which the concession is introduced by **bien sûr**, comes from a discussion of French culture as a generator of clear, simple and forceful ideas:

> Les idées simples, qu'un seul mot suffit parfois à exprimer, la France en a conçu plus d'une au cours de sa longue histoire. Bien sûr il serait grotesque de prétendre qu'elle détient là un monopole, ou même une prépondérance :

l'impérialisme intellectuel est à peine moins pire [*sic*] que l'autre. Mais c'est un fait qu'elle n'a guère cessé, depuis le temps de saint Louis et de la fondation de la Sorbonne, d'être ce qu'on est convenu d'appeler un foyer de civilisation.

(Fontaine, 1978: 212)

A mode like *de fait*

At other times, this more affirmative mode functions in a way close to *de fait*, at least in the expression *il est de fait que*. That is, it accompanies a confirming or reinforcing reminder of a previously stated point. In the following example, taken from near the end of a long development on the frequency with which derogatory terms in French are feminine, the author recurs to this general point just before exemplifying it:

L'attribution du genre grammatical relève, comme j'ai dit, de facteurs historiques et formels, qui d'ordinaire ne laissent pas place à un jugement de qualité ; mais ce qui reste libre, c'est, quand il s'agit de désigner une notion, le choix entre les possibles ; or c'est un fait que, quand le parler populaire adopte un péjoratif, celui-ci est le plus souvent féminin. Féminins sont les termes vulgaires par lesquels on nomme un être vil : *crapule, canaille*, [...]

(Marouzeau, 65–66)

In this mode, the function of the connector comes close to that of *le fait est que*.

d'ailleurs *

The French, who cannot speak or write for long without using this connector, are often taught when they learn English that it means 'moreover'. Thus the English spoken by many of them is full of a word which few native speakers of English, except the very educated, ever say. Among the most frequent equivalents of *d'ailleurs* in everyday English, whether spoken or written, are probably 'besides', 'in addition', 'also' and 'anyway', depending on function and place in the sentence. In some circumstances, an equivalent would be 'actually' or 'as it happens'; in others a mere tone of voice.

The structure derives from *ailleurs*, an adverb of place meaning 'elsewhere'. This is no doubt why French lexicographers continue to subjoin their entries about it to their entries on *ailleurs*, although the connector has long since parted semantic company with the latter. Some statements containing the structure can be misleading if it is used not as a connector but in the literal sense of 'from somewhere else': *Ces fausses solutions nous exposent à de graves mécomptes. C'est d'ailleurs que doit venir le salut.* And a statement like the following, dating from a century ago, would nowadays be made with **par ailleurs**: *Nulle œuvre, si admirable qu'elle puisse être d'ailleurs, n'est littéraire, à laquelle manque le style* (Alaux, 35).

The standard account

As a connector, this structure is probably the commonest of those which, like **au reste**, **du reste** and **d'autre part**, can add a further point to what precedes. According to the most authoritative sources (e.g. Ducrot, 193ff) the point introduced by *d'ailleurs* must be an argument. It would not accompany a mere extra item in a list of facts, after the fashion of, say, **de plus**. The point must be parallel, that is going in the same direction as what precedes, tending towards and supporting the same conclusion. In the first of the following examples, the opening sentence makes clear that Turkey has already raised its problem directly with the Kremlin. That is a sufficient condition for the latter to see it as important. The connector makes the second sentence into an appendix:

> Ankara a demandé à Moscou d'user de son influence auprès des autorités bulgares pour résoudre ce problème. Le ministre turc des affaires étrangères, M. Mesut Ylmaz, a d'ailleurs annoncé qu'il rencontrerait lundi l'ambassadeur d'URSS à Ankara.

In the next example, a point about contraception is added to a more important one about protection against disease:

> L'utilisation plus importante du préservatif masculin dans les pays industrialisés que dans ceux du tiers-monde tient, au-delà des données économiques et culturelles, à la perception de plus en plus claire des dangers que constituent les maladies sexuellement transmissibles. Cette méthode est d'ailleurs la seule à être à la fois contraceptive et préventive contre ces affections.

So the point added by the connector is usually supplementary: neither essential to the argument nor required by the conclusion. Sometimes it is added almost as an afterthought: « *À cette époque, étiez-vous membre du Parti communiste ?* » « *Bien sûr. J'avais ma carte. Je l'ai toujours d'ailleurs.* » There is thus a secondary nature in the function served by this structure, marking it off clearly from, say, **aussi**, which links two statements of equal importance.

More important links

To that standard account of the connector's primary function, it must be added that some writers use it to make a link of thought which is of more than subsidiary importance. Roland Barthes, for instance, uses it to open a whole new section of discussion which will define the difference he sees between a *texte de plaisir* and a *texte de jouissance* (Barthes, 1973: 36). In contexts like those in the next two examples, the connector functions more like *d'autre part*: it introduces a development which has greater significance than a mere supplement, which actually broadens the discussion of the point in the preceding paragraphs. The wider context of the first example is a discussion of banditry and violent lawlessness in nineteenth-century Sardinia, Naples and Sicily, to each of which regions the author has given two or more lengthy paragraphs. He ends his section on Sicily with the decrease in violence later in the century, then links in this way to what follows:

> Le taux des meurtres et assassinats reste élevé (dix-sept pour cent mille habitants), mais il a considérablement diminué par rapport à ce qu'il était dans la première moitié du XIXᵉ siècle : vraisemblablement de l'ordre de quarante ou cinquante, sinon davantage.
> À cette époque, d'ailleurs, l'Italie entière est en pleine transformation. S'il existe encore, dans la région de Rome des bourgs d'où toute autorité est bannie, où les crimes sont impunis, ceux-ci se font de plus en plus rares. [...]
> (Chesnais, 51)

Introduced by *d'ailleurs*, this new paragraph goes on to canvass the situation in the whole of Italy. A similar relation between a particular case and its broader implications is seen in the second extract, from an article on President Mitterrand's ambiguous attitudes towards the collaborationist Vichy government (*l'État français*) and its anti-Semitism:

> Depuis quelques mois déjà, de très nombreuses personnalités exigent du président de la République un « geste » reconnaissant la responsabilité de l'État français dans les crimes perpétrés contre les juifs de France. Vichy n'est d'ailleurs pas seulement une interrogation pour les juifs, mais pour tous les Français. En cela François Mitterrand a sans doute eu tort de choisir une radio juive pour s'expliquer à propos de la gerbe controversée sur la tombe du maréchal Pétain. Démarche dangereuse. Car elle suggère un distinguo entre les Français juifs et les Français non juifs quant à leur appréciation des années noires de la collaboration.

There it is clear that, with this connector, the author is not just appending a supplementary point about Vichy and the Jews but making a much farther reaching one about France as a whole. That point is so important that the link might even have been made with *or*.

Place in the sentence

As can be seen from the examples, *d'ailleurs* is often placed after the first verb. But it is also put first in the sentence. It is even, albeit rarely, used in the opening sentences of paragraphs. This infrequency is no doubt an effect of the supplementariness of the points which it usually introduces:

few afterthoughts deserve a paragraph. And when it does accompany the opening sentence of a paragraph, it is usually placed after the first verb or, as in the example from Chesnais above, the initial adverb: *Cela est d'ailleurs le cas en Europe...*; *Voici d'ailleurs l'importance de...*; *Dans la préface, d'ailleurs, l'auteur....*

Relation to *mais* and *et*

Because of its role in supporting an argument, it would be most unusual to find this connector combined with *mais*. On the other hand, and for the same reason, the combination of it with *et* is not infrequent. In this example, the author is explaining and excusing his digressive method of dealing with his subject:

> Bien que j'eusse un dessein très ferme et que je prétende aboutir à des conclusions formelles, j'ai fait peu d'efforts pour résister aux détours qui me tentaient. Peut-être mon récit gagnera-t-il en liberté ce que ce désordre lui fait perdre en évidence persuasive. Et d'ailleurs, en telle matière, une digression peut être un bon argument.
>
> (Blum, 5)

Accompanying an aside

It is when signalling what is no more than an aside or a brief interpolation that *d'ailleurs* either would have no equivalent in English or might be expressed by 'as it happens', 'actually', 'incidentally' or 'by the way': *Madame Mère, avec qui je déjeune demain, pour des raisons d'ailleurs sans rapport avec l'affaire... / Mon médecin – c'est d'ailleurs mon fils – voulait que je reste à la maison. / Cet homme est un Gascon. Yeux brillants, carrure de mousquetaire, verbe provocateur. D'ailleurs, il s'appelle Bordeaux, François-Xavier Bordeaux.*

Often the function of this aside is to add what can be seen as a personal opinion of the author to what is presented as a statement of fact, as in this extract from an article about the return of Mohammed Ben Bella to Algeria and the former President's hopes for

> un « come back » dans une Algérie devenue si différente de celle qu'il gouverna de 1963 à 1965, de manière d'ailleurs parfois imprévisible et brouillonne. Non seulement parce qu'un Algérien sur deux est aujourd'hui âgé de moins de quinze ans et que de nombreux jeunes ignorent jusqu'au nom même de Ben Bella pendant longtemps « gommé » des livres d'histoire. Mais surtout parce que [...]

There, the statement of fact is that Ben Bella was head of state during the period mentioned; and the judgment on his competence, announced by this connector, is no more than a passing comment of the journalist, interesting, related but incidental. This can be seen by the way the sentences following relate back not to the briefly interpolated judgment but to the substantive point in the first sentence quoted, about how different Algeria is nowadays from what it was in the early 1960s. In this incidental use, the connector is often found inside brackets: they contain the whole aside, which is linked to the surrounding statement by the connector: *mon éditeur avait publié ce livre (ce qui m'avait d'ailleurs totalement échappé)...*; *L'Alissa de* La Porte étroite *incarne un difficile (et peut-être d'ailleurs contestable) idéal de sainteté*. In such contexts, English would as often as not do without a connector of any sort.

d'autant que

This is one of the most commonly used of the adverbial conjunctions (like *de sorte que*, *si bien que* and *alors que*) which are often placed nowadays at the beginning of a *phrase dépendante*. As it sometimes has no obvious or natural English equivalent, it can be difficult for speakers of English to get a purchase on it.

The structure can strengthen a point by adding a second argument to a first, which is its more logical function; or it can introduce a single argument. It is quite often combined with a mode of *et ce*. It exists in two basic forms: *d'autant que* and *d'autant plus que*. The form with *plus* has several modes, including variants with *moins* and *mieux*. It can be replaced by a more spoken form *surtout que*, which some see as undignified, as in this excerpt from a book review:

> On regrettera seulement que M. Reymond [...] aille jusqu'à écrire *surtout que*, pour *d'autant plus*, ce qui étonne de la part d'un docteur ès lettres.
>
> (Henriot, 1954: 341)

English equivalents are sometimes given as 'all the more so since' or 'even more so because'. The most usual equivalent is probably 'especially because'.

d'autant que

This mode relates only to predicates: its usual function is to reinforce a preceding statement with a secondary circumstance. It can do this as part of the same sentence, as in this extract from an article on the dangers to human health of certain highly toxic substances:

> Les matériaux comme les hydrocarbures benzéniques et les pigments de peinture tels que le plomb, le cadmium, le chrome, sont une source de toxicité immédiate pour le système nerveux central, les muqueuses oculaires et respiratoires, d'autant qu'ils sont utilisés sans les précautions recommandées en milieu professionnel et en l'absence de surveillance médicale.

There, the structure functions in the straightforward way: it introduces a second proposition which strengthens the one preceding. The extract begins by saying the substances are toxic; then the proposition introduced by the connector adds that the dangers of their toxicity are increased by the careless ways in which they are used. This mode without *plus* is probably more often than not placed first in a *phrase dépendante*. This example is taken from an article on the nuclear disaster at Chernobyl:

> Plus de trente morts, environ sept mille irradiés, près de cent cinquante mille personnes évacuées, 9,3 milliards de roubles : le bilan de Tchernobyl ne s'oubliera pas de sitôt. D'autant qu'à ces chiffres s'ajoute une autre réalité, tout aussi cruciale pour l'avenir de la région : en dépit des importants crédits accordés par le gouvernement (900 millions de roubles, auxquels se sont ajoutés 240 millions en février dernier), la Biélorussie n'est toujours pas parvenue à réduire dans les proportions escomptées la pollution de son sol et de ses produits agricoles.

The first sentence having outlined the most memorable costs of the nuclear accident, the following one gives additional reasons why it will not be forgotten. In a more spoken register, the structure can be replaced by *sans compter que*. Unlike the modes with *plus*, *moins* and *mieux*, its parts are never separated by interpolated words.

d'autant plus que

This mode modifies verbs or adjectives. Littré and Grevisse stress the fact that it is often followed by a comparative, itself usually including *plus*. To this, Mauger (359) adds usefully that *La mer s'agite d'autant plus fort que le vent est plus fort* is another way of saying *Plus le vent est fort, plus la mer s'agite*. In fact, nowadays, this comparative combination does not appear to be as common as non-comparative combinations. However, it does occur, as in this statement about the roots of xenophobia: *L'étranger fait toujours peur, et d'autant plus qu'il est plus différent*; and as in this one expressing a view on a strike: *Elle est d'autant plus grave que ses motifs sont futiles* (Dutourd, 1985: 68).

The more usual non-comparative mode can take one of two different forms: either with its three parts unseparated from one another or with a complement interpolated between *plus* and *que*. In the first of these, it could be replaced by the mode without *plus*:

> Ce qui précède ne doit en aucun cas être considéré comme un motif supplémentaire de ne pas écouter l'argumentation allemande, d'autant plus que celle-ci, sur plusieurs points fondamentaux, est très forte, voire imparable.

From such structures *plus* could be omitted. This is so whether the structure is placed in the same sentence as the verb or begins the following sentence or paragraph.

In its second form, the words *d'autant plus* directly follow the verb but *que* is preceded by other words. In this example, the author argues against law-reformers and civil-libertarians who wish to abolish the institution of the *juge d'instruction*:

> Certains parlent de supprimer le juge d'instruction dont les pouvoirs feraient peser un danger permanent sur les libertés individuelles. Ils rêvent de cette procédure anglo-saxonne qu'ils parent d'autant plus de toutes les vertus qu'ils ne la connaissent pas.

Frequently, only an adverb or adverbial phrase will come between the two components: *Il a agi d'autant plus efficacement que...*; *Le gouvernement la prend d'autant plus au sérieux que...*; *Ces mesures étaient considérées avec d'autant plus de méfiance par les conservateurs que....* In theory, these interpolations can be quite long, as the expectation is that a *que* will necessarily arrive to complete the sense begun by the first part. In fact, few are longer than the one in the following example, which deals with terrorism and the taking of hostages in Lebanon:

> Cette démonstration de force, preuve supplémentaire d'un regain d'activisme iranien au pays du Cèdre avivera d'autant plus l'inquiétude de l'Occident quant au sort de ses otages, que l'enlèvement vendredi d'un ressortissant ouest-allemand relance le chantage dont ils sont l'enjeu.

Even if the interpolation includes another *que* of different function, the risk of ambiguity is not great, as in this comment on members of the Parti socialiste who are not sorry that their party's alliance with the Communists (*l'union de la gauche*) is now defunct:

> Il est d'autant plus compréhensible que les socialistes aient du mal à faire leur deuil de l'union de la gauche que malgré de nombreuses déconvenues, cette stratégie leur a permis d'accéder enfin au pouvoir et que la solution de remplacement n'est pas évidente.

When this mode modifies adjectives, it adds a second reason for their aptness. Here again it can adopt one or other of two forms. It can be placed in its entirety after the adjective; or it can incorporate the adjective into itself: *d'autant plus grand que*. The latter is probably more common. It can be seen in this example, linking two points about a new drug-fad, the second of which reinforces the danger indicated by the first:

> Cette drogue qui, comme la cocaïne, reste moins utilisée en France que dans les pays anglo-saxons, peut provoquer des lésions irréversibles de l'ensemble du système nerveux, d'autant plus dangereuses qu'elles apparaissent tardivement.

When placed wholly after the adjective, the structure varies depending on whether or not it is placed in the same sentence as the adjective. When it is in the same sentence, it amounts to a reordering of words as they would be used in the mode just discussed. The subject of the first of these examples is Georgian non-intervention in fighting taking place in a neighbouring state:

> Les Géorgiens restent à distance, préférant ne pas intervenir dans le conflit inter-ethnique de leurs voisins azéris et arméniens. Mais l'atmosphère leur est favorable, d'autant plus que les militants nationalistes, dont plusieurs ont été libérés de détention en 1987, ont commencé à se regrouper.

> Les dirigeants sont conscients de la montée des périls, d'autant plus que [...]

These sentences could have been structured as follows: *Mais l'atmosphère leur est d'autant plus favorable que...* and *Les dirigeants sont d'autant plus conscients de la montée des périls que...*. When the connector is placed in the sentence following that containing the adjective, it may link to it by means of the pronoun *le* and a part of *être*: *Ce jugement est catégorique. Il l'est d'autant plus qu'il n'a été ni improvisé ni précipité.*

In addition, this structure is commonly used not to introduce a second reason or factor reinforcing a first, but merely to stress a single one, as in this writer's comment on what he sees as the inordinate power wielded by a group of intellectuals:

> Je crois qu'un groupe d'intellectuels dispose désormais dans notre société d'un pouvoir d'autant plus grand qu'il formule en termes idéologiques et qu'il légitime les valeurs de cette société.

There, it is conceivable that what follows the connector is implicitly a second factor added to what precedes it. But it is likely that this author's meaning could be accurately expressed by *d'un grand pouvoir*, followed by either *notamment parce qu'il formule...* or *du fait qu'il formule...*.

d'autant moins que

This mode, less frequent than the form with *plus*, functions exactly like it. Preceded quite often by a negative structure, it stresses absence of reasons. Its function of adding a second factor to a first is well seen in the two following examples, the first of which is taken from an archeological text about our ignorance of the lives of ordinary people in ancient times. Here *moins*, itself reinforced by *et*, reinforces the preceding *très peu*:

> À part les informations données par certaines peintures des tombes et par quelques textes antiques, on ne sait que très peu de choses sur la vie des petites gens. Et d'autant moins que la population modeste vivait dans des cabanes de bois et torchis qui survivent mal à l'usure des siècles.

The second deals with Dutch Railways (*les NS*) and the unlikelihood that they will place orders for any rolling stock other than Alsthom and Talbot.

The first factor, their satisfaction, is strengthened by the second, the urgency of their need:

> Cinquante-huit locomotives Alsthom circulent, depuis le début des années 80, sur le réseau des Pays-Bas. De même, 75 unités à double niveau Talbot sont-elles déjà en service. Satisfaits de leurs fournisseurs, les NS ont d'autant moins de raisons d'en changer que leurs besoins sont pressants.

The form with adjectives (and comparative) is also used: *un réseau de corruption d'autant moins dénoncé qu'il est plus général et qu'il profite à tous.*

d'autant mieux que

This mode is probably the least used. Most often it is placed beside the verb; and unlike the others it is rarely placed in the sentence following. But it still usually introduces a second circumstance which it links to the preceding one. The first example deals with Moroccan peasants who learned in the mid-1970s from European tourists of the demand for cannabis and decided to supply it. The repetition of the same verb underscores the standard link made by the connector between two points:

> Accrochés à des bouts de terre pauvres et pentus, les paysans rifains comprirent le profit qu'ils pouvaient tirer de cette situation. Ils le comprirent d'autant mieux qu'à l'époque la sécheresse mettait à mal les cultures traditionnelles.

In this mode, too, the connector's two elements can be separated by interpolated words, as in this extract from a discussion of the future railway networks in Europe:

> Le TGV Rhin-Rhône peut jouer un rôle majeur dans la structuration du futur maillage du réseau européen. La logique des maillons manquants devrait en effet d'autant mieux fonctionner à partir de cette liaison que celle-ci est propice à la capture de flux nord-sud de voyageurs qui sont en Europe sensiblement plus importants que les flux est-ouest.

d'autre part *

The function of this connector is close to that of ***d'ailleurs*** and ***du reste***: like them, it adds a second point to a first. According to Robert, the function is: *introduire une phrase, un membre de phrase, un mot qu'on ajoute ou qu'on oppose à ce qui précède.* It says 'second' or 'for another thing'; it says 'not only that, but also this'; and in some contexts it says 'but on the other hand', 'but then again' or 'against that'.

Difference from *d'ailleurs*

The point introduced by this connector is more than the mere supplement that *d'ailleurs* usually accompanies. It can function separately or as the second part of the binary structure *d'une part... d'autre part*. In either case, it introduces a parallel point, usually one which reinforces what precedes, leads to the same conclusion and is of equal or at least comparable importance. It is not used to present only an aside. In force, it is thus closer to *de plus* or *en outre* than to *d'ailleurs*. A discussion of neo-Nazi groups in Germany identifies, one after the other, two symptoms of their increasing importance:

> Un cimetière juif a encore été profané ce week-end en Souabe. Les sondages montrent d'autre part que le poids électoral de l'extrême droite s'accroît.

Similarly, the connector is used to present the second of two equally remarkable reactions by French publishers and journalists to the *fatwa* by which in 1989 the Ayatollah Khomeini condemned the writer Salman Rushdie to death: first, the newspapers and magazines agreed to publish a chapter of the offending book; second, the publishers supported the idea of a joint edition of the whole book:

> Trois journaux, *Libération, le Nouvel Observateur* et *l'Événement du jeudi*, publient chacun un chapitre, jeudi 23 février, des *Versets sataniques*, « avec l'accord des ayants droit de Salman Rushdie ». D'autre part, l'appel à une coédition française du livre, lancé par Quai Voltaire, Arléa et *l'Événement du jeudi*, a reçu le soutien de nouvelles maisons d'édition (le Pré-aux-Clercs, les Presses de la Renaissance, Anne-Marie Métailié, Liana Levi) et de nouveaux organes de presse (*le Magazine littéraire*, les trois titres de Bauer-France : *Marie-France, Aujourd'hui Madame, Maxi*).

Combined with *mais*

When the connector introduces a point which runs counter to what precedes, it can be combined with *mais* (another way in which it differs from *d'ailleurs*), as in this excerpt from an essay on the origins of museums, in which the writer, speaking of private collections of curios and lists of these, focusses on the collection and list made by a gentleman named Borel:

> Aux XVIᵉ et XVIIᵉ siècles, les cabinets semblables à celui de Borel se comptent en Europe par centaines sinon par milliers. Borel lui-même en connaissait cent soixante-trois dans la France seule et quarante-quatre dans vingt-huit villes étrangères disséminées entre la Lituanie et l'Espagne. Il est vrai que parmi les cabinets qu'il mentionne certains n'existaient déjà plus de son temps. Mais, d'autre part, à la lumière de nos connaissances, pourtant fort incomplètes, sa liste apparaît comme très lacunaire et, ce défaut, elle le partage avec toutes les autres listes d'époque.

> (Pomian, 64)

In paired points and sequences

If the first of a pair of points is introduced by a connector, this structure may be used, again unlike *d'ailleurs*, to present the second. When a first point is introduced by *en premier lieu*, this connector is at times used for the following one. Some writers use it instead of **ensuite** when they have introduced the first of a pair by *d'abord*. Sometimes, as is often done with *d'une part... d'autre part*, these pairs are announced as such: *Ce principe du plein emploi a deux conséquences. Tout d'abord [...]. D'autre part [...].*

The connector can also make a point as part of a list. Thus, it can replace the standard *ensuite* in tripartite **sequences of points** – a sociologist discussing marriage in contemporary France says: *Plusieurs observations méritent d'être faites. D'abord [...]. D'autre part [...]. Enfin [...].* A second point introduced by this connector can be followed by a third introduced by *en outre* or even by *d'autre part encore*.

The structure quite commonly combines with **et**, as in this extract from an essay on the painter and writer Eugène Fromentin and the two reasons why he did not carry out his intention of writing a third book on North Africa:

Sa pensée était certainement de tirer de ses notes un troisième volume africain sur l'Égypte. Malheureusement le voyage avait été court et bousculé ; et la guerre, d'autre part, allait empêcher Fromentin de donner suite à son projet.

(Henriot, 1954: 141)

The connector is more often than not placed first in the sentence. The thematic significance of the points it introduces can be seen too in the frequency with which it opens a paragraph.

de ce fait *

This structure is related in meaning and function to *du fait* and *par le fait*. This function suggests it may derive from *à cause de ce fait*. Sometimes the *de* merely completes a verb which makes a straightforward semantic link with what precedes: *Il résulte de ce fait que...*; *Mais il serait insensé de conclure de ce fait à un progrès*.

When it functions separately as a connector, the structure is equally straightforward: it always introduces a consequence of what precedes. The *fait* in question is always what is stated in the preceding sentence or proposition. English equivalents could be 'because of this', 'thereby', 'hence', 'for that reason' or 'accordingly'. Some writers use this structure as a variant for *en conséquence*. At times, it could be replaced by **dès lors**; at others by *par là*. When it introduces a consequence that is mainly chronological, it can be a variant for **du même coup** or perhaps **du coup**, as in this extract from a discussion of the difficulty of timing the presidential election to be held in 1995:

> Comme il n'y a pas constitutionnellement moyen de faire autrement, les dates finalement retenues, malgré leurs inconvénients, seront fatalement celles des 23 avril et 7 mai.
> La date des élections municipales posera, de ce fait, un problème. Normalement prévues pour mars, elles devront forcément être déplacées.

The following example, in which the connector acts more like *par conséquent*, introducing what is more of a logical consequence, is taken from a discussion of class factors and their influence in perpetuating social inequalities in France:

> Raymond Boudon avait déjà constaté que le fils d'ouvrier avait plus de chances que son père d'accéder à l'université, mais pas plus que lui de rejoindre une catégorie sociale supérieure. Cette tendance, selon toute probabilité, va se renforcer.
> De ce fait, on ne retrouve pas dans notre société la mobilité – marque d'une véritable méritocratie – mais la stabilité – preuve de la dévolution héréditaire.

> (Closets, 1983: 189)

The structure is often placed at the beginning of the sentence, or even of the paragraph, where it is normally followed by a comma. Inside the sentence, it is often placed between commas, either with the verb or after *et*.

Reinforced modes

The connector is sometimes reinforced with the adjective *seul*, as in this extract from a report on a slack week's trading at the stock exchange:

> Le manque d'affaires a été particulièrement sensible au cours de cette semaine réduite à quatre séances par les fêtes du 14 juillet. De ce seul fait, le lent réchauffement observé depuis une quinzaine de jours à la Bourse de Paris a bien failli s'interrompre.

It can also be combined in a somewhat similar way with *même*, as in this sentence defining a consequence of the continuing relevance to contemporary sociological thought of Max Weber's ideas:

> De tous les grands sociologues du début du siècle, Max Weber est sans doute celui dont l'œuvre reste aujourd'hui la plus vivante, mais il est aussi, de ce fait même, celui dont la postérité est la plus divisée.

> (Raynaud, 7)

A variant

A variant mode, *par ce fait* or *par ce fait même*, is occasionally used, as in this example taken from an article on a meeting between officials of Communist China and Taiwan:

> Ils ont négocié les premiers accords formels jamais conclus entre les « deux Chines », portant sur le rapatriement des immigrants illégaux chinois dans l'île et celui des pirates de l'air – du moins ceux qui n'auront pas obtenu l'asile politique – et sur la résolution des conflits de pêche. Par ce fait, le régime de Pékin a, pour la première fois, reconnu une compétence juridique à un rival auquel il conteste toute légitimité.

As this example shows, the structure could be replaced in certain contexts by *ce faisant*. In others, it is a variant for *par là même*.

décidément *

This is one of those adverbs which, in addition to their common adverbial function, can have a different function when used as a connector. Rather like some spoken uses of English 'really' or 'there's no doubt about it', this one not only confirms a point but emphasizes it as well. Its tone can be familiar, conversational, even exclamatory. If placed first in the sentence, it is followed by a comma; inside the sentence, it is usually put between commas.

Recapitulative

The point emphasized is often one which the writer has discussed in a previous paragraph, in which case what is introduced by the connector may be a recapitulative statement in a final sentence. A satirical sally about Édouard Balladur's style as Prime Minister begins like this:

> La rondeur, voilà bien le maître mot de la stratégie Balladur. Les temps sont durs, la France va mal, alors il arrondit les angles.

The writer goes on to describe France as beset by unctuous muted softness, anaesthesia, fur-lined consensual cocoons, the reassurance of portly contours, *formes enveloppantes, dodues et rembourrées*, and eventually resumes the whole performance with a paragraph beginning:

> Décidément, notre Premier ministre peut se vanter d'avoir réussi son coup : la France en crise a choisi de lui ressembler, de s'identifier à ce docteur miracle qu'elle plébiscite à son chevet pour soigner ses plaies.

There, the function of the connector comes close to that of *bref*, *en un mot* or *pour tout dire*. Its tone, however, remains familiar.

Placed first in a discussion

The connector is often placed not at the end but at the very beginning of an argument, where it would not be replaceable by resumers such as *bref* or *en un mot*. Then it confirms by anticipation, as it were, a point which it seems to assume has already been made. It is especially in this position that a spoken and exclamative tone can be heard in it. It may resound too with a certain combative irony, since the writer who begins a discussion in this way may feign to assume the reader's agreement with a controversial or provocative proposition. Using it like this, the writer suggests the point is familiar, lying latent in the reader's mind, requiring no restating. An essayist expressing the view that the French are not gifted as sculptors can begin in this way:

> Décidément, l'idée que la sculpture est le plus souvent un art du toucher, du galbe, de l'effleurement et de la caresse n'est pas près de triompher en France.

This sort of sentence, presenting the idea not as a conclusion drawn from an argument, but as an introduction to one, could of course be transposed holus-bolus to the end of the discussion or to some other part of it. In the next example, dating from the Gulf War of 1991, a writer criticizes military men's liking for euphemism. The suggestion implicit in his use of the connector – that this practice is well known – is reinforced not only by *encore* in the opening sentence but also by the sentence following the one introduced by the connector:

> Qu'est-ce que c'est encore que cette histoire de « frappes aériennes » ? En français, jusqu'à nouvel ordre, cela s'appelle des bombardements. Décidément, la vogue de l'euphémisme bat tous les records. Ce n'est pas d'hier, notez, qu'elle sévit dans les choses militaires.

Reinforced

Whether placed before or after the discussion, the connector may be reinforced by another affirmative structure, such as *oui* or *bien*, as in this sentence summing up part of an article about how hard the times are for travelling entertainers: *Oui, décidément, les temps sont bien las pour les gens du voyage*; or as in this example taken from the beginning of a discussion of difficulties being experienced both by banks and the government with the *livret A*, a common form of savings account: *Décidément, le livret A est bien la bête noire des banques.*

de fait *

In the usage of the great majority, this connector is affirmative and does not function like *en fait* or *en réalité*, which are usually oppositive. Yet the bulk of the information given about it by the Robert dictionary is this: *Dans le fait, par le fait, de fait, en fait (loc. adv.) : en réalité*. This mixes up confirmatives and adversatives, obscures the functional differences between them and authorizes the erroneous inference that any of them can be used anywhere in the sense of *en réalité*. The following example neatly shows the usual difference between *de fait* and *en fait*; it quotes words spoken by Boris Yeltsin after meeting an official of the Chinese Communist Party, Jiang Zemin, and includes a journalist's gloss in square brackets:

> « J'avais peur que ce soit très formel et très rigide, les Chinois m'avaient traité de tous les noms quand j'ai quitté le PC soviétique. [De fait, M. Jiang avait refusé de le rencontrer lors de son séjour à Moscou, au printemps 1991.] Mais en fait ça a été très chaleureux. »

In the brackets, the reporter's *de fait* confirms the first statement: that the Chinese had been hostile to Yeltsin. After the square brackets, with *en fait*, Yeltsin himself says his expectation of a bad reception was contradicted in the event.

A non-connective mode

A non-connective mode of this structure can be adjectival or adverbial: in *une objection de fait*, *une question de fait* it is an adjective meaning 'of fact'. When applied to some other nouns, such as *situation* and *état*, it means 'de facto': *un gouvernement de fait* is one which is not recognized; *une partition de fait de la Bosnie* is a carving up of a state in the guise of some other arrangement. In the following sentence, describing the cover-up of a blood-transfusion scandal inside the Ministry of Health, the expression is adverbial:

> C'est la volontaire rétention d'informations, acceptée de fait par la dizaine de médecins aux plus hauts postes de la transfusion et du ministère, qui a entretenu le brouillard général.

Closeness to *en effet* and *effectivement*

When it is a connector, something of this value of undeniable fact remains in *de fait*. Although less often used than *en effet* or *effectivement*, its usual function is close to theirs: to corroborate and precise what precedes. It can be part of a longer structure: *il est de fait que*. In this example a writer discusses table-turning and spiritualism and the long-standing suspicion that such paranormal phenomena are mere trickery:

> On a cru longtemps qu'il fallait attribuer simplement ces mouvements à la supercherie, et il est de fait que dans bien des cas rien ne serait plus facile à simuler.

(Binet, 1892: 297)

This longer structure used to be more common than it has become, as in this excerpt from a discussion of the frequency of words of one syllable in English:

> Le monosyllabisme a été parfois considéré comme un trait caractéristique de l'anglais. Il est de fait qu'en général aux formes du vieil-anglais, encore chargées de syllabes, alourdies de suffixes et de désinences, l'anglais oppose des formes brèves, réduites à une syllabe unique.
>
> (Vendryes, 409)

When used as a confirmer, the connector could always be structured in that way; and there are writers who still use it like that (Caillois, 15; July, 27 & 83). However, most now prefer the shorter form, which is almost always placed first in the sentence, as in this pair of sentences about the French spoken by some non-French people:

> Ce qui distingue un étranger en France, c'est souvent la correction excessive de son langage. De fait, on peut voir des Syriens, des Turcs, des Égyptiens, qu'on ne reconnaît pour tels qu'à ce qu'ils parlent comme des livres.

It can even be placed first in the paragraph, as in this example taken from an article about a cancer specialist one of whose therapies relies on the restorative powers of the body:

> Le professeur Rosenberg est connu des spécialistes pour avoir apporté la preuve que l'organisme possède, en lui-même, les ressources nécessaires pour se débarrasser de ses tumeurs. Qu'il suffit, en somme, de lui donner un coup de pouce.
>
> De fait, le professeur Rosenberg a obtenu des rémissions et des guérisons spectaculaires sur quelques dizaines de patients en phase terminale, atteints de cancers réputés incurables.

In each of those examples, it would be possible, as it usually is with *en effet*, to put a finger, literally, not only on the words before the connector which are confirmed, but also on the words after it which repeat them more precisely. This mode, also like *en effet*, combines with *et*, an unambiguous sign of its confirmative nature:

> Le président égyptien, M. Hosni Moubarak, n'attendait « pas de miracle » de la première visite de M. Itzhak Rabin, mardi au Caire. Et, de fait, il n'y en eut pas.

An elliptic use

Despite its unambiguously confirmative function, however, the connector has two problematical features. First, some writers use it in ways which are elliptic: the link of thought they make is implicit, not clearly confirmative, as in this extract from a discussion of phonetic scripts, where it would be difficult to see the connector as replacing *en effet*:

Le linguiste demande avant tout qu'on lui fournisse un moyen de représenter les sons articulés qui supprime toute équivoque. De fait, d'innombrables systèmes graphiques ont été proposés.

(Saussure, 57–58)

Adversative *de fait*

Second, and more importantly, a minority of writers do use this connector like *en fait* or *en réalité*: not to confirm but to rectify a preceding statement. As one student of this connector has put it, dealing with this very aspect of its versatility:

...les intuitions linguistiques à propos de *de fait* manquent particulièrement de netteté. [...] La position de *de fait* par rapport à *en effet* et *effectivement* d'une part, et par rapport à *en fait* de l'autre, ne laisse pas d'être étonnante. Largement substituable à *en effet* et *effectivement* avec valeur confirmative, il l'est partiellement à *en fait* avec valeur oppositive.

(Danjou-Flaux, 137, 139)

The following example shows the connector clearly making such an adversative relationship between two statements: first, what seems to be the relation between a fish and the river it swims in, then the reality which contradicts the appearance:

Un poisson, dans l'eau, semble se mouvoir en un milieu où lui seul figure l'existence ; de fait, il est entouré d'une complexe animation vitale.

(Roule, 132)

This exemplar, since what is being structured is a contradiction, is replaceable by **au contraire** or **or**. A similar contradictive usage can be seen in the next example, taken from a discussion of the notion of latency in the early phases of certain illnesses:

On dit parfois de ces maladies commençantes, qu'elles sont à l'état latent ; mais de fait, elles sont déjà dûment installées, et elles ont commencé leur évolution et leur marche progressive.

(Héricourt, viii)

This combination with **mais** is a sure sign of adversativeness. Similarly, one finds *Il est de fait pourtant que* (Boucher, 549). It would be most unlikely for *en effet*, say, to be accompanied by *mais*. In the following example, there is no *mais*; but there could be. Taken from an article about the war between Russia and Chechnia in the early months of 1995, it reports that members of the Russian government said their army's lack of success was intentional, then contradicts this explanation in the sentence introduced by *de fait*:

Au point que Serguïe Chakraï, vice-Premier ministre, a accusé l'armée de saboter intentionnellement l'opération militaire en Tchétchénie (d'une durée annoncée de « quelques heures ») pour affaiblir le gouvernement. De fait, l'intervention a souffert d'un matériel vieilli interdisant toute frappe chirurgicale, de l'usure morale des hommes de troupe et du refus d'obéissance de nombreux gradés encadrant des corps d'élite.

These exemplars of *de fait*, idiosyncratic when compared with standard usage, show that certain native speakers of the language do not conform to majority usage. Some even use *de fait* in both ways, as a confirmer and as a rectifier (Roule, 172, 191; Héricourt, 12; Lejeune, 277, 269).

A variant

Among other rarer variants made from the noun *fait* is *par le fait*. Like *de fait*, it is used differently by different writers. Sartre uses it in his essay *Qu'est-ce qu'un collaborateur ?* Having said that ever since the Revolution, an anti-democratic *déchet* has survived into the present, he adds this:

> Il serait exagéré de soutenir, comme on l'a fait, que la France a été coupée en deux depuis 1789. Mais, par le fait, pendant que la majorité des bourgeois s'accommodaient d'une démocratie capitaliste qui consacrait le régime de la libre entreprise, une petite part de la classe bourgeoise est demeurée en dehors de la vie nationale française parce qu'elle a refusé de s'adapter à la constitution républicaine.
>
> (Sartre, 1949b: 48)

The presence of *mais* shows that the connector, rectifying as well as precising, stands either for *en fait* or for one of the idiosyncratic modes of *de fait* mentioned above. Other writers give to this variant the more usual confirmative function of *de fait*, as in this comment on the value of Saussure's *Cours de linguistique générale*:

> Du point de vue qui est ici le nôtre, son caractère éminent est d'avoir rapproché la langue de l'homme et d'avoir tenu compte – sans rien céder pour autant sur le principe d'autonomie de la linguistique – de la fonction humaine du langage.
> Les langues, par le fait, enregistrent quelques-uns des caractères sociaux des peuples qui les parlent.
>
> (Wagner, 20)

In the second sentence, with *caractères sociaux des peuples* the author confirms and precises the first sentence's mention of the *fonction humaine* of language.

Many English expressions could be used, depending on contexts, as equivalents for this connector, among them 'indeed', 'in fact', 'it is a fact that', 'it must be said that', 'there can be no doubt that'. Often, as happens with *en effet*, English would use no special connective structure.

de là *

Nearly always placed at the beginning of sentences or paragraphs, this structure is a specialized mode of *là*, which as a connector always designates the statement or the idea immediately preceding. It is very close in function to *d'où*: it introduces a conclusion or a statement of the consequences of what precedes, making a link akin to that made by English 'hence'. However, 'hence' is often followed by a structure with a verb; whereas this connector is mostly followed by a verbless noun (or pronoun): *De là une conséquence* is quite common. There is usually no comma between connector and noun, as in this description of aspects of the writing of Rabelais:

> Il ne déplaît pas à Rabelais d'user de termes savants, incompréhensibles au vulgaire. De là les étonnantes disparates de son vocabulaire. De là aussi celles de son style.

In the following example, the whole philosophical system of Descartes is seen as the outcome of his desire to prove the existence of God:

> Descartes prétend prouver l'existence de Dieu, rien de moins, et fonder sur cette vérité indubitable celle, jusqu'à lui douteuse, de nos sciences. De là le cartésianisme qui se voulait le système, fondé sur des vérités nécessaires, de toutes les vérités possibles.

Relation to a verb

Despite the lack of verb, the noun following the connector constitutes the subject of a sort of vestigial main clause. No doubt a verb is understood, one of those occasionally used with this structure, sometimes with inversion of the subject: *De là résulte une conséquence*; *De là je conclus que*; *De là dérive l'erreur*; *De là naissent des erreurs*; *De là est sortie une tendance à*; *Il suit de là que*; *De là vient l'idée de*. In the following example, *venir*, the most common of these verbs, is used with impersonal *il* understood as its subject. The author's point is the change of meanings brought about in words by the social context of their usage:

> Le mot « ascension », affiché à la porte d'une église, évoque une idée aussi précise, quoique différente, que le même terme entendu à la montagne dans un groupe d'alpinistes.
> De là vient que les mots ont une tendance à se spécialiser en raison du milieu social.
>
> (Dauzat, 1912b: 9)

Another quite common verb is *découler*, as in this example which speaks of the principles which Pierre Mendès France applied while in government:

La morale, pour Mendès, c'est d'abord le « respect du réel ». De là découle cet impératif catégorique : l'exercice du pouvoir commence avec celui de la vérité.

(July, 72)

de là que

This mode may be a variant of *de là vient que* minus the verb. Alternatively, it could be an abridgment of *de là le fait que*, which Foucault was fond of using (Foucault, 19–20). Albert Camus says of the woman-izer:

Ce n'est point par manque d'amour que Don Juan va de femme en femme. Il est ridicule de le représenter comme un illuminé en quête de l'amour total. Mais c'est bien parce qu'il les aime avec un égal emportement et chaque fois avec tout lui-même, qu'il lui faut répéter ce don et cet approfondisse-ment. De là que chacune espère lui apporter ce que personne ne lui a jamais donné.

(Camus, 1964: 97)

Another example comes from a comment on Virginia Woolf's novel *The Waves*, in which differences between the characters are marked, the author says, only by stylistic features, each of which is a *signe d'identité*:

Signe d'identité, mais signe seulement, car l'identité véritable et profonde du moi, sa permanence à travers la diversité qu'apportent les étapes du temps ne se fait pas sentir autrement que par ce moyen tout extérieur et formel. De là que cette œuvre – dont le titre même symbolise le mouvement perpétuel de flots sans cesse renouvelés – nous impose au contraire une impression de stagnation en chacun de ses chapitres.

(Cormeau, 111–112)

de là à

This is a very different structure. It is usually followed by the infinitive of a verb, never introduces a main clause and normally leads to another verb-structure completing the utterance. In this example, the subject is the rights and wrongs of the medical profession being a closed shop:

Qui voudrait en revenir aux temps où n'importe quelle personne « ayant le don » pouvait se proclamer guérisseur ? Le fait est que les pouvoirs publics se doivent de vérifier la compétence de ceux qui prétendent soigner leurs semblables. De là à demander qu'ils leur confèrent un statut corporatif, il n'y a qu'un léger biaisement du discours, qui n'est pas toujours remarqué.

(Closets, 1983: 440)

The completing verb-structures usually stress, as in that example, the fault-iness of the implied conclusion; they speak of jumping to conclusions or of the real distance separating the two ideas linked. Common ones are *c'est aller vite en besogne* (*De là à dire que tout va bien, c'est sans doute aller un peu vite en besogne*); and a range of expressions based on *il y a*, such as *il y a loin* (*De là à prétendre qu'elle est belle, il y a loin*); *il y a un saut*; *il y a un monde*; *il y a encore bien des gouffres à franchir*; and most often *il n'y a qu'un pas*, as in this excerpt from a discussion of the difference between anti-parliamentarians of the Right and of the Left – the former see politicians as *des grotesques*, the latter see them as *des fripons*:

> l'antiparlementarisme de gauche ne considère que le décalage entre les professions de foi du candidat et le comportement de l'élu : de là à penser que le milieu parlementaire est par excellence un milieu corrupteur, il n'y a qu'un pas, qui est vite franchi.
>
> (Julliard, 19)

This sequence is so common, in fact, that it is sometimes replaced by **points de suspension**, hinting that the consequence is so obvious or inevitable as not to need to be spelt out, as in this comment on the way prison officers can be a law unto themselves:

> En prison, l'évangile des gardiens et du directeur s'appelle « règlement intérieur ». De là à ce que l'arbitraire fasse force de loi et que l'humiliation devienne le lot quotidien...

At times *de là à* is followed not by an infinitive but by a noun, as in this extract from a discussion of how the heterosexual man whose experience of women has included a modicum of jaded debauchery sees homosexuals:

> Le bizarre de la pédérastie, pour lui, rejoint aisément ces jouissances contorsionnées et toutes dépourvues de fraîcheur sexuelle. De là à l'idée que le pédéraste est un pauvre, un infirme, un dément, la transition est insensible, et c'est pourquoi tout l'effort de compréhension de l'hétérosexuel le conduit d'ordinaire du malaise à la pitié.
>
> (Fernandez, 65)

de même

This structure could usually be replaced by *de la même manière*. However, it has a couple of other features which are not quite as self-evident. It can take two forms: either it is the second element of the binary construction *de même que..., de même*; or it functions without *de même que*.

The binary construction

This mode always structures a close comparison within a single sentence. The first element of it introduces a subordinate part of the sentence; the second element introduces the main clause. An example of it, taken from an article about Proust's *À la recherche du temps perdu*, adopts an aptly Proustian way of comparing the novel to a cathedral, ancient and full of meanings that have become more and more unclear to us:

> De même que nous ne savons plus lire les fresques ou les bas-reliefs des cathédrales, dont le sens était évident à nos ancêtres illettrés du Moyen-Âge – nous n'y voyons que des formes que nous trouvons « jolies », nous avons besoin qu'un guide nous déchiffre le message qu'ils nous adressent – de même, un jour, personne n'osera plus s'aventurer dans l'œuvre de Proust sans le secours d'un guide, équipé d'une lampe-torche.

This binary structure, the first part of which is cataphoric in function and the second anaphoric, corresponds to English 'Just as ..., so'. Often it compares like and like, even using the same key word in both parts, as in this dual statement about the belated adoption of two forms of duelling in England:

> de même que le duel judiciaire pénétra en Angleterre longtemps après avoir été adopté sur le continent, de même le duel privé n'y pénétra que fort tard.
> (Chesnais, 132)

And often the second element is structured with an inversion of subject and verb:

> De même qu'il avait assuré qu'il serait « honnête avec le suffrage universel », de même s'est-il montré honnête dans le traitement de ce scandale actuel.

Unaccompanied *de même*

When the anaphoric second part functions separately, it always begins the sentence. It signals more of a similarity than a close comparison and links to the preceding sentence. That apart, its features are similar to those it has as part of the binary: rarely followed by a comma; often followed by inversion of subject and verb. Its closest English equivalents might be 'similarly', 'likewise' or even one of the modes of 'also'. That is, it introduces a parallel point, clearly akin to the preceding one but often with a meaning closer to *ensuite*, adverbial *aussi* or *également*. This example comes from an article on the sentencing of senior medical officers of the national blood-bank (*le CNTS*) found guilty of having knowingly supplied blood-products contaminated with HIV to haemophiliacs:

> L'analyse du jugement rendu par la 16e chambre correctionnelle de Paris fait apparaître que, selon les juges, le docteur Garretta a délibérément appliqué

une politique destinée à tromper les hémophiles sur la qualité substantielle des produits sanguins vendus par le CNTS. De même, le tribunal indique-t-il précisément que l'information sur la contamination par le virus du sida des lots sanguins remonta complètement jusqu'au professeur Jacques Roux, ancien directeur de la santé, et jusqu'au docteur Claude Weisselberg, ancien membre du cabinet de M. Edmond Hervé, alors secrétaire d'État à la santé.

There, with minimal rearrangement of syntax, the connector could be replaced by *aussi*, as it could also in the next example, taken from a discussion of French cookery-books translated into other languages in the seventeenth century:

Le Cuisinier français est traduit en anglais dès 1653, deux ans après sa parution en France, puis en allemand et en italien (6 éditions jusqu'en 1815). De même en est-il du *Cuisinier royal et bourgeois* et de bien d'autres ouvrages.

(Pitte, 150)

This structure is sometimes used to introduce the second of two examples, the first of which is introduced by **ainsi** or **par exemple**. This example comes from a discussion of the revival of certain German customs which had all but died out:

Dans certaines régions, de lointaines traditions remontent en surface et redeviennent populaires. Par exemple les rites initiatiques étudiants pratiqués dans certaines universités et qui consistent en combats au sabre devant se solder par une balafre au visage redeviennent à la mode malgré les interdictions officielles. De même, le rituel du *Diener*, cet espèce de salut prussien (une inclinaison du buste raidi suivi d'un claquement des talons), est toujours enseigné dans la bonne société.

A variant

In some contexts, a variant for this structure with a more familiar or journalistic tone is *même chose*, as in this extract from a news report describing the end of the disastrous floods of 1993:

La situation connaît une nette amélioration. En Lorraine, dans le Pas-de-Calais et dans le Nord, la décrue est amorcée. Même chose dans les Ardennes, où les renforts de sapeurs-pompiers venus des départements voisins ont été désengagés et ont pu regagner leurs casernements dès hier.

de plus *

The adverb *plus* lends itself to many connective structures: unaccompanied *plus*, *il y a plus*, *de plus*, *qui plus est*, *bien plus*, *plus encore* and **en plus**. With slight variations depending on context, most of these are interchangeable with one another. They usually introduce a point which is to be taken in addition to the one before and is of similar importance. Most of them are equivalents of *en outre*. All of them except *en plus* are dealt with in this entry. The versatile 'also' is probably the most common English equivalent for most of them; others could be 'furthermore', 'in addition' or 'as well'. Some writers begin a sentence with mere 'More' followed by a comma.

plus

As an inter-assertional connector, *plus* is possibly a contraction of the more usual *de plus*. It is unknown to Robert; it may be symptomatic, along with similar contractions like *mieux* and *pis*, of recent developments in journalistic style. The potential for ambiguity requires it to stand first in a statement. It is usually followed by a *deux-points*. This example speaks of moles, exposure to sunlight and proneness to skin cancers:

> Les chercheurs australiens ont trouvé plus de grains de beauté chez les personnes qui avaient subi de cuisants coups de soleil dans l'enfance. Plus : ils ont démontré que les immigrants arrivés après l'âge de 15 ans en Australie ont moins de grains de beauté que les personnes nées sur place. Ils ont aussi un risque diminué de mélanome.

There, clearly, the connector could have been *en outre* or *de plus*. However, with either of them the writer would not have used a colon. The colon may indicate that this mode is rather an abridged form of *il y a plus*, which although less used now than it once was is often followed by one. The author of the following example discusses the self-interested socio-political behaviour of groups or classes of people:

> Chaque ordre ne tend qu'à un but : c'est de grandir lui-même, non d'accroître le bien commun. Il y a plus : même l'homme privé veille davantage à ses intérêts.

Some writers make a separate sentence of *Il y a plus* or *Mais il y a plus*. A fuller form of the latter is *Mais il y a plus que cela*. A further occasional variant is *Disons plus*, which is commonly followed by a colon or a full stop. The same goes for less frequent formulae like *D'autres remarques s'imposent* and for more emphatic or personalized variants such as *Allons plus loin*, *Je dirai plus* and *J'irai plus loin*.

A variant which functions as a brief sentence in a very similar way to *il y a plus* is *Ce n'est pas tout*. Though not as common as it once was, it is still used, sometimes combined with *mais* or *et*. In this example, the subject is a report by Amnesty International on the murder of children by semi-official death-squads in certain Latin American countries:

Soulignant que ces escadrons sont formés de policiers, l'organisation internationale indique qu'au nom du « nettoyage » (parfois entrepris à la demande
des commerçants que les larcins des gamins exaspèrent), ils ont tué, pour la
seule année 1991, plus de deux mille huit cents enfants en Colombie.

Ce n'est pas tout. Amnesty International rappelle que de nombreux enfants
sont également victimes de viols, de « disparitions » et d'assassinats politiques
[...].

An occasional variant for *plus*, favoured only by the writer who does
not fear being taxed with archaism, is unaccompanied *davantage*, usually
placed first in the sentence and followed by a colon (Bourgeois & d'Hondt,
93; Ricardou, 32, 35).

de plus

This mode is much more common than simple *plus*. It too introduces a
second or further point reinforcing an earlier one; but it can also present
a point which goes beyond the earlier one. It could often be replaced by
et or by ***d'autre part***. That is to say, unlike ***d'ailleurs***, it always accompanies a factor which is of at least the same importance as the one before;
and rather as ***ensuite*** follows *d'abord*, it can make the second point in the
pair made in English with 'For one thing ... For another ...'. It is often
followed by a comma and just as often it stands first in the statement:
*L'auteur du livre ne se nomme pas : de plus, il reste muet sur ses inten-
tions.* The argument that goes farther than a previous one can be seen
clearly in the paired points begun with *non seulement*, where this mode
can replace *mais aussi* or *mais encore*, as in this dual dissatisfaction with
the *Guide Michelin*'s allegedly incomprehensible and illogical star-rating
system for restaurants: *Non seulement le client ne s'y retrouve pas, ne
comprend pas, mais de plus il risque de se fourvoyer.* It should be bad
enough that the *Guide* is confusing; it is even worse that it is actively
misleading. A somewhat similar relation to a mode of ***encore*** is seen in a
sentence where *de plus* would be replaceable by ***encore faut-il***; the subject
here is the supposed frequency of 'hereditary suicides':

...ce n'est pas assez qu'ils soient plus ou moins fréquents. Il faudrait, de plus,
pouvoir déterminer quelle en est la proportion par rapport à l'ensemble des
morts volontaires.

(Durkheim, 1930: 71)

Frequently the statement following *de plus* is either a full sentence or
a paragraph. In this example, a demographer makes two points about the
huge mortality rates common in pre-modern societies. The second of them
may even be seen as stronger than the first:

Cette mortalité nous paraît aujourd'hui exorbitante : le quart des enfants
mouraient avant leur premier anniversaire, la moitié avant d'atteindre vingt

ans. À cet âge, l'espérance de vie ne dépassait guère vingt ans. De plus, la probabilité de mourir n'était pas concentrée à certaines phases de la vie : on pouvait décéder à tous âges.

As well as introducing the beginning of a whole new development, this mode can introduce a brief appendage, as with the adjectives of the following example: *J'ai donc lu, à mon tour, ces* Mystères galans. *C'est un ouvrage très médiocre, et, de plus, très bas.*

qui plus est

By definition, this says that what follows is additional to what precedes. The factor it introduces may not, of itself, be stronger than the one before. But by the addition of the two, the total argument is compounded. A writer discussing the changing role of wholesale fishmongers (*mareyeurs*) in the troubled fish trade identifies its two most salient features:

> La part des mareyeurs dans les achats de la grande distribution a tendance à reculer (elle représenterait désormais un peu moins de 48 % des quantités achetées) au profit des importations directes. Qui plus est, nombreux sont désormais les mareyeurs qui « mixent » achats à la criée et importations directes.

This mode is often placed first in the sentence or even the paragraph, and followed by a comma. Like *de plus*, it sometimes accompanies a brief adjectival appendage to a statement: *La noblesse ne se transmet que par filiation directe, qui plus est masculine.* And it is quite often combined with *et*: *Frappé, et qui plus est humilié.* Unlike *de plus*, it is at times placed at the end of statements, with an exclamatory tone, as in this ironic comment on an educational principle professed by two politicians of the centre-Right:

> Honnis soient ceux qui accuseraient Alphandéry et son président Méhaignerie d'opportunisme. Sur le dos de l'école libre, qui plus est !

An obvious English equivalent for this mode is 'what's more'.

bien plus

On the face of it, with its augmentative adverb, this mode is stronger than the preceding ones. In theory, it introduces a second factor which is deemed to be more telling than the first. Thus an account of Littré's constant attempts to keep ahead of his printers, who had started to typeset parts of the dictionary before he had completed them, identifies two features of the difficult situation he was in, the second of which actively aggravates it:

> L'imprimerie cependant avait commencé la composition des premiers feuillets. L'essentiel était de ne pas la laisser à court de copie ; bien plus, il fallait prendre

sur elle de l'avance, et lui préparer chaque semaine plus de manuscrit qu'elle n'en consommerait.

In practice, this mode is often used as nothing more than a variant for *de plus*, but one which may allow a writer to place the unobtrusive expression of a personal opinion. Unlike some of the others, it is found only at the beginning of statements; it is usually followed by a comma. An English equivalent could be 'more importantly'.

plus encore

Though often little more than a variant for *de plus*, this mode, at times reinforced by *et*, tends to be used to stress the fact that something which is already exorbitant can be seen to be even more exorbitant by the addition of what follows. Thus, a discussion of the huge profits made by some official receivers and liquidators goes from the outrageousness of this situation to something even more outrageous: that, by running a closed shop, they make their appointments marketable:

> les 60 liquidateurs les mieux payés atteignaient déjà, en 1978, 670 000 F d'honoraires et, tout en haut, les 5 plus gros d'entre eux gagnaient entre 1,2 et 2,2 millions de francs, rejoignant par là les premiers P.-D.G. de France.
> Plus encore : le *numerus clausus* a transformé les emplois en charges et permis, hors de tout statut légal, de créer une véritable vénalité [...]
> (Closets, 1983: 265)

Similarly, an article on the Chernobyl nuclear disaster, describing the construction of 'Shelter II', a new radiation-proof sarcophagus designed to supplement the first faulty covering put on the reactor, having noted the colossal dimensions of the thing, speaks of the gigantic feats of technology and engineering required to put it in place:

> Prévue pour empêcher toute agression extérieure (météorologique, sismique), son étanchéité sera à la fois totale et... relative. Car il lui faut favoriser l'évacuation des calories susceptibles de se dégager : tous les gaz rejetés dans l'atmosphère seront donc contrôlés et traités. Et plus encore, l'ouvrage est censé servir d'infrastructure pour le démantèlement ultérieur du réacteur accidenté : il est donc nécessaire d'installer des sas pour laisser passer hommes et robots ainsi que des emplacements ad hoc pour qu'ils puissent opérer.

Two variants of this mode, analogous to *il y a plus*, are *mais il y a plus encore* and *voici plus encore*.

dès lors *

This is one of those temporal expressions which, like *or* and *alors*, have extended their functions from the chronological to the logical: from expressing sequence in time they have come to express also consequence in reasoning.

Temporal adverb

In some contexts, narrative or historical, this one still functions more or less straightforwardly as an adverb of time, like *depuis lors*, with the meaning 'from then on'. The following example comes from a discussion of a phase of the Dreyfus Affair: *La Cour de cassation enfin, en octobre, décidait une nouvelle enquête : la révision, dès lors, était acquise* (Henriot, 1954: 300). However, even in this primarily temporal role, it can be difficult to say that there is no logical consequence implied by the connector: the certainty that the case will be reopened derives from the point in time called October; but it is also an outcome of the new state of affairs. This may be more evident in the next example, which comes from a discussion of the T.-P.G. (*trésoriers-payeurs généraux*), high Treasury officials in the *départements*:

> En 1953, le président de la Cour des comptes décide que l'inspection des trésoriers devra être faite d'après les documents fournis, sans vérification sur place de l'authenticité des faits présentés : les T.-P.G., dès lors, échappent pratiquement au contrôle de la Cour des comptes.
>
> (Closets, 1983: 233)

There, the connector can be seen to say 'ever since 1953' while also implying 'because of that ruling'. The French practice of narrating history in the present tense helps to conflate these two functions.

The logical sequencer

In other contexts, the connector functions unambiguously like a variant of ***par conséquent***: it could often be replaced by ***de ce fait***, one of the modes of ***cela étant*** or even the non-temporal *alors*. In English, one might say 'in these circumstances', 'in view of this' or 'that being the case'. The structure may link a conclusion back to a premiss, as in the two sentences of the following text, which from a general postulation about survivals of ancient Gaulish culture in modern French life argues to a particular consequence:

> Il n'est pas douteux que certains traits de la civilisation de la Gaule indépendante ont survécu dans des domaines aussi variés que la religion, la langue, la politique, le paysage, l'organisation de l'espace administratif, etc., et ce malgré les raz de marée culturels postérieurs : romain, germanique, italien, anglo-saxon, etc. Dès lors, il n'est pas absurde de formuler l'hypothèse d'une filiation entre l'intérêt marqué des Gaulois pour la nourriture et la gourmandise française.

Alternatively, it may link an enquiry back to the premiss: since what precedes is certain, how can the following be explained? In this example, which comes from a discussion of the scandal of the *vrai-faux passeport* allegedly issued illegally by the then Minister of the Interior, Charles Pasqua, the premiss is identified by *Il est établi que*:

> Il est établi aussi que le passeport a été rempli dans des conditions régulières (cachets, tampons, etc.), qu'il était de forme authentique bien que le nom de son titulaire fût un pseudonyme.
>
> Dès lors, les questions viennent d'elles-mêmes, qu'on le veuille ou non. Qui a fait cela ? Sur quel ordre ? Donné par qui ?
>
> (Boucher, 362)

This mode often accompanies verbs expressing understanding or explanation: *Dès lors, on saisit mieux pourquoi*; *On comprendra mieux, dès lors, pourquoi*; *Dès lors, cela ne peut être expliqué par*; *On a, dès lors, peine à croire que*; *Dès lors, force est bien d'admettre que*; *Dès lors, on s'étonnera moins que*; *Pas étonnant, dès lors, que*. It is also commonly used with questions, both direct and indirect: *On est dès lors en droit de se demander pourquoi*; *Dès lors, faut-il s'étonner que...?*; *Comment, dès lors, s'expliquer le fait que...?*; *Dès lors, une question se posait*; *Ne reste plus dès lors que la question de savoir si....*

dès lors que

As can be seen, when placed first in the sentence *dès lors* is followed by a comma; elsewhere it is usually put between commas. This punctuation helps differentiate it from the related *dès lors que*. The latter, although structuring only a single sentence, also functions in both temporal and logical ways. In this, it is very similar to another expression of time, *du moment que*. Both of them can express English consequential 'when' or 'since', a meaning akin to that of *puisque, vu que* or *étant donné que*. This example concerns the official relationship established by the constitution between the President of the Republic and his Prime Minister:

> Tous les chefs de l'État qui se sont succédé depuis plus de trente ans ont estimé qu'il était de leur devoir non seulement de contrôler l'action des premiers ministres qu'ils avaient nommés, mais aussi, et surtout, de définir les choix que ceux-ci mettaient en œuvre.
>
> Comment pourrait-il en être autrement, dès lors que chacun a accepté la réforme de 1962 qui fait de l'hôte de l'Élysée l'élu direct de tous les citoyens?

de [son] côté *

In this structure, *son* is variable. In theory, any other possessive adjective, *mon*, *ton*, *votre*, etc., could replace it. In practice, given the frequency of third-person statements in discursive prose, its most frequent variant is *leur*.

Whether placed first in the sentence or with the verb, the structure can function either as a contrastive or comparative connector or as a simple distributor of emphasis. Commonly used to introduce the second element in a pair of observations, it could often be replaced by *quant à [lui]*, the **pronom tonique disjoint** or **pour [sa] part**. English writers in the eighteenth century, and some who affected archaism in later periods, used 'on his side' in the same way:

> I had been too much perturbed to question him on the many points relating to the strange events as to which I was still completely in the dark, and he on his side had shown no desire to afford me any further information.
>
> (Falkner, 521)

The adversative link

The link made between the two elements is sometimes clearly adversative, as in this contrast between the two parts of France during the first phase of German occupation (1940–1942):

> Les habitants de Clermont-Ferrand et de Nice accusaient les Parisiens de pactiser avec l'ennemi ; les Parisiens, de leur côté, reprochaient aux Français de zone libre d'être des « mous » et d'étaler insolemment leur satisfaction égoïste de n'être pas « occupés ».

A contrast so marked could have been structured by **par contre** or **au contraire**. Sometimes a writer will stress oppositiveness by introducing the first element with the **si d'opposition**, as in this sentence from an article discussing differences of opinion between Greece and its partners in the European Union over the recognition of the former Yugoslav Republic of Macedonia as a sovereign state called Macedonia:

> Si l'Union européenne doute de la fiabilité hellénique, les Grecs, de leur côté, n'ont pas apprécié que leurs partenaires établissent des relations diplomatiques avec Skopje alors que la querelle du nom n'est toujours pas réglée.

The connector can signal also reciprocity, as in the next example, dealing with trade exchanges between the former USSR and Germany, where the writer could have used **alors que**, **en revanche** or **en retour**.

> Les Soviétiques ont établi à la mi-décembre un programme d'achat en Allemagne se montant à un milliard et demi de marks. De leur côté, les Allemands obtiennent de l'URSS de nombreuses et importantes matières

premières stratégiques, tournant ainsi le blocus naval instauré par la France et l'Angleterre.

In contemporary English, such a statement could be made with 'As for', 'As far as the Germans are concerned' or 'For their part'.

The implicit comparison

However, often the two factors stand beside one another in little more than an implicit or inert comparison. An article on freedom of the press opens like this:

> Le quotidien *le Monde* vient d'être condamné pour « apologie de crimes de collaboration avec l'ennemi » (nouvelle parue dans *le Monde* du 14 décembre 1993). Le quotidien *le Figaro*, de son côté, vient d'être condamné pour imputations diffamatoires « à l'égard d'un groupe en raison de son appartenance à une religion » (nouvelle parue dans *le Monde* du 15 décembre 1993).

As that example shows, this connector can signal mere concomitance between two points.

Distributor of emphasis

This structure is often used in narrative news items for no other reason than to show a change in the identity of the person or thing now being spoken of. This example describes the arrest of four men on charges of supplying drugs to prisoners:

> Lucien Ferrando, quarante-cinq ans, surveillant à la maison d'arrêt de Fleury-Mérogis et délégué régional du syndicat pénitentiaire FO, a été interpellé, mercredi 30 septembre, à Évry (Essonne), en compagnie de son fils, Stéphane. Considérés comme commanditaires du trafic, Jean Santoni, quarante-cinq ans, et Paul Tramoni, quarante-trois ans, ont, de leur côté, été arrêtés, jeudi 31 août, à Paris.

There, the connector does no more than mark the different times and places of the arrests. In English its function might be served by 'also' or 'however'; or more likely it would be omitted.

de sorte que *

This is one of those adverbial conjunctions ending in *que* which were traditionally placed inside sentences, but which are increasingly used at the beginning of a *phrase dépendante*. It is often replaceable by *si bien que* or *ainsi*: it looks as though it should describe the manner of a preceding action, but it really sets forth a consequence of what precedes. Among English equivalents of it are 'and so' and 'with the result that'.

Two modes

The structure exists in two modes which are interchangeable as connectors: *de sorte que*, the more frequently used, and *en sorte que*. Either of them could be replaced by *ce qui fait que*. In tone, the form with *en* is old-fashioned, literary and rarely to be found in the prose of journalists. Some of them, however, use both modes (Boucher, 84, 463). As part of the verb *faire en sorte que*, it also has a non-connective function which does not concern us. The first of these examples comes from an article commenting on what its author calls *l'une des plus célèbres aberrations de l'histoire littéraire contemporaine*, Sartre's preface to the *Œuvres complètes* of Jean Genet:

> Le commentaire sartrien occupe tout le premier volume de la série (qui est, de loin, le plus important). En sorte que si un lecteur non prévenu demande dans une librairie le premier tome des œuvres de Genet, il ressort avec un livre de Sartre.

The second example shows the relation that this connector can make between a preceding premiss, in this case a principle of speech and reasoning, and a consequence that follows from it:

> Tout ce qui est dit peut être contredit. De sorte qu'on ne saurait annoncer une opinion ou un désir, sans les désigner du même coup aux objections éventuelles des interlocuteurs.
>
> (Ducrot, 1972: 6)

As can be seen, the structure could also be replaced by one or other of the modes of **par conséquent** or by **c'est pourquoi**.

de telle sorte que

The mode with *de* quite often lends itself to a third variant: *de telle sorte que*. It functions like the other two modes. In the following example, dating from the 1960s, the subject is the moustache of Jean Ferniot, the gastronomic writer, whom the author, James de Coquet, dubs *cosmonaute de la gastronomie*:

> Sa séduisante moustache de magyar est en train d'éclipser celle de Brassens pour la bonne raison qu'on la voit tous les jours dans un journal du soir et qu'on l'entend – si j'ose ainsi parler – tous les matins à R.T.L. De telle sorte que, s'il s'assoit incognito à la table d'un restaurant, il est percé à jour comme l'était le futur Édouard VII lorsqu'il croyait s'affranchir du protocole en se faisant appeler le comte de Sandringham.

All three of these modes can be found in the work of a single writer (Launay, 100, 158).

de surcroît *

This structure is made from a noun, *le surcroît*, meaning roughly 'increase' or 'addition'. Related expressions are *pour surcroît* and *par surcroît*. Both of these have at different times done service as connectors, the former in the eighteenth century (see Rousseau, 108 & 353), the latter more recently.

Often replaceable by **en outre** and **de plus**, this connector usually introduces a second point going in the same direction as a first and reinforcing it. It can also introduce a later point in a series of three or more. The most common English equivalent is probably 'also'; others are 'in addition', 'furthermore' or 'as well'. A biographer, seeing two difficulties in trying to describe the character of Pierre Laval, the collaborationist Prime Minister of Marshal Pétain executed at the Liberation, uses this connector to link the second of them to the first:

> Faire son portrait n'est pas facile : il donnait l'impression d'un assemblage de personnages divers, ambigus. De surcroît, sa famille et ses proches se sont beaucoup dépensés pour contrer sa légende noire par une autre image, celle d'un enfant du peuple qui aurait conquis sa place par un travail acharné.

Points related by this connector are usually in consecutive sentences. However, it can link arguments over much longer distances of text. Here are two points separated by four paragraphs of discussion of the first one: *La position de la France est juste sur le plan économique. [...] De surcroît, et en dépit des apparences, la position de la France est juste sur le plan européen.*

When placed first in the sentence or paragraph it is always followed by a comma. In other positions, it is usually between commas: *Herriot, homme de poids, président de la Chambre des députés, et, de surcroît, historien de métier.*

As the last example suggests, some writers use this connector rather like *d'ailleurs*, that is to append a point that is less important than the preceding one, as in this excerpt from an article on French ignorance of Nazi Germany in the 1930s:

> Que savaient les Français de la place que pouvait bien réserver Hitler à la France vaincue ? Pas grand-chose, car ils l'avaient peu lu, comme tout ce qui venait de l'étranger, et n'avaient pu imaginer pareille issue à un conflit que, de surcroît, ils avaient cherché à éviter.

par surcroît

The mode with *par* was unknown to Littré. It may have been in the late nineteenth century that it evolved into a connective function. It was certainly much used then and by the first generation of twentieth-century writers. Now rare, especially among journalists, it probably has a more literary tone than the mode with *de*. It functions in ways broadly similar to the latter, with a meaning akin to 'into the bargain', though it may well be used more often to stress advantageous rather than negative or neutral points. The first of the following examples, adding a further point to a series of preceding points, comes from a discussion of the advantages that the French system of criminal justice has always seen in gaining a confession from the accused:

> L'idéal est, bien sûr, l'aveu. L'aveu, preuve suprême, dispense des autres. Il est économie de moyens, de temps. L'aveu assure au juge, comme au policier, la tranquillité d'âme : il efface la peur de se tromper. Par surcroît, il ouvre la voie à la réparation, à la rédemption. Il réconcilie la justice, le juge et l'accusé repentant.

The second example is a comment on the success of the unprecedented advertising campaign with which Bernard Grasset launched Radiguet's *Le diable au corps* in 1923:

> Faire une telle publicité pour un livre bref, de lecture excessivement aisée, et qui par surcroît choquait, c'était jouer sur du velours.

Used with other connectors

The mode with *par* is sometimes used in tandem with **avec**, flanked by commas, like *en prime* or **en plus**, as in this review of a recital by a choir:

> Le chœur de la Chapelle royale est à présent d'une qualité exceptionnelle : la beauté de la sonorité, la justesse extrême des intervalles, la souplesse sont celles que l'on a coutume d'admirer lorsqu'on entend de très grands orchestres... Avec, par surcroît, l'émotion des chanteurs eux-mêmes.

It also sees service as a replacement for the second half of the double structure *non seulement... mais aussi*, as in this statement about the catfish: *Non seulement il est laid, mais, par surcroît, il est dangereux* (Roule, 95).

de toute façon *

This connector is something of a variant for **de toute manière**. The point introduced by it is always presented as a fact or a certainty. The connector does this in one of two ways: either it follows a statement or a development implying something less than a certainty; or at a more intuitive level it dismisses what precedes as idle and implies that what follows, frequently a statement of more general scope, is more important, possibly only to be expected. In either case, what it introduces or accompanies is presented as more noteworthy and conclusive than what precedes. As often as not, it stands first in the sentence; and in that position it is usually followed by a comma. The spelling *de toutes façons* is favoured by a minority of writers. A longer version, *de toutes les façons*, is used by an even smaller minority.

The first of the two modes

This mode, the more common, suggests that what precedes may well be problematical or even invalid. It says 'at all events', 'anyhow' or 'anyway' in the sense of 'whatever the case may be on that, what follows is undeniable'. Robert defines it as *quoi qu'il en soit, quoi qu'il arrive* and gives references to **en tout état de cause** and *immanquablement*. Littré's definition includes *en dépit de tout*. The certainty introduced may follow a speculation, a hypothesis, a statement of theoretical desirability or future possibility: expressions typically found in the sentence preceding are *Je crois...*; *Si...*; *Tout se passe comme si...*; *Autre rumeur...*; *Selon les uns...*, *selon les autres...*; *Peut-être...*. The connector may follow a statement entertaining two competing possibilities: does a certain female character in Maupassant's novel *Notre Cœur* live in the rue du Général Foy or in the rue Lamennais?

> Ce sont deux rues du VIIIe arrondissement, peu distantes l'une de l'autre ; mais il ne convient pas de vérifier ces détails, car tout se passe, de toute façon, dans ces riches quartiers neufs que venait de créer le baron Haussmann.

Quite often what precedes is in the form of a question; and the connector could be replaced by **en tout cas**, as in this facetious comment on the difficulty of discovering the history of the condom:

> L'origine des préservatifs se perd-elle dans la nuit des temps ? Leur usage est volontiers nocturne, de toute façon.

Also like *en tout cas*, the connector can be placed last in the sentence, as that example shows.

The second mode

This mode also introduces a point seen as conclusive. But the conclusiveness now strengthens a first point which is not presented as overtly uncertain in any of the above ways. It says something like 'But then', as in this comment on a film:

> C'est très beau, presque pas ennuyeux, mais aussi guère original. De toutes façons, qu'est-ce qui est original de nos jours, au cinéma ?

In each of the two following examples, too, it is clear that the connector introduces a secondary argument reinforcing the gist of a preceding statement. The first one comes from a discussion of the procedures of the

Académie des sciences, in particular differences between it and the Académie française, many of whose members, unlike the *scientifiques*, enjoy dressing up and having a fancy sword:

> À la Française, tout le monde arbore une rapière, et les plus vernis, ceux qui ont beaucoup d'amis, l'ont bien longue, en cristal de roche ou incrustée de diamants. Les scientifiques, moins entourés de beau linge, la portent modeste ou pas du tout.
> De toute façon, les occasions de parader se font rares [...]

There the connector implies that, even if the scientists' rapiers were as impressive, they would still be useless, given the lack of opportunities of showing off. In this function, the sequence *De toute façon cela n'a aucune importance* is sometimes used (Sédouy & Bouteiller, 39). The second example is part of a discussion of the activities of certain illegal immigrants, some of whom are working as wood-cutters:

> Dans les sombres futaies qui entourent Bourganeuf, le travail clandestin fait rage. C'est même la principale activité dans un canton qui affiche 23 % de chômeurs. De toute façon, chacun vous le dira, le contrôle des chantiers en forêt est une opération hasardeuse, auprès de laquelle la quête du Graal fait figure d'aimable partie de campagne.

There, the connector links only partly to the sentence preceding it: the main link is, via that sentence, to the mention of *travail clandestin* in the one before it. This mention is followed by two sentences that adduce explanations of why so many illegal immigrants work in the district: unemployment is rife; and, in any case, even if it wasn't rife, it is very easy not to get caught. In contexts like these, the connector functions much after the manner of **aussi bien** or **d'ailleurs**. It may well be that this second mode is more often placed first in the sentence.

de toute manière *

This connector is a twin of **de toute façon**. Despite his comment on the difficulty of distinguishing *façon* from *manière* in certain contexts, Littré makes no mention of this structure, although it was in use before his time, albeit possibly in a different sense (Rousseau, 93). Robert pays little attention to it: no examples, no mention of plural forms and a definition saying only that it is equivalent to **en tout cas** and *quoi qu'il arrive*. In contemporary written French, it may be less used than *de toute façon*. The shades of expressiveness separating the two are akin to those one finds in English 'anyhow' and 'anyway': some speakers will use the two structures interchangeably; some will use one but not the other.

Three variants and two modes

Also like *de toute façon*, this connector exists in three variants which all function in the same ways as one another: as well as the singular form, there are two in the plural, *de toutes manières* and *de toutes les manières*. Some writers use more than one of them.

As for its two modes, the structure introduces a certainty, in one or other of two different ways: either it follows a statement or a development implying something less than a certainty, such as a question or a hypothesis; or, after a statement which is in no way uncertain, it implies that the certainty which follows, frequently a statement of more general scope, is more important than what precedes. With either mode, what it introduces or accompanies is presented as more conclusive than what precedes.

The first mode

With this mode, typical sequences are: *Il est certain de toute manière que...*; *De toute manière, il est entendu que...*; *De toute manière, il est manifeste que...*; *De toute manière, il n'est pas question que...*. English equivalents might be 'at all events', 'anyhow' or 'anyway' in the sense of 'whatever the case may be on that, what follows is undeniable'. It could usually be replaced by *quoi qu'il en soit* or *quoi qu'il arrive*. Thus, a writer speculating on the origin of the world-wide movement of unrest among students in the 1960s, locates it in the USA:

> Qu'il se soit répandu par contagion ou ait éclaté simultanément en divers foyers, de toute manière, c'est aux États-Unis qu'a été conçu et mis au point le *dissent* (mot que nous traduisons par « contestation »).

There, the author entertains first two hypotheses about how the movement may have originated; then, without pronouncing on the validity of either, he concludes, with the connector, to the substantive point about the place of origin. Similarly, a writer on the family wonders about an explanation of transformations in marital behaviour during the later 1960s:

> Sommes-nous, comme l'écrit Valéry, « vers le commencement de la fin d'un système social », dans ce « moment délicieux » où l'ordre d'hier rend possible les « premiers relâchements de ce système » ? C'est une hypothèse vraisemblable. De toutes manières, deux traits caractérisent la situation présente : nous sommes intellectuellement dans l'incertitude et, historiquement, à un moment où les jeux ne sont pas encore faits.
>
> (Roussel, 278)

There, although the writer appears to favour the hypothesis he has just entertained, his connector means 'whether one agrees with this or not, the fact remains that ...'

The second mode

The second mode is seen in the following extract from an interview: the speaker was asked his opinion of the practice among Parisian writers who also review books of using their newspaper column to puff the productions of their own publisher. First he deplores it; then with this connector he passes to a more important, farther-reaching statement:

> Il est choquant de parler des livres édités par sa maison d'édition. Moi-même, lorsque je suis entré chez Grasset, j'avais posé mes conditions qui étaient de ne pas parler de livres édités par Grasset. Par exemple, je n'ai pas écrit un seul article sur Bernard-Henri Lévy que j'aime pourtant beaucoup, et ce, depuis que je suis chez Grasset. De toutes les manières, je plains le critique qui parle des livres que publie la maison d'édition pour laquelle il travaille. Les attachés de presse et les auteurs eux-mêmes risquent alors de faire le siège de son bureau pour obtenir un article.

Even though what precedes the connector is in no way hypothetical or problematical, it is clear that its function is to introduce a point sensed to be more valid than anything just said. If the connector were to be replaced by *au reste* or *aussi bien*, the link of thought would probably be very similar.

deux-points *

Though only a punctuation mark, like the *points de suspension* the colon can relate sub-assemblies of sentences to each other. Some say *le deux-points*, some *les deux points*; on whether the term is singular or plural, the new Robert has no view. The new Grevisse gives also *le double point* (Grevisse, 1988, 177).

I discuss not the full range of its uses (see Drillon, 387–403), but only some which have a connective function. Like other French connectors, it tends to be more specific in its use than its English counterpart. The English use of a colon as a semicolon is not usual in French. This connector has, almost invariably, the special function which the semicolon does not have: 'that of delivering the goods that have been invoiced in the preceding words' (Fowler, 1965: 589). That is, in discursive prose, it usually presents what follows as an explanation of what precedes. This it does in two basic ways: by introducing either a complete statement or an alternative complement of a preceding verb. It can replace (or even accompany) *à savoir (que)*. At other times, it stands for *c'est-à-dire (que)*.

Before a complete statement

When introducing a complete statement, it is usual that the colon also follows one: *Une seule chose est sûre : Cuba est sur le qui-vive.* / *Leur constat est unanime : les certitudes sont rares.* / *On sait la suite : Franco envoie des renforts, fait régner la terreur et bombarde Guernica.* Grammatically, each of the paired statements could stand as separate sentences. Semantically, the colon makes them dependent on each other: it announces the second as justification or amplification of the first, as in this extract from a discussion of Peru's socio-economic ills:

> Le Pérou sombre insensiblement dans le quart-monde : le pouvoir d'achat des salaires a diminué de plus de moitié et les Nations unies estiment que si un tiers de la population se trouve déjà dans une situation de pauvreté critique, le dixième vit dans un état total d'indigence.

In such sentences, what precedes is the writer's judgment or conclusion; what follows gives the facts justifying the conclusion. A similar link can be made with *de fait* and *en effet*.

Sometimes the complete statement following the colon is of the order of a definition. Thus a discussion of religions and the European philosophical attitude to freedom of conscience states: *Cette philosophie a un nom, et déjà une tradition respectable : c'est le laïcisme.* An article on an Arab dictator, speaking of his dealings with other states, says: *Son principal atout pour parvenir à ses fins a un nom : c'est le terrorisme d'État.*

Quite often the complete statement preceding announces a question, which will be asked in the statement following:

> Partout la même question se pose : l'Occident évitera-t-il la répétition d'un choc pétrolier équivalent à ceux de 1973 et 1979 ?

At times what precedes the colon is a noun (or a short list of nouns) in apposition to the complete statement following. This noun can be accompanied by its article, as in *La suite* and *La cause.* Alternatively, it may have no article, as is often the case with *Conclusion* and, after a question, with *Réponse*; or when a consequence is introduced by *Résultat* or *Conséquence*, variants of *par conséquent.* At other times, what follows this noun in apposition is more clearly a justification of it:

> « Ultimatum », « guérilla » : le vocabulaire agricole a pris ces derniers jours un ton inhabituel et belliqueux qui traduit la vive inquiétude du monde paysan face à l'effet conjugué de la sécheresse et de la chute des cours de la viande, ovine et bovine.

This mode is sometimes used to structure *antithèses sans charnière*: *Nous avons perdu le paradis : gardons au moins l'enfer.* / *On ne naît pas femme : on le devient.*

Followed by a complement

In this second mode, the complement often takes the form of a noun-structure amplifying a noun which immediately precedes the colon. The following structure can be made of a single noun, as in this extract from an article about Romania and Bulgaria:

> Depuis dimanche 26 août, ces deux pays des Balkans ont un point commun supplémentaire : la violence politique, à laquelle les Bulgares, faisant montre d'une tolérance et d'un sang-froid exemplaires, avaient su échapper jusqu'ici.

It can be a pair of nouns, with or without articles: *L'économie française devra, dans la gestion de la crise, éviter deux écueils : l'inflation et la stagnation.* Or it can be a list of nouns, as in this ironic description of the Parti socialiste shortly before it was swept away by the general election of 1993:

> Depuis quelques mois, l'état de l'animal avait empiré sous l'effet de plusieurs maladies incurables : aboulie présidentielle ; lutte au couteau entre les prétendants au trône ; banalisation des scandales.

The list of complementary nouns in apposition can precede the colon rather than follow it, as in this example about the alleged responsibility of a Latin American President for corruption among his country's officials:

> Pots-de-vin touchés par de hautes personnalités, civiles et militaires, compromission de certains « hommes du président » dans des affaires louches : M. Carlos Andres Perez est largement responsable du malaise actuel.

Some writers use a comma instead of the colon (Colignon, 29; Drillon, 250). This can make for ambiguity, as can be seen in the comma following *pendantes* in the following example:

> La France était entrée en campagne à propos de l'Europe ; tous ses leaders politiques, ou presque, semblaient d'accord pour évacuer les questions pendantes, le septennat vieillissant, la crise de la représentation politique, le non-renouvellement des dirigeants, et tant d'aspirations ignorées.

As the comma replaces a colon, the nouns in apposition *septennat, crise* and *non-renouvellement* are examples of *les questions pendantes*. But the uncertainty created by the comma is such that they too could be read, like *questions*, as direct objects of *évacuer* – as could of course *tant d'aspirations ignorées* (but perhaps not). The use of a colon after *pendantes* would have avoided these unclarities.

Sometimes what precedes the colon is amplified not by a noun-structure but by a verb or verbs, as in this extract from an article about American military intervention in Haiti:

> Washington a clairement laissé entendre que les 225 « marines » qui, pour des raisons évidentes de sécurité, ont été placés « en situation de combat » n'avaient

qu'une seule mission : évacuer les ressortissants américains et protéger les installations sous bannière étoilée.

And of course other structures are possible, as in this extract from a discussion of how history is presented in certain schoolbooks: *L'histoire de la France s'y scinde en deux périodes : avant et après 1789.*

Sometimes the colon can be used to avoid a structure with *avec* and a past participle.

French printing practice is noteworthy: the colon is not only followed by a space as in English, it is also preceded by one, as is the case with certain other stops, including the semicolon.

donc *

This connector, which usually introduces a conclusion or a consequence of what precedes, is probably adequately dealt with by the dictionaries. In Le Bidois there is an enlightening discussion of its main functions, especially as they relate to *par conséquent* (Le Bidois, II, 245–246). Of its five modes (Zenone, 114) only one or two concern us.

Place in the sentence

Some native speakers of English tend to place this connector first in the sentence, possibly influenced by English 'so', which often occupies that position. However, *donc* is very often placed not first in the sentence but after the initial element: *Si donc l'on veut...*; *Le problème donc, c'est que...*; *Inutile donc de jouer les naïfs.* This initial element is very often a verb: *Le « oui » a donc gagné, mais pour autant la bataille de Maastricht ne fait que commencer. / En France, la littérature et le vin ont toujours fait bon ménage. On ne s'étonnera donc pas que plus d'un jury ait considéré qu'offrir un bon cru était encore la meilleure façon d'honorer un bon manuscrit.*

Not that it is never found at the beginning of statements. In the most celebrated example of its use as a marker of logical consequence, it stands first in the proposition: *Je pense, donc je suis.* It can of course also stand first in the sentence or the paragraph. A writer advocating a redesign of the constitution of the Fifth Republic says:

Qu'on me désigne un seul organe de la République, exécutif, législatif, judiciaire, une seule administration de l'État, un seul relais démocratique – parti, syndicat – qui remplisse à peu près convenablement sa mission. Donc il nous faut forger d'urgence de nouvelles institutions.

Similarly, a polemicist argues, early in 1993, that François Mitterrand should not remain President of the Republic after the foreseeable defeat of the Parti socialiste at the forthcoming elections, because he would be too old, too ill, too out of touch with contemporary France, which must

> relever les défis de la jeunesse en exorcisant les démons de la sénescence.
> Donc une remise à plat s'impose. Un redémarrage. Une nouvelle donne.
> Rapidement !

This conclusive mode is also used in combination with the consequential mode of **ainsi**, as in this extract from a discussion of Proust's concept of *la durée*:

> L'intensité de la durée présente compense le relâchement du passé de telle sorte que le Temps perdu est *retrouvé*, qu'il est même soustrait au flux du devenir et fixé par l'art dans une espèce d'éternité.
> Ainsi donc la durée se définit par la dilatation ou la contraction du temps extérieur dans le temps interne, c'est-à-dire, très simplement en somme dans l'âme des personnages.

> (Cormeau, 110)

Recapitulative

This mode means roughly 'as already mentioned' or 'as I was saying'. In the following list of singers' names, taken from a review of an anthology of French songs: *dont les interprètes sont Pierre Perret, donc, Michèle Bernard, Francis Lemarque, Robert Amyot, Marc Ogeret, Anne Sylvestre*, it reminds the reader that Pierre Perret was mentioned in that capacity in the preceding paragraph. It can recall by repetition the subject of the sentence, as in this extract from an essay on the prehistory of collection-making, which sees in the origins of this activity an attempt to link the visible world to an invisible world:

> Les collections, celles, du moins, que nous avons passées en revue, car l'interprétation de celles qui se forment dans les sociétés modernes de l'Occident reste à faire, les collections, donc, ne constituent qu'une composante de cet éventail des moyens mis en œuvre pour assurer la communication entre les deux mondes, l'unité de l'univers.

> (Pomian, 36)

A variation of this mode is heard in conversation: a speaker who has been interrupted may take up again a broken tale with initial *Donc*. Thus Swann, having begun a comment to *grand-père* on Saint-Simon's anecdote about Maulévrier and been diverted by the wittering of the maiden aunts, reverts to his subject a page later: « *Donc Saint-Simon raconte que Maulévrier avait eu l'audace de tendre la main à ses fils.* » (Proust, I, 25, 26).

d'où *

This connector, nearly always placed first in the sentence, and even in the paragraph, introduces a conclusion to be drawn from what precedes or a consequence of it.

Followed by a noun

The connector is close in function to English 'hence'. But it differs from 'hence' in that the latter is often followed by a verb; whereas *d'où*, when it functions as a connector, is usually followed by a verbless noun:

> Il est inconvenant, jusqu'à la fin du XIXe siècle, de sortir au restaurant en compagnie de son épouse... D'où le succès des salons particuliers.

> La France est une république où les titres sont interdits, mais pourtant ils sont encore utilisés. Par contre, en Allemagne, en Hollande ou dans les pays scandinaves, les titres sont autorisés mais personne n'a l'idée de les mentionner. D'où l'étonnement des étrangers.
>
> (Frischer, 45–46)

In English, these sentences might well begin with 'And so,' 'As a result' or 'Therefore' and contain a verb structure. This would not be the case with series of sentences in which the connector is repeated. These are quite common, either as a pair introduced by *D'où* and *D'où aussi* or in longer sequences, as in this criticism of certain provisions of the constitution of the Fifth Republic:

> Si nous vivons dans une sorte de monarchie républicaine, c'est parce que le grand problème en 1958 était d'en finir avec les excès parlementaristes de la IVe. D'où le mandat de sept ans renouvelable. D'où l'existence d'un Premier ministre tampon. D'où le droit de dissolution. D'où le 49-3.

At times the connector is placed not at the beginning of sentences but after a comma, as in this extract from a discussion of French farmers' ignorance of the real reasons for their financial losses: *Ils n'en savent rien, d'où leur colère.*

Followed by a verb

Not that this connector is never followed by a verb. Indeed, it can be seen as an abridged form of structures like *D'où résulte* and *D'où découle*, which are less used than the mode followed by a noun. This example is from a historical comment by a jaded observer on French politicians of the 1950s, overshadowed by events:

> Le grand homme est rabaissé, le médiocre est relevé, parce que, en dernière analyse, les mouvements lourds de l'histoire (la décolonisation en était un) se

jouent de la volonté de ceux qui sont censés conduire les peuples. D'où résulte le côté dérisoire de la politique politicienne, théâtre d'ombres, désopilante opérette [...]

There is also a set of impersonal verb-structures such as *d'où il suit que, d'où il résulte que, d'où il arrive que* or *d'où il ressort que*:

Le trait distinctif original de l'intellectuel n'est pas de penser mais de communiquer sa pensée. D'où il découle qu'Anthony Blunt n'est pas un intellectuel, mais simplement un grand historien de l'art et, très secondairement, un petit espion.

These structures with verb are usually in the present tense, but not always: *D'où il suivrait que....* Most of them can also be used without *il: D'où suit que....* To this set of impersonal conclusives can be added a set with personal subjects: *D'où je comprends que, D'où je conclus que* and *D'où l'on voit que* (as well as *Par où l'on voit que*).

Another mode of *d'où* followed by a verb is one which functions not as a connector, but as a plain preposition. It is not usually to be found at the beginning of a sentence. The verb is usually one of motion, such as *aller, émaner, émerger, procéder, venir, sortir*:

L'air de *Frou-frou*, composé dès 1889 par Henri Chatau pour un caf'-conc' parisien, avait été chanté à Vienne, d'où il revint revigoré.

Interrogative *d'où*

This is the *d'où* that is most commonly followed by a verb and is also placed first in the sentence: *D'où tenez-vous ce secret ? / D'où vient qu'ils puent donc tant ? / D'où vient l'argent pour financer ces coûteuses initiatives ?* It is no doubt the potential for ambiguity that makes *D'où vient que* rare as an initial non-interrogative connector. Despite which, Alain often used it. He could also write the following elliptical form of it, which shows the kinship between this structure and **de ce fait**. The writer's subject is how the brains of statesmen were addled in August 1914 by the trend of events towards war:

Les maux de l'an quatorze vinrent, à ce que je crois, de ce que les hommes importants furent tous surpris ; d'où ils eurent peur.

(Alain, 1956: *passim* & 449)

A structure that is almost identical to *d'où* in its connective function is **de là**.

du coup *

Although this structure, with its companion ***du même coup***, seems to have evolved in the later part of the nineteenth century, lexicographers have paid little attention to it. Dictionaries vary in their definitions: some separate it from *du même coup*, some treat the two expressions as one. Grevisse did not notice it until 1959: he speaks of the

> locution néologique *du coup* qui sert à annoncer un effet brusque et spontané, se produisant pour ainsi dire au même moment que l'action qui l'a causé ; le sens est voisin de celui de *du même coup* [...]

The latest edition rewords but does not much modify this outmoded view of the function as essentially dramatic and narrative: Du coup *exprime l'idée d'une cause agissant brusquement; il est proche d'*aussitôt (Grevisse, 1959: 808–809; 1988: 1473). Most of Grevisse's examples are unrepresentative of contemporary usage. Very common among writers of discursive prose nowadays, the structure is used as a substitute for ***par conséquent*** or *en conséquence*. Journalists favour it; so do historians (Braudel, 116; Le Roy Ladurie, 31, 62)

du coup and *du même coup*

The connector is most often placed first in the sentence or paragraph and followed by a comma. There does seem at times to be no great difference in function between it and *du même coup*. Literally, the latter should link simultaneous factors and the former successive ones. In practice, both structures link an effect to a cause and designate pairs of factors which it can be difficult to define as either simultaneous or successive. However, in many contemporary contexts ***ce faisant*** could replace *du même coup*; and ***de ce fait*** could often replace *du coup*.

Contemporary usage

The connector often introduces something seen as the immediate, automatic or inevitable result of what precedes. But just as often what follows is a mere consequence. When placed first in the sentence, a position which may stress more the consecutive nature of the factors it links, it usually has the sense of 'as a result', 'hence' or 'because of this', as in this comparison between different sorts of windows used in European countries:

> Alors que les Espagnols, Français et Italiens se protègent tant de la chaleur que des cambrioleurs derrière des volets, on ne connaît cet accessoire ni en Grande-Bretagne ni aux Pays-Bas ! Du coup, les fenêtres anglo-saxonnes sont nettement plus résistantes.

It is evident there is nothing of Grevisse's *cause agissant brusquement* or *aussitôt* in that. The same goes for this example, which speaks of the consequences of French eating habits:

> L'alimentation du Français moyen se compose de 4 % de légumes, 5,5 % de racines et tubercules, 8 % de graisses animales, 9 % de laitages, 9 % de graisses végétales, 11 % d'alcool, 12,5 % de sucre, 19 % de viande. L'horreur absolue. Bonjour, cholestérol ! Le parfait exemple de ce qu'il ne faut pas faire.
>
> Du coup, on a les maladies qu'on mérite. En 1983, sur 539 702 décès, on en compte 201 155 pour troubles cardiaques. Et 13 962 pour diabète sucré.

The lack of any immediacy in the consequence is seen too when the structure is combined with an expression like *tôt ou tard* in which there is nothing sudden, as in this extract from an essay on the unintended consequences likely to flow from a reduction of the term of office of the President of the Republic from seven years to five:

> En réalité, le quinquennat bouleverserait tout l'édifice. Élu pour une durée plus raisonnable, le président voudra gouverner directement le pays. Du coup, le poste de Premier ministre disparaîtra tôt ou tard pour cause de double emploi.

A similarity to **dès lors** is apparent. It may be only a vestigial narrative function in *du coup* which makes for a slight difference.

When the structure is not placed first in the sentence, it is usually between commas. Or it may be preceded by **et** or by **mais**, as in this example which speaks of an autobiography in which no proper names, whether of people or places, are given:

> On ne peut pas dire où cela s'est passé. Mais du coup on voit bien que cela pourrait se passer n'importe où.

du même coup *

This connector has points in common with **du coup**: the two structures may have a common origin; and the makers of some French dictionaries do not clearly distinguish between them. In practice, both structures are used to designate pairs of events or actions which are related as cause and effect but which it can be difficult to define as either concomitant or successive. The following comment on the relation between brevity of marriage and remarriage would be scarcely different if it contained *du coup*:

> ...le raccourcissement de la durée du mariage avant divorce constitue un facteur favorable à une augmentation de la fréquence des remariages, puisque la probabilité de ceux-ci diminue avec l'âge. Mais du même coup, le nombre des deuxièmes divorces risque, lui aussi, d'augmenter.
>
> (Roussel, 252)

However, there are differences. The consequence designated by *du coup* seems often more overt, important and direct; that designated by *du même coup* feels at times more implicit, more like a secondary or unintended side-effect of the first cause. If *du coup* is often replaceable by **de ce fait**, then *du même coup* is in many contexts replaceable by **ce faisant**. More often than not, too, this connector is placed not first in the sentence but with the verb. And a combination with *et* is not infrequent. In these features can be seen something of the concomitance of the factors linked: it is often placed with the second of two verbs which have the same subject, as is seen sometimes in sequences such as *non seulement... mais aussi*. In this example, a writer comments on Sartre's enunciation of a principle of fiction:

> En faisant à Mauriac la querelle que l'on sait (lui reprochant d'imposer à ses personnages une substance postiche et de les transformer ainsi en choses), Sartre n'a pas seulement affirmé une certaine conception – nouvelle somme toute, – du roman, mais il a aussi défini du même coup sa position en tant que critique.
>
> (Poulet, 1971: 264)

And a similar sequence can be seen when the connector accompanies the second part of two-part sentences structured with a mode of **c'est dire**:

> Dire que les langues naturelles sont des codes, destinés à la transmission de l'information d'un individu à un autre, c'est admettre du même coup que tous les contenus exprimés grâce à elles sont exprimés de façon *explicite*.
>
> (Ducrot, 5)

With similar effect it can accompany the second of two complements:

> Altérer le sens d'un mot, c'est en altérer la valeur représentative, et, du même coup, l'idée même qu'il est destiné à exprimer.
>
> (Vincent, xxix)

When the structure is placed first in the sentence, followed by a comma, it can indicate that the subject of the next verb will be different from that of the one before. However, this is not necessarily the case, as in this example which speaks of humans' exploitation of certain plants:

> L'homme, en les adoptant dans sa clientèle, leur a rendu ce service, il les a déliées. Du même coup, il a frayé la route à un cortège de végétaux ou d'animaux non conviés.
>
> (Vidal de la Blache, 14)

English equivalents, depending on context and taste, might be 'at one fell swoop', 'at one and the same time', 'thereby' or 'by the same token'.

The adverbial structure *dans la foulée* is often used by journalists as an approximate replacement for *ce faisant* or *du même coup*.

du moins *

This structure usually introduces something seen as surer than what precedes: like a mode of *en tout cas*, it restricts or attenuates a statement while precising it. What precedes is often hypothetical, interrogative or of dubious certainty. This way of making in the second place a more limited but more valid point than was made in the first place is common in speech: *Il est resté à la maison hier soir. Du moins, c'est ce qu'il m'a dit.* In the following example of this mode, taken from an article on the death of a boy who belonged to a gang, the fact that the statement is hearsay is made plain by the tense of the verb in the second sentence:

> Omar était un « Mendy ». Il aurait été tué par des « Black unis ». C'est du moins l'une des versions qui circulent dans le Paris des bandes à propos de cette bagarre.

In such statements, rectifying what is only a possibility, *en tout cas* could be used: *Officiellement, Michel Simon n'est plus communiste. En tout cas, il n'en fait jamais état.*

With inversion of subject and verb

When placed first in the sentence, the connector is usually followed by an inversion of subject and verb. Thus, a discussion of the hypothesis that other nations may join the EC makes the point that they may have to amend some of their fundamental national policies:

> L'Autriche, la Suède et la Finlande, si elles veulent entrer dans la Communauté, devront en principe renoncer à leur neutralité et adhérer à l'objectif de la politique de défense commune. Du moins est-ce la position de principe réitérée par les Douze.

A prehistorian, discussing cave-paintings which obliterate hand stencils dating from an earlier era speculates about what meaning this may have had for the painters:

> Comme si les auteurs des peintures, venant 7 000 ou 9 000 ans après ceux des mains négatives, avaient voulu neutraliser ces anciens signes. Du moins est-ce là une hypothèse vraisemblable, qui ne pourra, bien sûr, jamais être vérifiée.

With *sinon*

A very common use of the structure is in tandem with *sinon*: the latter states a possibility before *du moins* clarifies it, as in this comment on neglected artists:

Du début du dix-neuvième siècle, on avait, sinon oublié, du moins négligé, les œuvres et les artistes qui ne se fondent pas dans les catégories ordinairement en usage, néo-classicisme et romantisme.

A similar combination can be made with the *si d'opposition* and negative structure: *S'il n'a pas menti, du moins a-t-il caché l'essentiel.*

English equivalents for most of these uses would be 'at least' and 'at any rate'. Like those two expressions, this one can follow rather than precede what it modifies: *La crise s'aggrave, les gains diminuent – en valeur relative, du moins.* It can also be inserted into the possibly unreliable statement that it modifies: *Voici un accord qui, sur le papier du moins, fait date.*

Relation to *au moins*

This structure used to be closer to *au moins* than it tends to be today. Mascarille says in Molière's *L'étourdi*: *C'est, Monsieur, votre père, au moins à ce qu'il dit.* Rousseau says: *j'étais, sinon tout à fait inepte, au moins un garçon de peu d'esprit* (Rousseau, 124). For Littré, they were synonyms. A hundred years later, a lexicographer could still say they were *souvent interchangeables* (Bénac, 599). In contemporary usage, the main differences are that *du moins* is generally anaphoric in function and tends to concede a maximum, while *au moins* is usually cataphoric and tends to affirm a minimum. The same goes for the variants of the latter, *tout au moins*, *à tout le moins* and *pour le moins*. It is unlikely that *du moins* would be used for *au moins*, at least in the latter's quantitative function: *Ça coûtera au moins cinquante francs. / Trois personnes au moins ont trouvé la mort.* However, *au moins* is occasionally used for *du moins*: *Si ce n'est un fracassant coup de cymbales, c'est au moins une surprise de taille.* Some writers use both in similar contexts:

> Alain Girard fut le premier, en France du moins, à mener sur ce point une enquête systématique. [...] Des enquêtes plus récentes sembleraient montrer qu'en France au moins cette idée rallie encore la majorité des suffrages.
>
> (Roussel, 117 & 156)

If there is a difference between them, it may be that *du moins* says this is certain of France and implies nothing about anywhere else; whereas *au moins* says this is certain of France and implies that it could be true of elsewhere. Dupré (II, 1630) and Le Bidois (II, 609) have informative points on the relationship between this pair of structures.

d'un autre côté

Some dictionaries say nothing about this structure, some say little. Few identify it as a structure separate from the binary connector ***d'un côté...*** ***de l'autre***. Littré ignores it, though it existed long before the nineteenth century (Prévost, 46). Montaigne says *Mais, d'autre costé* and *et d'autre costé* (Montaigne, II, 76 & 550). The *Trésor de la langue française* sees it only as part of a binary. The older Robert said nothing; the newer gives an example which implies it is part of a binary. No definition is given, no notion conveyed that it might ever be used independently of *d'un côté*.

Used without *d'un côté*

The connector can be as independent of *d'un côté* as ***d'autre part*** is of *d'une part* and as English 'on the other hand' is of 'on the one hand'. It could often be replaced by *d'un autre point de vue*. Rather like English 'against that' or 'but then again', it marks off a second point from one preceding. This is often seen in the fact that what precedes contains a concessive, such as ***il est vrai*** or ***sans doute***. Addressing members of the *Alliance pour la propagation de la langue française*, Renan says that, on receiving their invitation to speak, he had been beset by doubts:

> Cette association est sûrement une des œuvres auxquelles je suis le plus dévoué. D'un autre côté, je m'étais imposé pour règle absolue, cet hiver, de ne plus faire de conférences [...]
>
> (Renan, 1087)

In the first sentence, *sûrement* concedes a positive aspect of his response; the connector counters that with a negative aspect. This adversative quality is seen in combinations like *d'un autre côté cependant* and when the connector is in tandem with ***mais***, as in this comment on what travel can teach:

> On s'instruit en voyageant, dit le Huron, et assurément cette diversité des peuples, des coutumes et des dieux est utile à considérer. Mais, d'un autre côté, l'on n'apprend jamais que ce que l'on sait déjà.
>
> (Alain, 1956: 413)

There may be some indeterminacy in usage of this structure. As some writers conflate the functions of the two binary structures *d'un côté... de l'autre* and ***d'une part... d'autre part***, so something similar may affect this one. In the following extract from a description of the premiere of Verdi's *Requiem* in Milan, a writer discusses why it took place not in the cathedral but in the church of San Marco. Here, following *d'abord* and saying little more than 'in the second place', the connector is replaceable by *d'autre part*, ***ensuite*** or even ***par ailleurs***:

Plusieurs raisons ont déterminé le choix de San Marco. D'abord San Marco est de petite dimension, les voûtes ne sont pas trop élevées ; l'acoustique y est meilleure qu'au Dôme. D'un autre côté, il paraît que le clergé du Dôme se serait montré peu disposé à admettre des chœurs de femmes dans la cathédrale.

Used after *d'un côté*

At other times, the connector does form the second part of a binary begun by *d'un côté*. This example is from an article on American policy in the war in Bosnia:

L'administration américaine a arrêté sa position après trois jours d'intenses discussions. D'un côté, les chefs militaires ont fait valoir les « limites » de ce que pouvaient réaliser des bombardements aériens.

D'un autre côté, les « politiques » ont observé que la crédibilité des États-Unis (et de l'OTAN) déjà passablement émoussée dans ce conflit, était devenue un des véritables enjeux de la crise bosniaque.

Such binaries tend to be less oppositive than those made with the more usual *d'un côté... de l'autre*. The latter canvasses two possibilities, often speaking of divergence, alternatives, irreconcilables. Whereas this connector, whether preceded or not by *d'un côté*, usually canvasses a possibility among others. It could sometimes be replaced by **au contraire** or **par contre**. This is not usually the case with the second part of *d'un côté... de l'autre*. Some writers link three points in this way: *d'un côté..., de l'autre..., d'un autre côté*; some writers use a plural mode: *d'autres côtés*. Against that, however, it is plain that some do use this connector exactly as most others use *d'un côté... de l'autre*.

Whether used as part of a binary or by itself, this connector nearly always follows a stop. When used by itself, it is often placed first in the paragraph.

d'un côté... de l'autre *

On this binary structure many dictionaries are uninformative. Robert gives it no entry; the reader must deduce its existence and something of its function from an incomplete example. In the *Trésor de la langue française*, the total entry, quite misleading, is: *Loc. adv. D'une part... d'autre part.* Yet most French writers distinguish between this binary and **d'une part... d'autre part**. This contrasts with English 'on the one hand ... on the other', commonly used for both antithetical and complementary binaries.

d'un côté... de l'autre and d'une part... d'autre part

The distinction usually observed between the two binaries is that, whereas *d'une part...* *d'autre part* links factors which reinforce each other, this one generally structures differences between points:

> Les anarchistes et les marxistes se disputent la direction du mouvement ouvrier. D'un côté l'incandescence nihiliste, de l'autre une froide passion.

> Des Croates tirent sur d'autres Croates. D'un côté, les troupes gouvernementales, de l'autre, les bérets noirs du HOS, le bras armé de l'extrême droite croate opposée à tout compromis avec Belgrade.

This oppositive link is often anticipated in the words preceding the connector, such as: *antinomie*; *cassure*; *clivage*; *conflit*; *confusion*; *contradiction*; *contraste*; *controverse*; *découpage*; *différence*; *dilemme*; *distinction*; *distorsion*; *divergence*; *division*; *divorce*; *écart*; *éclatement*; *incohérence*; *s'opposer*; *polémique*; *position ambiguë*; *affrontements idéologiques*; *des avis contraires*; *le vieux débat*; *fractures béantes*; *le paradoxe suivant*; *c'est l'empoignade*; *la bataille politique*; *confronté à un choix clair*; *une ligne de partage très claire*; *le pire côtoie le meilleur*; Solidarité *est désormais scindée en deux*; *un mur symbolique est mis en place*; *l'économie française est atteinte de schizophrénie*. That is, what is usually underlined by this binary is disparity, lack of congruity: *D'un côté, des avantages, de l'autre, des inconvénients*.

However, as a minority of writers use *d'une part... d'autre part* to make an antithesis, so conversely some use this present structure to link points which are more complementary than antithetical, as in this discussion of a decrease in cigarette smoking:

> Les indices sont fragiles, mais ils vont tous dans le même sens : la cigarette perd de la faveur en France. D'un côté, une consommation en (légère) baisse : 92 milliards de cigarettes vendues en 1988 dans l'Hexagone, contre 94,2 en 1987 et 96,2 en 1985. De l'autre, des jeunes qui sont de moins en moins nombreux à fumer. Et puis [...]

The presence of *deux* (or *double*) in the sentence preceding is less common with this structure than with *d'une part... d'autre part*. When it does precede this one, it is usually in a statement stressing opposition or disparity: *deux systèmes s'affrontent*; *deux attitudes extrêmes*; *deux choses bien distinctes*; *deux notions différentes*; *deux pôles*; *deux positions opposées*; *un double langage*; *deux projets de société inconciliables*.

Variable forms

The second part sometimes appears not as *de l'autre* but as *de l'autre côté*, if the first point is a long one, say. And some writers use **d'un autre côté**, either replacing the usual second half of this structure or in a less oppositive way. The placing of the two halves can vary: sometimes they begin separate sentences or paragraphs; sometimes both are in the same sentence; they commonly precede the statements they bear upon, but sometimes they follow them: *Une fracture entre le social et le culturel d'un côté, le politique de l'autre.* Often the antithesis is verbless, as in this series of contrasts between Israelis and Palestinians:

> D'un côté, cinq millions d'Israéliens, bien établis, bien ancrés dans la communauté internationale. De l'autre, environ quatre millions de Palestiniens dispersés dans le monde. D'un côté, une stratégie, l'encadrement. De l'autre, un rêve, l'indépendance. D'un côté, 12 000 dollars de PNB annuel par tête d'habitant. De l'autre, autant qu'on puisse l'établir, dix fois moins. D'un côté, une infrastructure sophistiquée, nucléaire, missiles, téléphone cellulaire, télé par câble. De l'autre, la houe, la charrette à mulet, routes défoncées, ateliers minables, éducation au rabais, chômage chronique [...]

Some writers, not just journalists in a hurry, having begun a binary with *d'un côté*, finish it with *d'autre part*. Bergson liked this sequence, frequently combining it with ***mais***, as in this extract from *Le rire*, discussing *le comique de caractère*:

> Nous revenons ainsi, par un long détour, à la double conclusion qui s'est dégagée au cours de notre étude. D'un côté une personne n'est jamais ridicule que par une disposition qui ressemble à une distraction, par quelque chose qui vit sur elle sans s'organiser avec elle, à la manière d'un parasite : voilà pourquoi cette disposition s'observe du dehors et peut aussi se corriger. Mais, d'autre part, l'objet du rire étant correction même, il est utile que la correction atteigne du même coup le plus grand nombre possible de personnes.
>
> (Bergson, 468)

It is clear that this sequence enables the writer to mark not only a sort of similarity between points but also a distinction. This is usually done with *d'un autre côté*.

In its usual antithetical mode, this connector is on occasion replaced by ***ici... là***.

d'une part... d'autre part *

A connector closely related to this one is ***d'autre part***; one from which it is usually differentiated is ***d'un côté... de l'autre***.

Majority and minority usage

As *d'autre part* can introduce the second of a pair of points which are of roughly equal importance, so this binary can structure both of such points. The definition of its function given in Robert requires some modification:

employé pour mettre en parallèle, pour opposer deux idées ou deux faits,
deux aspects d'un objet. Most writers nowadays do not use this connector
pour opposer deux idées. They use it to link two points which are parallel
or complementary to each other. With this structure, two things are usually
viewed together, as in this comment on the double meaning of the verb
tromper:

> Pourquoi la langue française désigne-t-elle par ce mot unique : tromper, d'une
> part, le fait d'avoir partagé les caresses d'un autre homme que son mari ou
> son amant, d'une autre femme que sa femme ou sa maîtresse, d'autre part, la
> dissimulation de ce fait à celui ou à celle qui pourrait s'en dire lésé ?
>
> (Blum, 94)

Whereas, with *d'un côté... de l'autre*, two things are generally seen as
separate from each other. However, some writers do at times use *d'une*
part... d'autre part contrastively, preceding it with words like *contraste*,
contradictoire, *dilemme*, *division*, *s'opposer*, etc.:

> L'univers se compose de deux parties : d'une part l'Amérique, citadelle de la
> réaction, et d'autre part le reste de la terre, composé du camp des résistants
> à l'Amérique.

Preceded by *deux* or *double*

Although the previous example is contrastive, it does show one way in
which this binary most differs from *d'un côté... de l'autre*: the much greater
frequency with which *deux* (or *double*) is used in what precedes. Used in
such a sequence, the connector often structures separate sentences or is
preceded by a colon:

> Dans le programme d'éradication mondial de l'hépatite B, deux phénomènes
> importants sont à noter. Il y a, d'une part, le développement d'une dynamique
> de santé publique, qui voit des spécialistes défendre et promouvoir l'idée qu'il
> faut absolument généraliser la vaccination. Il y a, d'autre part, la prise de
> conscience des principaux fabricants mondiaux qu'ils ne pourront trouver de
> nouveaux marchés qu'en s'intéressant au tiers-monde et en s'associant à notre
> action.

> L'enfant unique doit obéir à une « double contrainte » : d'une part, une dépen-
> dance affective où il voit la seule forme possible de loyauté à l'égard de ses
> parents, d'autre part, son besoin d'exister dans sa propre identité.

Examples of the type of statement with *deux* often placed in the sentence
preceding this connector are: *deux situations se présentent*; *deux principes*
s'imposent; *il n'y a guère que deux signes*; *et ceci pour deux raisons*; *il y*
a à cela deux causes principales; *deux constatations*; *deux idées fortes*
sous-tendent cette exposition; *cela s'explique de deux façons*; *ceci est ori-*
ginal à deux titres; *ce compromis tient en deux propositions*; *deux tendances*

s'annoncent; *en voici les deux conséquences*. Common expressions with *double* are: *à (un) double titre*; *doublement justifié*; *un double défaut*; *conséquences doubles*; *une double caractéristique*; *un double handicap*; *un double processus*.

Variable usage

The two parts of the connector usually precede the words they modify, but they can also follow them, as in this comment on the world's food crisis:

> Le déficit alimentaire mondial devient absolument dramatique, du fait de l'explosion démographique incontrôlée des « Tiers-Mondes » d'une part ; par le réchauffement global de la planète, d'autre part, dû à l'effet de serre.

Occasionally the second element of the connector is not *d'autre part* but *de l'autre*. If the second part is combined with a conjunction, this is often *et*, sometimes *mais*. Or the second part may be reinforced by *aussi*. As with *d'un côté... de l'autre*, one finds that a minority of writers, having begun a binary structure with *d'une part*, will complete it with *de l'autre côté* (or *d'un autre côté*), as in this comparison of airlines in the USA and in Europe:

> Regardez les forces en présence. C'est saisissant. D'une part, aux États-Unis, un transport aérien très concentré avec quatre ou cinq compagnies géantes exploitant des flottes de l'ordre de 400 à 500 appareils chacune. De l'autre côté, en Europe, plus de vingt compagnies, dont la plus importante exploite une flotte ne dépassant pas les 210 avions.

Other combinations are at times used: *d'une part... puis* (Braudel, 253); *d'une part... et par ailleurs* (July, 265); or *d'une part... mais aussi*, as in this oppositive comment on reasons why the Plateau d'Albion is well known:

> On le connaît deux fois, et pour des motifs bien distincts. D'une part y rôde, non loin du Contadour, une vieille odeur de pacifisme avec les fondateurs des Auberges de jeunesse. Mais c'est aussi là que gîte, en sous-sol, la force de frappe française : les missiles nucléaires.

In most contexts, the structure could be replaced by one of the duos which commonly introduce pairs or *sequences of points*, such as *D'abord... Ensuite* or *D'abord... Et puis*.

An English equivalent for some of the examples quoted above could clearly be 'on the one hand ... on the other'. Often a better equivalent would be 'in the first place ... secondly' or 'for one thing ... for another'.

du reste *

It is generally agreed by dictionaries that this structure and *au reste* are two modes of the same connector and that the *du* mode is less often placed first in the sentence than the *au* mode. According to Robert, the main dissimilarity between them is that: *« du reste », moins littéraire, est beaucoup plus employé que « au reste ».*

similarity to *d'ailleurs*

The structure usually functions much like *d'ailleurs*: to a preceding statement, it adds a point of lesser importance tending in the same direction. Sometimes this added point can restrict or clarify, as in this extract from a Swiss traveller's letter, written from Holland:

> Si le temps reste à la pluie il me faudra peut-être renoncer à la Belgique par laquelle je comptais revenir en Suisse. Ce serait bien contrariant, car on aime à utiliser un voyage et à rapporter au moins quelques connaissances, surtout si le but hygiénique est manqué. Tous les jours du reste nous avons des éclaircies et des coups de soleil, hier au soir un clair de lune superbe [...]

Sometimes the connector more clearly introduces a refinement or a supplementary factor, especially if combined with *et*, as in this comment on the style of a pedantic purist:

> Le purisme est souvent à la limite de l'archaïsme. Quand on emploie par exemple, *malice* dans l'acception de *méchanceté*, *énerver* au sens propre d'*affaiblir*, ce sont des archaïsmes évidents, et du reste un peu durs.

At other times, it is used to extrapolate from the particular to the general, reinforcing a preceding point by broadening it, making a link similar to English 'but then': *Il n'a pas de chance, Daniel Augereau. Du reste, ici, personne n'a de chance. / Le Code civil de Napoléon, pris comme modèle dans toute l'Europe, reconnaît peu de droits à la femme (le XIXe siècle sera, du reste, celui de la régression de la condition féminine).*

It can also, in a sort of aside, link two points which are similar but slightly different, in a way reminiscent of English 'by the way' or 'of course':

> La prose classique eut pour caractère général, comme du reste la poésie du même âge, de respecter une certaine ampleur oratoire, un certain balancement.

Introducing a more important development

Sometimes the link is more substantial and the connector may introduce not a passing remark but a development of similar importance to the thematic point preceding. This example comes from a discussion of alcoholism in the former USSR:

La consommation par adulte d'alcool *légalement* produit a doublé entre 1957 et 1972 ; pour les alcools forts plus dangereux, en particulier la vodka, les eaux-de-vie ou les spiritueux, l'accroissement est encore plus net. Quant à la distillation clandestine, elle est florissante ; c'est, du reste, la seule activité florissante en URSS : son produit est estimé à dix-huit milliards de roubles ! Mais l'alcool sorti de l'alambic familial est souvent de très médiocre qualité ; il est, en outre, hautement toxique. Cela pourrait expliquer la plus grande aggravation de la surmortalité masculine en milieu rural [...]

In this role, the connector can even serve to join paragraphs, introducing one which enlarges the scope of a preceding discussion. A paragraph on duelling in seventeenth-century France, and on Richelieu's edict against it, ends as follows and leads to one that broaches, via *du reste*, the wider European situation:

Privation de charge, confiscation de biens, peines de mort... rien n'y fit. La coutume, irréfragable, recula, mais perdura.

C'est, du reste, l'époque où tous les souverains d'Europe s'emploient, avec plus ou moins de bonheur, à combattre cette pratique qui, telle une épidémie, s'est brusquement répandue, et se maintient sans vergogne. On s'accorde à punir exemplairement le duel, comme acte pernicieux à la société ; [...]

(Chesnais, 127)

Semi-adversative

The connector belongs to the general field of 'and'. But it can serve a more adversative function, which brings it closer to 'but'. It often accompanies a brief adjectival insertion in a subsidiary clause, appending what is really an opinion of the author's to what can appear to be more like a statement of fact, as in this passing comment on the less than total anti-feminism of Balzac and Rabelais:

[Ils font preuve d'un] manque d'amertume contre les femmes malgré l'anti-féminisme, atténué du reste parfois, de l'un et de l'autre.

(Lecuyer, 18)

Or in this finely detailed judgment on an American newspaper:

Quoique l'un des journaux les plus complets et les mieux informés de la planète, quelles que soient par ailleurs ses préférences politiques, du reste variables et variées, le *New York Times* n'a pas pour autant été privé par la nature d'un des dons les plus distinctifs de l'*Homo sapiens*, celui de ne pas voir ce qui existe et de voir ce qui n'existe pas.

(Revel, 1988: 242–243)

In this use, the connector could be replaced not only by *au reste* or *d'ailleurs* but by **au demeurant**.

effectivement *

As a connector, this is a variant of *en effet* and, at times, of *de fait*. Variants, of course, help to avoid repetition of words, as in the following example (dating from 1989) in which the writer has used both *effectivement* and *en effet* in the same sentence:

> Un lecteur nous écrit pour s'étonner de l'utilisation du terme « emprisonné » pour qualifier la situation actuelle de Nelson Mandela. Ce terme, effectivement, peut prêter à confusion ; bien qu'il ne soit toujours pas un homme libre, le leader noir est en effet, depuis le début du mois de décembre, assigné à résidence.

This connector's usual function is to confirm a preceding statement while giving it more definition, as in this dry comment on a Prime Minister's comment on the wet weather:

> « Il pleut » : tel était le seul commentaire, lapidaire, que M. Balladur accordait à la presse en pleine crise monétaire, vendredi 30 juillet à Matignon. Effectivement, il pleuvait.

That example shows how an English equivalent could at times be 'sure enough'. Another one might occasionally be 'indeed'. However, English would often use no connector other than an intonation or its typographical translation, italics: 'It *was* raining'.

In spoken French, *effectivement*, meaning only *Oui* or 'I agree with what you say', but showing clearly its function of linking a second statement to a first which it confirms, is often uttered to express agreement with an interlocutor, much as the British say, 'Absolutely!' and the French themselves, *Absolument !*

As simple adverb

A difference with *en effet* is that *effectivement* is used at times not as an inter-assertional connector but as a simple adverb modifying a verb. In such contexts, as when a journalist speaks of the difficulty of quantifying the hours really worked by journalists: *Les horaires effectivement accomplis sont aussi difficiles à cerner que ceux des enseignants*, it corresponds to 'effectively', 'actually', 'in reality' or 'in effect': *Notre premier projet était plus vaste que celui que nous avons effectivement réalisé* (Bastide, 5).

également *

Like adverbial *aussi*, of which it is a less frequent variant, this connector is not placed first in the sentence. Variants help avoid repetitions, as in this pair of sentences about a police investigation, in which the writer uses both *également* and *aussi*:

> Les sièges des sociétés du Groupe Pierre Botton ont tous fait l'objet d'une ou de plusieurs perquisitions par les policiers du SRPJ, qui ont également visité, à Lyon, deux filiales de la Lyonnaise des eaux. Le juge d'instruction s'est aussi rendu en personne, avec une équipe de policiers, dans les résidences parisienne, lyonnaise et cannoise (la luxueuse villa « Helen Roc ») de M. Pierre Botton.

Pairing verbs

Robert defines this *également* as familiar in tone; the *Petit Robert* adds *de même* to the definition of it. It normally modifies the verb expressing the second of two points of roughly equal importance, which it adds to the first. Often the same verb, with the same subject, makes both points, as in this comment on a musical phrase, in which it is *on peut dire* which is repeated:

> Revenons à la phrase de Gounod. On peut en dire deux choses ; on peut dire que sa mélodie comporte vingt-six notes correspondant aux vingt-six syllabes ; on peut dire également qu'elle est chantée sur une seule note.
>
> (Backès, 28)

Alternatively, the paired verbs, even though not the same word, have very similar meanings and a common subject, as in statements like: *Les ministres ont décidé... Ils ont également confirmé... / Cette circonstance ne permet plus de... Elle impose également de...*; or as in this example containing *déclarer* and *indiquer*:

> M. François Mitterrand a déclaré vendredi 10 que l'élaboration d'une doctrine nucléaire européenne allait devenir « très vite l'une des questions majeures » pour les Douze. Le président de la République a également indiqué que « le Parlement sera saisi » des accords de Maastricht sur l'Union politique et l'Union économique et monétaire.

Other pairs

The connector can of course accompany other parts of speech. Again, the words linked are often identical or close in meaning: *Partout ailleurs... Partout également....* In the following example, with a repeated noun, from an article on Ireland's referendum approving the Treaty of Maastricht, the writer begins by saying Irish reactions to the result are dominated by *Un sentiment de fierté et de soulagement*. She reverts to *soulagement* a little later:

> Soulagement pour les quatre formations principales qui avaient appelé à ratifier Maastricht de vérifier que leur crédit n'était pas entamé.

Soulagement également de voir la manne européenne ne pas s'éloigner d'une île qui connaît un taux de chômage de près de 20 % et qui a grandement béné-ficié de son entrée dans l'Europe en 1972.

In combinations

The role of this connector as a variant for *aussi* extends to its use in tandem with the **si d'opposition** and in the dual structure *non seulement... mais également*. This example of the latter comes from an article about a baker who sold cheaper bread than his competitors, who then retaliated against him:

Les boulangers eurent vite fait de mettre à l'index non seulement leur confrère trop combatif, mais également les industriels qui lui avaient fourni un matériel plus productif.

en clair *

This connector functions as a variant for **autrement dit** and other clari-fiers which introduce a rewording of what precedes. Usually followed by a comma, at times by a colon, it is almost always placed at the beginning of the sentence, as in this extract from an account of relations between Japan and the USA just before the attack on Pearl Harbor:

Un message de Togo à Nomura lui enjoint d'obtenir du Département d'État, pour le 25 au plus tard, l'acceptation du plan japonais. Sinon, des événements qu'on ne précise pas, mais qu'il est facile de deviner, suivront leur « cours automatique ». En clair : ce sera la guerre.

The structure derives from an expression used by the decipherers of codes: a message decoded is a *dépêche en clair*; to decode is *écrire en clair* as opposed to *en chiffres*. Something of this sense was already present in older expressions such as *tirer au clair* and *mettre au clair*, which speak of clarifying obscurities or setting things out intelligibly.

The function of the connector can be to translate, as it were, into simpler language a complex technical statement, say, on a President and his prostate:

Cinq jours plus tard, les Français apprenaient que « l'examen histologique des tissus prostatiques a montré l'existence de lésions adéno-carcinomateuses. Le taux de l'antigène spécifique prostatique est au-dessus de la normale. En revanche, celui des phosphatases acides prostatiques est normal. Le président est traité en conséquence ». En clair, opéré en principe d'une tumeur bénigne de la prostate, François Mitterrand était atteint de cancer.

It can introduce a clarification of obscurities, often put inside quotation marks, implying that concision is superior to officialese:

M. Pomonti préconise une régionalisation de l'activité de création, notamment à travers FR3 qui deviendrait ainsi « un interlocuteur privilégié de l'action éducative sous réserve d'une évolution sensible de ses modes de fonctionnement et de son statut général ». En clair, cela signifie une part d'antenne plus grande pour le réseau régional.

Used like (or with) *c'est-à-dire*

This connector is favoured by those wishing to give the impression of being investigative journalists blowing the gaff on a secretive government. It is also used without any such intention, either by a venerable historian (Braudel, 235) or as a replacement for simple *c'est-à-dire*, in contexts like the following, dealing with the importation of foreign-made toys into France:

> Selon les statistiques officielles, les importations (7,7 milliards de francs, en progression de 25 % en 1991) ont représenté l'année dernière... 70 % du marché national. En clair, moins d'un jouet sur trois vendus en France provient de notre pays.

Indeed, some writers use *c'est-à-dire en clair*. Another connector of the same set sometimes combined with it is *soit*, as in this extract from an article about European Community regulations limiting bird-shooting to certain seasons:

> Le régime français laisse aux préfets la décision de fermer la chasse dans leurs départements à une date « qui s'inscrit dans les dix jours pendant lesquels un seuil de 10 % des oiseaux ont entamé leur migration nuptiale », soit, en clair, entre fin janvier et fin février.

Variants

A variant of the previous combination is *soit, pour être clair* (Wagner, 123); and a variant of the basic mode is *En termes clairs*. There may also be reinforcement by a redundant verb: *En clair, cela voulait dire que...*; *En clair, cela revient à dire que ...*; *En termes clairs, cela signifie....* Another variant, possibly tongue-in-cheek, certainly not to be found in the dictionaries, is *en décodé*:

> Même s'ils ne le disent pas, les socialistes ont choisi leur « nouvelle alliance » : ce sera « rouge-vert-rose ». En décodé, communistes, écolos et socialistes.

A different variant, making explicit the idea of a translation, can be seen in the next example, which comes from an article about economic restructuring in Russia:

> La priorité est donnée à la stabilisation macroéconomique de la Russie. Traduisez : la lutte contre l'inflation, qui était de 834 % en 1993.

Other variants of that variant are *Traduisons*, *Traduire* and *Traduction*, also followed by a colon.

English equivalents include 'in other words', 'in effect' or 'this means'.

en contrepartie

This contrastive structure, unknown to Littré, barely visible in Robert, is formed from a noun meaning 'compensation' or 'quid pro quo'. As a connector, it usually presents a positive point seen as counterbalancing a preceding negative one; but some use it to do the opposite. In texts dealing with negotiations or contracts on economic matters, it may speak of an actual financial benefit rather than present a point of view, being part of the information rather than a rhetorical linking of the information. This is most evident in the non-connective structure, *en contrepartie de*.

However, as a connector, the structure is most usually an occasional variant for **par contre**, **en revanche** or **à l'inverse**, shaping contrasts of any sort, between, say, paired antonyms like *acquérir* and *vendre* or, as in this example, *solitude* and *fidélité*:

> Dans le personnage de Lohengrin, Wagner avait voulu symboliser la solitude et l'incompréhension de l'artiste qui cherche sa place dans le monde des humains. Une place qui exige, en contrepartie, une fidélité absolue, exactement celle qui est demandée à Elsa [...]

In the following extract from a film review, the contrast is between a positive feature and a less positive one:

> Il est question de religion, de connaissance, de tolérance et d'amour sur un ton qui n'est pas celui que l'on s'attend à entendre dans une comédie de Gérard Oury. En contrepartie, le film est très lent et très bavard.

The structure is sometimes combined with **mais**, as in this extract from an article on an Algerian frontier settlement:

> Il est de notoriété que quelques-uns des frontaliers se livrent à une contre-bande anodine sur laquelle tout le monde ferme les yeux.
> Mais, en contrepartie, reconnaît *mezza-voce* un policier, ils peuvent être de précieux auxiliaires en signalant les anomalies qu'ils constatent.

Variants

On occasion, some writers use variants such as *en contrepoint*, *en compensation* or a mode of the latter favoured by the ironic Jules Renard, *par compensation*:

Le directeur du *Rire* tenant à Léandre un discours subtil pour lui prouver que, si désormais on lui prend moins de dessins, par compensation on les lui payera moins cher.

(Renard, 1965: 367; see also 360)

English equivalents include 'on the other hand'; 'but against that'.

encore *

Only three modes of this connector are discussed here. It can help to set out certain *sequences of points*. It can be a variant of *également* or adverbial *aussi*. And combined with *et* it can come close to the contrastive function it has in *encore faut-il que*.

In sequences of points

It can combine with *ou bien* or *soit* to make a sequence of alternatives beginning with *Ou... Ou bien... Ou encore* or *Soit... Soit... Soit encore*. A writer on traditional Buddhist architecture discusses three ways of digging a pit to judge the aptness of a site for building a temple; the second and third run as follows:

Ou bien on remplissait d'eau la fosse et l'y laissait toute une nuit; on évaluait la qualité du terrain à la quantité d'eau qu'on y retrouvait le lendemain matin. Ou encore, on descendait dans le trou une flamme vive ; selon qu'elle brûlait ou s'éteignait, le terrain était choisi ou abandonné.

Similar sequences of points are made with *de même... de même encore*.

A variant for *également* or adverbial *aussi*

Just as *également* can replace *aussi* in the binary structure *non seulement... mais aussi*, so can *encore*. It can accompany an inversion of subject and verb, as in Gide's description of his mother's shyness when young:

Non seulement elle se retirait sans cesse et s'effaçait chaque fois qu'il aurait fallu briller ; mais encore ne perdait-elle pas une occasion de pousser en avant Mlle Anna [...]

(Gide, 1954: 364)

This mode combines also with *là*: *là encore* is as common as *là aussi*. It functions like *aussi* in paired statements containing the same verb, like *il faut* in this extract from an essay on the genius of Rodin as compared with his twentieth-century successors:

Il faut, pour travailler ainsi, une virtuosité d'anatomiste qu'aucun des successeurs de Rodin n'a su atteindre. Il faut encore une logique du sujet et du

sentiment pour décliner, à partir d'une figure, ses virtualités expressives et allé-
goriques sans tomber dans l'absurde et le désaccordé.

Again like *également*, it can be used not only instead of *aussi* but as well
as it, to add not just a second point to a first, but a third to a second, as
in this judgment on a landslide election:

> C'est la fin d'un monde que les électeurs ont enregistrée : fin de l'après-
> guerre ; fin d'un univers balisé. C'est aussi la fin d'un mode de gestion qui
> voyait le « progrès » passer par toujours plus de redistribution ; la fin, encore,
> d'un mode de relation au reste du monde où un peu de tiers-mondisme tenait
> lieu de supplément d'âme, etc.

Usually with *et*

This third mode is restrictive. Usually in combination with *et*, it implies
that what precedes is exaggerated. Often the preceding statement is itself
no more than a concessive or partial affirmation:

> Éviter toute intervention étrangère dans le conflit irako-koweïtien est bien la
> seule chose sur laquelle paraissent s'accorder les chefs d'État arabes, au moins
> dans le discours et encore avec quelques nuances.

There the connector compounds the weakening effect of *au moins*,
which introduces a first dilution of the preceding statement, itself something less than a certainty by being no more than a deduction from
appearances. In the next example, three points are set out in three
sentences from an article about Algerian women's reactions to the
family-law act of 1984, which revived the Shariah's four-marriage rule for
men:

> Pourquoi diable aller légaliser une pratique en voie d'extinction ? Sur 100
> mariages en Algérie, 1,5 seulement relève de la polygamie. Et encore, dans la
> majorité des cas, il s'agit davantage d'abandonner une épouse sans en divorcer
> que d'en prendre une seconde.

In the third sentence, the connector reduces even further the limited extent
of the practice mentioned in the second, which precises, as though by
implicit *en effet*, the already restricted idea of the first. There is little
difference between this *encore* and *encore faut-il* except the presence of
et and the lack of inversion of verb and subject. And some writers do
invert, also omitting *et*, as in this extract from a discussion of unemployment throughout the world:

> Seuls des grands pays industrialisés, le Japon et la Suède ont réussi à main-
> tenir des taux de chômage minimes. Encore la Suède n'y est-elle parvenue
> qu'en contraignant les entreprises à garder du personnel en surnombre.
>
> (Fontaine, 1978: 220)

An abridged mode *et encore* sometimes restricts or casts doubt by leaving implicit the sceptical conclusion to be drawn. This is common in speech, with exclamative intonation. An exemplary sentence comes from an essay on the tributaries of the Rhône, unsuited to navigation: *Seule la Saône – et encore – faisait exception* (Braudel, 246). Another example is from a discussion of the USSR's huge stockpile of nuclear weapons, seen as useless to its Arab allies and ultimately to itself; the exclamative tone is conveyed by the combination with the ***points de suspension***:

> Boumediène avait raison qui, au lendemain du conflit d'octobre 1973 au Proche-Orient, dans lequel l'URSS avait observé une prudence de serpent, confiait à ses visiteurs : « Nous sommes arrivés à la conclusion qu'elle ne fera la guerre que pour l'Allemagne... et encore. »

The doubt implied by the expression is sometimes spelled out, as in: *Et encore ! Ce n'est pas si sûr !* (Poulet, 1971: 265); and as in this comment on the two major political parties in the USA: *L'un me paraissait vaguement à gauche, l'autre vaguement à droite, et encore je n'en étais pas bien sûr* (Dutourd, 1985: 88).

English equivalents for this third mode might be 'and even so' or 'and even then'.

encore faut-il (que) *

This connector has four modes, only three of which actually contain *falloir*. It can function adversatively or as a reinforcer; both ***mais*** and ***et*** can combine with it. The combination with *et* may be seen as a specialized mode of ***encore***. The tense is nearly always the present; the conditional is sometimes used, other tenses rarely. It is usual to place the structure first in the sentence and to invert subject and verb.

encore faut-il que

The three modes containing *falloir* speak of a lack. They usually shape oppositions between the desirable and the deficient. What precedes usually presents something as favourable; what follows implies a criticism: the advantage, though welcome, does not go far enough. Thus, from a review of a television interviewer's performance: *Elkabbach sait un peu poser des questions. Encore faut-il que les réponses méritent cette mise en scène.* And this, from a discussion of cheap consumer goods: *Il est bien de fabriquer des produits moins coûteux. Encore faut-il que ces produits aient une esthétique* (Renard, 1987: 21). The structure is sometimes preceded by ***certes***; it could often be replaced by *Certes, mais il faut aussi que....*

encore faut-il + **infinitive**

The model of this mode is a comment on a Prime Minister by a member of the opposition: *C'est bien d'écrire des Livres blancs, encore faut-il les appliquer.* In theory, this mode could contain the infinitive of any verb; in practice, the verb often expresses knowing with precision, stressing or distinguishing: *comprendre*; *savoir*; *s'interroger sur*; *noter*; *s'entendre sur*; *préciser*; *distinguer*; *souligner.* In this way a writer readjusts a focus, refines a concept, as in this excerpt from a discussion of the decline in infanticide and the growth of a new attitude towards children:

> Il a fallu attendre le XVIIIe ou le XIXe siècle en Europe occidentale, pour que soit reconnue la valeur de l'enfant et qu'apparaisse le souci de protéger sa vie. Encore faut-il souligner que le développement du sentiment familial à l'égard de l'enfant est d'abord le propre de la bourgeoisie urbaine et qu'il ne se diffuse que tardivement dans les milieux populaires.

What follows clarifies what precedes. If there is a contrast, it is between a broad definition and a much more detailed statement which particularizes and restricts the range of what precedes. Common in this function is *Encore faut-il nuancer.*

Rather than beginning a sentence, this mode quite often completes one. The first part of such sentences is often structured by the **si d'opposition**. The subject of this example is the under-representation of Frenchwomen in the nation's governing bodies:

> Au sein des assemblées élues, les Françaises brillent d'une obscure clarté : 6 % des députés, 3 % des sénateurs, 4 % des conseillers généraux. Une misère ! Et si leur présence est mieux affirmée dans les municipalités (14 %), encore faut-il préciser que moins de 4 % des mairies ont une femme à leur tête.

Even commoner than the combination with *si* may be one with *il ne suffit pas de.* It, too, often shapes the first half of a sentence: *Il ne suffit pas d'ajouter les territoires aux territoires, encore faut-il savoir les gouverner* (Brun, 80). It has variants, such as *On ne peut se contenter de, Ce n'est pas assez de, Ce n'est pas tout de* as in *Ce n'est pas tout de constater que les Français ont peur de la capote anglaise : encore faut-il savoir pourquoi.* Such binaries oppose not positive and negative but insufficient and necessary. Rare exemplars without inversion are found with this mode: *Il ne suffit pas de savoir parler; il faut encore savoir à qui l'on parle* (Reboul, 9).

encore faut-il + **noun**

This, the least common mode, also tends to follow structures like *il ne suffit pas de.* Here a writer speaks of the conditions necessary for the existence of fair and accurate reporting:

Comme le pluralisme, l'indépendance constitue *l'une des conditions* qui rendent *possible* une information honnête et exacte, mais qui ne la rendent pas certaine.

Les conditions favorables ne suffisent pas : encore faut-il les hommes capables et désireux de les mettre à profit pour produire de la bonne information.

(Revel, 1988: 241)

A journalist, discussing the leader of the extreme Right-wing Front national, says this:

Pour être un vrai démagogue, il ne suffit pas d'avoir la technique, la manière, l'absence de principes, la malhonnêteté, le fanatisme, la mégalomanie et le mépris du peuple que l'on flatte. Encore faut-il du caractère, de la volonté et du talent.

encore + inversion of any verb

Quite common in this mode are two verbs which function as variants of *falloir*: *encore convient-il* and *encore s'agit-il*. Like some of the other modes, this one can introduce the third in a trio of related points, as in this excerpt from an essay on French dislike of a French composer:

Les Français, c'est bien connu, n'ont jamais su vraiment rendre justice à Berlioz. Il faut remonter à P. Monteux pour trouver chez un interprète français cette force et cette légèreté à la fois, cette passion fiévreuse et cette précision dans le dosage des timbres, ce souffle romantique et ce modernisme aigu que demandent des pages aussi singulières que « Roméo et Juliette ». Encore l'enregistrement de cette étonnante « symphonie dramatique » avait-il été réalisé avec des forces anglaises et dans une ville, Londres, qui allait devenir la patrie d'adoption d'un compositeur voué à l'incompréhension des siens.

There the first sentence makes a general statement; the second confirms the negativity of it, half-mitigating, half-aggravating it; and the third invalidates the mitigation, thus reaffirming the truth of the initial point. In other contexts, this mode functions like the others in binary structures. An article comparing the very small numbers of women given winnable positions on the voting cards of political parties ends like this:

Actuellement, la lanterne rouge de la féminisation – mais ce n'est pas vraiment une surprise – revient aux chasseurs-pêcheurs, champions de la misogynie, qui sont dixièmes, et bon derniers avec seulement deux femmes pour soixante-dix neuf hommes. Encore sont-elles mal placées.

The second element of the binary says the bad situation mentioned in the first is actually worse.

It is possible to make this link of thought in other ways: *Ce n'est pas tout de mourir : il faut mourir à temps* (Sartre, 1964: 11). It would be possible to use **de plus** or a variant for it: *Il ne suffit pas à M. Nyssen*

d'écrire, sur le livre, des banalités, il lui faut en outre les rendre précieuses.
Or the idea may be phrased with ***aussi***: *Il ne suffit pas que* […]. *Il est nécessaire aussi que*....

English has no special equivalent for this connector. The first half of some binaries shaped by it might well include 'up to a point', 'that's all very well' or 'as far as it goes'. In the second half, one might say 'even so' or else fall back on 'but' or 'however'.

en d'autres termes *

The meaning of this connector is apparent: 'in other words'. Its function, like that of its English equivalent, is not only to introduce a different way of expressing what precedes. It also spells out consequences of it, puts a finer point upon it, clarifies an implication. It is one in a set of explicators or precisers which can serve as variants for ***autrement dit*** or ***c'est-à-dire (que)***. Indeed, the latter has on occasion been combined with it:

> M. Bayle a prétendu prouver qu'il valoit mieux être athée qu'idolâtre ; c'est-à-dire, en d'autres termes, qu'il est moins dangereux de n'avoir point du tout de religion que d'en avoir une mauvaise.
>
> (Montesquieu, 403–404)

Like ***en clair***, this connector is sometimes preceded by words in quotation marks, technical terms, esoteric language which the writer 'translates' for the reader. This example comes from an essay on supposed 'national characteristics', their possible contribution to clarity of discussion and the risk of over-simplification entailed by the concept:

> Il y a aussi un risque dans ce genre d'exercice. C'est que ces représentations reflètent, d'une certaine manière, ce que certains sociologues comme Michel Dobry qualifient d'« illusion culturaliste ». En d'autres termes, on n'est parfois pas très loin de la vieille idée selon laquelle chaque peuple a son caractère, son âme propre, son « génie ».
>
> (Frischer, 20)

Sometimes a longer form of words is used: *Pour le dire en d'autres termes.*

en définitive *

This connector introduces a conclusive statement, which can be either recapitulative or not. It comes close to being an all-purpose resumer-concluder, a sort of amalgam of 'in a word', 'in other words', 'when all's said and done' and 'in the last analysis', and can replace one or other of a sizeable set of related connectors. Some dictionaries include *pour conclure* among their definitions of it (Robert; Hanse, 1983: 312). That may mislead: for all its versatility, this connector would not replace *pour conclure* in its expository function (*Disons pour conclure...*), just as it would never replace **enfin**, say, in its enumerative function, or *en dernier lieu*.

Recapitulative

As a recapitulative it can function like **bref**, as in this extract from a discussion of reasons why a majority of Argentinians voted Peronist in the election of 1989:

> En 1989, l'Argentine est revenue au péronisme parce que ses pauvres sont plus pauvres que jamais, parce que sa classe moyenne rase les murs, parce que les progressistes, atomisés, n'ont pu briser la polarisation péronistes-radicaux. En définitive, l'Argentine est redevenue péroniste faute d'alternative, parce qu'elle ne pouvait se résoudre à ne plus croire en rien.

Like **en somme** or **en clair**, it can signal an interpretation or translation into simpler form of a detailed exposition. The next example of it is part of an ironist's discussion of what he says are Left-wing attitudes to racism – or rather the only racism deplored by the Left, which is, he says, white racism against non-whites:

> Et, pour être tout à fait complet, le racisme blanc n'est lui-même répréhensible que s'il vient d'une société capitaliste et démocratique. Le massacre d'Asiatiques ou d'Africains par des Européens socialistes est autorisé, de même que la discrimination à l'encontre des Noirs à Cuba. Le seul racisme, en définitive, est le racisme blanc capitaliste.

> (Revel, 1988: 114)

There, the connector could alternatively be replaced by **autrement dit** or **en un mot**.

At other times, it can function like **au total**, introducing a comprehensive statement which adds up a detailed sequence of amounts, as in this one about a play that flopped at the Amandiers theatre:

> Les recettes du Rond-Point (neuf cents places) ne couvrent pas le prix de la représentation : 85 000 F, dont 30 000 F pour la location de la salle. Les places coûtent 180 F et 140 F, 150 F pour les collectivités, et 90 F pour les onze mille abonnés des Amandiers. En définitive, *Retour au désert* aura coûté aux Amandiers 1,5 million sur lesquels le théâtre aura récupéré 500 000 F.

Non-recapitulative

The connector can also function like **au bout du compte**, **en fait**, **en fin de compte** or the non-temporal **finalement** which introduces a statement of a real outcome contradicting an expected one, as in this extract from a historian's discussion of a proposal that Descartes's remains be transferred to the shrine of national remembrance: *Mais, en définitive, la « translation des cendres de Descartes au Panthéon » n'eut pas lieu* (Bourgeois & d'Hondt, 174). English 'eventually' or 'in the end' could translate this contrastive and quasi-narrative use.

As in the last example, the structure is sometimes combined with *mais*. An example of it replacing *somme toute*, *au fond* or *tout compte fait* as a non-recapitulative concluder, comes from a discussion of a proposal to ban the possibility of medically assisted pregnancy for women past the age of menopause, in the alleged interest of *l'enfant à venir*. If there is a vestige of recapitulative function to this usage, it is the implicit summing up which accompanies the unargued judgment. English 'actually' and 'in fact' can function like this:

> L'enfant grandira auprès d'une femme âgée et sera, selon toute vraisemblance, tôt orphelin. Y a-t-il nécessité de légiférer ou faut-il s'en remettre au bon sens général et à la déontologie médicale ? L'erreur serait ici d'en rester à un problème certes spectaculaire, alimentant de nombreux fantasmes, mais en définitive relativement marginal.

Nowadays, *au final* could also replace this connector in many of the contexts illustrated above.

en effet *

This connector has a single function: to introduce a confirmation of what precedes. This it can do in two ways: either by precising a statement or by explaining it.

Precising

This mode introduces a more particular rewording of a preceding point. In what precedes, it is usually possible to identify quite precisely the words which are confirmed and particularized by equally identifiable words in what follows:

> Paris a une densité de lycées largement supérieure à la moyenne, qui attire bon nombre de banlieusards, voire de provinciaux. En effet, on estime qu'au moins 25 % des élèves parisiens n'habitent pas la capitale.

There, the second sentence both corroborates the first sentence's statement that a fair number of pupils in Paris *lycées* come from outside the city and precises that number by quantifying it: *bon nombre* it restates as *25 %*, and *banlieusards* and *provinciaux* as *n'habitent pas la capitale*.

Likewise, in the next example, *beaucoup moins* is quantified by the difference between 44.1% and 50.3%:

> Globalement, on peut dire que le Parisien paye beaucoup moins d'impôts directs que le citoyen des autres grandes villes. Dans le premier cas, en effet, ces impôts entrent pour 44,1 % dans l'ensemble des recettes du budget, dans le second pour 50,3 %.

It can be seen that the function of this connector is akin to but weaker than that of **autrement dit** or **en d'autres termes**, which do not just reword but also introduce an apter and more acutely analysed formulation of an idea. It is unlikely that in English these sentences would be linked by a connector.

The function of what precedes can often be to comment on the fact following it, to interpret or give an opinion on this fact. In the next example, taken from a weather forecast, the only factual statement is the one in the second sentence; the first sentence is more of a gloss by the writer:

> Samedi, les conditions météorologiques seront particulièrement dangereuses. En effet, les vents de sud et de sud-ouest souffleront en tempête.

It is in this way that *en effet* corresponds at times to the concealed editorializing effect of the 'with' combined with a present participle in the English written by some journalists. In this sentence: 'The BMA has split, with several hundred of its members demanding that the President resign', 'with' serves an *en effet*-like function by linking two statements which are two ways of saying much the same thing: a fact preceded by an opinion on the fact. The same English structure is often used to give two statements telling of two different facts. Is not the main objection to this 'with' that it thereby ambiguates the link of thought between two statements? The French connector makes for French clarity, although it must be said that **avec** is at times used in a similar way to this 'with'.

As a preciser, this connector can generally be replaced by **de fait** or **effectivement**.

Explaining

The second mode comes close to **c'est que** or **car**: what precedes is not only confirmed but explained. This example comes from an information leaflet issued by the Crédit lyonnais bank:

> Le code confidentiel de votre CARTE BANCAIRE est le garant de votre sécurité. Pour vous protéger totalement, personne d'autre que vous ne doit le connaître. En effet, en cas de perte ou de vol, l'utilisation de votre carte avec son code confidentiel engagerait votre responsabilité.

There, the links between *personne d'autre que vous* and *en cas de perte ou de vol*, and between *pour vous protéger* and *engagerait votre respon-*

sabilité, are less direct as translations than those seen in the previous examples. Again in the following one, it is with an implication, rather than with actual words, that the connector makes its link. What makes for the semantic logic is the reader's assumed knowledge of the penal code:

> Dans ce village de mille habitants, la moitié seulement des habitants votent : les autres sont privés de leurs droits civiques. Mauzac abrite, en effet, depuis 1986, un établissement pénitentiaire réservé aux « délinquants moyens ».

In each of these two examples, the second sentence could be introduced as follows: *C'est que, en cas de perte ou de vol* and *Car Mauzac abrite, depuis 1986*. The relationship between *en effet* and *car* has exercised many a French grammarian and purist. For some, the two expressions are synonymous and therefore the combination *car en effet* is an intolerable solecism; for others not. In any case, though denounced as a *pléonasme fréquent* (Hanse, 1983: 197), the combination of *car* and *en effet* is rare in contemporary written French.

It is only this second mode which introduces new information. In the following example, about a painting which may or may not be genuine, the second sentence does not just reword the information already given in the first:

> La polémique qui a resurgi à propos de l'authenticité du *Verrou* de Fragonard risque de prendre fin. Le tableau a subi en effet un examen approfondi dans les laboratoires du Louvre en novembre et décembre de l'année dernière.

en effet and *en fait*, 'in fact' and 'indeed'

This connector can be problematical for speakers of English who think it means 'in fact' or 'indeed'. They confuse a very specific French connector with two unspecific English ones; they also confuse *en effet* with **en fait**. On this, they could be misled by French lexicography: the first definition given of this structure in both the Robert and the *Trésor de la langue française* is *en réalité, en fait*. This misinformation derives from older dictionaries, like the Académie's, which also recorded the fact that, formerly, *en effet* sometimes functioned like present-day *en fait*. Vinay & Darbelnet give an enlightening note on the crucial difference between *en fait* and *en effet*:

> On notera que les dictionnaires ne peuvent pas donner de bons équivalents de « en effet », parce qu'il leur faudrait citer autant d'exemples que de situations. Beaucoup d'Anglais sont portés à traduire « en effet » par « in fact », qui correspond au français « en fait ». Mais en fait « en fait » est le contraire de « en effet » : *Il a dit qu'il s'en occuperait, en fait c'est moi qui ai tout fait / il a dit qu'il s'en occuperait, et en effet il a fait tout le travail.*
>
> (Vinay & Darbelnet, 227, n. 36)

Helpful as it is, this still equates *en fait* with 'in fact', which is also a faulty and misleading rule. The following extract from a discussion of the useful- ness of screening men for prostate cancer, containing both French structures, illustrates in another way the difference between them:

> Faut-il dépister le cancer de la prostate ? Un homme qui ne ressent aucun trouble a-t-il intérêt à chercher à savoir s'il en est atteint ? A priori, on pour- rait le croire. En effet, c'est un cancer fréquent (13 000 nouveaux cas chaque année) et pour lequel on dispose de techniques de dépistage. En fait, la réponse n'est pas simple. Le débat est ouvert et il a ses extrémistes.

Functioning here in its second mode, *en effet* introduces a statement confirming the implication of the previous sentence: that there might appear to be some point in screening for this cancer. Then *en fait*, the second element of the antithesis initiated by *a priori*, casts doubt on the validity of these appearances.

If a translator writing in English really needs an equivalent of *en effet*, the meaning expressed by it is usually 'sure enough'. But English sentences rarely need a connector serving this purpose; and if one added 'sure enough' to every translation of a statement with *en effet*, one would soon write non-English. It is with *en effet* that the frequency in English of the *charnière-zéro* becomes at times obvious. English often needs no connector at places where *en effet* is used in French. In the following example of English-language journalism, without *en effet* to show that the second statement only confirms and precises the first, it would be theoretically possible, but only theoretically, to believe that the two sentences spoke of two different events, instead of the same one:

> The Iranian Government has been asked to upgrade security at the Australian Embassy in Teheran because of fears of reprisals against Australia in the wake of the attack on the Iranian Embassy in Canberra. The Iranian Ambassador to Australia, Mohammed Abianeh, said yesterday he had asked his Government to put on extra security for Australian diplomats in Teheran, saying there was a danger.

One of the roles of *en effet* being to obviate that sort of potential ambi- guity, a good French translator would probably insert this connector in the second sentence.

Former usage

Readers of texts written in former times should beware the fact that, since the seventeenth and eighteenth centuries, the connective function of *en effet* has profoundly changed. As stated above, it once served two func- tions: not only its present confirming one but also the oppositive one now served by *en fait*. In Racine: *Reine longtemps de nom, mais en effet captive* (*Mithridate*, line 136) and Rousseau: *C'était en apparence la même situa-*

tion, et en effet une toute autre manière d'être (Rousseau, 21), this connector makes an adversative link. In French written two or three centuries ago, far from confirming anything, it contradicts, it does mean 'in fact', in opposition to the merely nominal (*de nom*) or apparent but misleading (*en apparence*). The combination with **mais** would be possible today only with *en fait*.

en fait *

This connector, essentially oppositive, introduces a statement of fact. It has two modes: overtly antithetical; and implicitly antithetical, stressing a precision.

Overtly antithetical

This mode structures the second element of binaries. It introduces a fact which rectifies a point seen as less than fact, unsure, ideal or theoretical; it contradicts a supposition or a falsehood. What precedes is at times introduced by *en principe*, *en droit*, *en titre* or *a priori*, making manifest the disparity between theory and fact:

> Secrétaire général du PCF, en titre depuis vingt et un ans, en fait depuis vingt-trois ans, Georges Marchais part vaincu par l'âge.

The antithesis often begins with an adverb such as *officiellement* or *théoriquement: Officiellement, rien n'a changé. En fait, le rapport des forces est bouleversé. / Ce problème, apparemment simple, est en fait d'une complexité extrême.*

The first element of the binary may express intention, imagination, promise, wish, hope, fear; and this potential outcome will be cancelled by the connector's statement of fact. This example comes from a description of life under the Occupation of 1940–1944:

> Nous espérions un avenir meilleur avec du pain blanc, du lait qui ne serait pas écrémé, des rues et des balcons tricolores, des guinguettes pour valser et des nuits de juin pour aimer – mais aussi et surtout survivre pour leur raconter l'inouï, l'intempestif que nous avions pourtant vécu. En fait, hormis quelques héros, de surcroît doués du verbe, nous ne pouvions pas dire grand-chose : que nous avions eu faim, que nous avions eu peur, que nous avions espéré, pleuré de tristesse et parfois de joie [...]

At other times, what precedes is a statement about pretence or falsehood, a reported claim, which is then contradicted: *Une armée prétendument fédérale, mais en fait serbe. / Le maire est « en vacances ». En fait, il a été proprement écarté, mais en douceur.* This relation of *en fait* to a revelation of truth is seen, too, when it contradicts an error:

On sait que Mérimée passait pour le père de l'impératrice Eugénie parce qu'il aurait été autrefois l'amant de sa mère, la comtesse de Montijo. En fait il ne connaissait pas encore celle-ci quand la petite Eugénie était née, et il n'y a plus aucun doute là-dessus.

(Henriot, 1954: 87)

The unsureness of what precedes may be expressed as an interrogation, direct or indirect, as in this excerpt from a preface to a novel once thought scandalous:

Pourquoi une réaction si passionnée devant un ouvrage écrit avec tant de pudeur et un sens remarquable de la suggestion ?
En fait, les protestations de vertu outragée ne datent point de cette époque ni les allusions à l'homosexualité féminine.

(Cantégrit, 6)

False impressions, too, are put right by *en fait*: it is at times preceded by statements containing nouns such as *impression, leurre, songe, rêve, rumeur*.

Marking the difference between hypothesis and truth, between a supposed state and a reality, this structure is akin to **en réalité**, **en vérité**, **au contraire** and in some contexts **or**. Indeed, it is at times combined with *au contraire* and *or*. It is its strong adversative quality which makes it combine also with **alors que** and **mais**.

Implicitly antithetical

This mode can combine with **et**, less to make an opposition than to precise a point by broadening it, as in this discussion of cities laid waste, such as Warsaw in 1944:

Un deuxième exemple a été découvert plus récemment dans toute sa tragique ampleur. C'est celui de Bucarest, dont un large tiers de la ville, et en fait la quasi-totalité des plus anciens quartiers, a été rasé, pour laisser place à de pseudo-Champs-Élysées.

This mode combines also with **c'est-à-dire (que)**. Here a writer makes the point that the real power on the waterfront does not lie with the shipowners or the statutory authority:

Les armateurs ne peuvent faire travailler sur les quais que les titulaires d'une carte professionnelle délivrée par le bureau central de la Main-d'œuvre docker – c'est-à-dire, en fait, le syndicat unique CGT.

That combination could be replaced by **autrement dit** or **en clair**. As indeed could at times the unaccompanied connector:

Les gardes-côtes ont annoncé qu'ils maintenaient leur dispositif d'« encer-clement » autour de l'île, en fait dix-sept bâtiments entre la Floride et Haïti.

Though this second mode is not preceded by an explicit theory, ideal, expectation or error, it can be seen as implicitly antithetical: the precision which follows it usually contrasts with the less precisely expressed point preceding. Thus, having noted that road deaths began to decline in the early 1970s, a writer introduces a more important point:

> Pour la première fois en temps de paix, le fléau reculait. En 1974, l'Europe compte sept mille morts et cent trente mille blessés de moins qu'en 1970. La rupture est, en fait, plus remarquable encore : si la mortalité routière avait suivi son rythme antérieur, le nombre des morts en 1974 se serait élevé à cent huit mille, au lieu des quatre-vingt-quatre mille enregistrés. Ainsi, pour la seule année 1974, le nombre de vies humaines sauvées a pu atteindre jusqu'à vingt-quatre mille.

en fait, en effet and 'in fact'

Some English-speakers confuse this structure and *en effet*. One of the most marked differences between them is that *en effet* never shapes an opposition, whereas *en fait* does. On the differences between the two, Vinay & Darbelnet are enlightening (227, n. 36). The confusion may be increased by the existence of *de fait* and the inadequate guidance of dictionaries on structures like *en fait* and 'in fact'. Both Harrap and Collins-Robert mention *de fait* as an equivalent for 'in fact' – this despite the fact that, although a few writers do use it like *en fait*, most use it like *en effet*.

If one translates *en fait* into English 'in fact', one will not go far wrong; but if one translates 'in fact' into French as *en fait*, one will more often than not mistranslate. Most of the following ten pairs of sentences show how inapt *en fait* is as an equivalent of 'in fact': 'She said she would come that afternoon, and she did turn up in fact at half past two': *Elle avait dit qu'elle viendrait cet après-midi-là et en effet elle est arrivée à deux heures et demie.* / 'This is the cleanest, niftiest, best performing model, in fact the best overall': *Ce modèle est le plus propre, le plus nerveux, le plus performant, bref le meilleur à tous égards.* / 'We see much less of him than we used to. In fact, he hardly ever comes at all now': *Nous le voyons beaucoup moins qu'autrefois. Il vient même très rarement.* / 'He declared that he would never again set foot in a house where he was treated like a boor. And in fact he never reappeared': *Il déclara qu'il ne remettrait plus les pieds dans une maison où on le traitait en paltoquet. Effectivement, il ne reparut plus.* / 'She said she would come on Tuesday and in fact she came on Wednesday': *Elle avait dit qu'elle viendrait mardi. En fait, elle est venue mercredi.* / 'These children are homeless – in fact, their parents have kicked them out': *Ces enfants sont des sans abri. A vrai dire, ils ont été chassés par leurs parents.* / 'The man's a cad, a bounder, in fact a scoundrel!': *Cet homme est un goujat, un mufle, voire un scélérat* / 'Many, in fact most, of these issues were first raised by Freud in his essay about Dora': *Beaucoup de ces questions, sinon la plupart, c'est Freud qui le premier les souleva dans son essai sur Dora.* / 'Daniel Augereau is out of luck. In fact, hereabouts, no one's in luck': *Il n'a pas de chance, Daniel Augereau. Du reste, ici, personne n'a de chance.* / 'She played a piece by Bach – in fact, two pieces': *Elle exécuta un morceau de Bach. Ou plutôt deux.* On the one hand, an English connector, versatile and unspecific, making many different conceptual links; on the other, ten French connectors, to which several more could be added, with discrete functions. Of these equivalents for 'in fact', only one is *en fait*.

dans les faits

En fait seems to have evolved relatively recently as a connector; but the unhistorical nature of much French lexicography makes it difficult to know. Napoléon Landais's dictionary (1851) gives it, but defining it as *en matière de* and without an example. It is unknown to Littré, who gives only *Dans le fait*, which he defines as *loc. adv. Réellement, effectivement*, and an example which shows it in the contrastive function now served by *en fait*: *Malgré les apparences, c'est, dans le fait, un homme dangereux.* Nowadays, the related *dans les faits* is sometimes used, as in this antithesis initiated by *sur le papier*:

> Sur le papier, la dérive droitière qui avait caractérisé les vingt dernières années de la vie politique israélienne peut paraître enrayée. Dans les faits, la situation est moins simple.

If 'in fact' can be seen as an English equivalent for many exemplars of *en fait*, perhaps this variant can be deemed to correspond to 'in actual fact'. Other similar variants are *dans la pratique* and *en pratique*.

Most often this connector is placed first in the sentence or with the verb. It can also go at the end, as in this extract from a discussion of fictional policemen:

> Quelle sorte d'hommes seraient-ils s'ils ne pouvaient montrer leurs muscles contre la racaille ? De bien piètres machines à fantasmes, en fait.

enfin *

Roughly speaking, this connector has two basic modes: one in which its function is influenced by its meaning of 'lastly'; and one in which, sometimes combined with other connectors, its function is more to add emotive precision or emphasis and has little to do with literal finality.

Finality

The first mode is used to present the last in a list of points, often three of them, as in this extract from a discussion of the conditions favouring rapid change in language:

> ...là où les populations se mêlent et où elles n'ont pas d'homogénéité, là où des idiomes différents se juxtaposent et où nombre de sujets sont amenés à adopter une langue nouvelle, là où enfin il se produit des changements sociaux importants et où les conditions de la vie se modifient profondément, les langues sont sujettes à se transformer avec une grande rapidité.
>
> (Meillet, 75)

Similarly, when all three are accompanied by connectors, it is used in *sequences of points*: *d'abord... ensuite... enfin*. In the final paragraph of a discussion, some writers combine it with *reste à*, even though it is redundant: *Il reste enfin à savoir*. In many contexts, this enumerative mode could be replaced by *finalement*, *pour finir* or *pour conclure*.

In a slight variant of this mode, it is used not only to conclude but to prioritize. Rather like *pour tout dire*, it can present an element of a statement, again usually the last one, as apter or more precise than the preceding ones, as in Bergson's sentence about human faces: no matter how regular or harmonious their lines and features, the balance among them will never be perfect:

> On y démêlera toujours l'indication d'un pli qui s'annonce, l'esquisse d'une grimace possible, enfin une déformation préférée où se contournerait plutôt la nature.
>
> (Bergson, 399)

One of the commonest functions of this mode is recapitulative: at the end of a longish development, a writer sums up the preceding points. This example is from an essay on the long *romans-fleuves* of the early twentieth century, in which novelists such as Galsworthy, Romains and Proust discuss, among other things, historical characters, decisive events and the problems these give rise to:

> On discute les problèmes que posent ceux-ci : la part de l'homme et de sa volonté, celle du destin, celle des masses anonymes et celles des minorités averties, celle des choses inertes, institutions ou mécanismes, qui précipitent les catastrophes par la seule action de leur pesanteur propre. Enfin, point de problème où l'homme a part qui ne soit, dans ces encyclopédies, abordé, traité, résolu.
>
> (Caillois, 157)

Without finality

This mode can be used without any hint of finality, in a way akin to its exclamatory absolute use in speech, to stress a strong objection or to precise a shade of criticism. Here, a purist, having rebuked users of archaisms, now conversely censures neologisms and what he calls *l'effort, que nous avons appelé futuriste, pour rénover la langue*:

> Il est infiniment plus nocif que le premier, plus arbitraire, plus absurde. Mais il procède au fond de la même inquiétude, de cette indocilité que marquent nos contemporains à l'égard de l'histoire, parce qu'ils l'ignorent entièrement, enfin d'une ignorance rare.

This emotional tone and spoken quality can combine with ***mais***, ***car*** or ***bref***. This example with *mais* is taken from a criticism of the reasons given in 1994 (the centenary of the start of the Dreyfus Affair) for the lack of official commemoration of it:

> Nulle initiative des pouvoirs publics. On dira peut-être : c'est mieux ainsi pour diverses raisons sur lesquelles je vais revenir. Mais les arguments avancés rendent un son surprenant. On ne commémore pas, dit-on, la condamnation d'un innocent, on ne commémore pas une injustice.
> Certes. Mais enfin, commémorer n'est pas célébrer.
>
> (Reberioux)

This mode is mainly a reinforcer of *mais*, which does the main job of countering the preceding concession. It has something of the force of ***après tout*** or a mode of ***quand même***, in that what it introduces is deemed to be close to self-evident; the writer, albeit with some emotional force, merely reminds the reader of this. In a different register, it expresses something of the spoken English 'I mean!', which hints a protest at having to state the obvious. This combination is sometimes printed as a separate sentence, with exclamation mark: *Mais enfin !* the better to show the warmth of feeling it expresses.

Combined with *car*, the connector can express something of the same indignation or irritation that comes from having to state or restate the self-evident, especially to those who will not listen. This example comes from the debate which in November 1993 encouraged the Balladur government to abort its proposal to reduce unemployment by creating a *Smic-jeunes*, a reduced wage for young people:

> Conclusion du gouvernement : pour sortir les jeunes de l'ornière, il leur faut un Smic sur mesure – assorti, pour la forme, d'un vague tutorat. CQFD. Mais non, justement, pas CQFD ! Car enfin, admettons. Admettons qu'il soit nécessaire de baisser le coût du travail des jeunes pour faciliter leur embauche (ce qui n'est d'ailleurs pas démontré). Était-il pour autant indispensable de diminuer leur maigre rémunération ? Certes pas.

The combination *enfin bref* also retains an echo of spoken tone. Unlike unaccompanied *bref*, the function of the combination is not necessarily recapitulative: it may be *bref* rather than *enfin* that is supplementary, shown perhaps by the placing of the latter before rather than after the other connector.

Still in a more spoken than written register, the connector can introduce a restriction or even half-retraction of a preceding point, as in this satire on the trendy young company-man in the modern office:

> Il se promène son « mug » de thé à la main. Le sachet d'Earl Grey est devenu universel. Tutoyer aussi il l'a appris : sa secrétaire et son directeur. D'ailleurs, il les appelle tous deux par leur prénom. Petit à petit, il a réussi à adopter les manies collectives qui font de lui un « homme maison ». Surtout pas de porte de bureau fermée, enfin quand il en existe, car évidemment les espaces sont paysagers [...]

Close to the restrictive mode, and still strongly tinged with a tone of speech, is another exemplified (and discussed) in an anecdote told by Gide about the painter Jacques-Émile Blanche. Gide has just told Blanche that friends now live in the rue Claude-Lorrain:

> ...il pressent que la rue Claude-Lorrain doit être une rue inavouable, impossible, dans un tout à fait inhabitable quartier. Il ajoute : « Je ne connais pas. » (Or il connaît tout ce qu'il sied de connaître.) « Où est-ce ? »
>
> – Elle donne dans la rue Michel-Ange, lui dis-je, sitôt après le viaduc d'Auteuil.
>
> – Enfin : Billancourt.
>
> Cet « enfin », d'après le ton, signifie : « osez le dire », « avouez-le » et « c'est bien ce que j'attendais »... « Comment peut-on habiter Billancourt ? »
>
> (Gide, 1951: 566)

If Blanche had said not *Enfin : Billancourt* but *Billancourt, quoi*, the effect would have been similar.

The connector is used too, with something of the force of ***donc***, in questions; and sometimes it is combined with *donc*: *Qu'est-ce donc enfin que ce christianisme de Gide ?* (Fernandez, 86). In some modes, it can be replaced by *à la fin*.

en fin de compte *

In this structure the *Trésor de la langue française* detects a familiar flavour of which other lexicographers make no mention. Like ***au bout du compte***, ***au total*** and ***en somme***, it derives from a noun which means adding things up. It has two modes: it can either round off points explicitly canvassed in what precedes; or it can remind the reader of implicit points. It is often replaceable by ***finalement***.

Explicitly rounding off

This mode introduces an ultimate consequence or definitive conclusion, often following either an extended development or a description of a lengthy process, involving possibly negotiations, disagreement or complex consideration. In a narrative, a writer describes a gourmet's search for the best wine to accompany a certain cheese:

> Confronté à un livarot somptueux, il sortit de sa cave un châteauneuf-du-pape, « vin droit, ouvert, puissant ». Résultat nul. Il fit alors appel à un vouvray « assez tendre, plein ». Rien à faire. Changeant alors tout à fait de boisson, il opta pour « un cidre pétillant et frais ». En vain. En fin de compte, il trouva son bonheur dans un calvados servi frais.

In such contexts, the connector is not quite replaceable by **enfin**: it does not just signal the end of a process, it also reminds about its cumulativeness. And in that it has a shade of recapitulative function.

Implicit resumer

In this mode, the connector quite often helps to define and categorize an ultimate outcome, in tandem with verbs which describe the end of a process: *mener à, aboutir à, finir par*. The hippy's refusal to join the acquisitive rat-race of contemporary society is seen as *le refus d'une agitation qui ne conduit, en fin de compte, qu'à moudre du vent* (Fontaine, 1978: 150).

It is used as a preciser, after the manner of **en définitive**, to introduce not only a conclusive point but a more accurate evaluation or redefinition of what precedes. In the following example, the writer discusses an objection sometimes made against the *nouveau roman*: that its supposed literary qualities are mere technical devices, what he calls *procédés*, an exemplar of which is Michel Butor's book *Transit*, which can be read front-to-back or back-to-front:

> La double entrée de *Transit* est un procédé ? Soit : comme toute mise en forme, comme toute écriture, comme toute production. Ce qui choque, ce qu'on reproche le plus vivement en fin de compte au nouveau roman, c'est que ces procédés s'affichent au lieu de se tenir cachés; qu'en place de [sic] nous montrer un corps décemment recouvert de sa peau, il nous propose un écorché, avec ses viscères et ses nerfs, ses agencements et ses jointures, ses graisses, ses viandes et ses liquides. Le roi ne se contente pas d'être nu, il est transparent.

There the connector helps to refocus the argument and to define a significant emendation to the objection: it is no longer only that the thing is full of *procédés*, it is that these devices are made flagrantly visible.

In this mode, the connector can allude not to points already discussed but to a subject assumed to be known to the reader. That is, as it resumes implications it reminds the reader of them. The following exemplar assumes in its reader the knowledge that Michel Noir, a politician of the Right, now seen to be seeking support from the RPR-UDF, had once tried to distance himself from this grouping, saying that the prevailing party arrangements of the Right were *obsolètes*:

> En difficulté à Lyon, Michel Noir est reparti depuis peu à la recherche d'appuis parisiens. Il considère que, en fin de compte, il ne lui serait pas inutile d'appartenir à une future majorité RPR-UDF. Et tant pis pour les partis « obsolètes » !

In such contexts, given that the reference is not to a past outcome but to a speculation involving second thoughts or second guessing, 'eventually' would not do as an English equivalent, as it would in a statement like *En fin de compte j'ai renoncé à mon dessein*. A better one here would be 'taking everything into account'. The example also shows that, when the statement speaks of possible consequences, the structure comes close to being replaceable by *après tout*. Nowadays, in most contexts it could also be replaced by *au final*.

English equivalents include 'after all', 'all things considered' or 'eventually'.

en la circonstance

This structure seems to be unrecorded by the makers of French dictionaries. The *Trésor de la langue française* uses it to define *en l'espèce* but nowhere defines it. It functions as a variant for *en l'espèce* and for *en l'occurrence*, while being much less common than either. Like them, it means roughly 'in this instance' and links the particular to the general, relating a single exemplar back to the broader category to which it belongs. A critic censures the proliferation of glossy coffee-table books and uses this connector to link the single case of Nathan to a set of Paris publishers:

> Comment s'étonner d'un penchant presque universel pour l'attractif et le divertissant ? Quand un éditeur, Nathan en la circonstance, publie un ouvrage dénommé *Orsay, le goût d'une époque*, il ne contribue pas à l'étude de la peinture académique, il flatte un engouement à grand renfort de papier glacé et de simplifications excessives.

By using this connector, the writer criticizes not only the case in point but implies that the whole group of publishers are equally responsible for this deplorable trend. This would not so clearly be the case if the connector had been *à savoir*, which some writers use almost interchangeably with *en l'occurrence*. In the next example, the broad category is the characteristic outspokenness of a French general in command of a United Nations peace-keeping force in Bosnia; the particular instance is an occasion when he made a bitter public criticism of the UN officials whose policy led to his men being killed for no apparent benefit to anyone:

> D'aucuns, qui ne l'aiment pas beaucoup, parlent de sa capacité à accumuler les gaffes ou les maladresses, emporté qu'il serait par sa fougue et son franc-parler. Il est vrai que le général Cot ne fait pas habituellement dans la litote. En la circonstance, dans une affaire qui devrait rester toute de diplomatie, il exprime les ressentiments et les amertumes des « casques bleus » lorsqu'il se fâche tout rouge contre l'attitude ambiguë de l'ONU dans « ses palais de Genève », où l'on discute sans considération pour ceux qui se font tuer.

A variant

Also unrecorded in the dictionaries is *en l'occasion*. If André Thérive uses it, it must be because he deems it worthy of the pen of the purist. Discussing an apparently novel usage of the noun *atteinte* which had provoked the quibbles of some who dislike neologisms (the implicit general category of which the word in question offers an instance of petti-fogging purism), he says: *Quant aux scrupules, en l'occasion, ils proviennent de ceci* [...] (Thérive, 1962: 171; see also 1923: 20).

en l'espèce

The older Robert gave no entry for this connector; in the newer, the sole information is *dans ce cas particulier*, and no example of its use is given. The structure derives from the legal sense of *espèce*: a case before a court of law. It continues to have its strict legal application, figuring in the texts of judgments and the like:

> Par arrêt du 7 juillet 1994 de la Cour d'appel de Paris (11ᵉ chambre), Monsieur Albert DU ROY, directeur de la publication du journal « L'ÉVÉNEMENT DU JEUDI » et Monsieur Guillaume MALAURIE, journaliste, ont été déclarés coupables du délit de diffamation publique envers un fonctionnaire public, en l'espèce Monsieur Michel GAGNEUX, Inspecteur des Affaires sociales [...]
> (Anon, 1994b: 14)

There, as sometimes with *en l'occurrence*, the difference between some uses of this connector and that of *à savoir* or *nommément* can be seen to be slight.

The extension of meaning is direct: just as, in law, the connector links the case to the rule, so in less technical contexts it relates the particular to the general, the single exemplar to a whole category of things or to a principle. In the previous example, the particular is *Monsieur Michel* GAGNEUX; the general is *un fonctionnaire public*. Like *en l'occurrence*, for which it is a not uncommon variant, and ***en la circonstance***, which is a less common one, this structure is generally an equivalent for English 'in this instance' or sometimes 'as it happens':

> Pour la première fois depuis 1967, un ressortissant occidental, en l'espèce un coopérant américain, a été enlevé dans la bande de Gaza.

There, the *coopérant américain* is the exemplar; the set to which he belongs is that of Western nationals. Similarly, in the next example, the *Cour de cassation* is the whole of which the part is the *chambre criminelle*:

> Le procès de Klaus Barbie devait amener la Cour de cassation, en l'espèce sa chambre criminelle, à donner une définition du crime contre l'humanité au regard de la loi française.

The rule to which the single case is linked may be left implicit: in the following example, it is the grammatical rule that certain French masculine forms are epicene. A commentator, writing on Marivaux's *La vie de Marianne*, posits that whenever a character in a first-person narrative says « *Je conte mon histoire* », there is always *une identité étroite entre celui (en l'espèce, celle) qui parle et ce dont il est parlé* (Rousset, 16–17) – his point being that in the novel under discussion the narrator is a woman-character.

Place in the sentence

The connector is usually placed by the verb; quite often in an interpolation; on occasion at the beginning of the sentence. It can even be placed at the end, as in this extract from an article on two senior police officers suspended by a government of the Right after being implicated in a charge of spying on a party of the Left. The journalist says the minister, Charles Pasqua, should now quickly reform the whole operation of the Renseignements Généraux department:

> Si M. Pasqua tergiverse, les deux têtes sacrifiées sembleront, dans le climat de rumeur ordinairement suscité par les affaires policières, de commodes boucs émissaires chargés d'endosser en lieu et place du pouvoir la responsabilité d'une mystérieuse manipulation, alors même qu'il n'y en a pas l'ombre d'une, en l'espèce.

There, the connector relates this particular occurrence to the general category of *affaires policières* or *mystérieuses manipulations* of political inspiration.

A variant

The form *dans l'espèce*, given without comment by the *Trésor de la langue française*, is possibly archaic, certainly rare nowadays: *C'est vrai en principe, mais pas tout à fait exact dans l'espèce* (Henriot, 1956: 276).

en l'occurrence *

The noun *l'occurrence* is, in most of its meanings, a *faux-ami* with English 'occurrence'; and outside this structure, it has little existence in modern French.

This can be a difficult connector for the English-speaker to get a purchase on. The meaning is clear enough : *dans le cas présent, dans le cas particulier*. But the conceptual link made between two statements can sometimes be difficult to grasp. It relates the particular to the general, the part to the whole. It is usually equivalent to 'in this instance' or sometimes 'to be precise'. Like 'instance', it relates, explicitly or implicitly, what it accompanies to a whole category of things, a generalization or a principle, of which the exemplar given is seen as a case in point, as in this comment on a childhood spent in colonial Africa: *On ne vit pas impunément « à la colonie » – le Sénégal en l'occurrence – quand on a huit-douze ans*. There, the general category is denoted by the collective *la colonie*; the single instance of it is *le Sénégal*. In the following example, the connector links the instance (the character of Lucien Leuwen) to a preceding category in the plural (writers and their fictional characters after whom streets are named):

> Stendhal, qui dispose d'un passage, d'une villa et d'une rue, est le seul à se voir décerner une plaque pour l'un de ses personnages, en l'occurrence Lucien Leuwen.

And the relation of a single case to a principle is seen here:

> Savez-vous en quoi les libertés ont reculé en France ces temps derniers ? En raison de cette pratique, incroyable pour un État de droit, de changer une loi au cours d'un procès – en l'occurrence le procès d'Action directe – et de continuer à délibérer en s'appuyant sur la loi qu'on vient de changer.

Differences with *à savoir*

At times, the difference between this connector and *à savoir* seems slight. Some writers use *en l'occurrence* where *à savoir* might appear to be more apt, i.e. with only tenuous reference from a particular case to a category. The essential difference between the structures is well shown in two sentences, in which, apart from the connector, only the first word differs:

Un président de la République, en l'occurrence François Mitterrand, n'a pas le droit de changer la Constitution. / *Le président de la République, à savoir François Mitterrand, n'a pas le droit de changer la Constitution.* In the first sentence, *Un* states an explicit rule. The second focusses only on the incumbent and leaves implicit the general principle. A further shade of difference in the use of these two connectors can be seen in this example, containing an interpolation:

> Le président du conseil régional, Noël Josèphe, élu du Pas-de-Calais, refuse de démissionner au milieu de son mandat, pour laisser la place à un homme du département du Nord – en l'occurrence Michel Delebarre – comme le prévoyaient les accords passés entre les deux fédérations.

The connector makes it clear that the agreement covering a replacement for Josèphe stipulated only that it be an *homme du Nord* and did not name Delebarre. Had it named Delebarre, the writer would have used *à savoir*. In such contexts, English might use 'as it happens' or 'to be precise', to isolate the contingent and relate it to the essential. A similar way of denoting an interpolation by the author is seen in this extract from an article in which a journalist, discussing the then minister Yvette Roudy, gives in brackets his opinion on two matters of fact:

> Jamais un ministre (en l'occurrence honnête et compétent) n'a essuyé autant de vannes qu'elle. Son physique (en l'occurrence plutôt plaisant) a été attaqué par des hommes excessivement tartes.

With *or*

The structure quite often functions in tandem with *or*. This formulaic sequence, in the form of a brief negation beginning with *or* and ending with *en l'occurrence*, makes the point that, despite a principle or a general expectation, the case being discussed contradicts the latter:

> La Constitution rend obligatoire la consultation des assemblées locales sur les projets de loi qui doivent s'appliquer dans les territoires d'outre-mer. Or cela n'a pas été le cas en l'occurrence.

Place

The structure is usually placed within the sentence, often as part of an interpolation. On occasion it is placed at the beginning, as in this extract from a comment on one particular prosecution launched by the Chemises Lacoste company for infringement of its copyright:

> Chaque fois que cela lui est possible, la société Lacoste engage des poursuites contre tous ceux qui utilisent comme « logo » un animal ressemblant, de près ou de loin, à son crocodile. En l'occurrence, les reptiles étaient deux, et le dessin ne laissait aucun doute sur leurs occupations...

This connector has two main variants: **en l'espèce**, which is more frequently used than **en la circonstance**. Occasionally a writer will use none of these, preferring *dans le cas qui nous occupe*, *dans le cas donné*, *dans le cas précis* or *dans le cas particulier*.

en outre *

This connector, very common, is one of a set, containing also adverbial **aussi**, **de plus** and **de surcroît**, which serve usually to introduce a further point, parallel and equal in value to the preceding one. In the first example, the author alludes ironically to two features required for success in the fine French art of ballot-rigging: talent and inventiveness. The second of these he introduces with this connector:

> La fraude électorale est, en France, considérée comme l'un des beaux-arts. Et, comme en toute noble matière, le talent n'est pas également réparti. Si charcuter une liste électorale n'est pas dénué d'élégance, jeter une urne au résultat défavorable à la mer est pour le moins vulgaire. En outre, les modes varient et l'invention est permanente, même si quelques valeurs sûres ont su traverser le siècle sans prendre une ride, comme l'inusable bourrage d'urne.

Similarly, the next example offers two reasons why the British authorities distrusted the French police system in the early nineteenth century: its recruitment of former criminals; and its political role. Again, the second of these points is presented by this structure:

> En France, jusque vers 1840, on est persuadé que pour attraper des voleurs, il faut d'autres voleurs, car eux seuls connaissent le langage, les mœurs et les techniques du milieu. Il existe donc une brigade spéciale de détectives conduite exclusivement par d'anciens détenus. En outre, et c'est ce qui trouble les esprits anglais, la police française est étroitement mêlée à l'activité politique ; elle surveille les garnis, pour lesquels elle a constitué un registre spécial ; elle épie, grâce à un réseau de mouchards, les moindres faits et gestes de tous les individus qui peuvent compter dans la vie publique.

In these contexts, the connector could be replaced by *de plus* or one of its variants.

In paired points

What precedes may be introduced by a connective structure such as *pour commencer* or *d'abord*, as in this ironic presentation of how an opponent of the Parti socialiste in 1991 might view the past decade of government dominated by it:

> Décidément, les socialistes, en dix ans de pouvoir, n'ont pas joué le jeu. D'abord, il était prévu qu'ils passeraient la main au bout de deux ans. Or, ils

sont toujours là, fût-ce en lambeaux. En outre, il était admis que leur « ouvriérisme » inconséquent, leur « gauchisme » larvé, leur « bolchevisme » intrinsèque, laisseraient les caisses vides, un franc à l'agonie, une inflation galopante, un déficit budgétaire record, une épargne lessivée et un grand patronat ruiné. Or, ce n'est pas Boulogne qui a mis la clé sous le paillasson, mais Billancourt.

There the connector's function could be served by adverbial ***aussi***: *Il était aussi admis que...* It can also replace *aussi*, or ***encore***, in the binary made of *non seulement... mais*, as in this extract from a discussion of Catholic reasons for disagreeing with Anglicans who favour the ordination of women as priests:

Les adversaires de l'ordination des femmes font une autre démonstration. Non seulement ils invoquent la tradition masculine bimillénaire de l'Église catholique, dont l'anglicanisme s'est séparé au seizième siècle, mais, en outre, au prix d'une interprétation plus littérale de la Bible, ils estiment que, si le prêtre est le représentant du Christ, l'« icône » du Christ sur la terre, il ne peut qu'être homme comme lui.

In sequences

This structure can make one in a ***sequence of points*** presented by a series of different connectors. The second point may be introduced by *aussi* or by ***d'autre part***, the third by *en outre*. The diarist Amiel, summing up a period of three months in his life, uses it to introduce a third point after a second introduced by *à côté de cela*:

J'ai fait connaissance d'un pays nouveau, d'une poésie nouvelle, observé des caractères variés, des types nationaux divers, pénétré dans une construction philosophique qui m'était encore étrangère (Herbert Spencer). À côté de cela feuilleté les mœurs françaises et beaucoup causé. En outre on m'a exercé aux échecs, aux dames, aux mots carrés, aux énigmes, aux acrostiches, aux anagrammes, aux chansonnettes [...]

(Vadier, 207)

The structure is usually placed first in the sentence or paragraph; but it can also accompany the verb.

English equivalents include 'in addition', 'besides', 'for another thing', 'furthermore', 'secondly' and, of course, 'also'.

en plus

Most dictionaries define this structure as essentially different from the other connectors based on *plus*, such as ***de plus***. For Littré, Robert and the *Trésor de la langue française*, *en plus* is a simple adverb and has no function as a connector. Littré separates *de plus* from *en plus*, yet gives *en outre* as an equivalent for both. Robert gives for *en plus* a set of equivalents or cross-references which are quite different from those given for *de plus*. Its definitions of the structures differ without clarity: DE PLUS *marque qu'on ajoute quelque chose à ce qu'on vient de dire. [...] En plus marque que la chose s'ajoute à la précédente, vient en complément.* However, the *Trésor de la langue française* does include this structure in a list of synonyms of *de plus*. Grevisse and Le Bidois take a minute interest in *en plus de* but not in *en plus*.

The functioning of *en plus* as a connector in contemporary usage makes it difficult to justify a distinction between it and *de plus*, *bien plus* or *qui plus est*. Though it has modes in which it does not interchange with them and though it is probably of less frequent occurrence, it is clear that as connectors the structures are largely interchangeable. Like the others, this one usually introduces a further point which either strengthens the one before or goes beyond it. After 'not only that' it says 'but also this'. Take this pair of points on a versatile and talented musician:

> Richard Thompson sait la musique soufie aussi bien que le blues et les jigs celtiques.
> En plus, c'est un grand guitariste, l'un des derniers à pouvoir encore inventer en jouant du rock.

The second of the points is clearly of equal importance with the first. It could have been phrased as *C'est aussi un...*; it could have been introduced by *de surcroît* or *en outre*. As a pair, the points could have been introduced by *d'une part... d'autre part*. All of that can be seen too in the linking of points in this extract from an article on the precarious working conditions of seamen employed in the coastal trade. Here the structure is combined with initial *et*:

> Ils louent leurs services pour des journées de dix-huit heures ou des semaines de cent à cent trente heures. Tous n'obtiennent même pas de leurs employeurs un contrat en bonne et due forme. Et, en plus, ces temps-ci, toutes ces heures passées en mer ne leur rapportent presque rien. Ils ne peuvent même pas se tourner vers les Assedic.

In pairs and sequences

Just like *en outre*, this connector sometimes does service as a variant for *aussi* or *encore* in the binary *non seulement... mais*, usually in a single sentence but also in two sentences, as in this report of unpleasant sailing conditions in the Mediterranean:

> La tempête a fait aussi passer un mauvais moment aux passagers des deux car-ferries *Kalliste* et *Monte Cinto* qui devaient assurer, samedi matin, les liaisons entre la Corse et Marseille. Car non seulement ils sont arrivés avec un retard considérable, 3 heures pour le premier, 9 heures pour le second. Mais en plus,

il leur a fallu supporter – très mal pour certains – des creux atteignant 8 à 10 mètres au large.

Also like *de plus* or *en outre*, the connector replaces the more usual **ensuite** or **puis** in **sequences of points**: an article by a financial journalist justifies a long-awaited lowering of interest rates: *Pour trois raisons. D'abord [...]. En plus [...]. Enfin [...].*

The connector is placed either first in the sentence or between commas with the verb, as in this comment on the growing unmanageability of the *baccalauréat* examination: *Déjà inefficace et ingouvernable, le bac est en passe de devenir, en plus, impraticable.* It is also placed between commas when combining with **avec**, like *en outre, en prime* or *à la clef*, often towards the end of the sentence or at the beginning of a **phrase dépendante**, as in this comment on a proposal to reform the constitution, seen as nothing more than a red herring in a time of unemployment:

Une fois encore, le serpent de mer de la réforme constitutionnelle n'est qu'un prétexte à une manœuvre politique. Avec, en plus, une dérobade : est-ce vraiment à cause du cadre institutionnel que les gouvernants ne parviennent pas à lutter efficacement contre le chômage ?

Even the structure *en plus de*, though not interchangeable with *de plus*, can function similarly in linking ideas, as in this extract from a speech by a coal-miner's wife on the dangers of the miner's life: *Mais les accidents ne sont pas tout. En plus de cela, il y a la maladie professionnelle qu'on appelle la silicose.*

English equivalents include 'in addition', 'besides', 'for another thing', 'furthermore', 'secondly' and, of course, 'also'.

en réalité

Like **en fait**, this connector introduces fact or truth to counter an alleged fact or truth: *La sauce dite hollandaise, bien française en réalité...*; *Beaucoup de mères, statutairement célibataires, sont en réalité des femmes « séparées » d'un ancien conjoint.* Its function is essentially oppositive.

Explicit antitheses

A contrast between misleading appearances and truth is often made visible in what precedes the connector by adverbs like *en apparence* or verbs like *sembler: On dirait des petits croûtons de pain rassis. Ce sont en réalité des fragments d'os humains.* Similar antitheses are made with statements of theory, often accompanied by adverbs like *apparemment, en théorie, nommément, prétendument* or *juridiquement: Théoriquement, l'Algérie est une république. En réalité, c'est le règne des féodalités.* In political contexts, this adverb may be *officiellement*. Likewise, the connector may be preceded by statements meaning 'supposedly': *selon la légende* or *on prétend que*:

> Les fromages français – on dit qu'il en existe autant que de jours dans l'année; en réalité il y en a beaucoup plus.

> La trilogie tomate-ail-huile d'olive, qui passe pour caractéristique de la cuisine provençale et la différencie du reste de la France, est en réalité très récente, et pas seulement pour la tomate, d'origine américaine.

Unfounded beliefs and errors of fact, often denoted by words like *erreur* or *se tromper*, are also rectified by this connector:

> Theodore Zeldin se trompe lorsqu'il ne fait remonter la réputation internationale de la cuisine française qu'au début du XIXe siècle. Celle-ci date, en réalité, du XVIIe siècle.

In similar vein, and again like *en fait*, this structure is used to precise or define terms: *Les « habits bleus », qui, en réalité, sont souvent des blouses grises* ; *En parlant des pays capitalistes, il voulait, en réalité, dire « les pays libéraux »*. Or it can introduce answers to questions, as in this canvassing of the supposed plight of French arms dealers after the end of the cold war:

> Faut-il compatir au « spleen » des « marchands de mort » ? Ou doit-on refuser d'avaliser le diagnostic pessimiste de beaucoup d'entre eux qui crient au loup pour qu'on s'apitoie ? La situation mondiale de ce commerce est, en réalité, plus contrastée et plus nuancée.

The connector's adversativeness is sometimes reinforced by **mais**: *L'armée obéit en apparence, mais en réalité gouverne*. A similar function can be served by **or** and by **alors que**, as in this comment on the slow unnoticed growing together of people who live as man and wife:

> Chacun de nous, durant des périodes plus ou moins longues, a éprouvé le sentiment que rien ne se passait dans son couple, alors qu'en réalité se renforçaient les goûts, les opinions et les désirs communs.

> (Roussel, 218)

Place in the sentence

As can be seen from the examples, the place of the connector is variable: at the beginning of statements, beside the verb and elsewhere. It is also put at the end:

> La France consent 3,1 % de son produit national à la défense. C'est à quelques décimales près ce que d'autres pays de sa dimension réservent à leur sécurité. La comparaison s'arrête là, en réalité.

dans la réalité

Less common, more concrete is *dans la réalité*. The differences and similarities between the two forms are analogous to those between *en fait* and *dans les faits*. In the more concrete form, the noun can function semantically in its own right, rather than as part of a procedural formula. The form with *en* relates to statements, usually defining certainties; the form with *dans* can relate to actions, describing the results of putting a plan into action. As well as being an equivalent for 'really', it has at times a sense close to 'in real life' or 'in practice'. But apart from those shades of difference, it functions in some of the same ways as the mode with *en*. It scotches pseudo-truths, as in Mme Smith's perceptive dictum, in *La cantatrice chauve*, on the vexed question of whether or not anyone is at the door when someone knocks: *Cela est vrai en théorie. Mais dans la réalité les choses se passent autrement* (Ionesco, 36). It is also opposed to expressions of intent or design, to inaccurate analyses and confusions of thought:

> Afin de stabiliser leurs revenus, les éleveurs de porcs ont bien créé une caisse de péréquation censée leur verser, certaines années, des subventions pour compenser la chute des cours et à laquelle, d'autres années, ils devraient cotiser lorsque les cours seraient au plus haut. Dans la réalité, le système s'est révélé impraticable : il marchait dans un sens mais pas dans l'autre.

English equivalents include 'actually', 'in fact', 'in reality', 'more accurately', 'really'.

en résumé *

As the noun *résumé* suggests, this structure usually functions as a recapitulative concluder. It is an infrequent variant for connectors like ***en un mot*** and ***bref***. It introduces a succinct summing up of a lengthy and detailed development; it is often to be found at the beginning of final sentences or paragraphs. In the nature of things, examples of this connector in full contexts are hard to give: it does seem to be reserved for quite extended developments, many of them a page and more in length (Moutote, 165); or else it introduces a general conclusion at the end of a whole article. One of the shortest examples, from a discussion of the earnings of French parliamentarians, finishes like this:

> Jean-Christophe Cambadélis, député socialiste de la 20e circonscription parisienne reçoit chaque mois, au titre des indemnités parlementaires, 33 899,93 F net avant impôts. Il reverse 7 000 F à son parti et 7 500 F pour les frais de sa permanence. Il perçoit également des aides pour son secrétariat et ses collaborateurs, soit respectivement : 25 109 F brut par mois et 25 446 F. Sommes dont il peut disposer à sa convenance. Le député parisien a choisi d'utiliser

intégralement cet argent pour la « bonne cause ». Ce qui lui permet d'employer quatre personnes, dont deux pour des activités dactylographiques à mi-temps. En résumé, il lui reste chaque mois pour vivre un peu moins de 20 000 F puisqu'il n'exerce pas d'autre mandat.

There the connector might be replaced by *au total*, *en fin de compte* or *tout compte fait*. Similarly, Durkheim, arguing against the view that the incidence of suicide increases towards the end of the year in different European countries, uses this connector to sum up a long and complicated paragraph dense with place-names, numbers, dates and conflicting rates of increase and decrease:

> Des chiffres mêmes donnés par Morselli, il résulte que, d'octobre à novembre, le nombre des suicides n'augmente presque dans aucun pays, mais, au contraire, diminue. Il n'y a d'exceptions que pour le Danemark, l'Irlande, une période de l'Autriche (1851–54) et l'augmentation est minime dans les trois cas. En Danemark, ils passent de 68 pour mille à 71, en Irlande de 62 à 66, en Autriche de 65 à 68. De même, en octobre, il ne se produit d'accroissement que dans huit cas sur trente et une observations, à savoir pendant une période de la Norwège [sic], une de la Suède, une de la Saxe, une de la Bavière, de l'Autriche, du duché de Bade et deux du Wurtemberg. Toutes les autres fois il y a baisse ou état stationnaire. En résumé, vingt et une fois sur trente et une, ou 67 fois sur cent, il y a diminution régulière de septembre à décembre.
>
> (Durkheim, 1930: 96)

Other structures which might be used in that context are *au bout du compte*, *autrement dit*, *c'est-à-dire*, *en clair* and *en d'autres termes*. Or it could be replaced by a *transition mécanique* : *Résumons-nous....*

One way in which most of the structures already mentioned differ from this one is that unlike them it can also precede the discussion, helping the reader to grasp a lengthy rigmarole by anticipating it: *L'affaire est, en résumé, la suivante.*

Among English equivalents are 'briefly', 'in short', 'in a few words' and 'to sum up'.

en retour

This is an adverbial expression, meaning roughly 'in return' or 'in exchange', which expresses the idea of reciprocal obligation. Article 1 of the *Code du travail* uses it in that straightforward non-connective way to define apprenticeship as a contract by which an employer

> s'oblige à donner ou à faire donner une formation professionnelle méthodique et complète à une autre personne qui s'oblige, en retour, à travailler pour lui [...]

Similarly, in a report of an industrial agreement signed by Renault and the American manufacturer John Deere, the structure's function is primarily semantic, although there is something of a similarity with *en revanche*:

> Celui-ci va fournir à Renault Agriculture des moteurs Diesel produits dans l'usine John Deere de Saran (Loiret). Ils seront montés sur la gamme des tracteurs Renault. En retour, Renault Agriculture fournira à John Deere des tracteurs équipés de moteurs John Deere, qui seront commercialisés sous la marque John Deere en complément des gammes actuelles du constructeur américain.

Semi-reciprocal semi-contrastive

It is no doubt because of the inverse symmetry which this structure makes between two points that it has come to lend itself to the shaping of antitheses. A usage already shading towards the less semantic, more contrastive function of a procedural connector is this, from a discussion of the former divorce between everyday speech and written style:

> Dans nos sociétés modernes un semblable phénomène ne serait plus possible : la langue écrite, pénétrant dans toutes les couches de la population, par les affaires, la science, la littérature, au moyen du journal, du livre, de la conférence, de l'école, etc., ne peut rester en marge de l'idiome parlé ; ceux qui écrivent doivent compter avec tout le monde ; en retour, la moyenne des sujets entre plus aisément dans l'état d'esprit que suppose une expression spéciale de la pensée.
>
> (Bally, 197)

Much the same could be said of two exemplars used in a discussion of the influences that the École normale supérieure and the philosopher Louis Althusser had on each other:

> Façonné par le style de l'institution, Althusser a largement contribué à entretenir en retour les réalités et les légendes de la Rue d'Ulm.
> [...] L'ineffable mélange de vide et d'absolu qui fait le charme de Normale sup' avait, à sa manière, profondément marqué le philosophe. Lui, en retour, donnait à cette tradition une nouvelle jeunesse, en proposant la révolution prolétarienne comme horizon aux enfants studieux.
>
> (Droit)

Sartre uses this mode twice in his essay 'Paris sous l'Occupation' (1945), contrasting the attitudes of peasants and city-dwellers:

> Les paysans, longtemps blessés par le mépris où ils croyaient être tenus, prenaient leur revanche et tenaient la dragée haute aux habitants des villes : ceux-ci, en retour, les accusaient d'alimenter le marché noir et d'affamer les populations urbaines. [...] Pendant quatre ans, les combattants de « 14 » reprochèrent à ceux de 40 d'avoir perdu la guerre et ceux de 40, en retour, accusèrent leurs aînés d'avoir perdu la paix. (Sartre, 1949b: 40, 41)

So symmetrical is the reciprocation that the structure could almost be replaced by *à l'inverse*. Something similar is seen in this extract from a discussion of Stendhal's 'double nature', partly logical, partly poetic:

> Le logicien se méfiait ainsi du poète, et le poète, en retour, dans ses moments de plein abandon, se méfiait de la logique et de l'analyse.
>
> (Blum, 540)

There it would be difficult to distinguish whether the structure, which clearly shapes a contrast, retains any of the original semantic function.

Adversative

Other writers use the structure as a straightforward variant of adversative connectors like *en revanche* and **par contre**, without a vestige of the idea of reciprocity, as in this discussion of a novel by Belot which got two very different critical receptions, unfavourable when it was first published as a serial in *Le Figaro*, then favourable when it came out as a book:

> le roman est d'une extrême discrétion. Pourtant il fit scandale. Des lecteurs indignés accablèrent Belot d'injures... Quand il parut en librairie, en retour, le livre fut un énorme succès : plus de 30 rééditions de 1870 à 1885 !!
>
> (Cantégrit, 6)

And in this example, a book reviewer speaks of the politician Edwige Avice's account of her relationship to her constituency, towards which, as an outsider and even after having lost her seat, she continued to have very warm feelings:

> Il semble que la parachutée ait atterri sur sa terre d'élection, plus que sur un filon électoral. La curieuse façon dont elle rend compte de son mandat montre, en retour, qu'elle a été plus sensible à sa rencontre avec le pays qu'à la possession durable d'un fief.

There, it is the position of the structure in the sentence that makes clear its connective rather than semantic function.

English equivalents are 'conversely' and 'on the other hand'.

en revanche *

This is one of the most used of the adversative structures of French discursive prose. It always introduces the second of two statements which it sets in contrast with each other, as in this comparison between common and uncommon genetic disorders:

> On recense environ 3 500 maladies génétiques, affections dues aux dysfonctionnements d'une zone spécifique du génome humain. Certaines, comme la

> trisomie 21 (ou mongolisme) et la myopathie de Duchenne, sont relativement
> fréquentes et bien connues. D'autres, en revanche, sont extrêmement rares
> (quelques dizaines de cas à travers le monde) et difficiles à diagnostiquer.

An English text marking such a simple distinction might well do without
a connector. This one could be replaced by *au contraire*. Alternatively,
in many instances of this quasi-neutral contrastiveness, where no judgment accompanies the comparison, it functions like the *pronom tonique
disjoint*, as in this pair of sentences discussing the European Community's
different arrangements on identity cards and drivers' licences, where it is
replaceable by *eux*:

> La perspective de l'Europe de 1993 n'abolit pas la nécessité de détenir une
> carte d'identité nationale. Les permis de conduire sont, en revanche, parfaite-
> ment harmonisés depuis le 1er janvier 1986.

en revanche and *par contre*

Some writers, seeing this connector as essentially different from *par contre*,
prefer to use it only when comparing something favourable in the statement following to a less favourable point in what precedes. That
negative–positive relation can be seen in this irony on Lebanon during its
civil war: *Sans président de la République depuis le 23 septembre, il a en
revanche deux gouvernements*; and in this excerpt from a discussion of a
man's reasons for marrying without love:

> Il s'estimait incapable d'aimer, au sens romanesque du mot, mais considérait,
> en revanche, qu'on ne saurait asseoir trop tôt la sécurité de la vie, et que,
> commise à Élisabeth, elle serait en bonnes mains.
>
> (Blum, 14)

Thus defined, the structure would be a variant for *en compensation*; it
could sometimes be replaced by *en retour*, especially in a context where
there is a reciprocal relation between the two points. In theory, what
follows *par contre* is more negative than what precedes. Grevisse quotes
Gide's comment on this distinction and his two examples which show the
sort of absurdity that can arise if it is not respected:

> Trouveriez-vous décent qu'une femme vous dise : « Oui, mon frère et mon
> mari sont revenus saufs de la guerre ; *en revanche* j'y ai perdu mes deux
> fils » ? ou : « La moisson n'a pas été mauvaise, mais *en compensation* toutes
> les pommes de terre ont pourri » ?
>
> (Grevisse, 1964a: 994)

In practice many writers neglect this distinction; and the two connectors
are nowadays well-nigh interchangeable in introducing a point which is
less favourable than what precedes:

> Durant les quarante dernières années, les Françaises ont fortement progressé dans la hiérarchie scolaire et professionnelle. En politique, en revanche, elles ont stagné, voire régressé.

Clearly, in such contexts, a writer's view on what is favourable or not lies implicit in the assumptions shared with the readership of the time. In the following example, since the principle that most concerns the author is equality of treatment of men and women, the favoured treatment of men mentioned in the second sentence is presented as deplorable:

> L'islam interdit le mariage de femmes musulmanes avec des non-musulmans. En revanche, le musulman peut librement épouser des chrétiennes ou des juives.

And the author of the following comparison of rates of imprisonment is not in favour of the relative leniency shown to drivers who kill:

> En France, en 1975, onze pour cent seulement des auteurs d'homicides involontaires liés à la circulation ont été condamnés à des peines de prison ferme ; en revanche, soixante-sept pour cent des individus condamnés pour délit de vagabondage ou de mendicité ont été emprisonnés.

With the *si d'opposition*

In binary sentences, the connector is often combined with the *si d'opposition*. The latter initiates an antithesis which is underscored in the second part of the sentence, as in this extract from an article about trade negotiations between Europe and the USA on cereals and soya beans:

> Quant aux protéagineux, s'il est vrai que l'Europe n'a rien obtenu sur les produits de substitution aux céréales, elle a, en revanche, limité les dégâts sur le soja.

This connector is placed first in the statement as often as it is put by the verb. Some writers combine it with *mais*.

English equivalents, depending on contexts, might be 'against that', 'on the other hand', 'whereas', the ubiquitous 'but' or 'however'. When it is used in the second half of sentences beginning with the *si d'opposition*, English writers would probably do without a connector.

en somme *

This connector is one of the set of resumers and concluders. It has two basic modes: the more common of them explicitly recapitulates what precedes; the other concludes without explicitly resuming.

Recapitulative

Like *bref* or *en un mot*, which could often replace it, the more explicit recapitulator is usually placed near the end of a development and sums up in briefer form a diversity of detail, analysing and condensing length and complexity into a single point:

> Les adversaires de François Mitterrand le présentent aujourd'hui comme un vieillard frileux, timoré, pusillanime, dépassé par les événements. En somme, un homme « fini ».

As that example shows, what precedes often resembles a list, of adjectives or nouns, say, or else it accumulates clauses or sentences of similar construction. This is also clear in the following quotation, where the sentence linked by the connector continues the repetition of the word which structures what precedes, *il faut*:

> Pour M. Mitterrand, « politiquement il n'y a pas d'Europe », « il y a un vide », « il faut des institutions », il faut des règles, il faut un lieu où les uns et les autres soient sur un pied d'égalité. Il faut en somme ce que, faute de mieux, il avait appelé il y a quelques années « la confédération ».

The reduction of preceding multiples to a single proposition is seen, too, when the connector is combined with *tout* or with ***tout se passe comme si***, a variant of which is seen in these sentences listing features of the counter-revolutionary measures once more governing private life under the Bourbon Restoration of the 1820s:

> Juridiquement, le divorce, d'abord rendu plus difficile par le Code civil, avait en fin de compte été abrogé en 1817. Les enfants illégitimes se trouvaient de nouveau exclus de la succession. L'autorité du mari sur la femme avait été rétablie comme celle des parents sur leurs enfants. L'Église avait retrouvé ses pouvoirs et s'efforçait de reprendre son contrôle sur la vie privée. Tout en somme semblait retourner à l'ordre ancien.

The similar structures preceding the connector intimate its function: to abstract the common from the apparently diverse.

The connector can also rephrase not an accumulation of similar structures but only the single idea immediately preceding, sharpening its point:

> Les pays que nous allons maintenant parcourir, en les étudiant du point de vue français, ce sont ces pays de l'Europe méridionale qui se groupent au nord de la Méditerranée, du détroit de Gibraltar à la côte d'Asie Mineure. Ces États sont, en somme, les riverains d'un grand lac.
>
> (Herriot, 97)

In such contexts, it sometimes has a confirmatory and precising function close to that of ***de fait*** or ***c'est-à-dire***. Indeed, at times it is used in combination with the latter:

Si l'écrivain ne voit pas ce qu'il décrit, ce qu'il raconte, paysages et figures, mouvements et gestes, comment aurait-il du style, c'est-à-dire, en somme, de l'originalité ?

A variant of this combination can be seen in *Ce qui veut dire, en somme, que*....

The unargued judgment

This mode does not restate anything or reduce many statements to one. It introduces a conclusive analytical judgment, the grounds for which may be personal and implicit, functioning like **enfin**, a mode of **finalement** or, nowadays, **au final**, as in this comment on Flaubert's *La tentation de saint Antoine*:

> Comme devant l'échec de *Bouvard et Pécuchet*, je me dis que ces deux cents pages de coruscation négative et trente ans de travail forcé, c'est beaucoup, pour aboutir, en somme, à un livre ennuyeux.
>
> (Henriot, 1954: 48)

> Nous vivons dans un relatif dont la circonférence n'est pas très grande ; le changement n'est qu'un retour au passé et le futur, plein d'inconnu, ne contient, en somme, que des vieilles lunes.

Place in the sentence (and *quoi*)

When it accompanies a main clause, this structure tends to be placed either first in the sentence or after the first verb. When it introduces a complement, it tends to be placed late in the sentence, often with the final element. It can even be placed last, accompanied by an exclamation mark, as in this satirical comment on military euphemisms:

> Le maquillage verbal des « bombardements » en « frappes » date de la guerre du Golfe. À l'époque, la « frappe » était dite « chirurgicale ». Il fallait comprendre qu'un bien sortirait du mal nécessaire, comme pour les individus poussés sur le billard, et qu'autour de la cicatrice il n'y aurait pas de bobo. Une intervention dans l'intérêt de l'ennemi, en somme !

When the connector is placed last, one can see its similarity to the familiarly spoken *quoi* appended to statements. Here the latter follows a list:

> Innocent et coupable, trop sévère et trop indulgent, impuissant et responsable, solidaire de tous et rejeté par chacun, parfaitement lucide et totalement dupe, esclave et souverain : je suis comme tout le monde, quoi.
>
> (Sartre, 1949a: 147–148)

In equivalent English contexts, writers would often not use a connector. Some that might be used are 'in fact', 'in short' and 'on the whole'.

ensuite *

This is one of the many expressions, like *alors*, *tandis que* or *dès lors*, which can have either a temporal or a logical function. In narrative, it usually tells what happens next. In discussion, it adds an argument of similar importance to what precedes.

Pairs of points, unannounced and announced

In the unannounced pair, the first point is not signalled as such to the reader. In this example, taken from a discussion of evolution in the design of micro-chips through technological leaps (*le leap frog*), a writer canvasses its drawbacks:

> Le *leap frog* a ses limites. Sauter loin ne sert pas à grand-chose si les débouchés n'existent pas. Commercialisée trop tard, une puce dont la mise au point a coûté des centaines de millions de dollars ne vaut plus rien. Mise sur le marché trop tôt, elle ne vaut guère mieux. Ensuite, la pratique du saut technologique est extrêmement onéreuse. Elle suppose de mobiliser des sommes colossales.

The *limites* referred to in the first sentence and spelled out by the following ones turn out to be two in number: the possible untimeliness of the advance; and the huge financial risks. It is the second of these which is introduced by the connector. It could have been introduced instead by *d'autre part*, *de plus*, *de surcroît*, *en outre*, *et* or *puis*. Or the pair of points could have been structured by *d'une part... d'autre part*. Or else the first point could be announced as such by *d'abord*, as in this extract from a discussion of the acute political difficulties caused by one of the most pressing financial problems of the 1990s:

> Maîtriser les dépenses de santé ? C'est d'abord accepter de prendre de front le lobby médicalo-hospitalier. C'est ensuite reconnaître que le sacro-saint principe d'égalité n'est pas toujours équitable.

In sequences

The connector is often used to introduce one in a *sequence of points*, as in the classic triad *d'abord... ensuite... enfin*. Sequences, like pairs, may be unannounced. In the next example, a writer disputes the idea that the press constitutes a *contre-pouvoir*, analogous to the judiciary or the legislative arm of government. He points out a series of fallacies in this analogy, the third (or fourth?) of which is presented by this connector:

> Tandis que les autres contre-pouvoirs, le judiciaire et le législatif, sont eux-mêmes des pouvoirs, recrutent leurs membres selon des critères de représentativité ou de compétence et de moralité définis par la Constitution, par les

lois ou par les règlements, rien de tel ne conditionne l'embauche des journalistes. Les diplômes professionnels que décernent les écoles de journalisme n'ont qu'une valeur indicative. Outre qu'ils ne garantissent pas grand-chose, ils sont facultatifs, contrairement aux titres que la loi exige des médecins, des avocats ou des professeurs pour qu'ils puissent exercer. Ensuite et par conséquent le corps journalistique est seul juge des capacités et de l'honnêteté de ses membres, de la qualité de leur travail [...]

(Revel, 1988: 236)

As the examples show, the connector is placed either first in the sentence or with the verb.

In English, the links made by *ensuite* might be made by 'and then again', 'in addition', 'moreover', 'furthermore', 'as well as that' or by the factotum 'also'.

en tout cas *

This structure always introduces the second element in a binary affirmation. It usually attenuates or restricts what precedes while certifying the basic validity of it: *Les mots français ne sont pas français. Pas de souche, en tout cas. / La deuxième phrase est plus élégante. En tout cas, elle est plus moderne.* It makes the point that, though there may be room for debate or doubt on what precedes, no one can disagree with what follows. It introduces a fall-back position, especially when combined with *ou*: *Il n'y a plus de nature humaine, ou, en tout cas, elle est inconnaissable.* It also combines with **mais** and even with **et**: *La politique de transfusion sanguine n'a pas été menée en France selon des critères scientifiques, et en tout cas pas selon l'éthique médicale.*

Like *de toute façon*

In some sequences, this connector functions like **de toute façon**, as in the combination with *ou* or when what precedes is a **question** or a series of questions. The uncertainty expressed by the interrogative is answered by the connector with what is known: *L'Allemagne est-elle en stagflation? En tout cas, la locomotive allemande a cessé de tirer l'Europe.* Similarly, the uncertainty preceding may be conveyed by a series of hypotheses, forms of questions without question marks:

Querelle de personnes, remise en cause des structures de commandement, course ouverte aux nominations : c'est en tout cas une grave crise de confiance qui ébranle les sommets de la hiérarchie militaire d'Israël.

This mode of the connector is likely to be used in a discussion of the reliability of evidence. It says, as on the problematical origin of the Etruscan civilization, that though it may not be possible to state X with any certainty, Y is undoubted:

> Pendant longtemps, on a attribué aux Étrusques une origine lointaine. Des légendes, qui circulaient dès l'Antiquité, les faisaient venir des pays égéens. On sait maintenant, sans doute possible, que les Étrusques ont une origine que certains qualifient d'indigène (alors que d'autres récusent cet adjectif). Certes, on ne peut dire quand les diverses populations dont ils descendaient sont arrivées en Étrurie, ni d'où elles venaient. En tout cas, la civilisation étrusque est en parfaite continuité avec celle du néolithique du nord de l'Italie [...]

This role of advancing a restricted certainty is seen in the frequency of the sequence **peut-être** followed by *en tout cas* and of sentences beginning: *Ce qui est certain, en tout cas, est que..., En tout cas, une chose est sûre...* or *Il est clair, en tout cas, que....*

Also like *de toute façon*, this connector can be placed last in the sentence, as in the very first example used above.

Like *du moins*

The structure is sometimes used after a statement which implies no uncertainty: « *Il ne faisait pas de politique. Il ne m'en a en tout cas jamais parlé* ». In such an exemplar (spoken, not written), it can be seen to function as a variant for **du moins**: the second sentence may be read less as an attenuation of the first than as the justification for it. The connector makes a reservation about what had previously been said to be certain. It could often be replaced by *ou plutôt*, as in this statement, also spoken, about a projected timetable for renovations of a building:

> « Les concours pour l'aménagement de ces salles se dérouleront en 1994, et les travaux eux-mêmes l'année suivante. C'est en tout cas ce que prévoit à l'heure actuelle notre calendrier. »

Also like *du moins*, the connector can function in tandem with **sinon**, validating at least what follows if not also what precedes, as in this statement by an editor about a manuscript: *Il semble avoir été écrit sinon d'un seul jet, en tout cas dans un court laps de temps* (Malicet, 51).

Variant forms

The spelling *en tous cas* was widely used in the early twentieth century – it is common in authors such as Brunot, Dastre, Delacroix, Durkheim, Launay, Le Dantec, Lévy-Bruhl, Proust, Rougemont. It is still used on occasion, as in this comment on tattooed women: *Aucune tradition, contrairement à la femme japonaise, ne prépare l'Européenne, la Française en tous cas, à se faire tatouer* (Braudeau, v). A third form, *en tous les cas,* was also used then (Depéret, 53) and is still used today by some speakers and writers. This is similar to the three forms of *de toute façon*.

dans tous les cas

Dictionaries mislead by continuing to define this different structure as interchangeable with *en tout cas* (Robert; Hanse, 1949: 156). It was once, as in this statement written a century ago about *la femme*:

> ...l'être le moins facile à connaître de la création, le plus intéressant et le plus mystérieux, le plus illogique peut-être, dans tous les cas le plus bizarre.
>
> (Fouquet, 252)

Nowadays it does not confirm what follows by attenuating what precedes. Its usual function is primarily substantive or semantic: it does not restrict a hypothesis but recapitulates the several concrete cases under consideration and draws a common conclusion from them. In the following example, taken from an article about an alleged swindler, it sums up three related facts which are presented in the standard tripartite *sequence of points*, *D'abord... Ensuite... Enfin*:

> René Trager s'est décidé à donner les noms des destinataires des fonds qu'on lui reprochait d'avoir détournés. D'abord, dans des déclarations faites sur procès-verbal. Ensuite, dans les confidences qu'il a faites directement à plusieurs reprises depuis sa mise en liberté. Enfin, dans le livre qu'il a fait paraître au début du mois de novembre. Dans tous les cas, il a donné les mêmes précisions et livré les mêmes détails sur cette affaire.

And even when what precedes is a series of hypotheses rather than realities, the function may be still recapitulative and conclusive rather than restrictive: *Première question [...]. Deuxième interrogation [...]. Troisième hypothèse suggérée [...]. Dans tous les cas, il va falloir [...]*. In contexts dealing with two possibilities, the conclusive summing-up is done by related expressions like *dans un cas comme dans l'autre, dans l'un et l'autre cas* and *dans les deux cas*.

English equivalents could include, depending on context, 'at any rate' or 'or if not, at least'. A similarity with 'certainly' is seen in the following statement about the date when Oscar Wilde's friendship with Lord Alfred Douglas probably began:

> Wilde always claimed that the intimacy sprang up in April 1892 after Douglas had written from Oxford requesting his help with a man who was blackmailing him over an indiscreet letter. Certainly they seem to have started seeing each other more regularly from that time.
>
> (Sturgis, 130)

en tout état de cause *

This connector is in some contexts replaceable by *en tout cas* or a mode of *de toute façon*. Unlike *en tout cas*, it does not usually qualify or restrict an initial affirmation. However, it does introduce the second element in a binary sequence; and its function is essentially contrastive. Following a statement of the potential, it introduces a statement of the actual: what precedes usually canvasses a hypothesis, discusses possible outcomes, speculates about alternative explanations, sketches interpretations of possibly inconclusive evidence; what follows is usually a statement of certainty, a conclusion which, despite the preceding possibilities, holds good in any event. An essay severely critical of de Gaulle's handling of the calamities of the Algerian war of independence raises two possibilities, abstains from judgment on them and arrives at a conclusion:

> Peut-être était-il impossible de faire autrement, peut-être seul de Gaulle pouvait-il éviter de plus graves dégâts encore, on ne le saura jamais. Mais, en tout état de cause, on ne saurait dire qu'il y a eu « miracle algérien » grâce à de Gaulle.

Similarly, a discussion of whether or not Franz Brüggen sees any of the nine symphonies of Beethoven, only one of which was written in the eighteenth century, as classical enough to be played by his Orchestra of the Eighteenth Century, discusses several possibilities, pronounces on the validity of none of them, then states a definite fact:

> Il y a quelque temps, Brüggen disait: « Notre orchestre est incapable de dépasser l'*Eroica* (Troisième Symphonie de Beethoven). Il peut donc jouer la Quatrième et la Huitième, qui sont d'une écriture plus classique. » Quelques mois plus tard, il nous disait : « Nous pouvons jouer toutes les symphonies de Beethoven sauf la Cinquième. » Dans un entretien accordé plus récemment à Patrick Szersnovicz, il déclare ne pas pouvoir jouer la Neuvième. En tout état de cause, lors de son concert parisien, il va diriger la Septième, qui est d'une écriture plus moderne, à l'évidence, que l'*Eroica* !

The conclusions do not cancel the hypotheses; they merely state what is certain in contrast to what is not. The connector implies suspension of judgment, saying: whatever may be the truth or untruth of the foregoing, the following *is* true. Also like *en tout cas*, the structure can introduce the answer to a *question*, as in this extract from a discussion of the conditions likely to be put on the regional distribution of government loan-funds:

> Les régions seront-elles totalement libres de fixer leurs propres priorités pour l'utilisation de l'emprunt Balladur, ou bien des priorités nationales seront-elles affichées ? En tout état de cause, il s'agit bien de l'emprunt prévu depuis six mois, et non d'une manne supplémentaire.

With *et*

As in the first example above, the connector can combine with ***mais***, reinforcing the contrast. It also combines with ***et***, as in this extract from an article about the decline of the French Communist party under its then Stalinist leader, Georges Marchais:

> La plus grande réussite de M. Marchais est d'avoir fait admettre, depuis 1984, au parti qu'il dirige, que les échecs électoraux ne sont pas catastrophiques et qu'en tout état de cause ils ne sont de nature à provoquer ni des remous internes ni des déchirements stratégiques.

There, the connector introduces a supplementary element in the reasoning and implies a doubt on the apparent certainty of what immediately precedes it: 'The results are not catastrophic, but even if they *were* ...'. Similarly, in the following extract from a discussion of economic recession in Europe, what precedes appears at first to be a statement of fact; but its supposed certainty is undercut by what follows:

> La reprise américaine et les quelques succès britanniques ne laissent pas envisager un décollage équivalent dans les autres pays de l'Europe, et, en tout état de cause, pas de sitôt.

In such contexts, the connector comes close to the function of the second mode of *de toute façon*. In English this link of thought might be made by adding 'certainly not' or by placing 'anyway' at the end of the sentence.

Littré recalls the legal origin of the expression (*une cause* = 'a lawsuit'): *En tout état de cause, quel que soit l'état du procès. Dans le langage général, en tout état de cause, quoi qu'il en soit.* It can certainly be used at times as a variant for *quoi qu'il arrive* or for *quelle que soit la situation*. Unlike *de toute façon* and *en tout cas*, it is not usually placed at the end of the sentence; either it begins a sentence or even a paragraph, and is followed by a comma, or it accompanies the verb.

Depending on context, English equivalents would be 'at all events', 'in any event', 'at any rate', 'in any case' or 'whatever the case may be'.

en un mot *

This is one of the set of resumers and concluders which includes also ***bref***, ***en définitive*** and ***en résumé***. Like *bref*, this one always recapitulates what precedes. Given the ostensible meaning of the words that make it up, one might expect that what follows would be briefer than what precedes. This is often not so; and like English 'in a word', it means 'in a few words'. The function, rather than signalling a reduction to fewer words, is close to that of ***autrement dit*** or ***en d'autres termes***: to indicate an analytical conclusion. Most of the conclusions it introduces run to no more than a single clause or a simple sentence. Many are lucid and lapidary; others are lengthy – *Le rire* contains one running not to one word but to more than eighty (Bergson, 396). The structure is probably less common now than it was in the early twentieth century. It may have a faint flavour of the literary or the old-fashioned. Its users are academics rather than journalists.

Followed by a complement

The connector does at times link a shorter following text, even a one-word text, to a longer preceding text, as in these two examples, the first of which comments on a production of Mozart's opera *Così fan tutte*, during the 1988 Festival of Aix-en-Provence:

> Le *Così* d'Aix 1988 est réussi ; Mozart était là. Loin de toute métaphysique – avouée –, ce spectacle portait à sourire constamment. C'était un vrai régal, un bonheur de chaque instant. Ce *Così* était drôle, touchant, subtil, libre, jeune, exempt de toute amertume et de tout sarcasme. En un mot : mozartien.

> Jusqu'à quel point notre vie privée est-elle à l'abri du regard indiscret de l'administration, de l'entreprise, du fisc, de la police, en un mot de l'État ?

Such brevity is usual when the connector introduces a complement. It tends then to be placed towards the end of the sentence. Unlike *bref*, this resumer can not only precede the complement it accompanies but also follow it, as in this extract from the preface to a handbook on style:

> Les étudiants pourront trouver ici des suggestions, des idées de recherches à faire, d'impressions et d'hypothèses à vérifier, des directions à suivre et à dépasser, des cadres à remplir, des points de départ, en un mot, et des bases pour leur travail personnel.

> (Lanson, 6)

Followed by a main clause

When what follows is a main clause, the connector is usually placed first, is followed by a comma and introduces a lengthier wordage, a whole sentence (or sentences), as in this comment on the image of the writer Louis-Ferdinand Céline as given by a new book:

> Qu'apprenons-nous de nouveau ? Que Céline était en 1930 un chaud lapin, exubérant, drôle, préoccupé par la misère sociale, voyant déjà arriver la prochaine guerre mondiale. On le découvre aussi émotif, nerveux, rigolo, travailleur acharné. En un mot, on retrouve un jeune homme socialiste, tout en nerfs. Avec des jugements très précis, très beaux sur l'ensemble de la littérature française.

> (Amette, 90)

In the following example, the writer is the nineteenth-century diarist Amiel and his view is that the image of humanity given by the poets of Greek antiquity is out-of-date:

> *Leur homme n'est plus le nôtre.* On reconnaît que le monde a changé, qu'un rideau a été tiré. Leur homme n'est pas devenu *faux*, mais il est *incomplet*, il n'est qu'une partie de l'homme de nos jours. Il se retrouve tout entier en nous, mais non pas nous tout entiers en lui. En un mot l'homme moderne et sa poésie *renferment* l'homme et la poésie antique, et les *débordent.*

(Vadier, 113)

Of course, the connector introducing a complement can still come first in the sentence (if it is a *phrase dépendante*), as in the very first example above. And conversely, it can accompany a whole sentence without coming first, though this is rare and often entails no more than putting it after the first verb: *Il s'agit, en un mot, de...* or *Voici en un mot comment on....*

Variants

A less frequent variant is *en deux mots*. It too can introduce a full sentence or a complement; and it can precede or follow the latter. This example deals with a stage designed during the 1930s by the actor and director, Louis Jouvet:

> Deuxième acte : Jouvet élabore en fond de scène un praticable fixe, mais, comme on dirait aujourd'hui, « polyvalent », c'est-à-dire apte à servir en toutes circonstances, qu'elles soient tragiques ou comiques. Il s'agit, en deux mots, d'une arche, sorte de pont vénitien sur et autour duquel passent et repassent des escaliers.

Other variants, sometimes combined with a *transition mécanique*, are: *Disons-le en un mot*; *Résumons en deux mots notre impression*; *Il s'agit de savoir, en quelques mots, si....* Dictionaries give also *en trois mots* and *en peu de mots*; but these expressions are rare nowadays.

A further set of variants is based on the expression *en un mot comme en cent*, as in this extract from a review of Wagner's *Die Walküre* produced during the Festival of Orange:

> Il arrive, à Orange, la même mésaventure qu'à l'Opéra de Paris : gâtés par certaines soirées exceptionnelles, nous attendons de pied ferme, chaque fois, le mouton à cinq pattes. Or, l'animal est particulièrement rare dans les prairies de l'opéra.
>
> En un mot comme en cent, *La Walkyrie* n'a pas été tout à fait l'événement « historique » qu'on se jugeait en droit de vivre, après les *Tristan*, *Norma* et *Salomé* des étés précédents.

This expression, old enough to be found in comedies by Racine and Molière, may retain from usages such as the assaulted Sganarelle's *en un*

mot autant qu'en deux mille a jocular or emotional flavour that lends it
to adaptations, with suggestions of cutting a long story short, the long and
the short of it and not beating about the bush. One finds also *en un mot
comme en mille* and even *en un mot comme en deux*: *...le parti des « pa-
triotes » et de « la France française » réunis, en un mot comme en deux, le
Front national.*

As well as 'in a word', English equivalents are 'briefly', 'in short' and
'in a nutshell'.

en vérité

This connector has two discrete modes: affirmative and adversative. Most
dictionaries see it solely as an adverb functioning within a sentence, rather
than as a connector linking whole ideas or statements. They say it serves
to *renforcer une affirmation, une assertion*, which is true; and they give
cross-references to **assurément**, *certainement*, *vraiment* and, in Littré, to
sincèrement. None of which says anything about its roles as an inter-assertional connector. Yet it is probably as a connector that it is used most
often in contemporary written French. The *Grand Larousse de la langue
française* of 1978 comes closest to defining this role:

> Sert à introduire une restriction, une mise au point : Ce n'est pas un mauvais
> garçon, mais, en vérité, il est un peu paresseux.

Affirmative

This mode can function like **décidément**, and that in two ways. Either it
reinforces a preceding idea, as in an essay on Renan where it recapitulates a long description of the beneficent influence of Italy upon the
writer's mind: *En vérité, c'est à Rome que Renan est né.* Or else, placed
in an opening sentence, it stresses by anticipation an idea which will be
expanded in what follows, as in this opening of an article about the fiftieth
anniversary of the D-Day landings in Normandy:

> Étrange jour en vérité que ce « jour J » de Normandie, en superproduction
> mondiale, mais dont le message n'est pas clair.

There it serves rather like an exclamation mark – indeed, this mode is
sometimes accompanied not only by an adjective like *étrange* or *singulier*
but by an exclamation mark: *Curieuse firme en vérité !* English might say
'all right' or 'right enough'. Also in affirmative mode, some writers use it
like **à la vérité**.

Adversative

However, the affirmative mode is less common than the second one, essentially adversative. At times it is so contradictive that it could be replaced by a mode of *or*. Like *en réalité*, it can be seen as a variant for *en fait*, although it is less used than either of these structures. In this mode, it casts doubt on what precedes; and what follows is always a statement of fact. Thus, the connector can serve to correct an error, as in this extract from a discussion of the hole in the ozone layer:

> L'un des plus impardonnables actes contre l'éthique scientifique est d'avoir prétendu que la découverte du « trou d'ozone » datait de 1984. En vérité le « trou d'ozone » avait été découvert par Gordon Dobson, de l'université de Cambridge, en 1956–57, durant l'Année géophysique internationale.

It can rectify a misapprehension or a false premiss, as in this answer to the contention that the national health scheme should be changed because it is a drain on the economy. The writer contradicts that argument, seeing the health scheme as a stimulus to growth:

> Tous les projets de réforme procèdent de deux hypothèses qui me paraissent infondées. La première serait que les dépenses constituent une charge pour la nation, un poids mort. En vérité, la santé tire la croissance et la tirera plus encore.
>
> (Sorman, 35)

The connector can countervail a misleading appearance or impression, as in Gide's description of his childhood games with a playmate under the dining-room table:

> l'on agitait bruyamment quelques jouets qu'on avait emportés pour la frime. En vérité nous nous amusions autrement : l'un près de l'autre, mais non l'un avec l'autre pourtant, nous avions ce que j'ai su plus tard qu'on appelait « de mauvaises habitudes ».
>
> (Gide, 1954: 349)

There, the connector stands in direct antithesis to *pour la frime*. As with *en fait*, the first element of this kind of antithesis sometimes contains an expression such as *officiellement, il apparaît que, en apparence* or *on dit que: On « relit » les grands classiques, dit-on; en vérité on les lit enfin un jour*; or a question: *Tristes, inquiets, furieux ou perplexes, les Algériens ? En vérité, à bout de réflexions et de commentaires*; or else a verb of believing: *Je pensais me donner à la Littérature quand, en vérité, j'entrais dans les ordres* (Sartre, 1964: 208).

Still like *en fait*, this connector can introduce a redefinition of inaccurate terms, such as the notion that there existed a single *nation juive* in France before the Revolution:

> Resserrée en quelques villes, ou plutôt en quelques quartiers, disséminée dans quelques centaines de villages, la « nation juive » est rien moins qu'unie. Une diversité extrême marque la condition des Juifs en France. Fruit d'une histoire

douloureuse, parfois cruelle, leur statut varie selon les provinces, les villes, les seigneuries. En vérité, ils ne forment pas une « nation », mais des communautés aux régimes multiples.

(Badinter, 1989: 19)

English equivalents, none as specific in their functioning as this structure, are 'actually', 'as a matter of fact', 'in fact', 'really', 'right enough', 'to tell the truth'.

et *

This entry discusses only initial *et* and the variant of it which introduces the *infinitif de narration*. Other modes are discussed at *encore*, *et ce* and *puis*.

Initial *et*

Many writers of English never lose the superstition, acquired in primary school, that conjunctions, especially 'and' and 'but', must not begin sentences. In some latitudes, the superstition attaches to other connectors: 'In Australia I was brought up never to use "however" at the beginning of a sentence' (James, 220). Such a superstition is known to some speakers of French: *Des esprits logiciens considèrent comme une faute le fait de mettre une conjonction de coordination après un **point**.* (Grevisse, 1988: 1566). However, generally speaking, it does not govern French usage. Descriptions of how conjunctions work derive from definitions of the sentence. English conjunctions often link ideas by bringing them together, French conjunctions by separating them. An English conjunction is often put in the middle of a longish sentence, linking two ideas and having little function other than punctuation. A French conjunction is often placed first in a short sentence, linking it to a preceding short sentence. Many of these sentences are *phrases dépendantes*: *L'écologisme ne fonctionne que comme refus. Ou rejet.* In the view of some French commentators on style, some writers, many of them journalists, overdo this type of sentence. It may be difficult to see the advantage of writing this: *Cela lui a valu des ennemis redoutables. Et de tous les bords* rather than this: *Cela lui a valu des ennemis redoutables et de tous les bords*. But the placing of a conjunction may be justified on grounds of clarity, proper emphasis, dramatic effect or the logic of a context.

Broadly speaking, the more analytical a French text, the more the ideas will be expressed in separate sentences with initial conjunctions. Although the following pair of sentences makes three points, in English they could well be written as one:

Toutes les prisons sont plus ou moins archaïques comme l'administration qui les régit, centralisée à l'excès. Et dans cette institution où tout est coercition, la formation aux sciences des relations humaines est inexistante.

In their context the major point made by these sentences is the second of them; and that is what justifies their setting out as two. In the following example, the more important point is the one, not about African women infected by HIV, but about their babies:

Actuellement, si l'on considère le million de personnes qui ont été nouvellement infectées au cours du premier semestre 1992, on s'aperçoit que la moitié sont des femmes. Et que par un phénomène quasi-automatique, le nombre de nouveau-nés séropositifs ne cesse de croître. 71 % de ces enfants [...]

Whereas, in the next sentence, the author's two points relate by comparison rather than by consequence, and the conjunction is better placed in the middle:

Janvier et octobre, février et août, en France, comptent autant de suicides malgré des différences énormes de température, et il en est de même d'avril et de juillet en Italie et en Prusse.

(Durkheim, 1930: 92)

The connector can function like *aussi*, *en outre* or *de plus*, as in this sequence of sentences about how it is possible for a democrat to belong to the political Right:

Très tôt il y a eu des hommes de droite républicains. Et il s'est trouvé de nombreux conservateurs dans la Résistance et dans les régiments de la France libre. En outre un très violent antigaullisme de droite a persisté sous la Ve République.

It is used in explanations adding a second cause or reason to a first, stating how logical or significant these are: variants of *Et il est naturel que* are not uncommon. The first of these examples explains the global necessity for collective security since the disintegration of the former USSR:

C'est pourquoi, dans cette logique, il était normal que la communauté internationale, l'an dernier, donne une leçon à Saddam Hussein qui voulait jouer les conquérants d'un autre âge. Et c'est pourquoi il est tout aussi normal que l'Occident accorde son aide à l'URSS, son ennemi d'hier, non par charité mais parce qu'elle est une superpuissance nucléaire menacée par le chaos.

The second, containing two consecutive exemplars, comes from an essay on the prevalence of divorce in the USA and its roots in popular culture:

Si donc l'on s'est marié à cause d'une *romance*, une fois celle-ci évaporée, il est normal qu'à la première constatation d'un conflit de caractères ou de goûts, l'on se demande : pourquoi suis-je marié ? Et il est non moins naturel qu'obsédé par la propagande universelle pour la *romance*, l'on admette la première occasion de tomber amoureux de quelqu'un d'autre. Et il est parfaite-

ment logique qu'on décide aussitôt de divorcer pour trouver dans le nouvel
« amour », qui entraîne un nouveau mariage, une nouvelle promesse de bonheur [...]

(Rougemont, 1962: 247)

Consecutive statements with *et* are quite common, either within sentences:
*Tout l'honneur de la culture est là, et sa raison d'être, et son utilité; et la
condition des progrès de l'esprit humain*; or between sentences, as in this
review of an exhibition of paintings done by artists in old age, the purpose
of which, the critic says, is

> pour nous inviter à revenir sur bon nombre d'idées reçues assimilant l'œuvre
> tardive des peintres à un déclin. Et à méditer justement sur ces trajectoires si
> différentes, si singulières, qui toutes s'achèvent autrement, pour finalement
> révéler l'homme, ses hantises de toujours, ses rêves, ses désirs, à travers de
> formidables leçons de liberté. Et cela nous concerne, et comment ! Et quoi
> qu'on puisse penser du dernier Renoir, du dernier Chagall, ou même du dernier
> Kandinsky, comment ne pas reconnaître l'or de leur dernier message.

A particular mode of this connector is *Et pourtant*. Another can begin
a *question*: *Et la France ?* is the opening sentence of a paragraph on unemployment in France, following one on Spain and another on the situation
in Italy.

The *infinitif de narration*

As the name says, the function of this mode, also called the *infinitif
historique*, is narrative. It often consists of initial *et* + a subject + the infinitive of a verb, as in the second sentence of this example, about a character
in a play listening to a recording of his own voice, made years before: *Il
écoute les mots de jadis. Et ceux-ci d'emplir la nudité de l'espace.* The structure usually replaces a past tense, although the infinitive is always in the
present. Grevisse once defined as follows the circumstances of its functioning:

> Dans des propositions affirmatives se rapportant au passé et commençant
> généralement par *et*, pour exprimer une action se déclenchant vivement, et
> conséquence d'une autre action qui précède.

(Grevisse, 1964a: 672)

Contemporary practice often largely conforms to this observation. But a
significant number of writers diverge from it. The frequency of its use,
especially by journalists, can distemper the purist and the grammarian:
*tour faussement élégant; tour correct, mais un peu archaïque et affecté dont
le retour bi-quotidien obsède* (Le Bidois & Georgin, quoted in Dupré, II,
1322).

Most frequently used in news reports, the structure usually begins a
new sentence, introducing the second part of a two-part statement. The

infinitive is commonly a verb of speaking, *affirmer, appeler, citer, commenter, conclure, déclarer, dire, expliquer, lancer, proposer, s'interroger,* most often *ajouter*:

> « Notre posture de défense est fondée sur la dissuasion », continue d'affirmer, péremptoire, Charles Hernu. Et l'ancien ministre de la Défense d'ajouter, dans une de ces belles envolées lyriques dont il a le secret : « La pièce maîtresse de la stratégie de dissuasion française, c'est le chef de l'État ; tout dépend de sa détermination. »

The infinitive is often unaccompanied by a subject; or rather, its subject is in the preceding sentence, as in this statement about the level of health care in the former USSR:

> Si le gouvernement n'achetait pas chaque année pour plus d'un milliard de roubles de préparations pharmaceutiques, les soins médicaux dans le pays « seraient pratiquement paralysés », souligne *la Pravda*. Et d'ajouter : « Les préparations médicamenteuses sont d'une piètre qualité, qui ne correspond pas aux normes internationales. »

At other times, the infinitive is accompanied by a subject which is different from the subject of the preceding verb, as in the oft-quoted line from 'Les animaux malades de la peste': *Ainsi dit le Renard, et flatteurs d'applaudir* (La Fontaine, 180).

Sometimes *et* is omitted, as in *Ma mère de dire* (Vallès, 191); *...ainsi Gracq de s'étonner* (Berthier, 34); *Aussitôt le berger de chercher les causes* (Alain, 1956: 490); and as in the second sentence of this excerpt from a discussion of disquiets inspired by natural (and unnatural) disasters:

> La déchirure de la couche d'ozone au pôle Sud inquiète tout un chacun, les conséquences climatiques possibles de la combustion des composés carbonés fossiles terrorisent désormais les citoyens, la télévision provoque des angoisses dans nos foyers en évoquant l'avenir de la forêt amazonienne, la pollution d'un golfe en Alaska semble menacer l'avenir du monde. Chaque commentateur, qu'il soit de profession ou homme politique, de prendre des airs informés et concernés pour commenter tous ces faits devenus d'actualité.

And sometimes there is little to confirm Grevisse's idea of *une action se déclenchant vivement*, as in this passage dealing with the history of art exhibitions on the Côte d'Azur:

> Renoir fut le premier à « descendre » en 1908, puis il y eut Dufy, Matisse et Bonnard et Picasso, et Chagall, et Magnelli, et bien d'autres. Ils y accomplirent une partie de leur œuvre, y laissèrent des traces indélébiles, firent des donations, eux ou leurs proches, si bien que, le coup de pouce de l'État aidant, des musées naquirent. Et la fondation Mæght.
>
> Et la Côte d'Azur d'être pendant longtemps le seul haut lieu des expositions d'été en France [...].

et ce

Like *ce faisant*, *pour ce faire* and *sur ce*, this is a fossilized expression in which *ce* replaces *ceci* or *cela*. Or rather, it exists in three basic forms: *et ce*, *et ceci* and *et cela*. The *ce*-form is said to be more literary, those with *ceci* and *cela* more spoken (Dupré, I, 381–382) – as is of course *et ça*. In fact, the forms with *ce* and *cela* are very common in current prose; the form with *ceci* is uncommon. The structure is placed inside the sentence more often than at the beginning. If it does begin a sentence, the latter is a *phrase dépendante*. Most writers use no comma after the structure. Variants lacking *et* are also used.

Adverbial complements

The basic function of this structure is sometimes defined as being to add a *circonstance aggravante*. More accurately, it introduces usually a second point to reinforce a first one, adding a striking feature to what is already notable. It adds adverbial complements; and, since many of these begin with prepositions, it is often followed by a preposition: *et ce à*, *et cela depuis*, *et ce sans*, *et cela en*, *et ceci pour*. In the first example, what is remarkable is that the grand master Karpov should be beaten twice; the connector signals the additionally noteworthy fact that he was playing white on both occasions:

> Stupeur au tournoi de Rotterdam comptant pour la Coupe du monde d'échecs : Karpov, en tête depuis le début grâce à un parcours admirable (sept victoires, cinq nulles) a subi deux défaites consécutives dans les treizième et quatorzième rondes, face à Salov, dix-sept ans, et à Ljubojevic et ce avec les Blancs dans les deux cas.

A critic makes two points about the French novel: everyone says it is in crisis; and this is not new: *En France, il est devenu banal de parler d'une « crise du roman ». Et ceci depuis longtemps* (Boisdeffre, 7).

The structure is sometimes used to introduce not a second remarkable point but a single one, as in this comment on the suicide of Pierre Bérégovoy, a former Prime Minister:

> Jamais il ne lui vint à l'idée de rendre *le Canard enchaîné* (puisqu'il s'agit de lui) responsable du terrible désarroi qui, à travers sa conscience lacérée par une névrose de remords, se transformait peu à peu en souffrance indicible. Et cela pour une raison très simple : c'est que les informations publiées, avec humour et sans hargne, par notre « insupportable » confrère étaient vraies.

Reasons and causes

In this role of introducing a reason or a cause, common sequences are *et ce parce que*, *et cela en vertu de*, *et cela afin de*. In presenting a second reason, the connector has an obvious similarity to ***d'autant que***. This may be why it is often used in the sequence *et ce d'autant plus que* (or *et ce d'autant moins que*):

> Le « trou » d'ozone ayant été constaté et, depuis 1985, mesuré au-dessus de l'Antarctique, il fallait, bien évidemment, voir si un phénomène semblable se produisait au-dessus de l'Arctique. Et ce d'autant plus que les hautes latitudes de l'hémisphère nord sont occupées en grande partie par des masses continentales où vivent des populations permanentes.

Conversely, the connector also helps to structure oppositions with *malgré* or *en dépit de*, giving the reasons notwithstanding which an act takes place. A discussion of the USSR's unpreparedness for the Nazi invasion of 1941 is rounded off as follows:

> Bref, Staline croit dur comme fer à la validité de son traité d'amitié avec Hitler. Et ce, en dépit des avertissements qui lui parviennent de tous côtés.

Other common sequences in this mode are: *et cela, bien que...*, *et cela, malgré...*, *et ce, sans compter...*, *et ce, alors que...*.

Time and place

Adverbs of time (as ***alors que*** can be) and adverbs of place are also introduced by this structure. The former emphasize temporal aspects of an event, its striking duration, the fact that it is timely, belated or premature. A critic, reviewing a play, stresses the sheer length of time occupied by one aspect of it:

> En fond de plateau, et ce durant toute la durée du spectacle, un homme peint une immense et très belle fresque à larges coups de brosse, en rouge, blanc, noir, des chiens, des hommes, un cheval au galop lancés dans une chasse à courre éperdue.

A writer discusses a new technology enabling predictions of the genetic health of foetuses:

> On pourra dépister des gènes responsables de maladies bénignes, guérissables, voire de simples défauts, comme la myopie, et cela dès la grossesse.

In this temporal mode, the structure can add a pointed irony to coincidences. Common sequences are: *et ceci alors même que*, *et cela au moment précis où*, *et ce le jour même où*, *et cela en une période de*.

Expressions of place are underlined in a similar way, so as to stress either their aptness or inaptness in relation to what precedes. The following example is from a discussion of dangers resulting from the nuclear disaster at Chernobyl:

> Danger aussi pour les populations environnantes qui vivent au quotidien les effets de la catastrophe et ce à des distances de parfois plusieurs centaines de kilomètres !

The combination with the exclamation mark adds emotional force to the monstrousness of the situation.

et tout cela

This reinforced form usually follows a point which is lengthy, complicated or seen as outrageous, as in this contribution to the debate, provoked by schoolgirls' wearing of the so-called *foulard islamique*, on whether religious tolerance entails tolerating an intolerant form of religion. The writer comments on the view of an Islamist that women's only valuable production is male Muslims:

> Dans cette religion patriarcale – elles le sont toutes ! –, la femme est soumise à la loi masculine. Le foulard est le signe de ce statut. Après l'avoir accepté, faut-il admettre l'excision, la polygamie et la vente des jeunes filles de 12 ans pour des mariages arrangés par les parents ? Et tout cela au nom du respect des différences culturelles, comme on disait, à gauche, dans les années 80.

Without *et*

This mode, less common than those with *et*, functions with the same range of adverbial complements: *Cela en dépit de...*, *Ce depuis cinquante ans...*, *Ce pour de multiples raisons...*, etc. This example comes from a letter written by Émile Zola during his exile in England in 1898:

> Vous me demandez de mes nouvelles. Les deux premières semaines ont été affreuses, je n'avais même ni linge, ni vêtements, cela dans un pays dont j'ignore la langue, et où j'étais forcé de me cacher.
>
> (Henriot, 1954: 299)

Here too the form with *ceci* is unusual. This *et*-less mode exists also in the form reinforced by *tout*. One difference between the form with *et* and this mode is that this one is placed first in the sentence more often.

English equivalents

Among English equivalents, 'and that' is used in exactly the way this connector is used, albeit much more seldom and in a register of obsolescent orotundity which is not that of the French expression. The indeterminacy of polyvalent 'that', variously adjective, pronoun, adverb or conjunction, no doubt inhibits this use in current English:

> 'Tis altogether impossible to give any definition of the passions of *love* and *hatred*; and that because they produce merely a simple impression, without any mixture or composition.
>
> (Hume, 329)

> And it remains scandalous that the Queen, again outside the law, should be able to pay only those taxes she agrees to pay, and that after a secret meeting with the Prime Minister.
>
> (Haseler, 17)

One could either add 'at that!' to the end of the sentence or make do with the exclamation mark which can accompany the French structure. In other circumstances, structures such as 'as well', 'and even then', an italicized 'and' or a dash with 'despite which' would do, although they would lack all the specificity of the French structure. How would an English-speaking journalist express a sentence like the following, describing two terrorist bomb attacks in the Basque country?

> Ce nouvel attentat intervient quelques heures après la mise en liberté de quatre militants membres présumés d'Iparretarrak et onze jours après l'explosion d'une autre bombe contre l'hôtel des impôts de Bayonne et ce, après plus de huit mois d'accalmie.

One possibility would be to put a full stop after Bayonne and begin another sentence with 'This comes at a time when'. And in the following text, dealing with some of the political difficulties faced by Gorbachev in the last days of the USSR:

> Il va falloir, en attendant, contenir les populistes, tenir l'appareil et ne pas décevoir les futurs alliés. Pas simple et cela d'autant moins que tout ou presque reste à faire.

would an English-speaking writer do anything but simplify the second sentence, with its composite connector *et cela d'autant moins que*, into 'This will not be easy, especially because ...'? It may well be that this structure is often an example of the *charnière zéro* phenomenon remarked on by writers on comparative syntax: French sometimes puts into words what English says without them.

finalement *

This concluder has three modes: analytical, enumerative and narrative. It can be difficult, perhaps pointless, to separate these functions; in a statement like the following, damning the rhetoric and self-presentation (*ce discours*) of the government supposedly of the Left which was voted out of office in 1993, all three may be present:

> ce discours, logomachique, angélique et finalement purement idéologique, qui a coupé le peuple réel de la gauche divine et fait le jeu du Front national.

There, the connector may express the author's considered point of view, introduce the third adjective in a triad or designate the last phase of the government's period in power.

Analytical

In this mode, this connector is used in a way akin to *en définitive*: it functions essentially as an analytical persuader, introducing a point which a writer wishes to isolate and emphasize as a definitive judgment on a certain subject. What it introduces is an opinion. In the following example, the author is describing the impression made by a politician during his first major appearance on television:

> Quinze millions de gens ont regardé M. Le Pen, l'ont trouvé homme de bon sens, plutôt sympathique, assez modéré finalement.
>
> (Dutourd, 1985: 58)

There the connector could be replaced by *à la fin*, *pour tout dire* or *somme toute*. It also expresses a shade of implicit contrastiveness, contradicting an expectation, as M. Le Pen was known to be anything but *modéré*. A second example comes from a debate on a modest suggestion by primary-school teachers to reform some aspects of French spelling. Here the connector, more clearly recapitulative, translates into a single statement the gist of the different objections made against the *instituteurs* by the individuals named; these opponents of reform, says the author, see spelling reform as foreboding social catastrophe:

> Être partisan de la réforme, c'est encourager le laisser-aller à l'oral et à l'écrit (André Frossard, Jacqueline de Romilly), c'est renoncer à toute exigence de savoir (Raymond Vilain, Pierre Perret), c'est aller dans le sens d'une société sans exigence, qui démissionne devant toute rigueur, permissive, laxiste (Philippe de Villiers, Jean Dutourd). Finalement, comme le dit expressément Philippe de Villiers, les instituteurs « réclament l'abolition de participes passés » comme on a réclamé l'abolition des privilèges en 1789.

As with English 'in the last analysis' or 'when all's said and done', this mode often introduces a conclusion deriving from what is at most an implicit examination of the points at issue. It hints that the analysis has been done or need not be done, that the reader participates in this unexpressed reasoning; and, after the manner of *après tout* or *somme toute*, it reminds about a shared assumption more than it resumes an explicit argument. In this way, it is often briefly inserted into passing references which purport to be reasoned judgments, like this one on literary critics: *les chroniqueurs littéraires, qui n'écrivent finalement que pour leurs pairs*. The following extract, transcribed from speech, contains two examples. It is taken from a discussion of whether French book reviewers should subscribe to a code of professional ethics in the hope of guarding against possible malpractice and undue exercise of influence; and the speaker makes a comparison with the practices of British and American book reviewers:

> Le problème là-bas se pose non en termes d'influence mais en termes d'argent. Le système français n'est finalement pas trop mauvais, il ne faut pas de règles strictes et inobservables. La vie littéraire se résume finalement à une série d'influences et une série de frottements humains.

Such judgments are preceded by no demonstration or argument of the point they help to make. The connector functions much like *au fond* or a mode of English 'really'.

Enumerative

In this mode, the connector can mean 'in the last place'. That is, its function, essentially expository, is to introduce the final point in a series. Littré, in the preface to his dictionary, speaks of the three phases of the usage of words:

> un usage contemporain qui est le propre de chaque période successive ; un archaïsme qui a été lui-même autrefois usage contemporain, et qui contient l'explication et la clef des choses subséquentes ; et, finalement, un néologisme qui, mal conduit, altère, bien conduit, développe la langue, et qui, lui aussi, sera un jour de l'archaïsme et que l'on consultera comme histoire et phase du langage.
>
> (Littré, I, 119)

Narrative

The third mode introduces an outcome or the final event in a series; that is, its function is essentially narrative or *chronologique* (Schelling, 70). Unlike the other two modes, the statement made by this one could be made by the verb *finir par*. The context of the following example, in which the connector occurs twice, is the successive stages that a proposed measure in the government's financial plans and changes had gone through:

> D'un coût de 3,5 milliards de francs, cette mesure avait finalement été retirée du projet gouvernemental, au profit d'une réduction d'impôt sur les frais de scolarisation, d'un coût identique pour l'État. Finalement, les mois passant, les

économies budgétaires ne figurent plus au sommet des priorités, et c'est une mesure ponctuelle, au profit de toutes les entreprises, qui a été annoncée jeudi.

Both of those exemplars contain a shade of *en définitive*, but they could also be replaced by *pour finir* or the most literal mode of *enfin*, 'lastly' or 'eventually'. In this mode, the connector often accompanies negative structures, and, again like *en définitive*; the outcomes it speaks of may be those which contradict expectations or intentions, as in this extract from an article alleging cannibalism in China during the 'cultural revolution':

En avril 1969, les délégués de la province du Guangxi avaient prévu d'offrir à Mao un flacon contenant de la chair humaine. Ils ne l'ont finalement pas fait parce qu'ils se sont rendu compte que l'atmosphère était en train de changer.

Even when no explicit negative structure is used, the connector often functions in a context of negative polarity and, as can be seen in some of the examples, has at times an oppositiveness akin to that of **mais**, a conjunction with which it is readily combined.

In most of its modes, this connector could nowadays be replaced by **au final**.

English equivalents, depending on context, are 'all things considered', 'in the last analysis', 'really' or 'when all's said and done' (usually analytical); 'finally' or 'lastly' (usually enumerative); 'eventually' or 'in the end' (usually narrative); 'ultimately' (either analytical or narrative).

force est de *

This is an old expression, in which *force* is an adjective meaning 'necessary'. Montaigne says *il est force que* and in a narrative context: *Force fut de [...]* (Montaigne, II, 137). This structure is thus a specialized example of *inversion de l'adjectif*. Semantically, it offers no difficulty: it stands for *il faut*.

It has two modes. In either of them, the connector is followed by the infinitive of a verb, most usually *constater*. Also common are *admettre*, *confesser*, *convenir* and *reconnaître*. When used in a narrative, other verbs are possible, as are tenses other than the present. Sometimes the structure includes a pronoun, most usually *nous*: *Force nous est d'accepter...*; *Force m'est bien de dire....* The infinitive is nearly always followed by *que*, occasionally by a noun: *Force est de constater l'incapacité de Washington et des anciennes puissances coloniales....* Whatever the verb, this connector usually introduces an idea presented as indisputable, a consequence seen as unavoidable.

Contrastive

This is the more common of the two main modes. Always presenting the second element of an antithesis, the connector is often placed in the first part of a sentence, introducing a statement in opposition to the sentence preceding. Contrasts between expected and real outcomes are quite common:

> On attendait beaucoup du livre d'Édouard Balladur. Force est de reconnaître qu'il ne tient qu'une partie de ses promesses.

> Au lendemain du krach boursier d'octobre 1987, les observateurs étaient nombreux à penser que l'heure de la récession économique était arrivée et que le glas avait ainsi sonné pour les sociétés du secteur informatique. Un an après, force est de constater que l'année 1988 a enregistré une forte croissance de l'économie mondiale et que les fabricants de biens d'équipement en ont largement bénéficié.

If the structure is placed in the second part of a sentence, it introduces a contrast with the first part:

> Le grand épidémiologiste anglais Richard Peto a beau répéter que 10 à 70 % des cancers pourraient avoir une origine alimentaire, force est de constater que rien aujourd'hui de scientifiquement établi ne permet d'étayer pareille affirmation.

When it occupies this second position in the contrastive sentence, the first part often begins with an oppositive structure: *Malgré*, *Quel que soit*, *Qu'on le veuille ou non*, *À moins de croire que* or the *si d'opposition*, as in this comparison between computerized catalogues in English and in French:

> S'il est déjà impossible de rendre compte de la diversité des catalogues en anglais, force est de reconnaître que les titres français sont encore rares.

In some oppositive sentences, the connector may be accompanied by *mais*, *cependant* or *pourtant*. A writer tracing the influence of Rabelais on Balzac's writing of *La physiologie du mariage* says this:

> Nous ne voudrions pas exagérer le rôle d'intermédiaire joué par Rabelais en l'occurrence. Mais force nous est de reconnaître cependant en lui une sorte de phénomène catalytique.

A common formula in such a context is *Force est pourtant de constater que.*

Consequential

If the first of the two discursive modes of this connector says roughly 'despite this, the conclusion is inescapable', conversely the second says 'because of this, the conclusion is inescapable'. It may be introduced by *car*, *dès lors* or *dans ces circonstances*. A discussion of the huge debts owed by poor countries says that much consultation on this problem is required:

> C'est davantage par la multiplication des discussions et des réflexions que par des grands-messes entre riches et pauvres, que des avancées sur la dette pourront être réalisées. En ce sens, la rencontre entre M. Mitterrand et M. Perez est importante. Car force est de reconnaître que les « négociations globales sur les relations entre pays industrialisés et pays en développement » lancées lors du dernier sommet Nord-Sud, il y a huit ans, à Cancun, ont produit de bien maigres résultats.

In either mode, the connector is quite often preceded by an absolute construction with a past participle: *Ces exigences posées, force est bien de convenir que...*; *Une fois oubliée la beauté des images, force est de se dire que....*

In an occasional variant, *est* is replaced by *reste*: *Force reste d'admettre que....*

In its function of introducing a conclusion, this expression can be seen as related to **qui ne voit que** and to **tout se passe comme si**. The latter tends to present conjectural conclusions arrived at by deduction from probabilities or appearances; the former presents conclusions which are seen as inescapable.

fût-ce

This connector can introduce certain restrictive or concessive statements, some of them hypothetical. It has, it is said, the force of **même** (Le Bidois, II, 174). But it is a specialized *même*: it is *même si c'est*, *même si c'était* or in certain circumstances *y compris même*. That not all writers sense it as synonymous with *même* is seen in the fact that some use the compound structure *fût-ce même*, as in this criticism of linguists who exclude certain written forms from their inventory of language-structures, because, they say, written language is less 'natural' than spoken:

> Ils réprouvent partout le « purisme », l'« archaïsme », tout ce qui est artifice et qui heurte, dit-on, la nature. Or il conviendrait plutôt d'enregistrer tous les faits, aux fins de statistique, et de les laisser parler, fût-ce même rien dire.

In that reinforced form, the connector functions in a way close to **voire**.

This structure can modify by restricting the scope of a previous statement, as in this comment on the result of a referendum: *Le « oui » a remporté une victoire, fût-ce à la Pyrrhus*. It can emphasize a disparity between, say, the importance of a rule preceding and a minimal exception following, as in this statement about Simone de Beauvoir and Jean-Paul

Sartre who, while both working as school teachers, designed their long-lasting relationship as a sort of anti-marriage:

> Beauvoir et Sartre ne souhaitaient pas que la société leur renvoie d'eux-mêmes l'image de « gens mariés » (fût-ce pour obtenir de l'éducation nationale un poste dans la même ville).

What follows can be seen as disproportionately remarkable: *Louis XIV enjoint à ses ministres d'en référer à lui pour toutes choses, fût-ce pour établir un passeport*; and it may be implicitly criticized as incongruous, exaggerated, improbable or grotesque: *...si l'on émettait devant moi l'hypothèse qu'un cataclysme pût un jour détruire la planète, fût-ce dans cinquante mille ans, je m'épouvantais* (Sartre, 1964: 208).

What follows the connector is usually brief and rarely runs to more than three or four words, the first of which is often a preposition. Nowadays, it even begins a *phrase dépendante*, as in this comment on the world of professional football, where money is so important that the profits to be made from a win increase the likelihood of corruption:

> Dès lors, comment s'étonner qu'un succès qui enclenche un tel processus d'avantages induits et provoque une telle marge d'enrichissement, largement partagée parce que largement redistribuée, doive être obtenu coûte que coûte, à n'importe quel prix ? Fût-ce, si c'est possible, par achat d'un arbitre ou corruption d'un joueur adverse.

The literary tone of the structure is attested by its frequency in Proust:

> Françoise accepta les compliments de M. de Norpois avec la fière simplicité, le regard joyeux et – fût-ce momentanément – intelligent, d'un artiste à qui on parle de son art.
>
> (Proust, I, 484)

Variants

In addition to the basic structure, there is a set of variants in which *ce* is replaced by *il(s)* or *elle(s)*, as in this view of American popular culture:

> Exiger de n'importe quel film, fût-il sur la bombe atomique, qu'il tienne une certaine dose de la drogue romanesque (plus encore qu'érotique) nommée *love interest*, c'est faire de la publicité pour les microbes, non pour le remède, de la maladie du mariage.
>
> (Rougemont, 1962: 246)

> Quatre millions de dollars (environ 20 millions de francs) pour une exposition, fût-elle de Matisse, c'est un luxe qu'à Paris on ne peut s'offrir.

This mode quite often introduces a single adjective: *La solution militaire, fût-elle « onusienne », n'est qu'un ultime recours, inapte à régler les conflits politiques.*

The only modes of this structure given by Littré are *fût-il* and *fût-elle*. Although he comments on the related form ***ne fût-ce que***, sometimes used nowadays as a more elevated variant for ***ne serait-ce que***, he does not mention *fût-ce*, which is as old as the hills:

> Je reviendrois volontiers de l'autre monde pour démentir celuy qui me formeroit autre que je n'estois, fust-ce pour m'honorer.
>
> (Montaigne, II, 425)

Occasionally, a writer abandons the imperfect subjunctive form in favour of the simple conditional, as in this excerpt from an article about the presidential election of 1995 during which Jacques Chirac, a candidate of the Right, declined to change the style of his campaign so as to please voters who might believe he had moved towards the Left:

> Pas question de mettre à mal sept mois de campagne parfaitement maîtrisée, serait-ce pour « plaire » à son électorat « naturel ».

See another example, p. 332, the quotation beginning *Jirinovski a eu beau jouer.* This conditional form is also used at times with the *il* and *elle* mode: *La définition d'une politique économique, serait-elle socialiste, se révèle singulièrement difficile.*

English equivalents, restricting a concession, are 'admittedly', 'albeit', 'even though'; and restricting a hypothesis, 'even', 'even if'. In a statement like the following, a writer might say 'though it may be':

> Si le surréalisme peut englober une pareille attitude à côté d'autres si radicalement opposées, c'est qu'il n'est qu'un mot et je désire tout de même qu'il ne soit pas cela, fût-ce à mes dépens.
>
> (Caillois, 37)

ici... là

This binary structure usually functions as an infrequent and more literary variant for ***d'un côté... de l'autre***.

It can structure simple contrasts in a brief interpolation, such as this comparison between the professional critic and the book reviewer, saying that despite their different methods they are really engaged in the same activity: *c'est bien au fond la même entreprise (ici vulgarisatrice, là systématique)*. Or it can shape antitheses between more substantial pairs of points, as in this extract from an essay on the role of the subject in painting:

> En peinture, il est clair que le sujet joue un rôle opposé dans tel ou tel tableau : ici, c'est une donnée que le peintre travaille à faire oublier au profit d'harmonies linéaires ou chromatiques ; là, c'est le résultat final à quoi tout moyen d'expression est subordonné : quelque chose à produire et non à reproduire.

Also like *d'un côté... de l'autre*, this structure can juxtapose whole series of antitheses, as in this sequence taken from a discussion of the diversity of marriage systems devised by different human societies:

> Ici l'épouse ne quitte pas sa famille d'origine et les enfants qu'elle a de son conjoint sont destinés à l'oncle maternel, son frère. Là elle abandonne son lignage pour celui de son époux. Ici le mari est souverain, là il est insignifiant. Ici l'homme épouse une femme de son âge, là une femme beaucoup plus jeune et, dans un cas extrême, une toute petite enfant. Ici l'on vit en unités domestiques nombreuses ; là, et point seulement dans les sociétés modernes, la famille conjugale est très largement dominante. Ici l'échange des femmes est très simple [...]
>
> (Roussel, 31)

A paragraph from another writer accumulates eight consecutive antithetical pairs of *ici... là*, structuring a development of almost 200 words.

Occasionally a writer inverts the order of the two parts of the structure. In this example, taken from a contrastive discussion of the relationships between the scientist's intellectual attitude and the technician's, the inversion is in accordance with the convention that structures with *ci* designate 'the latter', while those with *là* designate 'the former':

> La conversion de l'attitude de savant en attitude de technicien résulte d'une simple conversion d'intention ; leur objet reste le même : là, il s'agit de le connaître, d'apprendre à s'en servir, ici d'en faire effectivement usage.

Longer sequences

Sometimes, the structure is extended by *là encore* to set out not just pairs but longer *sequences of points*, as in this comment on the picture of Roman manners given by Petronius in the *Satyricon*:

> Notant à mesure les faits, les constatant dans une forme définitive, il déroulait la menue existence du peuple, ses épisodes, ses bestialités, ses ruts.
>
> Ici, c'est l'inspecteur des garnis qui vient demander le nom des voyageurs récemment entrés ; là, ce sont des lupanars où des gens rôdent autour de femmes nues, debout entre des écriteaux, tandis que par les portes mal fermées des chambres, l'on entrevoit les ébats des couples ; là, encore, au travers des villas d'un luxe insolent, d'une démence de richesses et de faste, comme au travers des pauvres auberges qui se succèdent dans le livre, avec leurs lits de sangle défaits, pleins de punaises, la société du temps s'agite [...]
>
> (Huysmans, 85)

With the addition of *là enfin*, the extension can run to four elements. Such sequences are no longer antithetical, but rather contrastive enumerations, as in the previous example and in this reading of the sign-language of the villain in troupes of all-in wrestlers:

Ici, le catcheur triomphe par un rictus ignoble lorsqu'il tient le bon sportif sous ses genoux ; là, il adresse à la foule un sourire suffisant, annonciateur de la vengeance prochaine ; là encore, immobilisé à terre, il frappe le sol à grands coups de ses bras pour signifier à tous la nature intolérable de sa situation ; là enfin, il dresse un ensemble compliqué de signes destinés à faire comprendre qu'il incarne à bon droit l'image toujours divertissante du mauvais coucheur, fabulant intarissablement autour de son mécontentement.

(Barthes, 1957: 16)

Similar structuring of pairs and sequences can be done with *tantôt... tantôt*.

When *là* is not the second part of this binary structure but a separate connector, its function is significantly different from the one it has here.

il est vrai (que) *

This structure has four modes: *il est vrai* and *il est vrai que*; *c'est vrai* and *c'est vrai que*. In any of these, it has two functions: to reinforce what precedes; or to concede a point that counters what precedes. In these functions, it is a variant for **certes**, **sans doute**, **bien sûr** and other concessives.

il est vrai que

As a confirmer, this form, usually placed first in the sentence or paragraph, introduces a point which precises and explains the preceding one, after the manner of **le fait est que**:

L'album Kiri Te Kanawa est un hommage à Mozart. Nul ne s'en plaindra. La soprano néo-zélandaise lui doit ses plus grands succès. Il est vrai que sa voix vibrante et généreuse s'y prête particulièrement avec des graves de velours.

There, the connector could almost be replaced by **c'est que** or by **de fait**. In this function, it is at times preceded by **et**.

Like the other concessives, this one can help to structure a coherent sequence of three propositions: the point it introduces, by definition secondary to an initial affirmation, is frequently followed by a third point introduced by an objecting expression, commonly **mais**, reaffirming the force of the first and outweighing the concession. This example, from a discussion of the decline of the Parti socialiste, dates from just before the party's landslide defeat in the elections of 1993:

Le sentiment prévaut qu'une période s'achève et que la réélection de François Mitterrand en 1988, suivie de la courte victoire des socialistes aux élections législatives, n'a offert à la gauche qu'un sursis sur la pente d'un déclin inéluctable. Il est vrai que si la droite l'emporte en mars le président de la République restera en fonctions. Mais chacun voit bien que les circonstances ne sont pas celles d'il y a sept ans et que la défaite de 1993, si elle doit avoir lieu, aura toutes chances de mettre fin à l'expérience socialiste, au moins sous la forme qui fut la sienne depuis près de douze ans.

Often, the concessive explicitly structures not three but only two overt propositions, as in this extract from an article lamenting Western appeasement of Syrian expansionism in Lebanon:

Depuis plus de dix ans, le Liban meurt dans l'indifférence, et l'Occident accepte la disparition d'un État qui portait témoignage de ses valeurs ! Il est vrai que les événements ne se répètent jamais. Cependant, comment ne pas se répéter la phrase de Churchill interpellant le gouvernement de son pays au moment de Munich : « Vous aviez le choix entre le déshonneur et la guerre ; vous avez choisi le déshonneur et vous aurez la guerre. »

il est vrai

This form is never placed first in the sentence, but usually after the first verb or its subject. It has the same functions as the form with *que*. It too can confirm and precise what precedes, as in this statement about the house in London where Freud lived:

Il est difficile d'imaginer qu'elle n'est plus habitée. Vue de l'extérieur, seule une plaque apposée sur la façade la distingue de ses voisines et, une fois la barrière franchie, on se sent comme un invité sur le point d'être accueilli. Anna Freud, il est vrai, vécut ici jusqu'en 1982.

And it can concede a secondary point as a qualification of a first, while foreshadowing an overruling of the secondary point, as in this discussion of the fame of Émile Zola in relation to the Dreyfus Affair:

La réputation de Zola était établie et ses positions prises avant l'Affaire, qui ne lui valut que des coups, dans ses derniers temps ; et le Panthéon, il est vrai. Mais cet avantage est posthume et il ne l'avait pas sollicité.

(Henriot, 1954: 296)

As can be seen in the last example, this form is sometimes placed at the end of the sentence: *Le franc français s'est à nouveau raffermi vis-à-vis d'un mark plutôt affaibli, il est vrai.* It is also found in brief restrictive interpolations, appended to adverbial or adjectival structures: *L'autre type de cancer dont la mortalité globale diminue (légèrement, il est vrai) est le cancer du poumon.* These forms introduce unretracted concessions, a function in which this concessive is probably used more often than *certes* and the others.

c'est vrai

This mode functions, with one difference, like the one with *il*. The following example comes from a discussion of the geographical and historical role of the Massif Central:

> Sa masse forme barrière entre les différentes Frances ; il les sépare, c'est vrai, mais, en même temps, il les joint, les nourrit de ses émigrations répétées, les plus abondantes de toute la France.
>
> (Braudel, 49)

The difference between the two modes is that this one, grammatically capable of being a ***brief interpolated main clause***, can begin a sentence. This example, taken from a discussion of how some floods and landslides could be avoided, begins with the opinion of an expert who says local politicians are often to blame for natural catastrophes:

> « Les élus n'ont pas le courage politique de décider l'investissement nécessaire aux travaux de prévention », a-t-il déclaré au *Dauphiné libéré*. C'est vrai, mais ils ont des excuses : les avis des experts, souvent, ne permettent pas de se faire une idée exacte du risque.

For the same reason, this mode can also be a separate sentence, as in this extract from an article on the narrow defeat of the 'no'-vote in the referendum on the Treaty of Maastricht:

> 49 % des Français ont, toute réflexion faite, tout bien pesé, pris le risque de casser la construction européenne, d'isoler et de décrédibiliser la France. Certes, on peut se rassurer : constater que la France du « oui » est dynamique, moderne, jeune, urbaine, que les départements frontaliers directement confrontés à la réalité européenne ont plébiscité le « oui ». C'est vrai. Mais l'autre France n'en est pas moins la France. La périphérie dynamique ne saurait nier un centre qui doute.

There, the connector acts as a redundant reinforcement of *certes* at the beginning of the preceding sentence.

c'est vrai que

More spoken than the form with *il*, this one is more and more used by writers nowadays. It may give a more familiar tone to the statements it accompanies, as in this one about residual resentment among residents of Vichy towards the town's invidious reputation as the seat of a collaborationist government between 1940 and 1944:

> L'opinion locale est persuadée que les Vichyssois « continuent de faire les frais » d'une période qu'ils ont « très mal vécue ». C'est vrai qu'elle n'a pas de chance, cette ville insouciante dont Valéry Larbaud disait qu'elle « ne daigne exister que lorsque l'existence est bonne ». « On n'a pas de pot », affirme, résigné, un commerçant.

Or the tone may be, as Mauger suggests (Mauger, 130), more emotive, as in this extract from a scathing critique of a tendency in design shared by certain younger architects:

> Ce qui reste à déplorer, c'est le motif à l'emporte-pièce, gesticulant, braillant comme si le bruit faisait sens. C'est vrai qu'il n'est pas simple, pour un jeune ou moins jeune architecte, de savoir donner un sens à son œuvre et à son métier.

Among English equivalents for the different modes of this structure, depending on context, are 'admittedly', 'granted', 'of course', 'it is true' and 'it must be said'. One also finds 'True' standing first in the sentence.

il faut dire que *

This structure usually introduces a statement which explains, clarifies or justifies the preceding one. It often functions rather like *car* or *en effet*. It is usually placed first in the sentence or the paragraph. It can have a confirming and precising function close to that of *le fait est que* or *de fait*; and it can come close to the concessive mode of *il est vrai (que)*.

Explaining

Very often, this connector says no more than *c'est que* and could be exactly replaced by it. In this example, a historian speaks of the *épuration* of members of the Milice in 1944:

> Les miliciens, en tout cas ceux qui étaient pris les armes à la main dans les combats de la Libération, subissaient de plein fouet l'épuration extrajudiciaire ; un exemple parmi tant d'autres : le 28 août, 77 des 109 miliciens qui s'étaient rendus, jugés par une cour martiale improvisée, étaient fusillés au Grand-Bornand (Haute-Savoie). Il faut dire que la Milice – tous les témoignages concordent – était, en dehors des cercles collaborationnistes ou des milieux de pétainistes musclés, profondément haïe.

In this mainly explanatory mode, the connector can function in tandem with *car*, as in this excerpt from a discussion of whether pluralism and tolerance are as deeply rooted in the French political system as politicians of both Left and Right seem to believe:

> Le pluralisme fait partie du vocabulaire de Georges Marchais aussi bien que de celui de Valéry Giscard d'Estaing. Mais on ne jurerait pas qu'ils s'en font tout à fait la même idée. Car il faut bien dire que les Français, malgré Voltaire, n'ont pas la tolérance dans le sang.

> (Fontaine, 1978: 265)

There, as is quite frequent, the connector is combined also with *bien*.

Justifying

Sometimes *c'est que* would not suffice as a replacement, as what precedes is not only to be explained but, because it may be seen as remarkable or close to incomprehensible, justified as well. It is as though the writer argues against an anticipated objection. This example comes from a discussion of the films of Almodovar, in particular of a day to be spent filming a paradoxical scene of 'comical rape':

> Demain, plateau fermé, « scène de sexe » au tableau de travail. Depuis le début, on entend parler de ce « viol comique », termes tellement antinomiques. Il faut dire que chez Almodovar, le sexe, c'est la vie. Il n'est pas tabou, il n'est pas puni. Chez Almodovar, on fait l'amour partout, sur le sol, dans les toilettes, au couvent, on est hétéro, homo, bi, nécrophage, masturbateur, jamais bestial ou triste.

There it is clearly the juxtaposition of the incongruous terms *viol* and *comique* which cries out for justification.

Conceding

This structure can also be used to make an unretracted concession, like the mode of *il est vrai que* which appends a restricting circumstance to an assertion. In this example, the writer is comparing the student protest movements of 1968 in France, where they were accompanied by violence, constitutional crisis and social upheaval, and in England, where they caused a broken window:

> Même à l'Université libérale d'Essex où la contestation fut très vive, elle conserva une haute tenue et l'esprit y fit prévaloir ses droits. Les dommages matériels se limitèrent à une vitre cassée. Il faut dire que nombre d'enseignants non professeurs s'associèrent aux étudiants progressistes dans leur réaction contre le Sénat.
>
> (Wagner, 155)

Variant forms include *il faut bien avouer que* and *il faut reconnaître que*.

English equivalents could be 'it is true that', 'the fact is', 'the point is' or 'one should add that'.

il n'est que de

This is a written equivalent of the more spoken *il n'y a qu'à* or *on n'a qu'à*. Like both of those expressions, it always introduces an infinitive. It means *il suffit de*; but, unlike that structure, it is never followed by a noun.

The function of this connector, which always follows an assertion, is to adduce the evidence of which the assertion is an interpretation. Implying 'if you don't believe me, just listen to this', it counters possible objections to a statement which the writer may feel will be disputed. It is normally placed first in the sentence, of which it constitutes the main subject and verb. This example, dating from about 1970, discusses the inequitable treatment of women under the divorce law then obtaining:

> Ce sont toujours les hommes qui ont un métier et les femmes des enfants ; l'homme qui gère la fortune et la femme la maison. Il n'est que d'écouter les femmes divorcées, groupées en associations, fédérations ou syndicats pour se rendre compte qu'elles émergent du divorce défaites, déçues et souvent tragiquement démunies, malgré la récente refonte des régimes matrimoniaux.

That example, containing *pour se rendre compte que*, shows another common feature of the usage of this connector: it often functions in tandem with the infinitive of a verb of believing or understanding introduced by *pour*, such as *pour comprendre cela*, *pour s'en convaincre* or *pour s'en assurer*. In the following extract from an essay on an episode in the love-life of Stendhal, defending the novelist against the charge of immorality, this verb is *se persuader*:

> Tel est l'épisode de sa vie amoureuse qu'il convient d'avoir le plus présent à l'esprit, si l'on veut demeurer juste à l'égard de l'auteur du *Rouge* et des *Chroniques italiennes*, et ne pas accepter aveuglément l'opinion défavorable que ne cessent de nourrir pour lui les personnes qui ne l'aiment point, et ne voient en lui, comme un certain nombre de ses contemporains, qu'un Don Juan parfaitement immoral, et d'ailleurs souvent ridicule. Il n'est que de lire sans prévention ses écrits autobiographiques, son *Journal*, sa *Correspondance*, pour se persuader rapidement du contraire, et découvrir en lui, sous une apparence parfois fanfaronne, une sensibilité naïve et l'âme la plus tendre qui se puisse imaginer.
>
> (Henriot, 1924: 23–24)

The verb immediately following this structure is often one which has the meaning of *lire* or *voir*, as in *il n'est que de parcourir*, *il n'est que de noter* or *il n'est que de regarder*. At times in an apparent conflation of *il n'y a qu'à* and *il n'est que de*, a writer will use *il n'est qu'à voir*.

English has no specialized equivalent for this connector. There is, of course, 'you only have to'; but the expression has none of the formulaic specificity of the French structure. And in a more familiar register, one could say 'Ask any…', 'Read any…' or 'Just think of…'.

inversement *

This connector is a less common variant for *à l'inverse*. Like the latter, it is one of a set of adversative or oppositive structures, which also contains *à l'opposé*, of which *au contraire* can be seen as the paradigm. It tends to be used to draw attention to a reciprocal relation or inverse symmetry in the things compared, as in the following extract from an essay on continuing class distinctions among the French, noticeable in the workplace:

> Dans la plupart de ces entreprises, on constate que le personnel de base qui va de l'OS au contremaître et de l'employé de bureau au gradé subalterne (c'est-à-dire le personnel pas ou peu diplômé) adopte automatiquement une attitude déférente pour ne pas dire humble devant un supérieur. Inversement, ce dernier leur répondra par une attitude de condescendance polie mais distante.
>
> (Frischer, 65)

The connector often functions like a mere replacement for *en revanche* or *par contre*. But a writer will use it to stress the neatness of an antithesis, as in this comment on the correlation between certain companies' attitudes towards women employees and the general up-to-dateness of the same companies' industrial practices:

> Dans le secteur privé, le taux de féminisation est devenu un indice de modernité. Inversement, les entreprises les plus désuètes sont les plus misogynes.

In the next example, the author's point is that, to be genuine, all revolutionaries against established political authority must also be in favour of sexual liberation:

> En effet, la répression sexuelle manifeste l'existence d'instances autoritaires dans des domaines aussi variés que la famille, la religion, les relations entre sexes, entre groupes d'âges, entre races et entre classes sociales. Inversement, l'apparition de la liberté sexuelle est le symptôme de l'éradication de la relation d'autorité dans ces divers domaines.
>
> (Revel, 1970: 226)

Variants

Occasionally, a writer adopts a variant of the structure, *en sens inverse*, as in this extract from an article on the need for the European Union, then composed of twelve countries, to admit more countries to membership and to make changes to its constitution:

> Elargir encore l'Union sans la réformer serait tuer l'idée européenne, mais, en sens inverse, il faut savoir que l'un des objectifs fondamentaux de la réforme sera d'adapter l'Union à un nombre de partenaires proche de deux fois douze.

Sartre uses another curious variant, *diversement*, to mark an inverse symmetry. Here, it is the symmetry between Right and Left in French politics. Having spoken first of certain fascists who did not collaborate with the Nazis during the Occupation, he goes on:

d'anciens Cagoulards sont passés à la Résistance. Diversement il s'est trouvé un certain nombre de radicaux, de socialistes, de pacifistes pour considérer l'occupation comme un moindre mal et pour faire bon ménage avec les Allemands.

(Sartre, 1949b: 44)

The connector is usually placed first in the sentence and followed by a comma; it is sometimes combined with *et*, **mais** or *ou*. Like *à l'inverse* again, it can be seen as an equivalent of English 'conversely'.

inversion de l'adjectif

This is the adjective placed first in the statement, usually a sentence, and separated from its noun by a verb, usually a part of *être*: *Nombreux sont ceux qui....* The new Grevisse, unlike the old, has an excellent article on this structure; however, as usual, most of the examples given are from literary prose, or verse (Grevisse, 1988, 368–369). The structure functions most obviously as a connector when the adjective is comparative or contrastive, as the statement it makes comments on the one which precedes. However, other adjectives are inverted in the same way for other reasons. One of the commonest of these structures is the fossilized formulaic **force est de**. Another, **tel est**, shows that to pre-position an adjective usually entails also the inversion of verb and subject. Indeed, it makes some sense to see the inverted adjective as merely a specialized mode of **inversion du verbe**.

Comparative and contrastive adjectives

The three most basic comparisons with a preceding statement are made with *plus*, *moins* and **aussi**. Thus many sentences or paragraphs commenting on the one preceding begin like this: *Plus graves peut-être seront les conséquences de...*; *Beaucoup moins contrôlables sont ces...*; *Tout aussi frappante est la phrase par laquelle....*

Comparisons or contrasts can be made with other words and expressions: *Significatif également est le refus de...*; *D'autant plus remarquable est cette persistance des traits, que...*; *Autrement graves seront les problèmes qui...*; *Bien pire est la situation des...*; *On ne peut plus caractéristique est à cet égard l'attitude du ministre...*; *Mieux accueillie du monde savant fut la théorie philologique de....* Of these, the most common is no doubt the variant with *autre*, often intensified by *tout*: *Autre est la situation de l'anglais. / Tout autres sont les résultats que nous avons obtenus.* A variant of the mode with *autre* is the use of *différent*: *Toutes différentes étaient l'analyse et la préoccupation de Simone Veil.* As some of the examples show, any tense of the verb is compatible with this structure.

Sometimes a contrast is made, or reinforced, by the juxtaposition of successive adjectival statements, as in the following opposition between two forms of fear, one seen as *indispensable*, the other as *nuisible*:

> [La peur du danger réel] est indispensable ; elle fait partie de l'instinct de la conservation, pourvu qu'elle se borne à la conscience du péril et conduise à trouver les moyens de l'éviter. Nuisible est au contraire la peur stupide qui, devant le danger imminent, paralyse l'individu et le livre à son ennemi, désarmé par un fatalisme impuissant.
>
> (Le Dantec, 107)

And sometimes, as with **au contraire** in that example, the connector combines with a contrastive: *Rares, en revanche, sont les gouvernements qui ...*; *Exceptionnels pourtant sont ceux qui...*; *Tout autre eût été par contre la situation en ce qui concerne la....*

Adjectives of outstandingness

Other adjectives are at times used in this structure, even though they make no comparison or contrast. The most common are those which express the idea of the extraordinary, the exceptional because of rarity or the important because of abundance. Again with these adjectives, *être* is almost the only verb used. Thus structures such as *Rares sont ceux qui* and *Nombreuses sont les jeunes filles qui* are frequent. This category includes adjectival declarations like the following: *Illustre est l'exemple de...*; *Significatif est le fait que...*; *Eloquente est en ce sens cette leçon de...*; *Minoritaires sont donc les éléments qui...*; *Fréquents furent les dons collectifs*; *Innombrables sont les traces de son activité*; *Immense est le nombre de telles observations*; *Exemplaire est à cet égard la stratégie de...*; *Superbes sont les moments du film où Emma semble se réveiller*; *Exceptionnels sont aujourd'hui les enfants qui échappent à l'obligation scolaire.* One of the most common adjectives used in this way is *seul*: *Seule nous intéresse la position de Claudel.* Adjectives modified by intensifiers are sometimes pre-positioned (*Très prudente est la manière dont il formule l'exigence*; *Particulièrement subtile est la lecture qu'il fait de...*) as in this sentence about Haussmann's transformation of districts of central Paris in the middle of the nineteenth century:

> Si denses sont les faubourgs, et si grande leur résistance physique à cette géométrie officielle qu'il faudra quinze ans pour tracer, en rasant la butte des Moulins, l'avenue joignant le nouvel Opéra aux guichets du Louvre.
>
> (Meyer, 17–18)

The anaphoric adjective

This is the repetition in what follows of a word occurring in what precedes. In this example, the link is made between *antithèse* and *antithétiques*. The writer's subject is the antithetical nature of certain relationships between characters in legends and folk-tales:

> Pour qui n'est pas au courant des recueils de légendes et de contes, ces divers thèmes semblent n'avoir que la valeur poétique qu'a la gradation de l'antithèse. Antithétiques sont l'offre que fait d'elle-même à un étranger la fille d'un roi, la méconnaissance des liens qui unissent le père et le fils, et surtout leur combat.
>
> (Van Gennep, 240)

Another example can be seen on p. 185, ...*féminin. Féminins sont les termes...*, in the quotation beginning *L'attribution du genre grammatical.*

The principle of contiguity of semantically related syntagms

In addition, whatever the adjective, there is a tendency to put it first in the sentence when the subject of the verb is lengthy or linked to another element such as a relative clause. A statement like 'Those people who are capable of identifying the candidates at the end of the campaign will have to be pretty clever' may be quite tolerable in English, even though it separates 'Those people' from 'pretty clever' by seventeen words. But in French dialectical prose *Bien malins seront sans doute ceux qui, au terme de la campagne, sauront identifier les candidats* makes a preferable structure, because it puts the plural adjective and the plural subject much closer to each other. Also, with some adjectives, such as *malin* or *heureux*, echoes of proverbs, biblical utterances or literary quotation (*Bien malin qui...*, *Heureux celui qui...*) influence the usage of writers. As with other forms of inversion, this way of structuring a statement brings together two interrelated elements of it. This also applies, of course, to some modes exemplified above, in particular those beginning with comparatives or with *Rares sont* and *Nombreux sont*. Thus, in an article on reactions of Israelis to the agreement between their government and the PLO about the evacuation of the Golan heights, one finds this sentence:

> Prévisible était donc la colère de la droite israélienne, pour qui céder un pouce de territoire tient du sacrilège, et celle des principaux intéressés, les quelque douze mille colons israéliens du Golan.

If this sentence began *La colère de la droite israélienne* and ended with *était donc prévisible* it would be just as intelligible. But it would contravene the rhetorical convention that syntagms which have a close semantic or grammatical relationship with one another tend to be placed close together. And so it might be sensed as clumsy or inept, not in accord with a style or register deemed more appropriate. The same goes for a sentence like the following, which rather than leaving verb and adjective to the end brings them to the beginning:

> Dramatique fut la confrontation entre Carlo Sama, ancien administrateur du groupe Ferruzzi, et l'ex-ministre de la Justice Claudio Martelli, amis de longue date et habitués à fréquenter les mêmes yachts.

Sometimes writers adopt this structure even when that principle of contiguity of semantically related elements would hardly be breached by the more usual word order: *Dure est la loi de la pesanteur économique, mais c'est la loi.* In the next example, the adjective is striking (and, it must be said, idiosyncratic) by being the first word not just in the sentence but of the whole article from which it is quoted. The article examines attitudes among the French nobility to the Dreyfus Affair: *Courante est, sous la plume des dreyfusards, l'assimilation de la noblesse et de l'antidreyfusisme* (Brelot, 339). (This article, by the way, shows how a particular writer can favour a particular structure much more than others: in a text of seventeen pages, this one occurs eleven times, four examples of it on a single page (Brelot, 342)).

Non-initial position

It is unusual to place this structure anywhere other than at the beginning of the sentence. When it is done, it is most often done with *rare* and *nombreux*: *On le dit imprévisible. Surtout parce que peu nombreux ont été ceux qui prévoyaient sa réussite.* But on occasion other adjectives are used:

> Lorsque aux îles Fidji, en mai 1987, le colonel Sitveni Rabuka renverse un gouvernement régulièrement élu parce qu'il est à dominante indienne et que le colonel veut réserver le pouvoir aux Mélanésiens, alors, en Occident, bien faibles sont les voix qui blâment la création de ce nouveau régime fondé sur un principe explicitement raciste.
>
> (Revel, 1988: 224–225)

> Pour fuir les problèmes de la localisation étroite, vive est alors la tentation de recourir à une procédure inverse.
>
> (Ricardou, 23)

And some adjectives are placed at the beginning of the second part of certain binary sentences, making a chiastic relation with the adjectival structure ending the first part: *Mais leurs dimensions sont plus restreintes, et différentes sont leurs habitudes* (Roule, 123).

Verbs other than *être*

Occasionally the verb is not *être* but another which is close to it in function and meaning, usually a verb of seeming or appearing: *Les Français le veulent-ils ? Rien n'est moins sûr. Plus sûre leur paraît la voie de... / Plus scabreuse se révélera peut-être une immense affaire qui... / Autrement plus importante et fondée apparaît la critique de l'inégalité.*

inversion du verbe

This structure consists of the verb placed before the subject in affirmative statements which usually begin the sentence or the paragraph: *Participent à ce projet une dizaine d'institutions européennes.* As with *inversion de l'adjectif*, which is at times a mode of this structure, many of these inversions function as connectors.

Inversion including pronoun

In this, one of the commonest modes, a pronoun, frequently *en* or *y*, introduces the structure: *On sait que la nature n'est pas bonne. Y règne la loi du plus fort.* It is more the pronoun which functions as the connector, but the verb is integral to it. An example comes from an article describing the facilities of the Juilliard School of Music:

> Le bâtiment comprend vingt-huit salles d'enseignement, quinze studios, quatre-vingt-quatre pièces pour les représentations individuelles ou à deux, trente-cinq studios d'enseignement... Y sont mis à disposition des étudiants quelque deux cent trente pianos de concert Steinway [...]

One verb commonly used in this way is *témoigner de*. This extract, from an essay on the long history of human interest in things seen not as things in themselves but as representational objects, contains two exemplars:

> Il est vrai que les premiers symptômes de préoccupations non utilitaires semblent être très anciens. En témoigne, probablement, un fragment d'ocre rouge et un morceau de lave verte découverts à Olduvai. En témoignent aussi, peut-être, les trouvailles faites dans la grotte n° 1 du Mas des Caves (Lunel-Viel, Hérault, France).

The initial pronoun is often part of a reflexive or pronominal verb, commonly *s'ajouter*, as in this extract from a discussion of Manet's painting *Le déjeuner sur l'herbe*:

> Le mélange de personnages nus et vêtus à la mode contemporaine est un premier sujet de scandale. S'y ajoute le pastiche délibéré d'œuvres protégées par la distanciation spatiotemporelle de l'exotisme ou de l'Antiquité.

The other most common pronoun combining as a connector with this structure is *le*, as in this comment on the theatrical qualities of Stendhal's unfinished novel *Lucien Leuwen*:

> Qu'il y ait mouvement dramatique dans *Lucien Leuwen*, c'est, me semble-t-il, incontestable. Le prouvent non seulement maints passages dialogués qui pourraient entrer tels quels dans une comédie, mais la technique même que Stendhal applique pour poser ses personnages et pour indiquer leur profession.

(Wagner, 179)

Subjects containing a demonstrative adjective often function in a similar way, as in this example from an discussion of intellectual fashions:

> Bien sûr, tout courant dominant n'est pas une mode. Ne mérite ce nom que le courant de pensée qui apparaît sans justification rationnelle et disparaît de même.

(Revel, 1988: 377)

Comparatives and contrastives

Like some modes of the inverted adjective, this structure is used in comparative statements containing *plus*, **aussi** or *moins*. Here too the connective function is clear, as the comparison is always made with the sentence preceding. An example comes from an article on a campaign of eradication of certain flies:

> Parmi les modes de lutte contre ces mouches figure surtout la stérilisation des mâles. Sont efficaces, elles aussi, les méthodes de traitement des plaies et de pulvérisation des animaux avec certains produits insecticides.

Similarly, other connective structures are sometimes combined with an inversion: *Existait toutefois une notion de*; *Sont évitées en particulier les questions de*; *De ce fait sont écartées des options*; *Joue dans le même sens le fait que*; *Perdure enfin le risque de*; *Sont ainsi suspendues les lois sur*; *Surtout subissent le même sort les dispositions de la loi Pasqua*; *Sera également restauré un bijou de salle cent pour cent 1937*. A contrast with a preceding sentence may be made with *Fait contraste*, as in this opening to a paragraph following one on the destruction of villages in Afghanistan during the war with the USSR: *Fait contraste l'énorme croissance des villes par rapport à l'avant-guerre*.

Definitions with *être*

One of the more precise modes, again showing the similarity with the inverted adjective, especially the anaphoric adjective, is that which serves to give a clear definition of a term, itself usually an adjective or a noun used in a preceding statement. The quotation given above from Revel, defining intellectual faddery, could be seen as belonging also to this category. But in this mode, the verb is more usually *être*:

> Aujourd'hui, le terme « populaire » est un terme piège. Au temps où la communauté existait encore, était populaire ce qui préservait l'individualité de chacun à l'intérieur de cette communauté.

> ...nous préférons parler de linguistique synchronique et de linguistique diachronique. Est synchronique tout ce qui se rapporte à l'aspect statique de notre science, diachronique tout ce qui a trait aux évolutions.

(Saussure, 120)

Inversions with *problème* and *question*

An equally specific mode is found with the verb *(se) poser* when its subject is *question* or *problème*. It is often accompanied by **dès lors** or **alors**: *Se posent, dès lors, plusieurs séries de questions...*; *Si se pose la question des effets bienfaisants de...*; *Se retrouve alors posée la question du pluralisme.*

Often these two nouns and other similar ones are also the inverted subject of **reste** (or *demeure*): *Demeure toutefois une interrogation...*; *Si un tel vaccin était découvert, resterait le problème de son coût a priori très élevé.*

Narrative inversions

In contexts where their connective function can be seen to have a narrative quality, verbs describing the onset of events which may have a dramatic character, including verbs like *venir* and its derivatives, are at times inverted in combination with adverbs such as *alors*, **enfin**, *soudain*, **ensuite**: *Arrivent les municipales*; *Éclatait alors une affaire qui...*; *Survient alors un deuxième coup de théâtre*; *Sont apparues les faiblesses graves de l'économie espagnole*; *Viendra ensuite le tour de la côte sud-est*; *Paradoxalement, devint crédible ce qui aurait paru absurde dans un passé proche*; *Sont arrivés vers les années 60 les fameux chalutiers à pêche arrière*; *Vient, enfin, le dernier stade*; *S'ensuivit un beau tollé*; *L'idée fut abandonnée. Naquit celle de....*

The principle of contiguity of semantically related syntagms

Most of the preceding modes also show one of the features often present in inversion of any sort: it avoids putting the verb at the end rather than at the beginning of a long subject-group. Speakers and writers of English customarily interpolate many words between subject and verb, as in this sentence taken from a sequence of sentences in which two authors acknowledge assistance from colleagues and friends:

> Conversations, even the briefest, with John Bowen, John Burrow, Debbie Cameron, Jenny Coates, Mick Comber, Barbara Crowther, Norman Fairclough (whose own forthcoming *Language and Power* was a great stimulus), Simon Frith, Peter Goodrich, Eamon Grant, Stuart Hall, David Hopkins, Debbie Johnson, Paul Kenny, John Lyon, Angela Lloyd, Peter Mack, Clifford Myerson, Jonathan Rée, Yvonne Rydin, Peter Stallybrass, Carolyn Steedman, and with numerous colleagues in the Department of English and Communication Studies at Birmingham Polytechnic and the Department of English at the University of Bristol, have helped to shape the project.
>
> (Leith & Myerson, ix–x)

In French, such a sentence would almost certainly be inverted. This is a way of ensuring that the syntagm subject–verb remains intact. Many such sentences, although longish, are simple in structure, being often in the form of lists, and the initial verb is therefore plural, as in these examples the first of which is from an account of Napoleon's departure for Saint Helena:

> L'ont suivi librement dans son exil : le grand maréchal Bertrand et son épouse Fanny ; le comte et la comtesse de Montholon ; le général Gourgaud ; Emmanuel de Las Cases ainsi que le premier valet de chambre Marchand, et les domestiques Ali, Cipriani et Noverraz.

> Ne peuvent, aux termes de la loi soviétique, recourir à la grève les salariés de l'ensemble des moyens de transports, des communications, des hôpitaux, de l'énergie, des usines fonctionnant en cycle continu, de la défense, des différents services de police et des administrations gouvernementales.

Without being in list form, other sentences beginning with a verb may have a lengthy subject-group composed largely of clauses qualifying the noun:

> Déboussolés, les acteurs économiques ont besoin de reprendre confiance. Manquent encore les signes capables de les convaincre que la barre est bien tenue et que les politiques économiques des grands pays industrialisés sont claires et cohérentes.

Writers sometimes conclude discussion of a capital point, a whole development or even a chapter with a brief inverted sentence. To a statement of analytical finality it can lend concision and a maxim-like tone of solemnity, as in this sentence ending an essay on a technician who, to explain obscurities in his speciality, uses language which is itself so technical as to be incomprehensible to laymen:

> Il n'a trouvé aucun intérêt à faire effort pour être compris d'un simple « honnête homme ». Si bien que son explication n'est accessible qu'à ceux qui sont déjà au fait. Ce qui, si l'on y réfléchit, est merveilleusement absurde. Ont seuls droit à l'explication ceux qui n'en ont pas besoin.

Formulaic inversions

Three other formulaic inversions belong to the technical terminology of particular fields: stage directions in the script of a play: *Entrent précipitamment Mme Dupont-Fredaine et le général tout rouges*; the lists of honours and promotions periodically published by decree in the *Journal officiel*:

> Sont élevés à la dignité de *grand officier* : Geneviève Anthonioz, présidente d'ATD-Quart Monde ; Jean-Louis Barrault, artiste dramatique, directeur de théâtre ; Émile Biasini, ancien ministre ; Marcel Wiltzer, préfet honoraire [...];

and the mathematician's way of introducing a hypothetical example for discussion or demonstration: *Soient deux équations algébriques à deux inconnues.* This third one, in the form *soit*, has been adopted into general prose as a variant for *par exemple*.

Non-initial inversions

When not placed at the beginning of the sentence, the structure is rarely preceded by more than a brief adverbial clause: *Dans le camp socialiste, s'affrontent une pléthore de brillants colonels. / En abondance sont réunies de nombreuses informations. / C'est dans ce contexte qu'ont été publiés il y a quelques jours....* Sometimes clauses with *si, quand* or *puisque* precede: *Ce document – incomplet puisque manquait la liste des participants – dévoilait l'attitude de....* Sometimes, too, like the brief inverted sentence mentioned above, a longer sentence will end with an inverted main clause, sharpening a concise statement of finality, as in this comment on the advent of technocrats in the political process, which the author sees as pernicious:

> L'égalité civique se retrouve trahie, car, là où le citoyen avait le droit de dire ce qui devait être, ne se font plus entendre que ceux qui savent et peuvent faire.

Finally, certain connective structures placed first in the sentence, among them *ainsi*, a mode of *aussi* and *aussi bien*, are usually followed by an inversion of subject and verb.

là *

This connector has two modes: a demonstrative one, by far the more common and variable; and a less frequent adversative one.

Demonstrative *là*

In structures like *celui-là* and *ces femmes-là*, this adverb designates, of course, not a place but an antecedent. Related to this use as a demonstrative reinforcer is *là*'s function as an expository connector. As such, it usually disambiguates an antecedent of impersonal verb structures or the pronoun *ce*. It combines mainly with verbs (mostly *être, il y a* and *s'agir*); and in meaning it is close to the stressed 'that' in 'To be or not to be, that is the question' or italicized 'that' in 'Since no one quite knows what a university ought to do, perhaps *that* should be the subject of our educational system' (Vidal, 214). The main variants of this mode are *c'est là, là est, là réside, il s'agit là de, il y a là, par là, là aussi, là encore* and *à partir de là*. And sometimes it functions like one of the modes of *voilà*.

c'est là

This is the most common of the demonstrative variants. In this mode, the connector can often appear to be redundant. However, since *ce* can be both anaphoric and cataphoric, it could often be read as anticipating a later element in the sentence, rather than repeating an antecedent. And it is such potential ambiguities, arising less in English partly because it offers the choice between 'this' and 'that', 'these' and 'those', that this connector serves to clarify by its explicit reference to what precedes. An article about the ending of the Cold War and some international anxieties that it created says this:

> Tout comme M. Gorbatchev, l'Occident a quelques raisons de regretter la fameuse « stabilité stratégique » d'antan. Mais c'est là le prix à payer pour la victoire de ses valeurs : les progrès de la liberté à l'Est.

There, *là* refers to the whole main clause preceding. But it can refer to shorter elements of statements, even to single words. In this extract from a discussion of the requirement for total accuracy in using computer technology, it refers to the noun *quantités de données* or even just to *données*:

> La technologie informatique consomme, produit, stocke et diffuse d'immenses quantités de données : c'est là un trésor de savoir écrit, auquel on ne peut accéder qu'en évitant la défaillance graphique, et l'à-peu-près.

It is used in the plural: *Ce sont là les...*; in all tenses of the verb: *ce serait là*; *c'était là, ce furent là*, etc.; and in negative and interrogative forms:

> « Ah, Monsieur Ledoux, vous êtes un terrible architecte ! » s'exclame Louis-Sébastien Mercier dans ses *Tableaux de Paris*. Ce n'est pas là un compliment.

> La connaissance intime de Maupassant est décevante : elle ne révèle pas un être supérieur par le cœur et l'intelligence, et n'ouvre qu'un jour incertain sur une âme dure et désolée. Est-ce là la raison de l'admiration limitée que nous inspire son talent ?

This mode is placed mainly at the beginning of sentences and is usually followed by a noun structure. However, it is also followed by verbs in a variant of *c'est dire (que)*:

> Qu'attendent les Français du gouvernement Balladur ? Une réduction du chômage ? Ils ne se font, hélas, aucune illusion. Un redémarrage de la croissance ? Ils sont plus nombreux qu'on ne croit à savoir que la fin de la récession ne se décrète pas. Du gouvernement Balladur, les Français n'attendent rien. Bonne occasion pour faire quelque chose. Est-ce là trop demander ?

The structure is sometimes reinforced by **bien** or **même**: *c'est bien là*; *c'est même là*. And it can itself be combined with **c'est le cas de**: *c'est là le cas de.*

là est

This mode could often replace *c'est là*, as in this ironic contribution to the national debate on the notion of level of achievement among schoolpupils (*le niveau*):

> Le niveau se célèbre ou se déplore, se décrète ou se refuse, s'élève ou s'abaisse, s'atteint ou se dépasse : il ne se mesure jamais. Là est sa force et son principe de norme sociale et scolaire. La mesure est d'autant plus rigoureuse qu'elle est en caoutchouc.
>
> (Baudelot & Establet, 20)

This mode, which is akin to *voilà*, has an emphatic force which makes it suitable for the expression of points seen as of particular pertinence, combined with, say, *vrai*, *véritable* or *essentiel*: *Car là est l'essentiel. / Et là est le véritable enjeu. / Là évidemment est la vraie question.* And it, or variants of it combined with *tout*, are used to express the idea of importance: *Là est tout le charme. / Là est toute l'ambiguïté de cette tentative. / Toute la contradiction est là. / Tout le débat est là !* It is common in the negative, saying 'That's not the point!': *Là n'est pas le problème. / La question n'est pas là. / L'important n'est pas là. / Mais l'essentiel n'est pas là.*

Variants of *là est* as the emphasizer of a point of significance are *là se trouve* and *là réside*. An article on Michel Noir, a politician of the Right, after pointing out that he is becoming more popular with voters on the Left, says: *Là se trouve son vrai problème.* A scientific article on ribozymes first points out the limitations of certain enzymes, then adds: *Là réside, précisément, l'immense intérêt des ribozymes.*

il s'agit là de

This mode too can function more or less as a variant of *c'est là* or *ce sont là*. It can be followed by a noun, as in this statement about the localized nature of certain crimes of violence, the author's case being that there is no generalized crisis of violence in France:

> Il y a une incontestable montée de l'insécurité *physique* objective dans certains villages ou dans certains quartiers de certaines villes à certaines heures. Mais il s'agit là de problèmes ponctuels, locaux, pour lesquels un traitement approprié ne peut être que local.
>
> (Chesnais, 22)

It can be followed by a verb, as in this extract from a discussion of a government white paper on urban planning:

> Ce document, devant lequel les collectivités locales devront réagir, présentera les grands choix d'aménagement de l'Île-de-France. Les grands travaux – types villes nouvelles – qui s'inscrivaient en rase campagne ne sont plus de mise. Il s'agit là de remodeler un tissu fragile, de réparer des espaces meurtris, mais qui sont loin d'être vierges.

This mode is commonest in the present tense; but, again like *c'est là*, it can adapt to any. It too can combine with *bien*: *il s'agit bien là de*.

il y a là

This mode is less common than *c'est là*. It is only ever followed by a noun. Rather than meaning 'that is', this one expresses the idea of 'therein lies' or 'in that fact lies'. An article on the relationship between European monetary exchange mechanisms and a possible lowering of interest rates in France says:

> La réduction tant souhaitée des taux d'intérêt pour alléger les frais financiers des entreprises... Il y a là, en même temps qu'une préoccupation permanente, quelque chose comme un grand échec.

A discussion of the improving popularity rating of the government of Michel Rocard in 1989 says:

> Sa base politique est large – ce qui lui assure d'excellents chiffres globaux – mais elle est très hétérogène et difficilement mobilisable dans une consultation électorale. Il n'en demeure pas moins vrai qu'il y a là un gain et non pas un recul.

A variant for this structure, in some contexts, could be *on voit là*.

par là, par là même

This mode is quite common. When it is placed first in the sentence, it often serves to mark a similarity or a difference: *Par là, elle ressemble à...*; *Par là, la France se distingue de ses partenaires*. When placed inside the sentence, it often introduces a precision or a definition of what precedes, expressed by verbs such as *s'expliquer*, *entendre*, *vouloir dire*. It could be replaced variously by ***ainsi***, *à cet égard*, *de cette manière*. It can designate the whole of the preceding statement or part of it:

> Je suis né paysan. Ce n'est pas un titre de gloire. Ce n'est pas non plus une métaphore. Je ne veux pas dire par là que mes grands-parents possédaient cinq cents hectares d'une riche province française et qu'ils faisaient cultiver leur bonne terre par des fermiers polis qui saluaient en ôtant leur casquette.

A stressed variant of this mode is *par là même*. It would at times be replaceable by **de ce fait**, **du coup**, or even by **du même coup**. The following example comes from an article on press coverage of violence in the Paris *métro* (a branch of the RATP), in particular two murders committed in a short space of time:

> Certains dirigeants de la RATP regrettent la « médiatisation » des meurtres, qui aurait donné des idées aux joueurs de lame. Explication un peu courte, dans la mesure où les deux crimes évoqués par la presse ont paraphé cette période rouge plus qu'ils ne l'ont inaugurée. Mais, par là même, ils ont décuplé l'inquiétude des agents et des usagers : chacun a eu l'impression qu'il aurait pu être le mort.

This variant is sometimes hyphenated: *par là-même*. It is not usually placed first in the sentence, except when preceded by **et** or **mais**. Another variant is *par la même occasion*, as in this comment on a book: *Il annonce l'avènement d'une nouvelle philosophie et par la même occasion la mort d'une autre*. There are also *par cela même* and *par ce fait même*:

> Pour plus d'un Britannique, Hitler était avant tout l'homme qui unifiait l'Europe à son profit et qui, par cela même, mettait l'Angleterre en péril.

Other structures with demonstrative *là*

After an earlier point introduced by *là*, the connector can combine with **aussi** or **encore** to make a second or further point: *là aussi, là encore*. And *à partir de là* can introduce a logical consequence, after the manner of **dès lors**: *À partir de là, il est clair que....* A structure which often serves as a variant for **au contraire** is *loin de là*, following a negative statement such as this about Amiel's weakened attachment to Christianity: *Non qu'il l'ait jamais abandonné ; loin de là, il resta pieux toute sa vie* (Vadier, 20).

Adversative *là*

The structure *là où* is sometimes used contrastively as a variant for **alors que**. The use of this temporally derived structure is akin to English 'where' which sometimes does service instead of contrastive 'while' or 'whereas'. It usually introduces the first half of a binary sentence, shaping a contrast with the second part, as in this statement about an important difference between Émile Zola's methods of observation of his society and those of most novelists of his time:

> Là où les écrivains de son temps se contentaient d'observer à distance, et plutôt les salons que les cuisines, les maisons de maîtres que les écuries, lui est allé au charbon.

Similarly, a philosopher defines the difference between *l'apologie* and *la fable*: *Là où l'apologie contredit et proteste, la fable jette un regard résigné et amusé* (Reboul, 155).

Two other connectors which this one helps to structure are *de là* and the binary structure *ici... là*.

le fait est que

This connector has two modes: a confirmative one in which it functions rather like *car*, *de fait* or *c'est que*; and a more adversative one akin to *en fait*. Hanse distinguishes between this structure and *c'est un fait (que)* (Hanse, 1983: 409), but without defining an essential difference, which is that the latter is usually concessive in function.

Confirmative

The prime function of the structure is to introduce a precision or a statement of fact, often one which resolves an uncertainty or a point which has been contested. It certifies what is not contestable in what precedes. This it can do either by justifying some earlier statement or implication or by correcting a doubt or an error. Sometimes it does the first more than the second, sometimes the second more than the first. An example of the first mode, dating from the period when cranium measurement was the latest science in the study of mankind, is taken from a discussion of the essential distinction which this new technique enabled the anthropology of the time to make between humans and animals:

> Les caractères crâniens ont été particulièrement invoqués, lorsqu'il s'est agi de mettre en relief la distance qui sépare l'homme de l'animal. Le fait est que, à ce point de vue plus qu'à tout autre, des différences profondes, – encore qu'elles ne soient pas irréductibles, – se manifestent entre les Primates.
>
> (Hovelacque & Hervé, 39)

There the second sentence confirms and precises the point made more generally in the sentence preceding. The connector functions rather like *il est de fait que* or even *en effet*. In such a context it is not very different from *il est vrai (que)*. Something similar is seen in the next example, which is part of a discussion of the distinction that can be defined between verbs and nouns, with special reference to the Finno-Ugric languages:

> Dans les langues finno-ugriennes, le verbe et le nom ont tant de points communs qu'on a pu dire, à tort d'ailleurs, qu'ils ne se distinguent point. Le fait est que le verbe y apparaît souvent comme d'origine nominale et est encore parfois affecté des mêmes éléments morphologiques que le nom.
>
> (Vendryes, 140)

These examples show another common feature: in each case, the point preceding the connector has been problematized, by *encore qu'elles ne soient pas irréductibles* and *à tort d'ailleurs*. The connector serves to resolve the uncertainty thus introduced into the assertion.

The dual nature of this connector is seen in the next example, which begins with a quoted prediction: that corruption among senior French businessmen will soon become so widespread that it will have political consequences:

> « Dans trois, quatre ou cinq ans, la corruption sera tellement généralisée que, comme en Italie, les premières investigations des juges bouleverseront l'échiquier politique. » Le pronostic se réaliserait-il plus tôt que prévu ? Le fait est que, depuis deux mois, les politiques ont cédé la place aux patrons en première ligne de la chronique à répétitions des « affaires ».

There, as before, the initial affirmation has been problematized by the question following it. The third sentence, introduced by the connector, tends to both confirm the implication of the first one and partially resolve the uncertainty of the second. If replaced by *en effet*, it would confirm; if replaced by *en fait*, it would resolve.

More adversative

In this mode, the connector, sometimes combined with **mais**, introduces a certainty which can contradict preceding affirmations which it deems to be erroneous. In this discussion of the artistic qualities of the pianist György Cziffra, the writer is concerned to correct what she sees as a misconception, the idea that his brilliance was merely technical:

> On lui reprocha des qualités exclusivement athlétiques, on en fit un technicien du clavier, un pianiste qui vivait uniquement des prouesses époustouflantes qu'un interprète doit mettre en jeu dans les *Rhapsodies hongroises* ou dans *Mephisto-Valse* ou dans les *Études transcendantales*. Cziffra répondit en enregistrant un répertoire plus « réfléchi », Beethoven, Schumann ou Mendelssohn, ainsi que les pans plus austères de Liszt, sans toujours convaincre. Le fait est que qualifier Cziffra de grand technicien est un contresens. C'était un pianiste dopé au courage, travaillant douze heures par jour pour préparer ses concerts et dominer les épreuves qu'impose le répertoire romantique.

There the connector functions rather like the adversative mode of *or*. The link made is to an idea discussed in a whole paragraph, rather than in just the preceding sentence. A similar link, containing *or*, is seen in the next example. The author's point is that the inter-ethnic wars in the Balkans can only be stopped by some foreign power strong enough to impose itself on the combatants, such as Russia (i.e. the sabre-rattling Jirinovski) and Germany, neither of which, he says, is appropriate:

Jirinovski a eu beau jouer les Picrochole de Vukovar à Belgrade, il n'est pas encore en mesure de mettre en route le « rouleau compresseur », d'ailleurs passablement rouillé pour le moment, de l'armée ex-rouge. Il ne suffit pas non plus que le deutschemark ait supplanté un dinar miné par une hyperinflation trillionesque pour que l'Allemagne, encore mal remise de sa réunification, envisage, serait-ce une seconde, d'aller rétablir l'ordre en Bosnie.

Or le fait est que les peuples yougoslaves, comme la plupart de ceux que l'Histoire a enchevêtrés, ont rarement vécu en paix sans y être fortement incités par quelque hégémonie musclée : ottomane, autrichienne d'abord, puis, successivement, serbe et communiste.

Place in the sentence

The most usual position for this connector is at the beginning of a sentence, or at least after a stop. But it also occurs as the second element of a sentence in which the first implies the uncertainty which the connector then resolves: *M. Pierre Botton peut dire ce qu'il veut, le fait est qu'il se trompe. / Contestable ou pas, le fait est que c'est là une idée dont il va falloir désormais tenir compte.* The same goes for the mode combined with *mais*, as in this comment by Gide on a literary acquaintance:

Il ne vous quittait point qu'il n'eût pris de nouveau rendez-vous, et j'admire qu'il lui restât quelque temps pour écrire ou lire ; mais le fait est qu'il écrivait beaucoup et qu'il avait tout lu.

(Gide, 1954: 540)

l'idée que

Though not a connector, this construction can be problematical for anyone learning to write contemporary French. It affects the structuring of a certain type of sentence.

A certain English 'that'

English 'that' is often straightforwardly translatable into French as *que*: 'The letter that I received...' can be said in a relative clause *La lettre que j'ai reçue....* But 'that' also does certain jobs that *que* does not do. In the following English sentence, 'an ancient regulation that' is unambiguous; but if it was expressed in French *un vieux règlement que* would be impossible:

Ko-Ko makes things worse by informing them that he has now discovered an ancient regulation that when a married man is beheaded his wife is buried alive.

(Scholes, 638)

If *que* were used, the French reader would take it as the beginning of a relative clause saying something of what happened to the ancient regulation. Whereas 'that' introduces a noun clause saying what the contents of the regulation are. Similarly, 'the inexorable law that ideas degenerate' is clear; but for a similar French statement to be clear, *que* is accompanied by a verb: *l'inéluctable loi qui veut que les idées tombent des milieux où elles ont été élaborées, dans la foule innombrable qui les reçoit aveuglément* (Autin, 10–11).

This type of 'that' is very common in English: 'It was a sign that political groups would maintain a united front.' / 'He said criticism that the government's policies towards low-income earners were unfair was unfounded.' / 'He had ample evidence that the Princess herself had divulged details of their marital rifts.' / 'The hearing of charges that he conspired to pervert the course of justice has been postponed.' This 'that' always follows a noun; but it does not introduce a relative clause; it spells out what the sign, the criticism, the evidence, the charge consists of. It could usually be replaced by 'saying that', 'maintaining that' or 'to the effect that'. With most nouns of this sort, *que* would create indeterminacy in the reader's mind. And yet, a noun like *l'idée* is often followed by *que*.

A noun like *l'idée*

By 'a noun like *l'idée*' I mean a noun expressing the idea of an opinion, a statement or an idea. When *que* is used after such nouns, it can be ambiguous. In this sentence: *L'idée que j'avais eue allait simplifier notre tâche*, there is no ambiguity: a relative clause is introduced by the pronoun *que*, which could be expressed in English with 'that' or 'which'. But in this sentence: *L'idée que Poil de Carotte est quelquefois distingué amuse la famille* (Renard, 1970: 713), *que* is not a pronoun introducing a relative clause but a conjunction introducing a noun clause. This clause does not say anything about what happens to *l'idée*, as a relative clause would do. It says what the idea is; it details the idea's contents, so to speak. In this structure, *que* is invariably followed by a noun (or pronoun), itself the subject of a clause which could stand as a sentence: *Poil de Carotte est distingué*. In English, this *que* could never be 'which', only 'that': 'The official announcement that the franc would be devalued was delayed.'

The potential indeterminacy of *que* arises when a noun like *l'idée, la rumeur, le principe* or *l'affirmation* is accompanied by the definite article. With the indefinite article, the problem does not usually arise. Similarly, when the noun is preceded not by an article but by a demonstrative adjective, most writers use *que*:

> N'oublions jamais ce principe élémentaire que le totalitarisme ne peut vivre que grâce au mensonge et la démocratie survivre que grâce à la vérité.

However, with *l'un des* or when there is neither article nor demonstrative, *que* is usually avoided: *L'un des principes selon lesquels, en Bourse, les mêmes causes produisent rarement les mêmes effets. / À la suite de rumeurs selon lesquelles la troupe pourrait intervenir.*

Avoidance of *que*

The structure *l'idée que* followed by a noun clause is frequently avoided. This is done at times with a colon: *je souscris volontiers au verdict d'un éminent psychanalyste : je n'ai pas de Sur-moi* (Sartre, 1964: 11), a statement which could be comfortably made in English with 'the verdict of an eminent psychoanalyst that I have no super-ego'. But by far the most common alternative to *que* is *l'idée selon laquelle* (occasionally *suivant laquelle*):

> Faire des émissions culturelles dans une télévision de masse signifie accepter les contraintes de l'outil, et le principe selon lequel le public peut accéder à tout.

> Dans l'opinion publique prévaut encore l'idée suivant laquelle les couples auraient une préférence pour les bébés mâles au détriment des bébés femelles.

A form *l'idée d'après laquelle*, common fifty to a hundred years ago, is rare nowadays.

que preceded by a verb

Sometimes the grammatical indeterminacy of *que* is avoided by the insertion of a verb structure between the noun preceding and *que*: *le préjugé qui consiste à croire que...*; *le mot de Bergson, statuant que....* The most common of these is *vouloir*: *l'adage qui veut que....* Or else the noun plays the part of a verb: a sentence beginning *Goffman fait l'hypothèse que* could have begun *Goffman suppose que*. Similarly, the common expression *on a l'impression que* could be replaced by a verb like *il nous semble que* or *on croit que*. Sometimes, too, as in structures like *faire la preuve* or *avoir le sentiment*, the noun preceding is really part of a verb: *Ils avaient la conviction qu'il existait une forme unique de régime politique.*

Similarly, if the noun is one which is phonetically or semantically related to a verb (*la pensée/penser* and *l'affirmation/affirmer*), *que* is clear: *Notre politique repose sur la constatation qu'il n'y a pas de progrès social dans la récession économique.* But with a noun such as *attitude*, sensed as unrelated to any verb, *selon laquelle* is the only way to make the link between it and the explanation of it that follows:

Cela ne peut que mettre en porte à faux l'attitude, trop répandue dans le patronat français, selon laquelle la pression sur les coûts salariaux des ouvriers est le palliatif à toutes les carences de gestion.

It is clear, too, that the more words separate the noun from *que*, the more uncertainty there must be about the latter's grammatical function. In these circumstances, *selon* is usually preferred:

La thèse du film d'Oliver Stone, *JFK*, selon laquelle le president américain John Kennedy a été la victime d'un complot militaro-industriel, ne repose sur aucun fait avéré.

There *que* would introduce ambiguity, albeit momentary – would its antecedent be Oliver Stone, *film* or *thèse*? In theory, another possibility would be to precede *que* with *à savoir*. However, this is much less used than formerly. Like the structure with *d'après*, it dates from a century ago. Nowadays, the structure with *à savoir que* is common only when the noun is accompanied by the indefinite article: *Une autre interprétation, à savoir que....*

The author's attitude to the idea

The most important variable affecting the choice of structure may be the author's argument. A writer disputing an idea tends to use *selon laquelle*, as in this criticism of the notion that all Arabs are potential Islamic-fundamentalist terrorists:

Les médias banalisent l'idée selon laquelle l'islam en soi est potentiellement criminel, et tout Arabe un vecteur supposé de cette idéologie meurtrière.

But a writer endorsing the idea that advertisers want us to believe happiness lies in buying things uses *que*: *La publicité dispense l'idée que tout est possible et qu'il suffit, pour vivre heureux, de savoir acheter.* This distinction applies all the more to *l'idée reçue*, by definition less believable:

Prenons l'idée reçue selon laquelle ce serait François Mitterrand qui, au moyen de l'Union de la gauche et du Programme commun, aurait provoqué l'effondrement du parti communiste français.

This tendency is confirmed by two exemplars written by the same author in the same article, one with *que* taking an idea seriously, the other with *selon*, disputing an idea. The subject is Georges Marchais, the reluctantly outgoing secretary of the Parti communiste, and his unclear relation to the incoming secretary:

Obnubilé par l'idée que son successeur pourrait engager rapidement le procès de la dernière période, M. Marchais a préféré rester. [...] Il ne fallait pas accréditer l'idée selon laquelle le nouveau secrétaire national serait sous sa tutelle, a-t-il expliqué en substance.

(Saux)

Counter examples

It should be noted that what is outlined above is a tendency only. It is contradicted by writers who use *l'idée que* when rebutting an idea: *l'idée reçue que* / *l'idée chimérique que* / *l'idée idiote, mais très répandue, que Pétain et de Gaulle étaient d'accord.* / *L'idée que la grande guerre, en bouleversant l'économie du monde, lui aurait imposé une orientation nouvelle, ne résiste pas à l'examen* (Demangeon, 52). And conversely, even when a verb is inserted immediately after the noun, one does not invariably find *que*, as one sees by comparing the two following examples, where the structure differs, although the meaning of the first few words of each sentence is the same, roughly *on dit que*:

> La rumeur court selon laquelle des soldats auraient fait irruption dans certains hôpitaux pour tenter de retrouver des meneurs du mouvement.

> La rumeur est déjà solidement établie que tout rassemblement libertaire dépassant deux personnes compte au moins en son sein un « indic » ou un flic.

Common words normally used only with *que* are: *assurance(s)*, *certitude*, *constat(ation)*, *conviction*, *illusion* and *sentiment*. Generally speaking, nouns meaning roughly 'private belief' are used with *que*: *intuition*, *pensée*, *perception*, *persuasion*, *prise de conscience*. Normally used only with *selon* are: *accusations*, *adage*, *argument*, *déclaration(s)*, *information(s)*, *légende*, *théorie* and *version*. Equally generally speaking, nouns meaning roughly 'system of beliefs' are used with *selon*, especially if the beliefs are voiced and the writer takes issue with them: *bruit*, *couplet*, *discours*, *doctrine*, *évaluation*, *idéologie*, *insinuation*, *lieu commun*, *message*, *mot*, *ragot*, *raisonnement*, *slogan*, *utopie*. Used with both *selon* and *que* are: *affirmation*, *annonce*, *croyance*, *démonstration*, *hypothèse*, *impression*, *opinion*, *préjugé*, *principe*, *rumeur* and *thèse*. And of course *l'idée*.

On this conjunctional *que* (but not on any of the variants for it canvassed here) the old Grevisse had a brief, interesting and partially inaccurate paragraph (Grevisse, 1964a, 1011–1012).

mais *

This entry makes no attempt at a definitive description of all the functions of this multifarious connector. Its many similarities to 'but' make it relatively unproblematical. Also, such analyses have been done elsewhere (e.g. Ducrot *et al.*, 94ff; Le Bidois, II, 240–242). The article is restricted to a few points on *mais* and a remark on some relationships between it and four other objectors or contrasters: *cependant*, *néanmoins*, *pourtant* and *toutefois*.

mais

As is the case with *et*, most users of this connector ignore the English superstition that sentences should not begin with a conjunction. In French, it is commonly placed first, functioning as a connector between full but separate propositions, sentences and even paragraphs, as in this extract from an article on the identification of the AIDS virus:

> La découverte capitale du professeur Luc Montagnier, qui identifie avec son équipe le virus LAV, intervient en février 1983. Un an plus tard, ce virus sera identifié comme le vecteur du SIDA.
> Mais les avancées scientifiques sont une chose, l'information une autre. [...]

However, it can also link two ideas by being placed in the middle of a sentence. Unlike *et* in this position, it is usually preceded by a comma: *Le journal « Le Monde » va mieux, mais il reste fragile.*

It combines with *aussi*, *également* and *encore* in the second half of binaries begun with *non seulement*. It combines with *voilà* as a variant for *seulement*.

One of the most common functions of this connector is to cancel out concessive propositions introduced by structures such as *certes*, *il est vrai que* and *sans doute*. Again it can be placed either first in the sentence following or in the second half of the same sentence, again after a comma:

> Le chef de l'État est âgé et malade. L'âge ajoute sans doute à la dignité et la maladie au respect, mais ni l'un ni l'autre ne constituent pour autant les plus performants attributs du pouvoir en période de tempête.

cependant, néanmoins, pourtant and *toutefois*

As the previous example shows, some writers reinforce connectors with another redundant one. Quite often *mais* is combined not only with *pour autant* as in that case, but with one or other of a range of other connectors, each of which is more or less close in meaning and function to it, and including *tout de même*, *quand même*, *cependant*, *néanmoins*, *pourtant* and *toutefois*. Here are some examples of it combining with the last four: *Là-dessus on va se récrier; mais rien n'est plus vrai cependant.* / *Cette enquête est forcément superficielle mais reste néanmoins très utile.* / *Mon grand-père était mort depuis longtemps lorsque je vins au monde; mais ma mère l'avait pourtant connu.*

> Au début du XXe siècle, peut-être du fait des succès wagnériens et de la mode des walkyries, on observe une tendance à un embonpoint marqué chez quelques-unes des divas qui peuplent alors les scènes lyriques, mais sans toutefois aucune hégémonie de la graisse.

There is a brief but useful article on *cependant* and the other three in Bénac (133). They are sometimes seen as belonging in two pairs:

pourtant with *cependant*, *néanmoins* with *toutefois*. The former pair are perhaps more often used with *mais* or *et* than the latter pair. Of the first pair, *pourtant* is stronger than *cependant*; but both of them cancel out what precedes. The other two do not cancel out the preceding statement; rather they imply its acceptance with some reluctance and foreshadow a restriction of it or a partial objection to it. This is especially the case with *toutefois*, as can be seen in the frequency of combinations like *sans toutefois que* or *à une condition toutefois* and in the substance of the following statement: *Nous nous rallions à cette théorie, en émettant toutefois une réserve*. Other distinctions among these four connectors have been defined as follows:

> *Cependant* et *pourtant* sont d'un usage courant. *Toutefois* et *néanmoins* appartiennent à une langue plus recherchée ; ils interviennent surtout dans une argumentation pour marquer fortement la restriction.
>
> (Dupré, I, 397)

With *toutefois* another difference is sometimes seen: the subject and verb following may be inverted, as in this comment on the alleged lack of psychological interest shown in French theatre of the nineteenth and twentieth centuries:

> L'incapacité d'observer sérieusement le cœur humain, dont l'étude avait fait l'honneur de la littérature française, éclate déjà chez les romantiques de 1830 précisément par le néant de leur théâtre, du moins chez Hugo, en tant que valeur psychologique. Toutefois prétendait-il à cette valeur.

Similarities to *mais*

Each of these four connectors is, under certain circumstances, interchangeable with *mais*; but under others, it is not. For instance, all four of them are more or less compatible with *et*, which is incompatible with *mais*: *et pourtant* is common; but *et mais* is unimaginable. Littré gives an example, at *cependant*, of a binary statement in which the second part could be introduced by any of the other three: *Il a bon visage, cependant il est malade*. To this example of *synonymie complète dans le sens*, he could have added that *mais* would also fit there. It is especially when placed first in the sentence that the other four can replace *mais*:

> Les mineurs sont des gens pudiques, qui ne parlent pas facilement du passé. Pourtant, une fois lancés, ils deviennent intarissables sur les rites, les fêtes et les patois.

> La princesse était forcée, si on lui parlait de quelqu'un ou si on lui présentait quelqu'un, de feindre une grande froideur pour maintenir la fiction de son horreur du monde. Néanmoins, avec l'appui de Cottard ou de Mme Verdurin, quelques nouveaux réussissaient à la connaître.
>
> (Proust, II, 879)

Se trouver à vingt-huit ans professeur à cette Académie de Genève, où depuis Calvin tant d'hommes illustres avaient enseigné, était un succès que beaucoup envièrent. Cependant les circonstances dans lesquelles le jeune professeur obtenait sa chaire ne furent pas sans lui créer des difficultés.

(Vadier, 85)

Il nous a semblé méthodologiquement raisonnable de chercher à définir la poésie où elle se trouve, c'est-à-dire dans ce type de littérature appelé poème. Toutefois, le mot « poème » lui-même ne va pas sans équivoque.

Differences from *mais*

However, all four of them are more mobile than *mais* and can adopt positions in which it would be impossible: *En elle-même, la justification est recevable. À condition, toutefois, de correspondre à la réalité. / Débordante d'ingéniosité, l'étude me paraît néanmoins pâtir un peu d'un excès de subtilité. / Dans ce livre, qui fut pourtant dénoncé comme immoral, nous retrouvons le moraliste. / ...il allait dans des maisons de rendez-vous, espérant apprendre quelque chose d'elle, sans oser la nommer cependant* (Proust, I, 373).

They can also combine with the *si d'opposition* in ways that would be impossible with *mais*: *Si le communiqué de l'Élysée et de Matignon ne tranche pas la question, on peut cependant observer qu'il en dessine le contour.*

There are, of course, plenty of other common ways of constructing simple oppositions of the sort which are often made in English with 'but', 'however', 'although', etc.: among them are the *si d'opposition* itself, ***alors que***, ***or***, ***pour autant***, ***reste que*** and ***n'empêche***.

malgré tout

This structure has a straightforward adverbial function, in the sense of 'despite everything', used in contexts which speak of success being won in spite of difficulties. That is the only function of it known to Littré. But it also has a connective function which, depending on context, makes it a variant of concessive or objecting structures such as ***quand même***, ***tout de même***, *néanmoins* or *pourtant*.

More adversative

It may be that there is always a detectable adversative polarity in this connector. Like *quand même*, it is used in two ways, one of which is more explicitly adversative than the other. It can structure a simple contrast, placed usually in the second half of a binary sentence: *Prudentes et raisonnables, ces conclusions soulèvent malgré tout un épineux problème.* There the contrast is between the favourable features of the first statement and the unfavourable one of the second part. The similarity with *quand même* or *néanmoins* is evident. In that context, the **n'en... pas moins** structure could also replace it. Or, with slight restructuring, the sentence could be made with the **si d'opposition**: *Si elles sont prudentes et raisonnables, ces conclusions n'en soulèvent pas moins....* Or else, still with *n'en... pas moins*, the first part of the contrast could be structured by *avoir beau* or the oppositive *pour*: *Ces conclusions ont beau être prudentes et raisonnables, elles n'en soulèvent pas moins...* or *Pour être prudentes et raisonnables, ces conclusions n'en soulèvent pas moins....* Much the same could be said of the next example, taken from a discussion of the indeterminacy, before the eighteenth century, of certain nouns used more or less indiscriminately to designate 'riot', 'disturbance', 'revolt' and 'revolution': *...les mots qui les désignent, sans être tout à fait interchangeables, alternent malgré tout au petit bonheur* (Wagner, 157).

Less overtly adversative

In this mode, there is no visible contrast or opposition such as there is in the examples quoted above:

> Pratiquer le terrorisme, c'est s'abstraire du respect, c'est même s'affranchir de ce que l'on nomme dans une formule malgré tout curieuse « les lois de la guerre ».
>
> (Boucher, 293)

There, the only contrast is the implicit contradiction between the accepted meaning of *les lois de la guerre* (rules for proper conduct of warfare) and the meaning that the writer suggests by interpolating the adverb: that, war being by definition improper, it is paradoxical that there should be rules for its conduct. The force of the connector comes close to that of *il faut l'avouer* or **à vrai dire**. It comes almost as close to **après tout**, which invites the reader to agree with what it implies is an assumption shared with the writer. Much the same goes for this exemplar, taken from an article about M. Balladur's reluctance to use the word *retrait* to describe his government's withdrawal of a proposal which had been strenuously opposed by organizations of young people:

> Ce refus de prononcer le mot fatidique, ce souci de camoufler ce qui est, malgré tout, une retraite sur des positions non préparées, risque d'empêcher Édouard Balladur de profiter pleinement du geste fait en direction des jeunes.

It hints that its fuller meaning is *malgré tout ce que l'on pourra dire contre ce que j'avance* and thereby forestalls a possible objection. What has been said about the attenuated adversative mode of *quand même* could be said of it: that it facilitates *la mise en acceptabilité d'une contradiction* (Moeschler & de Spengler, 1981: 110).

English equivalents, depending on context, might be 'even so', 'for all that', 'nevertheless', 'yet' or, in a more spoken register, 'let's face it'.

même *

Of the three sorts of *même*, adjective, pronoun and adverb, it is only the last, the one *traditionnellement qualifié d'enchérissant* (Anscombre & Ducrot, 57), which functions as a connector. It could be defined as an augmentative preciser: what it introduces goes farther or is apter than what precedes: *Camus naît loin de la capitale, loin même de la métropole. / Au cours de la décennie écoulée, et même peut-être depuis la guerre... / Il est légitime, il est même élémentaire de mettre en cause le monde auquel on appartient.*

Sometimes what is added does not just go farther than what precedes, it actually supersedes it: *Chaque violon a une âme. Il en a même deux.* The following extract from an acerbic review of an episode of a long-running music programme contains both modes:

> Cette diffusion entrait dans le cadre de « Musiques au cœur », et même du dixième anniversaire de cette émission. Soyons clair. Dix ans, ça suffit. C'est même beaucoup trop.

There, the first one clarifies the relation of this episode to the series and stresses the specialness of it. Whereas the second one does not just put a sharper point upon the preceding verb, it replaces it with a more pertinent expression. The combination with *et*, seen in the first one, is quite common.

et même

In this combination, the connectors usually stand side by side: *Il resta pieux toute sa vie et même longtemps orthodoxe. / Le parti socialiste conserve et même accentue sa large avance sur ses points forts tradition-nels. / La désaffection grandissante des Français envers les hommes politiques, et même envers la politique....* At other times, a verb comes between them: *Je n'en crois rien et je pense même le contraire.*

The combination can function like *voire*, introducing the last in a series of increasingly stronger or apter terms:

> « Le moment n'est-il pas venu de jeter le voile, d'oublier ces temps où les Français ne s'aimaient pas, s'entre-déchiraient et même s'entre-tuaient ? » demandait Georges Pompidou au cours de sa conférence de presse en 1972.

The same goes for the combination *ou même*:

> Le président du Front national s'est toujours gaussé des analyses ou des hypothèses qui portaient sur le recul, le déclin ou, même, la disparition de son parti.

A few writers continue to use this connector with *voire*, a combination now all but universally seen as archaic: *les comportements maternels (les formes) prennent des aspects différents, voire même contradictoires* (Badinter, 1980: 15).

même after negative structures

This connector is quite commonly used after a negative structure. It may not only cancel the negative statement but affirm more than the latter denied, as in this extract from an article about the Moscow police rounding up citizens of Caucasian republics, or anyone who looks like them, and expelling them from the capital:

> On aurait tort de penser que les Moscovites s'indignent de cette chasse au faciès qui se déroule dans leur ville et souvent sous leurs yeux. La plupart d'entre eux sont même plutôt satisfaits de ce « nettoyage ».

> Le bâtiment Grand Écran est-il si moche ? Non, au regard de maintes catastrophes urbaines. Il est même gracieux, si on le compare à ce qui s'achève ces temps-ci sur la dalle de la gare Montparnasse.

This mode combines well, of course, with ***au contraire***, as in the following extract from a discussion of a surprising outburst by the Russian President about the Estonian government's alleged discrimination against Russians:

> Aucun fait nouveau concernant la situation des populations russes dans les pays baltes ne s'est produit ces derniers jours pour justifier un tel coup d'éclat. Au contraire, même : la volonté manifestée par le gouvernement estonien de libéraliser la législation sur la citoyenneté en rendant plus facile l'acquisition par les russophones de la nationalité estonienne, comme la victoire des ex-communistes aux élections lituaniennes, étaient de nature à arrondir les angles entre Moscou et les capitales baltes.

mieux même

The combination in which the connector is itself reinforced by ***mieux***, not dissimilar to the one with *au contraire*, is usually placed after a stop and followed by a comma. This example concerns Baudelaire's preparations for translating the works of Edgar Allen Poe:

> Il en avait fait plus amplement connaissance, s'était procuré ses œuvres complètes et ses éditions les plus rares, entouré des renseignements les plus sûrs : mieux même, avait rappris l'anglais, qu'il prétendait avoir étudié dans son grand voyage des Indes.

In some contexts, this combination comes close to replacing *ou plutôt*, suggesting not just that what precedes is strengthened but that what follows is a more accurate form of words, as in this extract from an essay on alleged racism among French policemen:

> Le discours spontané des policiers français postule généralement qu'il n'y a pas plus de policiers racistes qu'il n'y a de racistes dans l'ensemble de la population française.
> Mieux même : les policiers demandent très spontanément un renversement complet de la perspective. À les suivre, en effet, les accusations de racisme à leur encontre sont excessives.

Place in the sentence

The position of this connector in the sentence can be quite variable: in addition to the range illustrated in the examples already used, it is sometimes placed at the end: *Une banque ne saurait être que propre. Impeccable même* (Closets, 1983: 61); *Les consonnes françaises sont articulées avec énergie, avec violence même.* And sometimes it is placed at the very beginning of the sentence or statement. This example deals with a collection of letters from Zola to the brothers Goncourt, the publication of which some people had tried to prevent:

> On ne comprend guère pourquoi la garde était si bien montée autour de ces papiers. Nous les avons lus à la loupe et n'y avons rien trouvé qui justifiât tant de prudence. Même, ils décevront grandement les amateurs de scandale, qui s'en promettaient des délices.
>
> (Henriot, 1954: 303)

It should be said that the placing of this connector at the beginning of sentences is these days unusual, perhaps because it is sensed as archaic or literary in tone. It is particularly in that position that it is now combined with *mieux*.

English equivalents, depending on context, include 'actually', 'even', 'indeed' and 'in fact'. In the *mieux même* combination, 'what's more' or 'or rather' would do.

quand bien même

This structure usually restricts a hypothesis, functioning with one difference like *même si*, with the meaning 'even if' or 'even though'. The difference is that, unlike hypothetical *si*, the verb it introduces is normally in the conditional. An example of it placed first in a *phrase dépendante* is this, taken from an article about a candidate in a presidential election and the unlikelihood that he will divulge the entire truth about a financial transaction: *On voit mal Balladur se résoudre à une telle extrémité.*

Quand bien même il n'aurait rien à cacher. An article about the alleged desire of the last President of the USSR to hasten reductions in conventional weaponry says: *Est-il en mesure, quand bien même il le souhaiterait, de précipiter les choses?* Some writers invert the subject and verb following. And at times the conditional is changed to an imperfect.

mieux *

This connector has two distinct modes: the first of them introduces an alternative to what precedes; the other introduces an addition to it. In some exemplars, it is difficult to separate the two. On the existence of these two modes, the main dictionaries (*Robert, Grand Larousse, Trésor de la langue française*, etc.) are either uninformative or misleading: either they define only one mode or the examples they give do not consist with their definition or both.

Alternative *mieux*

Grammatically, this mode is followed only by a complement of what precedes; and this complement serves as an apter substitute for what precedes. That is, like **autrement dit**, *plus précisément* or *ou plutôt*, it introduces what the writer deems to be a better form of words. English equivalents for it could be 'on second thoughts', 'more precisely', 'not to say' and 'or rather'. The first example is part of a columnist's compliment to an actress:

> Serait-il permis à un humble amateur, avant qu'il ne retourne à ses démons favoris que l'actualité lui sert à profusion, de faire part d'un enthousiasme, mieux, d'une admiration ? Celle qu'a suscitée le jeu d'une toute jeune comédienne qui a nom Julie Delpy.
>
> (Boucher, 533)

> Le désir de s'entendre – mieux, de faire les choses ensemble – n'est pas présent qu'au sommet de l'État.

It is because it introduces only a complement that this mode is usually found inside the sentence. Any sentence in which it is placed first will normally be a **phrase dépendante**.

This mode includes the form *ou mieux* – the *ou* making explicit that what follows is not an addition but an alternative. Sainte-Beuve uses it in his article on Mme Récamier:

> Non, elle n'a jamais aimé, aimé de passion et de flamme ; mais cet immense besoin d'aimer que porte en elle toute âme tendre se changeait pour elle en un infini besoin de plaire, ou mieux d'être aimée [...]
>
> (Sainte-Beuve, 125–126)

This first mode can be seen as an abridged form of *ou pour mieux dire*:

Les idées les plus fortes et les plus vraies qu'on ait eues sur l'univers sont restées inédites ou, pour mieux dire, non exprimées.

(Renan, 1141)

Among a range of variants for it in this function, some of which were once more used than they are now, are *pour mieux parler, pour dire plus vrai, plus exactement, disons mieux* and *disons*. Another is used in this comment on the political ideas of Condorcet: *Le fait rationnel (ou plutôt, il vaudrait mieux dire : le fait raisonnable) auquel Condorcet renvoie [...]*.

Additive *mieux*

Grammatically, this mode is usually followed by an independent sentence. It is a sentence which does not usually refine or replace what precedes; it adds to it a whole new point, as in this pair of observations on the effects of the Franco-Russian alliance of 1894:

En janvier 1894, l'alliance franco-russe est rendue officielle. Elle rééquilibre l'Europe, libère les appétits et accroît les énergies des deux partenaires. Mieux : elle durera, contre vents et marée, jusqu'en 1917.

It functions there like *de plus*: it is a positive variant of it, just as *pis* is a negative variant. That is, it introduces a point or factor which is to be taken in addition to the one before, but which is of greater importance than it and is presented as favourable. It shows the shade of difference from *de plus* that *qui mieux est* shows from *qui plus est*: it sees the added point as an advantage, from the point of view of either the writer or the subject. The usual position of this mode makes it visibly different from the first one: it stands first in the sentence, which the other rarely does, or even in the paragraph. And it is not combined with *ou*. English equivalents for it could be 'as well', 'better still', 'and secondly', 'what's more' or 'in the second place'. In the first of the following examples, the author has two distinct points to make about employment of women in Britain; he introduces the second of them with this connector:

Aujourd'hui, les femmes anglaises occupent les deux tiers des emplois flexibles, y compris en travail indépendant, qui rassemblent un tiers de la population active. Mieux, elles sont moins touchées que les hommes par le chômage de longue durée (25 % contre 57 % en France).

There it is clear that the connector does not merely refine what precedes: it announces a whole new factor of the discussion, after the manner of *en outre* or *de surcroît*. The same can be seen in the next example, which makes two points about an alleged pandemic of anorexia and bulimia in the USA:

Anorexie et boulimie, sœurs maudites, progressent tant qu'il n'est plus un hôpital aux États-Unis qui ne comporte un service spécialisé dans leur thérapie.

Mieux, dans certaines universités, des étudiantes se livrent ensemble à des pratiques de boulimie, avant d'aller se faire vomir séparément, de retour chez elles.

Again like *de plus* and *en outre*, this mode can not only introduce a second point but also function as one in a *sequence of points* presented by a series of augmentative or reinforcing connectors. In the following example, a political journalist, having four points to make about a group of Centrists who criticize both the Socialists (PS) and the Gaullists (RPR), introduces them with *non seulement, en outre, Et en plus* and *mieux*:

Non seulement les centristes ragaillardis sont repartis à l'offensive, mais ils ont en outre redécouvert un slogan redoutable, même s'il a beaucoup servi : « Vive l'État impartial ! » Autrement dit : « À bas l'État PS ! » et « À bas l'État RPR ! »... Et en plus, nos libéraux ex-mous n'hésitent plus à dénoncer publiquement les « magouilles » du RPR. Mieux, ils vont jusqu'à prendre des mesures de rétorsion contre les candidatures sauvages.

Occasional less journalistic variants for this mode are *Mieux que cela*; *Mais il y a mieux*; *Mais il y a mieux à dire*. The structure mentioned above, *qui mieux est*, is still given in Robert; but it seems to be as uncommon these days as *qui pis est*.

mieux encore

This combination can function in either mode, more or less like unaccompanied *mieux*. In the first mode, inside a sentence, it introduces an alternative, presented as a more accurate wording, replaceable by *ou plutôt* and in the form of a complement: *Rien ne vaut le français de nos pères – ou, mieux encore, celui de nos aïeux.*

The second mode is also similar in its functioning to that of unaccompanied *mieux* and is probably interchangeable with it: it adds a stronger point and is usually placed first in an independent sentence. It may appear more in the prose of journalists given to breathless hyperbole, as in this example taken from a description of the arrest of a member of a Moscow Mafia:

Surprise : l'agresseur se présente comme un parent de Rouslan Khasboulatov, le président du Parlement russe. Mieux encore, on apprend qu'il fait partie des gardes armés de la Maison blanche (police privée du Parlement dissoute officiellement par Boris Eltsine mais toujours en activité). Résultat : il est relâché quelques heures plus tard...

But it occurs also in academic prose, as in this discussion of three reasons for the regeneration of the Musée national des arts asiatiques (also known as the Musée Guimet), the third of which is introduced by this augmented form of the connector:

> Des expositions temporaires plus nombreuses ont permis d'attirer des visiteurs en nombre croissant. Des donations de premier ordre, telle la donation Fournier dans le domaine tibétain et celle que vient de consentir Mme Krishna Riboud en matière de textiles asiatiques contribuent à enrichir le fonds. Mieux encore : Guimet a désormais son annexe, dite du « panthéon bouddhique », collection de sculpture japonaise somptueusement installée dans un hôtel particulier de l'avenue d'Iéna.

This form also combines with *et*. And among occasional variants for it are *bien mieux* and *Il y a mieux encore*.

mieux même

This combination too is used in both functions, either to introduce an apter form of words putting a finer point upon what precedes; or, more usually, to add a further point which is clearly distinct from what precedes and goes further than it, as in this extract from a discussion of radical criticisms of the Senate, in which members of the Left say this upper house of the French parliament is unrepresentative and outdated:

> Une partie de la majorité sénatoriale se retrouve avec la gauche pour partager ces griefs ; mieux même, elle a tenté de lui redonner un sang neuf.

ne fût-ce que

This is a mode of *fût-ce*, the minimizing effect of which is reinforced by the addition of *ne... que*. The structure is also akin to *ne serait-ce que*. However, it is much less common than the latter, belonging to a more elevated and literary register – Proust, for instance, who often uses *fût-ce* and its variants, now and then uses this structure, yet never once uses *ne serait-ce que* in the whole of *À la recherche du temps perdu*. Not only Proust uses this form; some of those who write about him do so too: *Swann peut, ne fût-ce qu'un instant, oublier Odette.*

Apart from the difference in tone, the main difference between the two structures with *ne... que* lies in the sequence of tenses which they accompany: *serait* is usual when the accompanying main verb is in the present, conditional or future:

> Les sondages prouvent que ni les ouvriers français ni, même, les communistes n'entendent épouser, ne serait-ce que sur le plan économique, le mode de vie soviétique.

And the variant with *fût* is more usual when the accompanying verbs are in a past tense:

> L'autre année, un chercheur français appelé Benveniste a bouleversé toutes les notions admises en chimie et en physique. Selon lui, l'eau avait une

« mémoire », elle gardait le souvenir des corps immergés ne fût-ce qu'un instant en son sein.

However, despite the difference in tone, these two related connectors are often interchangeable, especially when the main verb is in the present tense. The writer of the first example, above, could have chosen either of them; as could the writer of the following one, a comment on the value of untruthfulness in politics:

> Il est banal de dire que le mensonge fait partie intégrante de la politique, qu'il constitue un moyen de gouvernement comme d'opposition, un instrument dans les relations internationales, qu'il est un droit, un devoir même, quand des intérêts supérieurs sont en jeu, une sorte d'obligation professionnelle, ne fût-ce que sous la forme du secret.

Like a specialized *même*, the connector often introduces a minimizing qualifier such as a small amount, an insignificant detail, a minimal or momentary condition, *une fois* or *un début de*. A literal meaning is 'even though only'. In English, 'if only' would often be used. Sometimes, 'even' would be more appropriate, as in this excerpt from a spoken interview with a journalist who had received expensive presents from a businessman called Botton and who denies that there is the slightest evidence of malpractice on his part:

> Si on avait pu trouver la moindre preuve que j'ai, ne fût-ce qu'une seule fois, renvoyé l'ascenseur à M. Botton, croyez-moi, on en aurait déjà fait état.

Like the form with *serait*, this mode is also used in statements explaining cause or reason, that is to say, before structures such as **parce que**, *pour* or *à cause de*:

> Nous avons vu une jeune fille indifférente, insolente au bord de la mer, nous avons vu une vendeuse sérieuse et active à son comptoir qui nous répondra sèchement ne fût-ce que pour ne pas être l'objet des moqueries de ses copines [...]

> (Proust, III, 142)

Unlike the form with *serait*, this one is not usually placed first in the sentence. However, there appears to be no reason why a writer making a statement like the one in the following example would not write it as two sentences, the second of which would be a **phrase dépendante** beginning with this connector. The subject is the authoritarian system of government favoured by one-party states:

> Or la cause, répétons-le, qui rend ce système mauvais n'est pas du tout d'ordre esthétique ou moral mais d'ordre pratique : une société qui fonctionne ainsi fait inévitablement faillite, ne fût-ce qu'en étant refusée comme modèle par tous ceux qui en connaissent une autre.

n'empêche *

This structure exists in four forms: *n'empêche*, *il n'empêche*, *n'empêche que* and *il n'empêche que*. In all four, *pas* is omitted from what is a negative structure. All of them function more like adverbs than verbs, which may be seen in the fact that, if a verb follows, it is in the indicative, not the subjunctive. Some dictionaries make a distinction between the two forms with *que* and the two without: the newer Robert, in an entry that marks off *n'empêche* from the two forms with *que*, says its tone is familiar and defines its meaning as *Ce n'est pas une raison*. The *Trésor de la langue française* does not separate the forms; but it confirms the familiarity of tone of the two without *que*. The *Grand Larousse de la langue française* (1972) ignores the forms without *que*. Likewise, Le Bidois (II, 355) and Grevisse discuss only the two with *que*: *véritables formules toutes faites avec la valeur de « en dépit de cela », « et cependant »* (Grevisse, 1964b: 82)

Difference of tone there clearly is – for two examples of *n'empêche* in its familiar conversational usage, see Duras (20 & 21). But in meaning and function it is apparent that general written usage makes little if any difference between the first pair of forms and the other two. As used nowadays, all four variants are replaceable by *malgré cela* and equate to English 'even so' or 'the fact remains that'.

n'empêche in tripartite concessive contexts

One of the commonest functions of this connector is to reaffirm an initial assertion to which objection has been made or might be made. It introduces a third stage in the discussion of a point: after a first assertion of the point by way of premiss, and a second, often beginning with a restrictive such as ***il est vrai que***, ***sans doute*** or ***certes***, which concedes a partial objection against it, the third, introduced by this connector, broadly restates the main point. In the three sentences of the following example about the wife of a presidential candidate, that pattern is clearly visible: first a sentence about the possibility that she might attract votes to her husband; then *certes* and its objection; finally, the connector introducing a substantial reassertion of the first point: *Vote-t-on pour l'épouse du présidentiable ? Certes non. Il n'empêche, elle peut être un argument.* A similar sequence can be seen in the following example, this time structured by ***bien sûr*** and *Il n'empêche que*. The passage deals with the proliferation of museums in France:

> Si on en croit un bruit persistant, il s'ouvrirait en France un musée par jour. C'est exagéré, bien sûr. Il n'empêche que, de la chaussure à la parfumerie, de l'archéologie à l'art contemporain, on n'aurait pas imaginé hier tout ce qui peut aujourd'hui faire l'objet de musées nouveaux.

Sometimes the second stage of concession or restriction is implicit, not marked by a *certes* type of structure. The subject of the following example is the increasing likelihood that official measures will be necessary to prevent reckless people from skiing in unfavourable conditions:

> Faudra-t-il dès lors fermer les pistes ou les remontées mécaniques dès que les conditions pour skier ne seront pas idéales ? Faudra-t-il mettre des gendarmes ou des CRS pour interdire l'accès à la montagne aux imprudents ? Cela est totalement irréaliste. Il n'empêche que l'on se dirige de plus en plus vers la rigueur et vers des précautions hier considérées comme inutiles.

n'empêche in binary oppositions

Less often these structures shape not a three-stage development but a simpler opposition in two parts. This example deals with Ezra Pound's attitudes to anti-Semitism:

> L'antisémitisme ? « Stupide préjugé banlieusard », dira Pound au jeune poète juif Allen Ginsberg, venu le voir à Venise. N'empêche : le « stupide préjugé » envahit ses pensées, ses fantasmes de régénération monétaire, ses jugements, de plus en plus excités, contre Roosevelt et l'Amérique.

Whether as part of a three-part or a two-part sequence, this connector usually functions in ways close to the *n'en... pas moins* structure and to *reste que*.

Relative infrequency of *n'empêche que*

Of the four forms, *n'empêche que* is the least used nowadays, at least among journalists. And among other writers, it appears to have been more current in the earlier twentieth century than it is now. Rare as it is, it functions like the others, structuring either a three-part sequence with concessive *certes* or, as in this example, taken from a discussion of relations between Édith Cresson, a short-lived Prime Minister, and graduates of the École nationale d'administration (*les énarques*), a simpler binary:

> Ce n'est pas un secret, Édith Cresson n'aimait pas les énarques. Leur école fut même la première victime de la délocalisation. N'empêche que dans son cabinet, à Matignon, les énarques avaient l'écrasante majorité.

Place and punctuation

All four forms are usually placed at the beginning of sentences or even paragraphs. Only one, *il n'empêche que*, is found with any frequency in the middle of sentences, and that only in sentences structured with the *si d'opposition*, as in this extract from a review of Alain Finkielkraut's book *La défaite de la pensée*:

> Mais si je reproche à *la Défaite de la pensée* une analyse critique qui me semble mal fondée et surtout trop étroitement limitée – cette manière de dire : c'est la faute à Herder ! c'est la faute à Lévi-Strauss ! – il n'empêche que je sens à l'origine de ce livre une vraie blessure, quelque chose de profondément sincère.

On occasion a writer combines the structure with *mais*, usually at the beginning of the sentence, but sometimes not, as in this example taken from a discussion of an official banquet given in the late 1890s for the 36,000 mayors of France, which had been objected to by some politicians of the Right:

> Ces gardiens de l'honneur avaient eu l'idée, eux aussi, de convoquer les maires de leurs amis à des agapes rivales. Waldeck-Rousseau l'a interdit d'un trait de plume, mais il n'empêche : l'avenir de la gauche républicaine passe par le succès du banquet.

Of the two forms without *que*, the one with *il* is often followed by a colon. The form without *il* is usually followed either by a colon or a comma. At times, the former even makes a sentence in itself, as in this example, dealing with the Israeli government's historic announcement that it might countenance partial evacuation of the Golan Heights:

> L'État juif ne tenait-il pas le Golan pour son « Himalaya », qui le mettait à l'abri des attaques syriennes et lui assurait de précieuses ressources hydrauliques, même si sa valeur militaire avait quelque peu décliné, à l'époque des missiles à longue portée ? Il n'empêche. Aujourd'hui, M. Rabin n'entend pas laisser échapper l'occasion d'un tournant historique ; la paix avec la Syrie vaut bien quelques concessions sur le chemin de Damas.

cela n'empêche

This is an occasional variant. Sometimes it includes *pas*, sometimes not; sometimes it is followed by a subjunctive, sometimes not. This example comes from an essay on languages of the future. The author takes the view that Esperanto will never be able to compete with 'real' languages, because it will never have

> des racines aussi profondes dans les âmes et dans les mœurs qu'un parler déjà existant, doué d'une force politique et historique. Des Chinois, des Malais paraissent de temps en temps aux congrès espérantistes et y font, paraît-il, merveille. Cela n'empêche qu'ils n'apprennent d'abord la langue britannique, et que celle de Zamenhof ne leur soit une simple langue « troisième ».

n'en... pas moins *

This structure is related to *reste que*: most of its modes are constructed with *rester*; and, in some of its ways of functioning, it is also similar.

It has six basic modes, in all of which, barring idiosyncrasies, three elements remain present at all times: *n'en*, *pas* and *moins*, always in that sequence. All six modes function in binary statements, establish the same antithetical relationship between the two elements of an opposition and express the sort of contrast that is made in English with 'even so', 'the fact remains that', 'nevertheless', 'notwithstanding'. Like the latter pair of English words, this expression, though in the form of a negative, is always used positively. That is, it states or reasserts an affirmative feature in contrast to a negative one, a true one as against a false one, a favourable one despite an unfavourable one – or else vice versa. Whichever side of an opposition it stresses, it affirms a fact; the *ne... pas* serves only to mark the contradiction with the preceding element of the binary and to say 'That may well be so; but it does not rule out what follows'. It is always anaphoric; even when placed first in a sentence, it completes an antithesis begun by what precedes. Any of its modes can be placed in the middle of the sentence; many of them can begin sentences – but it is more usually the first two, Modes 1 and 2 below, always containing impersonal *il* and *que*, which begin sentences or even paragraphs. Though not a separable pronoun standing for an antecedent noun, *en* does have a semantic function: meaning roughly 'despite what precedes' or 'for all that', it recapitulates the first half of the binary.

This structure should not be confused with *ne... pas moins*. A discussion of Racine's *Andromaque* says this:

> Oreste est avili en amour. Pyrrhus, son rival, en use avec lui de la façon la plus cavalière, le charge de ses messages amoureux. Hermione ne l'humilie pas moins.

There is no opposition; the relation between the third sentence and what precedes is one of comparison for reinforcement: 'Hermione too humiliates him just as much [as Pyrrhus].' The comparative function may be more patent in this sentence: *Le New York Times n'est pas moins lu, craint et admiré aujourd'hui que son homonyme londonien en 1938* (Revel, 1988: 242).

Mode 1: *il n'en reste pas moins que*

This mode begins with impersonal *il*, ends with *que*, uses the present tense of *rester* and is always followed by a subordinate completive clause containing at least a subject and verb. It is more formal in tone than Mode 2. An article about the Islamic *fatwa* sentencing Salman Rushdie to death in 1989 uses this mode to structure a contrast between reassuring aspects of the situation and a disquieting one. Speaking of a small number of extremists who demonstrated vehemently in Paris, the writer draws a favourable conclusion about how unrepresentative they are of French Muslims:

Le gros des bataillons les plus excités était formé d'intégristes pakistanais, l'une des plus faibles communautés islamiques en France, dont la police se félicite d'une certaine façon de la sortie dans la rue car elle a pu ainsi en détecter les meneurs les plus extrémistes.

Il n'en reste pas moins, et il faut le déplorer, que trop peu des responsables spirituels et politiques du monde islamique se sont clairement désolidarisés à ce jour de la « sentence » de l'imam Khomeiny.

Sometimes the verb used in this mode is *demeurer* rather than *rester*. A discussion of Prince Sihanouk's apparent reluctance to become too closely involved in talks aimed at solving Cambodia's political difficulties canvasses his possible reasons:

Attitude tactique de la part d'un prince qui a élevé la volte-face diplomatique à la hauteur d'un art, amertume d'un homme lassé de tant de malheurs ou bien prudence sur l'avenir de son pays ? Il n'en demeure pas moins que seul le dialogue peut donner à cette conférence une chance de succès.

There, the opposition is between the uncertainty implied by the questions and the certainty introduced by the connector. It could be replaced by ***toujours est-il que*** or *le fait demeure que*.

Like ***n'empêche***, this structure can be the third element in a sequence of three, reaffirming an initial proposition after a statement introduced by a concessive such as ***sans doute*** or ***certes***. This three-part structure is visible in the three sentences of the following example. The French Foreign Minister, in the thick of the Salman Rushdie affair, spoke of the desire of Iran to normalize its relations with other countries; to which a newspaper editorial replied as follows:

Les propos du ministre des affaires étrangères sont pour le moins optimistes. Certes, les luttes de factions vont bon train à Téhéran en vue de la succession de l'imam Khomeiny, et on peut y entendre des propos contradictoires sur la « réouverture » du pays. Il n'en demeure pas moins que pas un seul responsable iranien n'a pris ses distances par rapport à la « condamnation à mort » de Salman Rushdie et de ses éditeurs.

Occasionally a noun structure follows the variant with *demeurer*. An article on Arab–Israeli peace negotiations starts by saying that relations between the two sides remain hostile, then completes the tripartite sequence of propositions illustrated by the previous quotation:

Quelques compromis, certes, paraissent bien avoir été conclus, notamment sur les modalités de la représentation jordano-palestinienne et celles de la participation européenne à une éventuelle conférence de paix. Il n'en demeure pas moins de profondes divergences entre les dirigeants israéliens et certains pays arabes, notamment la Syrie.

Sometimes this mode is combined with initial ***mais*** or *cependant*. An idiosyncrasy of some writers is to omit *en*, as in Caillois (39), Henriot

(1954: 238) and the prose of some contemporary journalists, thus making an ambiguous similarity with comparative *ne... pas moins* mentioned above. A rare variant is the replacement of *rester* or *demeurer* by *subsister* (Blum, 60, 550).

Mode 2: *il n'en est pas moins vrai que*

Like Mode 1, this mode always contains impersonal *il* and *que*; and the tense of the verb is the present. But *rester* is replaced by *être*; and the adjective *vrai* is added. Though less formal in tone than the first mode, its functioning is similar: it introduces a point that countervails a preceding one; it establishes a certainty against an uncertainty; it reaffirms an initial proposition against which a restriction has been made. It is always followed, too, by a subordinate completive clause composed of at least a subject and a verb. An article discussing the trial of a police inspector by the name of Jobic makes the antithetical point that the favourable outcome, for him, is counterbalanced by a less favourable outcome for the public good:

> « L'affaire Jobic » est terminée et le principal intéressé peut se féliciter du résultat ; il n'en est pas moins vrai qu'elle aura contribué largement à désacraliser la fonction de justice et à jeter une lumière trouble sur les rapports qui régissent les divers piliers de l'État.

An essay on the correspondence of Guizot juxtaposes two contradictory views of the man's character:

> La bonne humeur de M. Guizot ! Cette phrase peut sonner comme un paradoxe pour qui se rappelle, du grand historien, seulement sa physionomie de sévère ancêtre. Il n'en est pas moins vrai que cette correspondance nous révèle un François Guizot bien plus complet que même ses admirateurs ne nous l'ont dépeint.

Modes 1 and 2 are interchangeable in function. However, they do not usually intermingle their forms: generally, if *rester* or *demeurer* is used, *vrai* is not; if the adjective is used, the verb is *être*. One does find exceptions, albeit infrequent, to this rule: *il n'en reste pas moins vrai que* is found, for instance, in Durkheim (1953: 106) and in Brunot (416), both of them writing in the early years of this century, and is frequent in the prose of Lucien Goldmann, writing much later. Both it and *il n'en demeure pas moins vrai que* are occasionally used nowadays by some journalists.

Mode 3: personal subject + *rester* **or** *être* **+ adjectival complement**

In this mode, any noun, common or proper, any personal pronoun and any adjective, are used with either *rester* or *être*. The tense is frequently the present; the adjective is frequently a past participle; *que* is absent: *Atypique, la situation économique nippone n'en est pas moins délicate.* / *Dans l'acception courante du terme, un mari qui connaît l'amant de sa femme, et qui tolère cette liaison adultère, n'en est pas moins un mari trompé.*

The verb is not always finite: *Les symboles peuvent être le fruit du hasard mais n'en être pas moins éloquents.* And here too *demeurer* is sometimes used instead of *rester*:

> Si nos compatriotes sont par raison, sentiment (et aussi parce qu'ils connaissent un peu l'histoire sanglante de ce siècle) réellement européens, ils n'en demeurent pas moins par toutes leurs fibres des Français assez contents au fond de leur pays.

Mode 4: personal subject + verb (not *rester* **or** *être***), no adjective**

In this mode, any noun can serve as the subject of any verb other than *rester* or *être*. The verb can be in any tense; and it is usually followed by an object, more commonly a noun, sometimes a clause with *que*, and usually no adjective – unless the verb is one of seeming or appearing (see the last example at Mode 5 below):

> « Soyez donc modéré pour ne plaire à personne », a dit un poète assez oublié aujourd'hui, mais qui n'en a pas moins exprimé dans ce vers une vérité toujours vraie.

> Aucun site n'a été retenu pour accueillir l'installation, aucun budget n'a été réservé pour financer le programme et aucune date n'a été fixée pour son démarrage. L'Allemagne fédérale, la France et le Royaume-Uni n'en ont pas moins signé, jeudi 16 février à Bonn, trois accords de coopération portant sur le développement des réacteurs surgénérateurs.

In this mode, *demeurer* is sometimes used absolutely:

> La fin de la grève des mineurs polonais permet au premier ministre, Mme Hanna Suchocka, d'entamer l'année sous de meilleurs auspices. Les causes profondes de ce conflit n'en demeurent pas moins.

Mode 5: with *avoir beau*

Here the connector usually completes a binary sentence of which the first element is *avoir beau*: *On a beau être critique, on n'en est pas moins homme.* In this mode, the semantic reference of *en* is to the contradiction introduced by *avoir beau*. This quasi-pleonastic combination shows how typical of French sentencing it is to structure a balanced antithesis, each of its parts strongly framed by a construction that regards the other. Any of the modes can combine with *avoir beau*. In the following example, which uses Mode 1, the subject of the initial proposition is the poor performance of Communist candidates in the first freeish elections in the then USSR:

> Guennadi Guerassimov, le porte-parole du gouvernement, a beau souligner que « seulement » 20 % des cadres du Parti ont été battus, il n'en reste pas moins que, dans un système aussi verrouillé et bloqué que celui de l'URSS, la chute d'autant de petits tsars locaux va provoquer bien des remous au Bureau politique et au Comité central.

The next example uses Mode 3. The subject is the strong position of the then Prime Minister, Michel Rocard, despite the fact that he led a minority government: *Rocard a beau être minoritaire à l'Assemblée, sa position n'en est pas moins solide.* An example of Mode 4 shapes the contrast of the militarily powerful USA's relative powerlessness against unorthodox military action:

> L'oncle Sam a beau avoir de quoi rouler des mécaniques, crouler sous les canons et les lance-roquettes, il n'en semble pas moins désarmé face au terrorisme moyen-oriental.

As the verb is one of seeming, the variant with adjective is possible.

Mode 6: with oppositive *pour*

Similar to the relationship made between two propositions by *avoir beau* is the one made with oppositive *pour* preceding an infinitive, usually *être*, meaning roughly 'although' or 'despite the fact that'. This similarity of structure and function can be seen by comparing the first example used in Mode 5 above: *On a beau être critique, on n'en est pas moins homme* with Corneille's original of it: *Ah! pour être Romain, je n'en suis pas moins homme* (*Sertorius*, IV, i, 1194) or with the many whimsical adaptations of the latter such as Molière's *Ah! pour être dévot, je n'en suis pas moins homme* (*Tartuffe*, III, ii, 966), *Pour être prince, madame, on n'en est pas moins homme* (Stendhal, II, 337), *Pour être romancier, on n'en est pas moins homme* (Caillois, 175), *Mais, pour être athée, on n'en est pas moins homme* (Le Dantec, 106) and from a review of *The Man without a Face*, a film by Mel Gibson, *Pour n'avoir pas de visage, Mel Gibson n'en est pas moins homme.*

Since this *pour* cannot grammatically relate to an impersonal subject, the combination is not found with Modes 1 or 2. Examples of it with others are:

Le vocabulaire de l'anglais a une double racine et la part provenant du latin, pour être moins usitée, n'en est pas moins importante.

Les Occidentaux et les Israéliens observent avec vigilance le réarmement de l'Iran qui, pour être « paisible », selon l'expression de certains analystes, n'en est pas moins préoccupant.

Son beau-frère le pasteur G***, pour avoir un caractère diamétralement opposé au sien, n'en était pas moins un homme de mérite.

(Vadier, 98)

With *si d'opposition*

In addition to these six modes, this connector is quite often used to structure the second half of binaries introduced by the *si d'opposition*. This example is a comment on aspects of Indian art:

Et si certaines de ses réalisations ne sont pas du meilleur goût pour un œil occidental, elles n'en demeurent pas moins la plus parfaite expression d'une technique ancestrale mise au service d'un élan religieux comme peu de peuples en ont connu.

See also the last example in mode 3 above.

ne serait-ce que

This structure is nowadays very common in written French. Littré makes no mention of it. It is clearly a variant of *quand ce ne serait que*, which Littré does use, but only as the definition of *ne fût-ce que* – which he gives, for some reason, in the form *Ne fût-ce... que*. This connector has been described as follows:

a formalized expression which stands for 'if only because'; it functions simply as a subordinating expression: *nous n'irons pas ne serait-ce que parce que c'est trop loin*. This expression is commonly used in the spoken language. It takes the indicative.

(Judge & Healey, 171)

Brief as this is, it is much more informative than Grevisse, who seems to make no mention of the structure. Robert glances at it in passing, without definition. In fact, the use of *ne serait-ce que* is both more diverse and more widespread than this meagre treatment would suggest. It functions in two contexts, in both of which it introduces a notion of mereness: before a statement of cause; and before a minimal restricting condition.

Followed by cause, reason or intention

It is only in this function that the structure acts like 'if only because'. It is true that it is frequently found before *parce que*, as in the following extract from a discussion of the politician Charles Pasqua. The writer says Pasqua, though of the Right, though given to rabble-rousing, is no fascist:

> Pasqua, qui ne lésine ni sur l'effet de manche ni sur le mensonge logomachique ou le gros rouge verbal, ne s'apparente pas, pour autant, à un Mussolini : ne serait-ce que parce qu'il s'arrête toujours au bord du Rubicon.

However, cause or intention is commonly expressed in some other form, for instance by *pour* with an infinitive, as in this comment on an attempt to censor some trifling obscenities in the published letters of Gustave Flaubert:

> Tout écrivain digne de ce nom a toujours, par quelque coin secret de son œuvre, sa place réservée au Parnasse satyrique. Dût la modestie publique en rougir, ces *erotica* de grand style méritent d'être retenus, ne serait-ce que pour montrer la différence avec les pauvres saletés de nos analphabètes du jour.
>
> (Henriot, 1954: 72)

Sometimes a related structure, *pour* plus a noun, is used, as in this extract from an editorial on a constraint on American policy towards Israel:

> Le chef de la Maison Blanche ne peut pas se livrer à des pressions trop flagrantes, ne serait-ce que pour des considérations de politique intérieure (encore que la communauté juive américaine n'ait voté pour lui, en 1988, qu'à moins de 30 %).

A noun introduced by *par* is also possible:

> Sartre dit à Simone de Beauvoir, en 1974, en parlant des *Chemins de la liberté* : « Le roman, c'est raté ». A la même époque, à nous qui avions meilleure opinion de ce roman, il tenait, ne serait-ce que par courtoisie, des propos moins auto-dépréciatifs.

The other main construction used to express cause or reason is *ne serait-ce qu'en raison de*. The writer of this example speaks of a group of American conservatives (*anti-Soviétiques viscéraux*) who, in the 1980s, were very much in favour of continuing the Cold War:

> Ces conservateurs d'un autre âge ont vu d'un très mauvais œil l'accession en 1978 de Jean-Paul II à la tête de l'Église catholique ; ils le soupçonnent de vouloir négocier, ne serait-ce qu'en raison de ses origines polonaises, avec le bloc de l'Est.

Followed by a minimal condition

In its other mode, this structure functions like the special 'even' in 'even just' or 'even the slightest'. Acting like a specialized sort of *même*, it usually introduces the object of a verb, containing either an adjective like *premier* or *seul*, or a noun phrase functioning as a qualifier and containing a minimizing element such as *un instant, une fois* or *un début de*. The first of these examples comes from a discussion of the uncertain medical consequences of the nuclear catastrophe at Chernobyl in the then USSR:

> Parviendra-t-on un jour à dire quelles ont été – quelles seront – les conséquences de la catastrophe de Tchernobyl ? Cinq ans après, rien ne permet d'établir ne serait-ce qu'un premier bilan concernant les populations exposées aux radiations dues au plus grand accident de l'histoire du nucléaire civil.

> Le fondamentalisme juif prophétise un cataclysme. Il se produira à l'instant même où Israël abandonnera ne serait-ce qu'un millimètre de la Terre promise aux juifs par le Dieu de la Bible.

Place in the sentence

Although usually anaphoric in its functioning, modifying a preceding verb, this structure is at times placed first in the sentence. This occurs in two ways: either it stands first in a *phrase dépendante* and therefore modifies the verb in the preceding sentence, as in this comment on drugs, dating from the early years of the French epidemic of addiction:

> Des mythes se sont créés de tout temps, fantômes qui engendraient une terreur indistincte et absolue. De même, aujourd'hui, hurlons-nous à la « drogue ». Il faudrait pourtant savoir de quoi l'on parle. Ne serait-ce que pour pouvoir en parler utilement avec les « drogués ».

Or else it functions cataphorically: modifying the verb that follows, introducing a full sentence, it makes a sense that is complete without reference to the sentence before, as in this extract from an article about France's diplomatic role in the Gulf War against Iraq:

> Ne serait-ce que par la manière dont elle contribua à placer la crise du Golfe sur le terrain de l'ONU et du droit international, la « voix de la France » ne fut jamais, dans le conflit avec l'Irak, l'écho passif des consignes de Washington.

quand ce ne serait que

The structure used by Littré, without the inversion of pronoun and verb, is literary in flavour, as in this sentence where Alain speaks of clumsiness:

> Le maladroit pèse de tout son corps sur le moindre mouvement, et chacun est maladroit d'abord, quand ce ne serait que pour enfoncer un clou.
>
> (Alain, 1956: 345)

This form is still extant. In this example, the subject discussed is the lessening of class differences in speech:

> Un OS est bien loin de s'exprimer comme un académicien. Mais ils ont moins de peine à se comprendre, quand ce ne serait que parce que l'argot a envahi les salons les plus collet monté.
>
> (Fontaine, 1978: 194)

English equivalents, introducing a cause or reason, are 'if only because', 'if only so as to', 'if for no other reason' and 'perhaps only'; and in other contexts, 'even though only', 'even', 'even just' and 'even the slightest'.

n'était

This is a fossilized negative structure without *pas* and without a subject. It is at least as old as Montaigne: *Ce conte d'un évenement si legier est assez vain, n'estoit l'instruction que j'en ay tirée pour moy* (Montaigne, I, 414). The dictionaries define it as an ellipsis for *si ce n'était*. When it follows a main clause, its usual position, it is preceded by a comma and followed by a noun structure. Meaning roughly 'were it not for', it introduces a condition which rules out a possibility canvassed in the main clause. This is why the verb in that clause is often in the conditional or the conditional perfect. In the first example, a book reviewer comments on an impassioned passage in an essay by Jean-François Revel, in which the latter strongly criticizes François Mitterrand's exercise of his presidential powers:

> L'on pourrait penser que Revel y cède au mouvement de la philippique, n'était le raisonnement qui suit : il est accablant parce qu'il est évident.

A discussion of the idea of flexible hours for office-workers says this:

> Il y a quelques années, un directeur de ministère prétendit instaurer les horaires variables dans ses services. Les employés y auraient été favorables, n'était l'obligation d'utiliser l'horloge pointeuse pour comptabiliser les horaires de chacun.
>
> (Closets, 1983: 115)

The related form *n'était que* ('were it not [for the fact] that') is followed by a verb, as in this comment on Robert de Montesquiou:

> On serait volontiers tenté de sourire de cet insupportable personnage dont la morgue et la vanité n'eurent d'égales que le goût du toc et du bizarre, n'était

qu'il écrivit d'assez amusantes satires, et, surtout, qu'il aima fastueusement les arts [...]

(Henriot, 1956: 40)

There is a plural form *n'étaient*, of which many examples can be found in Grevisse (1964a: 779, 850, 1087), and a form *n'eût été* used with compound tenses.

Variants

The structure is not frequently used, which may be why some idiosyncratic variants of it turn up from time to time in the prose of some journalists. An article on Paul Grüninger, a Swiss policeman who was punished by his superiors for helping Jews escape Nazi persecution in the 1930s, says: *Rien ne prédisposait ce Suisse moyen à sortir des chemins battus, n'était-ce les circonstances exceptionnelles du moment.* There the structure that the writer presumably meant to write was *n'étaient* or even *si ce n'est (que)*. Again in the next example, taken from a description of the house of a Catalan artist, *n'étaient* would have expressed the writer's idea, which seems to have been confused with *ne serait-ce que*:

Bruits et lumière au dehors. Repos et pénombre à l'intérieur. Des pièces qui sembleraient vastes, peut-être, ne seraient les meubles anciens et les œuvres d'art qui s'accumulent jusque dans le jardin suspendu [...]

English equivalents, much less compact, are 'were it not for' or 'had it not been for' (followed by a noun) and 'were it not for the fact that' and 'had it not been for the fact that' (followed by a verb).

oh

This interjection is sometimes used as a more familiar, more spoken, more emotionally intense concessive than *certes* and most others. Concessives, even *sans doute* or *il est vrai que*, are by definition interactive, if only with an imagined or implicit reader. By agreeing with an unstated point of view, they accept the existence of an interlocutor, however ideal. As a connector, this one functions broadly like the others; but it adds a shade of affectivity to the point it introduces. Like them, it is often placed second in a sequence of three propositions: the statement which it accompanies usually objects to or qualifies an initial assertion, before itself being cancelled out by a substantial reaffirmation of the first point. In the first example, that first point deals with the expectation that the end of the Cold War would bring a better world:

Avouons-le : quand le mur de Berlin fut abattu par les Berlinois en liesse, nous avons cru à la naissance d'un nouveau monde. Oh, pas d'un nouveau monde idéal qui aurait été pacifique, démocratique et prospère –, nous n'étions pas naïfs à ce point – , mais tout de même d'un monde libéré de la chape de plomb que faisait peser sur nous l'affrontement immobile entre l'empire capitaliste de l'Ouest et l'empire communiste de l'Est.

There, as is usual with this sort of concession, the third point, restating a version of the first one, is introduced by **mais**. A similar sequence is seen in this extract from an article on what the writer calls the new *tiers état*: a passive class participating in political life via television, expressing its views mainly through opinion polls:

Le tiers état des classes moyennes s'est mis sur le banc de touche. Cantonné à un rôle passif, lui qui est aussi parfois « inactif », il s'est ainsi peu à peu laissé tenter par le jeu de massacre. Oh, pas dans la rue, car la violence lui fait peur. Mais en qualité de spectateur interactif qui baisse et relève le pouce, applaudit puis conspue les têtes couronnables qui défilent sur le petit écran. « La démocratie émeutière et sondagière », comme l'appelle très justement Olivier Duhamel, nous y sommes déjà.

As can be seen in these examples, when it is part of this tripartite sequence, this connector usually introduces a negative statement.

Sometimes the emotiveness of the connector is enhanced by the addition of an exclamation mark, usually placed immediately after it, as in this extract from a discussion which tries to answer the question: *Quelle est la véritable inégalité qui sépare les Français ?* The writer uses **seulement** rather than *mais* to counteract the force of the concession:

Sa première caractéristique est de n'être pas seulement financière. Oh ! l'argent est important et je n'ai garde de l'oublier. Seulement le « reste » ne l'est pas moins et il serait tout aussi grave de l'omettre.

(Closets, 20)

Sometimes, too, a writer strengthens this connector by combining it with another concessive: *Oh ! certes*; *Oh ! bien sûr*; *Oh ! cela est vrai, sans doute* (Renan, 1150). And sometimes *Oh !* is replaced by the more passionate *Ah !* as in this extract from a book review discussing the propriety of republishing nowadays offensively anti-Semitic and pro-Nazi texts:

Ce livre s'apparente un peu trop à l'exploitation commerciale de Vichy et de la collaboration. Nous n'en sommes pas encore à voir *Mein Kampf* réédité « pour les amateurs (et les adversaires) d'Adolf Hitler », mais cela arrivera un jour. Espérons qu'il est encore éloigné. Ah ! évidemment qu'il ne faut pas ignorer les années noires et leurs acteurs ! Bien sûr qu'il faut savoir ce que Céline a écrit, pour mieux le connaître. Cela devrait aller sans le dire. Mais il y a l'art et la manière, l'analyse, le commentaire. Plus les textes sont sulfureux, plus il faudrait prendre de précautions.

or *

This connector can at times be troublesome for speakers of English, in which language it has sometimes no evident equivalent. For example, in logic, to introduce the second term of a syllogism, English has no technical term as French has in, say, Condillac's *argument cornu*: *Vous avez ce que vous n'avez pas perdu; or vous n'avez pas perdu de cornes; donc vous avez des cornes*. This mode is used outside the field of formal logic, as in this sequence of three sentences about the *foulard islamique* and the Minister for Education's opposition to its being worn by girls at state schools:

> Le ministre assure que le foulard est, en soi, un signe de discrimination. Or, la discrimination n'a pas sa place à l'école publique. Donc le foulard est interdit.

As an expository connector, *or* has two basic modes: not necessarily adversative; and mostly adversative. Quite often it introduces the second phase of a development, either the second sentence of a paragraph or the second paragraph of a discussion. At times, it marks the transition from a preamble to a first important point. Or else it focusses attention on an element in a discussion seen to be significant, whether contrastive or non-contrastive. Even when non-contrastive, it can retain something of a comparative function, if only at the implicit level. It is almost always placed nowadays at the beginning of the sentence. Despite rules such as this one: *Il n'est obligatoirement suivi d'une virgule que devant un complément* (Hanse, 1983: 652), the best one can say about punctuation usage is that some writers follow it with a comma and some do not.

Narrative *or*

In contexts such as the exposition of children's stories, *or* functions like narrative 'now': 'Once upon a time, there was a little girl called Little Red Riding Hood who lived in the forest with her father the wood-cutter. Now, one day ...'. The connector and the change of tense, which in French would be from imperfect to preterite, signal the end of the scene-setting and the beginning of the narrative proper. It still functions in that way:

> notre cuisinière, qui avait nom Delphine, venait de se fiancer au cocher de nos voisins de campagne. Elle allait quitter notre maison pour toujours. Or, la veille de son départ, je fus réveillé au cœur de la nuit, par les bruits les plus étranges.
>
> (Gide, 1954: 385)

In narrative contexts, as well as signalling a change of tense and the beginning of the action, it denotes an important development. It is this secondary function of the narrative mode which adapts to the first of the two expository functions, the non-adversative one.

Non-adversative *or*

Although basically non-adversative, this mode can still at times make a contrastive relationship, while retaining some narrative force. It announces a disparity, a difference, a contrast between a past and present state of things. The change may be apparent in the tense of the verb following, which will differ from the one preceding. Thus an article on the rapprochement between western and eastern forms of Christianity speaks first of the mid-1960s, before going on to contrast that period with a later one:

> En 1964, la rencontre entre le « pape de Rome » et le « pape de Constantinople » scellait alors la réconciliation, après neuf siècles de discorde et de persécutions, entre les deux grandes capitales de l'Europe chrétienne. Or, un quart de siècle après, à la faveur des événements en URSS et dans les pays de l'Est, le dialogue entre le catholicisme et l'orthodoxie traverse sa plus grave crise.

In other similar contexts, the connector structures what is in part a contrastive account of events and in part a discussion of arguments. The expository function is sensed as more important than the narrative:

> Sur le plan mondial, la France a eu la chance d'appartenir à un petit groupe de nations dominantes. Or, celles-ci ont perdu leur hégémonie. Le monde futur sera multipolaire et nul ne sait si l'Europe pourra en rester un centre majeur.
>
> (Closets, 1983: 495–496)

At times, even this vestigial narrative element is absent; and then the connector's sole function is to announce the beginning of a substantive discussion, as in these two sentences opening a new chapter in an essay on *Tristan et Iseut*: the author, having established that the plot of the legend is made of separations between the lovers, is going on to focus more closely on these separations:

> Nous avons vu que le progrès du roman a pour principe les séparations et les revoirs successifs des amants. Or les causes de séparation sont de deux sortes : circonstances extérieures, entraves inventées par Tristan.
>
> (Rougemont, 1962: 34)

At other times, this mode introduces not a lengthy development, but only a significant fact or a precision which must be attended to as part of an argument. Instead of being near the beginning of a text, this can be near the end, as in the final sentence of a discussion of links between violence and consumption of spirits in Finland:

> L'ivresse du samedi soir est un désastre ; les habitués du grand défoulement hebdomadaire absorbent, d'un coup, de grandes quantités de liqueurs fortes.

> La prise d'alcool est occasionnelle, certes, mais elle est immense, effrénée. Or,
> à la différence de la bière qui rend plutôt passif, les spiritueux excitent l'agres-
> sivité ; certaines libations s'achèvent en pugilats ou en duels au couteau.

In that example, English might use 'and'. But in many of the contexts
illustrated above, the statements if said in English would very likely be
introduced by no connective word.

Adversative *or*

This mode introduces a statement of fact which is at variance with what
precedes. What precedes is seen as less acute, less accurate, less certain,
less pertinent than what follows. Among French connectors, this one is
the great rectifier, one of the most didactic: it signals a precision, a principle, a definition of a key term or a distinction, as in the first of these
examples, discussing the relation between crimes against persons and
crimes against property, where the writer defines what 'violence' is:

> Ce que craignent nos concitoyens est moins l'agression que le cambriolage,
> moins la violence à proprement parler que la délinquance, ou la criminalité
> contre les *biens*. Or les délits (voire les crimes) contre les biens ne peuvent
> aucunement être qualifiés de violence.
>
> (Chesnais, 13)

The connector can introduce the real outcome of an expected or hoped
for state of things or the contradiction of a hypothesis. This often takes
the form of a brief sentence like *c'est le contraire qui s'est produit* or *il
n'en est rien*, as in Durkheim's way of dealing with the notion that seasonal
variations of suicide are to be explained by variations in temperature:

> Si la température était la cause fondamentale des oscillations que nous avons
> constatées, le suicide devrait régulièrement varier comme elles. Or il n'en est
> rien. On se tue beaucoup plus au printemps qu'en automne, quoiqu'il fasse
> alors un peu plus froid.
>
> (Durkheim, 1930: 91)

> Le nombre des avortements, disaient-ils, va croître énormément. Or, les statis-
> tiques officielles montrent une grande stabilité, sinon même une diminution
> depuis quelques années.

Two other common formulas in such contexts are *Or ce n'est pas le cas
en l'occurrence* and *Or, pas du tout, ce fut l'inverse*. What precedes often
contains a verb in the conditional or the conditional perfect, such as *il
faudrait, on eût pu s'attendre à* or a part of *devoir*: *on devrait voir; on
aurait dû*.

After a verb of seeming, *or* can clarify that an apparent state of things
is possibly misleading. In this context, the little sentence *Or rien n'est
moins sûr* is quite common, as in this extract from an editorial about the

British government's decision to negotiate with Sinn Fein over the status of Northern Ireland:

> Londres semble faire sienne la thèse selon laquelle toute une génération de militants de l'IRA serait lassée de la violence. Or, rien n'est moins sûr.

It can introduce a statement of the opposite of an ideal state of things:

> La véritable réussite de la Révolution, c'eût été d'implanter en France un système durable et paisible de liberté politique. Or elle parvint surtout à frayer le chemin à des formes aggravées de tyrannie.

There, as in many of these contrastive contexts, the connector could be replaced by *alors que*.

Contradictive *or*

This is a strong variant of the adversative mode. It introduces not merely a contrast but a statement roundly contradicting an error or disputing an inaccuracy. What follows is often a sentence like *il s'agit là d'une erreur d'optique* or *cela est faux, archifaux*, or else a negative construction such as *il n'en est rien* or *rien n'est plus faux*. In these contexts, the connector functions like **en fait** or **en réalité** and could often be replaced by **mais** or **au contraire**. In this example the author sets out to refute the view that Taine's study *Les origines de la France contemporaine* was hostile to the French revolution:

> Après avoir connu un grand succès de librairie à la fin du XIXᵉ siècle, les *Origines* cessèrent peu à peu d'être rééditées. Pourquoi ? L'essai de Taine s'était vu conférer le statut infâme de machine de guerre contre-révolutionnaire. Or c'est là, me semble-t-il, une erreur, pour une double raison.

A second example comes from an article discrediting the notion that between 1940 and 1944 the Vichy régime of Pétain and Laval was not really collaborating with the Nazis but working with de Gaulle's Free French in London:

> Une forme de « révisionnisme » à la française tend à faire croire qu'on ne saurait en rien comparer l'oppression nazie, spécifiquement allemande, à l'action désordonnée et improvisée d'un gouvernement sans idéologie précise qui ne cherchait qu'à sauver les meubles. Au fond, et cela a été écrit cent fois, de Gaulle aurait été l'épée et Pétain le bouclier. Son seul crime : avoir accepté le mauvais rôle.
> Or cela est totalement et indiscutablement faux.

In contexts where English would use an equivalent, it would often be 'but', 'whereas' or 'however'. At other times, contrastive 'and', 'yet' or 'and yet' would be used.

ou bien... ou bien

Like *soit... soit*, this is a common binary structure serving to set out the possible alternatives following from a preceding point. It is a reinforced form of *ou... ou* for which English has no special equivalent different from the basic 'either ... or'. English does have 'or else' as a variant for the second part of the binary; but there is no such reinforcer for the first part. In some contexts, 'alternatively' could be adapted. In French, too, the first part is sometimes not reinforced by *bien*; and writers use *ou... ou bien*. The connector is sometimes used to structure the two parts of a single sentence; but it often structures two consecutive sentences, or even paragraphs, of similar form, in which case a part of it usually stands first in each.

Preceded by an expression of choice

The structure is often preceded by an expression based on a noun such as *un dilemme*, *le choix* or *une alternative*, or the verb *choisir*, often in the form *il faut choisir*. A variant of this is used by a writer discussing European economic planning: first he sketches a scenario of a possible future Europe; then he adds this:

> Au bout de cette route, il faudra choisir : ou bien imiter un socialisme encore libéral mais incapable de créer des richesses, le travaillisme britannique ; ou bien emprunter au soviétisme les méthodes despotiques qui permettent au pouvoir non de satisfaire les peuples mais de nourrir de vastes ambitions.
> (Aron, 1977: 481)

Preceded by an expression containing *deux*

Alternatively, in what precedes this structure many writers use an expression containing *deux*, such as *Il peut y avoir alors deux cas* or *Il existe deux possibilités*. An example of this mode discusses possible cooperation between France and Russia in disposing of the latter's excess stocks of plutonium:

> Les Français pourront être amenés à prodiguer leurs conseils aux Russes sur la destinée de leurs lingots de plutonium. Deux voies sont ouvertes : ou les stocker avec toutes les sauvegardes possibles, ou bien les faire brûler dans des super-réacteurs nucléaires aptes au « crackage » du plutonium.

Sometimes, in any of the above cases, the writer may reinforce the second part of the binary with *au contraire*, as in this extract from a discussion of two possible outcomes of negotiations in the early twentieth century between Westminster and the Dominions on future relations within the British Empire:

Toutes ces dispositions étaient susceptibles de deux interprétations. Ou bien c'étaient autant de pas vers l'organisation fédérale de l'empire. Ou bien au contraire elles tendaient, par la constitution du secrétariat, à détacher d'avec le reste de l'empire les colonies autonomes.

(Halévy, 24)

Possibly the most common variant nowadays for this use of *deux* is the set phrase *de deux choses l'une*. This example comes from an article canvassing the possible outcomes of a negative vote in the French referendum on the ratification of the Treaty of Maastricht:

En cas de victoire du « non », de deux choses l'une : ou bien les champions du « non » gouvernent – mais comment ? Ou bien les partisans du « oui » continuent de tenir la barre, mais entre eux et l'opinion publique le fossé deviendra un gouffre.

In sequences of points

Occasionally a writer uses an extension of the last variant, *de trois choses l'une*, as in this extract from a discussion of the possibilities for democracy in Iran:

On ne voit guère, à court terme, comment l'Iran pourrait se doter d'un régime un tant soit peu démocratique. De trois choses l'une, en effet. Ou bien le pays reste dans son état actuel, soumis au rigorisme et au fanatisme des « docteurs du dogme religieux ». Ou bien, deuxième hypothèse, les leaders de l'opposition installés à l'étranger réussissent à renverser le régime khomeiniste, et dans ce cas ils ramèneront dans leurs fourgons les hommes du chah, et donc les méthodes dictatoriales de ce dernier. Dernière hypothèse : le Kremlin renouvelle avec Téhéran le « coup de Kaboul ».

Other **sequences of points** may take the form of *ou... ou bien... ou encore...* or else *ou bien... ou encore... ou enfin*. A fourfold repetition of *ou bien* is not unknown, as in this account of Gorgias's canvassing of reasons why Helen of Troy was carried off:

L'orateur, par une énumération complète, inventorie toutes les causes possibles de cet enlèvement : ou bien, il est dû aux arrêts des dieux et du destin ; ou bien, elle a été ravie de force ; ou bien, elle a été persuadée par des discours ; ou bien, elle a été vaincue par le désir.

(Reboul, 17)

The further concomitants of the consequences envisaged are themselves often spelled out, either singly after each part of the binary or together after the second part. Typically, they are introduced by combinations of expressions containing **alors** or *cas*: *et alors...*; *En ce cas...*; *Dans un cas... dans l'autre*; *Auquel cas... Auquel cas...*; *Dans le premier cas... dans le second cas...*; *Dans les deux cas...*; *Dans tous les cas...*; *Dans ce dernier* *cas....* A typical combination is seen in this example, taken from a discussion of possible solutions to the war in Bosnia in 1993:

> Ajoutons une ultime contradiction : ou bien on se résout à une partition ethnique, et dans ce cas il faut imposer aux Serbes l'autonomie du Kosovo à majorité musulmane. Ou bien on refuse cette logique infernale, et alors il faut rétablir l'intégrité territoriale de la Bosnie, mais ne pas encourager la sécession du Kosovo.

oui

Like *si l'on veut* or *oh*, this connector is sometimes used as a more familiar or conversational variant of concessives such as *certes*, *sans doute* and *il est vrai que*. Unlike *oh*, it does not usually introduce negative statements. However, like all these concessive structures, it always starts by agreeing with what precedes. It is then usually followed by a restriction of what precedes, seen by the writer as more important than the agreement. The frequency of the combination *oui, mais* shows the immediacy with which the restriction usually follows this connector, as in Jules Renard's comment on the coming of wireless to the French countryside: *Télégraphie sans fil, oui. Mais je me demande où vont percher nos gracieuses hirondelles ?* (Renard, 1965: 902) and this comment on the idiosyncratic style of the novelist Céline:

> Céline considère la langue des romans habituels comme morte. Il a confessé qu'il faisait de copieux emprunts à l'argot pour que sa langue à lui fût vivante. Vivante, oui, mais d'une vie factice et pour combien de temps ?
>
> (Georgin, 1956: 304)

The combination is reinforced by *voilà* in the next example, taken from an article about the ex-minister Lionel Jospin and his decision in 1993 to retire from politics:

> Battu aux législatives dans sa circonscription toulousaine, il décide, « par règle de vie personnelle et par nécessité », de renoncer à la politique. C'est l'adieu aux armes ! Oui, mais voilà, la traversée du désert annoncée ne durera que cinq mois et deviendra dans la bouche de ses ennemis « la traversée du bac à sable ». Cruel !

At other times, as with most of the other concessives, the statement introduced by *mais* does not immediately follow the connector, but comes later in the same sentence or in one of the sentences following. In this example, the writer, a naturalized Frenchman about to be shot by the Nazis, jots down the pros and cons of the country for which he is dying:

> J'aime la France. J'aime ce beau pays et j'aime son peuple. Oui, je sais combien il est mesquin, égoïste, pourri de politique et victime de son ancienne gloire,

> mais dans tous ses défauts, il reste infiniment humain et ne voulant à aucun prix sacrifier sa grandeur et sa misère d'homme [...]
>
> (Frischer, 9)

Sometimes the interlocutory tone of this connector is shown by its use in answer to a question asked by the writer:

> Mais Dreyfus et les siens pouvaient-ils refuser de jouer le jeu ? En droit, oui. En fait, on ne voit pas très bien comment une résistance aurait été possible.
>
> (Vidal-Nacquet, 1982: 42)

A less frequent variant of *oui*, equally spoken in tone, is *d'accord*, as in this comment by a columnist on a letter from a reader concerned about proper usage of the subjunctive:

> Mon [correspondant] conclut que la meilleure façon de sauver le subjonctif est de n'en point abuser. D'accord, mais à condition que nous n'ayons pas l'air de faire la part du feu.
>
> (Hermant, 156)

par ailleurs *

Like some other connectors, **par contre**, say, or **pour autant**, this one, of relatively recent origin, has been the focus of controversy, the butt of pedants' indignation:

> On ne doit pas, comme on le fait, l'employer soit en tête, soit dans le corps de la phrase, au sens de : *d'autre part, du reste, à d'autres égards, de plus*.
>
> (Georgin, 1961: 59)

Usage having gone on ignoring such injunctions, that is exactly how the structure is now used in one of its modes: ...*présidente de la Région Guadeloupe, Lucette Michaux-Chevry, par ailleurs ministre à l'Action humanitaire*. Grevisse has an interesting article on the purists' objections (Grevisse, 1964b: 115–121).

This can be one of the most difficult of French connectors for speakers of English to get a purchase on. It has two main modes: at times, it can have a function very similar to that of **d'ailleurs**: *Il est riche, et par ailleurs intelligent*. At others, it is used in a markedly contrastive way. Dictionaries and grammars have diverse views: some report the contrastive use; some say it is unusual; some say that some grammarians deplore it.

Non-contrastive

This is the more common mode, often used in news reports. Its function is at times quasi-narrative. It introduces a second point of information which adds something to a first. The second point tells of a different event from the first; but it is related to the first because it concerns the same subject. In the first example, that subject is Jacques Chirac, then leader of the RPR which was in opposition:

> M. Jacques Chirac s'est clairement prononcé, jeudi 24 septembre, pour un départ de M. François Mitterrand dans l'hypothèse d'une large victoire de l'opposition aux élections législatives.
>
> Par ailleurs, au terme d'une réunion extraordinaire du conseil national du RPR à huis clos, mercredi 23 septembre à Paris, M. Chirac a obtenu, avec 95 % des suffrages, la confiance de son parti.

The second example details two developments concerning the British Prime Minister:

> Plus de cent mille personnes ont manifesté, dimanche 25 octobre, à Londres, pour protester contre la politique économique de M. John Major. Par ailleurs, le premier ministre britannique engage une nouvelle épreuve de force avec les « eurosceptiques ».

One possible English equivalent for it in this role would be 'in another development'. The more minimal type of news report might make do with the all-purpose 'also'. More often than not, this mode is placed first in the sentence or paragraph; occasionally, it is placed after the first verb: *Faut-il rappeler par ailleurs que…*; *M. Gorbachev a par ailleurs affirmé que….* Its function is close to that of *de plus*, *du reste* or *d'autre part*. This is seen, too, in contexts where it is used not to link an account of two happenings but to report two statements. The following example, dealing with the crash of a United Airlines jumbo-jet, has two related points to make which are relevant in different ways to the presumed airworthiness of the aeroplane:

> Chez United, on affirme que le 747 concerné était âgé de dix-neuf ans et qu'il n'avait pas dépassé les 58 000 heures de vol, alors que certains appareils de ce type ont atteint les 79 000 heures de vol. Par ailleurs, il venait de subir une inspection assez approfondie et avait été déclaré bon pour le service.

That is, this mode introduces another aspect of the fact dealt with in what precedes; it looks at it from another point of view.

Contrastive

It is because of that otherness of the respect canvassed in the second statement that this connector also lends itself to a more contrastive function. Unlike the first mode, which is placed mainly first in sentences, this mode is often placed inside the sentence. But even in the initial position, it can structure statements which set a point in opposition to another, as in this extract from an article making two points about a meeting of the twelve member-states of the European Union:

Les Douze, réunis à Lisbonne, ont décidé de maintenir M. Jacques Delors à la tête de la commission. Cette décision était vivement souhaitée par la grande majorité des États membres. Par ailleurs, le désaccord entre les Douze sur le financement de la Communauté au cours des années à venir reste complet.

There, the contrast between a point of agreement and a point of disagreement could not be more pointed if made by *en revanche* or *par contre*. In this function, the connector is even combined with *mais*, as in this extract from an essay on national identity as supposedly shown through national history:

On célèbre, en 1987, le « millénaire » d'Hugues Capet, on prépare, pour 1989, le bi-centenaire de la Révolution. On édite des « Lieux de mémoire », des histoires de France en série. Le symbole Hugues Capet réunit pour des commémorations officielles les plus hautes autorités, des historiens, des journalistes éminents. Mais, par ailleurs, les interrogations sur notre identité collective se multiplient.

(Citron, 7)

This mode can also single out a difference among broader similarities, as in this extract from a discussion of a type of Victorian family, so protective as to be stifling:

On comprend bien que ces havres étaient aussi des prisons et que c'est probablement pour avoir vécu dans ces sortes de familles qu'André Gide et François Mauriac, deux écrivains si différents par ailleurs, ont gardé de leur famille des images aussi négatives.

(Roussel, 57)

Often the contrast is between an exception and a rule. In the next example, a writer uses this mode to comment on the disparity between the survival of capital punishment in France until 1981 and the country's own image of itself as enlightened:

Si les cas visés sont d'une extrême gravité – crime contre la sûreté de l'État, rapt d'enfant avec homicide prémédité, meurtres multiples – cette survivance d'un rite primitif dans un pays qui, par ailleurs, se targue d'être à la pointe du progrès, n'en prend que plus de relief.

A similar contrast is made in the next examples, first between the general admiring indebtedness of Aragon and his generation to the mind of Maurice Barrès and their particular repugnance at his wartime jingoism:

Aragon a dix-sept ans en 1914. Il fait partie des adolescents qui, se sachant voués au massacre, exècrent les homélies d'un barrésisme dont ils sont imprégnés par ailleurs, en particulier touchant le style.

Next, between the general cleanly prettiness of a province and the untypical grottiness of the town within it: *Dans une Alsace par ailleurs si proprette, si bien léchée, Mulhouse fait exception.*

Like contrastive *au demeurant*, this mode says 'despite this', 'in other respects' or 'for all that'. Depending on context, other English equivalents could be 'otherwise', 'in another connection' and 'incidentally'. For the non-contrastive mode, English would often use 'also', 'in addition', 'as well' or 'as well as that'. But the connector is sometimes used in ways which it would be difficult to replicate in English. For example, the pointed contrastive effect afforded by the French connector in structuring the following idea (that the right to criticize failings entails the duty of fair-mindedness towards achievements) could not easily be achieved in English: *L'on n'a autorité pour formuler ces objections que si l'on a par ailleurs l'honnêteté de donner acte à ceux contre lesquels on les formule de leurs bons résultats.* To express the same idea, an English author might use 'conversely', fall back on 'at the same time' or mere 'also', neither of which would give the same antithetical effect, or else use no connector at all.

parce que *

To the speaker of English this conjunction, which means 'because' and is sometimes used to link a *phrase dépendante* to a preceding sentence, is pretty straightforward. However, it can offer two minor difficulties and one which is possibly major.

The first of the minor ones is that its spelling, in two separate words, should be noted. The second is that there is a great difference between it and *par ce que* written in three words. In *par ce que*, there is no explanation of a cause; there is a relative pronoun; and *par* is a simple preposition. If the following statement were to be made in English: *Ce n'est pas par ce qu'elles montrent que les jolies femmes intéressent, c'est par ce qu'elles cachent*, it could be expressed like this: 'Pretty women are interesting not by what they show, but by what they do not show.' An extract from an essay on the origins of cinema contains an example of both structures. The author's point is that, unlike earlier forms of reproducing moving pictures, the cinematograph brought people together: *Le cinématographe est partage. Par ce que l'on voit, mais aussi parce que l'on en parle.*

Readers of sixteenth-century French must beware the vagaries of that period's spelling of *parce que* which frequently make of it *par ce que*, as in Montaigne's celebrated explanation of his friendship with Étienne de La Boétie:

Si on me presse de dire pourquoy je l'aymois, je sens que cela ne se peut exprimer, qu'en respondant : « Par ce que c'estoit luy ; par ce que c'estoit moy. »

(Montaigne, I, 204)

As for the potentially major difficulty, i.e. when to use *parce que* and when to use *car*, see the entry on the latter.

par conséquent *

This connector is unproblematical for any speaker of English who uses 'consequently'. An example of its use comes from a comment on the sources of English vocabulary:

> L'anglais, qui est une langue germanique, a subi à peu près la même influence du latin savant. On y trouve par conséquent une forme telle que *paternal* en face de *father*.
>
> (Meillet, 212)

However, the structure does have a range of variants which deserve some comment: *en conséquence, par voie de conséquence, par suite* and *partant*. Some lexicographers and grammarians see differences between some of these and *par conséquent* (Bénac, 35; Brunot, 833). But the views and practices of others lend support to the idea that, apart from differences of tone, they are more or less interchangeable in introducing the result of a state of affairs or a conclusion to be drawn from what precedes. This function is also served by simple apposition of the nouns *conséquence* and *résultat*.

en conséquence

Literally, this structure means 'as a consequence'. This slight difference in meaning is the basis for the shade of difference that some dictionaries make between it and *par conséquent*. The newer Robert, for example, keeps the two structures mostly well apart. On the other hand, Littré's sole definition of *par conséquent* is *en conséquence*. Some see the latter as *plus distingué* (Marouzeau, 31). Sometimes it is used in the structure *en conséquence de quoi*. In practice, it is a variant of *par conséquent* with the sense of 'for which reason'. This example comes from a discussion of education policies, in particular the reform of 1937 which raised the school-leaving age to fourteen: *Elle prolongeait la scolarité obligatoire à quatorze ans, et prévoyait en conséquence le budget de constructions scolaires que cette mesure impliquait.* Either it accompanies the verb, as in that example, or it is placed first in the sentence and followed by a comma, as in this extract from a discussion of Mexico's trade deficit and in particular the effects of a restrictive monetary policy adopted in 1992:

> Il s'agissait de limiter la progression de la demande intérieure, à l'origine de l'explosion des importations. Le résultat ne s'est pas fait attendre. La croissance du PIB, qui était déjà revenue à 2,6 % en 1992, contre 3,6 % en 1991 et 4,4 % en 1990, n'atteindra vraisemblablement pas 1 % en 1993. En

conséquence, le pouvoir d'achat du revenu par tête aura diminué pour la première fois depuis six ans.

par voie de conséquence

This mode is paid little attention by most dictionaries. But it is probably the most frequently used nowadays of the variants for *par conséquent*. Often it is placed first in the sentence, in which case it is followed by a comma, as in this extract from an article on the British conductor, Simon Rattle, written before he was knighted:

> Le jeune chef n'est pas Sir, mais il mériterait d'être adoubé pour le travail qu'il a accompli à la tête de l'Orchestre de la ville de Birmingham : il l'a hissé sur le podium des meilleures formations d'outre-Manche. Par voie de conséquence, les Philharmonies de Vienne et de Berlin lui déroulent un tapis rouge.

When not placed first, it is often preceded by *et*, as in this comment on what, in the days before television, used to be seen as good business for a football team:

> Hier, accéder en première division, finir en tête du championnat, disputer une finale, remplissait les stades et, par voie de conséquence, les caisses du club.

par suite

This variant is in Littré, who defines it as meaning *par une conséquence naturelle*, but not in Robert. In Le Bidois, at the entry for *par conséquent*, there is this:

> Une autre locution conjonctive, PAR SUITE, marque également une conséquence, mais qui peut très bien n'être que comme indiquée en passant : « On a supprimé cet article du projet de loi ; *par suite*, les dispositions qui s'y rapportaient sont supprimées aussi. »
>
> (Le Bidois, II, 245)

The connector was once much more used than it is today. It is common in writers from the 1890s to the 1930s. Nowadays it probably has a dated or literary flavour. Philippe Boucher uses it on occasion (Boucher, 376, 445), as do Bourdieu & Passeron (43, 76) and Jean Dutourd, as in this jaded comment on the moral degeneracy of France under Socialism:

> Avec les nationalisations, il n'y a plus de sanction pour les incapables, il n'y a plus de sélection naturelle des chefs d'entreprise. Par suite, il n'y a plus de morale commerciale.
>
> (Dutourd, 1985: 26)

Sometimes too a rare journalist remembers its existence, as in this extract from an article about unemployment and apparently unavoidable side-effects of salary rises as a stimulus to consumption and hence to job-creation:

Ce qui nous ramène immanquablement à une impasse. La difficulté à résoudre la question de l'emploi conduit, dans un réflexe keynésien, à préférer les effets immédiats et visibles de l'augmentation des salaires et, par suite, du pouvoir d'achat. Seulement voilà, les salariés profitent de cette manne pour épargner toujours davantage et se détournent de la consommation.

partant

Like *par suite*, this adverb used to be more widely used than it is now. However, it is much more present these days than *par suite*. It is usually preceded by *et*, either at the beginning of a statement or in the middle of it. This example comes from an essay on Saint-Simon's *Mémoires*, which were first published just before the Revolution, in 1788:

En ce sens, on peut soutenir qu'au moment où l'on commence à les lire, les *Mémoires* apparaîtront à plus d'un prophétiques, et partant, que la tradition contre-révolutionnaire, celle d'une mécanique sans dynamique révolutionnaire interne, commence avant la Révolution, avec la publication de 1788.

(Bourgeois & d'Hondt, 219)

The mode with *et* most often introduces the final element of a sentence: *...la meilleure garantie de la continuité du régime et, partant, de son pouvoir.* / *...leur jugement sur la politique gouvernementale : incohérente, incompréhensible et, partant, inquiétante.*

Some prefer to use it without *et*, even after a stop, as in this ironic comment on a certain French view of Christianity among Martians:

Les Martiens, a dit *le Progrès de Lyon*, ont eu nécessairement un Christ ; partant ils ont aussi un pape (et voilà d'ailleurs le schisme ouvert) : faute de quoi ils n'auraient pu se civiliser au point d'inventer la soucoupe interplanétaire.

(Barthes, 1957: 43)

Colignon says that certain uses of this adverb *coulent mieux en présence de la conjonction et* (Colignon, 26–27) and, because of the possibility of confusion with the present participle of *partir*, identical in spelling, counsels caution in the placement of commas.

conséquence and résultat

The use of these nouns in apposition, to present a statement of consequence, is very common these days among journalists. Not that there is anything deplorable, or even modern, in that – it is also found in the prose of books and in former times. Usually the noun is in the singular and followed by a **deux-points**; but plurals and commas are not unknown. Unlike the variant structures discussed above, this one is always placed first and what follows is always a whole sentence. An example of *résultat* comes from an article on the stimulus to car sales of a reduction in purchase-tax:

> À l'époque, la réduction fiscale s'était traduite par un boom des ventes. En décembre, les ventes atteignaient un record. Aujourd'hui, le Comité des constructeurs français d'automobiles estime entre 40 000 et 50 000 unités le volume supplémentaire de voitures vendues grâce à cette mesure. Mais le mois suivant, l'euphorie des consommateurs faisait place à la morosité. Résultat : en janvier 1993, la baisse des ventes était de plus de 36 %.

An example of *conséquence*, which is the more frequently used, comes from a discussion of why Champagne wine froths:

> La mousse résulte historiquement d'un double phénomène. Il y eut d'abord l'abandon de la futaille, la conservation dans le bois ne convenant nullement à ces vins septentrionaux. Conséquence : la Champagne eut, dès le dix-huitième siècle, progressivement recours au verre. Or, s'ils pouvaient vieillir dans les flacons de l'époque « hauts d'environ dix pouces, goulot compris », les vins y évoluaient fréquemment, le temps les enrichissant d'une effervescence naturelle.

Other possibilities

A variant for some of the modes of *par conséquent* is **de ce fait**. Also widely used these days, by journalists and other writers, is **du coup**. Sometimes the structure *il en résulte que* is used instead of one of the nouns in apposition.

English has many equivalents, depending on context: 'as a result', 'because of this', 'consequently', 'for this reason', 'for which reason', 'the result was', 'so', 'therefore'.

par contre *

This adversative structure, much used, much maligned, has been the focus of two debates in the twentieth century. In the first, purists made a pother about its alleged belonging to a shopkeeper's register of speech, a skirmish to which Grevisse seems to have put an end (Grevisse, 1964b, 108–114). The other one concerns the definition given of it by some of the dictionaries: that it is equivalent to *en compensation* and **en revanche**:

> Ce n'est pas toujours vrai. Ces deux expressions introduisent un avantage ; *par contre* peut introduire un avantage ou un inconvénient.
>
> (Hanse, 1983: 271)

However, despite that view and despite a lingering more or less superstitious dislike of this connector in the minds of some, it is used very much like *en revanche* – indeed, in the usage of many writers, the two connectors are all but interchangeable. Or rather, *par contre* is used in any context where *en revanche* would fit; but for some writers the converse may not necessarily hold good. It is also used like one of the modes of **au contraire**. However, unlike both *en revanche* and *au contraire*, it is not often used in the second part of antitheses structured by the **si d'opposition**.

The connector shapes direct contrasts or oppositions between pairs of statements. In the first example, from an article discussing the fortunes of a banker called Vernes, what precedes is a success, what follows is a failure:

> La Banque Vernes ayant été nationalisée en 1982, il réussira le tour de force de recréer une banque moins d'un an plus tard avec l'aide de Dassault et de Rothschild : c'est la BICM ou Banque industrielle et commerciale du Marais. Par contre, en 1986, il perdra le contrôle de Béghin Say, passé sous l'égide du groupe italien Ferruzzi.

In the second example, a historian of labour in the late nineteenth century discusses the gradual acceptance of the idea that workers should not be expected to work seven days a week:

> Dans les grands magasins – *le Bonheur des dames* de Zola le montre avec clarté – le repos du dimanche, « où l'on jette son argent » à la volée, est respecté. Par contre il est presque inconnu dans la petite entreprise urbaine – particulièrement dans l'alimentation, le vêtement – où la pression de la crise et de la concurrence exige des horaires de plus en plus longs.

Like many connectors, this one is used as much in speech as in writing. The following quotation comes from remarks reportedly made by a Muslim fundamentalist speaking in favour of international terrorism:

> « Ce n'est pas compliqué de tuer des Américains ou des Français, » a-t-il ajouté benoîtement, « il y en a tellement partout dans le monde ! Par contre, c'est un peu plus difficile de tuer des Israéliens. »

Often followed by a comma, the connector usually stands first in the sentence or even the paragraph. It can be placed elsewhere, as in this extract from a discussion of the scandal of the *collier de la reine* in 1785: *La responsabilité factuelle de Louis XVI et de Marie-Antoinette n'était pas engagée, celle des mœurs du système, par contre, l'était.*

English equivalents include 'but', 'however', 'on the other hand' and 'against that'.

par exemple

This connector is so close in function to English 'for example' or 'for instance' that it requires no special mention. However, it is only one among a group of various ways of saying the same thing; and the others, being perhaps less visible, do deserve a mention.

à titre d'exemple

This is no doubt the most common of the variants. It is frequently used with a *transition mécanique* in the first person plural:

> Ce qui a caractérisé plusieurs des premiers Nouveaux Romans, c'est une construction agressive. À titre d'exemple, observons trois de ces mécaniques.

It is used with variable syntax and punctuation, for example, as a verb-less apposition, as in this extract from a depreciative judgment on the poetry of Apollinaire:

> C'est le triomphe absolu du style subjectif. À titre d'exemple, ce passage d'*Alcools*, où l'on voit quel abîme sépare le verlainisme ou le mallarmisme de ce style qui n'est que débraillé ou sans contours.

It is used in the sequence *À titre d'exemple, on peut citer...* It is used in the plural (*Voici, à titre d'exemples...*) and it can be followed by a colon, as in this excerpt from an essay on the relationships between individuals and the society they belong to:

> Les individus exceptionnels expriment *mieux* et d'une manière plus précise la conscience collective que les autres membres du groupe et, par conséquent, il faut entièrement renverser la manière traditionnelle des historiens de poser le problème des rapports entre l'individu et la société. À titre d'exemple : on s'est souvent demandé dans quelle mesure Pascal était ou n'était pas janséniste.

A variant of this structure is *à titre d'illustration*, as used in this discussion of whether moonlighting is a greater social evil than corruption among local politicians:

> La question de la lutte contre le travail au noir en appelle une autre, préa-lable : celle de sa nocivité. Sur ce point, la réponse peut varier selon que l'on occupe le point de vue de la morale, du droit ou de l'économie. À titre d'il-lustration, prenons l'exemple de fausses factures qui permettent de construire une piscine privée dans le jardin d'un élu municipal.

exemple

The word *exemple* is quite often used unaccompanied. On this usage, perhaps more familiar in tone than *par exemple*, the new Robert dictio-nary says: *En fin de phrase, on emploie parfois* exemple(s) *dans le même sens que* par exemple. (Robert, 1986: IV, 279) If this is a rule, it seems to be more often breached than observed. This variant is certainly used; but it is usually placed at the beginning of sentences, not near the end.

It is used with and without an article, in the singular and in the plural, sometimes with a question mark:

> Un pays de taille modeste comme l'Irak peut produire des effets de terreur inimaginables dans le passé, grâce à la combinaison des techniques les plus modernes et des procédés les plus frustes ou les plus cyniques. Exemples : le terrorisme, la pollution généralisée, la dissémination de déchets nucléaires.

> Vénus, planète coquette, garde ses secrets. Mais les chercheurs, obstinés, ne perdent pas espoir. Le coup de théâtre, l'indice inattendu, est toujours possible. Un exemple ? Les dernières mesures de Pioneer montrent la présence de beaucoup de méthane dans l'atmosphère vénusienne. C'est extrêmement inattendu et tout à fait curieux.

And there are other possibilities with the word *exemple*, some of which also combine with a ***question*** or a *transition mécanique*: *Faut-il un exemple ? / En voici un exemple... / Jugeons-en par quelques exemples. / Les exemples abondent. / Citons par exemple le cas de... / Prenons l'exemple de... / Donnons un exemple de nos méthodes. / Supposons par exemple que... / L'on peut en tenir pour exemple l'entrefilet anonyme paru dans....*

Combinations

At times, the basic structure *par exemple* is combined with another which sometimes replaces it, such as ***ainsi***: *C'est ainsi par exemple que...*; or ***c'est le cas de***: *il arrive que l'intérêt historique d'un mot tienne à son flou même (n'est-ce pas le cas, par exemple, du mot « romantisme » ?)* (Backès, 25).

Others

There are other ways of introducing an example. They include *nommément*, *notamment*, ***voyez*** and ***soit***. There is ***en l'occurrence***, which some writers use in a way close to the usual function of this structure. There is also *témoin*, as in this extract from an article on an alleged increase of random violence:

> On vole peut-être légèrement moins, mais on agresse davantage, le plus souvent gratuitement. On détruit pour détruire. On casse. On défonce. Les vitrines, les voitures, le mobilier urbain, mais aussi les gens. Témoin cette agression dont fut victime il y a quelques jours un jeune étudiant, sur le boulevard Montparnasse à Paris, en plein après-midi. Témoin encore ce crime récemment perpétré dans l'enceinte du métro.

peut-être *

As a connector, this structure is one of the set of concessives which also contains **certes**, **bien sûr** and **sans doute**. This one differs slightly from most of the others in their first role, that of expressing some measure of agreement with a preceding proposition, since, literally, it expresses less than agreement. Rather like **admettons**, it expresses provisional acceptance of a point for the argument's sake. That difference aside, it too can serve to stitch together three propositions: an initial affirmation; a second point, introduced by the concessive, raising a restriction of the first or an argument against it; and a third, often introduced by an objector such as **mais**, which largely confirms the force of the first point. The first example shows this tripartite sequence, in a discussion of the report of a French Constitutional Commission which had been set up to examine and recommend on the functioning of the Fifth Republic, a political system seen by many as *un régime hybride, mi-parlementaire mi-présidentiel*:

> Le comité prétend ne pas avoir voulu trancher ce nœud gordien. Peut-être, mais sa principale novation – l'obligation d'un vote de confiance pour tout nouveau gouvernement – pourrait bien avoir ce résultat.

In that sentence it is clear that the connector could be replaced by *sans doute*. Again like the other concessives, this one can constitute in itself a whole sentence:

> L'accord secret signé dimanche 29 décembre à Téhéran par M. François Scheer, secrétaire général du Quai d'Orsay, devrait permettre aux entreprises françaises, estime-t-on en haut lieu, de revenir en force sur le marché iranien. Peut-être. Mais à deux conditions, qui sont encore loin d'être remplies.

At times it is combined with another concessive, such as *il est vrai (que)* in this extract from an ironic discussion about the survival of French Communists after the death of Communism, that is the end of the Soviet bloc and the steep decline in electoral support for the Parti communiste français. The sequence of points is the tripartite sort:

> Au même titre qu'il reste des croyants dans les églises alors que Dieu est réputé mort depuis longtemps, il reste en France des gens qui croient au communisme. Une expérience de soixante-dix ans sur un échantillon planétaire ne les a pas convaincus de ce qui semble relever pour d'autres de l'évidence. L'enterrement, il est vrai, a peut-être été un peu rapide. Comme si tout allait bien partout, le communisme a subitement été proclamé mort. Il a plu des épitaphes, des oraisons funèbres. Pourtant, les communistes français sont toujours là.

This connector can replace the *si d'opposition* or the *avoir beau* construction to make an antithetical sentence of which the second part is shaped by *n'en... pas moins*. This example compares the two major components of the French upper house (the RPR and the UDF) after the general election of 1993:

> Le RPR est peut-être le groupe le plus puissant au Sénat avec plus de quatre-vingt-dix élus – même s'il n'a pas progressé à l'occasion de ce dernier renouvellement, – il n'en demeure pas moins minoritaire face à l'UDF, émiettée au Sénat en trois groupes.

The opening statement about the RPR is no more hypothetical than it would be if made in English with 'The RPR may be ...'.

phrase dépendante *

The meaning of a sentence is usually related to what precedes. But the grammar and structure of a sentence are not usually related in such a way to what precedes. Many writers of French discursive prose make sentences which depend for all three, meaning, grammar and structure, on the sentence before. These sentences often seem to be little more than typographical artifices, in which the expectable punctuation, a comma or a colon, has been replaced by a full stop. By isolating a statement, they may make a dramatic point or try for a rhythm which is staccato rather than legato. One of the important features of such a sentence is that, being complementary to the sentence preceding, it contains no main verb of its own. Another is that, because it is dependent, its opening words have a strong connective function. Some of the structures most commonly used in that way are illustrated here.

Noun in apposition

This structure introduces a statement which qualifies what precedes. Sometimes the noun is accompanied by its article:

> Les capitaux français investis à l'étranger sont passés de 20 milliards de francs en 1985 à 107 milliards l'an passé. Un boom qui traduit les ambitions nouvelles des grands groupes et parfois de plus petits, sur des marchés devenus mondiaux.

However, often the noun in apposition is used without the article:

> Un communiqué de la présidence a précisé que le gouvernement déciderait de « ses actions futures en fonction du déroulement de la réunion ». Phrase lourde de sous-entendus.

Adjectives

Detached adjectives are used in somewhat similar ways. The first example describes an election at which rural constituencies voted strongly against the government: *La première leçon de ce scrutin, c'est la sécession de la France rurale. Massive. Évidente. / Matra Communication doit au total, pour rester dans la course, mobiliser 1 milliard de francs par an. Difficilement tenable pour cette structure.*

Pronouns

A range of relative pronoun structures is also used, such as *dont, que* and *lesquelles* in this extract from an article about Dutch research on greenhouses:

La Hollande développe actuellement d'extraordinaires programmes de recherche tendant à améliorer l'efficacité des serres. Des serres dont on élève le plafond pour permettre aux plantes de mieux respirer. Dont on améliore l'architecture, pour augmenter toujours davantage la transparence en minimisant les structures. Que l'on éclaire la nuit avec des lampes spéciales riches en ultraviolets. Pour lesquelles on met au point des laveuses de vitres automatiques.

Other structures with *que*

As well as the relative *que*, other modes of *que* or structures based on *que* are common in this function:

La Russie n'évitera l'hyperinflation qu'à trois conditions. Que le chemin vers la liberté complète des prix soit poursuivi. Que les autres réformes de structure qu'impose le passage au marché (fin des situations de monopole, développement de la propriété privée, création d'un système bancaire et financier) soient engagées simultanément. Qu'une stricte rigueur budgétaire et monétaire soit assurée.

Many other constructions incorporating *que* are used in this way. They include **à ceci près que**, *ainsi que*, **alors que**, *à moins que*, **au point que**, **d'autant que**, *de même que*, *encore que*, **ne serait-ce que**, **parce que**, *puisque*, *sauf que*, **si bien que**. The same goes, of course, for *ce que* and *ce qui*. Many of such structures are, of course, adverbial.

Other adverbial structures

Many different sorts of adverbial complements are structured in the same way:

Il s'était présenté bien sagement, à l'heure et au jour dits, devant le juge qui l'avait convoqué, en compagnie de son avocat, Mᶜ Pierre Jacquet. Avec la ferme volonté de se confesser.

Le président de la société, M. Jean-Luc Lagardère, l'a affirmé devant la presse jeudi 2 juillet. Avant de reconnaître le poids « relativement faible » de sa société. À juste titre.

Repeated preposition

The repeated structural preposition, often *à* or *de*, is another very frequent way of linking consecutive sentences. The first of the following examples was spoken by a Muslim fundamentalist:

> Si mon père et ses frères ont expulsé physiquement la France oppresseur de l'Algérie, moi je me consacre avec mes frères, avec les armes de la foi, à la bannir intellectuellement et idéologiquement. À en finir avec ses partisans qui en ont tété le lait vénéneux.

> On l'a accusé d'avoir sous-estimé l'événement. D'avoir mené un combat d'arrière-garde. D'avoir perdu pied.

> Soupçonné d'indécision depuis ses premiers flottements au début de la crise des pays de l'Est, le président Bush vient de passer aux actes. Et de frapper fort, comme l'indique l'envoi de plusieurs milliers d'hommes, de plusieurs centaines d'avions et de plusieurs dizaines de navires dans la zone du Golfe.

Initial *et*

Verbless sentences beginning with different types of *et* are common. There is the *infinitif de narration* introduced by *et de* in which the infinitive can have a different subject from the verb in the sentence preceding. There is *et ce*: *Tout le monde avait échoué. Et cela pour des raisons diverses.* There are also, of course, variants of the same structure without *et*, as in this example about Eugène Fromentin, the nineteenth-century painter-cum-writer, one of whose characters, in his novel *Dominique*, was based on a girl he had loved:

> Fromentin, sans plus d'espoir, continua d'aimer jeune femme celle qu'il avait aimée jeune fille. Cela, dans la vie comme dans le roman.

The verbless sentence with initial *et* is also used at the beginning of paragraphs. An account of a retrospective exhibition of paintings by Miró finishes one paragraph with a dependent sentence and begins the following one with another:

> Une centaine de tableaux dont beaucoup n'étaient pas sortis de leurs collections depuis longtemps. Des choses des années 20, de cette période cruciale au cours de laquelle le peintre se débarrasse de la terre qui lui colle aux semelles, se déleste du poids des formes que le cubisme ou le réalisme lui ont soufflées, fait le vide, découvre d'un pied léger le terrain de ses rêves.
>
> Et beaucoup de choses des années 30, quand le peintre, capable de broyer plus de noir qu'on ne l'imagine, se laisse gagner par une armada de monstres terrifiants, d'une laideur obscène et cruelle, à la Jarry. Un passage de l'œuvre peu connu.

Series of such sentences

As can be seen from some of the examples, some writers do not use just one of these sentences; they use them to make whole *sequences of points*. An article about the hotels of Vichy where the different ministries were housed during the German Occupation has ten consecutive sentences made on the model of *Au Carlton, les finances et la justice. Au Plaza, l'éducation nationale. Au superbe Aletti, la défense nationale.* Sometimes the structures in these sequences are identical with each other, as in that example or in the next, where the structure repeated is the future tense of the verbs:

> La « concentration républicaine » des opportunistes et des radicaux modérés a gagné les élections de 1889, elle gagnera celles de 1893. Signera l'alliance avec la Russie. Protégera l'agriculture par une solide barrière douanière à l'instigation de Jules Méline. Et sollicitera à bon escient le gros bas de laine des Français.

In the next one, the repetition is made by *en* with a present participle. The extract is from an article dealing with precautions to be taken by France against the risk that the Treaty of Maastricht will create bureaucratic structures unmindful of social justice or the needs and aspirations of Eastern Europe and the Third World:

> La France se doit de combattre ce risque. En veillant à la vitalité de la démocratie locale. En limitant à l'essentiel les directives communautaires. En luttant pour une distribution équitable de la « qualité » de la vie au sein de la Communauté. En contribuant à la mise au point de nouvelles formes de coopération avec l'Europe centrale et orientale. En veillant au développement des relations avec l'Afrique et le monde arabe.

Sometimes there is no similarity in the structures. The first example comes from a sardonic gossipy piece about power-sharing between President Mitterrand (a Socialist) and his last Prime Minister, Édouard Balladur, especially in the field of foreign policy, a power supposedly restricted by the constitution to the President but in which Balladur had just announced a personal initiative:

> Il ne reste plus à l'Élysée qu'à se féliciter avec un sourire contraint de cette initiative. Douloureuse modestie. Pas drôle non plus pour le président de voir son Premier ministre rendre visite, seul, à Helmut Kohl et en obtenir une baisse des taux d'intérêt allemands. Baisse que son « ami Helmut » n'avait jamais accordé à Pierre Bérégovoy. *O tempora, o mores...*
>
> Et tout cela dans la plus parfaite urbanité entre deux hommes dont l'un pense que l'autre n'est qu'un représentant (talentueux) des grands intérêts financiers, et l'autre que l'un n'est qu'un aventurier (surdoué) de la politique.

The subject of the next example is Pierre de Fermat, the seventeenth-century mathematician, and in particular his Last Theorem which until the 1990s no mathematician could demonstrate, much to the chagrin of all those who attempted it:

> Rien ne pouvait être plus agaçant pour les mathématiciens qui eurent à lire ce texte. D'autant que, tout magistrat qu'il fut, Pierre de Fermat était sans doute l'un des plus grands mathématiciens de son temps. Au même titre que Descartes, dont les travaux en géométrie firent la renommée. Fermat fut partout. Avec bonheur. En géométrie comme en théorie des nombres. Dans le calcul infinitésimal comme dans le calcul intégral [...]

Sometimes the sentences may be in the form of verbless questions, as in this extract from a discussion of the division of powers within the European Commission between those which belong to member-states and those which belong to the Commission:

> Mais qui décidera de ce qui est du ressort de l'État-nation ou de celui de la Commission ? Selon quels critères ? En vertu de quels principes ? Mystère.

pis *

Just as *mieux* can be seen as a specialized form of *de plus*, introducing an additional proposition that is presented favourably, so this adverb, its opposite, is used to introduce an additional adverse point or one that the writer presents unfavourably. It has several different modes.

Unaccompanied *pis*

This is the most frequently used mode, usually placed first in the sentence or paragraph. Thus, a writer dealing with aspects of unemployment in the French work-force comes to speak of long-term unemployment, on which he has two adverse points to make, the second of which he presents with this connector:

> Un tiers de ces chômeurs de longue durée sont inscrits depuis plus d'un an, soit près de 915 000, en augmentation de 16,2 % sur mai 1991. Pis, la durée moyenne de chômage s'établit désormais à 390 jours, c'est-à-dire à 8 de plus que l'année dernière.

Similarly, the author of an article on economic aspects of French biomedical technology sees two drawbacks in it, the second of which is seen as worse than the first:

> Efficace lors des grandes catastrophes, utile dans les opérations des organisations humanitaires, testée lors des exploits sportifs comme le dernier Paris-Dakar, la technologie biomédicale française ne se vend pourtant pas bien. Pis : elle achète beaucoup ailleurs.

This mode is quite commonly used in tandem with **même**: *pis même*.

As can be seen from the examples, the punctuation varies. The comma following is the most common. Positions other than first in the sentence are not unknown, too, as in the following combination with *ou*, taken from a discussion of overt political influence on broadcasters in the days of the state-owned ORTF:

> Le ministre de l'Information n'avait qu'à décrocher son combiné pour modifier, supprimer ou – pis – imposer un sujet au journal télévisé.

The similarity between this combination and **voire** is obvious.

qui pis est

The monosyllabic mode is presumably a vestige of one or other of two longer structures: *qui pis est* and *il y a pis*. The *Grand Larousse de la langue française* (1976) certainly sees it as an ellipsis of *qui pis est*. The latter, a visible analogue to *qui plus est* and *qui mieux est*, was still used by writers of the first generation of the twentieth century: *elle a mené une vie de débauches, épousé un forçat ou, qui pis est, un homme divorcé* (Proust, II, 152); *je ne sens en elle, à mon égard, qu'incompréhension, méjugement ou, qui pis est, indifférence* (Gide, 1954: 1151). Nowadays, like *qui mieux est* but unlike *qui plus est*, it appears to be in the process of becoming extinct. This is an impression which it is difficult to test in the major contemporary dictionaries: the entries in most of them allow the inference that *qui pis est* is alive and well in current French. The only one of them to hint in any way that this structure is anything other than extant is *Trésor de la langue française*, which gives it as *Vieilli ou littér.* As far as one can judge from the practice of contemporary writers, *qui pis est* is close to non-existent. It may (or may not) have been survived by several other variants which once coexisted with it: *et pis que cela, ce qui est pis, ce qui est pis encore.*

il y a pis

This mode is still used, usually preceded by **mais** or one of its variants such as *toutefois*. This makes it an analogue of modes of *de plus* such as *mais il y a plus* or *et ce n'est pas tout*. In the following example, a writer discussing 'morphing', a technique used in making video-clips, has two points to make about the totally synthetic nature of all the ingredients used in these productions, the second of which is introduced by this mode:

> La mise en lumière, les raccords, les maquillages... tout est artificiel. Le corps devient une sorte de pâte à modeler avec laquelle tout est permis. Rappelez-vous le spot Perrier de Jean-Paul Goude : une créature de rêve marche à quatre pattes dans la savane et tombe nez à nez avec un lion qui rugit. Elle rugit à

son tour et, grâce au *morphing*, sa bouche s'agrandit autant que la gueule du lion. Mais il y a pis : il arrive que les différentes parties d'un corps n'appartiennent pas à la même personne.

plus grave

This mode can be seen, like *il y a pis*, as another analogue of *il y a plus*. Sometimes combined with **encore**, it is used either in the form of the detached adjective *plus grave* or as a main clause *il y a plus grave*. Combined with *mais*, the latter sometimes makes a separate sentence. An article on scientology discusses some ways in which some scientologists allegedly respond to sceptical investigations of their activities:

> Un mois plus tard, les scientologues manifestent devant les portes de l'ADFI. À l'intérieur, mêlés aux congressistes, trois d'entre eux tentent d'enregistrer les travaux. Ils sont rapidement repérés.
> Plus grave : une journaliste se voit harcelée téléphoniquement à la même époque pour avoir dénoncé les cours de rattrapage et les écoles privées derrière lesquels se cache l'Église.

pis encore

The *encore* is clearly augmentative; and some writers reserve this mode for a point preceded by one introduced with *pis*. For others, this mode functions much like the others, introducing a second adverse circumstance. This example comes from an article on false marriages of Muslim women arranged by confidence men with the connivance of an imam:

> Ils n'ont jamais revu l'imam. Djaouida Jazaerli, avocate, qui se bat depuis plusieurs années contre ces pratiques, est formelle : « Lui et ses semblables se mettent hors la loi et risquent deux ans de prison. Mais le plus odieux à mes yeux de musulmane, c'est l'utilisation de l'islam à des fins de pur cynisme. » Pis encore, selon Dalil Boubakeur, recteur de la Mosquée de Paris, « même en droit musulman ces mariages ne sont pas valables ! »

pire

Unlike *pis*, which is usually an adverb, this is usually an adjective. Both words are so seldom used nowadays and restricted to such special structures that there is less than unanimity about their different functions. Robert says: *Pis tend à disparaître de la langue usuelle au profit de pire* (Robert, 1986: V, 217). Some speakers use the adjectival form in adverbial functions, despite the disapproval of normative commentators:

> Il faut noter que *pire* ne peut, en français correct, être adverbe. [...] Ces exemples témoignent certes d'une évolution, mais ne sont pas encore à imiter.
> (Hanse, 1983: 721)

Despite this, some writers use *pire* as a connector. Like *pis*, it is used unaccompanied and in forms like *pire encore* (Alain, 1956: 365; July, 65), *Il y a pire* and *Mais il y a pire*. A comment on Giscard d'Estaing's attempt in the early 1990s to unite the UDF and the RPR in a single opposition grouping called the RUR says this:

> Ce projet Giscard ne semble guère jugé, cette fois encore, plus réaliste que le précédent. Pire, au RPR comme à l'UDF, ce RUR fait déjà rire.

An academic essay on the diarist Amiel speaks of his attitudes to consciousness in relation to death:

> Une de ses comparaisons favorites est celle qu'il fait entre lui-même et Charles-Quint « entrant doucement dans le cercueil de son vivant ». Pire encore, comme Poe, Amiel s'imagine volontiers sous la forme effrayante d'un mort vivant, d'un être qui, même après sa mort, continue de vivre par le seul truchement de la conscience.
>
> (Poulet, 1977: 82)

And a critic, using a combination replaceable by *voire*, speaks of *des discours dont la signification et l'énonciation sont toujours problématiques, pire même : impossibles*.

English equivalents, other than those which serve for *de plus* ('also', 'furthermore', 'not only ... but also', 'in addition', 'as well as that', 'what's more'), might be 'worse' or 'worse still'.

plutôt *

Though Robert, Brunot and Grevisse discuss different usages of this word, they do not clearly define one of its two main expository functions. The *Trésor de la langue française* gives a partial account of the latter. The fact is that as a connector it can make two different types of relation between statements: either adversative or alternative.

Adversative *plutôt*

In adversative contexts, this connector functions like one of the rectifying modes of *au contraire*. That is, it is often used after a negative statement: first, the negative says what is not the case; then, introduced by the connector, the writer states what is the case. In the first example, a political journalist discusses the reasons why modern Sweden has had so many governments of the Left:

> Si plus de 40 % des Suédois votaient habituellement social-démocrate depuis un bon demi-siècle, ce n'est pas parce qu'ils étaient « socialistes ». C'était plutôt parce qu'ils faisaient confiance à un parti pragmatique, garant de la stabilité,

qui gérait bien les affaires et savait donner un coup de volant à droite ou à gauche selon l'état de l'économie et du débat d'idées.

Again like *au contraire*, but also like *en revanche* or *par contre*, this mode can structure an adversative link between statements in which, instead of a negative, there is only a strong contrast. It can do this in two separate sentences, as in this example taken from a discussion of two dominant French models of relations between the family and the wider society:

> Dans un cas les conjoints se jettent dans le mouvement général, s'y investissent directement et à travers leurs enfants, et tentent d'avoir d'eux-mêmes une image sociale rassurante. Les autres se replient plutôt sur le ménage pour y trouver des gratifications que la société ne pourrait jamais leur accorder.
>
> (Roussel, 58)

Alternatively, it can make the contrast within a single sentence, as in this shapely antithesis taken from a discussion of Europeans' and Americans' divergent attitudes towards divorce:

> Là où l'Européen voit surtout une rupture créant un désordre social, et la perte d'un capital de souvenirs et d'expériences communes, l'Américain a plutôt l'impression qu'il met de l'ordre dans sa vie et qu'il s'ouvre un nouvel avenir.
>
> (Rougemont, 1962: 247)

Also like *au contraire*, sometimes the opposition is reinforced by *bien*, as in this extract from a discussion of the increasing readership attracted to works of fictionalized history and biography:

> Il n'est pas vraisemblable que le désir de s'instruire joue un grand rôle dans cet engouement. Il s'agit bien plutôt de la contagion de la curiosité romanesque à des domaines qui semblaient devoir en rester préservés.
>
> (Caillois, 161)

In some of these contexts, the connector could be replaced by *en fait* or *en réalité*.

Alternative *plutôt*

Usually combined with *ou*, this mode is used like the substitutive mode of *si l'on veut* or *mieux* – *Ça me chatouille, ou plutôt, ça me gratouille* (Romains, 1924: 70) – to introduce a better definition of a point or just a word that seems apter:

> La cuisine française des années 50 remettait ses pieds dans les traces, ou plutôt ses mains dans les casseroles, de jadis.
>
> (Ferniot, 1995b: 102)

Instead of the combination with *ou*, a writer may use a *transition mécanique*, as in this extract from an essay on the common *héritage idéologique* of the Parti communiste français and the Parti socialiste:

Il ne tient pas seulement au tronc commun originaire : le socialisme du XIXe siècle. Disons plutôt que le terme de « tronc commun » est impropre.

(Morin, 1984: 30)

When unaccompanied by *ou*, the connector is usually placed after the wording that it affects. A page of Proust, describing the pregnant skivvy dubbed by Swann *la Charité de Giotto*, provides an example of both forms:

la pauvre fille, engraissée par sa grossesse jusqu'à la figure, jusqu'aux joues qui tombaient droites et carrées, ressemblait en effet assez à ces vierges fortes et hommasses, matrones plutôt, dans lesquelles les vertus sont personnifiées à l'Arena. [...] Par une belle invention du peintre elle foule aux pieds les trésors de la terre, mais absolument comme si elle piétinait des raisins pour en extraire le jus ou plutôt comme elle aurait monté sur des sacs pour se hausser [...]

(Proust, I, 81)

Among English equivalents for the adversative mode are 'in fact', 'instead' and 'really'; and for the alternative mode, 'or rather', 'to be precise'.

points de suspension

Like the **deux-points**, a mode of this punctuation mark functions as a connector. Writers of French use it in two different ways, only one of which is normally used in written English. In French, it is placed either at the end of the sentence or inside the sentence. It is only the latter that can be considered as a connector.

In final position

Even this non-connective mode is more used in French than in English. It often leaves a statement incomplete, inviting the reader to fill in what is unexpressed; and even at the end of a complete sentence, the writer may use it to suggest what Grevisse calls *une sorte de prolongement inexprimé de la pensée*, as in the fine example which he quotes from Gide: *C'est à partir de Khartoum que je voudrais remonter le Nil...* (Grevisse, 1964a: 1118).

Inside the sentence: expecting the unexpected

The main function of this connective mode is to make the reader expect something unexpected. With it, a writer hints a brief comment on what follows, introduces a small paradox, invites the reader to see a slightly surprising aspect of the statement made. Words like *paradoxe* and *surprise* are not uncommon in the immediate context; and the point being made may be further signalled by an exclamation mark, as in this comment on a recital by a cellist:

> Après l'entracte, quelle surprise ! Le programme nous promettait la *Première Sonate en mi mineur* op. 38, de Brahms, et Yo Yo Ma attaque la *Troisième Sonate en ré mineur*, op. 108... pour violon !

The writer is drawing attention to the fact that a work for violin was played on a cello. Although points discussed in a serious tone may be signalled in this way, it is more usually done with an apparently whimsical intent: *Dans l'état actuel des connaissances, la prévision des climats reste... dans les nuages. / Ainsi la question de la liste centriste est-elle au... centre de tous les scénarios et des discours.* Like a comedian telegraphing a joke, it says 'Wait for it' – and thereby risks spoiling the comic effect. Its justification may be that, if it was not used, a reader might think the writer's bathos was unintended, rather than intended. The old Grevisse mentioned this usage (Grevisse, 1964a: 1118); the new omits it. Jacques Drillon draws attention to the rather corny humour which sometimes informs the practice: *Il s'agit là d'un « truc » assez facile, reposant sur une convention plus que sur une réalité littéraire* (Drillon, 408). Despite which, there is a lot of it about. Most of it is to be found in journalism; but it is not absent from publications of more durable interest.

Inside the sentence: the pun

Sometimes the punctuation accompanies, and as it were tries to excuse, a feeble play on words. In a discussion of the continuing prevalence of duelling among military officers in Restoration France, a historian says: *On règle ses comptes entre soi, sur-le-champ, ou plutôt... sur le pré* (Chesnais, 126). In a history of the restaurant business at about the same period, another writer, professing not to be punning, says: *En quelques années, de la prise de la Bastille à la... Restauration, sans jeu de mots, un bouleversement s'est produit.* A description of the universal exhibition of 1889 introduces a mention of the Eiffel Tower in these terms: *Le clou en sera... un clou d'acier : une tour métallique de trois cents mètres de haut.* In such contexts, the connector could be replaced by *si l'on ose dire*, as in this comment on the author of a book about the dancer Loie Fuller and her use of light on stage:

> C'est tout le mérite de ce spécialiste des avant-gardes que d'avoir mis en lumière – si l'on ose dire – la portée historique et l'impact artistique des danses de Loïe Fuller.

Inside the sentence: the paradox

In a slightly different way, the punctuation comments on what is seen as a contradictory or paradoxical feature of the point under discussion, as in this example, taken from an article about people who do not use condoms despite being informed about the protection they afford against HIV:

> Voilà des gens bien informés, qui ont peur du sida (69 % redoutent personnellement cette maladie), qui savent que le préservatif est un moyen de protection (83 % le citent spontanément) et qui, en majorité..., ne s'en servent pas.

> Döbritz, qui dessine pour *le Figaro*, *la Croix* et *Témoignage chrétien*, a été encouragé par le prix de « jeune talent » qui lui a été décerné à... trente-trois ans.

Inside the sentence: the preposterous

It can also introduce and act as a comment on something seen as exorbitant, a figure, an amount, a preposterous word. It thrives in astronomical contexts among others: *Le satellite Phobos s'écrasera un jour sur Mars, mais dans... trente millions d'années. / Cet objet céleste, nommé 1989PB, s'est approché vers 5 heures (heure française) à... quatre millions de kilomètres de la Terre. / Le « magic acid » est connu des chimistes comme le... pentafluorure de fluorohydrogénoantimoine. / Ainsi, ce qui, au chapitre quatre, sera nommé transits analogiques relèverait, à en croire les texticiens, de la catégorie des... parachorodicranotextures isologiques.*

Inside the sentence: the hesitation

A writer sometimes punctuates in this way to hint a doubt or an uncertainty, as in this statement by a drama critic a century ago wishing to compare Shakespeare to some writers of his own day:

> [...] un trait de ressemblance entre Shakespeare et... dirai-je les *symbolistes* ou les *décadents* ? Je le dirais si je ne craignais d'être mal compris.
>
> (Brunetière, 220)

In earlier positions

As most of the examples show, this punctuation is most often used just before the final element of the sentence. On occasion it is placed much earlier, as in this extract from an article about the great number of MPs wishing to speak on an item of business before the parliament of the then USSR:

> A quinze bonnes minutes par orateur, cela devrait faire... plusieurs semaines encore de débats car des centaines d'autres députés souhaiteront intervenir quand le président du conseil des ministres sortant, M. Ryjkov, demandera la

confiance et qu'il faut, surtout, à cette première session du nouveau Parlement soviétique, compter avec l'inattendu.

English usage

In either mode, this punctuation is unusual nowadays in English. English usage is to place it, if at all, at the end of the sentence. Even among readers and writers, there is hardly a recognized name for it: dictionaries and style manuals give 'points of suspension', 'dots', 'French dots', 'suspension dots', 'suspension periods', 'suspension points', 'three points'. Most people say 'three dots'. The connective mode is a good example of the *charnière zéro*: the structure making a relationship between French statements which has no English equivalent. In English, a writer may occasionally telegraph a point by preceding it by a dash. It is very rare to find a writer using this French practice in English, as in this example from a description of Samuel Beckett's reluctance to lend himself to Parisian social gatherings, lecture tours and interviews:

> Beckett, quite unaffectedly, had no truck with any of this, neither in self-advertisement nor in participating in occasions which reinforce status... and increase sales.
>
> (Lennon, 215)

It is worth noting that the writer from whose book that quotation comes spent a decade living and writing in France.

Points of omission

A form of this punctuation known as 'points of omission' is used in English to denote words deleted from quotations. This could not be done in French without ambiguity, as the dots already serving the connective function could not clearly serve another one at such variance from it. In French prose, omissions are signalled by dots inside square brackets, thus: [...].

pour autant *

This adversative structure has three main modes: placed first in the sentence (and usually affirmative); in negative constructions; and in interrogative constructions. In all three, it is anaphoric in its functioning: it never introduces the first but only the second of two related ideas. Meaning 'all that', *autant* refers to the idea immediately preceding, against which the second idea is contrasted. It is often combined with **mais**. The meaning of the structure, depending on its context and on which of the modes is used, can be roughly 'despite that' or 'because of that' or 'even allowing for what has just been said'. A close English equivalent in many contexts is the concessive 'for all that' which Burns uses in 'A man's a man for a' that'. In some of its functions, it is a variant of *pourtant*, which once had the same meaning and was two words, as this structure is now.

Affirmative, first in the sentence

The new Grevisse says, erroneously, of this structure: *ne s'emploie que dans des contextes négatifs* (Grevisse, 1988: 1499). But the structure is frequent nowadays in affirmative statements, most of which are placed first in the sentence.

This mode introduces either an objection to a favourable state of affairs or an advantage that partially countervails a disadvantage; it could usually be replaced by *néanmoins* or *malgré cela*. It links the two ideas in an 'even so' or 'although' sort of relationship. It is normally followed by a comma; it is frequently placed at the beginning of a paragraph. The first of these examples deals with the Nazi concentration camp of Buchenwald at a time when it was becoming clear that Germany was losing the war:

> Dans ce camp, comme dans les autres, on savait que la puissance nazie avait déjà essuyé des revers. La reddition de von Paulus à Stalingrad, les difficultés éprouvées par Rommel en Cyrénaïque, quelques autres piétinements significatifs avaient chaque fois apporté un peu d'espoir à ce peuple de matricules.
>
> Pour autant, de nouveaux « convois » amenaient toujours des quatre côins de l'Europe occupée leurs cargaisons de bétail humain.

The second is an extract from an article on the fortunes of Oliver North, a former officer in the US Army who, having been implicated in allegedly illegal arms-trading under the presidency of Reagan, was selected as a Republican candidate for election to Congress:

> Il empoche 25 000 dollars chaque fois qu'il donne une conférence. Et il est très demandé, car il demeure le héros de la droite américaine. Sa renommée remplit les salles, et le courant passe.
>
> Pour autant, Oliver North demeure un candidat encombrant, même pour son propre parti.

Even in this position, the connector can combine with a negative structure or else it can combine with a statement which, though grammatically affirmative, has a negative polarity, as in this extract from a discussion of writers whose names contains the particle of nobility *de*:

> L'Académie française compte toujours dans ses rangs d'authentiques aristocrates, tels le comte Jacques de Bourbon-Busset ou Jean d'Ormesson, dont l'anoblissement remonte au XVIe siècle.
>
> Pour autant, tous les écrivains à particule sont loin de pouvoir prétendre aux quartiers de noblesse que leur nom laisse imaginer.

Other affirmatives restricting or partially negating a preceding statement of apparent success or partial agreement are: *Pour autant, ce serait peut-être aller un peu vite en besogne. / Pour autant, il serait absurde de crier victoire. / Pour autant, les désaccords subsistent. / Pour autant, de réelles divergences sont apparues.*

On occasion, the connector with an affirmative statement is placed not first but beside the verb. This example comes from an article about an inventor of the ball-point pen:

> Aristocrate égaré dans l'industrie, mais la pratiquant avec un sérieux et un flair certains, le baron Bich se tient pour autant à l'écart de l'establishment des affaires.

In negative statements

In this mode, the most frequent, the structure also sets two ideas in an 'even so' or 'although' relationship. It may occupy different positions in the sentence, being placed most usually after the word of negation: *C'est en alexandrins, mais ce n'est pas pour autant d'un goût noble et relevé.* It can also be placed at the end, as in this sentence about an aspect of Nazi medicine surviving after the war in other parts of the world:

> Après les atrocités et les perversions du régime hitlérien (plusieurs centaines de milliers de personnes furent stérilisées pour « purifier la race »), ces pratiques ne furent pas abandonnées pour autant.

This mode quite often introduces the second element in a binary statement of which the first is structured with the *si d'opposition*. This makes for a very forceful and pointed contrast. An example comes from a discussion of the anomalous constitutional relations between Puerto Rico and the USA:

> Ce qui signifie en gros pour les quelque trois millions et demi de Portoricains que, si les liens de dépendance économique restent très forts, ils ne sont pas assortis pour autant d'une représentation politique pleine et entière.

A variant of this negative mode is the structure *Ce n'est pas pour autant que*. In the following example, taken from a spoken interview, the subject is President Mitterrand and his relations with women:

> Il n'aime rien tant que faire parler les femmes qu'il rencontre, ses amies de cœur comme son entourage féminin. Ça n'est pas pour autant qu'il estime décisif de les faire participer à la vie politique.

With *sans*

In many negative statements, the connector combines not with a *ne* construction but with *sans*. These oppositions can be made in two ways:

with *sans* and the infinitive of a verb, as in this extract from the debate on legalization of certain drugs: *Légaliser les drogues risque de provoquer une explosion catastrophique de leur consommation, sans pour autant réduire le trafic.* Or else with *sans que* and a verb in the subjunctive. This example concerns a postman whom the post office deemed to be over-weight:

> M. Victor Garnier s'est montré le premier surpris de l'oukase administratif qui lui enjoint d'avoir à maigrir dans les six mois. Après quoi on le pèsera de nouveau, sans qu'il ait pour autant été précisé, semble-t-il, le poids idéal que l'agent Garnier devrait atteindre.

With superfluous *en*

Some writers combine the negative mode with a superfluous reinforcing pronominal *en*, similar to the one in **n'en... pas moins**. Superfluous, because *en*, by resuming what precedes, says no more than *pour autant* itself. The first example is taken from a historian's discussion of exemptions from military service granted to young men by Breton bishops in the nineteenth century:

> Les évêques bretons dispensaient avec libéralisme des certificats de vocation au sacerdoce : les bénéficiaires de ces faveurs épiscopales échappaient ainsi au service militaire. Ils n'en devenaient pas pour autant serviteurs de Dieu dans tous les cas.
>
> (Le Roy Ladurie, 46)

> Douze ans après la découverte du sida, l'épidémie continue à progresser. En France, les premières vagues ont été freinées : les homosexuels ont appris à se protéger et les toxicomanes à ne plus partager la seringue. Mais le virus n'en a pas disparu pour autant.

A significant number of examples of this usage occur in the second part of binaries begun by the oppositive *pour*, itself commonly used with the *n'en... pas moins* structure: *...une présence militaire qui, pour n'être pas énorme, n'en est pas pour autant négligeable. / Pour être matière à débat, l'idée n'en est pas pour autant scandaleuse. / Les hommes, pour opprimés qu'ils soient, n'en deviennent pas pour autant des choses.* Those who foster this development are roundly taken to task by Hanse and others:

> on prendra garde, quand on surveille son langage, de ne pas employer *pour autant* quand il est tout à fait inutile. [...] C'est une faute de dire et d'écrire : *[Elles n'en cessent pas pour autant de nous étonner]*.
>
> (Hanse, 1983: 128; see also Thérive, 1962: 258)

In interrogative statements

In this mode, one of the commonest combinations is *Faut-il pour autant...?*
It is often placed at the beginning of paragraphs. This example concerns
new gynaecological technologies and the possible terminations of pregnancy which they may lead to:

> Avec les outils dont elle dispose, notre société pratique déjà l'eugénisme.
> Des couples interrompent une grossesse lorsque l'échographie révèle que le fœtus
> a un bec-de-lièvre ou un pied-bot. Faut-il pour autant interdire l'échographie ?

Verbs of saying, *dire, affirmer, soutenir*, are also common: *Peut-on laisser
affirmer pour autant que...?*; *Est-ce qu'on peut dire pour autant que...?*
Like the mode with negative structures, this one is also combined with
concessive *si*:

> Si le système copernicien s'est depuis longtemps réconcilié avec le dogme chré-
> tien, le procès de Galilée est-il pour autant terminé ?

In current English, many of these questions might well be asked in the
form: 'Does this mean that ...?' Other English equivalents, depending on
context, could be 'therefore', 'because of that', 'for that reason' or 'despite
that'.

pour autant and *pour cela*

Controversy once attended this connector. Apart from its newness, two
aspects of it were deplored: the combination with redundant *en*, mentioned
above; and the suggestion that *pour autant* was itself redundant, being an
exact replacement for ***pour cela***:

> On a les oreilles non pas rebattues, mais surbattues de cette formule difficile
> à expliquer. L'expression traditionnelle : *pour cela* (ou *pour cette raison*) peut
> sembler un peu plate, mais elle a le mérite d'être sans prétention.
>
> (Georgin, 1961: 63)

Against this, some pointed out that the structure was, in fact, more precise
than *pour cela*:

> La plupart des dictionnaires le font synonyme de « pour cela ». En fait, il a le
> sens de « uniquement pour cela », qui est important.
>
> (Dupré, III, 2041)

> [*Pour autant*] n'est pas exactement l'équivalent de *Pour cela, pour cette raison*,
> sur lesquels il renchérit.
>
> (Robert, 1953: V, 380)

The fact is, however, that *pour cela*, much used until the early twentieth
century, has nowadays been all but replaced by this connector in negative and interrogative structures.

pour ce faire

This structure, like *et ce* and *ce faisant*, is one of those in which a fossilized pronominal *ce* has the sense of *ceci* or *cela*. A second anomaly in its construction is that, again like *ce faisant*, the object pronoun precedes the verb. In that survival of an older French form, it is analogous in structure to English 'so to do' or 'so to speak'. It offers little difficulty to the English-speaker; its sole function as a connector is evident in its meaning: 'to that end' or 'for that purpose'.

The structure, followed by a comma, is often placed first in the sentence, where it is sometimes preceded by either *et* or *mais*. The first example comes from an essay on a king, the potato and an Apothecary Royal:

> Louis XVI contribue à la popularité de la pomme de terre, aliment de base pour le peuple, destiné à éloigner le spectre de la disette. Mais, pour ce faire, il organise avec Parmentier une cérémonie gastronomique d'anoblissement du tubercule méprisé par les Français : un repas au menu duquel figurent plusieurs plats de pommes de terre.

It can also be placed in the middle, with or without commas, as in the following extract from an article about the village of Jouques (Bouches-du-Rhône), pleasant and unremarkable, and a scheme designed to eliminate unemployment there:

> Par la volonté d'un « jouquard » d'origine, dont l'un des ancêtres fut le maire de la commune et lui dédia une fontaine, Jouques va peut-être, pourtant, sortir de cet anonymat plaisant. Christian Ménard, en effet, veut en faire « le premier village de France sans chômeur ». Il a créé une association pour ce faire, en novembre, et ne désespère pas d'y adjoindre une fondation.

Grammatically, the antecedent of *ce* is the verb-structure preceding: in the first example above, *éloigner le spectre*; in the second, *en faire*. Sometimes a writer makes the connector relate not to a verb but to a noun, usually one derived from a verb (*amélioration, formation*). The first of these examples comes from a contribution to the debate of the early 1990s on the relative merits of public schools and private schools:

> Les Français veulent-ils remplacer une école centralisée et égalitaire par une école concurrentielle et inégalitaire ? Rien n'est moins sûr. Plus sûre leur paraît la voie de l'amélioration prioritaire de l'école publique, dût-on pour ce faire froisser corporatismes et bureaucratie.

> L'humanisme rabelaisien concerne avant tout la formation de l'homme. Pour ce faire, la nature de l'enfant doit être convenablement dirigée, car la vertu n'est que conquête.

This structure can be replaced by the affirmative mode of *pour cela*; and in certain contexts is varied by *à cette effet* or *à cette fin*.

pour cela

This connector has two quite different modes: one straightforwardly affirmative; the other adversative. Unlike some other structures which include a demonstrative pronoun, such as *à ceci près que* and *cela dit*, this one has no variant form in *ceci*.

Affirmative

As part of a simple affirmation, often one which envisages a future or conditional state of affairs and which may be accompanied by a mode of *il faut*, the *pour* is one of intention and the structure can stand for *pour ce faire*. In these contexts, the meaning is 'to that end' or 'for that purpose':

> La loi d'orientation quinquennale de redressement des finances publiques est une nécessité. Elle s'imposera avant toute autre préoccupation dès que recettes fiscales et cotisations sociales recommenceront à remplir les caisses de l'État et de la Sécurité sociale. Il faudra pour cela attendre le retour de la croissance.

In other contexts, usually with reference to a past or an existing circumstance, the meaning is 'because of that' and the structure could be replaced by *pour cette raison*. This example deals with the first generation of office-workers using computers:

> Dans les années 75–85, marquées, comme on sait, par l'émergence de l'informatique de bureau, et qui, selon les experts, devaient pour cela s'avérer fatales aux secrétaires, la profession où s'est créé le plus grand nombre d'emplois a été celle de... secrétaire.

Sometimes the structure is used in a way which makes it replaceable by *ce faisant*, as in this extract from a comparison of de Gaulle and François Mitterrand, written when the latter had been in power for ten years:

> La décennie Mitterrand peut dès lors être mieux confrontée à la décennie de Gaulle, et les empreintes des deux hommes plus équitablement comparées. C'est l'objet de ce livre, même s'il doit pour cela hérisser les dévots de l'un et courroucer les zélotes de l'autre.
>
> (Duhamel, 15)

And occasionally a variant *pour ce* is used, as in this extract from an essay on the theory of interpretation:

> Il est nécessaire de redéfinir les fondements et les buts de l'interprétation, si l'on veut garder celle-ci comme activité scientifique. Pour ce, il faut d'abord différencier nettement l'interprétation de la réception.

Adversative

Used adversatively, in a negative or interrogative statement, this connector has the force of 'for that' or 'for all that'. Thus, one New South Welshman might say to another, proffering a glass: 'This is only a home-bottled red from Mudgee. But you shouldn't think any the less of it for that.' This mode was once much more common than it is nowadays. Texts dating from the earlier years of this century show it was ubiquitous in the type of negative and interrogative contexts in which writers now use *pour autant*: *Nos gens de sport, dont la langue est farcie de mots anglais, ne savent pas pour cela l'anglais* (Meillet, 341). Vital as it was up to two generations ago, this connector has been all but rendered extinct in these contexts by *pour autant*. The controversy which attended this evolution, some elements of which can be seen in Dupré (I, 208–209), did not prevent it from happening. When the structure is used, it is very rare indeed to find it accompanying a negative structure made with *ne*. It is slightly less rare in negative contexts containing *sans* or *sans que*, as in this example in which François de Closets says his book *Toujours plus !* offered *une analyse économique dont j'avais lieu de craindre qu'elle rebute le grand public sans intéresser pour cela les spécialistes* (Closets, 7). In the following example, a writer refers to the death of the Chinese dictator Mao Zedong and to reports published long afterwards which told of his enormous sexual appetite:

> C'est bien longtemps après qu'il ait tiré sa révérence, et sans pour cela cesser de lui tresser des couronnes (image audacieuse pour un tyran marxiste !) qu'on se hasarde à lancer la rumeur selon laquelle il se serait fait feuilleter le petit Livre rouge dans toutes sortes de positions par des milliers de jeunes Chinoises plus ou moins consentantes. (Bedos, 7)

The interrogative mode is equally infrequent these days; but it too occasionally turns up, as in this extract from an unfavourable review of a recording by the soprano Jessye Norman:

> Comme une traînée de poudre, le nom de Jessye Norman est devenu une légende. Faut-il pour cela tout lui faire enregistrer ?

And a pair of authors, writing on homosexuality, say their own private experience of bisexuality has helped them understand their subject:

> Notre expérience personnelle nous a préservé des préjugés habituels de tant d'auteurs qui parlent de ce qu'ils ignorent sans l'avoir vécu et sans même l'avoir observé. Va-t-on pour cela refuser de prendre en considération notre étude ?
> (Bon & d'Arc, 17)

When a contemporary writer does use this structure with *ne... pas*, it is hardly ever replaceable by the adversative function of *pour autant*, but only by the mode defined above as a replacement of *pour ce faire*, as in this extract from an article about research in prehistoric climatology and habitat:

> Depuis longtemps, déjà, certains chercheurs spécialisés sont capables de décrire avec force détails le climat et le paysage au milieu duquel vivaient nos ancêtres, *Homo habilis* ou de Cro-Magnon. Ils ne craignent pas, pour cela, de mettre le nez dans la poussière et dans les... excréments fossilisés des hommes et animaux.

The difference between adversative *pour autant* in a negative structure and contemporary *pour cela* in a negative structure is flagrant in an example like the following, spoken by a Member of Parliament, François Baroin, about Jacques Chirac, the leader of his party, the RPR:

> « Chirac et mon père étaient très proches. Quand mon père est mort, Chirac a été bien avec moi. Mais je ne m'engage pas avec lui pour ça. Il correspond à une vision que j'ai de la société française... »

If Baroin's *pour ça* was replaced by *pour autant*, it would make him say 'Despite the fact that Chirac was kind to me, I don't support him', which would be the opposite of his meaning. What he means is that he does support Chirac, but not because the latter was kind to him.

With redundant *en*

It is interesting to note that the combination of a redundant *en* with *pour autant* in negative structures, much deplored by some commentators, was already common with its predecessor *pour cela*, and that in the prose of the erudite, the literary and the academic (Henriot, 1924: 222): *Profondément scientifique d'intention, l'œuvre n'en sera pas pour cela moins vivante* (Berr, 15); *[Ce principe] provient, à n'en pas douter, du système de H. Spencer, mais il n'en est pas plus certain pour cela* (Lévy-Bruhl, 11).

> Les jeunes gens, dans leur ensemble, lisent-ils moins que naguère et autrefois? Je ne sais. J'en connais plusieurs qui n'ouvrent jamais un livre à l'exception de ceux qu'ils sont obligés d'étudier. Ils n'en sont pas pour cela incultes. (Mauriac, 43)

The *en* is redundant because its only meaning is *pour cela*.

pour le reste

Perhaps it is premature to see this structure as a connector. However, it may be on the way to becoming one. Like *au reste* and *du reste*, it is formed from the common noun *le reste*; and it is nowadays used in a way reminiscent of how *au demeurant*, formed from the now obsolete noun *le demeurant,* which meant *le reste,* seems to have been used in the sixteenth century. It is usually placed first in the sentence and may be combined with *car*, *et* or ***mais***; it closes a discussion of certain aspects of a subject by introducing a conclusive statement about other aspects which will not be canvassed at such length. This example is taken from an article on the prehistoric skeletal remains known as 'Boxgrove man':

> Une étude morphologique attentive du précieux tibia fournira peut-être quelques indications sur les postures favorites de son propriétaire en montrant, par exemple, s'il avait l'habitude de s'accroupir pour se reposer ou travailler. Des analyses chimiques pourraient également dévoiler le comportement alimentaire de cet Anglais moyen d'il y a un demi-million d'années. Pour le reste, l'homme de Boxgrove gardera sans doute longtemps encore ses secrets les plus intimes.

At present, the usual function of this structure is as straightforwardly semantic as can be seen in that example. However, what Dupré says about *à part ça* could clearly apply to it: that, apart from a single difference, *à part ça* is indistinguishable from *au reste*; and that the latter and *au demeurant* are the equivalent of *à part ça* (Dupré, I, 639). And in certain contexts, the unitary structure and functioning of *pour le reste*, the frequency of its use and the instrumental quality of the link which it makes hint that it could well be developing into a procedural connector capable of functioning in ways less closely related to its ostensible meaning. This may especially be the case when it is not placed first in the sentence. In the following example, written before 1950 and taken from the discussion of a speech delivered in Moscow by A. Zhdanov, the relationship made by the structure is not quite as semantically uncomplicated:

> Dans ce discours, pour le reste très insignifiant, l'épithète « objectif » est constamment prise en mauvaise part.

> (Caillois, 143)

There it is clear that the structure, opposing the generality (of the speech) to the particular (of the single point of interest), could be replaced by *au reste* or *du reste*; but perhaps also by ***par ailleurs*** or the contrastive mode of *au demeurant*. The main difference between the latter pair of connectors and this structure is that they have both departed from their original literal meaning, whereas this one retains it.

In many contexts, an English equivalent could be 'that apart'; in others, it could be 'otherwise'. Occasionally, a writer uses 'for the rest' as an exact analogue of this structure. Aldous Huxley, for instance, albeit a Francophile and not as contemporary as he once was:

> What readers has the Divine Comedy now? A few poets, a few lovers of poetry, a few strayed cross-word puzzlers, and, for the rest, a diminishing band of culture-fans and erudition-snobs.

> (Huxley, 37–38)

pour [sa] part *

In this structure, as in *de [son] côté* and *quant à [lui]*, one element varies according to context. In this case, as in *de [son] côté*, the variable is the possessive adjective, which can be replaced by any other. In practice, this adjective is usually either *ma*, *sa* or *leur*. The connector has a contrastive function, not commonly noted by dictionaries. It marks off the opinion, speech or act of the person or entity designated from the opinion, speech or act of some preceding person or entity. It is sometimes placed first in the sentence or paragraph; but it is probably more often placed after the first element or with the first verb. It does not usually introduce the first part of a contrast; and when the subject is *je*, it may be only a way of emphasizing a personal view, as in this extract from a discussion of whether or not Heidegger's philosophy could be deemed 'totalitarian thinking':

> Le nazisme de l'individu Martin Heidegger découle-t-il de sa philosophie ? Cette philosophie même est-elle donc un échantillon de pensée totalitaire ? Pour ma part, je l'ai toujours pensé, je l'ai écrit en 1957 dans *Pourquoi des philosophes ?*
>
> (Revel, 1988: 369)

In the next example, it structures a comparison between *banques étrangères* and *banques françaises*:

> Jusqu'à présent, seules des banques françaises ont dirigé des euro-emprunts en francs. Quelques banques étrangères souhaiteraient être autorisées à en faire autant.
>
> Pour leur part, les banques françaises n'auraient guère à redouter d'être sur leur propre terrain exposées aux vents de la concurrence internationale.

The connector often has a quasi-narrative function, being used in news items which report one after the other the sayings or doings of different people. This example comes from the report of a debate inside the Parti socialiste on the subject of a strike by workers in the Ministries of Finance and Taxation. First, the views of the *jospinistes* (a group of Socialist MPs led by Lionel Jospin) are canvassed; then the view of M. Jospin himself:

> Ce que les jospinistes avaient en tête a été précisé par l'intervention d'un militant engagé dans le conflit des fonctionnaires des finances, M. Jean-Claude Guillaume, qui a déclaré : « La politique, ce n'est pas seulement la distribution technocratique des surplus de la croissance. Ce peut être aussi la prise en compte de phénomènes irrationnels. » M. Jospin avait souligné, pour sa part, que les animateurs de la grève des agents des impôts sont des socialistes.

In this sort of use, the function of the connector could be served in English by 'As for M. Jospin', 'As far as M. Jospin is concerned' or 'M. Jospin, on the other hand'. But it would often have no explicit equivalent in English; and the contrastive effect, implicit in the sense of the words, would be marked only by the reader's inner voice.

As a distributor of contrastive emphasis, this connector need not introduce only a second point. In the following example, it introduces the third of three points relating to the trial and acquittal of Alain Boublil:

> L'instruction judiciaire avait porté ses soupçons sur Alain Boublil. Le ministère public l'avait promu coupable et traître. Le tribunal lui octroie pour sa part une relaxe empoisonnée de mille griefs.

Sometimes this structure introduces the second element of a binary begun by the *si d'opposition*. And in certain contexts, it would be replaceable by one of the two structures mentioned in the first sentence or by the *pronom tonique disjoint*. This can be seen in the following extract from a tongue-in-cheek discussion of what has become of two traditional symbols of France, *la baguette et le béret*:

> Las ! si le béret ne couvre plus nos chefs pollués, la baguette connaît pour sa part un très net ramollissement du croûton.

There, the second part of the binary could be structured either as *la baguette, quant à elle, connaît un très net ramollissement du croûton* or *la baguette, elle, connaît...* or even *la baguette, de son côté, connaît....*

pour tout dire

This structure has two functions: rather like *bref*, it can recapitulate or resume; and rather like *voire*, it can add a precision, an apter word, an expression putting a finer point upon what precedes. Littré gives it only in the forms *c'est tout dire* and *c'est tout dit* which he defines as *il n'y a rien à ajouter, cela achève, complète*. Robert gives it as equivalent to *en somme* and *en résumé*. In the first example, its final position in the sentence could certainly be occupied by *en somme* or the colloquial coda *quoi*:

> Voilà quelques années, un homme a « découvert » que Sartre et Beauvoir auraient été des pétainistes sournois, de vagues « collabos » pour tout dire.

However, it combines with *et*, which is not normally used with either of those resumers. It is often found in one or other of two positions: introducing the final element in a list; or first in the sentence or paragraph.

Introducing a final element

This mode, close to a mode of *somme toute*, precedes or follows the last in a list of usually three elements, often nouns or adjectives. These often express criticisms; and the one modified by this connector is thereby deemed to be the strongest or most adverse. When it precedes, it is commonly combined with *et*. For example, Mitterrand's systematic opposition to de Gaulle's governments in the 1960s is described as having seemed to some *bien stérile, bien agaçante et, pour tout dire, bien puérile* (Nay, 269). A theatre critic writing about the repertoire of what she calls *les pièces de Boulevard* says the theatre-goer cannot help being aware of three aspects of it: *de son extravagante grossièreté, de sa monotonie, et pour tout dire de sa laideur*. A commentator on the architecture of the Centre Pompidou after seventeen years of poor maintenance details four adverse aspects of the building's condition:

> ...ce bâtiment stupéfiant que ses détracteurs continuent d'appeler « la raffinerie », « le bastringue », ou « Notre-Dame-des-Tuyaux » et qui, à dix-sept ans, accumule les rides autant que les points de rouille, victime de quelques partis pris audacieux sinon imprudents dans le choix des matériaux, de légèretés coupables lors de sa livraison, d'un contentieux ancien qui le priva longtemps de l'entretien minimum des peintures ; et, pour tout dire, d'un furieux décalage d'époque entre la fin des années 60, date de sa conception, et les années 90, où la notion de précarité n'est plus vraiment au goût du jour [...]

When used without *et*, the connector often follows the final element. A theatre critic comments on unsatisfying aspects of the ending of a play: *un dénouement un peu anodin, un peu sentimental, faible pour tout dire*. A critic expresses dislike for some of Brahms's music: *la polyphonie recherchée, complexe, un peu vaine pour tout dire, de ses pièces religieuses*. In this position, the connector is akin to the mode of **enfin** which precises the aptness of a shade of expression: *Il se rend insupportable, odieux, nuisible enfin*.

It is used to introduce praise as well as dispraise, albeit less often. In this example, a writer dedicating a book to Antoine Augustin Cournot, whom he admires, compares him to Sainte-Beuve and eventually to Auguste Comte, both of whom he also admires:

> [Cournot], ce Sainte-Beuve de la critique philosophique, cet esprit aussi original que judicieux, aussi encyclopédique et compréhensif que pénétrant, ce géomètre profond, ce logicien hors ligne, cet économiste hors cadres, précurseur méconnu des économistes nouveaux, et pour tout dire, cet Auguste Comte épuré, condensé, affiné [...]

(Tarde, xxiv)

A variant for the basic mode is *pour dire le mot*, with which a writer, as though trying to attenuate or apologize for a certain word, warns of the severity of the criticism to come: *Votre livre sera, je le crains, bien technique, difficile à lire et, pour dire le mot, assez rébarbatif* (Georgin, 1951: 13–14).

Depending on context, the expressions 'frankly', 'to put a finer point upon it', 'to be blunt' and 'to be precise' could serve as English equivalents for this mode.

First in the sentence

In this position, the connector does not round off a list; it initiates a recapitulation. It is especially this mode which could be replaced by *en somme*. A writer begins the opening sentence of his conclusion: *Pour tout dire, trois propositions principales résument les faits précédents*; and those three *propositions* he then sets out (Binet, 1892: 315). This mode often stands first in a paragraph, the function of which is to sum up what precedes, as in this extract from a profile of an Italian businessman and corporate raider, Giancarlo Parretti:

> il ne lit pas, n'écoute pas de musique, ne va jamais au théâtre ni au cinéma et baragouine difficilement quatre langues, « dont l'italien », disent méchamment ses compatriotes. Un seul sujet de conversation : les femmes et *l'amore*. Parretti a un fort penchant pour les plaisanteries grivoises. Dans une interview, à la question « Votre hobby ? », il répond : « Faire l'amour. » Un sport ? « Faire l'amour. » Une manie ? « Faire l'amour », etc. Il parle haut et fort, serre toutes les mains, tape sur l'épaule, conclut des affaires à la manière d'un maquignon, et rit toujours de ses bonnes plaisanteries.
>
> Pour tout dire, Parretti donne dans le flamboyant : « Les affaires, c'est comme les femmes, quand quelque chose m'intéresse, je fonce. »

English equivalents for this mode might be 'in fact', 'in short', 'in a word'.

précisément *

This adverb is used as an emphasizing connector, mainly to recall a point in what precedes and to stress it. This it can do either by way of confirmation, giving point to a coincidence, or by way of counteraction, showing oppositeness or irony in a paradox. In either mode, it can function like one of the many modes of 'actually'. Other equivalents for it are structures with 'very': confirming ('What happened next was the very thing he expected') or contradicting ('What happened next was the very thing he didn't expect'). The form *plus précisément* can replace a mode of **mieux**, introducing a word or expression sensed as more accurate, as in this sentence on the industry of the town of Bort: *L'industrie est celle du cuir – de la tannerie, plus précisément* (Closets, 1983: 303).

Confirming

What follows this mode reinforces a point of similarity with what precedes. In the first example, the writer combines it with **or** to stress that what explains the vogue for Heidegger's philosophy among French intellectuals is its covert totalitarianism:

> [Heidegger] accumule les affirmations pour répéter la même idée de cinq ou six manières différentes, et en se bornant à placer un « donc » avant la dernière phrase du paragraphe, alors qu'il n'existe aucun enchaînement déductif entre les propositions antérieures et leur prétendue conclusion. Ce procédé caractéristique, que j'appellerai la « tautologie terroriste », se retrouve dans les discours de Hitler comme dans les écrits dits « théoriques » de Staline. Or c'est précisément ce procédé qui fit le succès de Heidegger chez les philosophes.
>
> (Revel, 1988: 369)

Other connectors sometimes combined with this mode are *bien*, itself an emphasizer, and *là*. In the first of these examples, André Gide tries to remember three recitals by Rubinstein which he had heard as a child,

> dont j'ai gardé souvenir si lumineux, si net, que je doute parfois s'il s'agit bien du souvenir de Rubinstein lui-même, ou seulement des morceaux que, depuis, j'ai tant de fois relus et étudiés. Mais non ; c'est bien précisément lui que j'entends et que je revois […]
>
> (Gide, 1954: 465)

And in the following example with *là*, the writer says that some of the most enlightening critical comment on writers is written by other writers, so that when Valéry writes on Stendhal it is doubly rewarding:

> La critique littéraire apparaît comme étant la seule, peut-être, des formes légitimes de l'autobiographie, parce qu'elle seule échappe au paradoxe du Narcisse : se perdre en son reflet, pour s'être trop cherché. Et c'est précisément là où elle est le plus personnelle, qu'elle est le plus enrichissante, le plus « objective » : c'est en parlant de Beyle comme de l'un des êtres qu'il aurait pu être, que Valéry nous éclairera le mieux la *Chartreuse* ou *Lucien*.

Sometimes the connector can both confirm an expectation and contradict one, as in this sentence of Proust's, again combined with *or*: *Or, la princesse des Laumes, qu'on ne se serait pas attendu à voir chez Mme de Saint-Euverte, venait précisément d'arriver* (Proust, I, 330). There, it acts not only as a reminder that, on the previous page, the absence of the Princess from Mme de Saint-Euverte's soirée had seemed likely but also, since her usual practice is to stay away, as a sign of contradiction.

Contradicting

This mode emphasizes an untoward or paradoxical coincidence of points. Proust again, much given to showing the unexpected and the curious in human affairs, often uses it to give point to an irony: *elle était devenue si chère à Swann au moment pour ainsi dire où il la trouvait précisément bien moins jolie* (Proust, I, 291).

This connective function of the adverb arose, say the lexicographers, in the eighteenth century. A writer of that period who was struck by the paradoxes and *bizarreries* of his own character combines it with a mode of *et ce* to tell of how spankings in childhood affected his adult sexuality:

> Qui croirait que ce châtiment d'enfant, reçu à huit ans par la main d'une fille de trente, a décidé de mes goûts, de mes désirs, de mes passions, de moi pour le reste de ma vie, et cela précisément dans le sens contraire à ce qui devait s'ensuivre naturellement ?
>
> (Rousseau, 15–16)

In a discussion of leaf-mimicry in insects, a writer wonders whether the real phenomenon might not in fact be the opposite of the one apparently observed:

> Des êtres sont imitateurs, d'autres gardent intacte leur apparence hétéroclite. On peut donc se demander si le mimétisme n'est pas une illusion ; si les insectes qui sont des feuilles, mantes et phyllies, sont devenus tels parce qu'ils vivaient au milieu des feuilles, ou s'ils ne furent pas attirés par les feuilles, comme par des sœurs, précisément par cette analogie de forme et de nuances.
>
> (Gourmont, 1902: 58)

This mode commonly combines with *mais*. Another common combination is with *parce que*, as in this remark on the dangers and inefficacies of Muslim fundamentalism:

> L'intégrisme musulman a toujours eu des adeptes – et toujours échoué : soit, en ne réussissant pas à prendre le pouvoir ; soit, quand il le prenait, en ne parvenant pas à mettre en place une société viable. Mais, tant qu'il se cantonnait aux pays musulmans, l'Occident ne s'en préoccupait guère. Si les mollahs d'Iran ont beaucoup inquiété, c'est précisément parce qu'ils prétendaient exporter leur révolution aux quatre coins du monde.

justement

A variant for this connector is *justement*. In this example, the writer draws attention to the contradiction between a Ministry of Culture newly inspired by a belief in progress and the real needs and nature of culture which, he suggests, are at variance with such a doctrine:

> Par là, l'administration nouvelle s'accordait plus ou moins à l'esprit du temps, utilitaire, fonctionnel, efficace. En France, elle s'est voulue le moteur même du progrès.
>
> Mais lorsqu'il s'agit de culture, c'est-à-dire au sens plénier du mot, d'une œuvre d'amour et de connaissance qui, justement, devrait faire contrepoids aux

effets pervers du progrès et de l'efficacité à tout prix, n'y a-t-il pas antinomie entre cette administration envahissante et activiste et la fin idéale dont malgré tout elle se réclame ?

(Fumaroli, 194–195)

pronom tonique disjoint *

To call this pronoun *disjoint* is something of a misnomer: at times all that separates it from a verb is a comma. As a connector, it functions like a short version of *quant à [lui]*. Though a pronoun, it does not replace a noun, it accompanies one. The basic function is contrastive: it usually shapes pointed oppositions; and it can distribute emphases in a list, marking off different elements from each other. It does not usually accompany the first element of a contrast. By the nature of discursive prose, its most common forms are *elle* and *elles*, *lui* and *eux*.

Pointed oppositions

Such contrasts are all the sharper when they make an antithesis within a single sentence: *La muleta du matador peut bien être rouge, le taureau, lui, n'y voit que du gris.* / *Monsieur Jourdain prenait des leçons; M. Nyssen, lui, en donne.* But they can equally well occupy two consecutive sentences, as in this contrast between two Marseilles newspapers:

> *Le Provençal* était la palissade électorale de la mairie et de la gauche. *Le Méridional* finit par devenir, lui, le tract de la droite.

The oppositions marked by this connector are often reinforced by combination with one of three others: ***mais***, ***alors que*** and the ***si d'opposition***.

With *mais*

This combination is sometimes used to mark the beginning of the second part of the contrast. In this extract from an interview, a speaker distinguishes between *racialisme*, an outdated theory of superiority of one 'race' over others, and *racisme*, a behaviour:

> Le racialisme ne peut resurgir que s'il change de contenu, en remplaçant par exemple la notion de race par celle de culture : évolution qu'a étudiée Taguieff dans *la Force du préjugé*. Mais le comportement raciste, lui, pour perdurer n'a pas besoin d'une doctrine scientifique : il lui suffit que des différences sociales se superposent aux différences physiques.

A discussion of traditional conceptions of the family contrasts the individual's impermanence with the family's durability: *La vie de l'individu était précaire, mais la famille était, elle, en principe immortelle* (Roussel, 242).

With *alors que*

Either the first or the second element can be reinforced by the addition of *alors que*. In this extract from a discussion of the differences between societies based on a free market and others on some degree of state control of the economy, the first element is reinforced:

> Alors que le système du marché est essentiellement multipolaire, avec ses milliers d'entreprises en lutte les unes contre les autres, le système de solidarité est, lui, focalisé sur l'État, générateur de l'ordre social.
>
> (Closets, 1983: 474–475)

In this example, taken from a discussion of homosexuality as seen by heterosexuals, it is the second element which contains not only the connector but the reinforcer:

> Sans le vouloir, l'hétérosexuel ne peut percevoir l'élan sexuel du pédéraste qu'au moment où il retombe et se déforme en vice, alors que le pédéraste, lui, garde la mémoire émerveillée de son exaltation.

Sometimes this combination is also made with **tandis que**.

With *si d'opposition*

This combination is much more common than the other two. The *si* always introduces the first element of the comparison. It is rare to find it anywhere but at the beginning of a sentence:

> Si l'Opéra de Paris a aujourd'hui trois théâtres, mais des équipes en piteux état, l'Opéra de Lyon, lui, est « hors les murs » de son théâtre qui ne sera pas reconstruit avant 1992, en raison d'atermoiements successifs!

> Si le film américain augmente sans cesse sa part de marché, le cinéma français, lui, ne parvient plus à attirer les spectateurs.

The contrast is almost always made in a single sentence, except in a juxtaposition like the following, where the *si d'opposition* not only structures the contrast between Buzzati and Kafka but also introduces the explanation of Kafka's hold upon his reader:

> Buzzati est souvent comparé à Kafka. Erreur. Si Kafka tient son lecteur, c'est qu'il l'enferme dans des espaces clos, qu'il lui ouvre des chemins labyrinthiques, qu'il le piège et l'emprisonne. Buzzati, lui, fait naître l'angoisse de l'espace, de la solitude, de ses « déserts »…

Punctuation and position

The most usual punctuation is to set the pronoun between commas. An obvious advantage of this, with *lui*, is to avoid uncertainty about the function of the pronoun: without commas, it could appear to be an indirect object. However, in a significant minority of cases, writers nowadays use no commas: *...les juifs venus d'Orient, par opposition aux ashkénazes qui eux viennent d'Europe. / Si Bagdad a pour lui l'avantage des canons, le Koweït lui n'a qu'un atout : son énorme poids économique et financier.* The position can also vary. Since the pronoun accompanies a noun which is always the subject of a verb, it is natural that it should precede the latter. But at times it is put after the verb, as in this comparison between humans and animals:

> C'est l'intelligence conceptuelle et créative, faculté unique au sein du monde vivant, qui a donné à l'homme la possibilité de s'autodétruire. Un lapin n'a jamais réussi, lui, à inventer le produit susceptible de tuer tous les lapins.

Less pointed contrasts

In most of the contexts illustrated above, this connector could be replaced by *au contraire*, *en revanche* or *par contre*. However, sometimes the connector serves as much to structure a series of points as to shape a comparison. In the following quotation, it is one in a sequence of three contrastive structures – the *si d'opposition* and *de [son] côté* are the other two – used to link and mark distinctions in a sequence of four political views on a matter (those of Balladur, Fabius, Bérégovoy and Aubry):

> Si M. Balladur se tait, le PS et M. Fabius se prononcent favorablement, sans dire clairement si les revenus seront proportionnellement réduits. M. Bérégovoy, lui, le laisse entendre. Mme Aubry, de son côté, fait une double observation [...]

Sometimes, too, there may be no great contrast or disparity between the two entities compared; and, as in this statement on the life and works of a painter, the connector serves merely to underline a comparison, to show in fact a similarity rather than a difference:

> La carrière de Frédéric Bazille tient en peu de temps, entre 1863 et 1870. Son œuvre, elle, tient en peu de tableaux et quelques dessins.

English equivalents would include 'on the other hand', 'however', 'as for ...' and simple 'but'. Quite often a contrast would be made without the use of an explicit connector.

puis

Like many other logical connectors, this one derives from an expression of time. In its most basic temporal use, it means simply 'next'. In the forms *puis* and *et puis*, it is used in narrative, denoting an act or event occurring after the preceding one: *Elle a vécu avec lui cinq mois et puis, un matin, il l'a ramenée chez ses parents.* Some English-speakers manage to mislearn one of the logical functions of *puis*: they believe it serves the function served by **alors**. Its temporal meaning of 'next' they transpose to a logical 'then', introducing a conclusion. It does not function like that. As a connector, *puis* indicates that what precedes is about to be reinforced by a further point. It adds a second argument or reason. In most of its modes and variants, the usual value is roughly 'not only that but also this'. Littré gives it as equivalent to **d'ailleurs** and **au reste**; to this, Robert adds **en outre**. It has two modes: usually placed first in the sentence or paragraph; and in pairs or **sequences of points**.

Initial *puis*

When it stands first in the sentence, it occurs either alone or more usually combined with **et**. In this mode, although the writer is by definition introducing a second point, the first one has not been signalled as such to the reader. In the following example, taken from a popular-science article colloquially discussing the essential requirements for life to develop, the writer says two things are essential, water and oxygen; the discussion of the second of these is introduced by *Et puis*:

> Pour être habitable, une planète doit proposer le confort minimal indispensable à une vie décente : elle doit avoir l'eau courante et de l'oxygène à gogo. Sans solvant pour dissoudre les petites molécules et les faire évoluer vers des composés complexes, pas de chimie organique possible. Une soupe primitive tiède est la seule recette connue pour cuisiner des organismes vivants. Et puis, il faut absolument de l'oxygène pour aérer les méninges et faire tourner la machine cérébrale.

In a different tone, a critic of Flaubert argues two reasons for the superiority of the story *Hérodias* over the novel *Salammbô* and uses *Et puis* to present the second of them:

> Le roman est trop long, avec des fragments admirables : mais le conte l'est de bout en bout. Et puis, il y a dans le sujet même une différence capitale, que Thibaudet avait très bien vue.
>
> (Henriot, 1954: 54)

In some exemplars of this mode, one senses a shade of 'and anyway', of a more spoken form of **après tout** or **aussi bien**, suggesting that the

writer is merely reminding the reader that the following point is under-
standable.

In pairs of points

This mode functions like the previous one. The only difference is that the
first point is announced as such, usually by *d'abord*. *Puis* sometimes
replaces **ensuite** in the expository duo *d'abord... ensuite*, as in this extract
from an article on an American poetess:

> Ce qui frappe tout d'abord dans l'art d'Elizabeth Bishop, c'est l'incomparable
> puissance de ses descriptions, et à quel point les mots répondent à l'acuité de
> son regard. « Si elle parle d'une chaise on peut presque s'asseoir dessus quand
> elle a fini », disait, à ce sujet, Mariane Moore. Et puis, avec quelle exactitude
> n'exprime-t-elle pas cette « merveilleuse pluralité du simple » dont parlait
> Bachelard, qui met si souvent au défi nos ressources d'expression !

In such paired points, the connective structures are replaceable by **d'une
part... d'autre part**.

In sequences of points

This connector can also replace *ensuite* in the triad *d'abord... ensuite...
enfin*. In this extract about a stressful period in the Prime Ministership of
Michel Rocard, the writer announces this tripartite structure with the
adverb *triplement*:

> La tempête actuelle oblige Michel Rocard à se faire triplement violence.
> D'abord, en parlant publiquement de l'immigration, alors que cela ne lui parais-
> sait jusqu'ici ni nécessaire ni très sain. Puis en renforçant un dispositif spécifique
> aux immigrés, au lieu de s'en tenir à une politique de droit commun. Enfin,
> en sacrifiant un petit peu à l'effet d'annonce, par un prochain catalogue de
> mesures volontairement long.

In such triads, this mode is sometimes used to replace not *ensuite* but
enfin:

> Trois secteurs sont particulièrement touchés. Il y a d'abord les matières
> premières. Ensuite, il y a la déprime boursière. Puis il y a la crise immobilière
> mondiale.

In some sequences, for cumulative effect, the basic structure is not
varied. In this example, where it occurs three times, the writer tries to
tell the truth about who among the French fought against the Nazis and
who collaborated with them during the Second World War:

> Il y a eu de Gaulle, voilà. Et puis une poignée d'hommes et de femmes, parfois
> fort humbles, qui ont sauvé un lambeau d'honneur et qui représentaient, tous
> ensemble, environ 1 % de la population. Les comptes ont été faits. Et puis il

y a eu les purs salauds, qui ont été, sans doute, plutôt moins nombreux. Et puis, entre les deux, des millions de gens qui ont vécu le moins mal qu'ils ont pu, en essayant de ne pas se compromettre [...]

(Giroud, 432)

A spoken tone

One tends to think of *et puis* as a reinforcement of *puis*. But sometimes, especially in conversation, it makes more sense to see it as a reinforcement of *et*. In the following example, transcribed from speech, its function could be served by *et aussi*:

Ce sont surtout les gros fermiers du Middle West qui en tireront profit. Et puis, bien sûr, les grandes compagnies céréalières qui règnent sur le commerce mondial du grain.

This spokenness can be heard too in Bornier's celebrated fustian: *Tout homme a deux pays, le sien et puis la France !* (Bornier, 57). In this function, one finds also *puis aussi*. Here is André Gide giving two reasons why as an adolescent he liked the diary of Amiel, introduced to him by M. Richard:

...pour moi, je ne laissais pas d'être sensible au charme ambigu de cette préciosité morale, dont les scrupules, les tâtonnements et l'amphigouri m'exaspèrent tant aujourd'hui. Puis aussi je cédais à M. Richard et j'admirais par sympathie [...]

(Gide, 1954: 481)

In such contexts, it is clear that *puis* is little more than a mode of *et*. The same goes for *puis ensuite*, seen introducing the second of a pair of points in the next example, which comes from a rather technical discussion of certain tertiary assessment procedures:

Les concours doivent parallèlement être simplifiés. Une double approche : d'abord des QCM de qualité sur différentes disciplines (mathématiques et sciences, histoire, géographie, langues vivantes, etc.), puis ensuite éventuellement pour ceux qui auront atteint un certain niveau, des épreuves qualitatives en fonction des différentes banques d'épreuves existantes [...]

(*Le Monde*, 15.12.93)

Anyone planning to use any of these combinations should probably attend to Hanse's dire injunction about the imitation of intellectuals:

On peut dire : *Et puis* ou, en interrogeant : *Et puis ?* Mais on n'imitera pas les intellectuels qui disent : *(et) puis après, (et) puis ensuite, puis alors, puis ensuite.*

(Hanse, 1983: 772)

English equivalents are 'in addition', the versatile 'also' or 'as well as that'. In pairs and sequences, 'for one thing ... for another' or 'in the first place ... in the second place' would do.

quand même *

As a connector, this structure has two modes: one of them is mainly adversative; the other is more familiar in tone, implicitly reminding the reader of a shared assumption. Anscombre & Ducrot (107ff) give a good discussion of it. In either mode, it could often be replaced by *tout de même*.

More adversative

This mode functions much like *cependant* or *néanmoins*. It can introduce a positive feature in opposition to a negative one or vice versa. It is placed only in the second element of oppositions. A critic reviewing a recording of a Beethoven piano concerto (Wilhelm Kempff with the Berlin Philharmonic under Leitner), first detracts, then praises:

> Dans une intégrale réalisée au début des années soixante, l'Orchestre Philharmonique de Berlin n'apparaît pas génial. Faut-il incriminer la prise de son ou la direction d'orchestre ? Difficile à dire ! Relevons quand même toute la vie qui parcourt cet enregistrement. Kempff séduit par son sens des contrastes, son toucher magnifique, son tempo approprié et son inventivité.

Similarly, a discussion of the First International, based in London, weak in funds and membership, first points out the organization's relative insignificance, then counters this with a point in favour of its relative influence:

> En 1870, la cagnotte de l'Internationale contient 50 livres et sa liste rassemble 385 adhérents. Tout juste de quoi remplir un pub... Notons quand même que l'Internationale apporte aux nordistes une aide précieuse pendant la guerre de Sécession américaine.

Quite often this mode combines with *mais*, as in this extract from a newspaper report on resignations of ministers from the government of John Major in the early 1990s:

> Tim Yeo, quarante-huit ans, est ainsi le quatrième ministre de John Major (après David Mellor, Norman Lamont et Michael Mates) à être obligé d'abandonner ses fonctions. Comme David Mellor, il part accablé de compliments et de regrets, mais il part quand même.

Sometimes, the adversativeness of this connector is underscored by a first element containing a structure anticipating a contrast, such as *avoir beau* in this discussion of the idea that the recession of the early 1990s is as disastrous as the great Depression:

> Les oiseaux de mauvais augure vont jusqu'à comparer la situation actuelle avec celle des années 30. Nul signe pourtant de déflation généralisée avec une baisse

de l'indice des prix. La désinflation mondiale a beau être spectaculaire, elle n'a quand même pas totalement supprimé la hausse des prix à la consommation.

A similar relation is established by **avec** in this extract from a report of a NATO decision to carry out limited bombing-raids during the war in Bosnia:

La menace est brandie « en soutien aux négociations de Genève, mais elle ne constitue pas une politique alternative ». Avec sa prudence de rigueur et son langage diplomatique, l'OTAN vient quand même de prendre un engagement de nature à peser sur les négociations de Genève.

Less adversative

This mode has a familiar tone, more spoken than the first. Robert's definition is *il faut l'avouer, à vrai dire, on en conviendra.* To that list one should probably add: *Je sais que je ne devrais pas le dire, mais....* In speech, it is a tactical gambit which, by sketching an apparent attenuation of what might be sensed as the impropriety of an affirmation, can enable the reinforcement of the latter. It facilitates what has been called *la mise en acceptabilité d'une contradiction* (Moeschler & Spengler, 1981: 110). That is, it offers a justification for the statement it accompanies, even a sort of excuse or apology for it. But thereby it too has an adversative quality, faint and implicit, in that it hints at contradicting an assumed objection, a hint which in speech may be conveyed by the intonation. Not unlike **après tout**, this mode anticipates a reader's reluctance to agree with what is being said; or else it implies that the statement it introduces is so obvious that it should go without saying, as in this exchange in which a television journalist asked a customer why she was buying shoes in a discount-shop: « *Pourquoi achetez-vous ici vos chaussures ?* » « *C'est moins cher, quand même...* » The implied meaning is, 'I shouldn't have to say this'. A spoken English equivalent might be 'Well, I mean'. Something of this meaning is heard too in the exclamatory *Oh ! quand même !* pronounced in a tone which protests against a statement or an act, rather like 'Really!' and 'Do you mind!' rebuking the objectionable.

An echo of this tone can be read in examples such as the following one, taken from an article, ironic in tone, on the then Prime Minister, Pierre Bérégovoy. The journalist says that the Prime Minister's cabinet colleagues will not allow their leader to co-ordinate the Government's policy strategy for the 1993 general election and that M. Bérégovoy must do no more than

se contenter de coordonner la participation des ministres à la campagne électorale. C'est quand même le moins que l'on puisse attendre d'un chef de gouvernement. Comme l'a fait comprendre M. Bérégovoy, lundi, être premier ministre demande du courage... et de l'abnégation.

If it is true that this mode of the connector is always an implicit reminder of a social norm which is infringed by the mention of what it accompanies (Moeschler & de Spengler, 1981: 107–110), there the norm invoked is no doubt that one does not treat a Prime Minister like that – or perhaps that one does not say this sort of thing about him. A rather similar example comes from a discussion of the policy of President Mitterrand towards the independence movement in New Caledonia. The writer has presented Mitterrand as for ever wishing to make manifest that his way of doing things is quite different from the way de Gaulle did them:

> Mais comme on n'échappe pas à l'Histoire et que l'histoire de la décolonisation est quand même profondément marquée par de Gaulle, c'est à un ancien ministre du Général que Mitterrand fait appel pour imposer l'idée d'une nécessaire « décolonisation de la Nouvelle-Calédonie » : Edgard Pisani.
>
> (July, 209)

There, the connector reminds both Mitterrand and the reader about the awkward fact that, however much Mitterrand might wish it not to be the case, to do such things differently from de Gaulle is difficult. An awkward fact is also what is signalled by the following example, taken from a comparison of Yves Montand, a man of the Left, and Jean-Marie Le Pen, a man of the extreme Right, whose relative popularity is based, says the author, on their common ability to speak in everyday language:

> Leurs paroles touchent directement les cœurs. Il est quand même révélateur que les seules personnalités nouvelles dans notre paysage politique si connu soient ces deux-là.
>
> (Dutourd, 1985: 65)

The connector's implicit invitation to the reader to agree with what is being said is sometimes seen more clearly, as in the coda *vous en conviendrez*, appended to this sentence about the undesirability of the nation being split into two clans, one as posh and smooth as a genteel Prime Minister, the other as vulgar as an uncouth comic genius:

> Mais l'alternative entre le tout-Balladur et le tout-Coluche ne devrait quand même pas être le seul choix possible, vous en conviendrez.

English equivalents for the more adversative mode might be 'even so', 'still' or 'none the less'; and for the other mode, 'really'.

quand bien même

Comments on this structure can be read in the entries for ***alors que*** and ***même***.

quant à [lui] *

Like *de [son] côté* and *pour [sa] part*, this is a structure in which one element varies according to context. In this one, the variable is the tonic pronoun, which agrees in number and gender with the subject it refers to. Also like those two structures, the basic function of this connector is contrastive: it can make a pointedly oppositive link between two statements; and as a distributor of emphasis, it can identify persons or things worthy of note in a comparison or a list. It goes almost without saying that it never introduces the first element of a contrast. In many of its functions, it can be seen as a longer version of the *pronom tonique disjoint*; it shares with the latter the fact that, though pronominal, it does not replace a noun but usually accompanies one. Given the nature of much discursive prose, the most common pronouns used are *elle* and *elles*, *lui* and *eux*. However, writers may refer to themselves: *Nous croyons, quant à nous, que...*, a formula which they may vary with *Nous croyons, pour notre compte, que...*.

Pointed oppositions

This mode makes sharp binary contrasts between statements. It can structure a neat antithesis between the different behaviour of two rivals in the same circumstance: *Jean-Pierre Lafond se dit serein. Bernard Tapie, quant à lui, reste silencieux.* In a consideration of the Indian economy, it can sharpen the distinction that a writer makes between two opposites, *industrie privée* and *secteur public*:

> En Inde, les réformes accélèrent la croissance, qui passe à 5 % par an. L'industrie privée, malgré certaines entraves, profite des mesures de libéralisation. De nouvelles générations d'entrepreneurs vifs et débrouillards montent en ligne. Le secteur public, quant à lui, présente des résultats mitigés, allant d'entreprises en net progrès à celles qui battent encore d'une aile.

In the next example, too, it is opposites which are contrasted (*poivre blanc* and *poivre noir*); but this time the connector underscores a similarity:

> Cela a débuté en septembre 1993 : les cours du poivre blanc, qui ne dépassaient guère 1 000 dollars la tonne au cours des deux années précédentes et atteignaient 4 000 dollars en automne, chutaient à 2 700 dollars la tonne à la mi-décembre pour remonter à 3 100 dollars en ce début d'année.
> Le poivre noir, quant à lui, suivait la même trajectoire. Il montait jusqu'à 1 600 dollars la tonne en septembre [...].

Like the *pronom tonique disjoint*, this mode is sometimes used in the second half of binaries which begin with the *si d'opposition*. In this example, a writer discusses a divergence of opinion between doctors and diabetics about treatment with insulin:

> Reste le problème des voies d'administration de l'insuline sur lequel s'opposent parfois médecins et malades. Si le malade rêve d'échapper aux contraintes de la piqûre d'insuline et des contrôles sanguins quotidiens, les spécialistes, quant à eux, exigent des contrôles stricts et des injections d'insuline fréquentes.

The more distributive mode

Perhaps because in contemporary journalism this mode is found more often in news reports than in discussions of propositions, past tenses often accompany it. That is, it tends in that respect to be quasi-narrative as well as expository in its function. It is especially in contexts such as the following, taken from a report of views expressed by members of the parties of the Right, that it could serve as a variant for *de [son] côté*:

> « Il est temps de réaliser, a déclaré M. Bernard Pons, que l'adversaire ne se trouve pas dans nos propres rangs mais face à nous. »
> M. Jacques Toubon s'est, quant à lui, proposé de créer un courant « majoritaire ».

There the function of the connector, rather than pointing a contrast, is to draw attention to points of view which are concomitant and separate but not necessarily at variance with one another. Similarly, in the next example, the connector which flags the attitude of France could be replaced by either *de son côté* or *pour sa part*. It merely identifies a new point of view which differs little from the one preceding it:

> Les États-Unis ont tout lieu, dans cette affaire, de se féliciter de la cohésion de la communauté internationale, et d'abord de la fermeté de leurs alliés. La Grande-Bretagne a donné, jeudi, une nouvelle preuve de son soutien sans réserve à Washington en annonçant l'envoi dans le Golfe d'une escadrille supplémentaire de chasseurs-bombardiers Tornado. La France, quant à elle, un moment soupçonnée – à tort, semble-t-il – d'avoir voulu faire bande à part, a réaffirmé avec force sa détermination.

Differences from the paradigm *quant à*

This connector is a particular variant of the contrastive paradigm *quant à*, which can be followed by a noun, a demonstrative pronoun, an adjective or the infinitive of a verb. There are three main ways in which this structure differs from the paradigm. One is that the latter, when followed by a noun or a demonstrative pronoun, may relate either to a subject or an object; but this connector only ever refers to a subject. Another is that the paradigm is almost always placed at the beginning of a sentence, whereas this connector normally comes later in the sentence, after the subject or even after the verb. The third difference is that, while the paradigm tends towards a basically narrative function, this variant with tonic pronoun, at least in its more contrastive mode, is little used in story-telling – in *À la recherche du temps perdu*, for instance, of the 191 occurrences of *quant à*, only seven could be said to bear some resemblance to it (Brunet, III, 1158–1159).

As can be seen from the examples, the majority view on the punctuation of this connector is to flank it with commas (see also Drillon, 205).

English equivalents include 'on the other hand', 'however', 'as for ...' and simple 'but'. Quite often a contrast would be made without the use of a connecting word.

question

The connective function of the question is obvious: it usually asks something about what precedes; and an answer to it can structure an entire following paragraph, even initiate a whole development. A form of question by which an author invites a reader to participate in the exposition of a point of view is still widely used in French dialectical discourse, much more so than in English. A writer sometimes reinforces this interlocutory relation by using the possessive adjective: *Comment alors justifier notre schématisation historique ?* In questioning his or her own way of discussing the subject, it is as though the writer were asking on the reader's behalf.

The question and the paragraph

A question can structure a paragraph in two ways. When asked in the final sentence of a paragraph, as it often is, it can serve as an explicit link to the following one which then gives a detailed answer to it. Or else it is asked in an opening sentence, announcing the structuring idea of the paragraph, which sets about answering it: *D'où tenait-il ces six volumes ? Très probablement de son père. / Que dit Toldo dans cet article ? En voici l'essentiel. / Qu'en est-il exactement du naufrage de ce sous-marin soviétique ? Nul ne le sait. Mais une chose est sûre.* Among the most common interrogative structures used are: *Est-ce à dire que...?* and *S'agit-il de...?*

Brief questions, brief answers

The initial answer to a question is often a verbless sentence. Many questions are very brief, often taking the form of a noun in apposition. Many answers, too, are very brief; and they are often in negative form: *Rentiers contre productifs ? Pas si simple. / Débat purement hollywoodien ? Non. Débat national. / La vie de Rabelais ? Prétexte à de plaisantes légendes. /*

*Constatation banale ? Que non pas ! | Snobisme inconscient ? Que nenni.
| Machiavélisme ? Point n'est certain. | Sujet menu ? Voire ! | Est-ce à dire
que le marxisme est condamné à la fixité absolue ? Nullement.* Other typical
brief answers, with or without verbs, are: *Loin s'en faut. | Nul ne le sait.
| On ne peut l'exclure. | Rien n'est moins sûr. | Pas si sûr. | Sans doute
pas. | C'est probable.* Quite common, too, is the single word *Réponse.* The
following example of such a question and answer constitutes the first two
sentences of a long article about the end of the cold war and the problem
of what to do about the excessive arsenals of nuclear weapons which had
been accumulated during it, especially those in Russian hands:

> De son interminable duel avec le monde occidental, que reste-t-il aujourd'hui
> à l'ex-« patrie du socialisme », en dehors d'une idéologie morte, d'une économie
> naufragée, d'un empire perdu, d'un pouvoir contesté ? Réponse : des armes,
> rien que des armes.
>
> (Fontaine, 1990)

Sequences of questions

Some writers ask several questions one after the other. These sequences
of questions and answers can go so far as to occupy a whole paragraph,
as in this review of French political history:

> De tous les régimes qu'a connus notre peuple, pas un n'a su éviter la cata-
> strophe. La royauté absolue ? Elle a sombré dans la plus sanglante des
> révolutions. La première République ? Dans l'anarchie et le coup d'État. Le
> premier Empire ? Dans deux invasions et deux abdications. La Restauration ?
> La monarchie de Juillet ? En quelques journées de barricades. La seconde
> République ? Dans le césarisme. Le second Empire ? À Sedan. La IIIe
> République ? À Sedan aussi. Vichy finirait à Sigmaringen, et la IVe République
> par le coup d'Alger.
>
> (Peyrefitte, 19)

Sequences of questions very similar to those are sometimes used to structure brief series of ***antithèses sans charnière***.

A series of such questions, standing first in consecutive paragraphs, can
even structure a whole article or argument. Thus, early in a discussion of
the style of Rabelais, a paragraph comes down to this statement defining
its three most salient qualities: *les caractères essentiels de l'art de Rabelais :
la vérité, la variété, la fantaisie.* This is immediately followed by three
further paragraphs, the first of which begins *La vérité ?*; the second, *La
variété ?*; and the third, *La fantaisie, enfin....* Similarly, an article about
the lack of anxieties facing Michel Rocard, then Prime Minister, first asks
these questions:

> Quelles raisons aurait-il, d'ailleurs, d'être inquiet ? Une mauvaise situation
> économique, des mouvements sociaux, une opposition forte, une majorité
> délabrée, des rapports difficiles avec le président de la République ?

The writer of the article then answers these questions in consecutive paragraphs each of which begins with a similar verbless question introducing an answer to the point previously raised: *La situation économique ?*; *Des mouvements sociaux ?*; *L'état de l'opposition ?*; *L'état de la majorité ?* etc.

Followed by *en tout cas* or *en tout état de cause*

Unlike the question which is asked only so as to introduce the certainty of its answer, some are asked so as to canvass no more than a hypothesis or to express uncertainty on a point. This may be done with single questions, or more usually with series of questions, to which the writer can give no firm answer. The sentence following such a question often contains *en tout cas*, which limits the uncertainty without answering the question, as in this extract from a discussion of the possibility that an ancient reluctance to be married in the month of May may have persisted into more recent times:

> Ce tabou a-t-il traversé les siècles et perduré pendant le moyen âge ? Il est difficile de le savoir. Il est en tout cas dénoncé par les autorités ecclésiastiques au XVIIᵉ siècle.

> (Besnard, 58)

A similar uncertainty or hypothesis expressed in interrogative form can at times be followed by *en tout état de cause*, a structure with which a writer does not resolve the uncertainty but introduces a statement of fact which is true despite the uncertainty. This example comes from a discussion of Russia's continuing expenditure on defence items for the purpose of protecting the economy of regions traditionally dependent on the manufacture of weapons, and despite the fact that the budget can hardly afford them:

> De manière significative, l'augmentation de 3 500 milliards de roubles qui figure au budget ira presque intégralement à l'industrie de défense. Ces recettes supplémentaires sont-elles réelles ou imaginaires ? En tout état de cause, si cette « solution-miracle » se révélait illusoire, l'État serait contraint, comme d'habitude, de trouver en cours d'année une autre source de revenus pour l'armée, fût-elle délibérément inflationniste.

Non-interrogative hypotheses

The rhetorical question is at times a variant for the non-interrogative inversion of subject and verb expressing a hypothesis: *Voudrait-il le faire, il ne le pourrait pas.* / *Restait-on dehors, on fondait au soleil* (examples borrowed from Grevisse, 1964a: 1075 & 1087). This type of inversion means nothing more than 'if'; and it can structure a single sentence of which the second element, the main clause, is introduced by *que* and does not end with a question mark:

> Apparaît-il que Havas a testé en Bourse les défenses du groupe Hachette désta-bilisé par la débâcle de la Cinq (et qui s'apprête pour cette raison à fusionner avec Matra), que nulle autorité morale ne s'en est offusquée.

The similarity in function can be seen in sentences which do end with question marks. In this example, the writer says François Mitterrand turns nasty if he is doubted or opposed:

> Se sent-il soupçonné, comprend-il qu'on le jauge, qu'on le juge ou qu'on le désapprouve ? Aussitôt, comme s'il était piqué par une mygale, il se cabre et déploie ses défenses : le regard se durcit, la moue gourmée devient babine cruelle...

> (Nay, 324)

Questions without answers

The question can also be used in a rhetorical way which serves no connecting purpose. A discussion of medieval architecture contains this one: *Si elle n'est pas exempte de mièvrerie, n'est-ce pas une merveille que l'église Saint Maclou de Rouen ?* There it requires no answer, being used merely for the paradoxical purpose of intensifying the expressive-ness of an affirmation while couching it in a form that appears to atten-tuate it. An analogous role is played by *Que dire de...*, **qui ne voit que**, *Comment ne pas voir que...* and the common formula *Est-il besoin de dire que...*, which is commonly printed without a question mark and is sensed as a variant for *Inutile de dire que...* and other formally interrogative modes of **ajoutons que**, such as *Faut-il ajouter...*. An expres-sive affirmation in interrogative form is seen in the next example too. The writer's point is that, although the Spanish Prime Minister, Felipe González, used arguments normally used by the extreme Right to oppose the immigration of poor foreign workers, this does not make him a fascist:

> Felipe González croyant, sans doute, protéger les intérêts des travailleurs espa-gnols n'en a pas moins commis sur ce point, à mon avis, une erreur économique et une mesquinerie morale. Est-ce pour ce motif qu'on aurait le droit de le traiter d'émule d'Eichmann ?

> (Revel, 1988: 73)

Sometimes a writer will attenuate an affirmation into a rhetorical ques-tion as though to guard against a possible objection or because the evidence may not appear to support the affirmative conclusion. A histo-rian discussing differences between groups of young men from the north of France and from the south in the early nineteenth century wonders whether the northerners are possibly more modern in their outlook on the world and in their view of themselves:

> Oserons-nous dire que ces mentalités septentrionales nous apparaissent plus modernes, et plus en conformité avec les caractéristiques professionnelles de régions actives et en expansion ?
>
> (Le Roy Ladurie, 53)

Punctuation

Two small but important points about French punctuation: firstly, like some other stops (the ***deux-points***, the semicolon, the exclamation mark), the question mark is normally preceded by a half-space, what is known to French typographers, for whom *espace* in this sense is feminine, as « *une* » espace « *fine* » *(sauf quand il est placé entre parenthèses)* (Drillon, 349). Secondly, as with the exclamation mark, it can be placed in the middle of a sentence and followed by a small letter:

> Est-il besoin de l'ajouter ? *quitte*, simple adjectif, dans des phrases comme : « Nous voilà *quittes* », « Je les tiens *quittes* », s'accorde.
>
> (Grevisse, 1962: 168)

qui ne voit que

This structure is one of those with a function which is as plain as its apparent meaning. It is used much less now than it was once. In the earlier years of this century, its function was to introduce a self-evident conclusion. Thus, Roger Dion, discussing the idea that the Rhine constitutes one of France's 'natural frontiers', says the river does not separate two peoples as much as it joins them, agreeing with Lucien Febvre's view that the 'natural frontier' notion is untenable and derives ultimately from Caesar's *Commentaries*:

> Il serait vain d'espérer cependant qu'un historien ou un géographe osât aujourd'hui prendre à son compte le thème suranné de la « frontière naturelle du Rhin » et professer ainsi son adhésion à ce que M. Lucien Febvre a joliment appelé « le vieux mythe forgé sur l'enclume des Commentaires ». Qui ne voit que la fonction naturelle du Rhin est d'unir bien plus que de séparer les peuples des deux rives ?
>
> (Dion, 1947: 59–60)

The structure, though couched in the form of a ***question***, is one of those formal interrogatives like *Comment ne pas voir que* and *Est-il besoin de dire que* which, by functioning as it were affirmatively, are often printed without a question mark.

In addition to the two last-named structures, replacements for this one used nowadays with greater or lesser frequency include: *Il est clair que*;

Il est évident que; *Il est incontestable que*; *Il est facile de voir que*; *Il est aisé de voir que*; *Il ne fait aucun doute que*; *Il ne fait pas de doute que*; *Il va de soi que*; *Il va sans dire que*; *Chacun le sait*; *Tout le monde sait que*; *Nul ne le conteste*; *Nul ne l'ignore*; *Qui pourrait le nier ?*

Conclusions introduced by this structure are clearly much firmer than those introduced by **tout se passe comme si** and probably even than those introduced by **force est de**.

quitte à

This structure is in most respects relatively unproblematical: it is almost always followed by an infinitive; and the link it makes often has a semi-adversative quality suited to the expression of irony or paradox. Its main interest lies in the fact that more and more writers these days like to use it as a way of linking a **phrase dépendante** to the sentence preceding. It has different shades of meaning, all of them suggesting possible conse-quences of a preceding action: *au risque de*, *avec la possibilité de*, *en se réservant de*.

Inside the sentence

Normally the structure is preceded by a comma and connects parts of a single sentence. The subject of the verb following is also the subject of the main verb preceding. The combination of connector plus what follows functions as a second or final complement of the main verb, as in this comment on the use that politicians of the Right make of Joan of Arc:

> Depuis un siècle, les tenants de l'idéologie d'extrême droite en France se sont fait un porte-drapeau de Jeanne d'Arc. Jean-Marie Le Pen s'est contenté en l'occurrence d'exacerber jusqu'à la caricature cette tradition, quitte à s'identi-fier à la sainte.

A dash preceding the connector can make for a contrastive effect, as in this extract from a discussion of Paul de Saint-Victor, deemed by the writer to be more of a romancer than a reliable historian of the theatre:

> Rappelons-nous que Saint-Victor est un romantique, et qui aurait quelquefois tendance à regarder ses sujets de page brillante avec les mêmes yeux que Victor Hugo regardait Richelieu ou François Ier. Il y a plus de littérature que d'his-toricité dans ces vues, mais si la page est belle, admirons – quitte à ne pas croire.

> (Henriot, 1954: 190)

As these examples show, what follows is often short, containing no more than a single proposition.

The examples show, too, that the adverbial relation is regressive, that is, the structure modifies the main verb preceding; and the complement it introduces is frequently the final element in a sentence. However, the adverbial relation can also be made with the main verb following, in which case the connector begins a statement rather than bringing up the end of one, as in this extract from a discussion of French disquiet about the financial power of a reunified Germany, at a time when the German Chancellor, Helmut Kohl, was reluctant to commit himself to European monetary union:

> François Mitterrand et quelques autres qui, comme lui, pressent le chancelier, ne dissimulent pas l'objectif : quitte à vivre dans une « zone mark » où la puissance allemande sera encore renforcée à terme par la réunification, mieux vaut avoir la possibilité d'y dire son mot ; autant amener la Bundesbank à partager un pouvoir qu'elle exerce et exercera sinon de façon hégémonique.

The structure can combine with *même*, as in this extract from a discussion of the reasons for the defeat of Giscard d'Estaing and the victory of François Mitterrand in the presidential election of May 1981. The writer says that many voters felt out of touch with things and had had enough of Giscard's far-fetched explanations:

> Des fractions entières de l'électorat en étaient toutes déboussolées. Dès qu'un problème se posait, la solution ou la cause était à chercher aux antipodes. La réalité finissait par devenir incontrôlable. Les électeurs avaient manifestement envie de revenir en France, de rompre avec la culture et le style des multinationales, de parler de la France aux Français, quitte même à se replier sur l'horizon hexagonal.
>
> (July, 50)

In *phrases dépendantes*

If there is a difference between the structure placed inside the sentence and placed first in the sentence (or even paragraph), it may be in the length and complexity of what follows in relation to what precedes. When placed first in a *phrase dépendante*, it is often followed by more than a single proposition. This example is from an article about the RPR, in which MM. Pasqua and Séguin, it is alleged, intend to undermine Jacques Chirac and supplant him not as leader but as the real power within the party:

> MM. Pasqua et Séguin mèneront non pas une campagne législative en dehors du RPR, mais une campagne autonome, car leur objectif est bel et bien de vider le RPR de sa substance chiraquienne, pour en prendre eux-mêmes le contrôle. Quitte à garder Jacques Chirac comme chef, mais à la condition qu'il les suive, qu'il devienne, ou redevienne, un instrument entre leurs mains.

Another example comes from a discussion of the decision by M. Fillon,
then Minister for Higher Education, to placate his back bench by limiting
the autonomy of certain new universities and their power to experiment
with courses:

> Après avoir, au creux de l'été, envisagé de reporter l'examen de ce dossier
> après 1995, le ministre paraît donc désormais décidé à ne pas renoncer à cette
> revendication permanente de sa majorité, impatiente jusqu'à l'obsession de
> casser le cadre de la loi Savary. Quitte, pour ne pas s'exposer à la même
> fausse manœuvre que cet été, à suivre les recommandations du Conseil consti-
> tutionnel : les expérimentations proposées seront, a précisé M. Fillon, « limitées
> dans le temps et dans l'espace ».

quitte à ce que

If the subject of the verb following is not the same as the subject of the
verb preceding, this structure augmented with *ce que* is adapted to a
subjunctive. This example comes from a discussion of the legal situation
of the former *maire* of Nice, Jacques Médecin, after his extradition from
Venezuela: although his criminal activities, both proved and alleged, made
it illegal for him to bear certain public offices, they did not prevent him
from standing for election to them: *Il ne semble pas que l'on puisse lui
interdire de faire acte de candidature, quitte à ce que son élection soit par
la suite annulée.* This mode is also placed first in a *phrase dépendante*.

As for possible English equivalents, the basic meaning of the connector
is 'even though (or even if) a possible consequence of this may be ...'
The Mansion dictionary offers an admirable range of them, all longer than
the very compact French construction, some of them based on 'even if'
or 'even though'. One could add to the list, say, 'with the proviso that'.
In a context like the following, first in a *phrase dépendante*:

> Contrairement aux chroniqueurs littéraires, qui n'écrivent finalement que pour
> leurs pairs, à l'instar des députés qui ne parlent qu'aux députés, les critiques
> de cinéma et de théâtre continuent, bon gré, mal gré, de s'adresser au public.
> Quitte, d'ailleurs, à le rudoyer, le provoquer, l'exaspérer, ou au contraire le
> flatter.

one might express its sense in English with 'This may mean, mind you,
browbeating etc ...'.

reste

This is one of three connectors made from the third person of the verb
rester. The other two are **reste à** and **reste que**. These three structures are
similar in some ways; but their differences justify treating them separately.

Three of the distinguishing features of this one are that the tense of the verb is variable, which never happens with *reste que*; that the subject of the verb is rarely impersonal, whereas in the other two it is always impersonal; and that the verb can be plural, which is never the case with the other two. In addition, it is almost always, unlike the others, an **inversion du verbe**.

The subject

This connector's basic function in argument is to announce a point that remains to be discussed. Of several factors considered in a discussion, it therefore usually introduces the last one: *Reste Mars*, says the author of an article on the planets of the solar system, after having dealt with the other eight. The structure is completed by a noun, which immediately follows the verb and functions as its inverted subject. Hence, if the noun is singular, the verb is singular: *Reste l'Italie*, says the last part of a discussion of some of the countries of Europe; if the noun is plural, so is the verb: *Restent les députés, vingt-six au total*, says an article on the decline of the French Communist Party.

The place in the sentence and the paragraph

Here is an example of the connector showing its relation to the paragraph which it helps to structure; in a consideration of the earnings of three groups of French peasants, it introduces the third of these:

> Un tiers des paysans français ont des revenus agricoles misérables mais ne se débrouillent pas trop mal grâce à des aides directes, dans les montagnes surtout, ou en développant d'autres activités. Un tiers d'exploitants sont très riches. Ce sont eux qui réalisent 80 % du chiffre d'affaires de l'agriculture française. Reste un tiers de paysans qui vivent avec des revenus moyens et fragiles, sans aides directes suffisantes. Ces derniers n'ont pas les reins assez solides pour s'en sortir.

The connector is almost invariably placed first in the sentence, often at the beginning of paragraphs, many of which, given its usual function, are final paragraphs. Here are the last two paragraphs of an article on possible ways of reducing the number of people whose rash behaviour leads them to be killed each year on French ski-slopes:

> Faudra-t-il dès lors fermer les pistes ou les remontées mécaniques dès que les conditions pour skier ne seront pas idéales ? Faudra-t-il mettre des gendarmes ou des CRS pour interdire l'accès à la montagne aux imprudents ? Cela est totalement irréaliste. Il n'empêche que l'on se dirige de plus en plus vers la rigueur et vers des précautions hier considérées comme inutiles.
>
> Reste l'information : c'est sans doute l'arme la plus réaliste pour dissuader les inconscients.

Typical ways of introducing a final sentence or paragraph are: *Reste un dernier point à régler* and *Reste posé un problème fondamental et non encore résolu.*

The tense

The present tense is commonest. But other tenses are sometimes used, as in the example following. It comes from an article on Gorbachev's normalization of relations with China in 1989: having begun by considering three of the four important areas in which Gorbachev had significantly altered Soviet policy in the late 1980s – the USA, Western Europe and the Third World – the author comes eventually to deal with the fourth of them:

> Restait la Chine, l'autre géant du socialisme, l'autre puissance communiste à siéger au Conseil de sécurité des Nations unies, le [...]

The next extract, containing the conditional, comes from an article on the great difficulties in the way of producing a vaccine against HIV:

> Il est très peu probable qu'un vaccin puisse être applicable à de larges populations avant, au minimum, la première décennie du vingt et unième siècle.
>   Si un tel vaccin était découvert, resterait le problème de son coût *a priori* très élevé, ce qui rendrait pour le moins difficile son utilisation à une large échelle dans les pays en voie de développement.

That sentence is also a rare example of the connector being placed later than the beginning of the sentence. When combined with *ne... que*, too, it is not actually the first word: *Ne restera plus dès lors que la question de savoir si....* There, the similarity to *Ne reste plus qu'à* shows how close this structure can come to being a variant of *reste à.*

With an adverb of time

The connector is sometimes combined with an adverb of time, such as *alors* or *dès lors* whether used temporally or logically. The most frequent of these adverbs is no doubt *maintenant*, as in this extract from an article on the Belgian government's devolution of some powers to the Wallonie region: *Voilà donc la Wallonie en partie maîtresse de son destin. Reste maintenant l'essentiel : pour quoi faire ?*

The addition of *enfin*, though no doubt redundant, is not unknown. In newspapers, *enfin* is at times replaced by its modish substitute *au final*: *Reste au final une question sans réponse à ce jour....*

Variations

On occasion, a writer uses this connector in a way reminiscent of one of the modes of *reste que*: to introduce the third point in a sequence of three, so as to reaffirm an initial proposition to which a possible objection has been raised in the second proposition. Thus a discussion of a similarity between Guilleragues's *Les lettres d'une religieuse portugaise* and aspects of the plays of Racine makes these three points: there is a similarity of tone; it is not evidence of an influence; but still the similarity is there. And it is that third point which is presented by this connector:

> ...la passion mélancolique et fière qui s'exprime dans les *Lettres* a pour nous un son « racinien » incontestable [...]. Je repousserai, pour ma part, toute idée d'influence, Racine étant Racine avant la publication des *Lettres*. Reste une ressemblance profonde.
>
> (Mauron, 254)

On occasion, too, a writer will use impersonal *il* as the subject of the verb, as in this extract from a discussion about the end of the international Communist movement:

> Quant au mouvement communiste international, l'effondrement du mur de Berlin, l'émancipation des pays de l'Est et la défaite de Mikhaïl Gorbatchev ont donné le signal de ses funérailles. Il reste bien la Chine, géante et ambiguë, mais elle ne peut prétendre devenir la capitale mythique du communisme mondial.

In such circumstances the grammar may change: the following noun, being now the object of the verb, may be plural without the verb being plural: *Il reste cependant deux grands contrastes....*

A further variation is sometimes found: *rester* is replaced by *demeurer*. Near the end of her review of a film, a critic speaks first of a powerful scene, then raises a question of morality. The scene, she says,

> ravit le spectateur, l'amenant aux confins de la fascination horrifiée. Le point de bascule qui entraîne les protagonistes dans l'horreur se joue à l'instant où Jean avoue à Laura – son amante – qu'il est séropositif. Est-ce cet aveu (il n'avait pas porté de préservatif) qui joue un rôle dans la folle passion qui embrasera Laura ?
>
> Demeure une question éthique : ce très beau film, en quelque sorte inaugural, ne risque-t-il pas de céder au piège d'un « Pardonnez-leur, ils ne savent pas ce qu'ils font » ?

English equivalents include 'finally', 'lastly' or 'There remains ...'.

reste à

This connector is one of three made from the third person of the verb *rester*. The other two are **reste** and **reste que**. Despite some similarities, these three structures present important differences: like *reste*, the tense of this one is variable; like *reste que*, it always has an impersonal subject; in function, it is close to *reste* and usually quite different from *reste que*.

Basic functions

Unlike *reste*, which is followed by a noun, this structure is followed by the infinitive of a verb. It has two forms, *reste à* and *il reste à*, which are interchangeable, except that the latter can combine with a pronoun: *Il nous reste à voir ce qui résulte de notre analyse.* Its function, similar to that of *reste*, is to introduce a statement about something that remains to be done, said or shown. And for reasons similar to those which obtain with *reste*, it is often placed near the end of a discussion, at the beginning of a final paragraph, say. An article about difficulties created by a proposal to have certain degrees and diplomas recognized in all countries of the European Community begins its last paragraph: *Reste à résoudre le problème des formations plus longues.* Another way of making this statement would have been with *reste* + noun: *Reste le problème des formations plus longues.*

The verb following

The verb most commonly used to complete this structure is *savoir*. An article about what is to become of the nuclear reactor at Chernobyl, a source of grave disquiet and danger since the accident there, says this:

> Sur le principe, tout le monde est d'accord depuis longtemps : il faut fermer Tchernobyl. Reste à savoir comment et dans quelles conditions, et à trouver le financement nécessaire.

Reste à savoir si... and *Il reste à savoir pourquoi...* are quite common forms. Almost any verb could combine with this structure. It tends to be used with verbs which, like *savoir*, express the idea of clarifying a fact: *Il reste à définir*; *Il reste à déterminer*; *Il reste à voir*.

With an adverb

The use of an adverb is common, perhaps more so than with *reste* + noun. It is often **enfin**, a combination which reinforces the connector's finalizing function. Adverbs of time such as **dès lors** or *maintenant*, used either temporally or logically, are also common. The adverb always stands between the verb and the preposition: *Reste maintenant à attendre le jugement. / Restera ensuite à tenter de... / Il reste désormais à savoir comment... / Le plan de bataille est, dans ses grandes lignes, arrêté. Reste encore à définir les modalités pratiques. / Certains motifs dont la pertinence apparaîtra progressivement nous incitent à choisir le second de ces deux modes de classification. Reste dès lors à assumer la tâche immédiate que ce choix comporte.*

Sometimes an adverb gives a sharp adversative focus to the relation between what precedes and what follows, as *toutefois* does in this comment on self-styled defenders of the French language. The writer says they are not very successful in 'defending' it:

> Mais ils ont certainement réussi à convaincre à peu près tout le monde qu'il convient de défendre la langue. Il reste toutefois à définir exactement ce qu'est cette langue française qu'il faut défendre et contre qui et contre quoi.
>
> (Martinet, 26)

Place in the sentence

Like the other two structures with *reste*, this one is rarely found anywhere but at the beginning of sentences. Sometimes it is placed in the second part of a sentence, as in this extract from an article on research on new interferons being developed to combat multiple sclerosis:

> La physiopathologie fine de la sclérose en plaques n'étant toujours pas élucidée, il reste enfin à savoir comment s'organisera la compétition commerciale entre les deux fabricants d'interféron.

A similar sequence is made when the connector is preceded by a **cela dit** type of structure: *Ce principe acquis, il restait à « découper » le pays en neuf régions.*

Apart from those sequences, the closest it comes to losing that initial position is when it is preceded by a single word, as in *Ne reste plus qu'à...* or when used in tandem with another connector such as **de même** or **mais**. The first of these examples is an extract from a discussion of negotiations between political groupings in South Africa:

> Aujourd'hui la question des frontières régionales n'est pas totalement tranchée. De même reste à régler le futur statut de Pretoria, dont la vocation de capitale est contestée par l'ANC.

> Émise par le ministre saoudien, M. Hisham Nazer, l'idée ne pouvait qu'être prise au sérieux. Elle l'a été. Mais il reste à la mettre en musique.

Variants

Occasionally a writer uses *de* with this structure instead of *à*, as in this extract from an article on the refurbishment of Jacques Copeau's former

Vieux-Colombier theatre under the new auspices of the Comédie française:

> Ce qui était un théâtre de bric et de broc devient donc un outil performant, mais qui garde, de la charpente de la salle au long couloir qui la sépare de la rue, toute l'histoire et tout le charme du Vieux-Colombier de Copeau. Reste aux sociétaires de la maison Molière non pas de prouver leur talent, mais de préserver un peu de cet esprit d'aventure qui pouvait jeter toute une troupe dans la rue, sur les traces du jeune Poquelin.

This writer's choice of *de*, a mode defined as *vieilli* more than a generation ago (Hanse, 1949: 637), may have been affected by the interpolation of an indirect object between the verb and the preposition. However, even then, the structure with *à* is usual: *Il reste aux socialistes et aux écologistes à engager une véritable discussion sur les projets d'avenir. / Il restera – plus tard – aux diplomates et aux experts à imaginer sur le terrain un compromis.*

Two further variants (*la question reste de savoir* and *le tout est de savoir*) can be seen in the following pair of examples. The first comes from a discussion comparing Flaubert's novel *Madame Bovary* with the so called *nouvelle version* of the text (in fact an earlier draft of the published work):

> Je dois renvoyer le lecteur à l'étonnant texte produit, si intéressant à considérer page à page, dans sa gangue compacte, avec le texte décanté que Flaubert a voulu définitif. La question reste de savoir aujourd'hui si l'on aime mieux ce grand Flaubert avec sa maîtrise ou avant ; à l'état de brouillon ou définitif ; le chef-d'œuvre en train de se faire ou le chef-d'œuvre fait.

> Il apparaît peu probable que les agriculteurs des différents pays de la CEE acceptent d'aller au-delà des sacrifices déjà consentis avec la réforme de la politique agricole commune. Le tout est maintenant de savoir si les demandes américaines sont compatibles avec cette réforme.

Unlike *reste* + noun, this one, because its subject, implicit or explicit, is always impersonal *il*, is hardly ever used in the plural. However, occasionally a writer does make the verb plural, to agree with nouns following, as in this extract from an article about the development of the part of Paris known to town-planners as Seine-Rive gauche, opposite the new Bibliothèque de France:

> Tout est prêt depuis plusieurs mois : les terrains ont été achetés, les projets d'architectes sélectionnés après concours et les maîtres d'ouvrage désignés, qu'ils soient publics ou privés. Restent à obtenir le permis de construire et les financements publics.

English equivalents would mainly use the verb 'remain'. They would include 'What remains to be established is …'. There is an evident similarity between 'It remains to be seen whether' and the quite common *Il reste à voir.*

reste que *

This is one of three connectors made from the third person of the verb *rester*. The other two are *reste* + noun and *reste à* + verb. They are similar to each other in some ways; but the differences between them outweigh the similarities. This one is similar to *reste à* in that it exists in two modes: *reste que* and *il reste que*. It is different from the two others in that the verb-form *reste* is invariable: both of the others can vary in tense, one of them in person. The greatest difference of function between this one and the other two is that they rarely make an adversative link, whereas this one never does anything else.

In binary oppositions

This connector is at times closer in function to *n'empêche* and to the *n'en... pas moins* structure than to the two other structures made from *reste*. The similarity between it and *n'empêche que* can be seen in the way it structures straightforward binary oppositions. The following example is from an article on the disquiet felt by some politicians in the early 1990s at the cost of the library then known as the TGB (Très Grande Bibliothèque), designed by Dominique Perrault and in the course of being built:

> Arrêter brutalement les travaux est difficilement imaginable. Quai de la Gare, le bâtiment de Dominique Perrault commence à sortir de terre. Les salles de lecture se dessinent peu à peu. Que pourra-t-on remettre en cause ? La taille des tours, l'aménagement du jardin central ? Les élus de l'opposition sont aujourd'hui fort prudents. Reste que le prix de la TGB (Très Grande Bibliothèque) paraît exorbitant à certains d'entre eux.

There, the structure introduces, as *n'empêche que* frequently does, the second element in a contrastive pair: first, the statement about the parliamentarians' caution; then, introduced by the connector, the countervailing statement about their concern over the cost. In such contexts, the connector could also be replaced by *mais* or *il n'en reste pas moins que*.

Apart from the ubiquitous 'but', English equivalents for this mode could be 'even so', 'however', 'the fact is, though' or 'the fact remains that'.

Following a concession

Also like *n'empêche que*, this connector can introduce the third part of a tripartite development, reaffirming the gist of an initial assertion which has been restricted by a second part beginning with a concessive such as *certes* or *sans doute*. The following example comes from a discussion of the Parti socialiste which, the writer says, having been routed at the general election of 1993, could think of nothing better to do than vote down Michel Rocard, a leader who would have been capable of revitalizing it:

> Le Parti socialiste n'a rien trouvé de mieux que d'écarter sans ménagement, un an après son échec électoral, celui qui avait commencé à lui rendre un certain dynamisme. Certes, Michel Rocard n'est pas exempt de toute responsabilité dans la perte de confiance des Français à l'égard des socialistes. Il reste qu'il avait engagé la gauche sur la voie du redressement et qu'il a bel et bien été « abattu en plein vol ».

The next example, in which the three-part sequence is only slightly less evident, comes from a discussion of the extent of the time-honoured French custom of ballot-rigging, which the writer calls *une honte de la démocratie dans ce pays*. Again, it introduces a third sentence which reaffirms the general import of the first one, after the partial objection to it introduced by *sans doute* in the second sentence:

> En novembre dernier, Michel Sapin (PS), le rapporteur de la loi antifraude adoptée à l'unanimité par l'Assemblée nationale, soulignait qu'il n'était « pas possible d'apprécier l'importance quantitative » du « phénomène » de la fraude. Il est sans doute faible. Reste que qualitativement, si l'on peut dire, le « phénomène » ne peut être tenu pour anecdotique.

After statements of uncertainty

The structure can also function after the manner of ***toujours est-il que***, introducing a statement of certainty after a development implying uncertainty. In the following example, the subject of the article is the sentencing to death, in 1989, by the imam Ayatollah Khomeini of the writer Salman Rushdie; and the uncertainty is expressed by the preceding ***questions***:

> S'agit-il d'une manœuvre politique contre le clan « libéral », que l'imam vient encore de dénoncer violemment ? D'un signe de démence sénile ? De la volonté de réaffirmer une autorité battue en brèche ? Laissons aux experts le soin de trancher. Il reste que, au nom d'une religion qui n'est celle que d'un humain sur cinq, un théocrate sans mandat politique s'arroge le droit de condamner à mort un étranger.

Lack of certainty may be expressed not only by questions. In the next example, much of it is expressed by the repeated *Peut-être*. But the sequence of propositions is very similar to that in the previous example: first, the uncertainty; next, an admission of the author's inability to resolve the uncertainty, analogous to *Laissons aux experts le soin de trancher* in the previous example; thirdly, the statement of what *is* certain, introduced by the connector. The subject under discussion is what the author calls *la spécificité des sexes*: whether the masculinity and femininity of men and women who form couples are behaviours learned and transmitted through culture or determined genetically, and whether this mystery can ever be solved scientifically:

> Peut-être les observations ne démontreront-elles jamais d'une manière irrécusable la spécificité des sexes. Peut-être ne parviendrons-nous jamais à reconnaître scientifiquement ce qui à la fois sépare et réunit les deux principes tant nature et culture sont radicalement mêlées. Faut-il admettre avec certains psychologues que les sexes correspondent à deux attitudes fondamentales et différentes, l'une de vive reconnaissance du réel, l'autre de désir de modifier celui-ci ? Nous n'avons pas la compétence pour en décider. Il reste seulement que pour beaucoup le couple demeure le lieu d'une plénitude, dont ils n'imaginent pas pouvoir trouver un équivalent.
>
> (Roussel, 238)

Place in the sentence

As is apparent from all the examples quoted above, this structure, whether containing *il* or omitting it, is commonly placed first in the sentence or paragraph. When a writer does put it elsewhere, which is rare, it is the mode with *il* which is preferred: *Tout cela accordé, il reste que....* It is sometimes placed in the second half of sentences begun by a *si d'opposition*. In this example, an editorialist deplores methods employed by Russia and the USA to force the Ukraine to agree to divest itself of nuclear weapons which the newly independent state had retained after the dissolution of the former USSR:

> Si, en fin de compte, on peut se féliciter d'un accord qui restreint le nombre des puissances nucléaires de la planète, il reste que la pression exercée par les Américains et les Russes pour faire céder Kiev a eu quelque chose de choquant.

Or it may be used following *mais* or a *cela dit* type of structure, as in this extract from an essay on the continuing importance of the four seasons in French life. The author makes two basic points: that, though the seasons are not all of the same length, we have the impression that they are. And that contrast is made by this connector, after a variant of *cela dit*:

> Les quatre saisons ne sont pas de même longueur : actuellement, dans l'hémisphère nord, l'été compte près de 94 jours, devançant le printemps, l'automne, enfin l'hiver qui ne dure que 89 jours. Et la durée des saisons varie lentement au fil des siècles. Ces précisions étant faites, il reste que nous nous représentons communément, sans commettre une grosse erreur, que les quatre saisons se partagent également l'année.
>
> (Besnard, 14)

Often, when placed second in such sequences, the connector could again be replaced by *il n'en reste pas moins que*.

Variants

A less common mode is *Il demeure que*. In the following extract, in which again the connector is not placed first in the sentence, the writer is ending a paragraph in which he has been concerned to point out that later French anti-Semitism does not alter the fact that it was in revolutionary France that Jews were first emancipated and accorded political equality with other citizens of the republic:

> Et même si, après un siècle, éclatait l'affaire Dreyfus, et, cinquante ans plus tard, la plus terrible épreuve qu'aient jamais connue les Juifs, il demeure que c'est en France – et non pas ailleurs en Europe – et pendant la Révolution française – et non pas sous l'Ancien Régime – que les Juifs furent proclamés, par une assemblée souveraine, « libres et égaux ».
>
> (Badinter, 1989: 16)

Sometimes this connector is combined with other *mais*-type objectors and contrastives in redundantly reinforced structures like *Mais il reste vrai que*, *Reste pourtant que*, *Il reste tout de même que*, *Reste seulement que* and *Reste néanmoins que*. Such combinations make apparent its closeness to *n'en... pas moins*. In the following sentence, Alain reinforces it with *toujours*, speaking about the person who, though his opinion is correct, is frowned upon for being right but inferior to those who frown upon him: *On reconnaît qu'il avait raison, mais il reste toujours qu'il a déplu ; il reste toujours qu'il a osé déplaire* (Alain, 1956: 342).

s'agissant de

This structure is something of an oddity, on two counts: it is one of only four parts of the defective verb *s'agir* to have survived into modern French, the others being the infinitive, the past participle and the tenses of the third person singular with impersonal *il*; and although a present participle, it neither needs a subject nor conforms to the rule that present participles agree with the subject of an accompanying main verb.

On this structure, the older Grevisse (1964a: 740–741) followed Littré's definition: *vu qu'il s'agit, puisqu'il s'agit*. For the speaker of English, this clarifies little and covers only about a third of the structure's most common usages. Nowadays, though it may retain something of the *teinte archaïque* that Grevisse discerned in it, it is extremely popular with journalists. It has evolved into two (if not three) quite distinct modes, which are at times related to its position in a statement: when first in the sentence, it is often an expository connector, a variant for *quant à*, *pour ce qui est de* or *en ce qui concerne*; and, when placed in the middle (or often, near the end) of a statement, it sometimes has the value of Littré's and Grevisse's *vu qu'il s'agit* and sometimes not.

First in the sentence, in sequences of points

There is in France a verbal superstition that dissuades some of the French from beginning a sentence with a present participle. This inhibition, possibly of primary-school origin, and akin to the English one about a-preposition-being-a-bad-word-to-end-a-sentence-with, is contradicted in speech and print every day of the week. This connector, nowadays ubiquitous, is very often placed at the beginning of sentences and paragraphs. In this position, it can signal discussion of a point previously mentioned. An article beginning *Il y a une Europe du chômage et de l'emploi* discusses first the unemployment for two paragraphs. Then the third paragraph opens with *S'agissant de l'emploi*, not only announcing the beginning of discussion on the second subject but also reminding the reader of the relation of this paragraph to the whole argument. English might say, 'As for the' or 'Turning now to the question of'. Something similar is seen in an extract from an article discussing anti-American violence of French farmers distempered by the GATT negotiations on trade in agricultural produce:

> Le premier réflexe de l'agriculteur lourdement pénalisé par les accords du Gatt a été de s'en prendre à tout ce qui semble venir des États-Unis d'Amérique : le Coca et les McDo. S'agissant du Coca, les jeunes, adeptes inconditionnels de cette boisson un rien pharmaceutique, comprennent mal que l'on touche à leur dada favori. Tous les jeunes, y compris les fils d'agriculteurs. Pour les McDo [...]

There, the writer broaches in the second sentence the first of two points mentioned in the sentence preceding. In this usage, the connector could clearly be replaced by *concernant*, as in this example taken from an article about two troublesome provisions in negotiations between Israelis and Palestinians: the extent of the area to constitute the autonomous territory of Jericho; and crossing-points between Jericho and Israel. The writer discusses first the crossing-points, then begins a new paragraph: *Concernant l'étendue du territoire autonome de Jéricho [...]*.

In such a **sequence of points**, whether introducing a point which has been foreshadowed or not, the connector can function as a straightforward variant of procedural formulæ such as *En premier lieu* or *En ce qui concerne*. When President Mitterrand addresses his government on three matters, which he announces as *les aspects suivants*, he gives a paragraph to each: the first paragraph begins *En matière de dépenses*, the second *S'agissant en second lieu des ressources* and the third *En troisième lieu*. He could have replaced this threefold expository sequence with *D'abord... Ensuite... Enfin*. A discussion of the low opinion many French citizens have of their parliamentary institutions deals in three consecutive paragraphs with three aspects of the subject: *Quant au débat politique [...]*; *S'agissant de l'initiative des lois [...]*; *En ce qui concerne l'organisation du débat politique*.

First in the sentence, exemplifying

This mode is used also to focus on a particular item, seen as exemplifying a broader category in the sentence immediately preceding. In the following example, *la fiscalité* is the broad category, *impôts indirects* the particular:

> Des progrès devraient aussi être accomplis sur le terrain si sensible de la fiscalité. S'agissant des impôts indirects, et en particulier de la TVA, les positions en présence – qu'on pensait jadis inconciliables – se sont rapprochées.

In the following extract from a discussion of political neglect of unsatisfactory conditions in the Île-de-France region, the writer uses this mode to link a general theoretical preamble to the concrete instance which concerns him:

> En théorie, gouverner c'est prévoir. En pratique, à voir se comporter nos princes, c'est trop souvent se laisser prendre à la gorge et s'en sortir comme on peut. Il y a (heureusement) dans les affaires publiques un seuil d'inacceptabilité à partir duquel ils sont contraints d'agir. S'agissant des conditions de vie en Île-de-France, le seuil est atteint.

In this particularizing use, it is sometimes accompanied by ***par exemple***, as in this extract from an article on arrangements made by the Parti socialiste (PS) to include certain non-members on their ticket for elections to the European Parliament:

> M. Lionel Jospin avait souligné que ces places devraient être attribuées à des personnalités représentatives et non simplement porteuses d'une étiquette. S'agissant, par exemple, de SOS-Racisme, le PS ne devrait accepter aucun autre candidat que M. Harlem Désir lui-même.

First in the sentence, contrasting

At times, just like *quant à* when it signals an adversative relationship, this mode presents a contrast between a set of similar things and a set of different things: in an article dealing with the European Community's plan to approve banks operating inside member countries, a paragraph on one sort of approval of one sort of bank is followed by a paragraph on a different sort of approval of banks of another sort:

> L'agrément unique, ouvrant la possibilité d'exercer sur tout le territoire de la CEE, serait accordé sans restriction aux banques possédant déjà une filiale dans la Communauté.
> S'agissant des banques encore absentes dans la CEE et désirant s'y installer, l'agrément communautaire serait accordé de façon automatique, sans enquête préalable sur la réciprocité.

In few of the preceding examples could the structure be replaced by the Littré-Grevisse *vu qu'il s'agit*. However, it could often be replaced by *s'il s'agit* or *quand il s'agit*.

Inside the sentence

It is mainly with this mode that the Littré-Grevisse definition still applies, but only partially. A news item about the third accident in three years to happen to one of the nuclear-powered submarines of the USSR contains this sentence:

> Forte de trois cent cinquante sous-marins de tous les types, qui représentent la moitié de son tonnage global, la marine soviétique ne peut plus se dispenser d'une autocritique, s'agissant du comportement à la mer de ce qui constitue son « fer de lance ».

There, the connector could clearly be replaced either by *vu qu'il s'agit* or *puisqu'il s'agit*. The element introduced by it is the final one of the sentence, which is often the case. The same points could be made about many other exemplars of this mode, including this one:

> Pour construire son restaurant de mille mètres carrés sur le toit du théâtre des Champs-Élysées, à Paris, la Caisse des Dépôts, propriétaire, s'est passée de permis de construire en arguant qu'il n'en était pas besoin, s'agissant d'un immeuble classé.

This mode can also function like the one at the beginning of sentences when it is nothing but a stylistic variant for structures like *pour ce qui concerne* or *en ce qui concerne*: *J'ai de tout temps répugné à me relire, même s'agissant de pages que j'avais écrites avec plaisir.* / *Peut-être la brouille sino-britannique était-elle inévitable compte tenu des priorités différentes des deux pays s'agissant de l'avenir de Hongkong.* There, it could not be replaced by the Littré-Grevisse *vu qu'il* (or *puisqu'il) s'agit*. An apter replacement would be *sur la question de*. Elsewhere, it could be replaced by simple *sur*:

> Boris Eltsine et Bill Clinton se sont gardés de faire allusion à leurs divergences s'agissant de la question de l'élargissement de l'OTAN aux pays de l'Est.

Nor could the structure be replaced by *puisque* or *vu que* in statements where it means something like 'in the case of' or 'as far as they are concerned': *82 % des enfants lisent des livres au moins une fois par mois, contre 57 % s'agissant de leurs parents.* The implausibility of replacing the connector with *vu que* is flagrant when one compares the next example (which speaks of the arrest in Honduras of six terrorists to be handed over to the government of Nicaragua) with the one following it, where *pour* does the same job:

> Les coupables ont été remis aux autorités de Tegucigalpa pour cinq d'entre eux, et à celles de Managua s'agissant de l'auteur du meurtre.

> Les ravisseurs n'ont pas exécuté leurs trois victimes, réussissant l'exploit de les garder cachées pendant sept jours (huit jours pour Mme Thévenot).

sans doute *

This structure, like other concessives such as *assurément*, *bien sûr* or *certes*, has two basic modes. Either it straightforwardly confirms a proposition or it agrees with it while foreshadowing a point that partially counters it.

Affirming and confirming

This mode can reinforce a writer's point of view. Yet, since the expression means only 'presumably', 'probably' or 'I daresay' and not 'without a doubt', it signals also that the writer is not promulgating a certainty but is in fact attenuating an affirmation, as in this extract from a historian's discussion of vineyards in the Paris region two hundred years ago, where the attenuated affirmation is restricted even further by what follows:

> Ce vignoble faubourien est sans doute le plus grand vignoble de France. Celui, en tout cas, qui fournit le plus haut revenu à l'hectare, plus que le meilleur cru de Bourgogne, de Champagne ou de Bordeaux, selon une statistique de 1817.
>
> (Braudel, 229)

Often, as in that example, the connector accompanies an interpretation, an attempt to explain, a speculation offered as a working hypothesis rather than as hard fact. In the following extract from an essay on the growing unenjoyableness of much twentieth-century music and the gulf separating composers from listeners, its function is to posit a fairly firm interpretive answer to the preceding question:

> Pourquoi donc tout s'est-il gâché depuis les années 50, qui ont consacré la fracture de plus en plus marquée entre la musique dite « contemporaine » et le public ? Sans doute parce que l'avant-garde musicale a voulu évacuer la notion de *plaisir* et parce qu'elle a trop souvent érigé la *cacophonie* en art.

Like *absolument* and *effectivement*, this mode is commonly used in conversation, to murmur an encouraging modicum of agreement with an interlocutor's point of view.

Concessive, foreshadowing objection

That willingness to agree is still perceptible when the connector introduces a concession. Rather than contesting the validity of what precedes, it accepts it; and what it introduces may only affirm that something else is more important, or at least in the writer's view more pertinent, as in this extract from a discussion of relations between religious belief and scientific knowledge, in which a writer first agrees that it is a good thing that science and organized Christianity have nowadays ceased to dispute each other's claims, before introducing with *mais* a far more important point:

> La science et la religion ne sont pas pour autant à l'abri de toute nouvelle tentation totalisante. L'Église n'a sans doute pas tort d'affirmer que l'homme de science se trompe à vouloir résoudre des questions qui échappent à sa compétence. Mais il faudrait s'empresser d'ajouter que l'homme de religion qui prétendrait diriger le monde au nom d'une révélation divine – il n'en manque pas par ces temps d'intolérance et d'intégrisme – serait un danger pour l'humanité.

There, one sees the standard sequence: *sans doute* expressing agreement with the proposition it accompanies, followed by *mais*, introducing a point seen as more valid.

In three-part developments

Like other concessives, this one can help to construct a sequence of three propositions: it occupies second place, introducing a partial objection to what precedes, an objection which will be followed by a restatement of the gist of the first. In the following example, these three parts fit into two brief sentences in which a man of the Right teases men of the Left for their dislike of a man of the extreme Right:

> Les cris d'horreur de la gauche dès que M. Le Pen se manifeste sont authentiques. Exagérés, sans doute, mais sincères.
>
> (Dutourd, 1985: 62)

In the next example, the reaffirming function of *mais* is served by the *n'en ... pas moins* structure. Here again the sequence is tripartite: the writer expresses displeasure at a particular notion; he then accepts, with this mode of the connector, that the displeasing notion is partly valid; and finally he restates his distemper in a modified form:

> J'avoue que j'ai moi-même éprouvé du dépit à voir l'un des commentateurs de la légende de Tristan la définir « une épopée de l'adultère ». La formule est sans doute exacte, si l'on se borne à considérer la donnée sèche du Roman. Elle n'en paraît pas moins vexante et « prosaïquement » restrictive.
>
> (Rougemont, 1962: 19)

Repeated *sans doute*

Like *certes* and some other concessives, this mode is at times repeated in successive sentences to structure *sequences of points*. In this extract from a review of works displayed in two new galleries of the Louvre, the critic starts by saying they are not quite as good as they are cracked up to be; then, inverting subject and verb after the connector as some do when it is first in the sentence, he adds this:

Sans doute, la *Descente de croix* de bois peint exécutée au XIIIᵉ siècle en Ombrie ou dans le Latium a-t-elle de la grandeur, suite de figures émaciées et anguleuses. Sans doute encore, l'ensemble de terres cuites émaillées signé des della Robbia brille-t-il de l'éclat de ses verts et de ses bleus intenses. Sans doute enfin, convient-il de rendre hommage à l'ampleur décorative de la *Nymphe de Fontainebleau*, bronze spectaculaire de Benvenuto Cellini, et à la grâce du *Mercure volant* de Giambologna.

Il n'empêche : bien des musées européens et américains ont, en ces matières, des collections supérieures à celles-ci, plus denses, plus variées, plus riches, par exemple, en bronzes de la Renaissance italienne, en retables gothiques, en terres cuites baroques, en marbres néoclassiques.

There the third element's reaffirmation of the initial proposition is made by **n'empêche**. Among other variations of the usual *mais* are *sans doute... mais cependant*; *sans doute... et pourtant*; *sans doute... mais pour autant*; *sans doute... il reste que.*

sauf à

This structure, like *quitte à*, introduces a subordinate clause and is normally followed by the infinitive of a verb. Also like *quitte à*, the verb following it canvasses a hypothetical eventuality which restricts the scope of the action expressed by the main verb. Both structures can either precede or follow the main clause and could at times be replaced by *au risque de*.

Nowadays, after the manner of *à moins de* the structure is often used to restrict a negative statement. The negative statement often precedes, as in this extract from a discussion of the effect thermo-nuclear weapons have had on international relations and of the wisdom of the choice France made of belonging to the group of nuclear powers:

Comment ne pas s'interroger sur la sagesse qu'il y a eu pour la France à vouloir à tout prix faire partie du club ?

La réponse n'est pas simple, sauf à rappeler que, quoi qu'on fasse et qu'on dise, Hiroshima a eu lieu et a transformé du tout au tout, en y introduisant la menace de l'Apocalypse, la nature des rapports internationaux.

(Fontaine, 1990)

However, the negative statement can also follow; or else it can be interpolated into the main statement, as in this example, taken from the same discussion but focussing this time on the factors which caused the break-up of the Soviet empire in 1989–1990:

Et ce n'est pas une pression militaire – sauf à ranger sous cette définition le poids économique de la course aux armements et la crainte inspirée par l'épée de Damoclès de la guerre des étoiles – qui a bouleversé le *statu quo*, c'est la révolte de peuples qui avaient cessé d'avoir peur de leurs maîtres.

(Fontaine, 1990)

The structure can also be placed first in a ***phrase dépendante***, as in this extract from an article on the rise of political movements of the extreme Right such as the Front national, the failure of conventional methods and arguments to combat them and the need for new ideas:

> C'est l'échec même des stratégies employées qui commande aujourd'hui un effort de lucidité, fût-il cruel, une remobilisation qui soit – enfin ! – réaliste. Sauf à considérer comme allant de soi que la France devienne peu à peu le dernier espace occidental où puisse se refonder une extrême-droite antiparlementaire et néofasciste.

The subject of the infinitive following is often the same as that of the main verb, as in this extract from the Declaration of the Rights of Man of 1789:

> La libre communication des pensées et des opinions est un des droits les plus précieux de l'homme : tout citoyen peut donc parler, écrire, imprimer librement, sauf à répondre de l'abus de cette liberté dans les cas déterminés par la loi.

However, as can be seen from the earlier examples, the subject of the infinitive following may not be the same as that of the main verb. It is often grammatically indeterminate, implicitly the *on* which, in the last quotation but one, say, would be used with a finite verb in the construction *sauf si l'on considérait*.

sauf à ce que

Again like *quitte à*, this variant is followed not by an infinitive but by a verb in the subjunctive. This example comes from a criticism of a decision by a Minister of the Interior, Jean-Louis Debré, to support mayors who outlawed begging in their towns:

> En voulant donner satisfaction à des maires, dont certains se prétendent de gauche, pour lesquels une image « propre » de leur ville passe avant le respect des droits de l'homme, M. Debré laisse accroire que les beaux discours du chef de l'État et du premier ministre ne sont que des mots. Sauf à ce qu'il soit clairement et rapidement désavoué.

English has no all-purpose equivalent for this structure. In some contexts, a mode of 'unless' would do. In others, 'short of' would fit, followed either by a noun or a present participle. In this sentence, taken from an article advocating closer integration of immigrant Muslim communities into the fabric of French society – *Sauf à laisser la voie libre au couple intégrisme-Front national, il n'y a pas d'autre choix* – 'short of leaving' could be used, as could 'apart from leaving' or 'other than leaving'.

sequences of points *

The shortest sequence of points is a pair. They can be either announced as such to the reader or unannounced.

The unannounced pair

Often no connecting structure is placed before a point to intimate that it is in fact the first of a pair. It is only with the second one that the reader sees the relation between them, because it is signalled by an additive or augmentative such as *aussi*, *de plus*, *encore*, *en outre*, *ensuite*, *puis* or, as in these two points made about French politics near the end of the Mitterrand years, moribund and overly affected by the imminent presidential election, *d'autre part*:

> Le pouvoir est fatigué. Le président, en fin de mandat, donne l'impression de jouer les prolongations. « C'est injuste », dit-il. Mais qu'y faire ? Une fin de mandat, en France, c'est une fin de règne. D'autre part, la compétition présidentielle stérilise la vie des partis, verrouille des positions où l'antagonisme, bien souvent, est purement tactique.

At times, two consecutive paragraphs may begin with structures such as *quant à* or *s'agissant de*, at most implying a series of related points, as in this pair taken from an article on budgetary matters: *Quant au financement du fonds de garantie* and *S'agissant des économies budgétaires*.

The announced pair

Among the commonest binary structures introducing paired points are *soit... soit*, *ou bien... ou bien*, *d'un côté... de l'autre* and *d'une part... d'autre part*. A little less common is *ici... là*. Such pairs are often explicitly anticipated by phrases such as *de deux choses l'une*; *l'alternative suivante*; *pour deux raisons*; *à double titre*.

Many other pairs, some of them preceded by a statement containing *double* or *deux*, are introduced by *d'abord*. The paradigm of this sort of pairing is *d'abord... ensuite*, as in this sentence about the two reasons for the breakdown of a relationship:

> Ils ne peuvent plus être amant et maîtresse comme ils l'ont été, d'abord parce qu'ils ne s'aiment plus, ensuite parce qu'ils n'en ont plus le goût.

Variants of this paradigm are *d'abord... mais surtout*; or *d'abord... aussi*, as in this description of the refusal of a trades union to sign an agreement:

> Ce refus est doublement symbolique. Symbolique d'abord d'une méfiance ancienne à l'égard de tout ce qui, de près ou de loin, conduit à introduire plus

> de flexibilité dans les conditions d'emploi. [...] Symbolique, ce refus l'est aussi du recentrage de la politique contractuelle auquel procède la centrale.

Many other variations include *d'une part... ensuite*; *d'une part... en outre*; *d'abord... et puis*; *d'abord... de plus*; *tout d'abord... qui plus est*.

Paired points are sometimes numbered: *À cela, deux explications. Premièrement [...] Deuxièmement [...]*. A close variant of this sequence is seen in the following: *Pourquoi cette angoisse ? Pour deux raisons. La première, c'est que [...] La seconde est que [...]*. Quite a common way of pairing points, *en premier lieu... en second lieu*, occurs in this extract from an essay on Balzac's debts to Rabelais, again preceded by a mention of *deux*:

> Dans son appendice l'auteur signale deux faits : en premier lieu il indique les moyens employés par Balzac dans ses *Contes drolatiques* pour imiter le procédé rabelaisien de création de mots, en second lieu il signale que le style de Balzac dans ses autres œuvres se ressent également de l'influence de Rabelais.

En premier lieu is sometimes paired either with *La deuxième raison* or with one of the modes of ***d'autant plus***.

Another possibility is to imply a sequence by the use of key words, unshaped by a procedural connective structure. In the following example, taken from a discussion of a difficult stage in negotiations between North Korea and the United Nations on nuclear inspections, the reader who reaches the first word in the second sentence, *Difficultés*, knows to expect *Menaces* a little farther on:

> Mais cette étape, diplomatique encore, est lourde de difficultés et de menaces. Difficultés : pour des raisons différentes, ni la Chine ni la Russie, membres permanents du Conseil de sécurité avec droit de veto, ne sont favorables à la coercition. Menaces : le régime de Kim Il-sung a haussé le ton en déclarant que des sanctions seraient vues et traitées comme une « déclaration de guerre ».

Sequences of three points

Sequences of three points are common. Sometimes they are only implicitly signalled as such. Thus, a newspaper article about a government report on ways of improving European access to Strasbourg contains three paragraphs which begin:

> En ce qui concerne les transports aériens, le rapport reste réaliste [...]. Pour ce qui est des liaisons ferroviaires, le rapport préconise [...]. En matière d'hébergement, le rapport suggère notamment [...].

However, triads of points are often signposted by the addition of ***enfin*** to *d'abord... ensuite* or to *d'une part... d'autre part*. The more common of these is used in the following example setting out the three main achievements generally credited to de Gaulle:

> De quoi crédite-t-on normalement ou traditionnellement le général de Gaulle ? D'abord d'avoir résolu le problème algérien et plus généralement réussi la décolonisation. Ensuite d'avoir doté la France d'institutions stables et aujourd'hui incontestées. Enfin d'avoir édifié une politique étrangère et une politique de défense « indépendante » et propres à redonner au pays son rôle de grande puissance, ou, du moins, de « puissance moyenne de premier plan ».

Variants of this sequence include *D'abord... puis... enfin*; *D'abord... en plus... enfin*; *D'abord... en outre... enfin*; *D'abord... aussi... enfin*; *D'abord... en second lieu... enfin*; *D'abord... ensuite... enfin et surtout.* This last, a way of emphasizing the importance of a point in a sequence, is at times varied by *D'abord et avant tout.* The related signallers of points need not stand first in the sentence or paragraph:

> La fantaisie éclate dans la conception même de l'ensemble, d'abord. Dans la composition de chaque livre aussi. Dans l'invention de maints épisodes enfin.

Triads may be preceded by statements containing *Pour trois raisons* or *triplement.* Or they may be combined with a repetition of a key word or similar structure, as in a sequence of three lengthy paragraphs which begin like this: *On en tirera d'abord la conclusion que [...] On notera ensuite que [...] On jugera enfin que [...].*

As for triads based on *d'une part... d'autre part*, the most common, also with *enfin*, is used in this extract from a discussion of the predicament of some only children:

> On le coince entre plusieurs discours contradictoires : d'une part on le plaint – quelle tristesse d'être seul ! ; d'autre part on l'envie pour ses réussites parfois imaginaires ; enfin on le déteste pour son statut d'« élu ».

This sequence, too, lends itself to variations: an article on three sources of anxiety flags them as follows: *D'une part...*; *La deuxième source d'inquiétude...*; *Enfin....* A critic convinced of the unoriginality of twentieth-century French poetry makes three points:

> D'une part, aucun style nouveau à proprement parler. D'autre part, une transposition du style mallarméen. En troisième lieu, le dépouillement du romantisme *extérieur.*

Some writers combine elements of both these basic sequences, such as *d'abord, d'autre part, enfin.* Others use parts of them, as in this sequence from a discussion of M. Le Pen and his Front national:

> On peut donc ne pas avoir peur de M. Le Pen. À trois conditions. À condition de ne pas sous-estimer la gravité du mal social qui l'a produit. À condition, aussi, de ne pas formuler un diagnostic incomplet. À condition, enfin, de le combattre sur tous les terrains.

A variant used in some triads is *encore*, as in this sequence of alternative interpretations of the unemployment figures:

Selon la manière dont on les interprète, on peut dire, au choix, que le nombre des demandeurs d'emploi s'élève à 2 899 000 (au sens du Bureau international du travail), ou bien à 2 819 200 (selon les nouvelles règles françaises, en données brutes), ou encore à 2 911 700 selon ces mêmes règles, mais en données corrigées des variations saisonnières) ou enfin à 3 214 100 (selon les anciennes règles, en vigeur jusqu'en juin).

Other possibilities include this: *Prenons trois exemples. Primo [...]. Secundo [...]. Tertio [...].* Or *Primo... Secundo... Enfin.* Or, in a colloquial variant, *Primo... Deusio... Tertio.*

The repetition, mentioned above, of a grammatical structure or key expression, can be done without explicit connecting structures, as in this way of beginning three consecutive paragraphs on problems facing the USSR in its final days: *Première difficulté... Deuxième difficulté... Troisième difficulté....* This type of visible replication of structures is often adopted in a text where the points are separated from each other by longish paragraphs: *D'où l'importance de... D'où aussi l'idée de... D'où enfin l'annonce de....*

Sequences of more than three

Sequences of more than three elements, perhaps because they are less common, tend to show less regularity than most three-part sequences or to appear rather improvised. They may be preceded by a statement like *une série de facteurs.* Medleys such as the following are used: *D'abord... D'autre part... De plus... Ensuite... / D'une part... D'autre part... Enfin et surtout... Sans compter que... / Tout d'abord... D'autre part... Troisièmement... Enfin... / En premier lieu... En second lieu... Ajoutons-y... Enfin... / En premier lieu... Ensuite... Enfin... Ajoutons que... En dernier lieu... Sans oublier....*

A final example of a sequence of four points shows that it too may be announced by a statement to the effect that there are in fact four of them. It comes from a discussion of possible explanations of the fact that the French birth-rate has seasonal variations; the four points are linked by *d'abord* and *ensuite*, an ***inversion du verbe***, an ***inversion de l'adjectif*** and ***reste***:

> Regroupons-les en quatre genres. Il y a d'abord celles qui font appel à des causes « naturelles » ou biologiques : les oscillations éventuelles au cours de l'année des inclinations érotiques [...].
> Viennent ensuite les explications que l'on peut appeler « occasionnelles » ou sociales, fondées sur la disponibilité pour les accouplements. [...]
> Non moins plausibles sont les explications « rationnelles » fondées sur un calcul utilitaire qui évalue les avantages et les inconvénients des dates de naissance et de grossesse. [...]
> Restent les explications « culturelles ».

(Besnard, 33)

seulement *

As a specialized variant for **mais**, this connector, sometimes accompanied by **voilà**, can link whole sentences or paragraphs. In the following example the word occurs twice: the first is a simple adverb meaning 'just', the second an inter-assertional connector. After a state of affairs presented positively (the idea that, as television-watchers, the French are discriminating), it introduces objections to that satisfaction (the mess allegedly created by President Mitterrand's policy on the privatization of some French television):

> Les Français ne regardent pas seulement la télévision, ils sont aptes à la juger. Et à faire, entre les quatre chaînes privées et les deux publiques, le choix qui leur convient. Seulement voilà : la télévision française a atteint ce qu'on pourrait appeler l'âge démocratique en payant le prix fort. On ne fait pas d'omelettes, surtout en direct, sans casser des œufs. Crises, palinodies, pièges, bourdes, complots, cadavres : le mitterrandisme appliqué à la télé figure un triste feuilleton.

The use of this connective mode is deplored by one normative authority on usage:

> Dans l'usage parlé de notre époque, *seulement* est très couramment utilisé au sens de « mais », surtout en tête de phrase. Cet emploi appartient à un style négligé. En langage soigné, on ne l'admettra que si l'abverbe *seulement* peut garder son sens propre : *il n'a pas de gros défauts, seulement, il est bête* (= « son seul gros défaut est d'être bête »).
>
> (Dupré, III, 2373)

This view, it must be said, is not shared by most other commentators. It is disregarded, too, by the great majority of writers.

The connector is usually placed, as Dupré says, first in the sentence, or at least after a stop. Its function is to raise a difficulty, to present an objection to what precedes or an exception overlooked, a snag, a weakness, a contradiction; and it is used especially after a description of an apparently advantageous state of affairs. It does this by dramatizing an argument. It implies that the objection is of great pregnancy; it says, 'Unfortunately' or 'The trouble is, though ...' and could often be replaced by *Le problème est que* or *L'ennui, c'est que*. It can have a certain irony or sardonic tone, possibly a touch of smugness, as it prepares to contradict. An author may set out a point of view in fine detail; then, before demolishing it, will say something like this: *Presque trop beau pour être vrai. Seulement, il y a un hic. / Seulement, il ne s'agit pas du tout de cela. / Seulement, il y a aussi des inconvénients. / Seulement, la difficulté réside dans... / Seulement voilà : il y a une difficulté de taille. / Seulement, c'est ici que se trouve le point faible du système. / Seulement, il se trouve que*.... Thus, intending to attack the argument that government influence on French television news services was not (in 1968) a matter for concern, a writer first feigns agreement with it, then antiphrastically introduces a huge objection to it:

> On entend souvent dire en France que l'esclavage officiel de la télévision n'a pas tellement d'importance, ou du moins que tous les régimes se valent à cet égard parce que la IVᵉ République ne laissait pas plus de liberté aux moyens de communication de masse que ne le fit ensuite la Vᵉ. C'est parfaitement exact. Seulement il y a un petit détail qui n'est pas sans intérêt : à la veille de la prise du pouvoir par de Gaulle, il y avait environ 600 000 télérécepteurs en France, dix ans plus tard il y en avait environ 12 millions.
>
> (Revel, 1970: 46)

After a concessive

In the last example, the short sentence *C'est parfaitement exact* represents a concession. In that type of relation between points, this connector, again like *mais*, is often preceded by explicit concessive structures like *il est vrai que* and *sans doute*, as in this extract from an article on the then leader of the French Communist Party, Georges Marchais:

> Georges Marchais a l'art d'oublier ce qui le dérange, par exemple son soutien inconditionnel à Leonid Brejnev, pour ne se rappeler que ce qui l'arrange. Il est vrai, s'il faut en croire Emmanuel Berl, que le souvenir repose sur la « digestion » du passé. Seulement, il est des choses qui demeurent difficiles à digérer.

Like other objectors (*pourtant*, *cependant*, etc.), this one enables a writer to avoid repeating the same one. In the following example, the *seulement* is little more than a *mais*; but, having used *mais* only two brief sentences before, the author now varies the connector. Commenting on French regional languages in 1934, he describes a linguistic situation which, it must be said, has much changed nowadays in important respects:

> La France est divisée aujourd'hui en deux parties par la limite qui sépare l'occitan et le français. Mais le sens de cette limite n'est plus le même qu'autrefois. Actuellement on parle français au nord comme au sud. Seulement au nord les patois régionaux, qui sont une langue seconde, sont beaucoup plus entamés par la langue nationale qu'au sud, où ils appartiennent à un type de langue très différent du français.
>
> (von Wartburg, 274–275)

Punctuation

The form without *voilà* is almost always followed nowadays by a comma. This is an apt way of distinguishing the function of the connector from the very different adverbial usage found in contexts like this excerpt from an article on an issue in American politics which threatened to split both major parties:

> Si le Parti démocrate sort de cette bataille exsangue, les républicains sont moins partagés. Seulement une quarantaine d'élus de l'opposition ont rejoint le camp des « anti ».

The form with *voilà*, too, is often followed by a comma, but more usually by a colon. Clearly, without a stop of some sort after *voilà*, a statement beginning *Seulement voilà la femme de Socrate* could confuse by implying that *la femme* is the object of *voilà*, when it might really be the subject of a following verb.

simplement

This is an occasional variant for the connector, more or less equivalent in function. In the following example, about a reform of procedures for dealing with applications for French citizenship, one sees the same relationship between ideas as with the modes of *seulement*: first a statement about the advantages of the reform, then the disadvantage:

> Que les acquisitions de la nationalité française soient désormais transférées du ministère des Affaires sociales aux instances judiciaires est plutôt une bonne nouvelle. D'autant que l'appel sur des décisions contestées sera plus transparent qu'auparavant. Simplement, les tribunaux d'instance sont en l'état totalement incapables, en termes à la fois de compétence et de moyens, de faire face à l'afflux des dossiers. 23 500 en 1991 !

In other contexts, *simplement* is still used in the older sense of *seulement* recommended above by Dupré, merely to identify a difference which is single, as in this comic colloquial comment on how best to see in the New Year:

> C'est ça, serpentins et confettis ! T'es pas malade ? Ça aurait l'air de quoi ? Les douze coups de minuit, moi, je les attends toute seule au fond de mon lit. Simplement je remplace mon verre d'eau par une bouteille de whisky. Un bon conseil : fais pareil !

si bien que *

This is one of those adverbial and conjunctional structures, like *de sorte que* or *à ceci près que*, which, although they introduce a complementary statement, nowadays are often placed first in the sentence, thus making a *phrase dépendante*. It is in that position, linking two ideas that a writer has separated, that their function as connectors is most apparent. This placing is no doubt to be explained partly by the fact that these statements, although complementary, are also of the nature of independent clauses and, without the connector, could stand as sentences in their own right.

Traditional usage

This structure introduces a complement of consequence. Its meaning is not what its appearance might lead one to believe: it could usually be replaced by *ce qui fait que* or indeed by *de sorte que*. And English equivalents for it could be 'with the result that', 'to such effect that' or even 'which means that', as can be seen in a sentence like this:

> Prenant acte de cet échec, M. Jacques Delors a retiré ses propositions de compromis, si bien que la discussion devra reprendre pratiquement à zéro.

That sentence shows the form of this structure which used to be standard: placed inside the sentence, following a comma and introducing a complement of the preceding main verb. Texts dating from before the contemporary period rarely show any other form.

Contemporary usage

Nowadays that traditional form appears to be favoured by a minority of writers. Much more frequent, not only among journalists, are sentences which make a clearer separation between this structure and what precedes it, by the use of a semicolon, say, or brackets, as in this extract from an essay on the puppetlike view of humanity given by the characters in the novels of Aldous Huxley:

> Au plan humain, nous ne sommes qu'un paquet d'impulsions, de sentiments et de notions contradictoires, sans cohérence intérieure ni liberté : il n'existe rien en nous qu'on puisse appeler l'âme (si bien que le romancier est parfaitement fondé à nous représenter comme de pauvres marionnettes).

Or else, more commonly, the sentence (or even the paragraph) begins with this structure, as in this example taken from an essay on polemics among French journalists and the inevitable political dimension taken by such controversies, even when their differences of opinion concern only ways of writing French:

> Car, chose bouffonne au plus haut point, la politique s'en mêle. Les uns tiennent à marquer leur soin d'être conservateurs, les autres leur foi religieuse au Progrès. Si bien que sur ce terrain, comme sur bien d'autres, il y a une *gauche* et une droite.

The relation made between what precedes and what follows remains the same as when the structure is placed inside a single sentence. But by being separated from what precedes, it enables a writer to shorten a sentence which otherwise might get out of hand and to focus attention on a conclusion, as in this extract from a discussion of French reactions to manifestations of Muslim fundamentalism:

> Il est vrai que l'Islam en est aujourd'hui au stade de la religion catholique sous l'Ancien Régime. Il envahit la société et n'est pas considéré comme une affaire privée par ses fidèles, et donc heurte le sens commun. Il est vrai aussi qu'au moment où l'Est et l'Ouest paraissent solder leur querelle de près d'un siècle un autre conflit, qui remonte à la naissance du prophète, envahit de nouveau l'imaginaire collectif avec son cortège de tueries libanaises, d'attentats et de totalitarisme intégriste. Si bien qu'après avoir refusé le trop-plein d'immigrés la société française est en passe de refuser l'intégration elle-même.

In such sentences, the connector could clearly be replaced by **ainsi** or by the **aussi** which expresses logical consequence or introduces a conclusion.

tant et si bien que

Like the shorter mode, this expanded variant used to be placed after a comma in mid-sentence, as in this extract from a discussion of how the historical transfer of negativity from the word *ne* to the word *pas* deprived the latter of its original meaning: *la valeur négative s'est communiqué à ce mot régime, tant et si bien qu'elle en a étouffé la valeur propre* (Vendryes, 199). Nowadays this mode too is usually placed first in the sentence. The contexts in which it appears tend to be slightly more narrative than discursive; and the consequences it introduces may be more chronological than logical, less a conclusion drawn by the writer than an objective result of a preceding event. The addition of *tant*, which adds a degree of intensity, is apt in descriptions of cumulative effects or sequential circumstances. The first of these examples is taken from a discussion of birds of prey and their vulnerability to residues of chemical insecticides:

> Placés en bout de chaîne alimentaire, les oiseaux carnivores accumulent les produits organo-chlorés absorbés par leurs proies, au point que le processus inhibe leur production de calcium. Leurs œufs, dès lors, ont des coquilles trop molles pour résister aux épreuves de la couvaison. Et c'est l'hécatombe par non-reproduction – elle fut totale aux États-Unis pour le faucon pèlerin. Tant et si bien que, jusque dans les années 60, la France s'est constamment appauvrie en représentants de la gent ailée dite rapace.

And the second comes from an essay on the expansion of the French absinthe trade in the nineteenth century, from its origins in the army:

> La conquête de l'Algérie offrit à l'absinthe l'occasion de son véritable triomphe : aux soldats du corps expéditionnaire qui avaient peine à se procurer, aux marches du désert, de l'eau assurément potable, on conseilla d'ajouter quelques

gouttes à celle dont ils se désaltéraient. Le goût leur en parut agréable. Les doses furent bientôt augmentées, et la mode de cette boisson neuve rapportée par eux au pays.

Tant et si bien que sous la IIIe République la progression de la consommation fut vertigineuse : 7 000 hectolitres d'alcool en 1873, plus de 10 000 en 1880, 105 000 en 1890. Les chiffres culminent à 238 000 en 1900 [...]

(Jeanneney, 87)

si ce n'est (que)

This is one of a set of *expressions figées*, like **fût-ce** and **ne serait-ce que**, made from *ce* and a part of the verb *être*, and usually functioning like a single word. One of its main functions is to restrict the scope of a preceding statement, after the manner of 'unless' or 'except that'. In some of these restrictive uses, it can be replaced by one of the modes of **sinon**. The structure exists in two forms, one with *que*, the other without.

Without *que*

This mode, the more common, always introduces a simple complement. It can restrict a preceding statement, often one phrased as a negative or implying negation. It is not usually placed first in the sentence. Hence, it is normally preceded by a comma. An article about Pierre Mendès France, speaking of his prestige and his brief tenure of the Prime Ministership in the mid-1950s, says:

> Sur les estrades d'une IVe République déjà vermoulue, un homme nouveau était passé, avisé autant que prompt, hardi, enthousiasmant, s'imposant à la gauche non communiste comme son leader incontesté. Pourtant, « P.M.F » qui suscita tant d'élan ne revint jamais au pouvoir, si ce n'est le temps très court de se morfondre dans un gouvernement Guy Mollet sans lustre.

An essay on the young Renan during his time in Italy says this:

> Sur l'intérêt scientifique de la mission italienne de Renan il n'y a pas lieu de s'étendre, si ce n'est pour noter le zèle et l'ardeur au travail de ce savant de vingt-six ans.

Sometimes what precedes is not negative but restrictive, as in this statement, part of an enumeration of the artists represented in an exhibition of paintings: *Qui encore ? Peu de maîtres d'autrefois, si ce n'est quelques expressionnistes allemands.* In all of the examples so far quoted, the structure could be replaced by *sinon* or even by *sauf*.

The similarity to *sinon* is seen too in contexts where the connector functions in tandem with **du moins**, often linking two adjectival expressions: *une thématique si ce n'est de « gauche », du moins aux accents* *progressistes.* Sometimes this closeness to *sinon* also shows when the connector functions like **voire**: *à l'âge de l'adolescence, si ce n'est de la majorité.* And also functioning like *voire*, it can combine with **même**, as in this sentence from a humorous account of awkward encounters you may make on aeroplanes:

> ...les rencontres aériennes sont en général du genre de celles qu'on voulait éviter comme la peste : l'admirateur éperdu qui vous prend pour un autre, le voisin de dîner qu'il aurait été légitime, ce soir-là, d'étouffer avec les arêtes du turbot sauce mousseline, si ce n'est même une passade amoureuse classée depuis longtemps par pertes et profits.
>
> (Boucher, 502)

This mode has been described as *un vrai mot composé* (Brunot, 128). And it is usual for *est* to remain invariable, even when followed, as in the example above about the German expressionists, by a plural. Indeed, the older Robert dictionary says: *Le verbe* Être *est toujours au singulier dans certaines expressions figées,* Si ce n'est *[...]* (Robert, I, 671), a view implicitly confirmed by Le Bidois (II, 174). However, at times writers do make the verb plural, as in this comment on the theory of global warming:

> L'on parle d'un réchauffement de l'atmosphère, d'une montée de la « température de la planète » comme d'un fait d'observation, d'un phénomène dûment constaté. Or, rien à l'heure actuelle ne permet pareille affirmation, si ce ne sont les allégations de scientifiques qui cherchent à le faire croire (car ils y trouvent des intérêts assez divers).

With *que*

This mode always introduces an independent clause capable of forming a sentence in its own right. It too usually restricts a preceding negative statement. In some contexts, this mode can replace *à ceci près que* or *sauf que*, restricting what precedes by introducing a slight exception to it, as in this comment about Jesus Christ seen as a faith-healer whose gift sometimes deserts him:

> Nul n'est parfait. Il lui arrive même de connaître quelques échecs. Souvenez-vous de son retour au pays, à Nazareth. Jésus est mal accueilli parce qu'« il ne pouvait faire aucun miracle, si ce n'est qu'il guérit quelques infirmes en leur imposant les mains ». Dixit saint Marc !

A comment spoken on Jacques Chirac, a candidate of the Right in the presidential election of 1995, says first that neither the Right nor its candidate have changed, then modifies this:

> La droite n'a pas changé. Jacques Chirac non plus, si ce n'est que, pour son dernier tour de piste, il déploie sans retenue ses talents indéniables de démagogue.

One marked difference with the functioning of *à ceci près que* is that it is rare for this mode to introduce a ***phrase dépendante***.

quand ce n'est pas

This is a variant which in certain contexts replaces the mode without *que*. Unlike the latter it is not usually preceded by a negative. It too is formulaic, functioning as a semantic unit: the tense of the verb is always the present; *pas* is always part of it. It usually stands for *ou même* or the *sinon* which is akin to *voire*, as in this statement about newspaper and radio reporting in the days before television, and especially the vogue for *le récit de voyage*:

> Ce genre journalistique satisfaisait une curiosité du public dont on a peu idée aujourd'hui, alors qu'il suffit d'allumer un récepteur de télévision pour se retrouver à l'autre bout de la planète, quand ce n'est pas dans l'espace sidéral.

In the following example, it helps to make a dispirited comment on the futility of protesting against abuses of authority or power when those responsible just ignore the protest:

> À quoi sert en effet, du moins en France, de s'élever contre des actes ou des propos que la morale, quand ce n'est pas la loi, réprouve ?

(Boucher, 421)

si d'opposition *

The name given to this structure, to differentiate it from the hypothetical *si*, is something of a misnomer, as some of its important functions are not oppositive. The main difference between this *si* and the hypothetical one is that whereas the latter introduces a possibility (*Si tu te trouvais chez toi à midi, je passerais te prendre*), this one introduces either what is assumed to be fact for the purpose of an argument or, more commonly, a simple statement of fact – the following statement: *Si Paul Touvier est condamné à mort, c'est qu'il est impliqué dans une série de crimes* does not imply that Touvier may or may not have been sentenced to death. The factual nature of the statement made by this *si* is one reason why the tense accompanying it is usually the present.

Simple oppositions

In this mode, it is one of the most common adversative structures in French. Its frequency is rivalled only by ***n'en... pas moins*** and ***alors que***: the former is sometimes used with it; the latter can often replace it. Its most basic mode establishes a contrastive, adversative or oppositive relationship between two statements in a single sentence. Normally, it is placed first in the sentence, introducing a noun subject; and the second part of the sentence, which is the main clause, will contain a semantic element which is clearly opposed to an element in the first part. The other feature which distinguishes this simplest use of the structure is that the second element of the contrast is unaccompanied by a connector. It is the meaning of the statement which shapes it in relation to the first one, as in this comment on French use of condoms as protection against HIV: *Si, pour huit Français sur dix, le préservatif est le seul moyen efficace, son usage reste très limité.* The opposition between 'Many know' and 'Few do' could be structured by *alors que* and is expressed in the two semantic elements *huit sur dix* and *usage très limité.* The same features are visible in the following example, which deals with recordings of music by Mahler: the opening statement could be introduced by *alors que*; and the contrast is made by the semantic elements *une vingtaine en 1953* and *en 1960, quatre-vingts*:

> Si l'on recensait une vingtaine de disques Mahler en 1953 (toutes les œuvres éditées étaient disponibles sur disque, ni plus ni moins), en 1960, quatre-vingts disques figurent au catalogue, dont dix pour les *Kindertotenlieder*.

This opposition between the two elements is frequently made more pointed by being couched in pairs of antonymous subjects and verbs: *Si la gauche les a perdues, ces élections, la droite ne les a pas gagnées. / Si l'animal vit dans le présent, l'homme a toujours voulu connaître l'avenir.*

Occasionally, the structure, though still introducing the first element of the contrast, is placed not quite at the beginning of the sentence. In that case, it is usually interpolated between the subject and the verb of the main clause; the statement it introduces begins with a pronoun repeating the subject: *Les grandes grèves, si elles ont débuté à Anvers, enflamment les bassins ouvriers wallons. / On aura compris, je pense, que ce livre, s'il échappe au résumé, n'échappe pas au ridicule.*

In many other modes, the second part of the binary combines with some other connector – **force est de**, say, or **tout de même** – helping to reinforce the relation between the two statements. It may be **alors**, linking a principle to an instance:

> Si l'exercice du pouvoir est d'abord un face-à-face sincère avec la réalité, alors le nouveau président américain, le démocrate Bill Clinton, ne s'y dérobe pas.

The other main combined structures are as follows.

si... aussi

This combination is sometimes used in long complex sentences, where **aussi** serves as a reminder of the contrast initiated by *si* at the beginning. However, it can also be used to structure simple sentences: *Si Hanson sait* *acheter, il sait aussi vendre.* This is adverbial *aussi*, often used with the same verb, or verbs of similar meaning, in both parts of the binary. Given this similarity in the verbs, it is usually the complements of them that carry the contrast. An example comes from an obituary on the film-maker André Cayatte: *S'il eut l'audace de s'attaquer à de grands sujets, il eut aussi à essuyer bien des sarcasmes.*

At times *aussi* is varied by **également**, as in this comment on French road accidents:

> Si tout le monde est d'accord pour déplorer le nombre et la gravité des accidents de la route en France, chacun, ou presque, est également prêt à considérer qu'il s'agit là d'une fatalité ou, en tout cas, d'un phénomène si bien ancré dans les mentalités qu'il n'est guère raisonnable d'espérer le modifier.

And in negative statements, other analogous arrangements are used, such as with *non plus*:

> Si nul n'entrevoit le moindre risque de « choc » pétrolier à la hausse, nul ne prévoit non plus désormais une rechute durable des prix aux niveaux bas des trois dernières années.

si... n'en pas moins

With this combination, a writer can define a proper shade of distinction to be made between two statements. The concessive relation made is akin to that made in English by 'Although on the one hand ..., on the other ...', as in this comment on Marxists' attitudes to egalitarianism and equality: *Si Marx et les siens rejettent l'égalitarisme, ils n'en font pas moins de l'égalité une des caractéristiques de leur utopie.*

A cognate sort of binary is sometimes made with some of the modes of **reste**: *Si Matignon s'estime en phase avec l'Élysée sur l'essentiel, les différences d'appréciation restent importantes.*

si... du moins

In a somewhat similar way to the previous combination, this one can define a concessive relation and a shade of distinction between two statements. The first example comes from a discussion of the role of the trial of Émile Zola in advancing the cause of justice during the Dreyfus Affair:

> Si la lumière ne s'est pas faite, comme l'espérait Zola, du moins les paroles ont-elles jailli des lèvres : Picquart a pu faire la démonstration de l'innocence de Dreyfus.

The second, showing one of the modes of *au moins* which on occasion function like *du moins*, is taken from an article on the declining electoral support for the Front national:

Si le niveau très élevé des abstentions dans les villes de plus de trente mille habitants incite à être prudent sur l'exacte signification de cette « dégringolade », celle-ci démontre, à tout le moins, que le message extrémiste, qu'il soit de droite ou de gauche, passe décidément mal.

si... pronom tonique disjoint

This combination, which is frequently used, allows for very direct antitheses: *Si les mots ont changé, les idées, elles, sont inchangées.* / *Si Verlaine, surtout comme poète sentimental, a laissé des héritiers qu'on n'écoute pas sans plaisir, Stéphane Mallarmé, lui, est mort sans postérité.*

The fuller form, **quant à [lui]**, is also used, as are at times the other two structures which can function like these ones, **pour [sa] part** and **de [son] côté**.

si... en revanche

Another commonly used combination, this one also makes for pointed oppositions, as in this extract from a discussion about access of working-class students to university places:

Si l'on peut estimer que le nombre des diplômés issus des milieux populaires ira croissant, le nombre des places offertes risque, en revanche, de se restreindre considérablement.

S'il est exact que le nombre des homicides crapuleux est passé de 181 à 172 entre 1975 et 1979, on constate, en revanche, une augmentation constante des autres formes de criminalité et de délinquance.

A similar combination with **par contre** is rarer than that with *en revanche*.

si... au contraire

This combination, less common than *si... en revanche*, is sometimes used instead of it. The subject of this example is the savage self-criticism of Michel Leiris writing about himself:

Si la plupart des autobiographies semblent sottement nombriliques, celle de Leiris, au contraire, fut un véritable sabordage : cet Arlequin du verbe n'a cessé de se peindre sous les traits d'un Paillasse dérisoire, pour dire quelle déroute fut son existence, quelle bouffonnerie se dissimule sous les falbalas de la comédie littéraire.

si... pourtant

Under this heading, I include combinations not only with *pourtant*, but also connectors such as *cependant*, *néanmoins*, etc. Their ability to be combined with *si* is one of the things which most marks them off from *mais*. Indeed, the whole combination could often be replaced by *mais* placed at the beginning of the second element of the sentence. The first example comes from the preface to a study of prose stylists:

> Si j'ai pensé d'abord au grand nombre des gens instruits qui ne lisent que par plaisir, j'espère pourtant que cette esquisse rapide d'un grand sujet ne sera pas inutile aux étudiants qui s'appliquent spécialement à l'histoire de la littérature française.

> Si tout n'est pas mauvais ni absurde, dans ce décret, il faut cependant convenir qu'en son ensemble il manque de logique et de clarté.

> Si les opérateurs sont dans leur ensemble persuadés que les autorités monétaires américaines ne procéderont pas prochainement à un nouvel assouplissement du crédit, ils ont néanmoins salué la baisse de cet indice, qui suggère un ralentissement de la croissance.

si... pour autant

This combination is similar to that with *pourtant*, but is usually reserved for sentences of which the second half is couched in negative form:

> Si l'on comprend le souci de la France d'encourager M. Arafat à poursuivre dans la voie de la modération et du dialogue, il ne serait pas pour autant judicieux de considérer dès maintenant que l'OLP est définitivement convertie à l'idée d'une coexistence future entre Israël et un État palestinien.

Non-contrastive modes: with *c'est bien*

In the first of these modes, the *si*-statement is completed by an assertion beginning *c'est bien*. The verb form used with *si* is commonly *il est*, in the sense of *il y a*, lending to the statement a formality of tone appropriate to a dictum: *S'il est un reproche que nul ne peut adresser à Édouard Balladur, c'est bien celui de l'inconstance. / Toute langue est échange et vit d'échanges. S'il est une langue qui devrait envisager sans complexe les intrusions linguistiques, c'est bien la nôtre.* English might complete such a statement like this: 'then surely it is ours' or 'it must be ours'.

Non-contrastive modes: with *c'est que*

This mode is explanatory: it introduces a statement of cause or reason. It exists in several variant forms, as the second element of the sentence can be structured in three different ways: by *c'est que*, by *c'est parce que* or by some other way of expressing cause. The first two of these can mostly function interchangeably:

Si neuf passagers du vol 811 d'United Airlines ont été éjectés hors de la cabine, avant d'être aspirés, pour certains d'entre eux, par le réacteur droit, c'est qu'une déchirure s'est produite dans le fuselage.

Si la littérature arabe n'a pas eu de tradition romanesque, si le roman arabe n'est apparu qu'au début du vingtième siècle, c'est parce que la société arabe ne reconnaît pas l'individu en tant qu'entité.

The second part of the structure can be interrogative; and it can of course be negative, if a potential reason or cause for the first fact is being denied rather than affirmed:

Si *l'Express* connaît aujourd'hui des difficultés économiques, ce n'est pas qu'une éventuelle baisse de qualité aurait entraîné un recul de sa diffusion.

Sometimes this mode is combined with the mode with *bien* described above: *Au fond, si Maupassant est devenu écrivain, c'est bien parce que Flaubert a passé des années à lui inculquer les règles du métier.*

The third variant of this explanatory mode uses neither *c'est que* nor *c'est parce que.* There are many other ways of stating explanation or cause: *Si Giscard se déclare candidat, aujourd'hui et maintenant, c'est pour au moins trois raisons.* / *Si l'ONU est réhabilitée, quarante-cinq ans après sa naissance, elle le doit d'abord à M. Gorbatchev.* / *Si le cinéaste d'Au revoir les enfants a fait une entorse à ses principes, c'est à cause de l'événement.* However, even in statements of this sort, the second part mostly begins with *c'est.*

English usage

Though this structure corresponds in theory to the English concessive 'if', in practice it is very much commoner. Unlike 'if', which is educated and written, the French structure belongs to an everyday register and is used in speech. Truer English analogues for the oppositive modes would be 'although', 'while' or 'whereas'; and even the all-purpose 'but', after a construction with 'may', often serves its function – the example used above about French use of condoms could be phrased 'Eight out of ten Frenchmen may well know that condoms offer the only proper protection, but very few of them ever use any.' In statements of explanation or cause, English would tend to avoid 'if' and use simple 'because' or else begin the sentence with 'The reason why ...'. The quotation used above about the novel in the Arab world would be phrased in common English either as: 'The reason why there is no tradition of the novel in Arab literature is that ...' or 'There is no tradition of the novel in Arab literature because ...'.

si l'on veut

This expression exists in two modes: one introduces a concession; the other introduces an alternative form of words. Both of these are usually placed inside the sentence, between commas.

Concessive

As *certes*, *sans doute* and the other concessives can do, this mode starts by agreeing with what precedes. But that agreement is then followed and in some measure contradicted by a further point, often introduced by *mais*, which the writer deems to be more pertinent. As a concessive, this one is no doubt closer to *admettons* than to *assurément*, say, in that the agreement it expresses is less than whole-hearted. The reader's expectation of the objection which it foreshadows is correspondingly stronger. In the first example, the writer, discussing supposedly autobiographical elements in Gustave Flaubert's *Trois contes*, uses this connector to give grudging and brief credence to the view of Thibaudet that the central character of *Un cœur simple*, Félicité, is based on Flaubert himself, before restricting that agreement to a sort of disagreement:

> Albert Thibaudet allait jusqu'à retrouver Flaubert lui-même dans le morne destin de la servante Félicité. Si l'on veut : mais seulement dans la mesure où il était aussi madame Bovary. N'exagérons rien.
>
> (Henriot, 1954: 53)

Similarly, a writer discussing Rousseau's concepts of the body politic and the natural group considers whether the family is a natural group rather than an entity held together by reason. The writer combines this mode with concessive *bien* to express his provisional acceptance of the point he is contesting:

> Ce n'est pas seulement le corps politique qui est un être de raison, mais aussi la famille. Elle est bien, si l'on veut, un groupe naturel en ce sens, en tant que les enfants sont unis aux parents par le besoin qu'ils ont d'eux pour pouvoir se conserver. Mais ce besoin ne dure qu'un temps. Quand l'enfant est en état de se suffire, il ne reste attaché à ses parents que s'il le veut bien.
>
> (Durkheim, 1953: 138)

A cognate structure, less impersonal in tone, is *je veux bien* or *je le veux bien*, used here in a discussion of whether or not Napoleon was a war-monger:

> Dans mon enfance, quelques historiens s'échinaient à démontrer que Napoléon avait horreur de la guerre, mais qu'il y était sans cesse acculé par les coalitions qui se formaient contre lui. Je le veux bien. Cependant, il faut convenir qu'il

ne faisait pas grand-chose pour éviter les conflits et qu'il prenait quelquefois
la décision de les déclencher lui-même.

(Dutourd, 1985: 110)

Substitutive

This mode, introducing or accompanying the replacement of a word by
another, derives from the straightforward meaning that the expression can
have in, say, a recipe: *Ce plat, poché dans le bouillon, agrémenté de beurre
et, si l'on veut, de gruyère, est un délice.* Rather like the substitutive mode
of **mieux** or **plutôt**, it says that what follows is a more appropriate expression. It has a shade of courtesy that the other structures do not have. In
the following example, the writer is discussing the disproportionate role
played in a polity like France, often evenly divided into those who vote
for the Left and those who vote for the Right, by the small number of
voters who are committed to neither of the major groupings. He uses this
mode to suggest that they are more aptly described by *frange* than by
marge, the word he has been using:

> Or, compte tenu de la stabilité d'un corps électoral coupé en grandes masses,
> c'est de cette marge-là, de cette frange, si l'on veut, que dépend et continuera
> selon toute vraisemblance, de dépendre le résultat des grandes consultations
> électorales.
>
> (Fontaine, 1978: 157)

In this function, the structure is sometimes replaced by *ou si l'on préfère*:
L'histoire, ou, si l'on préfère, la mémoire du passé.... And it is also used,
as it were, to excuse a liberty taken with the language, rather like *si j'ose
dire, si je puis dire, si l'on passe ce mot* or *si l'on peut dire*: a historian
makes up a word to describe the twelve largest French cities as *ces sur-
villes, si l'on veut* (Braudel, 224).

In English, equivalents for the concessive mode could be 'I daresay',
'if you like' or 'possibly'. The other mode could be expressed by 'if you
prefer', 'or rather' or 'to be more precise'.

sinon *

Some of the major lexicographers are less than wholly clear on this multifarious connector. As Joseph Hanse says in a lengthy, interesting and
informative note, its functions and meanings are *non toujours définis avec
assez de précision par les dictionnaires* (Hanse, 1983: 867). Only four of
its modes are discussed briefly here: at the beginning of statements; in
combination with **du moins**; as a restrictive akin to **si ce n'est (que)**; and
a mode which is close to **voire**.

First in the sentence or statement

This mode means 'otherwise' in the sense of 'if that were not to be the case' and could be replaced by *autrement, sans quoi* or *faute de quoi*. It is usually placed first in the sentence and followed by a complete statement introduced by a subject and verb; but it can be placed elsewhere. Frequently accompanied by a verb in the conditional, it comes between two statements of possibility: the one following envisages a possibility opposite to the one preceding. It is sometimes followed by a comma, sometimes not. The first example is from a facetious article on people whose well-laid plans lead to resounding failures:

> Avant, ce qu'il est joli, le futur flop, quand il monte vers le ciel ! Une bulle irisée, une montgolfière peinte aux couleurs de l'espérance, un feu d'artifice... Le décideur-prophète est sûr que ça va marcher, qu'on va gagner la bataille, la fortune, les élections. Sinon, il ne se serait pas embarqué dans cette galère.

And a discussion of progress towards European union canvasses the pros and cons of federal systems of government:

> Ce n'est pas que le système fédéral soit mauvais en soi, au contraire. Sinon, il n'aurait pas été adopté par plus de la moitié de la planète.
>
> (Fontaine, 1978: 288)

When the statement which it accompanies comes in the middle or near the end of a sentence, the connector is usually put between two commas, as in this extract from an article about the influence of contraceptive technology on the sexual behaviour of individuals and on the population of the planet:

> En dépit des discours religieux interdisant le recours aux méthodes contraceptives modernes, il existe aujourd'hui une très forte demande pour les techniques permettant de dissocier la procréation de la sexualité, et peut-être de maîtriser une démographie planétaire qui, sinon, conduirait à la catastrophe.

In tandem with *du moins*

In this mode, the connector accompanies the first part of a two-part affirmation. It admits doubt on the accuracy of the first of these two statements; the second part, introduced by *du moins*, certifies the accuracy of the second of them: *Certaines œuvres de jeunesse, Balzac les a, sinon reconnues, du moins avouées plus tard*. In this sequence, *sinon* is often replaced by *si ce n'est*. The equivalent English combination is 'if not ... at least'. Here, an author discusses change in moral attitudes now that more and more couples choose to live together without marrying:

> Presque partout, ce qui était encore vers 1960 une situation fortement stig-
> matisée est devenu aujourd'hui comportement sinon majoritaire du moins
> largement admis.
>
> (Roussel, 95)

Some writers vary the shade of meaning of *du moins* by replacing it with
au moins, as in this extract from a theatre critic's review of a contemporary work entitled *Enfonçures*:

> *Enfonçures* est une représentation splendide du théâtre d'aujourd'hui, d'un
> théâtre qui empoigne les contradictions bruyantes de son environnement pour
> essayer d'en rendre compte sinon justement, au moins honnêtement.

A similar combination is made with **en tout cas**.

The placing of a comma before this mode of *sinon*, as in one of the
examples above, is deemed inappropriate by some:

> Dans les constructions avec « au moins » ou « du moins », il ne faut pas de
> virgule avant *sinon*, car cela hacherait la phrase de façon illogique.
>
> (Colignon, 27)

The view of Drillon on appropriate punctuation is more detailed (Drillon,
186–187).

Restrictive like *si ce n'est*

In the sense of 'except' or 'with the possible exception that', this mode
can introduce a statement restricting the scope of what precedes. The
preceding point is usually couched in the negative. Like the previous mode,
this one too can be replaced by *si ce n'est*; unlike the previous mode, it
can combine with *que*: *De son enfance, on ne connaît pas un seul fait avéré,
sinon qu'elle fut marquée par la guerre*. It could often be replaced by *sauf*.
In this example, a writer speaks of Left and Right in post-Revolutionary
politics:

> Entre les Enragés et les Ultras, il n'y avait rien de commun, sinon la volonté
> de se liquider mutuellement.
>
> (Duverger, 20)

This mode is used too in a **question** or in the answers to questions, as
in this excerpt from a historian's essay on what might constitute the identity of France:

> Alors qu'entendre par identité de la France ? Sinon une sorte de superlatif,
> sinon une problématique centrale, sinon une prise en main de la France
> par elle-même, sinon le résultat vivant de ce que l'interminable passé a
> déposé patiemment par couches successives, comme le dépôt imperceptible de
> sédiments marins a créé, à force de durer, les puissantes assises de la croûte
> terrestre ?
>
> (Braudel, 11)

Close to *voire*

This mode is as potentially ambiguous as English 'if not'. In a statement like 'The elections will have to be postponed, if not cancelled', two quite different meanings are possible: The elections will at least have to be postponed, and possibly even cancelled; and: If the elections are not cancelled, they will have to be postponed. Sometimes the context clarifies the reader's dilemma; sometimes not. Likewise, *sinon* may invalidate either the meaning preceding it (the usual function); or else it invalidates the one following it. And in some contexts the reader must guess which it does. In sentences like the following two, there can be no doubt that the connector functions, after the manner of *voire*, by replacing a preceding less apt term by a following apter one:

> La photographie aérienne montre encore distinctement la marque sur l'herbe de constructions détruites depuis des siècles sinon des millénaires.
>
> (Fontaine, 1978: 164)

> Les exploitants de la centrale de Creys-Malville voient le redémarrage de l'installation repoussé à plusieurs mois, sinon à un an ou plus.

And conversely, in the next example, the final sentence of an article criticizing the ways in which the original design of the Bibliothèque de France has been tampered with, cheesepared and diluted, so as to turn it into little more than a conventional library, a reader who has followed the arguments and tone of the writer may have little difficulty in seeing that the relationship made by the connector is the opposite of that made in the previous examples, i.e. it validates what precedes, not what follows:

> On peut s'interroger sur la méthode adoptée pour arriver à un résultat qui sera vraisemblablement honorable, sinon original.

This ambiguity is sometimes avoided by a combination of the connector with *même*:

> Le nombre des avortements, disaient-ils, va croître énormément. Or, les statistiques officielles montrent une grande stabilité, sinon même une diminution.

soit *

This word, a 'crystallized' subjunctive, has its entry in dictionaries separate from the verb *être*. It has three connective functions: in concessive statements; in a mode cognate with ***par exemple***; and in a sense akin to ***c'est-à-dire que***, sometimes combined with ***au total***.

Concessive

Like *sans doute* or *il est vrai*, this is one of a set of concessives more or less replaceable by *certes*. All of these structures, in varying degrees, express provisional agreement with a preceding proposition, while fore-shadowing a partial objection to it, which is usually introduced by a word like *mais*. This one, basically an interjection, expresses strong agreement; but the objection following it is one which the writer deems to be perti-nent none the less. In this example, the writer uses it to accept the validity of de Gaulle's dictum on the Fourth Republic; then she broaches a point about one of that period's Prime Ministers which the dictum leaves out of account:

> Le général de Gaulle disait de la IVe République : « La France souffre d'un système qui fait porter aux hommes politiques des responsabilités injustifiées. » Soit, mais d'où vient que Guy Mollet ait été plus sévèrement jugé que d'autres, qui n'ont pas fait mieux ?

Unlike some other concessives, this one, rather than introducing a whole sentence of concession, is usually followed directly by *mais*. On occasion it does introduce a separate sentence. And often it forms a whole sentence by itself, which enhances its usual brevity and interjective abruptness, as in this example, taken from a discussion of the possible role of chance among other factors making for a profound and sudden evolution of moral values in recent times:

> Les partisans de cette thèse rétorqueront qu'on ne saurait, parmi les facteurs d'évolution, écarter le hasard et que précisément l'ampleur exceptionnelle des changements exigeait des convergences exceptionnelles. Soit.
> Pourtant, à rester à ce niveau d'explication, des difficultés subsistent.
>
> (Roussel, 192)

And quite often, too, in keeping with the peremptory way this interjec-tion is often uttered in conversation, a writer will add an exclamation mark. The following example is taken from a comment on the biograph-ical study by Pierre Péan, *Une jeunesse française : François Mitterrand 1934–1947*. The book discusses the question of whether the Socialist President had been, in his teens, a member of the Cagoule, a violent orga-nization of the extreme Right:

> Donc, Pierre Péan l'établit, François Mitterrand, malgré une adolescence immergée dans les milieux d'extrême-droite, n'a jamais été membre de la Cagoule. Soit ! Mais il a longtemps fréquenté les cagoulards amis de sa famille.

In speech, the final *t* is pronounced, thus expressing some of the emphasis that the word conveys, as well as disambiguating this mode from others. In writing, this clarifying function is done by punctuation: as can be seen from the examples, it is always followed by a stop; other modes never are.

Cognate with *par exemple*

This mode, being always followed by a noun which is its subject, is therefore also a mode of *inversion du verbe*. It derives from a technical usage in mathematics: *Soit un triangle ABC* ('Given a triangle ...' or 'Let ABC be a triangle'). In that technical use, it posits a hypothesis. Adapted first by logicians, as a connector in discursive prose it has rather the sense of 'for instance' that one finds in expressions like 'Let us consider', 'Let us imagine' or 'Take'. It usually stands first in the sentence or paragraph and could always be replaced by *Prenons comme exemple*. A variant is *Soit le cas de*. A writer discussing elementary things in music begins a paragraph: *Soit la phrase que chante Marguerite dans le* Faust *de Gounod* (Backès, 27). Sometimes it is combined with the word *exemple*, as in *Soit un exemple simple*, or with *par exemple*, as in this extract from a discussion of whether there is any such thing as a 'beautiful' language and in particular the impression a foreign language may make on someone who does not understand a word of it:

> Il n'est pas rare que s'impose à l'attention de l'étranger un certain type articulatoire, inconnu ou peu usité dans sa langue, mais d'une grande fréquence dans celle sur laquelle il doit se prononcer. Soit, par exemple, les consonnes palatalisées du russe ou du polonais.
>
> (Martinet, 54)

As can be seen in that example, this connector has evolved so far from the usual functioning of the verb *être* that there is no agreement between it and the plural noun following.

Combined with *au total*

Used with or without *au total*, this mode can mean roughly *c'est-à-dire* or *autrement dit*, as in the following extract from an essay on the patriotic mythic bias given to French history in primary-school textbooks, of both the present and the past, and the distortions of truth that this entails:

> Les manuels actuels, édités depuis le « rétablissement » de l'enseignement de l'histoire à l'école élémentaire, restent inspirés par la même logique du passé : France immémoriale, ancêtres gaulois, justification implicite des guerres qui « agrandissent » la France.
>
> Soit une histoire qui ne soulève jamais la problématique *dreyfusarde* des rapports entre la Vérité et la Raison d'État et qui ne donne pas la parole aux vaincus du pouvoir (monarchique ou républicain).
>
> (Citron, 15)

With *au total*, it is used in conclusive statements which add up amounts or recapitulate the force of preceding points. Some writers place commas before and after *au total*; some use none. The statement introduced is sometimes appended to the end of the sentence; sometimes it makes a sentence on its own. In either case, it usually contains no verb. An example comes from an article about the computerization of the policing of Europe's new frontiers; writing at a time when the EC consisted of twelve countries, the author discusses the replacement of old national borders by *des frontières électroniques*:

> Cela suppose en premier lieu la création d'un fichier central, rassemblant et connectant entre elles l'ensemble des données informatiques des polices des Douze, tant sur les étrangers déclarés « indésirables » que sur les personnes recherchées et les objets volés (billets, papiers d'identité, véhicules). Soit, au total, quelques dizaines de millions de données, susceptibles d'être accessibles à tout policier européen en quelques minutes.

At times *au total* is replaced by *un total*, as in this extract from an article about the number of people going to see films in Paris in a particular week. The writer, having said that the Walt Disney film *Aladdin* was the most popular, goes on like this:

> Loin derrière, *Little Buddha* se maintient assez bien en deuxième semaine, à 75 000 dans 32 salles (soit un total de près de 200 000). Également en quinze jours, *Tout le monde n'a pas eu la chance d'avoir des parents communistes* fait lui aussi preuve de bonne santé, avec 35 000 amateurs de chœurs de l'Armée rouge, soit un total de plus de 85 000.

soit... soit

This structure is usually a variant for *ou bien... ou bien*. It introduces pairs of alternatives, choices to be made, incompatible consequences that might arise from circumstances previously mentioned.

Announced alternatives

Like other structures which introduce paired points, for example *d'une part... d'autre part*, this one is frequently preceded by an announcement to the effect that there are two points to be made. This is sometimes done by a mention of *deux possibilités* or by placing the adjective *double* in the sentence before, as in this extract from an editorial critical of the government's handling of the so-called 'Uruguay Round' of international trade negotiations. The piece was written at a time when the European Community could still be referred to as *les Douze*:

> Le pilotage des intérêts de la France dans l'Uruguay Round n'est pas apparu comme un modèle de cohérence, ni d'efficacité, face à un double danger : soit elle devait se résigner, dans le secteur sensible des exportations agricoles, à des concessions politiquement et économiquement insupportables ; soit elle prenait le risque de l'isolement parmi les Douze.

Unannounced alternatives

At times the alternatives are not announced in what precedes. Equally, they may not structure a single sentence or be preceded, as in the previous example, by a *deux-points*, but may begin a separate *phrase dépendante*, as in this extract from a discussion of two possible ways in which the then Prime Minister, Pierre Bérégovoy, might reduce France's dependence on foreign-sourced investment:

> Le financement de la dette de l'État dépend en définitive du jugement que portent les grands investisseurs étrangers sur l'avenir de la France. Dépendance inévitable, sans doute, mais qui peut être réduite. Soit en diminuant le déficit budgétaire, et donc les besoins à financer. Soit en augmentant l'épargne intérieure. M. Bérégovoy préconise un cocktail des deux.

Sequences of more than two

This structure may be adapted to the presentation of more than two points by the addition of a third *soit* to the other two. Here a writer, speaking of apparent regionalisms in the prose of the Provençal writer Jean Giono, says that each of them needs to be carefully inspected:

> ...identifiée soit comme transcription francisée d'un terme indigène, soit comme équivalent français d'un mot du pays, soit comme mot français introduit par les routes et implanté en provençal [...]
>
> (Wagner, 196)

A variant of that three-part sequence (*soit... soit... soit encore*) is seen in the following extract from an essay on the importance of speaking and writing without clichés:

> Les clichés abondent dans la langue des parlementaires, dans celle de l'administration, dans les reportages de faits-divers et dans les conversations courantes. Ils portent soit sur deux noms associés : les leviers de commande, un brandon de discorde, les arcanes de la science, le maquis de la procédure, un métier de chien ; soit sur le groupe nom-adjectif : la pierre angulaire, un charme pénétrant, un repos bien gagné, la chute verticale, des doses massives, le point crucial ; soit encore sur les locutions verbales : prodiguer ses soins, offrir ou présenter un aspect, réserver un accueil favorable, revêtir de sa signature, procéder à un échange de vues ou à un tour d'horizon, attenter à ses jours, prendre des mesures (quand il ne s'agit pas d'un tailleur).

Also used are *soit... soit... ou* and *soit... soit... ou encore*.

Hanse's note

On this structure, Hanse has an interesting note:

L'alternative marquée par *soit... soit* ne peut porter sur des verbes ou des propositions. C'est *ou... ou* qui s'emploie alors : *Ou vous viendrez, ou j'irai vous voir.*

(Hanse, 1983: 875)

It must be said that this rule is widely disregarded. It is contradicted by one of the quotations used above and by the following one, taken from an editorial discussing the possible outcomes of Iraq's decision, during the Kuwait crisis of 1991, to retaliate against the actions of Western governments by blockading their embassies in Baghdad:

Tout dépendra d'abord du comportement de l'Irak : soit ses soldats se contentent, dans un premier temps, d'encercler les chancelleries ; soit ils en délogent aussitôt les diplomates « manu militari ».

The structure is even used in a way which separates subjects from their verbs, as in this comment on British political movements of the extreme Right and Left:

En Grande-Bretagne, les bruns du National Front et les rouges du Militant Tendency soit ont disparu de la scène politique, soit sont en très nette perte de vitesse.

soit que... soit que

This combination is used with points dependent on a preceding verb. According to the nature of that verb, the two verbs following may be in the subjunctive: *S'agissant de Mac-Mahon, Gambetta voulait soit qu'il se soumette, soit qu'il se démette.* Or they may be in the indicative: *De deux choses l'une : Monsieur le ministre montre soit qu'il est un paresseux indécrottable, soit qu'il est monstrueusement ignorant.*

somme toute *

This structure usually puts a finer point upon what precedes, functioning at times as a resumer or a concluder akin to **bref**, **finalement** or **en définitive**; and at others as a preciser, such as **autrement dit**. One of its modes, introducing a considered but undemonstrated judgment, is close to **au fond** and **pour tout dire**.

Recapitulative

This mode can introduce a restatement, in more analytical terms, of information given in what precedes. In the following example, the author first makes two points, in a two-part sentence, about Freudian aspects of the tragedies of Racine; then, with this connector, he reduces them to a single more pointed diagnosis:

> Le film des tragédies placées côte à côte nous montre d'une part une poussée libidinale (celle du moi amoureux), qui se révèle incestueuse et se charge de culpabilité, d'autre part, le développement d'une conscience désexualisée et bientôt punitive. Il nous retrace, somme toute, une crise œdipienne, presque normale dans ses grandes lignes, avec apparition d'un sur-moi.
>
> (Mauron, 179)

When placed beside the verb, this mode often functions within a single sentence. But as an inter-assertional connector it is also placed first in the sentence, with a comma, as in this extract from an ironic discussion of the idea that the dignity of the office of President of the Republic requires the existence of the death penalty:

> Ah, ça ! Rétablir la peine de mort pour restaurer le prestige du président de la République, il fallait y penser ! Mme Marie-France Garaud y a pensé puisqu'elle affirme que M. Mitterrand, ayant « pris la mesure de sa charge », n'abolirait plus aujourd'hui la peine de mort. En effet, dit Mme Garaud, cette sanction est « le signe le plus profond de [la] fonction, le symbole – le symbole le plus fort ». Somme toute, c'est la faculté de donner la mort (ou de l'épargner, ce qui, philosophiquement, revient au même) qui justifierait de présider à la vie de ses concitoyens.
>
> (Boucher, 132–133)

There, with minimal rearrangement of syntax, the connector could be replaced by *c'est-à-dire*. Indeed, it is sometimes used in the combination *c'est-à-dire, somme toute*.

With an unargued judgment

In this mode, it would be unusual for the connector to be placed first in the sentence. Sometimes what follows is of the nature of a definitive judgment, not explicitly canvassed in what precedes; and the connector signals it in passing, as it were, in an adjective:

> En faisant à Mauriac la querelle que l'on sait (lui reprochant d'imposer à ses personnages une substance postiche et de les transformer ainsi en choses), Sartre n'a pas seulement affirmé une certaine conception – nouvelle somme toute, – du roman, mais il a aussi défini du même coup sa position en tant que critique.
>
> (Poulet, 1971: 264)

This mode, after the manner of ***au fond*** or at times *finalement*, is really introducing an opinion. It is usually an opinion based on no previous demonstration and at most implying that the mature reflection justifying it has been done by the writer but is left implicit. The opinion is often a criticism, a statement of disappointment expressed in a depreciative adjective such as *banal*, making the point that the *somme* that the whole judgement adds up to is in fact no great sum. The first of these examples is taken from a review of a performance by a pop-group from Orléans known as *les Burning Heads*:

> Le quatuor orléanais a imposé – en bermuda – son expérience de la scène. Leur parfaite cohésion propulse une fureur qui prend la salle d'assaut. La hargne et le tempo convainquent enfin le public de s'adonner aux joies du pogo (un emballement qui fleure bon les années punk). Dommage pourtant que cette frénésie ne remette pas plus en question les formes d'un rock somme toute conventionnel et trop linéaire.

A similar descent to a final unsupported adverse opinion is seen in this comment on Jean-François Revel's book, *La tentation totalitaire*:

> Malgré ses vertus pédagogiques, ce livre fut d'emblée, et cruellement, hypothéqué par les défauts de ses qualités : c'était utile, plein de bon sens mais, somme toute, banal.

That example shows the similarity of this mode with the ***pour tout dire*** rounding off a criticism, as does the following one taken from an entry in Gide's *Journal*, giving a judgment on a re-reading of Dostoyevsky's *A Raw Youth*:

> Nous lisons à haute voix *l'Adolescent*. À la première lecture, le livre ne m'avait pas paru si extraordinaire, mais plus compliqué que complexe, plus touffu que rempli, et, somme toute, plus curieux qu'intéressant.
>
> (Gide, 1951: 135)

It functions, too, like the *à la fin* which at times replaces modes of ***enfin*** or *finalement*, as in this extract from a judgment on the style of Colette, in which the criticism is similarly signalled:

> Il y a chez Colette, sous tant de grâces, de bonheur à dire, à conter, sous tant d'art à la fin un peu précieux et raffinant sur le choix des mots, un sens et un goût de la vérité qui la mettent à part.
>
> (Henriot, 1956: 337)

These examples show two other things: the criticism follows praise, and the connector therefore has a partly contrastive function; and, by implying that this is a considered judgment, it presents what it accompanies as the outcome of a process. The verb accompanying it is quite often one which expresses the idea of reaching a conclusion. In the following example, this verb is *conclure*; and the contrast shaped by the connector is that between the summariness of the trial and the comparative leniency of the sentence:

> Si expéditif qu'il ait été, accusés et défenseurs refusant de participer aux audiences, le procès des deux « stars » de l'ex-Front islamique du salut, s'est somme toute conclu, mercredi 15 juillet, devant le tribunal militaire de Blida, par un verdict de relative clémence.

The verb in the next example is *finir par*; and the contrast between a process and its outcome – that the diarist's impersonality eventually is his solipsism – is underscored by the connector:

> Par un détour bien étrange, l'impersonnalité d'Amiel le conduisait insensible-ment au plus inconscient, mais au plus complet égoïsme. Sous le prétexte qu'il se considérait, suivant son expression, comme une boîte à phénomènes, il finit par ne plus s'inquiéter que de ses propres états d'âme, et, somme toute, à [*sic*] ne voir que lui dans le monde, lui, avec ses hésitations et ses langueurs, lui, avec ses efforts incertains et ses insuffisances, mais lui uniquement, et lui toujours.
>
> (Bourget, 271)

English equivalents for the first mode could often be 'all things consid-ered', 'in short' or 'in fact'; and for the second mode, 'actually', 'on the whole' or 'really'.

tandis que

This is one of a pair of temporal structures – the other is *alors que* – which can also function interchangeably as contrasters. It is analogous to English 'while' (or 'whilst'): basically a word for linking two actions happening at the same time, it can have the sense of 'whereas' or 'though' in adversative sentences. Like *alors que*, the function of this structure can be either anaphoric or cataphoric, depending on its place in the sentence.

In mid-sentence

Like *alors que*, the structure is placed either in the middle of sentences or at the beginning. In the middle, it is always anaphoric, constructing the second part of a contrast initiated by the first part of the same sentence, as in this extract from an article on the predicaments in which two types of displaced African intellectuals find themselves:

> Dans leurs tentatives d'échapper à la crise sociale et à l'effondrement économique engendrés par le détournement des ressources africaines, de nombreux Africains participent à la fuite des cerveaux vers l'Occident, tandis que d'autres se retrouvent dans les camps de réfugiés installés en Afrique par des agences occidentales d'aide internationale.

At times, the function is more temporal than contrastive, at other times, less temporal. In the following example, which makes a comparison between two sorts of glaciers, there is clearly a temporal element; but equally clearly, that element is less important than the contrast of the *petits* with the *gros*:

Les conditions climatiques qui ont régné ces dernières années en montagne ont ainsi entraîné un recul de tous les petits glaciers, tandis que les plus gros voyaient leur avancée se réduire ou être stoppée.

First in the sentence

Again like *alors que*, when it is first in the sentence, the structure can function either anaphorically or cataphorically. When it is anaphoric, introducing the second element of a contrast, it stands first in a *phrase dépendante*. The first element of the contrast is then contained in the sentence before, as in this extract from a comparison between two works of historical fiction by Flaubert, the novel *Salammbô*, set in ancient Carthage, and the novella *Hérodias*, set in biblical Palestine:

L'histoire de la princesse carthaginoise laisse le lecteur indifférent ; elle n'engage que l'art de l'auteur et sa compétence historique. Tandis que la légende d'*Hérodias*, s'insérant, à l'aube du christianisme, à l'intersection du monde judaïque et du monde romain, excite une curiosité bien plus vive dans l'esprit du lecteur moderne et de formation chrétienne.

(Henriot, 1954: 54)

When its function is cataphoric, it introduces not the second element of a contrast but the first. The second element is contained in the same sentence, as in this comparison between the two branches of the Rhône in spate, the Grand and the Petit, one of which threatens to flood the town of Arles and the other floods the countryside of the Camargue:

Ils se séparent en amont d'Arles, juste au-dessus du village de Fourques, pour embrasser la Camargue, au sud. Mais tandis que le Grand Rhône roule ses eaux boueuses en vagues furieuses sous le pont de Trinquetaille, à ras bord des murailles en maçonnerie qui l'enserrent dans la traversée de la ville, le Petit Rhône étale sournoisement les siennes entre les branches des arbres qui le bordent.

In that position and function, the structure could be replaced by the *si d'opposition*.

Less oppositive comparisons

The structure is used to make not only marked antitheses of the sort illustrated above but also simpler comparisons. In the following extract from an article about the lack of uniformity on certain matters among countries of the European Community, the connector merely juxtaposes condoms and homing pigeons much as *et* might do:

Les Italiens refusent encore de laisser entrer chez eux les préservatifs britanniques, pas assez longs, disent-ils, pour leur morphologie. Tandis que les Belges et les Allemands ne laissent toujours pas circuler librement les pigeons voyageurs.

Although interchangeable with *alors que* as a contrastive, this structure is much less common than the latter. It may well be less used nowadays than it was when it shared the contrastive function mainly with *au lieu que*. However, it is much more common than two other temporal conjunctions marking simultaneity of events, *pendant que* and *cependant que*, which used to function contrastively, but which hardly ever do so nowadays.

tant il est vrai que

Containing a verb and subject, this structure can function rather like a main clause at the beginning of the sentence. And because of the adverbial link made by *tant*, it can function rather like a subordinate clause inside the sentence. The latter positioning may be more frequent than it once was. The connector is of commoner occurrence than its scant treatment in dictionaries might lead one to suppose. The statement it introduces supports or explains what precedes and can come close to stating the obvious. With it, the writer often reminds the reader of an assumption of a general nature which they share. At other times, the writer does not remind but rather informs the reader of something more particular related to the matter under discussion. Although it contains *il est vrai (que)*, the structure has none of the concessiveness of that connector.

Assumptions of a general nature

These assumptions are expressed either as historical fact, generally known, or as principles of common experience. A journalist commenting on French unionism draws on an argument which is common knowledge as historical fact: that only a small minority of French workers have ever joined a union:

> Croire à la vertu du syndicalisme dans un pays comme la France est certes une gageure, tant il est vrai que les syndicats ont su y briller avec une belle constance par leur médiocrité.

There, the historical nature of the truth alleged by the connector is seen in the use of a past tense. More often the tense used is the present; and then the statement introduced by the connector comes closer to being a general principle, as in this extract from a discussion of the conditions responsible for the economic recession of the early 1990s, which identifies *la consommation des ménages* as a vital factor in any possible recovery:

Car ce sont bien les ménages qui depuis deux ans, en modifiant leur attitude vis-à-vis de l'épargne, ont beaucoup aggravé la crise, craignant le chômage et s'inquiétant de l'avenir de leur retraite. Tant il est vrai que ce qui est vertu en période de prospérité – l'épargne – peut devenir calamité nationale en période de dépression.

Sometimes the truth which is invoked with this structure belongs to a more specialized domain and can be assumed to be known only to the reader to whom that domain is familiar. Here too, though, the writer generalizes to remind rather than to inform, as in this extract from a review of the art of a weaver, Nicole Martin, which the writer links to a spiritual world, a *tradition mythique*:

L'art de tisser n'est qu'enfantement de formes, souffle expansif du flux vital reliant entre eux tous les états du monde. L'esthétique de Nicole se dévoile progressivement comme art de vivre, cheminement philosophique, Tao lumineux, tant il est vrai que le travail du tissage présuppose une communion absolue entre le corps et l'esprit, entre la pensée et la matière.

In this mode, the function is akin to that of *au fond* or *après tout*.

Information of a particular nature

In this mode, the structure introduces a statement which informs rather than reminds the reader. It still serves to corroborate what precedes or to explain why the previous statement was made; but what follows is no longer a gnomic dictum. It could be more aptly replaced by *étant donné que*, *aussi bien*, even by *car*, or at least by *car enfin* or *car, il faut bien dire que*. In an example like the following one, rather than assuming that the reader already knows about the work-habits of President Clinton, the writer is telling his reader something:

Dans le feu de la bataille électorale, Bill Clinton avait annoncé que son équipe serait à même de présenter au Congrès un programme économique et social complet dès son arrivée à la Maison Blanche. On en est loin ; pareil document devra sans doute attendre la fin février, tant il est vrai que le sudiste Bill Clinton a montré, depuis le 3 novembre, qu'il n'entendait pas travailler au rythme effréné qu'affectionnent les gens de la côte est.

It is noticeable that the statement still contains a vestigial generalization, as these alleged work-habits are related to the man's southern origins. However, with this mode it is more usual that what follows is not assumed to be known to the reader, as in this extract from a description of Longwood, the house where Napoleon spent the years of his exile on the island of St Helena:

Cette maison biscornue ne ressemble à rien. De loin, elle fait songer à un hôpital de fortune pour pays de tiers monde. De près, à un bungalow mal fichu, mi-cabanon, mi-fermette, tant il est vrai que tout n'est fait qu'à moitié dans cette résidence-prison.

tant with other adjectives

At times, *tant* is used with adjectives other than *vrai*, in ways which show that the connector is a crystallized mode of a construction of more general application. Sometimes, like *vrai* in the connector, the adjective can combine with impersonal *il*, as in these two extracts from an article about conflicts which may arise during periods of *cohabitation* between the President and a Prime Minister such as Édouard Balladur:

> Quand diplomatie et action militaire sont étroitement associées, comme dans le dossier bosniaque, M. Balladur ne peut qu'apparaître en retrait, tant il est évident que les décisions essentielles se prennent à l'Élysée.

> Les vraies difficultés, le premier ministre les a rencontrées dans le domaine militaire, tant il lui est difficile de contester le rôle de chef des armées du président de la République.

At other times, the adjective relates to a personal subject:

> L'ancien premier ministre polonais, Tadeusz Mazowiecki, rapporteur spécial de la commission en ex-Yougoslavie, doit présenter un nouveau rapport qui risque d'être le dernier, tant son auteur est découragé du fait que ses recommandations n'ont jamais été suivies d'effet.

As for English equivalents, there appear to be none fixed in the same function. Harrap gives 'so true is it that', an expression that it might be difficult to document from current English usage, although one can find 'to such an extent is this true that' (Leith & Myerson, 87). In the first mode, 'of course' would be apt. With modifications of syntax, 'after all', 'as is well known', 'it is a fact that', 'it must be said that' or 'it is common knowledge that' would also fit in certain contexts. But 'for', as in this extract from late nineteenth-century fiction, would probably fit them all:

> Like other people who have always been idle, he did not consider his idleness a vice. He rather plumed himself upon it, for the man who has done nothing all his life naturally looks down upon people who have done something or are doing something.
>
> (Howells, 358)

tel est *

This structure is so formulaic in its functioning that the two words which make it are rarely separated by any other. However, each of them can vary: *tel*, always an adjective, agrees in gender and number with the noun it qualifies; and the verb may be any third-person part of any tense of *être*. Indeed, the verb need not even be *être*. The order of the words, however, is invariable, making of this structure a specialized mode of **inversion de l'adjectif**. Thus the noun qualified by *tel* is always placed after the verb. The connector is usually first in the sentence, or even the paragraph, which it links to the preceding one. It has a marked dramatic tone: by its brevity, the accumulation of structures which often precedes it and the unusual place of the inverted adjective, it is suited to contexts which stress the solemnity of arresting circumstances. In some of these contexts, it is at times replaceable by *c'est là* or a mode of **voilà**.

After a question

What precedes this connector is commonly a **question** or a sequence of questions. The noun following is then often *problème* or *question*. If *Hamlet* had been written in French, the line beginning 'To be or not to be?' might well have been completed with *Telle est la question*. The first example deals with an attempt by the Interparliamentary Union to address one of the inequalities between women and men:

> Les femmes représentent près de la moitié de la population mondiale mais ne détiennent que 12,7 % des sièges parlementaires. Que faire pour que ce chiffre soit (au moins) doublé en l'an 2000 ? Telle était l'une des principales interrogations du premier symposium sur « la participation des femmes au processus de décision dans la vie publique » organisé par l'Union interparlementaire.

Usually, as in that example, the connector does no more than identify the question. In the following example, it helps to answer one. The quotation is from an essay on the possibility that the art of Nazism may soon come to be seen as no more objectionable than any other form of artistic expression:

> Au nom de l'art, bientôt les sculptures d'Otto Freundlich, mort en déportation à Maidanek en 1943, à côté de celles du nazi Breker, mort à quatre-vingt-dix ans dans son lit ? En clair, oui, tel est bien ce qui nous est promis.

After an infinitive

It is equally common to find this structure following the infinitive of a verb or a sequence of infinitives. In this mode, the structure more usually introduces the final part of the sentence rather than standing first in a new sentence: *Reconstruire la gauche, tel est le pari de Michel Rocard. / Concentrer, neutraliser : tels ont été les deux maîtres mots du nouveau premier ministre.*

> Maintenir vaille que vaille le cap vers la convergence des économies et l'union monétaire, mettre en place les rouages administratifs nécessaires au fonction-

nement du traité, réfléchir collectivement au problème de la récession, bref essayer d'éviter que l'ensemble communautaire continue de se déliter, tels sont les seuls objectifs pour l'instant à la portée des Douze.

As can be seen, these verbs often designate a purpose, which is presented as an objective or a challenge. In such contexts, *Tel est l'enjeu* is not uncommon.

After a list

As with the sequence of infinitives, this mode often recapitulates a set of diverse qualities which may run to a whole paragraph. A common sequence is the list of qualifiers. These are often nouns, as in this judgment on Communist governments throughout the world:

> Cinquante millions de morts, un milliard d'hommes maintenus en servitude, 350 dollars de revenu par habitant. Tel est, dans sa simplicité, le bilan de quarante ans de communisme.

This mode is also used to sum up an accumulation composed mainly of adjectives, as in this valedictory review of the roles played by a film-actress of the 1930s:

> Brune, coiffée en frange sur le front, l'œil noir hardi, la bouche aux lèvres épaisses, fardée, lourde de promesses... Telle était, dans le cinéma français des années 30, Ginette Leclerc, vouée, comme bien d'autres, à l'emploi de « petite femme » ignorant le sens du mot vertu, de garce accrochée au premier homme venu, comme si elle avait le feu au corps.

At times, too, this structure sums up a series of full independent statements, a list of sentences or, as in the following example, a single long complex sentence. This one, composed mainly of clauses qualifying *la France*, comes from a review of a history of the last years of the Fourth Republic:

> De Dien-Bien-Phû à Suez, des Aurès à Sakhiet, de l'affaire des fuites aux complots du 13 mai, la France, plongée en pleine tourmente, assaillie sans relâche par les tempêtes, a connu un des moments les plus agités de son histoire : hésitant entre un passé glorieux mais révolu et un avenir aux contours brumeux et encore incertains, écartelée entre mendésisme, communisme, poujadisme et gaullisme, déchirée par la querelle de l'Europe, tandis que le régime accumule, après une brève embellie au temps du gouvernement Mendès France, les échecs et les déceptions, puis agonise lentement jusqu'au jour où il est emporté par la crise algérienne. Telle est la période dramatique dont Georgette Elgey nous conte l'histoire avec verve et avec talent sous un titre bien trouvé, *la République des tourmentes*.

After a single circumstance

Often no list precedes and a single significant circumstance justifies the use of this dramatic structure:

> Il lui faut remettre en ordre les finances publiques. Tel est son objectif politique principal.

> Une armée malade au secours d'un régime malade, tel est l'un des aspects qui, avant même les affrontements sanglants de dimanche, compliquait terriblement la tâche de Boris Eltsine dans son bras de fer avec le Parlement.

With a verb other than *être*

At times, instead of *être* a verb of seeming is used, *sembler*, *paraître* or *apparaître*. An analysis of why the electorate turned to the Socialists in May 1981 says that among the reasons was a generalized dissatisfaction with Mitterrand's predecessor, with his attitudes and style of government:

> L'attitude et le style, tels paraissent être les moteurs de la vague rose dont François Mitterrand fut l'habile stratège.

> (July, 50)

A description of some of the qualities of a nineteenth-century statesman says this:

> À travers les lettres où il raconte, soit à sa mère, soit à sa femme, les phases diverses où se développe son activité, la joie circule, joie intense et profonde de l'homme encore jeune qui participe à l'œuvre de son temps et qui l'aime. Tel nous apparaît M. Guizot avant que la révolution de Juillet ne le porte aux affaires, tel encore après cette révolution et dans l'exercice de son rôle de ministre ou d'ambassadeur.

In most of its modes, the most common English equivalent is probably only a stressed 'that' or 'this'. In a more sententious tone, 'such is' might be used, as in the age-old dictum, 'Such is life!'

toujours est-il que *

This structure is nearly always placed first in the sentence or paragraph. As it contains a subject and verb, albeit inverted, the sentence it heads is independent, unlike those made by other structures containing *que* such as *si bien que* or *au point que*. It is basically a contrastive, serving a very particular purpose: it introduces a certainty which stands in contradistinction to a preceding uncertainty. According to Le Bidois, speaking of the fact that some modes of the adverb *toujours* depart from its original temporal meaning:

La locution *toujours est-il* paraît réunir le sens proprement temporel et le sens oppositif, (*en tout cas*, *quoi qu'il en soit*).

(Le Bidois, II, 620)

The affinity with *quoi qu'il en soit* is usually clear: the connector implies 'Whatever the case may be on the foregoing, the fact remains that …'. An author can even begin a sentence *Quoi qu'on pense à ce sujet, toujours est-il que [...]* (Durkheim, 1930: 15). But if the connector does retain temporal force, it is surely minimal, no greater than that of **n'empêche** or **reste que**, which can sometimes replace it.

Following a question

The uncertainty preceding is often expressed in the form of a *question* or questions. The connector usually introduces not an answer but a countervailing certainty which leaves the question unresolved and is seen as more important than it. The first of these two examples comes from the column of a television reviewer who cannot remember why he watched a certain channel:

Comment a-t-on abouti, ce soir-là, sur la chaîne câblée Planète ? Une fausse manœuvre de télécommande ? Un bouton pressé à la place d'un autre ? Toujours est-il, arrivant sur Planète, que l'on eut dès les premières secondes l'étrange certitude d'avoir traversé un miroir.

(Schneidermann, 21)

The second recounts an exploit of three Paris policemen:

Au commissariat du 11e arrondissement, ne confond-on pas Paris et Los Angeles ? Dimanche 18 octobre, vers 15 heures, Athmane Kharouni, 22 ans, partiellement tétraplégique, est interpellé rue Sedaine pour « épanchement d'urine sur la voie publique ». Les trois fonctionnaires de police qui ont constaté le délit s'estiment « menacés ». Par l'urine ? Toujours est-il qu'un brigadier fait illico usage d'une bombe lacrymogène sur Athmane et sa sœur Magda.

Following a hypothesis

Lack of certainty can, of course, be expressed in other ways. For instance, a hypothesis or different hypotheses may be entertained. This extract from an article about a Chinese delegate to the annual congress of the French Communist Party also shows one of the few sequences in which the structure is not placed first in the sentence:

L'envoi, comme chef de la délégation au congrès du PCF, du responsable du Parti communiste chinois pour le Tibet, Chen Kuiyan, indique le peu de cas fait par les dirigeants chinois des préoccupations des démocraties occidentales à propos des droits de l'homme sur le Toit du monde. Insensibilité ou provocation, toujours est-il que seule la plus grande prudence sera de mise, si Paris veut éviter de paraître céder aux sirènes chinoises.

There, the two nouns in apposition, *insensibilité ou provocation*, offered as possible explanations of the Chinese act, could clearly be followed by question marks.

Following a statement of ignorance

The uncertainty may be expressed by a plain statement of ignorance, as in this extract from one of the first reports about the assassination of the President of Algeria, Mohamed Boudiaf, which starts by saying what is not known:

> On ne distingue pas vraiment si c'est la mince silhouette de Mohamed Boudiaf ou sa veste fripée qui gît sur la table devant le micro. On ne connaît pas encore les circonstances précises de l'interpellation du meurtrier, ni le nombre de ses éventuels complices. Toujours est-il qu'une dizaine de minutes après l'assassinat du président, une fusillade nourrie a éclaté de nouveau à l'intérieur de la maison de la culture.

Following a statement of disagreement

Or else there may be a mention of disagreement, evidence of differences of opinion. This example deals with conflicting evidence given to a police inquiry by two men, Jean-Claude Gaudin, *président du conseil régional*, and Fernand Saincené, allegedly one of his temporary employees:

> Saincené affirme que Jean-Claude Gaudin et son plus proche entourage sont à l'origine de ses activités. Le président du conseil régional rétorque qu'il s'agit là d'affabulation et qu'il en fournira les preuves au juge Murciano. Toujours est-il que Saincené a vu son contrat renouvelé chaque mois et à cinquante-sept reprises ; il a bénéficié de plus de trois cents ordres de mission signés « Jean-Claude Gaudin ».

With a concessive

What precedes sometimes includes a concessive such as **certes** or **sans doute**. The full adversativeness of this connector, functioning as the variant of **mais** which often cancels concessions, is then seen. In this example, the writer discusses the poor relationship between Togo and France, recently exacerbated by remarks made by a former French minister speaking out of turn:

> Au Togo, Paris est regardé désormais avec suspicion. D'autant que la visite de M. Charles Pasqua, venu apporter son soutien au chef de l'État togolais fin décembre, a été considérée comme une provocation. L'ancien ministre n'a-t-il pas laissé entendre qu'en cas de victoire de la droite aux prochaines législatives, le président Eyadéma serait assuré du soutien de la France ? Sans doute

M. Pasqua a-t-il outrepassé son rôle. Toujours est-il que la cote des Français au Togo est au plus bas.

Apart from 'the fact remains that', English equivalents might be, depending on context, 'all the same', 'anyway', 'even so', 'nevertheless', 'none the less' or simple 'but'.

tout compte fait *

This is one of several conclusive expressions deriving from the noun *le compte*, which means a sum or an account. The standard dictionaries use the same terms, *tout bien considéré*, to define the meaning of both this structure and **au bout du compte**; and the only difference they see between them is one of tone, the latter expression being more familiar. Some dictionaries see no difference between this structure and **en fin de compte**. Littré, who includes the other two as well as the archaic *de compte fait*, says nothing about this one. It has a single main function: to introduce a definitive judgment. Sometimes it introduces a summing up of reasons already given; sometimes it presents the judgment based on implicit reasons.

Recapitulative

The connector may introduce a conclusion summarizing points which a writer has made previously. In this mode it is typically placed near the end of a development. The following example is the final paragraph of a comparison between two works of Flaubert, *La tentation de Saint Antoine* and *Salammbô*. The connector in the second sentence is a reminder of the reasons touched on in the first justifying the author's preference for *Salammbô*:

> Que si l'admirateur de *la Tentation* affirme que Flaubert est toujours sauvé par son style, je me permettrai d'observer qu'elle n'est pas mieux écrite que *Salammbô*, qui, paré des mêmes prestiges de vocabulaire, de musique et de coloris, a tout de même plus d'allant, de mouvement et de vibration humaine, sous le vernis archéologique et l'excès de documentation. L'ayant relue, pour m'en assurer, tout compte fait, j'aime mieux *Salammbô*.
>
> (Henriot, 1954: 48)

The structure is commonly placed either in the middle of a sentence, as in the previous example, or at the beginning, as in this extract from an article about an injustice directly deriving from a system of justice which works in favour of the rich, the clever and the unscrupulous: too many laws enable too many lawyers to slip through too many loopholes:

Cet excès de lois et la confusion qu'elle entraîne nécessairement est pain béni pour les petits malins et manne céleste pour les escrocs et les mafieux. Avec de bons juristes, plus il y a de textes, plus on a de chances de passer entre les gouttes, d'opposer une loi à une autre, de profiter des contradictions entre deux réglementations ou des superpositions de deux règles. Tout compte fait, cela donne deux France. Celle qui subit la loi et celle qui en profite.

Introducing an unargued judgment

As with one of its possible English equivalents 'all things considered', this expression is sometimes used without any intention to sum up preceding points. It implies that the judgment it introduces has been arrived at after mature reflexion. In this mode, it could be replaced by *à tout prendre*, *pour tout dire* or *somme toute*, as in an example like the following one, taken from a profile of a Chinese politician:

> On s'interroge sur la sincérité de ce vieux roublard qui se présente comme un bon catholique, un patriote, et tout compte fait un honnête homme.

Or it may even foreshadow points, introduce an anticipatory conclusion which is justified not by what precedes but by what follows. It is in the sentences after the one in this example, taken from the beginning of an article in a weekly, that the points implicit in the connector are spelled out:

> Est-ce le bon moment pour proclamer, comme nous le faisons cette semaine, que tout compte fait c'est peut-être en France que ça va le mieux ?

Spelling

A variant spelling, quite common these days but unrecorded in the standard dictionaries, has all three elements in the plural, as in this extract from a report of demonstrations:

> Au lendemain du vote au Sénat, trois mille manifestants pacifiques mais révoltés avaient défilé dans les rues d'Albi pour clamer leur indignation. Cette semaine, tous comptes faits, ils seront sept cents au départ.

This form may be used more often than the singular in contexts where the meaning is literal, that is to present an amount or a number as the total of a numerical calculation, as in the previous example and in the following one, taken from an account of Stendhal's arrangements for the first publication of *Rome, Naples et Florence* in 1817:

> Imprimé aux frais de l'auteur, par Egron, le livre se vendit assez convenablement. En 1821, Stendhal avait remboursé l'imprimeur ; tous comptes faits l'édition lui rapportait 120 francs.

(Henriot, 1924: 165)

However, it is also used when there is nothing arithmetical about its precising function.

Variants

A range of other variants, quite often used, includes forms like *tout pesé* (or *tout bien pesé*), *tout bien réfléchi* and *tout bien considéré*. These forms may be placed first in the sentence more often than the basic structure. But, like it, they are also placed in the middle, as in this comment on the unpredictable but fair distribution of gratifications and dissatisfactions in our lives:

> Le *bon* qu'on attendait n'arrive pas, mais celui qu'on n'attendait pas arrive. Il y a une justice, mais celui qui la rend batifole. C'est un juge jovial, qui se moque de nous, nous attrape, mais qui, tout pesé, ne se trompe jamais.
>
> (Renard, 1965: 255)

Some writers use more connectors than others. The usefulness of having a range of different ones functioning in similar ways can be seen in the following extract from a discussion of data on dangers to life and limb in early nineteenth-century Paris. The writer begins his three consecutive sentences with three resumers, all different, all more or less interchangeable with one another:

> Finalement, l'analyse est plus complexe qu'il n'y paraît. À tout prendre, le bourgeois risque moins de mourir trucidé par le prolétaire que le prolétaire d'être écrasé par la diligence du bourgeois.
> Tout bien pesé, Paris n'est pas le coupe-gorge que l'on imagine au travers de certains récits. La montée de la violence y est aussi mythique que la vague de violence actuelle [...]
>
> (Chesnais, 78)

In some of its functions, English equivalents for this structure could be 'altogether', 'all in all', 'all things considered', 'on the whole' or 'taking everything into account'.

tout de même *

In many contexts, this connector is interchangeable with **quand même**. Two main similarities are that it functions in adversative statements and can be said to have two slightly different modes, one of them more logical, the other more emotional. In the recent past it has changed its meaning; and it has developed from being seen as familiar in tone, even improper to some purists, into a perfectly acceptable expression belonging to written register. Echoes of the polemics which attended these developments can be detected as recently as Dupré (II, 1583), Hanse (1983: 938) and Le Bidois (II, 242).

Logical adversative

In English, the contrastive or adversative function can be done by 'even so' or 'all the same'. That is to say, this mode introduces not a negation of what precedes, but a countervailing certainty which stands beside a preceding affirmation without cancelling it out. In the first example, after a list of adverse comments usually made by critics on the books of Philippe Sollers, the connector introduces a point of praise:

> L'inventaire de ses recettes est dressé par les critiques chaque fois qu'il « sort » un livre, dont il leur faut bien hélas, parler. Beaucoup de « cul », autant de narcissisme, l'exploitation des nostalgies, un parisianisme exacerbé, un zeste de méchanceté, enfin, et tout de même, une grande qualité d'écriture.
>
> (Sédouy & Bouteiller, 302)

In combination with *mais*, etc.

Even though it can combine with *et*, as in the previous example, the structure can be seen to be something of a 'but'. It is often used restrictively with *mais*. In this example, the subject is a general election in Spain, at which the party of Felipe González, the PSOE, narrowly lost its majority on the floor of the Cortes:

> Lors des dernières élections législatives, le PSOE avait, d'extrême justesse, perdu la majorité absolue, mais Felipe González était tout de même parvenu à constituer un gouvernement quasi homogène en s'appuyant sur de petites formations régionalistes.

A particular mode of this combination is used to confirm a point against which a concession has been made, usually with a repetition of a word just used, as in this extract from a comment written about a century ago on two French translations of Homer, the most recent of which in those days was Leconte de Lisle's. The word repeated is *miroir*:

> Depuis plus de trente-cinq ans, la France voit Homère dans Leconte de Lisle; c'est un meilleur miroir que Bitaubé, mais tout de même, c'est un miroir.
>
> (Gourmont, 1902: 111)

Combinations are also made with other *mais*-like connectors such as *pourtant*, *cependant* and *reste que*.

In combination with *si d'opposition*

In a similar way, the connector can structure the second part of contrasts initiated by the *si d'opposition*, as in this extract from a discussion of the disparate origins of the regional style of the Provençal writer Jean Giono, in which it restricts the force of the first part of the binary:

> Si Manosque a été le milieu naturel de son enfance, Giono est tout de même issu d'une famille dont les deux membres étaient, originellement, étrangers à cette petite ville.
>
> (Wagner, 194)

Emotional adversative

In its second mode, slightly less adversative than the first one, this structure can lay an emphasis on a single statement rather than shape an opposition between two. If it has oppositive force, this comes from the unstated objection which it counters with a justification. Like the second mode of *quand même*, it can accompany an implicit criticism, an objection, a reproach, the frankness of which it attenuates; rather like *après tout*, it can add a shade of excuse for having to state the obvious. In the following example, all of this is perceptible in the reproach of the no longer quite so young wife, Mariette, whose husband, Abel the narrator, rather fancies Annick, one of two teenagers in bikinis who pass him on the beach:

> Simone repasse, avec Annick flanquée d'un éphèbe blond assez agaçant. Mes yeux font le travelling.
>
> « Tout de même, Abel, devant moi, regarde-la un peu moins », dit soudain Mariette.
>
> Il y a de l'amusement dans sa voix plutôt que du reproche.
>
> (Bazin, 357)

Even when it accompanies an opposition, its function may be less that of marking the contrast than of underscoring some emotional force implicit in the statement. It often has too a slightly more familiar or spoken tone. This example, clearly adversative but equally clearly implying a criticism of Zola (who liked to present himself as the 'inventor' of the literary mode he called *le naturalisme*), comes from a discussion of the latter's criticisms of Hugo:

> Tout y est, et le morceau pourrait paraître tout entier dans quelque factum d'un de nos modernes hugophobes ; en dépit de l'admiration pour l'artiste – et encore ? – Zola est sans pitié pour le penseur ; mais il a oublié seulement *les Misérables*, où le naturalisme a tout de même été devancé, ne serait-ce qu'aux chapitres des égouts et de Waterloo.
>
> (Henriot, 1954: 292)

The spoken tone is heard in the autobiography of Gide, who sometimes describes scenes in language suggestive of the point of view of the child he was. Here he is hoping to be 'inadvertently' seen by M^{mc} Bertrand as he goes into the aviary:

> En entrant dans le poulailler, j'avais moins d'yeux pour mes tourterelles que pour Mme Bertrand ; je la savais dans le salon, dont je surveillais les fenêtres ; mais rien n'y paraissait ; on eût dit que c'était elle qui se cachait. Comme c'était manqué ! Je ne pouvais tout de même pas l'appeler.
>
> (Gide, 1954: 448)

One hears the spoken tone too, tinged with impatience or self-righteousness, in combinations with **car** and **enfin** such as *car enfin tout de même*. Here, a writer speaks of pre-school children's hysterical enjoyment in pronouncing certain 'naughty' words:

> Quand les enfants de trois, quatre ou cinq ans hurlent de rire pendant des heures simplement en disant « cacaboudin », grand classique des cours de maternelles, c'est fou ce que ça agace. On tolère cinq minutes, et puis on se lasse. D'accord ce sont des enfants, on les excuse, mais enfin tout de même, quel plaisir peuvent-ils bien trouver à prononcer ces grossièretés ineptes ?

Exclamative

The less contrastive, more familiar mode shades into an exclamatory usage, in which the connector may be placed late or last in the sentence, accompanied by an exclamation mark or both: *Curieuse histoire, tout de même!* At times it is reminiscent of the emotion-charged English 'You must admit!' or the colloquialism 'I *mean*!' which are strong invitations to share the speaker's critical attitude or feeling. This example describes Barbey d'Aurevilly at the age of twenty-two in 1830, trying to be a dandy:

> Que de naïveté, chez Barbey ! Il faut lire ses *Memoranda*, son journal de 1830 ; voir tout le souci qu'il se donne, en son narcissisme ingénu, mi-convaincu, mi-ironique, tout ce temps passé en toilette, en frisures, en essais de gilets et de redingotes, en arrachements de cravates. Il se moque, je le veux bien ; mais avec quel sérieux, quelle gravité, tout de même !
>
> (Henriot, 1954: 244)

A final example, without exclamation mark, speaks an eloquent word of reproach to the wise: the three words constitute a whole sentence full of implicit reminders to the knowing reader about anti-Semitism and music. It is taken from an article about the German concentration camp at Theresienstadt, where, for the benefit of Nazi propaganda, Jewish prisoners were encouraged to sing in choirs and play in an orchestra as though they were being spoiled by their captors:

> On organisa des représentations théâtrales, on monta des opéras à Terezin. Un piano fut apporté. Il n'avait pas de pieds, on le posa sur des caisses. Mahler, Schoenberg, interdits ailleurs, côtoyèrent Bizet, Schubert, Brahms, Zemlinsky, Chopin, Debussy et la musique des compositeurs internés. Mais l'on ne jouait ni Richard Strauss ni Wagner. Tout de même.

Enough said.

tout juste

Among its various adverbial usages, *juste* also has a sentence-connective function, especially in the combination *tout juste*. This function can be slightly adversative, in that the connector often restricts the scope of a preceding negative statement by admitting a faint shade of positivity in what follows.

The basic structure can be seen in this statement about a young tennis-player who, despite his apparent unreadiness for high-level competition on grass courts, has just won the junior final at Wimbledon: *Il n'exulte pas. Il pense juste qu'il a bien fait de forcer son destin.* The negativity of what precedes need not be couched in a grammatically negative structure. In the following example, dealing with Austria's objection to the require-ment that in order to join the European Union it abandon its policy of neutrality, the negative polarity of the statement lies in the verb *insistent sur*:

> Le chancelier Franz Vranitzky et son parti insistent sur le maintien du statut de neutralité aussi longtemps que l'Union européenne n'offre rien pour garantir la sécurité militaire de ses membres. Ils ont tout juste accepté l'adhé-sion de l'Autriche au « Partenariat pour la paix » (PPP), se réservant le droit de ne pas faire participer l'armée autrichienne à des manœuvres militaires communes.

With inversion of subject and verb

Instead of being placed beside the verb, as in the preceding examples, the structure is often placed at the beginning of the sentence. It is then usual for it to be followed by an inversion of subject and verb. This inversion may be of the simple sort, in which the subject is a pronoun standing for a noun in what precedes, as in this extract from an account of the trial of Marshal Pétain:

> Impavide, insensible aux bruits de la salle, Philippe Pétain ressemble à un petit soldat de bois perdu dans une bataille qui ne le concerne plus. Tout juste réagit-il lorsque le bâtonnier Payen demande à Édouard Daladier, l'ancien président du Conseil : « Monsieur le président, je pose une question à votre conscience. Le maréchal Pétain a-t-il d'après vous trahi la France ? » À ce moment seule-ment, le vieillard se soulève un peu de son fauteuil.

Or the inversion may be of the more complex variety, in which the subject-group contains both the noun and the pronoun. This example comes from an article about the lack of a significant response by the Banque de France to a sluggishness in investment and a worrying budget deficit:

> Après avoir salué la présentation du collectif budgétaire en rétablissant le taux de ses pensions de 5 à 10 jours, suspendu depuis le 8 mars, le Conseil de la

politique monétaire de la Banque de France (CPM) s'est abstenu de tout geste significatif.

Tout juste le Conseil a-t il consenti, jeudi 29 juin, à baisser d'un seizième de point son loyer de l'argent au jour le jour.

c'est tout juste si

A variant of the inverted structure placed first in the sentence is the form *C'est tout juste si* without inversion. This example comes from a discussion of astronomy and the measures taken by different countries to limit or reduce light emitted by towns near observatories:

> Aux États-Unis, par exemple, l'éclairage public de la ville de Tucson (Arizona) est réglementé pour protéger l'observatoire voisin de Kitt Peak.
> Mais en France, rien ! C'est tout juste si les amoureux du ciel ont obtenu que les rayons lasers émis par les discothèques de campagne soient soumis à autorisation préfectorale.

In this mode, there is an evident similarity both of form and function with *c'est à peine si*. The latter structure could often replace this connector. The functional closeness of *à peine* and *tout juste* can be seen in the following sentence, which speaks of the near-nakedness of some fashions for young women in the early summer of 1995:

> C'est à peine voilé d'un souffle de mousseline, tout juste masqué d'une brume de dentelle, voire dans le simple appareil d'une beauté que l'on vient d'arracher au sommeil que le corps s'avance, à la veille de l'été.
>
> (Boulay, 22)

tout au plus

Another structure which could often replace *tout juste* is *tout au plus*. Like *tout juste* this one can stand beside the verb: *L'air est invisible pour nous ; nous pouvons tout au plus sentir s'il est froid ou chaud.* Or it can stand first in the sentence, followed usually by an inversion of subject and verb, as in this extract from a discussion of air pollution and the ineffectiveness of French legislation on the subject, authorities having only an advisory function without any power to limit, say, the use of private cars:

> Aujourd'hui encore, les recommandations du préfet n'ont pas valeur de décret, pas plus qu'elle n'ont un pouvoir coercitif. Pas question de limiter, comme à Mexico ou à Athènes, les trajets automobiles domestiques ! Tout au plus peut-on encourager la population à utiliser les transports en commun ou à grouper ses déplacements.

au mieux

Much the same goes for *au mieux*, as in this comment on a stage in the negotiations aimed at ending the civil war in Bosnia: *Le plan de paix est obsolète. Au mieux pourrait-il servir de document de discussions.* And *tout au mieux* is used in the same way, as in this second extract from Anne Boulay's article on the transparency and semi-nakedness of young women's summer clothes:

> ...la mode en transparence est aux antipodes de celle de la triche. Là où certains vêtements promettent au corps de le conformer à une silhouette idéale, les voiles glorifient le travail de la nature. Tout au mieux offrent-ils la sécurité d'une deuxième peau, parfois plus élastique, moins fragile, peut-être plus colorée que l'épiderme d'origine.
>
> (Boulay, 22)

English has no equivalents of such pointed functionality. 'At (the) most' and 'at (the) best' serve similar purposes. At times, 'all' with part of the verb 'do' also sees service – in the last quotation, *Tout au mieux offrent-ils* could be expressed in English as 'All they do is'; and in the one about air pollution *Tout au plus peut-on* could become 'All that can be done is'. In the extract about Austrian neutrality, *Ils ont tout juste accepté* might translate as 'The most they have accepted is' or 'They have gone no further than accepting'.

tout se passe comme si *

Long as it is, this structure is a connector. Like the related expression **force est de**, it has in recent years become a very common way of making certain links of thought. It has a few variants, mostly structured with the verbs *penser* or *croire*. Although it derives from the technical discourse of the sciences, a rough equivalent for it in everyday English might be 'One could be forgiven for thinking that'. That is, it is something of a resumer: it usually introduces a quasi-conclusion, one based not upon arguments from certainty but upon probabilities or appearances. Like *on a l'impression que* or *on dirait que*, it conjectures a possible explanation for something which, by its nature, cannot be proved. This example comes from an essay in which an ironist discusses a disparity between the theory and the practice of French Socialist governments of the 1980s, compromised by economic forces and obliged to enact policies which are at variance with their principles:

> Mais si l'action « pragmatique » (pur pléonasme) des socialistes a dû et su, sauf exception, se rapprocher de la réalité, leur vision du monde, comme par compensation, s'en est encore davantage éloignée. Tout se passe comme s'ils

mettaient les bouchées doubles dans la sphère de l'idéologie, afin de rattraper des privations qu'ils doivent, à leur corps défendant, s'infliger dans la sphère de la gestion.

(Revel, 1988: 130)

Sometimes, in say a historical context, the tense varies, as in this extract from a discussion of the celebration of Bastille Day in 1939:

Les cérémonies, au demeurant peu nombreuses, organisées depuis le 5 mai 1939, manquaient tout à la fois d'imagination, de ferveur et de public. Tout se passait comme si les responsables politiques adoptaient volontairement pour cette célébration une ligne avant tout défensive, prudente politiquement, et la plus neutre possible idéologiquement.

Occasionally writers vary the tense as follows *Tout s'est passé comme si* or *Tout se passerait alors comme si.*

Variants with *penser*

A variant tending towards a more positive certainty is *Tout laisse à penser que*, as in this extract from a report on the early vintage of 1989 in the Bordeaux region:

Dans quelques jours, du Médoc à Pomerol et Saint-Émilion, ce sera l'heure des rouges : merlot, cabernet franc, puis cabernet-sauvignon. Et tout laisse à penser que, à l'exception des vins liquoreux de sauternes, loupiac et sainte-croix-du-mont, qui s'enfonceront crânement dans l'automne en quête de pourriture noble, la cueillette, aujourd'hui malheureusement mécanisée (70 % des vignes sont récoltées à la machine), des 100 000 hectares du plus grand vignoble de vins fins du monde, sera terminée dans les premiers jours d'octobre.

This variant is also used as *Tout laisse penser que.* Both versions are also used with *supposer: Tout laisse supposer que; Dès lors, tout laissait à supposer que.* The statement is sometimes made as *Tout donne à penser que* or *Tout incite à penser que*, as in this example taken from a discussion of the apparent disintegration of the Communist state in China in the spring and early summer of 1989:

Il ne m'appartient pas d'interpréter une conjoncture historique et de prévoir quelle sera la réponse du régime et sa capacité de répression. Mais tout incite à penser qu'en Chine comme en Pologne, il ne peut pas y avoir de normalisation à la tchèque et que l'histoire de la Chine continuera à être celle de la désagrégation accélérée d'un régime qui fut totalitaire.

It is clear that the shade of certainty expressed by these variants with *penser* and *supposer* is different from that expressed by the basic structure. With them, the writer is surer of the ground, the justification for the conclusion drawn is more solid. It gives the impression of being a deduction from experience rather than a guess from appearances. Much the same goes for variants with *indiquer*: *Tout indique que* and *Tout semble indiquer que*.

Variants with *croire*

The most common form of the other main variant, structured with *croire*, is *Tout porte à croire que*, as in this extract from an article about Salman Rushdie, the writer sentenced to death in 1989 by the Ayatollah Khomeini:

> Ce n'est pas que Rushdie, hélas ! soit un cas isolé : tout le monde sait qu'il est d'autres écrivains, d'autres intellectuels, notamment en Algérie, en Égypte, en Turquie, au Pakistan, à avoir été condamnés à mort par l'intégrisme « islamique », et que nombre d'entre eux ont déjà été exécutés.
>
> Mais tout porte à croire que, si Rushdie focalise ainsi l'attention, si son sort est perçu *autrement*, ce n'est pas par indifférence envers les autres victimes réelles ou potentielles. C'est d'abord parce que son cas fut en quelque sorte inaugural.
>
> (Scarpetta, 2)

This variant can lend itself to expressing both the quasi-certainty of the basic structure and the more reasoned sureness of *laisser penser*. In *À première vue, tout porte à croire que*, it introduces a temporary hypothesis which may be contradicted in what follows. And in *Tout me porte à croire que*, *Tout porte à croire cependant que* or *Tout porte à croire au contraire que*, the addition of personal pronoun or objecting connector gives greater authority to the conclusion being advanced. A variant, with *pousser*, is *Tout me pousse à croire que*. The form *C'est à croire que* is also used. A shortened variant of it is seen in this extract from a description of a part of Armenia recently devastated by an earthquake:

> C'est une ville de fantômes, un amoncellement de cabanons faits de bric et de broc, où erre une population brisée, désœuvrée. À croire que l'aide humanitaire s'est volatilisée.

Other variants

These include: *Il est à penser que*; *On peut penser que*; *Tout démontre que*; *J'ose croire que*; *Il est permis de supposer que*; *Il y a lieu de présumer que*; *Selon toute apparence*. The paradigm for all these modes is probably *il semble que*. Roger Caillois uses it and another variant in a single paragraph. He is speaking about the rise of the European novel:

> Il semble qu'à toutes les époques un genre littéraire bien défini possède sur les autres une suprématie manifeste. [...] On est tenté de reconnaître en lui un symptôme d'agonie [...]
>
> (Caillois, 154)

A variant which can suggest not probability but improbability is used in this conclusion drawn from a discussion of whether students can be seen as a set, sharing defining characteristics:

> Tout conduit donc à douter que les étudiants constituent en fait un groupe social homogène, indépendant et intégré.
>
> (Bourdieu & Passeron, 55)

A variant of the basic structure is *Tout semble se passer comme si* (Frischer, 13), which introduces a more tentative conclusion, if not a pleonasm.

The place in the sentence

The structure is always placed first in the sentence, except when accompanied by an expression of time, say: *Et parfois, tout se passe comme si*; or by another connector, usually a *mais*-type objector or one like ***donc*** or ***en somme***, reinforcing the conclusive function: *Ainsi tout se passe comme si*. Occasionally, the structure makes the second half of a binary initiated by the ***si d'opposition***, as in this extract from a discussion of a new and apparently successful technique for artificial insemination, where the writer contrasts uncertainty with probable certainty:

> Si l'on ne peut encore situer avec précision l'origine de tels succès, tout laisse à penser que les derniers résultats observés proviennent d'une série d'aménagements techniques (forme, taille et biseautage de la pipette, milieu de conservation des spermatozoïdes, gestuelle maîtrisée du biologiste, etc.).

transitions mécaniques

This is Antonin Vannier's name for injunctions to the reader:

> [...] ce qu'on appelle des transitions mécaniques. Exemples : – *Examinons maintenant l'autre argument... Passons à la question suivante*, etc.
>
> (Vannier, 290)

These structures consist of procedural hints to the reader about what comes next in the setting forth of a ***sequence of points***, the exposition of an argument, the development of a point of view. They are usually placed first in the sentence and very often in the paragraph. Grammatically, the verbs which introduce them are imperatives, most usually first person plural; and the statements they make are injunctive sentences.

Followed by a stop

Sometimes the injunction constitutes the entire sentence and is followed by a full stop: *Regardons les faits. / Insistons sur ce point. / Prenons le cas de la métaphore. / Jugeons-en par quelques exemples. / Posons maintenant le problème des ministres communistes. / Ouvrons ici une parenthèse. / Nuançons tout de même. / Marquons ici une pause avant de reprendre le fil du débat.* Sometimes the injunction is followed by another type of stop, usually a **deux-points**: *Comprenons : ils ont ceci de commun. / Précisons : il va de soi que... / Sachons-le : il faudra bientôt....* This form with colon is used especially with pronominal verbs: *Résumons-nous : ... / Entendons-nous bien : ....*

Not followed by a stop

More often the structure is not followed by a stop but introduces a substantive statement which constitutes most of the sentence. This extract from a discussion of the history of medecine invites the reader to consider the idea that hand-me-down theory supplanted empirical observation of the body for about a thousand years:

> Interrogeons-nous d'abord sur cette occultation du corps qui aurait, au Moyen Âge, entraîné une parenthèse de mille ans dans l'évolution des techniques thérapeutiques.

Other verbs more or less frequently used in this way are: *Abordons maintenant le grand problème de*; *Commençons par*; *Concluons que*; *Constatons néanmoins que*; *Contentons-nous d'établir que*; *Disons d'emblée que*; *Essayons toutefois de*; *Laissons de côté pour le moment*; *Notons que*; *N'oublions pas que*; *Parlons d'abord de*; *Passons vite sur*; *Rappelons brièvement que*; *Remarquons que*; *Reprenons cependant notre analyse de*; *Revenons maintenant à notre schéma du chapitre II*; *Serrons maintenant la question qui*; *Soulignons que*; *Supposons maintenant que*; *Tournons-nous maintenant vers*; *Venons-en à*. One of the most common of these structures is **ajoutons que**.

If not placed first in the sentence, these injunctions are usually placed after the first element: *À titre d'illustration, prenons l'exemple de...*; *Enfin, pour terminer ce paragraphe, rappelons que....*

Variants

An occasional variant of the first person plural imperative is the third person impersonal subjunctive form with *que*: *Qu'on nous permette, avant de terminer ce chapitre, de...*; *Qu'on me comprenne bien : je ne m'oppose pas à...*; *Avant tout, qu'il me soit permis de reconnaître ici quelques dettes et d'exprimer ma gratitude.* This mode is itself variable: *On nous permettra de préciser la portée de ce qui précède.*

Another variant, more personally addressing the reader, is the imperative form in the second person plural, as in this sentence from a study of the tragedies of Racine:

> Supposez Agrippine encore régnante, autrement dit confondez en ce personnage féminin Agrippine elle-même et Néron, faites-lui naturellement aimer Britannicus – et vous obtenez le motif de *Bajazet*.
>
> (Mauron, 94)

French rhetorical protocol

The use of these injunctive connectors can be seen as part of a broader traditional protocol of structures by the use of which the French writer may still treat the reader as more of an active interlocutor than does the contemporary writer of English. This would include the more frequent use of the **question**; less use of passive structures; references to the reader (*Le lecteur avouera que...*; *Cette confusion choquera le lecteur*); references to the writer in the first person: *je veux dire, si j'ose dire, pour ma part*; a greater frequency of interpellative or vocative structures like **oh**, **oui** and **voyez**; and a wide range of non-imperative statements such as: *Nous venons de parler de... / Nous croyons utile de commencer par... / Nous nous permettons de citer le texte en question... / Nous touchons ici à une question cruciale... / Nous nous proposons de suivre dans ce chapitre le chemin inverse. / Nous pouvons laisser de côté... / Nous pourrions clore ici ce chapitre. / Nous voici ainsi revenus au point de départ. / Il nous reste à envisager un dernier problème. / Avant d'aborder l'analyse du texte lui-même, nous voudrions insister sur... / Il nous faut enfin examiner... / Ceci nous pose un tout autre problème. / Comme on le voit... / On ne s'étonnera pas si nous essayons de montrer... / On voit déjà toute l'importance de... / Voici terminée l'analyse sommaire de... / Voilà un point acquis. / Je me contenterai de signaler...*:

> N'ayant pas l'intention de suivre Pascal dans toutes les analyses concrètes où il retrouve l'opposition des vérités contraires, nous nous limiterons à trois points qui nous paraissent particulièrement importants.
>
> (Goldmann, 279)

These procedural statements will sometimes take the form of the **brief interpolated main clause**: *La forme de cette aventure, nous l'avons montré, est... / Une telle analyse eût demandé, remarquons-le, une disposition toute contraire. / L'idée principale, nous venons de le dire, c'est... / Nous avons dans les pages qui précèdent, et nous le ferons encore dans les prochains paragraphes, cherché surtout à... / L'un des éléments les plus significatifs, il convient de le noter, est celui qui....*

And sometimes they are put as questions, as in the opening sentence of Mauron's study of the plays of Racine: *Comment allons-nous aborder l'œuvre de Racine ?* (Mauron, 17).

voilà *

This word functions in a range of different modes, mainly as a declarative preciser. In some of these modes, it is also close to other connectors such as *là*, *c'est pourquoi*, *seulement* and *tel est*. It is usually placed first in the sentence and often preceded by structures in the form of a list.

Introducing a noun

The connector functions anaphorically in most of its modes: with something of a resuming function, it identifies and defines points of importance in what precedes. It often acts as a more demonstrative or dramatic form of *c'est* or *c'est là*, say, in contexts where it introduces a noun or a pronoun structure. In the following excerpt from a discussion of the nexus between a popular conception of romantic love and the rising rate of divorce the writer uses this mode to identify a point of significance:

> De fait, si l'amour romanesque triomphe d'une quantité d'obstacles, il en est un contre lequel il se brisera presque toujours : c'est la durée. Or le mariage est une institution faite pour durer – ou il n'a pas de sens. Voilà le premier secret de la crise actuelle, crise qui peut se mesurer simplement par les statistiques de divorce, où l'Amérique tient le premier rang.
>
> (Rougemont, 1962: 246)

Whether the connector stands first in the sentence or not is largely a question of punctuation. Here an author, defining what he sees as the proper subject of history, precedes it with a dash:

> ...les modalités et le progrès de la vie, sous la forme humaine, dans les sociétés, – voilà l'objet propre de la science historique.
>
> (Berr, 16)

After an infinitive

Again like *c'est là* (or *tel est*), this mode is often preceded by an infinitive or a list of infinitives; and it is this element in what precedes that it resumes. It often introduces the last element of the sentence. Its function of defining or identifying a point of great pertinence is seen in the combination with an analytical concluder like *en somme* or *en définitive*, as in this comment on the state of mind of the true Marxist: *Croire au pouvoir illimité de l'homme sur la création, voilà en définitive le plus puissant ressort de la religion soviétique.*

With *pour* and *pourquoi*

A resuming or defining function can also be served with *voilà pour* and *voilà pourquoi*. The first of these structures is used, followed by a noun, to round off discussion on one point in a series, while foreshadowing the broaching of the next: *Voilà pour la leçon d'histoire. Reste la leçon esthétique.* It is English 'So much for ...'. In the next example, the writer is pointing out that the employees of the Banque de France enjoy many advantages not enjoyed by people who work in other comparable jobs. He deals with the first of these, their higher salaries, before moving on to discussion of the others:

> En 1980, les employés y gagnaient en moyenne mensuelle 7 272 F, les caissiers 8 212 F et les cadres 16 542 F. C'est dire que le salaire de l'employé était exactement le double de la moyenne nationale pour sa catégorie et que le caissier gagnait à peu près autant qu'un cadre supérieur dans la fonction publique. Voilà pour l'argent : ce n'est là qu'un début.
>
> (Closets, 1983: 73)

As for *voilà pourquoi*, it is a common substitute for *c'est pourquoi*. In this example, Durkheim discusses the conditions in which the word 'hereditary' might be properly used to describe an illness. Again the defining role of the connector is apparent:

> Pour avoir le droit de soutenir qu'une affection est héréditaire, à défaut de la preuve péremptoire qui consiste à en faire voir le germe dans le fœtus ou dans le nouveau-né, à tout le moins faudrait-il établir qu'elle se produit fréquemment chez les jeunes enfants. Voilà pourquoi on a fait de l'hérédité la cause fondamentale de cette folie spéciale qui se manifeste dès la première enfance et que l'on a appelée, pour cette raison, folie héréditaire.
>
> (Durkheim, 1930: 77)

voilà qui

With this mode, too, always followed by a verb, a writer can marshal together a set of preceding points. In a discussion of the decay of parliamentary government under the French constitution, a writer begins by listing several pressing priorities, then defines the role of parliament towards them:

> Le développement des libertés publiques, la lutte contre l'inégalité, mais surtout contre l'humiliation, l'élargissement de la responsabilité des citoyens sur les lieux de leur travail et de leur existence, voilà qui demande à entrer progressivement dans le domaine de la loi et qui redonnerait à la fonction parlementaire, non son lustre – on n'en a cure – mais sa nécessité sociale.
>
> (Julliard, 227)

An article on alleged extravagances among Brazil's governing class at a time of supposed austerity in economic policy lists the details of some of these before rounding off the paragraph with this mode:

> Le voyage de M. Sarney à Paris, en juillet, a été rien moins qu'austère : selon la presse, il a emmené avec lui une suite de cent cinquante personnes, alors que la délégation d'un pays riche comme le Japon n'en comportait que quatre-vingts. On cite le cas d'un conseiller présidentiel invité avec femme et enfants. « La moitié des accompagnateurs du président sont allés se promener », affirme l'hebdomadaire *Veja*. Voilà qui cadre mal, assurément, avec les difficultés économiques du pays et l'utilisation qui en est faite dans les forums internationaux.

voilà tout

This mode is often placed last in the sentence. It can serve to make for precision in definition, by being appended, say, to the second element of a contrastive binary. Again it could be replaced by a mode of *c'est*. Here, an author defines the proper distinction between a seventeenth-century view of Homer and a contemporary one:

> Nous nous figurons aujourd'hui mieux comprendre Homère que le dix-septième siècle ; nous le comprenons différemment, voilà tout.

(Gourmont, 1902: 111)

voilà que

More dramatic than the others, this mode has a more narrative function. It tends to act cataphorically, looking forward to the consequences of a new development, one additional to what had seemed enough. It is often combined with initial *et* or *or*. An article on a politician, presented as *ce forcené de travail*, gives instances of his activities, then, with this mode, envisages the future:

> Cet activiste se jette à corps perdu dans toutes sortes d'études, pond d'innombrables notes, intervient de colloque en colloque, anime des instituts, crée des organismes de réflexion... Et ce n'est pas tout : voilà qu'il envisage aujourd'hui de lancer un journal, pour défendre ses idées. Toujours les mêmes.

It is sometimes combined with *maintenant*. Here a satirist (of the Right) comments on what he sees as a malady of the Left, much worse, he says, than the destruction of the legions of Varus during the reign of Augustus:

> La gauche en France souffre d'une affection beaucoup plus grave, d'une anémie pernicieuse et implacable, d'une étrange leucocytose : ses globules rouges deviennent des globules blancs. Et voilà maintenant que le mal s'attaque au cerveau. Nous entrons dans l'agonie.

(Dutourd, 1985: 16)

mais voilà

The combination with *mais* differs from most of the preceding modes by being basically cataphoric and adversative. A variant of *seulement* or *seulement voilà*, it usually follows a description of a favourable state of affairs and announces a drawback. The contrastive effect shows clearly in this evocation of the enviable life of the novelist Philip Roth:

> Pourquoi est-il si malheureux, Philip Roth ? Il vit dans une très belle maison du Connecticut, couvre chaque matin six kilomètres au pas de course, nage dans sa piscine une demi-heure, puis se met devant son Macintosh pour rédiger un roman qui se vendra à des milliers d'exemplaires. Il est un des écrivains américains les mieux payés depuis 1969. Mais voilà, sa célébrité ne lui cache pas la vérité : il est un homme en procès. L'accusé ? Son sexe.

This mode almost always stands first in the sentence and is followed by a comma. It too can often follow an accumulation of similar structures, as in the previous example and in this extract from an article about a police inspector called Philippe Vénère, widely rumoured by his colleagues to be corrupt:

> Les confidences distillées dans les couloirs de la préfecture de police et de l'Intérieur le présentent comme un « caïd ». Pêle-mêle, on affirme que son épouse aurait été la compagne d'un truand ; que la pizzeria et le bar dont elle est la gérante serviraient de rendez-vous à la pègre. Et, pour faire bonne mesure, on n'oublie pas de rappeler que Vénère eut sous ses ordres le commissaire Jobic – impliqué dans une affaire de corruption, puis blanchi. Mais voilà, rien dans cette histoire ne résiste vraiment à l'examen des faits.

Sometimes this mode functions with *oui* in the combination *oui mais voilà*, usually followed by a *deux-points*.

voici and *voilà*

The *Petit Robert* says the old distinctions between *voilà* (normally anaphoric) and *voici* (normally cataphoric), when used in their more literal senses, have been largely abandoned: *L'opposition classique entre* voici *et* voilà *(proche et éloigné) n'est plus guère respectée.* The versatility of *voici* can be seen in anaphoric usages where *voilà* might be expected. A chapter begins: *Voici le lecteur instruit de mon système*, a reference back to the preceding chapter's exposition of the author's method. The final paragraph of a chapter begins like this, reminding the reader of what immediately precedes:

> Voici donc, brièvement résumés, les principaux problèmes qui se posent quant à la genèse de l'art indien et à ses plus anciennes réalisations.
>
> (Auboyer, 18)

A more conventional *voici*, designating not what precedes but what follows, is this: *Voici donc la définition que nous proposons : la rhétorique est l'art de persuader par le discours.* (Reboul, 188)

voire *

The function of this adverb is usually described as affirmative. More precisely, it introduces a term which reinforces and outpasses the value of what precedes. When it functions within a single sentence, which it does almost invariably, it usually links two terms, of the same part of speech, and it implies that the one following is apter than the one preceding. In former times, English had in 'nay' an exact equivalent for it: 'The fellow's a bounder – nay, a cad!' Nowadays, we would probably say 'if not' or 'not to say'. Sometimes 'or even' or 'or rather' would be used.

With numerals

With numerals, the second of the quantities linked by this connector is usually higher than the first: *Les recherches sur l'embryon sont possibles pendant sept, voire quatorze jours après la fécondation. / La plupart des grands équipements à Paris ont été réalisés il y a dix ou vingt ans, voire davantage.* However, this is not always the case, as the connector introduces not necessarily a higher quantity but one which is more pertinent, even if lower. This is the case in the first of these examples, the subject of which is an agreement to reduce arsenals of nuclear warheads:

> S'il est appliqué, l'accord fera passer le nombre d'ogives possédées par les deux pays de quelques 21 000 à 7 000, voire 6 000, en onze ans.

The same goes for its use in a discussion of the economically profitable number of farmers that France needs to produce its food: *500 000, voire 350 000 agriculteurs très performants pourraient à eux seuls nourrir le pays.*

With nouns

Of the other parts of speech linked by this structure, nouns are probably the commonest. They are often used in pairs, the weaker one preceding, the stronger following: *Le marxisme était en train de prendre un sérieux coup de vieux, voire d'archaïsme. / Des risques d'hépatite, voire de sida....*

Sometimes, *voire* follows not a single noun but a list of them, as in the next example's description of the barricades erected in Peking against the army during the failed pro-democracy movement of May–June 1989:

Pendant trois nuits, les Pékinois leur ont barré la route. Avec des autobus placés en travers des avenues, des chicanes faites de collecteurs d'égouts, de barrières de circulation, de tas de graviers, de camions de charbon ou de sacs de ciment, voire, dans un quartier fleuri, des arbres en pots artistement disposés sur toute la largeur de la chaussée.

And an ironist can use this structure to paradoxical effect at the end of a list of nouns:

Il y a autant de penseurs de gauche, notamment après 1945, que de penseurs de droite qui ont employé leur talent à justifier le mensonge, la tyrannie, l'assassinat, voire la sottise.

(Revel, 1988: 326)

With adjectives

Used with adjectives, *voire* most commonly links no more than two of them: *Des réalités très différentes, voire incompatibles*; *En faisant vibrer chez l'électeur la corde xénophobe, voire antisémite*; *Certaines forces, pour le moment fort discrètes, voire secrètes*; *Ses adversaires socialistes sont assez inconsistants, voire pour certains nullissimes.*

But it is also used to round off lists of more than two: *Un ton passionné, quelquefois emphatique, voire déclamatoire.* / *Interminable, inéluctable, irréversible, voire incompressible, le chômage s'installe dans la société.*

With verbs

Verbs also tend to be used in twos, one preceding, the other following: *Ce coup d'éclat risque de compromettre, voire d'annuler, tout le processus.* / *Un singe est capable d'utiliser, voire de préparer des instruments simples.* / *Modeste, capable de sourire jusqu'aux oreilles, voire d'éclater de rire....* But the connector can also round off a longer list of verbs, as in this comment on how, even in an open pluralist society where information may in theory circulate freely, information is never neutral or unselected:

[Le « pluralisme »] trie les informations, il leur barre la route, il les passe sous silence, les nie, les ampute ou les amplifie, voire les invente.

With adverbs and other structures

Here are some examples of the connector being used with adverbs and other constructions: *Les interventions réactives peuvent être aussi complexes, voire davantage.* / *Dans des conditions plus, voire beaucoup plus difficiles....*

Si les notions de criminalité et de délinquance ont un contenu juridique et pénal précis, celles de violence et, *a fortiori*, de « sentiment d'insécurité », encore plus souvent utilisées, surtout dans le langage public et politique actuel, n'en ont guère, voire aucun.

(Chesnais, 12)

As can be seen from the examples used so far, the two terms linked by *voire* are usually the same part of speech. Proust provides an exception to this rule:

...elle a soif d'une orangeade, d'un bain, voire de contempler cette lune épluchée et juteuse qui désaltérait le ciel.

(Proust, II, 645)

First in the sentence

At times, *voire* is placed first in a ***phrase dépendante***. This is often frowned upon for being a dismembered non-sentence, severed from its body: *Cette technique essaimera partout en France. Voire ailleurs.* However, the complexity of a structure or the subtlety of an idea may justify such a separation, on grounds of clarity of exposition. A discussion of people's small quirks of behaviour, such as those of dentists who are forever washing their hands or people who carry two watches, says this:

Les manies vestimentaires ont aussi la vie dure. Une secrétaire, par exemple, toujours tirée à quatre épingles, qui assortit invariablement ses catogans avec ses tenues, et qui, lorsqu'elle part en vacances, emporte une valise pleine de nœuds pour ses shorts. Voire un cadre qui, seule concession pour montrer qu'il n'est pas au bureau, accepte en congé de ne pas lacer ses chaussures...

In this position the connector can be momentarily misleading: it might be mistaken for the other *voire*, the sceptic's *voire* which does not introduce anything but, as in this comment on a fiscal measure designed to encourage spending, says: 'A likely story!'

Coûteux, inopportun et intempestif, le cadeau ainsi fait au contribuable permettra-t-il au moins de relancer la consommation ? Voire.

voire même

This combination has been the focus of debate among grammarians since at least Vaugelas in 1647. In more recent times, they have tended to condemn it as pleonastic:

« Voire » et « même » ont le même sens ; c'est le mot ancien et le moderne. Les juxtaposer, c'est un peu comme si l'on disait « suffisamment assez » ou « trop excessivement ». Les écrivains attentifs emploient l'un de ces termes seulement.

(d'Harvé, 294)

Nowadays it is widely held to be archaic and is much less used than fifty to a hundred years ago. However, some writers, historians, academics, who seem no less responsive than others in matters of style, continue to use it. Intellectuals and government ministers can be heard using it on television. Some journalists also use it, as in this extract from an article in *Le Monde* dealing with the repression of dissidents by the Chinese authorities in the summer of 1989:

> Un silence officiel répond aux rumeurs d'arrestations, d'envois « à la campagne » – en clair déportation ou camp de travail – voire même d'exécutions.

même

A mode of *même* itself still functions with more or less the same value as *voire*. Unlike *voire*, it can follow what it modifies: *Il rend la musique vivante, agissante, agressive même*. Sometimes a writer will use *ou même* for the same purpose, as in this example about a medieval marriage-tax payable by any bridegroom seeking exemption from a rule *exigeant la chasteté durant la première nuit, ou même les trois premières* (Enckell, 84). The combination *et même* can function in the same way. And some writers do without any connector when introducing an apter word: *le rôle important, essentiel, que joua son « penchant naturel » dans la formation de sa pensée.*

sinon, pour ne pas dire, que dis-je and others

One of the modes of *sinon* functions as a variant for this connector: *Il est extrêmement difficile, sinon impossible, de préciser exactement la date de composition.* So does *pour ne pas dire*: *Il est sans doute nécessaire, pour ne pas dire indispensable, de....* An obituary commenting on an Italian actress, famous for her performances in pornographic films, says this: *Selon un journal très sérieux elle avait « laïcisé », pour ne pas dire « démocratisé » le sexe.*

There is also *que dis-je*. This example comes from a profile of Robert Sabatier: *Il y a trois Robert Sabatier, que dis-je, quatre ou cinq au bas mot.* Sometimes this structure is accompanied by an exclamation mark; sometimes it precedes a repetition of the term it deems insufficiently expressive or accurate: *Nous admettrions, que dis-je ! nous admettons les reconstitutions d'argot.* / *Avez-vous vu ces deux femmes du monde, la Bordelaise et la Parisienne, enchantées d'elles-mêmes, que dis-je enchantées : grisées, saoules, ivres mortes.*

Sometimes *allons plus loin*, an occasional variant for *de plus*, is used like *voire* (Reboul, 51). Other equivalents or part equivalents for this connector are particular modes of *mieux, plutôt* and *pour tout dire.*

voyez

This is an occasional variant for ***par exemple***, more familiar or emotive in tone. It is akin to the English usage of 'Take' or 'Look at' in a statement like 'British football is in the doldrums nowadays – take Arsenal, or look at the World Cup!'

Relation to *par exemple*

Though not exactly equivalent to *par exemple*, this connector has a very similar function. One difference is that it always precedes the example, whereas *par exemple* may follow it. An equally important difference is that *par exemple* can combine with many different parts of speech, whereas this one is always followed by a noun or a pronoun. It could not be exactly replaced by *par exemple* in an example like the following. The author's subject is the prehistory and evolution of human languages:

> La multiplicité des langages, qui étonnait tant les Anciens et passait volontiers pour un phénomène d'ordre surnaturel destiné à confondre l'orgueil humain – voyez l'allégorie de la tour de Babel – s'explique rationnellement et de la façon la plus simple, par la tendance du langage à se transformer incessamment.
>
> (Dauzat, 1912b: 39)

For *par exemple* to be appropriate in that context, either it would have to be combined with *voyez* or else the latter would have to be replaced by something like *comme on le voit par exemple dans*. But the following extract from a discussion of scientific tampering with the genetics of edible plants could more easily accommodate *par exemple*:

> Un légume oublié, archaïque, médiéval même, genre crambé (ou crambe) maritime ou cerfeuil tubéreux, réapparaît-il subitement sur les marchés ? Soyez sûr qu'un clônage sophistiqué a téléguidé sa résurrection. Endive douce et craquante ? Manipulation génétique ! Fruit tropical ? Serre hollandaise ! Petits pois du jardin ? Brevet américain ! Et ainsi de suite...
>
> Voyez la cerise : depuis dix ans, tandis que les cerises ont doublé de volume, la hauteur des cerisiers a été réduite de moitié.

Place, punctuation and the interlocutory style

The connector is usually placed first in the sentence. Quite often the noun which it introduces is a proper noun: *La dérision est tout un art. Voyez Molière*. Quite often, too, it is repeated in a sequence of sentences or statements, as in this extract taken from an article about certain French regions of the Central West and of the North, traditionally of the Left, and the contradictory votes they cast in the referendum on the

Treaty of Maastricht, some confirming old loyalties, some going against them:

> Dans toutes ces terres laïques et souvent tentées par le nationalisme, ouvriers et paysans n'ont pas suivi les élus socialistes, tandis que, pour la première fois depuis longtemps, le Parti communiste s'est retrouvé en phase avec ses électeurs d'antan, qu'ils aient ou non dérivé vers le lepénisme. Voyez le Limousin, vieille terre rouge, où ni Chirac et ses élus ni les socialistes ne peuvent contenir le « non ». Voyez, dans le bassin houiller, Lens ou Liévin, voyez Dunkerque.

Being an imperative, it is often followed by an exclamation mark, as in this sequence taken from an essay on how difficult it is even for great writers to achieve *l'idéal*:

> [...] les grands écrivains eux-mêmes n'y sont pas parvenus sans effort [...]. Voyez Lamartine ! [...]. Voyez Molière ! [...]. Voyez Racine ! [...].
>
> (Vannier, 68)

The use of *voyez* is sometimes not the only feature of interlocutory style favoured by a writer. In the example about cherries used above, the writer has used **questions** and exclamations, as well as another imperative, *soyez*. Similar features are seen in this extract from an essay on the importance of reading, and reading everything:

> Savoir lire, c'est aussi pouvoir tout lire sans rejets et sans préjugés : Claudel et Céline, Artaud et Proust, Sade et la Bible, Joyce et Mme de Sévigné. Prouvez-le, montrez que vous n'êtes pas un esprit religieux. Savoir lire, c'est vivre le monde, l'histoire et sa propre existence comme un déchiffrement permanent. Savoir lire, c'est la liberté. La biographie des écrivains ? Mais oui ! Ce qu'on devrait y trouver, ce sont les traces de cette passion permanente. Voyez la vie quotidienne de Voltaire : quel roman fabuleux, risqué, sinueux, nerveux !
>
> (Sollers, iv)

Variants

An occasional variant is *Voir*, especially in a reference to a text or an author: *Cet écrivain étonne sans cesse. Voir, par exemple, dans les* Contes, *le passage consacré à* [...]. Another is *Voyons*. The following example comes from an article about French companies in difficulties and gives in a sequence of similar statements examples of some whose employees have accepted reductions of working-hours or job-sharing schemes so as to avoid redundancies:

> Voyons la cristallerie Daum. Quatre mois déjà que les salariés ont accepté de partager le travail pour éviter une soixantaine de licenciements. Voyons Montabert, entreprise lyonnaise en difficulté. Sur proposition des syndicats, la semaine de travail a été diminuée de quatre heures et les rémunérations de

10 %. Voyons Potain, le premier fabricant mondial de grues de chantier. 91,05 % des salariés ont approuvé le plan de partage du travail proposé par les syndicats, qui sauvegarde 278 emplois.

The similarity with English 'Take' can be seen in another occasional variant, *Prenez*, as in this satirical metaphor about French attitudes to television and the annual television awards:

Les Français aiment les alchimistes, ceux qui s'échinent à transmuer le vil métal en or. Prenez la télévision : ses succès, ses échecs, ses jalousies et ses nostalgies, elle les exorcise chaque année dans le rituel baptisé Sept d'or.

(Procyon, 30)

A selection of sources used

[Note: If unstated, the place of publication is Paris.]

Books (in editions used)

Acollas, É. (1891) *Le contrat de mariage*, Librairie Ch. Delagrave.
Adam, M. (1975) *Essai sur la bêtise*, Presses universitaires de France.
Adler, L. (1983) *Secrets d'alcôve*, Hachette.
Alain (1956) *Propos*, Gallimard Pléiade.
—— (1970) *Propos II*, Gallimard Pléiade.
Anouilh, J. (1967) *La valse des toréadors*, London: Harrap.
Anscombre, J.-C., & Ducrot, O. (1983) *L'argumentation dans la langue*, Brussels: Mardaga.
Aron, R. (1968) *La révolution introuvable*, Fayard.
—— (1977) *Plaidoyer pour l'Europe décadente*, Robert Laffont.
Assouline, P. (1985) *L'épuration des intellectuels*, Éditions Complexe.
Auboyer, J. (1965) *Introduction à l'étude de l'art de l'Inde*, Rome: Is.M.E.O.
Autin, A. (1930) *Le « Disciple » de Paul Bourget*, Société française d'éditions littéraires et techniques.
Backès, J.-L. (1994) *Musique et littérature*, Presses universitaires de France.
Badinter, E. (1980) *L'amour en plus*, Livre de poche.
Badinter, R. (1973) *L'exécution*, Grasset.
—— (1989) *Libres et égaux*, Arthème Fayard.
Bally, C. (1926) *Le langage et la vie*, Payot.
Balzac, J.-L. G. de (1665) *Œuvres*, 2 vols.
Barthes, R. (1957) *Mythologies*, Seuil.
—— (1973) *Le plaisir du texte*, Seuil.
Bastide, R. Morin, F. Raveau, F. (1974) *Les Haïtiens en France*, Mouton.
Baudelot, C. & Establet, R. (1989) *Le niveau monte*, Seuil.
Bazin, H. (1984) *Le matrimoine*, Livre de poche.
Beaumarchais (1965) *Théâtre*, Garnier-Flammarion.
Beauvoir, S. de (1958) *Mémoires d'une jeune fille rangée*, Gallimard.
Bénac, H. (1956) *Dictionnaire des synonymes*, Hachette.
Benda, J. (1970) *La France byzantine*, 10/18.
—— (1975) *La trahison des clercs*, Livre de poche Pluriel.
Bénichou, P. (1977) *Le temps des prophètes*, Gallimard.
Berget, A. (1912) *La vie et la mort du globe*, Flammarion.
Bergson, H. (1959) *Œuvres*, Presses universitaires de France.

Berr, H. (1934) *En marge de l'histoire universelle*, La Renaissance du livre.
Berthier, P. (1990) *Julien Gracq critique d'un certain usage de la littérature*, Presses universitaires de Lyon.
Besnard, P. (1989) *Mœurs et humeurs des Français au fil des saisons*, Balland.
Binet, A. (1892) *Les altérations de la personnalité*, Félix Alcan.
—— (1910) *Les idées modernes sur les enfants*, Flammarion.
Blum, L. (1962) *Du mariage & Stendhal et le beylisme* in *L'Œuvre*, tome II, Albin Michel.
Bohn, G. (1910) *La naissance de l'intelligence*, Flammarion.
Boillot, F. (1930) *Psychologie de la construction dans la phrase française moderne*, Presses universitaires de France.
Boisdeffre, P. de (1972) *Où va le roman?*, Del Duca.
Bologne, J.-C. (1986) *Histoire de la pudeur*, Hachette Pluriel.
Bon, M. & d'Arc, A. (1974) *Rapport sur l'homosexualité de l'homme*, Éditions universitaires.
Bonnier, G. (1907) *Le monde végétal*, Flammarion.
Bornier, H. de (1930) *La fille de Roland*, Dent.
Bory, J.-L. & Hocquenghem, G. (1977) *Comment nous appelez-vous déjà?*, Calmann-Lévy.
Boucher, P. (1993) *Journal d'un amateur*, Belfond.
Boulenger, J. & Thérive, A. (1924) *Les soirées du grammaire-club*, Plon.
Bourdieu, P. & Passeron, J.-C. (1964) *Les héritiers*, Minuit.
Bourgeois, B. & d'Hondt, J. (1993) *La philosophie et la Révolution française*, Vrin.
Bourget, P. (1926) *Essais de psychologie contemporaine*, tome II, Plon.
Bouty, E. (1908) *La vérité scientifique*, Flammarion.
Braudel, F. (1986) *L'identité de la France*, Arthaud-Flammarion.
Brogan, D. (1961) *The French Nation*, London, Arrow Books.
Brun, A. (1973) *Recherches historiques sur l'introduction du français dans les provinces du midi*, Geneva: Slatkine.
Brunet, E. (1983) *Le vocabulaire de Proust*, Slatkine-Champion, 3 vols.
Brunot, F. (1926) *La pensée et la langue*, Masson, 3ème édition.
Brusini, H. & James, F. (1982) *Voir la vérité*, Presses universitaires de France.
Caillois, R. (1974) *Approches de l'imaginaire*, Gallimard.
Camus, A. (1964) *Le mythe de Sisyphe*, Gallimard.
—— (1965) *Essais*, Gallimard Pléiade.
Carroll, L. (1965) *The Annotated Alice*, London: Penguin.
Charle, C. (1990) *Naissance des « intellectuels »*, Minuit.
Chervel, A. & Manesse, D. (1989) *La dictée*, INRP/Calmann-Lévy.
Chesnais, J.-C. (1982) *Histoire de la violence*, Hachette Pluriel.
Citron, S. (1987) *Le mythe national*, Éditions ouvrières.
Closets, F. de (1977) *La France et ses mensonges*, Denoël.
—— (1983) *Toujours plus !*, Livre de poche.
Cohen, J. (1966) *Structure du langage poétique*, Flammarion.
Colignon, J.-P. (1992) *Un point c'est tout!* CFPJ.
Coquet, J.-C. (1973) *Sémiotique littéraire*, Tours: Mame.
Cormeau, N. (1966) *Physiologie du roman*, Nizet.
Coupry, F. (1991) *L'énorme tragédie du rêve*, Robert Laffont.
Dastre, A. (1903) *La vie et la mort*, Flammarion.
Dauzat, A. (1908) *La langue française d'aujourd'hui*, Armand Colin.
—— (1912a) *La défense de la langue française*, Armand Colin.
—— (1912b) *La philosophie du langage*, Flammarion.
—— (1949) *Le génie de la langue française*, Payot.

Delacroix, H. (1918) *La psychologie de Stendhal*, Félix Alcan.
—— (1927) *Psychologie de l'art : essai sur l'activité artistique*, Félix Alcan.
Delage, Y. & Goldsmith, M. (1911) *Les théories de l'évolution*, Flammarion.
Delas, D. & Filliolet, J. (1973) *Linguistique et poétique*, Larousse.
Demangeon, A. (1942) *Problèmes de géographie humaine*, Armand Colin.
Depéret, C. (1907) *Les transformations du monde animal*, Flammarion.
Derrida, J. (1967) *De la grammatologie*, Minuit.
Dion, R. (1934) *Essai sur la formation du paysage rural français*, Tours: Arrault.
—— (1947) *Les frontières de la France*, Hachette.
Drillon, J. (1991) *Traité de la ponctuation française*, Gallimard.
Ducrot, O. (1972) *Dire et ne pas dire*, Herman.
Ducrot, O. *et al.* (1980) *Les mots du discours*, Minuit.
Duhamel, A. (1991) *De Gaulle-Mitterrand*, Flammarion.
Duprat, G.-L. (1924) *Le lien familial*, Félix Alcan.
Dupré, (1972) *Encyclopédie du bon français dans l'usage contemporain*, Éditions de Trévise, 3 vols.
Duras, M. (1958) *Moderato cantabile*, Minuit.
Durkheim, E. (1930) *Le suicide*, Félix Alcan.
—— (1953) *Montesquieu et Rousseau précurseurs de la sociologie*, translated by Armand Cuvillier, Marcel Rivière.
Dutourd, J. (1956) *Les taxis de la Marne*, Folio.
—— (1985) *La gauche la plus bête du monde*, Flammarion.
Duverger, M. (1982) *La République des citoyens*, Ramsay.
Étiemble, (1973) *Parlez-vous franglais ?*, Gallimard Idées.
Falkner, J. (1954) *The Lost Stradivarius*, Oxford: OUP.
Febvre, L. (1922) *La terre et l'évolution humaine*, Albin Michel.
Fernandez, R. (1985) *Gide, ou le courage de s'engager*, Klincksieck.
Fikry, A. (1974) *L'art roman du Puy et les influences islamiques*, Soest: Davaco.
Fontaine, A. (1978) *La France au bois dormant*, Fayard.
Foucault, M. (1976) *La volonté de savoir*, Gallimard.
Fouillée, A. (1890) *L'avenir de la métaphysique fondée sur l'expérience*, Félix Alcan.
Fowler, H.W. (1965) *A Dictionary of Modern English Usage*, Oxford: OUP, 2nd edition.
Fowler, H.W. & Fowler, F.G. (1918) *The King's English*, Oxford: OUP.
Franck, D. (1991) *La séparation*, Seuil.
Frédérix, P. (1948) *Washington ou Moscou*, Hachette.
Frischer, D. (1990) *La France vue d'en face*, Robert Laffont.
Fumaroli, M. (1991) *L'état culturel*, Fallois.
Furetière, A. (1690) *Dictionnaire universel*, La Haye.
Georgin, R. (1951) *Pour un meilleur français*, André Bonne.
—— (1961) *Le code du bon langage*, Éditions sociales françaises.
—— (1956) *La prose d'aujourd'hui*, André Bonne.
Gide, A. (1951) *Journal 1889–1939*, Gallimard Pléiade.
—— (1954) *Journal 1939–1949*, Gallimard Pléiade.
—— (1958) *Romans, récits et soties, œuvres lyriques*, Gallimard Pléiade.
Girard, P. (1983) *Les Juifs de France*, Bruno Huisman.
Giroud, F. (1973) *Une poignée d'eau*, Robert Laffont.
Goldmann, L. (1959) *Le dieu caché*, Gallimard.
Gourmont, R. de (1902) *Le problème du style*, Mercure de France.
—— (1955) *Esthétique de la langue française*, Mercure de France.
—— (1964) *La culture des idées*, Mercure de France.

Gowers, E. (1954) *The Complete Plain Words*, London: HMSO.

Gray, B. (1977) *The Grammatical Foundations of Rhetoric*, The Hague: Mouton.

Greer, G. (1970) *The Female Eunuch*, London: Macgibbon & Kee.

Grevisse, M. (1959) *Le bon usage*, 7ème édition, Bruxelles: Duculot.

—— (1964a) *Le bon usage*, 8ème édition, Bruxelles: Duculot.

—— (1988) *Le bon usage*, 12ème édition refondue par A. Goosse, Paris–Gembloux: Duculot.

—— (1962) *Problèmes de langage*, 2ème série, Presses universitaires de France.

—— (1964b) *Problèmes de langage*, 3ème série, Presses universitaires de France.

Gros, B. (1983) *Presse : la marée rose*, Albatros.

Gros, D. (1994) *Les seins aux fleurs rouges*, Stock.

Guignebert, C. (1910) *L'évolution des dogmes*, Flammarion.

Guisnel, J. (1990) *Les généraux : Enquête sur le pouvoir militaire en France*, La Découverte.

Halévy, E. (1932) *Histoire du peuple anglais au XIXe siècle Épilogue 1895–1914 II*, Hachette.

Hanse, J. (1949) *Dictionnaire des difficultés grammaticales et lexicologiques*, Bruxelles: Baude.

—— (1983) *Nouveau dictionnaire des difficultés du français moderne*, Bruxelles: Duculot.

d'Harvé, G.-O. (1923) *Parlons bien !*, Bruxelles: Office de publicité.

Henriot, E. (1956) *Maîtres d'hier et contemporains nouvelle série*, Albin Michel.

—— (1954) *Réalistes et naturalistes*, Albin Michel.

—— (1924) *Stendhaliana*, Crès.

Héricourt, J. (1910) *Les frontières de la maladie*, Flammarion.

Hermant, A. (1929) *Remarques de Monsieur Lancelot pour la défense de la langue française*, Flammarion.

Herriot, E. (1933) *La France dans le monde*, Hachette.

Houssaye, F. (1933) *Les industries des animaux*, Librarie J.-B. Baillière & Fils.

Hovelacque, A. & Hervé, G. (1887) *Précis d'anthropologie*, Adrien Delahaye et Émile Lecrosnier.

Howells, W. (1989) *Novels 1886–1888*, New York: Library of America.

Hume, D. (1888) *A Treatise of Human Nature*, Oxford: Clarendon.

Huxley, A. (1960) *Music at Night*, London: Chatto & Windus.

Huysmans, J.-K. (1975) *A rebours*, 10/18.

Ionesco, E. (1954) *Théâtre I*, Gallimard.

Irigaray, L. (1984) *Ethique de la différence sexuelle*, Minuit.

James, C. (1994) *The Metropolitican Critic*, London: Jonathan Cape.

Jeanneney, J.-N. (1987) *Concordances des temps*, Seuil.

Judge, A. & Healey, F. (1983) *A Reference Grammar of Modern French*, London: Arnold.

Julliard, J. (1981) *La IVe République*, Pluriel.

July, S. (1986) *Les années Mitterrand*, Grasset et Fasquelle.

Kahn, J.-F. (1987) *Les Français sont formidables*, Balland.

La Bruyère (1962) *Les caractères*, Garnier.

Laclos (1961) *Les liaisons dangereuses*, Garnier.

La Fontaine (1962) *Fables*, Garnier.

Landais, N. (1851) *Dictionnaire général et grammatical des dictionnaires français*, Au Bureau central.

Lamand, F. (1986) *L'Islam en France*, Albin Michel.

Lanson, G. (1968) *L'art de la prose*, Nizet.

Launay, L. de (1910) *L'histoire de la terre*, Flammarion.

Le Bidois, G & R. (1967) *Syntaxe du français moderne*, Auguste Picard, 2 vols.
—— (1931) *Bases scientifiques d'une philosophie de l'histoire*, Flammarion.
Le Dantec, F. (1917) *L'athéisme*, Flammarion.
Le Gal, E. (1932) *Cent manières d'accommoder le français*, Nouvelle Librairie Française.
Leith, D. & Myerson, G. (1989) *The Power of Address*, London: Routledge.
Lejeune, P. (1980) *Je est un autre*, Seuil.
Lennon, P. (1994) *Foreign Correspondent: Paris in the Sixties*, London: Picador.
Le Roy Ladurie, E. (1973) *Le territoire de l'historien*, Gallimard.
Lesage, A. (1911) *Théâtre*, Garnier.
Lévy-Bruhl, L. (1922) *Les fonctions mentales dans les sociétés inférieures*, Félix Alcan.
Leygues, G. (1903) *L'école et la vie*, Calmann-Lévy.
Littré, E. (1971) *Dictionnaire de la langue française*, Gallimard/Hachette.
Mach, E. (1913) *La connaissance et l'erreur*, translated by M. Dufour, Flammarion.
Mansuétus (1902) *Le milieu social : étude sociologique*, Guillaumin et Cie.
Marestan, J. (1927) *L'éducation sexuelle*, Marseille: Editions Jean Marestan.
Marouzeau, J. (1950) *Aspects du français*, Masson.
Martinet, A. (1969) *Le français sans fard*, Presses universitaires de France.
Mauger, G. (1968) *Grammaire pratique du français d'aujourd'hui*, Hachette.
Mauron, C. (1969) *L'inconscient dans l'œuvre et la vie de Racine*, José Corti.
Maurras, C. & Daudet, L. (1927) *L' « Action Française » et le Vatican*, Flammarion.
McCarthy, P. (1982) *Camus*, London: Hamish Hamilton.
Meillet, A. (1918) *Les langues dans l'Europe nouvelle*, Payot.
Merlin, O. (1989) *Tristan Bernard, ou le temps de vivre*, Calmann-Lévy.
Meyer, P. (1977) *L'enfant et la raison d'État*, Seuil.
Moisson-Franckhauser, S. (1974) *Serge Prokofiev*, Publications Orientalistes de France.
Montaigne (1962) *Essais*, Garnier, 2 vols.
Montesquieu (1907) *De l'esprit des lois*, Garnier.
Morin, E. (1969) *La rumeur d'Orléans*, Seuil.
—— (1984) *Le rose et le noir*, Éditions Galilée.
Moutote, D. (1968) *Le Journal de Gide et les problèmes du moi*, Presses universitaires de France.
Nabert, J. (1943) *Éléments pour une éthique*, Presses universitaires de France.
Nay, C. (1984) *Le noir et le rouge*, Grasset.
Ollivier, E. (1911) *Philosophie d'une guerre 1870*, Flammarion.
Orwell, G. (1961) *Down and Out in Paris and London*, New York: Harcourt Brace Jovanovich.
—— (1968) *The Collected Essays, Journalism & Letters*, London: Secker & Warburg, 4 vols.
Ory, P. (1983) *L'entre-deux-mai*, Seuil.
Paulhan, F. (1920) *Les transformations sociales des sentiments*, Flammarion.
Peyrefitte, A. (1976) *Le mal français*, Plon.
Picard, E. (1908) *La science moderne et son état actuel*, Flammarion.
Picard, G. (1994) *De la connerie*, José Corti.
Pittard, E. (1924) *Les races et l'histoire*, Albin Michel.
Pitte, J.-R. (1991) *Gastronomie française*, Fayard.
Pomian, K. (1987) *Collectionneurs, amateurs et curieux*, Gallimard.
Poulet, G. (1971) *La conscience critique*, José Corti.
—— (1977) *Entre moi et moi*, José Corti.

Prévost (1967) *Manon Lescaut*, Garnier-Flammarion.
Proust, M. (1954) *À la recherche du temps perdu*, Gallimard Pléiade, 3 vols.
Rabelais, F. (1962) *Œuvres complètes*, Garnier, 2 vols.
Raynaud, P. (1987) *Max Weber et les dilemmes de la raison moderne*, Presses universitaires de France.
Reboul, O. (1991) *Introduction à la rhétorique*, Presses universitaires de France.
Renan, E. (1948) *Œuvres complètes*, tome II, Calmann-Lévy.
Renard, Jacques. (1987) *L'élan culturel: la France en mouvement*, Presses universitaires de France.
Renard, Jules. (1965) *Journal 1887–1910*, Gallimard Pléiade.
— (1970) *Œuvres I*, Gallimard Pléiade.
Revel, J.-F. (1970) *Ni Marx ni Jésus*, Robert Laffont.
— (1988) *La connaissance inutile*, Grasset et Fasquelle.
Rey, A. (1908) *La philosophie moderne*, Flammarion.
Ribot, T. (1897) *La psychologie des sentiments*, Félix Alcan.
Ricardou, J. (1990) *Le nouveau roman*, Seuil.
Robert, P. (1953) *Dictionnaire alphabétique et analogique de la langue française*, 7 vols.
— (1986) *Dictionnaire alphabétique et analogique de la langue française*, 9 vols.
Romains, J. (1924) *Knock*, Gallimard.
— (1966) *Lettre ouverte contre une vaste conspiration*, Albin Michel.
Rougemont, D. de (1936) *Penser avec les mains*, Albin Michel/La Baconnière.
— (1962) *L'amour et l'occident*, 10/18.
Rougier, L. (1929) *La mystique démocratique*, Flammarion.
Roule, L. (1930) *La vie des rivières*, Stock.
Roulet, E. (1991) *L'articulation du discours en français contemporain*, Bern: Peter Lang.
Rousseau, J.-J. (1964) *Les confessions*, Garnier.
Roussel, L. (1989) *La famille incertaine*, Odile Jacob.
Rousset, J. (1973) *Narcisse romancier*, José Corti.
Said, E. (1993) *Culture and Imperialism*, London: Chatto & Windus.
Sainte-Beuve, C.-A. (1858) *Causeries du lundi, I*, Garnier.
Sansot, P. (1985) *La France sensible*, Champ Vallon.
Sarcey, F. (1863) *Le mot et la chose*, Ollendorff.
Sartre, J.-P. (1949a) *La mort dans l'âme*, Gallimard.
— (1949b) *Situations, III*, Gallimard.
— (1957) *La nausée*, Livre de poche.
— (1964) *Les mots*, Gallimard.
— (1976) *Situations, X*, Gallimard.
Saussure, F. de (1916) *Cours de linguistique générale*, Payot.
Schneider, M. (1985) *Voleurs de mots*, Gallimard.
Scholes, P. (1978) *The Oxford Companion to Music*, Oxford: Clarendon.
Sédouy, A. de & Bouteiller, P. (1987) *Les voix de la France*, Calamann-Lévy.
Stendhal (1922) *La Chartreuse de Parme*, Crès.
Stone, L. (1990) *Road to Divorce England 1530–1987*, Oxford: OUP.
Sturgis, M. (1995) *Passionate Attitudes*, London: Macmillan.
Tarde, G. (1895) *Les lois de l'imitation*, Félix Alcan.
Thérive, A. (1923) *Le français, langue morte?*, Plon-Nourrit.
— (1962) *Procès de langage*, Stock.
Thomas, A. (1956) *Dictionnaire des difficultés de la langue française*, Larousse.
Thomas, M. (1989) *Esterhazy, ou l'envers de l'affaire Dreyfus*, Vernal/Philippe Lebaud.

Trouillas, P. (1988) *Le complexe de Marianne*, Seuil.
Vadier, B. (1886) *Henri-Frédéric Amiel : étude biographique*, Fischbacher.
Valéry, P. (1960) *Œuvres II*, Gallimard Pléiade.
Vallès, J. (1964) *L'enfant*, Éditeurs Français Réunis.
Van Bruyssel, E. (1907) *La vie sociale et ses évolutions*, Flammarion.
Van Gennep, A. (1910) *La formation des légendes*, Flammarion.
Vannier, A. (1907) *La clarté française*, Librairie classique Fernand Nathan.
Vendryes, J. (1921) *Le langage : introduction linguistique à l'histoire*, La renaissance du livre.
Vidal, G. (1993) *United States*, London: André Deutsch.
Vidal de la Blache, P. (1922) *Principes de géographie humaine*, Armand Colin.
Vidal-Naquet, P. (1987) *Les assassins de la mémoire*, La Découverte.
Vinay, J.-P. & Darbelnet, J. (1958) *Stylistique comparée du français et de l'anglais*, Marcel Didier.
Vincent, Abbé Cl. (1910) *Le péril de la langue française*, Ancienne Librairie Poussielgue.
Voiture, V. (1855) *Œuvres, lettres et poésies*, Ubicini.
Voltaire (1960) *Romans et contes*, Garnier.
Wagner, R. (1980) *Essais de linguistique française*, Nathan.
Wartburg, W. von (1958) *Evolution et structure de la langue française*, Berne: Francke.
Zola, E. (1969) *L'assommoir*, Garnier-Flammarion.

Articles

Alaux, J. (1888) 'Qu'est-ce qu'une littérature ?', *La revue littéraire et artistique*, janvier 1888.
Amette, J.-P. (1994) 'Céline, encore...', *Le Point*, 29 janvier 1994.
Anon (1994a) 'Communiqué de l'Évêché', *Agglo Troyenne* 78, décembre 1994.
Anon (1994b) 'Communiqué judiciaire', *L'Événement du jeudi*, 8–14 septembre 1994.
Anscombre, J.-C. (1983) 'Pour autant, pourtant (et comment) : à petites causes, grands effets', *Cahiers de linguistique française* 5: 37–84
Bedos, G. (1994) 'Mauvaises pensées', *Libération*, 10 janvier 1994.
Bénéton, P. (1993) 'Sur la correction du style', *Famille chrétienne* 809, 15 juillet 1993, 48–49.
Boulay, A. (1995) 'L'été du prêt à dévoiler' *Libération*, 30 juin 1995.
Braudeau, M. (1994) 'Un papillon pour deux', *Le Monde*, 19 février 1994.
Brelot, C.-I. (1994) 'Entre nationalisme et cosmopolitisme : les engagements multiples de la noblesse', in P. Birnbaum (ed.), *La France de l'affaire Dreyfus*, Gallimard.
Brunetière, F. (1890) *Revue des deux mondes* 97, 1 janvier 1890.
Canovas, F. (1992) 'En déclinant *Paludes* : sur les traces de Virgile et de Dante', *Essays in French Literature*, 29, November 1992: 105–120.
Cantégrit, C. (1978) 'Préface' in A. Belot, *Mademoiselle Giraud, ma femme*, Garnier.
Carcassonne, G. (1994) 'Un budget flatteur', *Le Point*, 8 janvier 1994.
Coulet, H. (1967) 'Préface', in Prévost, *Manon Lescaut*, Garnier-Flammarion.
Cournot, M. (1994) 'Recopier n'est pas jouer', *Le Monde*, 19 janvier 1994.
Danjou-Flaux, N. (1980) 'À propos de « de fait », « en fait », « en effet » et « effectivement »', *Le français moderne* 48: 110–139.
Droit, R.-P. (1994) *Le Monde*, 20 octobre 1994.

Enckell, P. (1995) 'Le droit de cuissage, mythe ou réalité ?', *L'Événement du jeudi*, 2–8 mars 1995.
Ferniot, J. (1995a) 'Au nom du vin', *L'Événement du jeudi*, 26 janvier–1 février 1995.
—— (1995b) 'Autant en emportent les modes culinaires', *L'Événement du jeudi*, 9–15 février 1995
Fontaine, A. (1990) 'Le tas de bombes,' *Le Monde*, 28 juillet 1990.
François, F. (1968) 'Le langage et ses fonctions', in *Le langage*, Encyclopédie de la Pléiade.
Genette, G. (1981) 'Le journal, l'antijournal', *Poétique*, 47: 1981.
Grieve, J. (1995a) '*Au final* : a connector in the making', *Cahiers AFLS* 1 (1) Spring 1995a, 13–18.
—— (1995b) 'From *le finale* to *au final*', *Journal of French Language Studies* 5 (2) Autumn 1995.
Guichard, L. (1964) 'Introduction' in R. & C. Wagner, *Lettres à Judith Gautier*, Gallimard.
Haseler, S. (1993) letter to editor, *Times Literary Supplement* 4708, 25 June 1993.
Le groupe λ-l (1975) 'Car, parce que, puisque', *Revue romane* 10: 248–280.
Lerner, M. (1973) 'Introduction' in, E. Rod, *Le sens de la vie*, Geneva: Slatkine.
Le Saux, B. (1993) 'Faux « de » mais vrais écrivains', *L'Événement du jeudi*, 23–29 décembre 1993.
MacNamara, M. (1994) 'Text Type and Sentence Form in Three *Le Point* Articles', in J. Coleman, & R. Crawshaw (eds.), *Discourse Variety in Contemporary French*, AFLS/CILT.
Malicet, M. (1970) '*Introduction*', in P. Claudel, *Richard Wagner rêverie d'un poète français*, Les belles lettres.
Mauriac, C. (1969) *Le Figaro littéraire*, 1191, 3–9 mars 1969.
Moeschler, J. & de Spengler, N. (1981) '*Quand même* : de la concession à la réfutation', *Cahiers de linguistique française*, 2: 93–112.
—— (1982) 'La concession ou la réfutation interdite', *Cahiers de linguistique française*, 3: 8–36.
Poirot-Delpech, B. (1993) 'Noël de l'impuissance', *Le Monde*, 22 décembre 1993.
Polac, M. (1994) 'Du coup de foudre', *L'Événement du jeudi*, 15–21 septembre 1994.
Procyon (1993) 'Alchimie', *Le Monde*, 16 décembre 1993.
Reberioux, M. (1994) 'Quelle affaire !', *Le Monde*, 13 janvier 1994.
Rodriguez, P. (1982) 'L'éveil des sens dans *Le petit chaperon rouge*', *Littérature*, 47, octobre 1982.
Saux, J.-L. (1994) 'La prunelle de ses yeux', *Le Monde*, 2 février 1994.
Scarpetta, G. (1993) 'Comment défendre Salman Rushdie ?', *Le Monde*, 29 décembre 1993.
Schelling, M. (1982) 'Quelques modalités de clôture, les conclusifs : *finalement, en somme, au fond, de toute façon*', *Cahiers de linguistique française*, 4: 63–106.
Schneidermann, D. (1994) 'Sale gosse milliardaire', *Le Monde*, 13 janvier 1994.
Sollers, P. (1994) *Le Monde*, 11 février 1994.
Sorman, G. (1994) 'Sauver la solidarité en détruisant le monopole', *L'Événement du jeudi*, 15–21 décembre 1994.
Troyat, H. (1993) *Le Point*, 22 mai 1993.
Vidal-Naquet, P. (1972) 'Préface', in M. Marrus, *Les Juifs de France à l'époque de l'affaire Dreyfus*, Calmann-Lévy.
—— (1982) 'Dreyfus dans l'Affaire et dans l'histoire', in A. Dreyfus, *Cinq années de ma vie*, François Maspero.
Zenone, A. (1983) 'La consécution sans contradiction : *donc, par conséquent, alors, ainsi, aussi*', *Cahiers de linguistique française*, 5: 107–141 & 189–214.

End-list

This list contains structures not given as separate entries in the dictionary. Most of them are mentioned or discussed in the entry or entries printed in bold.

absolument : **effectivement; sans doute**
à cause de ce fait : **de ce fait**
à cela près que : **à ceci près que**
à ce point que : **au point que**
à cet effet : **pour ce faire**
à cette fin : **pour ce faire**
a contrario : **au contraire**
à côté de (cela) : **au-delà (de); sequences of points**
à deux titres : **d'une part... d'autre part**
à dire (le) vrai : **à vrai dire**
à double titre : **d'une part... d'autre part; sequences of points**
ah : **oh**
ajoutons-y : **ajoutons que; sequences of points**
à la clé : **avec**
à la différence de : **au contraire**
à la fin : **enfin; finalement; somme toute**
à la suite de quoi : **du coup**
allons plus loin : **de plus; voire**
alors même que : **même**
à moins de : **sauf à**
à moins de croire que : **force est de**
à part ça : **au demeurant; pour le reste**
à partir de là : **là**
à peu près : **à ceci près que**
à propos : **au fait**
à quoi il faut ajouter : **ajoutons que; sequences of points**
à telle enseigne que : **au point que**
à tel point que : **au point que**
à titre d'exemple : **par exemple**
à titre d'illustration : **par exemple**
à tout considérer : **à tout prendre**
à tout le moins : **du moins**
au mieux : **tout juste**

au moins : **du moins**

au point de : **au point que**

à un tel point que : **au point que**

auquel cas : **alors; ou bien... ou bien; soit... soit**

au résumé : **en résumé**

au risque de : **quitte à; sauf à**

aussitôt : **du coup**

autant vaut dire (que) : **autant dire (que)**

autrement : **sinon**

avoir beau : **malgré tout; n'en pas... moins; peut-être**

bel et bien : **bien**

bien plus : **de plus**

ce à quoi : **ce qui**

ceci dit : **cela dit**

ceci étant : **cela étant**

cela étant dit : **cela dit; cela étant**

cela n'empêche : **n'empêche**

cela parce que : **et ce**

cela posé : **cela dit**

cela va sans dire : **brief interpolated main clause**

cela veut dire que : **cela étant; c'est dire (que)**

ce n'est pas assez de : **encore faut-il (que)**

ce n'est pas le cas : **or**

ce n'est pas tout : **de plus**

ce n'est pas tout de : **encore faut-il (que)**

cependant : **à ceci près que; ce faisant; force est de; mais; n'en... pas moins; quand même; sans doute; seulement; si d'opposition; tout de même**

ce pourquoi : **c'est pourquoi**

ce pour quoi : **c'est pourquoi**

ce que : **ce qui; phrase dépendante**

ce qui fait que : **de sorte que; si bien que**

ce qui revient à dire que : **autant dire (que); c'est dire (que)**

c'est : **c'est le cas de; par exemple**

c'est à croire que : **tout se passe comme si**

c'est ainsi que : **ainsi**

c'est aller vite en besogne : **de là**

c'est à peine si : **tout juste**

c'est à savoir : **à savoir**

c'est assez dire : **c'est dire (que)**

c'est au point que : **au point que**

c'est bien : **si d'opposition**

c'est dire combien : **c'est dire (que)**

c'est entendu : **bien entendu; brief interpolated main clause**

c'est là : **là; voilà**

c'est parce que : **c'est que; si d'opposition**

c'est peu dire : **c'est dire (que)**

c'est pour cette raison que : **c'est pourquoi**

c'est tout dire : **brief interpolated main clause; c'est dire (que)**

c'est tout juste si : **tout juste**

c'est un fait : **brief interpolated main clause**

c'est un fait admis : **qui ne voit que**

c'est vrai (que) : **il est vrai (que)**

comment ne pas voir que : **question; qui ne voit que**
complément absolu : **cela dit**
comprenez : **autrement dit**
concernant : **s'agissant de; sequences of points**
conclusion : **deux-points**
conséquence : **de ce fait; deux-points; du coup; par conséquent**
d'abord : **en outre; ensuite; puis; sequences of points**
d'accord : **oui**
dans ce cas : **alors**
dans ces circonstances : **cela étant; dès lors; force est de**
dans la foulée : **ce faisant; du même coup**
dans la réalité : **en réalité**
dans le cas particulier : **en la circonstance; en l'espèce; en l'occurrence**
dans le cas présent : **en la circonstance; en l'espèce; en l'occurrence**
dans le cas qui nous occupe : **en la circonstance; en l'espèce; en l'occurrence**
dans l'espèce : **en l'espèce**
dans le fait : **aussi bien; de fait; en fait**
dans le fond : **au fond**
dans les faits : **en fait**
dans tous les cas : **en tout cas**
d'autant mieux que : **d'autant que**
d'autant moins que : **d'autant que**
d'autant plus que : **d'autant que**
d'autres remarques s'imposent : **de plus**
davantage : **de plus**
de cette façon : **ainsi**
de deux choses l'une : **ou bien... ou bien; sequences of points; soit... soit**
de là à : **de là**
de la sorte : **ainsi**
de là que : **de là; d'où**
de là vient que : **de là; d'où**
de même que : **phrase dépendante**
de telle sorte que : **de sorte que**
de toute évidence : **bien évidemment**
de toutes façons : **de toute façon**
de toutes les façons : **de toute façon**
de toutes les manières : **de toute manière**
de toutes manières : **de toute manière**
deuxièmement : **sequences of points**
deux possibilités : **d'une part... d'autre part; sequences of points; soit... soit**
de vrai : **au vrai**
dit autrement : **autrement dit**
diversement : **inversement**
d'où l'on voit que : **d'où**
d'où résulte : **d'où**
d'où suit que : **d'où**
du fait : **de ce fait**
d'un autre point de vue : **d'un autre côté**
en bref : **bref**
en ce cas : **ou bien... ou bien; soit... soit**
en ce qui concerne : **s'agissant de; sequences of points**
en compensation : **en contrepartie; en revanche**

en conséquence : **de ce fait; du coup; par conséquent**
en contrepoint : **en contrepartie**
encore convient-il : **encore faut-il (que)**
encore que : **phrase dépendante**
encore s'agit-il : **encore faut-il (que)**
en dehors de : **au-delà (de); sequences of points**
en dépit de : **et ce**
en dernier lieu : **en définitive; sequences of points**
en deux mots : **en un mot**
en faisant cela : **ce faisant**
en fin de parcours : **au final**
en peu de mots : **en un mot**
en premier lieu : **d'autre part; s'agissant de; sequences of points**
en prime : **avec; de surcroît**
en sens inverse : **à l'inverse; inversement**
en sorte que : **de sorte que**
en témoigne : **inversion du verbe**
entendez : **autrement dit**
en termes clairs : **en clair**
en tous cas : **en tout cas**
en tous les cas : **en tout cas**
en tout : **au total**
en tout et pour tout : **au total**
en un mot comme en cent : **en un mot**
est-ce à dire que ? : **c'est-à-dire (que)**
est-il besoin de dire que : **ajoutons que; question; qui ne voit que**
étant donné que : **tant il est vrai que**
et ceci depuis longtemps : **et ce**
et même : **même**
et puis : **ensuite; et; puis; sequences of points**
et tout cela : **et ce**
évidemment : **bien évidemment**
faute de quoi : **sinon**
faut-il ajouter que : **ajoutons que; sequences of points**
finir par : **finalement; somme toute**
fût-il, fût-elle : **fût-ce**
gnomic contrasts : **antithèses sans charnière; deux-points**
il demeure que : **reste que**
il est aisé de voir que : **qui ne voit que**
il est à penser que : **tout se passe comme si**
il est clair que : **qui ne voit que**
il est de fait que : **c'est un fait (que); de fait; le fait est que**
il est facile de voir que : **qui ne voit que**
il est permis de supposer que : **tout se passe comme si**
il faut : **force est de**
il ne fait pas de doute que : **qui ne voit que**
il n'en est rien : **or**
il ne suffit pas de : **encore faut-il (que)**
il n'y a qu'à : **il n'est que de**
il n'y a qu'un pas : **de là**
il s'agit là de : **là**
il semble que : **tout se passe comme si**

il s'ensuit de là que : **c'est dire (que)**
il suffit de : **il n'est que de**
il va de soi que : **qui ne voit que**
il va sans dire que : **qui ne voit que**
il y a lieu de présumer que : **tout se passe comme si**
il y a là : **là**
il y a loin : **de là**
il y a pis : **mais; pis**
il y a plus : **de plus**
il y a plus grave: **pis**
infinitif de narration : **et; phrase dépendante**
inutile de dire que : **ajoutons que; sequences of points**
je dirai plus : **de plus**
je le répète : **brief interpolated main clause**
je veux bien : **si l'on veut**
je veux dire : **à savoir (que); autrement dit; c'est-à-dire (que); transitions mécaniques**
jusqu'à : **voire**
justement : **précisément**
là aussi : **là**
la conviction que : **l'idée que**
l'adage selon lequel : **l'idée que**
là encore : **ici... là; là; sequences of points**
là enfin : **ici... là; là; sequences of points**
l'alternative suivante : **ou bien... ou bien; sequences of points**
là où : **alors que; là**
la question reste de savoir : **reste à**
là se trouve : **là**
la théorie selon laquelle : **l'idée que**
le fait demeure que : **n'en... pas moins**
l'ennui, c'est que : **seulement**
les uns... les autres : **au contraire**
le tout est de savoir : **reste à**
l'illusion que : **l'idée que**
loin de là : **brief interpolated main clause; là**
loin s'en faut : **brief interpolated main clause**
maintenant : **reste à**
mais il y a plus : **de plus**
mais voilà : **voilà**
malgré : **avec cela; et ce; force est de**
malgré cela : **n'empêche; pour autant**
malheureusement : **seulement**
même chose : **de même**
même si c'était : **fût-ce**
mieux même : **même; mieux**
mieux encore : **mieux**
mis à part : **au-delà (de); sequences of points**
néanmoins : **cela étant; certes; mais; quand même; reste que; sans doute; si d'opposition**
n'est-ce pas ? : **après tout**
n'est-ce pas le cas ? : **c'est le cas de**
n'eût été : **n'était**

noblesse oblige : **brief interpolated main clause**
nombreux sont ceux qui : **inversion de l'adjectif**
nommément : **à savoir (que); par exemple**
non plus : **si d'opposition**
non seulement : **au-delà (de); mais; sequences of points**
notamment : **c'est le cas de; par exemple**
n'oublions pas que : **transitions mécaniques**
nul ne le conteste : **qui ne voit que**
nul le l'ignore : **qui ne voit que**
on a l'impression que : **tout se passe comme si**
on dirait que : **tout se passe comme si**
on le voit : **brief interpolated main clause**
on n'a qu'à : **il n'est que de**
on peut penser que : **tout se passe comme si**
on s'en doute : **brief interpolated main clause**
oppositive *pour* : **malgré tout; n'en... pas moins; pour autant**
ou alors : **alors**
ou même : **même; voire**
ou plutôt : **autrement dit; à vrai dire; mieux; plutôt; précisément**
outre : **au-delà (de); sequences of points**
paradoxe : **autant... autant**
par ce fait : **de ce fait**
par ce que : **parce que**
par compensation : **en contrepartie**
par-delà : **au-delà (de)**
par là, par là même : **de ce fait; là**
par le fait : **de ce fait; de fait**
par le fait même : **du coup**
par où : **d'où**
par suite : **de ce fait; du coup; par conséquent**
par surcroît : **de surcroît**
partant : **de ce fait; du coup; par conséquent**
par voie de conséquence : **de ce fait; du coup; par conséquent**
pendant que : **alors que; tandis que**
pire : **pis**
plus : **de plus**
plus encore : **de plus**
plus exactement : **au vrai; à vrai dire; mieux; pis; plutôt**
plus grave : **pis**
plus... plus : **antithèses sans charnière**
plus précisément : **autrement dit; mieux; plutôt; précisément**
pour ce : **pour cela**
pour ce qui est de : **s'agissant de**
pour commencer : **en outre**
pour conclure : **en définitive; enfin; finalement**
pour de multiples raisons : **et ce**
pour deux raisons : **d'une part... d'autre part**
pour dire (le) vrai : **à vrai dire**
pour dire la vérité : **à vrai dire**
pour être tout à fait précis : **au vrai; à vrai dire**
pour finir : **enfin; finalement;**
pour le moins : **du moins**

pour ne pas dire : **voire**
pour ne rien dire de : **ajoutons que**
pour notre compte : **quant à [lui]**
pour s'en convaincre : **il n'est que de**
pour surcroît : **de surcroît**
pourtant : **cela étant; certes; et; force est de; mais; pour autant; reste que; sans doute; seulement; si d'opposition; tout de même**
premièrement : **sequences of points**
prenez : **voyez**
prenons le cas de : **transitions mécaniques**
primo : **sequences of points**
puisque : **aussi bien; car; parce que; phrase dépendante**
puisqu'il s'agit : **s'agissant de**
quand : **alors que; si ce n'est (que)**
quand bien même : **alors que; même**
quand ce ne serait que : **ne serait-ce que**
quand ce n'est pas : **si ce n'est (que)**
quand il s'agit : **s'agissant de**
quant à : **quant à [lui]; s'agissant de**
que dire de : **ajoutons que; question**
que dis-je : **voire**
quelle que soit la situation : **en tout état de cause**
quel que soit : **force est de**
quel que soit le cas : **aussi bien**
qu'est-ce à dire ? : **c'est-à-dire (que)**
qui l'ignore (?) : **brief interpolated main clause**
qui mieux est : **mieux**
qui pis est : **pis**
qui plus est : **de plus; sequences of points**
quitte à ce que : **quitte à**
quoi : **en somme; pour tout dire**
quoi qu'il arrive : **au final; en tout état de cause**
quoi qu'il en soit : **toujours est-il que**
qu'on le veuille ou non : **force est de**
qu'on nous permette : **transitions mécaniques**
rappelons que : **transitions mécaniques**
rares sont ceux qui : **inversion de l'adjectif**
répétons-le : **brief interpolated main clause; transitions mécaniques**
réponse : **deux-points**
résultat : **de ce fait; deux-points; du coup; par conséquent**
rien n'est moins sûr : **or**
sans compter que : **d'autant que; sequences of points**
sans oublier : **ajoutons que; sequences of points**
sans parler de : **ajoutons que**
sans que : **pour autant**
sans quoi : **sinon**
sauf : **si ce n'est (que); sinon**
sauf à ce que : **sauf à**
sauf que : **à ceci près que; phrase dépendante; si ce n'est (que)**
savoir : **à savoir**
secundo : **sequences of points**
selon toute apparence : **tout se passe comme si**

s'entend : **c'est-à-dire (que)**
serait-ce : **fût-ce**
si j'ose dire : **si l'on veut; transitions mécaniques**
si l'on ose dire : **points de suspension**
si l'on passe ce mot : **si l'on veut**
si l'on peut dire : **si l'on veut**
simplement : **seulement**
soit dit en passant : **brief interpolated main clause**
soit que : **soit... soit**
sous-phrase : **brief interpolated main clause**
sur la question de : **s'agissant de**
surtout que : **d'autant que**
s'y joint : **inversion du verbe**
tant et si bien que : **phrase dépendante; si bien que**
tantôt... tantôt : **antithèses sans charnière; ici... là**
témoin : **par exemple**
toujours : **reste que**
tout au moins : **du moins**
tout au plus : **tout juste**
tout bien considéré : **à tout prendre; au final; en définitive; finalement; tout compte fait**
tout bien pesé : **à tout prendre; au final; en définitive; finalement; tout compte fait**
tout bien réfléchi : **à tout prendre; au final; en définitive; finalement; tout compte fait**
tout cela : **et ce**
tout cela dit : **cela dit**
tout démontre que : **tout se passe comme si**
toutefois : **certes; mais; sans doute; si d'opposition**
tout incite à penser que : **tout se passe comme si**
tout indique que : **tout se passe comme si**
tout laisse penser que : **tout se passe comme si**
tout porte à croire que : **tout se passe comme si**
traduction : **en clair**
traduisez : **en clair**
voici : **voilà**
voici plus encore : **de plus**
voilà pourquoi : **c'est pourquoi; voilà**
voir : **voyez**
voyons : **voyez**
vrai : **n'en... pas moins**
vu que la chose est ainsi : **cela étant**
vu qu'il s'agit : **s'agissant de**
y compris même : **fût-ce**